Rhett Lyons

HOUGHTON MIFFLIN LITERATURE SERIES

PHILIP McFARLAND

SHARON BREAKSTONE

WILLIAM A. JAMISON

MORSE PECKHAM

REFLECTIONS IN LITERATURE

HOUGHTON
MIFFLIN
COMPANY

BOSTON
Atlanta
Dallas

Geneva, Illinois
Hopewell, New Jersey
Palo Alto

Printed in the U.S.A.

Library of Congress Catalog Number: 75–144318

ISBN: 0–395–20073–3

ABOUT THE EDITORS

Philip McFarland is a novelist and teacher of English at Concord (Mass.) Academy. A graduate of Oberlin, he holds a master's degree from Cambridge University, where he received First Honors in English Literature. Before becoming a teacher, Mr. McFarland edited textbooks for classes in secondary school English.

Sharon Breakstone is a teacher of English in the Newton (Mass.) school system. She is an honors graduate of the University of Iowa, where she was elected to Phi Beta Kappa. Winner of the Pi Lambda Theta Prize, Mrs. Breakstone holds an MAT degree from Harvard University. She has published articles in *Education Times* and *Reading Newsreport*.

William A. Jamison is teaching in the Humanities Division of Kirkland College, Clinton, New York, and has taught in the Department of English, University of Rochester. Dr. Jamison did his undergraduate work at the University of Pittsburgh, and has his M.A. and Ph.D. in English from Princeton. His background includes extensive experience in publishing, and he is the author of the critical study *Arnold and the Romantics*.

Morse Peckham has spent many years studying the relationship among the arts of literature, painting, and music, and evolving a new theory of art. The result can be seen in two recent volumes—*Beyond the Tragic Vision* and *Man's Rage for Chaos*. Dr. Peckham has taught at the Citadel, Rutgers, the University of Pennsylvania, and the University of South Carolina, where he now serves as Distinguished Professor of English and Comparative Literature.

CONTENTS

COMING TO TERMS

THE SHORT STORY

POETRY

DRAMA

THE GENERATIONS

EPIC POETRY

THE NOVEL

REFLECTIONS
IN
LITERATURE

COMING TO TERMS

THE UNEXAMINED LIFE is not worth living." These are the words of Socrates, and what that Greek philosopher meant by so blunt a pronouncement is this: to get up in the morning and brush your teeth and eat your breakfast and go to school and come home and do your homework and brush your teeth once more and go to bed without ever asking yourself what it is all about—why am I doing these things?—means that you are leading a life without much interest or purpose. For it is only by questioning: Why am I here? What should I do with the years of my life? What meaning can I make of these years?—it is only by asking such questions that we can live beyond the level of animals and become fully human.

Occasionally a person begins to examine his life seriously before the ninth grade. Sometimes he starts that examination as a senior in high school. A number get around to it finally when they are thirty-five or so and are deeply embroiled in a job that may seem suddenly not very important. And some don't get around to making such an examination at all. For you can live, after a fashion, without questioning your life in any way. But you will live more fully if you do question it: if you come to terms with it, and with its relationship to all the other lives that you encounter.

What kind of world is this we have been set down in, with moments of intense happiness, yes, but with moments of injustice and cruelty and agony and loneliness? What can you make of such a confusion of different values and vices and possibilities? And how, in particular, do you fit into such a world? It is about that question, above all others, that these selections may lead you to wonder.

Philip McFarland

1

"He was a beautiful child. This was the brother I killed."

SHERREL
WHIT BURNETT

I DO NOT KNOW whether I can do this thing or not. Maybe it is just a thought; maybe I just think it is necessary to do it. I mean about the name. I have thought about it a lot though and it keeps urging at me. It is not easy to understand. But I must try to understand and explain it.

You see, I actually did have a brother. People sometimes asked me, Are you the only boy in the family? And I've said, Yes. This wasn't a lie wholly. I was the first born in my family. But there were others, two others. One died in long clothes.[1] We have his picture at home. The other was named Sherrel.

It is easy to remember him. My mother had us photographed together, for instance. And one especial print was transferred onto little smooth discs the size of a saucer. The discs fit into small twisted wire easels and my brother and I used to sit on the easel like that on my mother's bureau in the bedroom.

He was, as I said, younger than I. This is important. The neighbors used to say, It's the difference in their ages. They tried to explain in that way why I was so mean. And you can see the difference clearly enough on the picture discs. We both stood by the photographer's chair, a plush chair. But I was up to the top of it. My brother's hand rested on the arm. It looks pretty small to me now because I'm twice as old

as I was then. We both wore black velvet tam-o'-shanters and dark red velvet coats and pants. My mouth was a little open, too, looking at the photographer. I did not touch my brother. He had one hand, which was very small, on the chair, and the other one had hold of me. His hair was lighter than mine and softer and his eyes wider and bluer. He had a small mouth like a flower and it was smiling. He was a beautiful child. This was the brother I killed.

I am not telling you about a melodrama. I won't be arrested and hanged. I did not kill him yesterday. It was a long time ago, in fact, and I do not remember it all the time, only sometimes when something suggests the way I was then or when someone asks, Have you any other brothers? And I say, No. And here too in this other town at this school except for a girl I know I am quite alone in certain ways and in the winter as now I have seen any number of things to remind me. There is, for example, an epidemic of smallpox here, and instead of smooth, fast automobile hearses they still have funeral carriages that drag along slowly through the streets. Only once have I ridden in such a carriage. And that was then.

There are some things difficult to remember out of childhood. I do not remember when my brother was born. There was not so much difference then. Only four years before, I had been born. But I remember clearly when I was nine. My brother then was five. And we were two in the family. But I was the first.

[1] IN LONG CLOTHES: in infancy.

Do you know how this is? Nine and five? Well, nine is somebody. Five is still curls. At nine I have seen something of the world. What have you seen at five? Go on, you can't come with us! Go on back to the house! We're going down to the store. You'll get run over. Go on, you can't play with us. You ain't big enough. Go on, grow up some before you come tagging around after us. Who asked you along? Beat it! I know how that is. I said all that, more brutally even. He didn't say anything. He didn't cry or whine or crab. I probably would have. He stopped following simply, and stood there. And then we ran off. He stood alone. Sometimes I found him other places alone, sitting still in a corner thinking quietly about something. I am always a little puzzled now I am older. I have talked it over with others. He would have been important. . . . But at nine one is a weed, growing wild. Five is still in the hothouse.

We lived near the sand hills. It wasn't until several years later that I really got into the hills exploring them with a cousin of my own age. Sherrel never did get there. And there was a great liking in both of us for the hills, his maybe different from mine. I often found him sitting dreaming looking at them. But one day late in the spring the hills in a way came down to our house. A cloudburst drenched them, rolling down soft sand, cutting great ditches in the road in front of our place. We weren't long in discovering that, I'll tell you. When Sherrel wandered out of the kitchen the ditch was full of us kids. It was a peach of a ditch as high as our head, gnawed with caves and dangers.

I started the discoveries. There's some hole, I yelled. And down I had gone, doing what the others wanted to do, the first to absorb their wishes. Then they followed, yelling too. Sherrel, I suppose, could hear my voice coming up out of the ground. He came over to the ditch and looked down, standing alone above us. Go on back, I shouted, you'll fall in. He moved away. I paid no more attention then to him, and the rest of us ran racing, hiding, searching, together in the wash.

And then, separated from the others for a moment or so, I noticed something odd about my hands. Hey, kids, I cried, lookee! Look at my hands! They looked. They stood back in wonderment. They looked at their own hands. No, they couldn't, they said. It was something funny. Look what Martin can do! Lookee, he can peel off his hands! It was true, something had happened to my hands. I took hold and pulled off long shreds of skin. I amazed them all They stood astounded.

Let me see, said somebody. It was Sherrel.

Say, I yelled, didn't I say not to come down here? You ain't big enough to be in this here ditch. Let me see your hands, he said. The kids were all looking at me. I'll let you see, all right! I said. He stood his ground and didn't go. That makes me mad, I felt. No, I said. I took him by the shoulder and talked straight in his face, hard. How many times do I have to tell you to get out of this ditch! He turned around and walked up the gorge to a shallower spot and climbed slowly out.

A day or so later Sherrel stayed in bed. There's something the matter with him, my mother said. She didn't know what. Then he took a high fever, they said, and was delirious. I thought it was strange about delirious. Sherrel's eyes were shut and he looked as if he was sleeping but he was talking without any sense. We'll have to have a doctor, my mother said. And that afternoon the doctor came to our house, wiping his feet at the door and entering with a serious look. Let's see the other young fellow, he said. Anything wrong with him? He had a little sore throat, my mother said, but he's all right. He looked down my throat. Look at my hands, I said, ain't they funny?

What I thought, he said.

The same afternoon a man from downtown came and nailed up a yellow flag. It was a cloth sign saying, black on orange, Scarlet Fever. I couldn't go out of the yard. That's sure tough, the kids said, peering through the pickets. I even had to keep back from the fence, too. It was catching.

I sat on the steps fronting north from our bare two-room brick house and looked at the hills. I had had the Scarlet Fever and hadn't even known it. Why, my mother said, he was playing around all the time. Why, he was out there playing in the ditch with all those children. That's bad, said the doctor. But my brother was worse. He had it good.

I remember the windows in the front room were darkened and my mother never went to bed. She never took her clothes off. And my father didn't go to work. My aunt came to the fence with a bag of oranges and bananas. How is he? she asked. If he isn't any better Dr. Anderson says he'd better have a consultation, said my mother. How is Dr. Anderson? asked my aunt. He is the best doctor in town, my mother said.

I sat in the sun all tired now and weak. But I wasn't sick. I was big and nine.

I remember the consultation. There were four doctors in the kitchen standing around and talking low and sitting down and getting up. I could see in from outside. My mother was nervous and walking around and my father, who was a big heavy man, stood around too and sat down and then got up. They were waiting for something definite they spoke of that I could not understand. It was the Crisis. I asked what it was, and my mother had said, Sherrel will get better then. I didn't know what a Crisis would be like and I opened the door

slowly and got into the house quietly, past the doctors.

My father and mother were in the front room by the bed where Sherrel lay. He was still and wasn't talking deliriously. And then my mother, who was standing by him with my father waiting, suddenly cried terribly for a minute or so, and then she took hold of my father and pulled him down by the bed to the floor. I didn't know what was happening. I was frightened, too. Pray, she sobbed. Pray, if you never prayed before. O God, she began . . . and she was crying more and more. My father was kneeling heavily and strangely in a big dark bulk. He put his arm around my mother. There, there, he said. I never saw them like that before. My father is English; my mother is German. I did not think about that though then. I thought, I am scared; this is all different, and dark. I stood in the doorway, too frightened to move.

Come in, Martin, my mother suddenly cried out to me. Come in to your brother. Come here with us. I came over, and there we were all kneeling down together.

Do you want your brother to die? she asked. No, I said. I was frightened at her, at the strange heavy silence on my father, at my brother even. Go and look at him, she told me.

I got up and looked at my brother's white face. It was like a face of ivory with pale lips. I looked hard. He was different too. What do I do? I thought. I am rough, not like that. My mother is looking at me terribly. Kiss him. I bent over and touched his face. His lips opened with a quiet breath, like a little flower bursting on my cheek.

The crisis came and passed. It came while we were in the room there. My mother could not wait. She went to the bed, trying to wake up my brother. Look, Sherrel, she whispered, we are going to get you the nice pearl-handled pocketknife tomorrow. You won't have to wait till Christmas. Tomorrow. You just get well, now. Sherrel! Do you hear me, Sherrel?

Or, he can have mine, I thought.

But he didn't hear us. He didn't hear anybody. Then my mother went to sleep suddenly, it seemed, and drooped down by the bed and they put her in the other room on a couch.

I stood in the dark by a curtain when the doctors came in. Too bad, said Dr. Anderson. He leaned over my brother. Remarkable head, said one of the others. Isn't it! spoke up another one. Artist's head, said the one with the beard. Yes. . . . Then the doctors walked out together into the room where my mother was and in a little while they all left the house.

A few days later there were the strange preparations for the funeral. I don't want to dwell on the funeral. That is not the point. But we rode in a carriage shut in by ourselves, still quarantined, the others following slowly behind us. I remember we passed the Watson's place. They were standing at the gate, the family, staring stupidly at the procession as the horse carriages jogged down the hilly street rolling off to the cemetery.

This is all strange, I thought, riding along past the Watson's house in a carriage like this. My mother and my father and myself. I was taken up with the thought and looked back out of the carriage window now and then at the carriages behind me. My mother pulled me back to sit up straight. My mother's face was drawn and tired and she was crying. My father's eyes had tears in them too. I could not cry. I thought, I ought to cry. How can I cry? I am not hurt any place where I can feel. I squeezed into the corner of the carriage opposite them, pressing up against one hand hard to make it hurt. It turned numb and pained but not in a crying way. You cry easy differently, I thought. Onions, for instance, make you cry. Would it have been a trick, I thought, or right and honest if I had put an onion in my handkerchief, no one seeing me, and

then smelt it now and then in the curtained shadows of the carriage? I would have cried then. I wanted to cry. But all I could think was, Sherrel was a queer kid. Were we brothers sure enough? Am I anybody's brother? Why don't I cry? . . .

You see, he would sit in a corner quiet and frailly beautiful. I was nine and active. It's the difference in their ages. Maybe so. There were the Elwell brothers, now. They were twins. They had a carpenter's shop. It was a peach of a shop, down in a cellar, and they worked together great, making book ends and rabbit hutches and things like that.

I gave him that sickness. I knew that. That killed him. That is why my brother is dead. But I am trying to remember, to clear things up. I am trying to remember if I thought that then. I remember I thought, It's funny just he got it. Why not Leona Eads, Ed or Billy Simons? They touched my hands. I wondered if I hadn't forced my sickness on my brother out of hatred for him, out of my own peculiar older-brother hatred. Did I slap him, maybe strike him in the face with my peeling hand? Perhaps I did. I wondered over this for many weeks now and then.

I'm not even sure now. I might have. It's funny how mean, you see, a person can be. I've thought of that. I've got a girl. I've talked things over with her, not everything, but generally you know. She doesn't like meanness either. I remember when I was about twelve, my sister was just coming along then. She was about two and I had to tend her occasionally. I didn't like it. Once my mother said to me, Do you want your little sister to die too? Well, no, I said. She might even have said, Do you want to kill your little sister too? Maybe this was it, because I asked myself that a lot later, trying to be better. I said, Do you want to kill your sister too? No, I said.

I didn't, either. But I remembered what I'd said when she was born. I said, There's enough in this family already. But I didn't want to kill her. Still I had killed my brother. I had killed Sherrel. Not only by giving him sickness. But by meanness.

This is how I figure it now. I killed my brother by meanness. And it is too bad. I wouldn't do it now. I am not that way. I could have got him a job here in this other town where I am now after he got out of school. I'll be out of school here pretty soon. I'm eighteen next week. Then I'll go on a paper where I've got a stand-in.[1] I'd have said, Now you keep on at school and read a lot of good things, good books you know, poetry and good things and learn how to write. You've got good stuff in you, I can tell. You're going to be an artist. So am I. We'll be two artists, brothers, maybe different, but we can help each other. You've got a poetic style, and I've got a stronger style. I see things more as they are. I'm a little tougher. I can digest more. But that's all right. When I get going, I'll help you. You've got fine things in you. I'll help you bring them out.

That's the kind of a person he would have been. He would have been an artist. There's nothing any bigger than that. Nothing finer. It's the best, in a holy way. It has to be in you first. It hides sometimes and doesn't get a chance to come out where people are.

I've talked that over with people, with that girl I spoke of. I want to be an artist. A writer. I can see back from where I am, though. I've been pretty mean, pretty contemptible. It's funny to look back like that and see yourself in old pictures and things. It's hard to think you had the same name, even.

---

[1] STAND-IN: person with influence.

And that's what I'm puzzling over now. There's nothing wrong with my name, actually. Mark. Mark Stowe. It was first Martin. It was even Martin Tilton Stowe. I didn't like it. All that, I mean. I cut it down to Mark Stowe. It made me feel surer, quicker, stronger.

But even that doesn't quite go. It doesn't all fit. I'm not all blunt, like that. Mark. Mark Stowe. I've got other things. I've written poems, even, and I wouldn't kiss a girl hard. I know how my brother was. He would have been like that too, only a lot more.

And, you know, about the name. . . . My folks are getting along now. Sisters don't count, the way I mean, that is. I'm the only boy in the family. And I've been thinking, what if I should write a poem, a long, good one—here I am, alive and everything—and sign it not Mark Stowe, but, well, Sherrel Stowe? Do you see what I mean? And then by and by there would be another poem, and after a while I would just go ahead and use it right along. Can you understand that? How I would be more him too, then—Sherrel?

FOR DISCUSSION

1. Why would Mark like to write a poem in Sherrel's name? How would that help him to feel better about himself?

2. At eighteen, Mark feels that he is different from the person he was nine years before. How has he changed in his feelings about himself? How has he changed in his feelings about Sherrel?

3. Do you think Mark really killed his brother? Why does he feel that he did?

4. In the first paragraph of the story the narrator Mark is trying to decide what to do about his name. This is also where the story ends. Why is his name so important to him? What does it have to do with the rest of the story?

FOR COMPOSITION

• Pretend Mark has told you, his friend, this story. What would you say to him? Could you make him feel any better? Write your answer as a letter to him, using the informal language in which the story is written.

There is an old saying, "There are two kinds of people in the world: suckers and phonies." Pete discovers it is possible to be both at once.

SUCKER

CARSON McCULLERS

IT WAS ALWAYS like I had a room to myself. Sucker slept in my bed with me, but that didn't interfere with anything. The room was mine, and I used it as I wanted to. Once I remember sawing a trap door in the floor. Last year, when I was a sophomore in high school, I tacked on my wall some pictures of girls from magazines, and one of them was just in her underwear. My mother never bothered me, because she had the younger kids to look after. And Sucker thought anything I did was always swell.

Whenever I would bring any of my friends back to my room, all I had to do was just glance once at Sucker, and he would get up from whatever he was busy with and maybe half smile at me, and leave without saying a word. He never brought kids back there. He's twelve, four years younger than I am, and he always knew without me even telling him that I didn't want kids that age meddling with my things.

Half the time I used to forget that Sucker isn't my brother. He's my first cousin, but practically ever since I remember he's been in our family. You see, his folks were killed in a wreck when he was a baby. To me and my kid sisters he was like our brother.

Sucker used to always remember and be-

lieve every word I said. That's how he got his nickname. Once a couple of years ago I told him that if he'd jump off our garage with an umbrella, it would act as a parachute, and he wouldn't fall hard. He did it and busted his knee. That's just one instance. And the funny thing was that no matter how many times he got fooled he would still believe me. Not that he was dumb in other ways—it was just the way he acted with me. He would look at everything I did and quietly take it in.

There is one thing I have learned, but it makes me feel guilty and is hard to figure out. If a person admires you a lot, you despise him and don't care—and it is the person who doesn't notice you that you are apt to admire. This is not easy to realize. Maybelle Watts, this senior at school, acted like she was the Queen of Sheba and even humiliated me. Yet at this same time I would have done anything in the world to get her attentions. All I could think about day and night was Maybelle until I was nearly crazy. When Sucker was a little kid and on up until the time he was twelve, I guess I treated him as bad as Maybelle did me.

Now that Sucker has changed so much, it is a little hard to remember him as he used to be. I never imagined anything would suddenly happen that would make us both very different. I never knew that in order to get what has happened straight in my mind I would want to think back on him as he used to be and compare and try to get things settled. If I could have seen ahead, maybe I would have acted different.

I never noticed him much or thought about him, and when you consider how long we have had the same room together, it is funny the few things I remember. He used to talk to himself a lot when he'd think he was alone—all about him fighting gangsters and being on ranches and that sort of kids' stuff. He'd get in the bathroom and stay as long as an hour, and sometimes his voice would go up high and excited, and you could hear him all over the house. Usually, though, he was very quiet. He didn't have many boys in the neighborhood to buddy with, and his face had the look of a kid who is watching a game and waiting to be asked to play. He didn't mind wearing the sweaters and coats that I outgrew, even if the sleeves did flop down too big and make his wrists look as thin and white as a little girl's. That is how I remember him—getting a little bigger every year but still being the same. That was Sucker up until a few months ago when all this trouble began.

Maybelle was somehow mixed up in what happened, so I guess I ought to start with her. Until I knew her, I hadn't given much time to girls. Last fall she sat next to me in general science class, and that was when I first began to notice her. Her hair is the brightest yellow I ever saw, and occasionally she will wear it set into curls with some sort of gluey stuff. Her fingernails are pointed and manicured and painted a shiny red. All during class I used to watch Maybelle, nearly all the time except when I thought she was going to look my way or when the teacher called on me. I couldn't keep my eyes off her hands, for one thing. They are very little and white except for that red stuff, and when she would turn the pages of her book, she always licked her thumb and held out her little finger and turned very slowly. It is impossible to describe Maybelle. All the boys are crazy about her, but she didn't even notice me. For one thing, she's almost two years older than I am. Between periods I used to try and pass very close to her in the halls, but she would hardly ever smile at me. All I could do was sit and look at her in class—and sometimes it was like the whole room could hear my heart beating, and I wanted to holler or light out and run for hell.

At night, in bed, I would imagine about Maybelle. Often this would keep me from sleeping until as late as one or two o'clock. Sometimes Sucker would wake up and ask me why I couldn't get settled, and I'd tell him to hush his mouth. I suppose I was mean to him lots of times. I guess I wanted to ignore somebody like Maybelle did me. You could always tell by Sucker's face when his feelings were hurt. I don't remember all the ugly remarks I must have made, because even when I was saying them, my mind was on Maybelle.

That went on for nearly three months, and then somehow she began to change. In the halls she would speak to me, and every morning she copied my homework. At lunch time once I danced with her in the gym. One afternoon I got up nerve and went around to her house with a carton of cigarettes. I knew she smoked in the girls' basement and sometimes outside of school —and I didn't want to take her candy, because I think that's been run into the ground. She was very nice, and it seemed to me everything was going to change.

It was that night when this trouble really started. I had come into my room late, and Sucker was already asleep. I felt too happy and keyed up to get in a comfortable position, and I was awake thinking about Maybelle a long time. Then I dreamed about her, and it seemed I kissed her. It was a surprise to wake up and see the dark. I lay still, and a little while passed before I could come to and understand where I was. The house was quiet and it was a very dark night.

Sucker's voice was a shock to me. "Pete? . . ."

I didn't answer anything or even move.

"You do like me as much as if I was your own brother, don't you, Pete?"

I couldn't get over the surprise of everything, and it was like this was the real dream instead of the other.

"You have liked me all the time like I was your own brother, haven't you?"

"Sure," I said.

Then I got up for a few minutes. It was cold, and I was glad to come back to bed. Sucker hung onto my back. He felt little and warm, and I could feel his warm breathing on my shoulder.

"No matter what you did, I always knew you liked me."

I was wide awake, and my mind seemed mixed up in a strange way. There was this happiness about Maybelle and all that— but at the same time something about Sucker and his voice when he said these things made me take notice. Anyway, I guess you understand people better when you are happy than when something is worrying you. It was like I had never really thought about Sucker until then. I felt I had always been mean to him. One night a few weeks before I had heard him crying in the dark. He said he had lost a boy's beebee gun and was scared to let anybody know. He wanted me to tell him what to do. I was sleepy and tried to make him hush, and when he wouldn't, I kicked at him. That was just one of the things I remembered. It seemed to me he had always been a lonesome kid. I felt bad.

There is something about a dark cold night that makes you feel close to someone you're sleeping with. When you talk to-

gether, it is like you are the only people awake in the town.

"You're a swell kid, Sucker," I said.

It seemed to me suddenly that I did like him more than anybody else I knew— more than any other boy, more than my sisters, more in a certain way even than Maybelle. I felt good all over, and it was like when they play sad music in the movies. I wanted to show Sucker how much I really thought of him and make up for the way I had always treated him.

We talked for a good while that night. His voice was fast, and it was like he had been saving up these things to tell me for a long time. He mentioned that he was going to try to build a canoe and that the kids down the block wouldn't let him in on their football team and I don't know what all. I talked some too, and it was a good feeling to think of him taking in everything I said so seriously. I even spoke of Maybelle a little, only I made out like it was her who had been running after me all this time. He asked questions about high school and so forth. His voice was excited, and he kept on talking fast like he could never get the words out in time. When I went to sleep, he was still talking, and I could still feel his breathing on my shoulder, warm and close.

During the next couple of weeks I saw a lot of Maybelle. She acted as though she really cared for me a little. Half the time I felt so good I hardly knew what to do with myself.

But I didn't forget about Sucker. There were a lot of old things in my bureau drawer I'd been saving—boxing gloves and Tom Swift books and second-rate fishing tackle. All this I turned over to him. We had some more talks together, and it was really like I was knowing him for the first time. When there was a long cut on his cheek, I knew he had been monkeying around with this new first razor set of mine, but I didn't say anything. His face seemed different now. He used to look timid and sort of like he was afraid of a whack over the head. That expression was gone. His face, with those wide-open eyes and his ears sticking out and his mouth never quite shut, had the look of a person who is surprised and expecting something swell.

Once I started to point him out to Maybelle and tell her he was my kid brother. It was an afternoon when a murder mystery was on at the movie. I had earned a dollar working for my Dad, and I gave Sucker a quarter to go and get candy and so forth. With the rest I took Maybelle. We were sitting near the back, and I saw Sucker come in. He began to stare at the screen the minute he stepped past the ticket man, and he stumbled down the aisle without noticing where he was going. I started to punch Maybelle, but couldn't quite make up my mind. Sucker looked a little silly—walking like a drunk with his eyes glued to the movie. He was wiping his reading glasses on his shirt tail, and his knickers flopped down. He went on until he got to the first few rows where the kids usually sit. I never did punch Maybelle. But I got to thinking it was good to have both of them at the movie with the money I earned.

I guess things went on like this for about a month or six weeks. I felt so good I couldn't settle down to study or put my mind on anything. I wanted to be friendly with everybody. There were times when I just had to talk to some person. And usually that would be Sucker. He felt as good as I did. Once he said: "Pete, I am gladder that you are like my brother than anything else in the world."

Then something happened between Maybelle and me. I never have figured out just what it was. Girls like her are hard to understand. She began to act different to-

ward me. At first I wouldn't let myself believe this and tried to think it was just my imagination. She didn't act glad to see me any more. Often she went out riding with this fellow on the football team who owns this yellow roadster. The car was the color of her hair, and after school she would ride off with him, laughing and looking into his face. I couldn't think of anything to do about it, and she was on my mind all day and night. When I did get a chance to go out with her, she was snippy and didn't seem to notice me. This made me feel like something was the matter—I would worry about my shoes clopping too loud on the floor, or the bumps on my chin. Sometimes when Maybelle was around, a devil would get into me, and I'd hold my face stiff and call grown men by their last names without the Mister and say rough things. In the night I would wonder what made me do all this until I was too tired for sleep.

At first I was so worried I just forgot about Sucker. Then later he began to get on my nerves. He was always hanging around until I would get back from high school, always looking like he had something to say to me or wanted me to tell him. He made me a magazine rack in his Manual Training class, and one week he saved his lunch money and bought me three packs of cigarettes. He couldn't seem to take it in that I had things on my mind and didn't want to fool with him. Every afternoon it would be the same—him in my room with this waiting expression on his face. Then I wouldn't say anything, or I'd maybe answer him roughlike, and he would finally go out.

I can't divide that time up and say this happened one day and that the next. For one thing, I was so mixed up the weeks just slid along into each other, and I felt like hell and didn't care. Nothing definite was said or done. Maybelle still rode

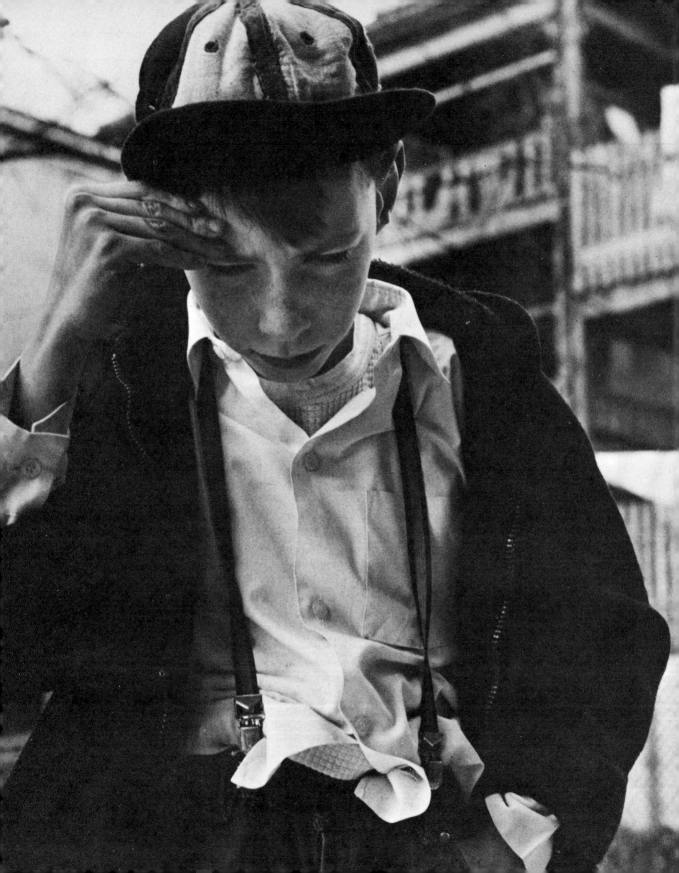

around with this fellow in his yellow roadster, and sometimes she would smile at me and sometimes not. Every afternoon I went from one place to another where I thought she would be. Either she would act almost nice and I would begin thinking how things would finally clear up and she would care for me—or else she'd behave so that if she hadn't been a girl, I'd have wanted to grab her by that white little neck and choke her. The more ashamed I felt for making a fool of myself, the more I ran after her.

Sucker kept getting on my nerves more and more. He would look at me as though he sort of blamed me for something, but at the same time knew that it wouldn't last long. He was growing fast and for some reason began to stutter when he talked. Sometimes he had nightmares or would throw up his breakfast. Mom got him a bottle of cod liver oil.

Then the finish came between Maybelle and me. I met her going to the drugstore and asked for a date. When she said no, I remarked something sarcastic. She told me she was sick and tired of my being around and that she had never cared a rap about me. She said all that. I just stood there and didn't answer anything. I walked home very slowly.

For several afternoons I stayed in my room by myself. I didn't want to go anywhere or talk to anyone. When Sucker would come in and look at me sort of funny, I'd yell at him to get out. I didn't want to think of Maybelle, and I sat at my desk reading *Popular Mechanics* or whittling at a toothbrush rack I was making. It seemed to me I was putting that girl out of my mind pretty well.

But you can't help what happens to you at night. That is what made things how they are now.

You see, a few nights after Maybelle said those words to me, I dreamed about her again. It was like that first time, and I was squeezing Sucker's arm so tight I woke him up. He reached for my hand.

"Pete, what's the matter with you?"

All of a sudden I felt so mad my throat choked—at myself and the dream and Maybelle and Sucker and every single person I knew. I remembered all the times Maybelle had humiliated me and everything bad that had ever happened. It seemed to me for a second that nobody would ever like me but a sap like Sucker.

"Why is it we aren't buddies like we were before? Why—?"

"Shut your damn trap!" I threw off the cover and got up and turned on the light. He sat in the middle of the bed, his eyes blinking and scared.

There was something in me, and I couldn't help myself. I don't think anybody ever gets that mad but once. Words came without me knowing what they would be. It was only afterward that I could remember each thing I said and see it all in a clear way.

"Why aren't we buddies? Because you're the dumbest slob I ever saw! Nobody cares anything about you! And just because I felt sorry for you sometimes and tried to act decent, don't think I give a damn about a dumb bunny like you!"

If I'd talked loud or hit him, it wouldn't have been so bad. But my voice was slow and like I was very calm. Sucker's mouth was part way open, and he looked as though he'd knocked his funny bone. His face was white, and sweat came out on his forehead. He wiped it away with the back of his hand, and for a minute his arm stayed raised that way as though he was holding something away from him.

"Don't you know a single thing? Haven't you ever been around at all? Why don't you get a girl friend instead of me? What kind of a sissy do you want to grow up to be anyway?"

I didn't know what was coming next. I couldn't help myself or think.

Sucker didn't move. He had on one of my pajama jackets, and his neck stuck out skinny and small. His hair was damp on his forehead.

"Why do you always hang around me? Don't you know when you're not wanted?"

Afterward I could remember the change in Sucker's face. Slowly that blank look went away, and he closed his mouth. His eyes got narrow and his fists shut. There had never been such a look on him before. It was like every second he was getting older. There was a hard look to his eyes you don't see usually in a kid. A drop of sweat rolled down his chin, and he didn't notice. He just sat there with those eyes on me, and he didn't speak, and his face was hard and didn't move.

"No, you don't know when you're not wanted. You're too dumb. Just like your name—a dumb Sucker."

It was like something had busted inside me. I turned off the light and sat down in the chair by the window. My legs were shaking, and I was so tired I could have bawled. The room was cold and dark. I sat there for a long time and smoked a squashed cigarette I had saved. Outside the yard was black and quiet. After a while I heard Sucker lie down.

I wasn't mad any more, only tired. It seemed awful to me that I had talked like that to a kid only twelve. I couldn't take it all in. I told myself I would go over to him and try to make it up. But I just sat there in the cold until a long time had passed. I planned how I could straighten it out in the morning. Then, trying not to squeak the springs, I got back in bed.

Sucker was gone when I woke up the next day. And later, when I wanted to apologize as I had planned, he looked at me in this new hard way so that I couldn't say a word.

All of that was two or three months ago. Since then Sucker has grown faster than any boy I ever saw. He's almost as tall as I am, and his bones have gotten heavier and bigger. He won't wear any of my old clothes any more and has bought his first pair of long pants—with some leather suspenders to hold them up. Those are just the changes that are easy to see and put into words.

Our room isn't mine at all any more. He's gotten up this gang of kids, and they have a club. When they aren't digging trenches in some vacant lot and fighting, they are always in my room. On the door there is some foolishness written in Mercurochrome saying "Woe to the Outsider who Enters" and signed with crossed bones and their secret initials. They have rigged up a radio, and every afternoon it blares out music. Once as I was coming in, I heard a boy telling something in a low voice about what he saw in the back of his big brother's automobile. I could guess what I didn't hear. For a minute Sucker looked surprised, and his face was almost like it used to be. Then he got hard and tough again. "Sure, dumbbell. We know all that." They didn't notice me. Sucker began telling them how in two years he was planning to be a trapper in Alaska.

But most of the time Sucker stays by himself. It is worse when we are alone together in the room. He sprawls across the bed in those long corduroy pants with the suspenders and just stares at me with that hard, half sneering look. I fiddle around my desk and can't get settled because of those eyes of his. And the thing is I just have to study because I've gotten three bad cards this term already. If I flunk English, I can't graduate next year. I don't want to be a bum, and I just have to get my mind on it. I don't care a flip for Maybelle or any particular girl any more, and it's only this thing between Sucker and me that is the trouble now. We never speak except when we have to before the family. I don't even want to call him Sucker any more, and unless I forget, I call him by his real name, Richard. At night I can't study with him in the room, and I have to hang around the drugstore, smoking and doing nothing, with the fellows who loaf there.

More than anything I want to be easy in my mind again. And I miss the way Sucker and I were for a while in a funny, sad way that before this I never would have believed. But everything is so different that there seems to be nothing I can do to get it right. I've sometimes thought if we could have it out in a big fight, that would help. But I can't fight him, because he's four years younger. And another thing—sometimes this look in his eyes makes me almost believe that if Sucker could, he would kill me.

FOR DISCUSSION

1. At the end of the story, Pete refers to Sucker by his real name, Richard. Why?

2. In what ways were both Richard and Pete "suckers"?

3. Compare the way Pete treated Sucker with the way Maybelle treated Pete.

4. Compare the two boys' reactions when each of them learned that the person he admired despised him.

FOR COMPOSITION

• The basic meaning or message of a story is called the *theme*. Pete summed up the theme of this story: "If a person admires you a lot, you despise him and don't care—and it is the person who doesn't notice you that you are apt to admire." Write a composition based on your own experiences in which you agree or disagree with this theme.

In the plains country of northeastern Colorado, young Hal's imagination created a "time machine."

FROM

HIGH, WIDE AND LONESOME
HAL BORLAND

IT WAS LATE April before Spring really came. It came first as a greenness in the hollows beside the shallow ponds of snow-melt, but soon it began to spread like a faint green mist on all the hillsides and across the flats. After that the chilly days and the raw nights didn't seem quite so raw or chilly.

Timbered country has Spring subtleties:[1] rising sap and first buds, florets on trees and bushes, half-hidden flowers among the rocks and leaf mold. But the plains are a vast simplicity at any season, their moods and changes swift, evident, and decisive. On that boundless open grassland neither Spring nor any other season can hide or creep up slowly. Spring comes in a vast green wave rolling northward, a wave as evident as were the buffalo millions that once swept northward with new grass, as evident as the Winter-hungry Indians that once swept northward with the buffalo. Spring on the plains has little more subtlety than a thunder storm.

Winter ends, March drags its cold, muddy feet but finally passes, and there is Spring, a rebirth that assaults all your senses. The surge of life at the grass roots penetrates your soles, creeps up through your bones, your marrow, and right into your heart. You see it, you feel it, you smell it, you taste it in every breath you breathe. You partake of Spring. You are a part of it, even as you were a part of Winter. Spring is all around you and in you, primal, simple as the plains themselves. Spring is, and you know it.

I rode over to the Bromleys to return *David Copperfield* and get *A Tale of Two Cities*. . . . On the way home I saw a badger cleaning out his den. He was down in the hole kicking dirt out with his hind feet almost as fast as a man could toss it out with a shovel. Then I saw a flock of meadowlarks. Most of them were busy looking for beetles, but two of them were so full of song they just strutted around whistling at each other. And when I got to the head of our draw I saw the first of the lark buntings, which we called prairie bobolinks. Half a dozen of them flew up, singing on the wing, and I knew that before long I would be finding their nests in the grass, and light blue eggs in the nests.

A few days later I rode over to the big prairie dog town. Even there, where the prairie dogs had eaten the soil bare last Summer, the grass was beginning to come

---

[1] SUBTLETIES (sŭt'əl·tēz): aspects so delicate or slight as to escape notice.

back. The prairie dogs were out by the hundred, chipper and noisy as though they hadn't an enemy in the world. Over at the far side of the town an old badger was waddling along, watching me over one shoulder. The dogs over there were all out of sight, but a hundred yards from the badger other prairie dogs paid him no attention.

Two little owls were bobbing and screaming at each other; they saw me and forgot their own quarrel and screamed at me, but the minute I was past they began hopping at each other again.

Most of the old mother prairie dogs were fat with pup. The pups would be born in another week or two, but would stay in the dens for a month. The thin old males were feeding greedily on the grass, truculent and quarrelsome among themselves.

I dismounted to watch an ant hill, and I saw two tumblebugs pushing each other around in the grass. They butted and rolled and nipped and got to their feet and butted each other again, until one of them drove the other off. The victor pursued a little way, then came back and began rolling the ball of dung over which they probably had been fighting. They were strange creatures with the mark of antiquity on them, though I didn't know then that they were close cousins of the ancient Egyptian scarabs. All I knew was that these big, dark, timeless-looking beetles fashioned balls of cow manure three quarters of an inch in diameter and rolled them from place to place, walking backward and rolling the balls with their hind legs. They laid eggs in the balls and the eggs hatched into grubs which ate their way out and eventually turned into beetles which laid their own eggs in other dung balls. It seemed to me that the way the birds did it, laying eggs in nests, eggs with shells on them and food inside, was much simpler.

I watched the tumblebug maneuver his ball to the edge of the bare space around the ant hill, and I watched the ants gather to repel the invader, who paid almost no attention to them. The tumblebug rolled his ball across the little clearing and into the grass beyond, the ants rubbed feelers in a conference as though telling each other that they had driven off a major threat to the colony, and everybody went back to work.

The sun was warm. Even the ground was beginning to lose its March chill. I lay there thinking about the beetles and the ants and the prairie dogs and the badgers and the owls and the meadowlarks. They had been here a long time, all of them. They were here when the buffalo first came, and that was so long ago that the Indians couldn't remember that far back. Time was a strange thing. It was days and nights and months and years, and then it stretched out into something else. Into grass, maybe, or into clouds. Or into the earth itself. You lay watching a cloud overhead, and you closed your eyes and pretty soon the cloud moved over the sun. You felt the coolness and the darkness of the shadow. You lay and waited for the brightness and the sun's warmth again. You could count, slowly, and that was time. You counted slowly, and the cloud passed the sun. The shadow was gone.

Time was strange. A prairie-dog pup was born in May, and by Fall it was practically grown up. A meadowlark laid an egg in a nest in May and before frost in the Fall the baby bird hatched from that egg was as big as its mother and it flew south with the other birds. But it took years for a boy to grow up.

We had been out there two years. When we first came I was so short I had to stand on a manger or a cut-bank to get on a horse. Now I could mount Mack from the ground, just put my hands on his withers and jump and throw my leg over his back.

I wondered how many ants had grown old and died while I was growing up enough to get on a horse from the ground. A year must be a long time to an ant. Or a beetle. Or a prairie dog. Even a day must be a long time. Maybe time was like distance. If an ant got twenty feet away from the ant hill, he was a long way from home, much farther than I was right now from the house. And it probably would take a tumblebug all day to roll that ball of dung fifty feet, especially with all the obstacles it had to get over or around.

Some day, I told myself, I would find a tumblebug early in the morning and watch him all day and see just how far he did go. I would catch him and tie a thread around him, or mark him some way, so I could be sure to know which one he was if he had a fight with another beetle.

But not today. I caught Mack and whistled to Fritz, who was still trying to catch a prairie dog, and I rode west, to circle back toward our place.

I rode only a little way when a kit fox jumped not fifty yards ahead of me. He had been catching ground squirrels until I startled him. A kit fox was like a small coyote with a very bushy tail. He was really a fox, but not much bigger than a good-sized cat. There weren't many of them around, and most of them were here on these South Flats. This one jumped and ran like a streak, its bushy tail floating behind, graceful as a bird. It ran maybe twenty yards; then, without slackening pace, it veered and ran off at an angle another twenty-five yards or so, then changed directions again. That's the way a kit fox always ran, zigzag. Dogs would seldom run kit foxes, and anyone who ever watched one knew why. It made you dizzy just watching that zigzagging. I yelled, and

the kit veered again. One more turn and it vanished in a little hollow.

I rode over to the hollow, but I couldn't find the kit fox. It must have darted down the little wash and out onto the flats again where I wasn't watching. But as I rode down the hollow I came to a fresh cut-bank that had washed out in the Spring melt. The grass had caved away, leaving a bank of fresh gravelly soil. Such a place was always worth searching for arrowheads. I got off and began poking through the gravel.

It was different from the gravel on our land, coarser and full of lumps of sandstone. The sandstone was grayish-yellow. There was a thin ledge of it reaching back under the grass. I sifted a few handfuls through my fingers and stood up, about to leave. Then I scuffed at it with my toe and a smooth, rounded flat piece caught my eye. It wasn't a pebble. It was almost the size of a silver dollar, but smooth and rounded.

Even as I picked it up, I sensed that here was something out of time so remote that my mind could not quite grasp the distance. It was a fossil clam, and the place I found it was fifteen hundred miles from the nearest ocean.

There it was, a clam turned to stone, a petrified clam with fluting around the edges of the twin shells, with bits of sandstone still clinging to it. Different from the freshwater clams of the Missouri River, but still a shellfish, something from an ocean that once had been where I stood. And somehow, standing in the warm Spring sunlight on the high plains, I comprehended the matter of eons and ages. Without knowing geology, I sensed geologic time. I touched the beat of the big rhythm, the coming and going of oceans and the rise and fall of mountains. And, for a little while, I was one not only with the Indians who had

been there before me, but with those who were there before the Indians; not only with the grass which had greened with a thousand Springs, but with that which was there before the grass.

There had been ranchmen before we came, and Indians before the ranchmen, and buffalo before the Indians. And long before the buffalo there had been an ocean, and clams. Back, back—how far back? And how far ahead? Time was indeed a strange thing. The time of the ant, the time of the tumblebug, the time of the prairie dog, the time of a boy. The time of a fossil clam.

I got on my horse and rode slowly home in the late afternoon of that Spring day, with a strange, hard, smooth fragment of time in my pocket.

Mother said, "You've just got time to get the chores done before supper."

FOR DISCUSSION

1. What kind of time did each of the following suggest to Hal: the tumblebug, the ants, the fossil clam, his mother?

2. Which of these made the strongest impression on Hal? Why?

3. The terms *simile* and *metaphor* both refer to comparisons of unlike objects. The simile is a direct comparison using the words "like" or "as." ("Spring . . . spread like a faint green mist.") The metaphor is an implied or suggested comparison and does not use "like" or "as." ("March drags its cold muddy feet.") In this story Hal Borland uses several other metaphors to describe the coming of spring. Can you find them?

FOR COMPOSITION

• Choose a season of the year that you especially like or dislike. In a brief composition describe that season, and use several metaphors that will convey your like or dislike.

Early settlers almost destroyed the civilization of the Indians by slaughtering their buffalo and taking their land. Buffy Sainte-Marie, an American Indian singer and composer, sees that destruction continuing even today.

NOW THAT THE BUFFALO'S GONE
BUFFY SAINTE-MARIE

Can you remember the times
That you have held your head high
And told all your friends of your Indian claims,
Proud good lady, and proud good man?
Your great, great grandfather from Indian blood sprang,   5
And you feel in your heart for these ones.

Oh it's written in books and in songs
That we've been mistreated and wronged;
Well, over and over I hear the same words
From you, good lady, from you, good man.   10
Well, listen to me if you care where we stand,
And you feel you're a part of these ones.

When a war between nations is lost
The loser we know pays the cost;
But even when Germany fell to your hands   15
Consider, dear lady, consider, dear man,
You left them their pride and you left them their land
And what have you done to these ones?

Has a change come about Uncle Sam
Or are you still taking over our land   20
A treaty forever George Washington signed
He did, dear lady, he did, dear man,
And the treaty's being broken by Kinzua Dam*
And what will you do for these ones?

Oh it's all in the past you can say   25
But it's still going on till today;
The government now wants the Iroquois land
That of the Seneca and the Cheyenne.
It's here and it's now you must help us, dear man
Now that the buffalo's gone.   30

²³ KINZUA DAM: To build this dam ten thousand acres of land were taken from the Seneca Indians by the U.S. Army Corps of Engineers. The Seneca's rights to this land that they held sacred had been guaranteed by treaty.

FOR DISCUSSION

1. Who are the "dear man" and the "good lady" to whom this song is addressed? In what tone of voice do you think Buffy Sainte-Marie would pronounce "dear" and "good"?

2. Who are "these ones"? What is happening to them that the author is protesting?

"I can turn my wrist slightly, put a bit more pressure on the blade, let it sink in. . . . There is nothing more tender than a man's skin, and the blood is always there, ready to burst forth."

LATHER AND NOTHING ELSE

HERNANDO TELLEZ

HE CAME IN without a word. I was stropping my best razor. And when I recognized him, I started to shake. But he did not notice. To cover my nervousness, I went on honing the razor. I tried the edge with the tip of my thumb and took another look at it against the light.

Meanwhile, he was taking off his cartridge-studded belt with the pistol holster suspended from it. He put it on a hook in the wardrobe and hung his cap above it. Then he turned full around toward me and, loosening his tie, remarked, "It's hot as the devil. I want a shave." With that he took his seat.

I estimated he had a four days' growth of beard. The four days he had been gone on the last foray after our men. His face looked burnt, tanned by the sun.

I started to work carefully on the shaving soap. I scraped some slices from the cake, dropped them into the mug, then added a little lukewarm water and stirred with the brush. The lather soon began to rise.

"The fellows in the troop must have just about as much beard as I." I went on stirring up lather.

"But we did very well, you know. We caught the leaders. Some of them we

Reprinted from *Americas*, monthly magazine published by the General Secretariat of the Organization of American States in English, Spanish, and Portuguese. Reprinted by permission of Pan American Union.

brought back dead; others are still alive. But they'll all be dead soon."

"How many did you take?" I asked.

"Fourteen. We had to go pretty far in to find them. But now they're paying for it. And not one will escape; not a single one."

He leaned back in the chair when he saw the brush in my hand, full of lather. I had not yet put the sheet on him. I was certainly flustered. Taking a sheet from the drawer, I tied it around my customer's neck.

He went on talking. He evidently took it for granted I was on the side of the existing regime.

"The people must have gotten a scare with what happened the other day," he said.

"Yes," I replied, as I finished tying the knot against his nape, which smelt of sweat.

"Good show, wasn't it?"

"Very good," I answered, turning my attention now to the brush. The man closed his eyes wearily and awaited the cool caress of the lather.

I had never had him so close before. The day he ordered the people to file through the schoolyard to look upon the four rebels hanging there, my path had crossed his briefly. But the sight of those mutilated bodies kept me from paying attention to the face of the man who had been directing

23

it all and whom I now had in my hands.

It was not a disagreeable face, certainly. And the beard, which aged him a bit, was not unbecoming. His name was Torres. Captain Torres.

I started to lay on the first coat of lather. He kept his eyes closed.

"I would love to catch a nap," he said, "but there's a lot to be done this evening."

I lifted the brush and asked, with pretended indifference: "A firing party?"

"Something of the sort," he replied, "but slower."

"All of them?"

"No, just a few."

I went on lathering his face. My hands began to tremble again. The man could not be aware of this, which was lucky for me. But I wished he had not come in. Probably many of our men had seen him enter the shop. And with the enemy in my house I felt a certain responsibility.

I would have to shave his beard just like any other, carefully, neatly, just as though he were a good customer, taking heed that not a single pore should emit a drop of blood. Seeing to it that the blade did not slip in the small whorls. Taking care that the skin was left clean, soft, shining, so that when I passed the back of my hand over it, not a single hair should be felt. Yes. I was secretly a revolutionary, but at the same time I was a conscientious barber, proud of the way I did my job. And that four-day beard presented a challenge.

I took up the razor, opened the handle wide, releasing the blade, and started to work, downward from one sideburn. The blade responded to perfection. The hair was tough and hard; not very long, but thick. Little by little the skin began to show through. The razor gave out its usual sound as it gathered up layers of soap mixed with bits of hair. I paused to wipe it clean, and taking up the strop once more went about improving its edge, for I am a painstaking barber.

The man, who had kept his eyes closed, now opened them, put a hand out from under the sheet, felt of the part of his face that was emerging from the lather, and said to me: "Come at six o'clock this evening to the school."

"Will it be like the other day?" I asked, stiff with horror.

"It may be even better," he replied.

"What are you planning to do?"

"I'm not sure yet. But we'll have a good time."

Once more he leaned back and shut his eyes. I came closer, the razor on high.

"Are you going to punish all of them?" I timidly ventured.

"Yes, all of them."

The lather was drying on his face. I must hurry. Through the mirror, I took a look at the street. It appeared about as usual: there was the grocery shop with two or three customers. Then I glanced at the clock: two-thirty.

The razor kept descending. Now from the other sideburn downward. It was a blue beard, a thick one. He should let it grow like some poets, or some priests. It would suit him well. Many people would not recognize him. And that would be a good thing for him, I thought, as I went gently over all the throat line. At this point you really had to handle your blade skillfully, because the hair, while scantier, tended to fall into small whorls. It was a curly beard. The pores might open, minutely, in this area and let out a tiny drop of blood. A good barber like myself stakes his reputation on not permitting that to happen to any of his customers.

And this was indeed a special customer. How many of ours had he sent to their death? How many had he had mutilated? It was best not to think about it. Torres

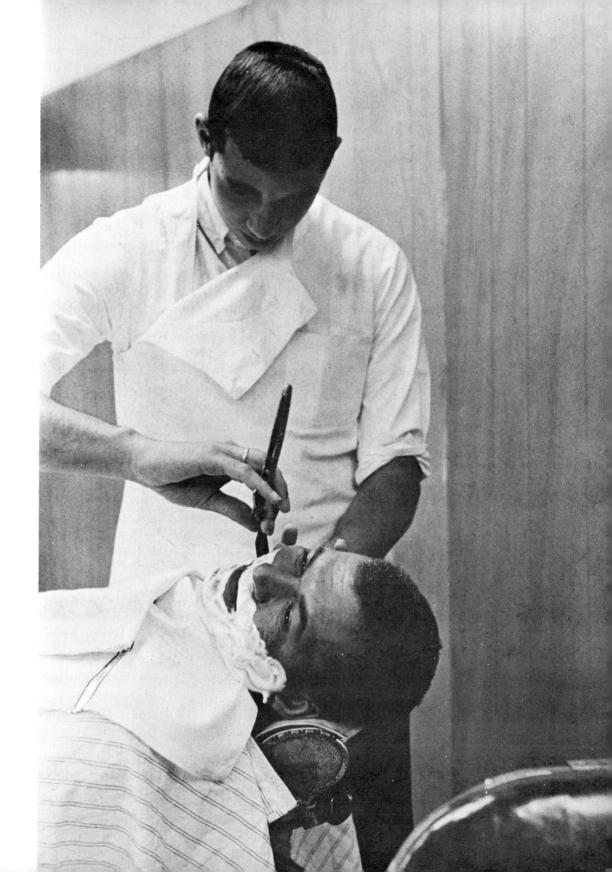

did not know I was his enemy. Neither he nor the others knew it. It was a secret shared by very few, just because that made it possible for me to inform the revolutionaries about Torres' activities in the town and what he planned to do every time he went on one of his raids to hunt down rebels. So it was going to be very difficult to explain how it was that I had him in my hands and then let him go in peace, alive, clean-shaven.

His beard had now almost entirely disappeared. He looked younger, several years younger than when he had come in. I suppose that always happens to men who enter and leave barber shops. Under the strokes of my razor Torres was rejuvenated; yes, because I am a good barber, the best in this town, and I say this in all modesty.

A little more lather here under the chin, on the Adam's apple, right near the great vein. How hot it is! Torres must be sweating just as I am. But he is not afraid. He is a tranquil man, who is not even giving thought to what he will do to his prisoners this evening. I, on the other hand, polishing his skin with this razor but avoiding the drawing of blood, careful with every stroke—I cannot keep my thoughts in order.

Confound the hour he entered my shop! I am a revolutionary but not a murderer. And it would be so easy to kill him. He deserves it. Or does he? No, damn it! No one deserves the sacrifice others make in becoming assassins. What is to be gained by it? Nothing. Others and still others keep coming, and the first kill the second, and then these kill the next, and so on until everything becomes a sea of blood. I could cut his throat, so, swish, swish! He would not even have time to moan, and with his eyes shut he would not even see the shine of the razor or the gleam in my eye.

But I'm shaking like a regular murderer. From his throat a stream of blood would flow on the sheet, over the chair, down on my hands, onto the floor. I would have to close the door. But the blood would go flowing, along the floor, warm, indelible, not to be stanched, until it reached the street, like a small scarlet river.

I'm sure that with a good strong blow, a deep cut, he would feel no pain. He would not suffer at all. And what would I do then with the body? Where would I hide it? I would have to flee, leave all this behind, take shelter far away, very far away. But they would follow until they caught up with me. "The murderer of Captain Torres. He slit his throat while he was shaving him. What a cowardly thing to do!"

And others would say: "The avenger of our people. A name to remember"—my name here. "He was the town barber. No one knew he was fighting for our cause."

And so, which will it be? Murderer or hero? My fate hangs on the edge of this razor blade. I can turn my wrist slightly, put a bit more pressure on the blade, let it sink in. The skin will yield like silk, like rubber, like the strop. There is nothing more tender than a man's skin, and the blood is always there, ready to burst forth. A razor like this cannot fail. It is the best one I have.

But I don't want to be a murderer. No, sir. You came in to be shaved. And I do my work honorably. I don't want to stain my hands with blood. Just with lather, and nothing else. You are an executioner; I am only a barber. Each one to his job. That's it. Each one to his job.

The chin was now clean, polished, soft. The man got up and looked at himself in the glass. He ran his hand over the skin and felt its freshness, its newness.

"Thanks," he said. He walked to the wardrobe for his belt, his pistol, and his cap. I must have been very pale, and I felt my shirt soaked with sweat. Torres finished adjusting his belt buckle, straightened his gun in its holster, and, smoothing his hair mechanically, put on his cap. From his trousers pocket he took some coins to pay for the shave. And he started toward the door. On the threshold he stopped for a moment, and turning toward me he said:

"They told me you would kill me. I came to find out if it was true. But it's not easy to kill. I know what I'm talking about."

FOR DISCUSSION

1. Was there any clue that Torres might know what was going through the barber's mind?

2. What effect did the ending have on your impression of Torres?

3. How did the barber justify his decision not to kill his enemy? Would Torres agree that this was the real reason for his decision?

FOR COMPOSITION

• Should the barber have killed Torres? Answer yes or no and defend your position with reasonable and logical arguments.

War makes enemies of strangers who might have been friends.

THE MAN HE KILLED
THOMAS HARDY

"Had he and I but met
By some old ancient inn,
We should have sat us down to wet
Right many a nipperkin!*

"But ranged as infantry,   5
And staring face to face,
I shot at him as he at me,
And killed him in his place.

"I shot him dead because—
Because he was my foe,   10
Just so—my foe of course he was;
That's clear enough; although

"He thought he'd 'list, perhaps,
Off-hand like—just as I—
Was out of work—had sold his traps—   15
No other reason why.

"Yes; quaint and curious war is!
You shoot a fellow down
You'd treat if met where any bar is,
Or help to half-a-crown."   20

4 NIPPERKIN: a half pint of ale.

FOR DISCUSSION

1. Why did the young man speaking in this poem decide to enlist?
2. What feelings of his about war and killing are revealed in the third stanza? Does the rest of the poem confirm or deny the poet's thoughts in the third stanza?

Reprinted with permission of The Macmillan Company from *Collected Poems* by Thomas Hardy. Copyright 1925 by The Macmillan Company.

One of the most glamorous jobs a nineteenth-century American boy could imagine was piloting a Mississippi River steamboat. Samuel Clemens loved the work so much that when he later became a writer he took his pen name from the riverman's call for safe water: "Mark Twain!" In this excerpt from his book Life on the Mississippi *he tells about coming to terms not only with the treacherous Mississippi, but with his own courage and a faultfinding teacher as well.*

FROM

LIFE ON THE MISSISSIPPI
MARK TWAIN

THERE IS ONE faculty which a pilot must incessantly cultivate until he has brought it to absolute perfection. Nothing short of perfection will do. That faculty is memory. He cannot stop with merely thinking a thing is so and so; he must *know* it, for this is eminently one of the "exact" sciences. With what scorn a pilot was looked upon in the old times if he ever ventured to deal in that feeble phrase "I think," instead of the vigorous one "I know!"

One cannot easily realize what a tremendous thing it is to know every trivial detail of twelve hundred miles of river and know it with absolute exactness. If you will take the longest street in New York and travel up and down it, conning its features patiently until you know every house and window and lamppost and big and little sign by heart, and know them so accurately that you can instantly name the one you are abreast of when you are set down at random in that street in the middle of an inky black night, you will then have a tolerable notion of the amount and the exactness of a pilot's knowledge who carries the Mississippi River in his head. And then, if you will go on until you know every street crossing, the character, size, and position of the crossing-stones,[1] and the varying depth of mud in each of those numberless places, you will have some idea of what the pilot must know in order to keep a Mississippi steamer out of trouble. Next, if you will take half of the signs in that long street, and *change their places* once a month, and still manage to know their new positions accurately on dark nights, and keep up with these repeated changes without making any mistakes, you will understand what is required of a pilot's peerless memory by the fickle Mississippi.

A pilot must have a memory, but there are two higher qualities which he must also have. He must have good and quick judgment and decision and a cool, calm courage that no peril can shake. Give a man the merest trifle of pluck to start with, and by the time he has become a pilot he cannot be unmanned by any danger a steamboat

From pp. 109–118 in *Life on the Mississippi* by Mark Twain, (Harper & Row). Reprinted by permission of Harper & Row, Publishers, Inc.

[1] CROSSING-STONES: flat stones placed in unpaved streets to keep pedestrians out of the mud.

can get into; but one cannot quite say the same for judgment. Judgment is a matter of brains, and a man must *start* with a good stock of that article or he will never succeed as a pilot.

The growth of courage in the pilothouse is steady all the time, but it does not reach a high and satisfactory condition until some time after the young pilot has been "standing his own watch" alone and under the staggering weight of all the responsibilities connected with the position. When an apprentice has become pretty thoroughly acquainted with the river, he goes clattering along so fearlessly with his steamboat, night or day, that he presently begins to imagine that it is *his* courage that animates him; but the first time the pilot steps out and leaves him to his own devices he finds out it was the other man's. He discovers that the article has been left out of his own cargo altogether. The whole river is bristling with exigencies in a moment; he is not prepared for them; he does not know how to meet them; all his knowledge forsakes him; and within fifteen minutes he is as white as a sheet and scared almost to death. Therefore pilots wisely train these cubs by various strategic tricks to look danger in the face a little more calmly. A favorite way of theirs is to play a friendly swindle upon the candidate.

Mr. Bixby served me in this fashion once, and for years afterwards I used to blush, even in my sleep, when I thought of it. I had become a good steersman, so good, indeed, that I had all the work to do on our watch, night and day. Mr. Bixby seldom made a suggestion to me; all he ever did was to take the wheel on particularly bad nights or in particularly bad crossings,[1] land the boat when she needed to be

landed, play gentleman of leisure nine tenths of the watch, and collect the wages. The lower river was about bank-full, and if anybody had questioned my ability to run any crossing between Cairo and New Orleans without help or instruction, I should have felt irreparably hurt. The idea of being afraid of any crossing in the lot, in the *daytime,* was a thing too preposterous for contemplation.

Well, one matchless summer's day I was bowling down the bend above Island 66, brimful of self-conceit and carrying my nose as high as a giraffe's, when Mr. Bixby said, "I am going below a while. I suppose you know the next crossing?"

This was almost an affront. It was about the plainest and simplest crossing in the whole river. One couldn't come to any harm, whether he ran it right or not; and as for depth, there never had been any bottom there. I knew all this perfectly well.

"Know how to *run* it? Why, I can run it with my eyes shut."

"How much water is there in it?"

"Well, that is an odd question. I couldn't get bottom there with a church steeple."

"You think so, do you?"

The very tone of the question shook my confidence. That was what Mr. Bixby was expecting. He left, without saying anything more. I began to imagine all sorts of things. Mr. Bixby, unknown to me, of course, sent somebody down to the forecastle[2] with some mysterious instructions to the leadsmen,[3] another messenger was sent to whisper among the officers, and then Mr. Bixby went into hiding behind a smokestack where he could observe results. Presently the captain stepped out on the hurricane deck; next the chief mate ap-

---

[1] CROSSINGS: places where the steamboat had to cross from one side of the river to the other, in order to stay in navigable water.

[2] FORECASTLE (fōk′ səl): section of the forward part of the boat.

[3] LEADSMEN (lĕdz′ mən): men who determine the depth of the water by using a line weighted with lead and marked off in fathoms.

peared; then a clerk. Every moment or two a straggler was added to my audience, and before I got to the head of the island, I had fifteen or twenty people assembled down there under my nose. I began to wonder what the trouble was.

As I started across, the captain glanced aloft at me and said, with a sham uneasiness in his voice, "Where is Mr. Bixby?"

"Gone below, sir."

But that did the business for me. My imagination began to construct dangers out of nothing, and they multiplied faster than I could keep the run of them. All at once I imagined I saw shoal[1] water ahead! The wave of coward agony that surged through me then came near dislocating every joint in me. All my confidence in that crossing vanished. I seized the bell rope; dropped it, ashamed; seized it again; dropped it once more; clutched it tremblingly once again, and pulled it[2] so feebly that I could hardly hear the stroke myself.

Captain and mate sang out instantly, and both together, "Starboard lead there! and quick about it!"

This was another shock. I began to climb the wheel like a squirrel; but I would hardly get the boat started to port[3] before I would see new dangers on that side, and away I would spin to the other; only to find perils accumulating to starboard, and be crazy to get to port again.

Then came the leadsman's sepulchral cry: "D-e-e-p four!"[4]

Deep four in a bottomless crossing! The terror of it took my breath away.

"M-a-r-k three! M-a-r-k three! Quarter-less-three! Half twain!"

This was frightful! I seized the bell ropes and stopped the engines.

"Quarter twain! Quarter twain! *Mark twain!*"

I was helpless. I did not know what in the world to do. I was quaking from head to foot, and I could have hung my hat on my eyes, they stuck out so far.

"Quarter-*less*-twain! Nine and a *half!*"[5]

We were *drawing* nine![6] My hands were in a nerveless flutter. I could not ring a bell intelligibly with them. I flew to the speaking-tube and shouted to the engineer, "Oh, Ben, if you love me, *back* her! Quick, Ben! Oh, back the immortal *soul* out of her!"

I heard the door close gently. I looked around, and there stood Mr. Bixby, smiling a bland, sweet smile. Then the audience on the hurricane deck sent up a thundergust of humiliating laughter. I saw it all now, and I felt meaner than the meanest man in human history.

I laid in the lead, set the boat in her marks, came ahead on the engines,[7] and said, "It was a fine trick to play on an orphan, *wasn't* it? I suppose I'll never hear the last of how I was ass enough to heave the lead[8] at the head of 66."

"Well, no, you won't, maybe. In fact I hope you won't, for I want you to learn something by that experience. Didn't you *know* there was no bottom in that crossing?"

"Yes, sir, I did."

"Very well, then. You shouldn't have allowed me or anybody else to shake your

---

[1] SHOAL: shallow.
[2] PULLED IT: to direct a leadsman to measure the water depth on the starboard (right) side of the boat.
[3] PORT: the left.
[4] DEEP FOUR: four fathoms (24 feet) deep.

[5] NINE AND A HALF: feet.
[6] DRAWING NINE: The boat was displacing nine feet of water, leaving only six inches of water between its keel and the river bottom.
[7] LAID IN . . . ENGINES: had the depth-measuring lines pulled on board again, set the boat on course (according to the landmarks used for steering through this stretch of the river), and called for more speed.
[8] HEAVE THE LEAD: request that depth measurements be taken.

confidence in that knowledge. Try to re-member that. And another thing: when you get into a dangerous place, don't turn coward. That isn't going to help matters any."

It was a good enough lesson, but pretty hardly learned. Yet about the hardest part of it was that for months I so often had to hear a phrase which I had conceived a par-ticular distaste for. It was "Oh, Ben, if you love me, back her!"

During the two or two and a half years of my apprenticeship I served under many pilots and had experience of many kinds of steamboatmen and many varieties of steamboats, for it was not always conven-ient for Mr. Bixby to have me with him, and in such cases he sent me with some-body else. I am to this day profiting some-what by that experience, for in that brief, sharp schooling I got personally and famil-iarly acquainted with about all the different types of human nature that are to be found in fiction, biography, or history. The fact is daily borne in upon me that the average shore-employment requires as much as forty years to equip a man with this sort of an education. When I say I am still profiting by this thing, I do not mean that it has constituted me a judge of men—no, it has not done that, for judges of men are born, not made. My profit is various in kind and degree, but the feature of it which I value most is the zest which that early experience has given to my later reading. When I find a well-drawn character in fic-tion or biography, I generally take a warm, personal interest in him, for the reason that I have known him before—met him on the river.

The figure that comes before me often-est, out of the shadows of that vanished time, is that of Brown, of the steamer *Pennsylvania.* He was a middle-aged, long, slim, bony, smooth-shaven, horse-faced,

ignorant, stingy, malicious, snarling, fault-hunting, mote-magnifying tyrant. I early got the habit of coming on watch with dread at my heart. No matter how good a time I might have been having with the off-watch below, and no matter how high my spirits might be when I started aloft, my soul became lead in my body the mo-ment I approached the pilothouse.

I still remember the first time I ever entered the presence of that man. The boat had backed out from St. Louis and was "straightening down." I ascended to the pilothouse in high feather and very proud to be semiofficially a member of the execu-tive family of so fast and famous a boat. Brown was at the wheel. I paused in the middle of the room, all fixed to make my bow, but Brown did not look around. I thought he took a furtive glance at me out of the corner of his eye, but as not even this notice was repeated, I judged I had been mistaken. By this time he was picking his way among some dangerous "breaks"[1] abreast the wood-yards; therefore it would not be proper to interrupt him; so I stepped softly to the high bench and took a seat.

There was silence for ten minutes; then my new boss turned and inspected me de-liberately and painstakingly from head to heel for about—as it seemed to me—a quarter of an hour. After which he re-moved his countenance, and I saw it no more for some seconds; then it came around once more, and this question greeted me: "Are you Horace Bixby's cub?"

"Yes, sir."

After this there was a pause and another inspection. Then: "What's your name?"

I told him. He repeated it after me. It was probably the only thing he ever forgot, for although I was with him many months, he never addressed himself to me in any

[1] "BREAKS": places where the surface of the water is broken by snags, rocks, or other objects.

other way than "Here!" and then his command followed.

"Where was you born?"

"In Florida, Missouri."

A pause. Then: "Dern sight better stayed there!"

By means of a dozen or so of pretty direct questions, he pumped my family history out of me.

The leads were going[1] now in the first crossing. This interrupted the inquest. When the leads had been laid in, he resumed: "How long you been on the river?"

I told him.

After a pause: "Where'd you get them shoes?"

I gave him the information.

"Hold up your foot!"

I did so. He stepped back, examined the shoe minutely and contemptuously, scratching his head thoughtfully, tilting his high sugar-loaf hat well forward to facilitate the operation, then ejaculated, "Well, I'll be dod derned!" and returned to his wheel.

What occasion there was to be dod derned about it is a thing which is still as much of a mystery to me now as it was then. It must have been all of fifteen minutes—fifteen minutes of dull, homesick silence—before that long horse-face swung round upon me again—and then what a change! It was as red as fire, and every muscle in it was working. Now came this shriek: "Here! You going to set there all day?"

I lit in the middle of the floor, shot there by the electric suddenness of the surprise. As soon as I could get my voice, I said apologetically, "I have had no orders, sir."

"You've had no *orders!* My, what a fine bird we are! We must have *orders!* Our father was a *gentleman*—owned slaves—and *we've* been to *school*. Yes, *we* are a gentleman, *too*, and got to have *orders!* ORDERS, is it? ORDERS is what you want! Dod dern my skin, *I'll* learn you to swell yourself up and blow around *here* about your dod-derned *orders!* G'way from the wheel!" (I had approached it without knowing it.)

I moved back a step or two and stood as in a dream, all my senses stupefied by this frantic assault.

"What you standing there for? Take that ice pitcher down to the texas-tender![2] Come, move along, and don't you be all day about it!"

The moment I got back to the pilothouse Brown said, "Here! What was you doing down there all this time?"

"I couldn't find the texas-tender; I had to go all the way to the pantry."

"Derned likely story! Fill up the stove."

I proceeded to do so. He watched me like a cat. Presently he shouted, "Put down that shovel! Derndest numskull I ever saw—ain't even got sense enough to load up a stove."

All through the watch this sort of thing went on. Yes, and the subsequent watches were much like it during a stretch of months. As I have said, I soon got the habit of coming on duty with dread. The moment I was in the presence, even in the darkest night, I could feel those yellow eyes upon me and knew their owner was watching for a pretext to spit out some venom on me. Preliminarily he would say, "Here! Take the wheel."

Two minutes later: "*Where* in the nation you going to? Pull her down![3] Pull her down!"

[1] THE LEADS WERE GOING: Depth measurements were being taken.

[2] TEXAS-TENDER: waiter on the texas, or top deck.

[3] PULL HER DOWN: Brown was directing Sam to pull down hard on the steering wheel in order to turn the boat. At other times the cub helped the pilot turn the wheel.

After another moment: "Say! You going to hold her all day? Let her go—meet her![1] Meet her!"

Then he would jump from the bench, snatch the wheel from me, and meet her himself, pouring out wrath upon me all the time.

George Ritchie was the other pilot's cub. He was having good times· now, for his boss, George Ealer, was as kindhearted as Brown wasn't. Ritchie had steered for Brown the season before; consequently he knew exactly how to entertain himself and plague me, all by the one operation. Whenever I took the wheel for a moment on Ealer's watch, Ritchie would sit back on the bench and play Brown, with continual ejaculations of "Snatch her! snatch her! Derndest mudcat I ever saw!" "Here! Where are you going *now*? Going to run over that snag?" "Pull her *down!* Don't you hear me? Pull her *down!*" "There she goes! *Just* as I expected! I *told* you not to cramp that reef. G'way from the wheel!"

So I always had a rough time of it, no matter whose watch it was, and sometimes it seemed to me that Ritchie's good-natured badgering was pretty nearly as aggravating as Brown's dead-earnest nagging.

I often wanted to kill Brown, but this would not answer. A cub had to take everything his boss gave in the way of vigorous comment and criticism; and we all believed that there was a United States law making it a penitentiary offense to strike or threaten a pilot who was on duty. However, I could *imagine* myself killing Brown; there was no law against that; and that was the thing I used always to do the moment I was abed. Instead of going over my river in my mind, as was my duty, I threw business aside for pleasure, and killed Brown. I killed Brown every night

for months, not in old, stale, commonplace ways, but in new and picturesque ones— ways that were sometimes surprising for freshness of design and ghastliness of situation and environment.

Brown was *always* watching for a pretext to find fault, and if he could find no plausible pretext, he would invent one. He would scold you for shaving a shore, and for not shaving it; for hugging a bar, and for not hugging it; for "pulling down" when not invited, and for *not* pulling down when not invited; for firing up without orders, and for waiting *for* orders. In a word, it was his invariable rule to find fault with *everything* you did, and another invariable rule of his was to throw all his remarks (to you) into the form of an insult.

One day we were approaching New Madrid,[2] bound down[3] and heavily laden. Brown was at one side of the wheel, steering; I was at the other, standing by to "pull down" or "shove up." He cast a furtive glance at me every now and then. I had long ago learned what that meant; viz., he was trying to invent a trap for me. I wondered what shape it was going to take. By and by he stepped back from the wheel and said in his usual snarly way, "Here! See if you've got gumption enough to round her to."[4]

This was simply *bound* to be a success; nothing could prevent it, for he had never allowed me to round the boat to before; consequently no matter how I might do the thing, he could find free fault with it. He stood back there with his greedy eye on me, and the result was what might have been foreseen: I lost my head in a quarter of a minute and didn't know what I was about; I started too early to bring the boat around, but detected a green gleam of joy

---

[1] MEET HER: turn the wheel in the other direction.

[2] NEW MADRID: in southern Missouri.
[3] BOUND DOWN: going downstream.
[4] ROUND HER TO: dock the boat.

in Brown's eye and corrected my mistake. I started around once more while too high up, but corrected myself again in time. I made other false moves, and still managed to save myself; but at last I grew so confused and anxious that I tumbled into the very worst blunder of all—I got too far *down* before beginning to fetch the boat around. Brown's chance was come.

His face turned red with passion; he made one bound, hurled me across the house with a sweep of his arm, spun the wheel down, and began to pour out a stream of vituperation upon me which lasted till he was out of breath. In the course of this speech he called me all the different kinds of hard names he could think of, and once or twice I thought he was even going to swear—but he had never done that, and he didn't this time. "Dod dern" was the nearest he ventured to the luxury of swearing, for he had been brought up with a wholesome respect for future fire and brimstone.

That was an uncomfortable hour, for there was a big audience on the hurricane deck. When I went to bed that night, I killed Brown in seventeen different ways—all of them new.

Two trips later I got into serious trouble. Brown was steering; I was "pulling down." My younger brother appeared on the hurricane deck, and shouted to Brown to stop at some landing or other a mile or so below. Brown gave no intimation that he had heard anything. But that was his way: he never condescended to take notice of an underclerk. The wind was blowing; Brown was deaf (although he always pretended he wasn't), and I very much doubted if he had heard the order. If I had had two heads, I would have spoken, but as I had only one, it seemed judicious to take care of it, so I kept still.

Presently, sure enough, we went sailing by that plantation. Captain Klinefelter ap-peared on the deck and said, "Let her come around, sir, let her come around. Didn't Henry tell you to land here?"

"*No*, sir!"

"I sent him up to do it."

"He *did* come up, and that's all the good it done, the dod-derned fool. He never said anything."

"Didn't *you* hear him?" asked the captain of me.

Of course I didn't want to be mixed up in this business, but there was no way to avoid it, so I said, "Yes, sir."

I knew what Brown's next remark would be, before he uttered it. It was: "Shut your mouth! You never heard anything of the kind."

I closed my mouth, according to instructions. An hour later Henry entered the pilothouse, unaware of what had been going on. He was a thoroughly inoffensive boy, and I was sorry to see him come, for I knew Brown would have no pity on him.

Brown began, straightway, "Here! Why didn't you tell me we'd got to land at that plantation?"

"I did tell you, Mr. Brown."

"It's a lie!"

I said, "You lie, yourself. He did tell you."

Brown glared at me in unaffected surprise, and for as much as a moment he was entirely speechless; then he shouted to me, "I'll attend to your case in a half a minute!" then to Henry, "And you leave the pilothouse; out with you!"

It was pilot law, and must be obeyed. The boy started out, and even had his foot on the upper step outside the door, when Brown, with a sudden access of fury, picked up a ten-pound lump of coal and sprang after him; but I was between, with a heavy stool, and I hit Brown a good honest blow which stretched him out.

I had committed the crime of crimes—I had lifted my hand against a pilot on

duty! I supposed I was booked for the penitentiary sure and couldn't be booked any surer if I went on and squared my long account with this person while I had the chance; consequently I stuck to him and pounded him with my fists a considerable time. I do not know how long; the pleasure of it probably made it seem longer than it really was; but in the end he struggled free and jumped up and sprang to the wheel—a very natural solicitude, for all this time here was this steamboat tearing down the river at the rate of fifteen miles an hour and nobody at the helm! However, Eagle Bend was two miles wide at this bank-full stage, and correspondingly long and deep; and the boat was steering herself straight down the middle and taking no chances. Still, that was only luck—a body *might* have found her charging into the woods.

Perceiving at a glance that the *Pennsylvania* was in no danger, Brown gathered up the big spyglass, war-club fashion, and ordered me out of the pilothouse with more than Comanche bluster. But I was not afraid of him now, so instead of going, I tarried. He presently laid aside his glass and took the wheel, muttering and shaking his head, and I retired to the bench. The racket had brought everybody to the hurricane deck, and I trembled when I saw the old captain looking up from amid the crowd. I said to myself, "Now I *am* done for!" for although, as a rule, he was so fatherly and indulgent toward the boat's family and so patient of minor shortcomings, he could be stern enough when the fault was worth it.

I tried to imagine what he *would* do to a cub pilot who had been guilty of such a crime as mine, committed on a boat guard-deep with costly freight and alive with passengers. Our watch was nearly ended. I thought I would go and hide somewhere till I got a chance to slide ashore. So I slipped out of the pilothouse and down the steps and around to the texas door, and was in the act of gliding within, when the captain confronted me! I dropped my head, and he stood over me in silence a moment or two, then said impressively, "Follow me."

I dropped into his wake; he led the way to his parlor in the forward end of the texas. We were alone now. He closed the after door, then moved slowly to the forward one and closed that. He sat down; I stood before him. He looked at me some little time, then said, "So you have been fighting Mr. Brown?"

I answered meekly, "Yes, sir."

"Do you know that that is a very serious matter?"

"Yes, sir."

"Are you aware that this boat was plowing down the river fully five minutes with no one at the wheel?"

"Yes, sir."

"Did you strike him first?"

"Yes, sir."

"What with?"

"A stool, sir."

"Hard?"

"Middling, sir."

"Did you knock him down?"

"He—he fell, sir."

"Did you follow it up? Did you do anything further?"

"Yes, sir."

"What did you do?"

"Pounded him, sir."

"Pounded him?"

"Yes, sir."

"Did you pound him much? That is, severely?"

"One might call it that, sir, maybe."

"I'm deuced glad of it! Hark ye, never mention that I said that. You have been guilty of a great crime; and don't you ever be guilty of it again on this boat."

FOR DISCUSSION

1. What caused Sam finally to fight Mr. Brown? What had kept him from doing so sooner?

2. How did Mr. Brown make Sam's life miserable? Did he treat others in the same way?

3. Mr. Bixby also humiliated Sam. How were the traps that the two men set for their apprentices different?

4. Looking back, what did Mark Twain feel that he had gained from working with these two men?

FOR COMPOSITION

1. Write a character description which, like Mark Twain's description of Brown, exaggerates one main characteristic. You might begin with a trait—greed, laziness, talkativeness, timidity, forgetfulness—and exaggerate it in every part of his appearance and behavior to a ridiculous extreme.

2. Instead of describing your character, as suggested above, *show* what he is like by writing a dialogue between him and another person. Again, emphasize one main characteristic to a comic degree.

"When it is seventy-five below zero, a man must not fail in his first attempt to build a fire—that is, if his feet are wet."

TO BUILD A FIRE

JACK LONDON

DAY HAD BROKEN cold and gray, exceedingly cold and gray, when the man turned aside from the main Yukon[1] trail and climbed the high earth-bank, where a dim and little-traveled trail led eastward through the fat spruce timberland. It was a steep bank, and he paused for breath at the top, excusing the act to himself by looking at his watch. It was nine o'clock. There was no sun nor hint of sun, though there was not a cloud in the sky. It was a clear day, and yet there seemed an intangible pall over the face of things, a subtle gloom that made the day dark, and that was due to the absence of sun. This fact did not worry the man. He was used to the lack of sun. It had been days since he had seen the sun, and he knew that a few more days must pass before that cheerful orb, due south, would just peep above the skyline and dip immediately from view.

The man flung a look back along the way he had come. The Yukon lay a mile wide and hidden under three feet of ice. On top of this ice were as many feet of snow. It was all pure white, rolling in gentle undulations where the ice-jams of the freeze-up had formed. North and south, as far as his eye could see, it was unbroken white, save for a dark hairline that curved and twisted from around the spruce-covered island to the south, and that curved and twisted away into the north, where it disappeared behind another spruce-covered island. This dark hairline was the trail—the main trail—that led south five hundred miles to the Chilcoot Pass, Dyea, and salt water; and that led north seventy miles to Dawson, and still on to the north a thousand miles to Nulato, and finally to St. Michael on Bering Sea, a thousand miles and half a thousand more.

But all this—the mysterious, far-reaching hairline trail, the absence of sun from the sky, the tremendous cold, and the strangeness and weirdness of it all—made no impression on the man. It was not because he was long used to it. He was a newcomer in the land, a chechago,[2] and this was his first winter. The trouble with him was that he was without imagination. He was quick and alert in the things of life, but only in the things, and not in the significances. Fifty degrees below zero meant eighty-odd degrees of frost. Such fact impressed him as being cold and uncomfortable, and that was all. It did not lead him to meditate upon his frailty as a creature of temperature, and upon man's frailty in general, able only to live within certain narrow limits of heat and cold; and from there on it did not lead him to the conjectural field of immortality and man's place

[1] YUKON: river flowing from Canada through Alaska to the Bering Sea.

[2] CHECHAGO: tenderfoot, a Chinook Indian word.

in the universe. Fifty degrees below zero stood for a bite of frost that hurt and that must be guarded against by the use of mittens, ear flaps, warm moccasins, and thick socks. Fifty degrees below zero was to him just precisely fifty degrees below zero. That there should be anything more to it than that was a thought that never entered his head.

As he turned to go on, he spat speculatively. There was a sharp, explosive crackle that startled him. He spat again. And again, in the air, before it could fall to the snow, the spittle crackled. He knew that at fifty below spittle crackled on the snow, but this spittle had crackled in the air. Undoubtedly it was colder than fifty below—how much colder he did not know. But the temperature did not matter. He was bound for the old claim on the left fork of Henderson Creek, where the boys were already. They had come over across the divide from the Indian Creek country, while he had come the roundabout way to take a look at the possibilities of getting out logs in the spring from the islands in the Yukon. He would be in to camp by six o'clock; a bit after dark, it was true, but the boys would be there, a fire would be going, and a hot supper would be ready. As for lunch, he pressed his hand against the protruding bundle under his jacket. It was also under his shirt, wrapped up in a handkerchief and lying against the naked skin. It was the only way to keep the biscuits from freezing. He smiled agreeably to himself as he thought of those biscuits, each cut open and sopped in bacon grease, and each inclosing a generous slice of fried bacon.

He plunged in among the big spruce trees. The trail was faint. A foot of snow had fallen since the last sled had passed over, and he was glad he was without a sled, traveling light. In fact he carried nothing but the lunch wrapped in the handkerchief. He was surprised, however,

at the cold. It certainly was cold, he concluded, as he rubbed his numb nose and cheekbones with his mittened hand. He was a warm-whiskered man, but the hair on his face did not protect the high cheekbones and the eager nose that thrust itself aggressively into the frosty air.

At the man's heels trotted a dog, a big native husky, the proper wolf-dog, gray-coated and without any visible or temperamental difference from its brother, the wild wolf. The animal was depressed by the tremendous cold. It knew that it was no time for traveling. Its instinct told it a truer tale than was told to the man by the man's judgment. In reality, it was not merely colder than fifty below zero; it was colder than sixty below, than seventy below. It was seventy-five below zero. Since the freezing point is thirty-two above zero, it meant that one hundred and seven degrees of frost obtained. The dog did not know anything about thermometers. Possibly in its brain there was no sharp consciousness of a condition of very cold such as was in the man's brain. But the brute had its instinct. It experienced a vague but menacing apprehension that subdued it and made it slink along at the man's heels, and that made it question eagerly every unwonted movement of the man as if expecting him to go into camp or to seek shelter somewhere and build a fire. The dog had learned fire, and it wanted fire, or else to burrow under the snow and cuddle its warmth away from the air.

The frozen moisture of its breathing had settled on its fur in a fine powder of frost, and especially where its jowls, muzzle, and eyelashes whitened by its crystalled breath. The man's red beard and mustache were likewise frosted, but more solidly, the deposit taking the form of ice and increasing with every warm, moist breath he exhaled. Also, the man was chewing tobacco, and the muzzle of ice held his lips so rigidly that he was unable to clear his chin when he expelled the juice. The result was that a crystal beard of the color and solidity of amber was increasing its length on his chin. If he fell down it would shatter itself, like glass, into brittle fragments. But he did not mind the appendage. It was the penalty all tobacco chewers paid in that country, and he had been out before in two cold snaps. They had not been so cold as this, he knew, but by the spirit thermometer at Sixty Mile he knew they had been registered at fifty below and at fifty-five.

He held on through the level stretch of woods for several miles, crossed a wide flat and dropped down a bank to the frozen bed of a small stream. This was Henderson Creek, and he knew he was ten miles from the forks. He looked at his watch. It was ten o'clock. He was making four miles an hour, and he calculated that he would arrive at the works at half-past twelve. He decided to celebrate that event by eating his lunch there.

The dog dropped in again at his heels, with a tail drooping discouragement, as the man swung along the creek bed. The furrow of the old sled trail was plainly visible, but a dozen inches of snow covered the marks of the last runners. In a month no man had come up or down that silent creek. The man held steadily on. He was not much given to thinking, and just then particularly he had nothing to think about save that he would eat lunch at the forks and that at six o'clock he would be in camp with the boys. There was nobody to talk to; and, had there been, speech would have been impossible because of the ice muzzle on his mouth. So he continued monotonously to chew tobacco and to increase the length of his amber beard.

Once in a while the thought reiterated itself that it was very cold and that he had never experienced such cold. As he walked along he rubbed his cheekbones and nose with the back of his mittened hand. He did this automatically, now and again changing hands. But rub as he would, the instant he stopped his cheekbones went numb, and the following instant the end of his nose went numb. He was sure to frost his cheeks; he knew that, and experienced a pang of regret that he had not devised a nose strap of the sort Bud wore in cold snaps. Such a strap passed across the cheeks as well, and saved them. But it didn't matter much, after all. What were frosted cheeks? A bit painful, that was all; they were never serious.

Empty as the man's mind was of thoughts, he was keenly observant, and he noticed the changes in the creek, the curves and bends and timber jams, and always he sharply noted where he placed his feet. Once, coming around a bend, he shied abruptly, like a startled horse, curved away from the place where he had been walking, and retreated several paces back along the trail. The creek, he knew, was frozen clear to the bottom,—no creek could contain water in that arctic winter,—but he knew also that there were springs that bubbled out from the hillsides and ran along under the snow and on top of the ice of the creek. He knew that the coldest snaps never froze these springs and he knew likewise their danger. They were traps. They hid pools of water under the snow that might be three inches deep, or three feet. Sometimes a skin of ice half an inch thick covered them, and in turn was covered by the snow. Sometimes there were alternate layers of water and ice-skin, so that when one broke through he kept on breaking through for a while, sometimes wetting himself to the waist.

That was why he had shied in such panic. He had felt the give under his feet and heard the crackle of a snow-hidden ice-skin. And to get his feet wet in such a temperature meant trouble and danger. At the very least it meant delay, for he would be forced to stop and build a fire, and under its protection to bare his feet while he dried his socks and moccasins. He stood and studied the creekbed and its banks, and decided that the flow of water came from the right. He reflected a while, rubbing his nose and cheeks, then skirted to the left, stepping gingerly and testing the footing for each step. Once clear of the danger, he took a fresh chew of tobacco and swung along at his four-mile gait.

In the course of the next two hours he came upon several similar traps. Usually the snow above the hidden pools had a sunken, candied appearance that advertised the danger. Once again, however, he had a close call; and once, suspecting danger, he compelled the dog to go on in front. The dog did not want to go. It hung back until the man shoved it forward, and then it went quickly across the white, unbroken surface. Suddenly it broke through, floundered to one side, and got away to firmer footing. It had wet its forefeet and legs, and almost immediately the water that clung to it turned to ice. It made quick efforts to lick the ice off its legs, then dropped down in the snow and began to bite out the ice that had formed between the toes. This was a matter of instinct. To permit the ice to remain would mean sore feet. It did not know this. It merely obeyed the mysterious prompting that arose from the deep crypts of its being. But the man knew, having achieved a judgment on the subject, and he removed the mitten from his right hand and helped tear out the ice particles. He did not expose his fingers more than a minute, and was astonished at the swift numbness that smote them. It certainly was cold. He pulled on the mitten hastily, and beat the hand savagely across his chest.

At twelve o'clock the day was at its brightest. Yet the sun was too far south on its winter journey to clear the horizon. The bulge of the earth intervened between it and Henderson Creek, where the man walked under a clear sky at noon and cast no shadow. At half-past twelve, to the minute, he arrived at the forks of the creek. He was pleased at the speed he had made. If he kept it up, he would certainly be with the boys by six. He unbuttoned his jacket and shirt and drew forth his lunch. The action consumed no more than a quarter of a minute, yet in that brief moment the numbness laid hold of the exposed fingers. He did not put the mitten on, but, instead, struck the fingers a dozen sharp smashes against his leg. Then he sat down on a snow-covered log to eat. The sting that followed upon the striking of his fingers against his leg ceased so quickly that he was startled. He had had no chance to take a bite of biscuit. He struck the fingers repeatedly and returned them to the mitten, baring the other hand for the purpose of eating. He tried to take a mouthful, but the ice-muzzle prevented. He had forgotten to build a fire and thaw out. He chuckled at his foolishness, and as he chuckled he noted the numbness creeping into the exposed fingers. Also he noted that the stinging which had first come to his toes when he sat down was already passing away. He wondered whether the toes were warm or numb. He moved them inside the moccasins and decided that they were numb.

He pulled the mitten on hurriedly and stood up. He was a bit frightened. He stamped up and down until the stinging returned into the feet. It certainly was cold, was his thought. That man from Sulphur Creek had spoken the truth when telling how cold it sometimes got in the country. And he had laughed at him at the time! That showed one must not be too sure of things. There was no mistake about it, it *was* cold. He strode up and down, stamping his feet and threshing his arms, until reassured by the returning warmth. Then he got out matches and proceeded to make a fire. From the undergrowth, where high water of the previous spring had lodged a supply of seasoned twigs, he got his firewood. Working carefully from a small beginning, he soon had a roaring fire, over which he thawed the ice from his face and in the protection of which he ate his biscuits. For the moment the cold of space was outwitted. The dog took satisfaction in the fire, stretching out close enough for warmth and far enough away to escape being singed.

When the man had finished, he filled his pipe and took his comfortable time over a smoke. Then he pulled on his mittens, settled the ear flaps of his cap firmly about his ears, and took the creek trail up the left fork. The dog was disappointed and yearned back toward the fire. This man did not know cold. Possibly all the generations of his ancestry had been ignorant of cold, of real cold, of cold one hundred and seven degrees below freezing point. But the dog knew; all its ancestry knew, and it had inherited the knowledge. And it knew that it was not good to walk abroad in such fearful cold. It was the time to lie snug in a hole in the snow and wait for a curtain of cloud to be drawn across the face of outer space whence this cold came. On the other hand, there was no keen intimacy between the dog and the man. The one was the toil-slave of the other, and the only caresses it had ever received were the caresses of the whiplash and of harsh and menacing throat-sounds that threatened the whiplash. So the dog made no effort to communicate its apprehension to the man. It was not concerned in the welfare of the man; it was for its own sake that it yearned back toward the fire. But the man whistled, and spoke to it with the sound of whiplashes, and the dog swung in at the man's

heels and followed after.

The man took a chew of tobacco and proceeded to start a new amber beard. Also, his moist breath quickly powdered with white his mustache, eyebrows, and lashes. There did not seem to be so many springs on the left fork of the Henderson, and for half an hour the man saw no signs of any. And then it happened. At a place where there were no signs, where the soft, unbroken snow seemed to advertise solidity beneath, the man broke through. It was not deep. He wet himself halfway to the knees before he floundered out to the firm crust.

He was angry, and cursed his luck aloud. He had hoped to get into camp with the boys at six o'clock, and this would delay him an hour, for he would have to build a fire and dry out his footgear. This was imperative at that low temperature—he knew that much; and he turned aside to the bank, which he climbed. On top, tangled in the underbrush about the trunks of several small spruce trees, was a high-water deposit of dry firewood—sticks and twigs, principally, but also larger portions of seasoned branches and fine, dry, last year's grasses. He threw down several large pieces on top of the snow. This served for a foundation and prevented the young flame from drowning itself in the snow it otherwise would melt. The flame he got by touching a match to a small shred of birch bark that he took from his pocket. This burned even more readily than paper. Placing it on the foundation, he fed the young flame with wisps of dry grass and with the tiniest dry twigs.

He worked slowly and carefully, keenly aware of his danger. Gradually, as the flame grew stronger, he increased the size of the twigs with which he fed it. He squatted in the snow, pulling the twigs out from their entanglement in the brush and feeding directly to the flame. He knew there must be no failure. When it is seventy-five below zero, a man must not fail in his first attempt to build a fire—that is, if his feet are wet. If his feet are dry, and he fails, he can run along the trail for half a mile and restore his circulation. But the circulation of wet and freezing feet cannot be restored by running when it is seventy-five below. No matter how fast he runs, the wet feet will freeze the harder.

All this the man knew. The old-timer on Sulphur Creek had told him about it the previous fall, and now he was appreciating the advice. Already all sensation had gone out of his feet. To build the fire he had been forced to remove his mittens, and the fingers had quickly gone numb. His pace of four miles an hour had kept his heart pumping blood to the surface of his body and to all the extremities. But the instant he stopped, the action of the pump eased down. The cold of space smote the unprotected tip of the planet, and he, being on that unprotected tip, received the full force of the blow. The blood of his body recoiled before it. The blood was alive, like the dog, and like the dog it wanted to hide away and cover itself up from the fearful cold. So long as he walked four miles an hour, he pumped that blood, willy-nilly, to the surface; but now it ebbed away and sank down into the recesses of his body. The extremities were the first to feel its absence. His wet feet froze the faster, and his exposed fingers numbed the faster, though they had not yet begun to freeze. Nose and cheeks were already freezing, while the skin of all his body chilled as it lost its blood.

But he was safe. Toes and nose and cheeks would be only touched by the frost, for the fire was beginning to burn with strength. He was feeding it with twigs the size of his finger. In another minute he would be able to feed it with branches the size of his wrist, and then he could remove his wet foot-gear, and, while it dried, he could keep his naked feet warm by the fire, rubbing them at first, of course, with snow. The fire was a success. He was safe. He remembered the advice of the old-timer on Sulphur Creek, and smiled. The old-timer had been very serious in laying down the law that no man must travel alone in the Klondike after fifty below. Well, here he was; he had had the accident; he was alone; and he had saved himself. Those old-timers were rather womanish, some of them, he thought. All a man had to do was to keep his head, and he was all right. Any man who was a man could travel alone. But it was surprising the rapidity with which his cheeks and nose were freezing. And he had not thought his fingers could go lifeless in so short a time. Lifeless they were, for he could scarcely make them move together to grip a twig, and they seemed remote from his body and from him. When he touched a twig, he had to look and see whether or not he had hold of it. The wires were pretty well down between him and his finger-ends.

All of which counted for little. There was the fire, snapping and crackling and promising life with every dancing flame. He started to untie his moccasins. They were coated with ice; the thick German socks were like sheaths of iron halfway to the knees; and the moccasin strings were like rods of steel all twisted and knotted as by some conflagration. For a moment he tugged with his numb fingers, then, realizing the folly of it, he drew his sheath knife.

But before he could cut the strings it happened. It was his own fault, or, rather, his mistake. He should not have built the fire under the spruce tree. He should have built it in the open. But it had been easier to pull the twigs from the brush and drop them directly on the fire. Now the tree under which he had done this carried a weight of snow on its boughs. No wind had blown for weeks, and each bough was fully freighted. Each time he had pulled a twig he had communicated a slight agitation to the tree—an imperceptible agitation, so far as he was concerned, but an agitation sufficient to bring about the disaster. High up in the tree one bough capsized its load of snow. This fell on the boughs beneath, capsizing them. This process continued, spreading out and involving the whole tree. It grew like an avalanche, and it descended without warning upon the man and the fire, and the fire was blotted out! Where it had burned was a mantle of fresh and disordered snow.

The man was shocked. It was as though he had just heard his own sentence of death. For a moment he sat and stared at the spot where the fire had been. Then he grew very calm. Perhaps the old-timer on Sulphur Creek was right. If he had only had a trailmate he would have been in no danger now. The trailmate could have built the fire. Well, it was up to him to build the fire over again, and this second time there must be no failure. Even if he succeeded, he would most likely lose some toes. His feet must be badly frozen by now, and there would be some time before the second fire was ready.

Such were his thoughts, but he did not sit and think them. He was busy all the time they were passing through his mind. He made a new foundation for a fire, this time in the open, where no treacherous tree could blot it out. Next he gathered dry grasses and tiny twigs from the high-water flotsam. He could not bring his fingers together to pull them out, but he was able to gather them by the handful. In this way he got many rotten twigs and bits of green moss that were undesirable, but it was the best he could do. He worked methodically, even collecting an armful of the larger branches to be used later when the fire gathered strength. And all the while the dog sat and watched him, a certain yearning wistfulness in its eyes, for it looked upon him as the fire-provider, and the fire was slow in coming.

When all was ready, the man reached in his pocket for a second piece of birch bark. He knew the bark was there, and, though he could not feel it with his fingers, he could hear its crisp rustling as he fumbled for it. Try as he would, he could not clutch hold of it. And all the time, in his consciousness, was the knowledge that each instant his feet were freezing. This thought tended to put him in a panic, but he fought against it and kept calm. He pulled on his mittens with his teeth, and threshed his arms back and forth, beating his hands with all his might against his sides. He did this sitting down, and he stood up to do it; and all the while the dog sat in the snow, its wolf-brush of a tail curled around warmly over its forefeet, its sharp wolf-ears pricked forward intently as it watched the man. And the man, as he beat and threshed with his arms and hands felt a great surge of envy as he regarded the creature that was warm and secure in its natural covering.

After a time he was aware of the first faraway signals of sensation in his beaten fingers. The faint tingling grew stronger till it evolved into a stinging ache that was excruciating, but which the man hailed with satisfaction. He stripped the mitten from his right hand and fetched forth the birch bark. The exposed fingers were quickly going numb again. Next he brought out his bunch of sulphur matches. But the tremendous cold had already driven the life out of his fingers. In his effort to separate one match from the others, the whole bunch fell in the snow. He tried to pick it out of the snow, but failed. The dead fingers could neither touch nor clutch.

He was very careful. He drove the thought of his freezing feet, and nose, and cheeks, out of his mind, devoting his whole soul to the matches. He watched, using the sense of vision in place of that of touch, and when he saw his fingers on each side the bunch, he closed them—that is, he willed to close them, for the wires were down, and the fingers did not obey. He pulled the mitten on the right hand, and beat it fiercely against his knee. Then, with both mittened hands, he scooped the bunch of matches, along with much snow, into his lap. Yet he was no better off.

After some manipulation he managed to get the bunch between the heels of his mittened hands. In this fashion he carried it to his mouth. The ice crackled and snapped when by a violent effort he opened his mouth. He drew the lower jaw in, curled the upper lip out of the way, and scraped the bunch with his upper teeth in order to separate a match. He succeeded in getting one, which he dropped on his lap. He was no better off. He could not pick it up. Then he devised a way. He picked it up in his teeth and scratched it on his leg. Twenty times he scratched before he succeeded in lighting it. As it flamed he held it with his teeth to the birch bark. But the burning brimstone[1] went up his nostrils and into his lungs, causing him to cough spasmodically. The match fell into the snow and went out.

The old-timer on Sulphur Creek was right, he thought in the moment of controlled despair that ensued: after fifty below, a man should travel with a partner. He beat his hands, but failed in exciting any sensation. Suddenly he bared both hands, removing the mittens with his teeth. He caught the whole bunch between the heels of his hands. His arm muscles, not being frozen, enabled him to press the hand-heels tightly against the matches.

[1] BRIMSTONE: sulphur.

Then he scratched the bunch along his leg. It flared into flame, seventy sulphur matches at once! There was no wind to blow them out. He kept his head to one side to escape the strangling fumes, and held the blazing bunch to the birch bark. As he so held it, he became aware of sensation in his hand. His flesh was burning. He could smell it. Deep down below the surface he could feel it. The sensation developed into pain that grew acute. And still he endured it, holding the flame of the matches clumsily to the bark that would not light readily because his own burning hands were in the way, absorbing most of the flame.

At last, when he could endure no more, he jerked his hands apart. The blazing matches fell sizzling into the snow, but the birch bark was alight. He began laying dry grasses and the tiniest twigs on the flame. He could not pick and choose, for he had to lift the fuel between the heels of his hands. Small pieces of rotten wood and green moss clung to the twigs, and he bit them off as well as he could with his teeth. He cherished the flame carefully and awkwardly. It meant life, and it must not perish. The withdrawal of blood from the surface of his body now made him begin to shiver, and he grew more awkward. A large piece of green moss fell squarely on the little fire. He tried to poke it out with his fingers, but his shivering frame made him poke too far, and he disrupted the nucleus of the little fire, the burning grasses and tiny twigs separating and scattering. He tried to poke them together again, but in spite of the tenseness of the effort, his shivering got away with him, and the twigs were hopelessly scattered. Each twig gushed a puff of smoke and went out. The fire-provider had failed. As he looked apathetically about him, his eyes chanced on the dog, sitting across the ruins of the fire from him, in the snow, making restless, hunching movements, slightly lifting one forefoot and then the other, shifting its weight back and forth on them with wistful eagerness.

The sight of the dog put a wild idea into his head. He remembered the tale of the man, caught in a blizzard, who killed a steer and crawled inside the carcass, and so was saved. He would kill the dog and bury his hands in the warm body until the numbness went out of them. Then he could build another fire. He spoke to the dog, calling it to him; but in his voice was a strange note of fear that frightened the animal, who had never known the man to speak in such way before. Something was the matter, and its suspicious nature sensed danger—it knew not what danger, but somewhere, somehow, in its brain arose an apprehension of the man. It flattened its ears down at the sound of the man's voice, and its restless, hunching movements and the liftings and shiftings of its forefeet became more pronounced; but it would not come to the man. He got on his hands and knees and crawled toward the dog. This unusual posture again excited suspicion, and the animal sidled mincingly away.

The man sat up in the snow for a moment and struggled for calmness. Then he pulled on his mittens, by means of his teeth, and got upon his feet. He glanced down at first in order to assure himself that he was really standing up, for the absence of sensation in his feet left him unrelated to the earth. His erect position in itself started to drive the webs of suspicion from the dog's mind; and when he spoke peremptorily with the sound of whiplashes in his voice, the dog rendered its customary allegiance and came to him. As it came within reaching distance, the man lost his control. His arms flashed out to the dog, and he experienced genuine surprise when he discovered that his hands could not clutch, that there was neither

bend nor feeling in the fingers. He had forgotten for the moment that they were frozen and that they were freezing more and more. All this happened quickly, and before the animal could get away, he encircled its body with his arms. He sat down in the snow, and in this fashion held the dog, while it snarled and whined and struggled.

But it was all he could do, hold its body encircled in his arms and sit there. He realized that he could not kill the dog. There was no way to do it. With his helpless hands he could neither draw nor hold his sheath-knife nor throttle the animal. He released it, and it plunged wildly away, with tail between its legs, and still snarling. It halted forty feet away and surveyed him curiously, with ears sharply pricked forward. The man looked down at his hands in order to locate them, and found them hanging on the ends of his arms. It struck him as curious that one should have to use his eyes in order to find out where his hands were. He began threshing his arms back and forth, beating the mittened hands against his sides. He did this for five minutes, violently, and his heart pumped enough blood up to the surface to put a stop to his shivering. But no sensation was aroused in the hands. He had an impression that they hung like weights on the ends of his arms, but when he tried to run the impression down, he could not find it.

A certain fear of death, dull and oppressive, came to him. This fear quickly became poignant as he realized that it was no longer a mere matter of freezing his fingers and toes, or of losing his hands and feet, but that it was a matter of life and death, with the chances against him. This threw him into a panic, and he turned and ran up the creekbed along the old dim trail. The dog joined in behind and kept up with him. He ran blindly, without intention, in fear such as he had never known in his life. Slowly, as he plowed and floundered through the snow, he began to see things again,—the banks of the creek, the old timber-jams, the leafless aspens, and the sky. The running made him feel better. He did not shiver. Maybe, if he ran on, his feet would thaw out; and, anyway, if he ran far enough, he would reach the camp and the boys. Without doubt he would lose some fingers and toes and some of his face; but the boys would take care of him, and save the rest of him when he got there. And at the same time there was another thought in his mind that said he would never get to the camp and the boys; that it was too many miles away, that the freezing had too great a start on him, and that he would soon be stiff and dead. This thought he kept in the background and refused to consider. Sometimes it pushed itself forward and demanded to be heard, but he thrust it back and strove to think of other things.

It struck him as curious that he could run at all on feet so frozen that he could not feel them when they struck the earth and took the weight of his body. He seemed to himself to skim along above the surface, and to have no connection with the earth. Somewhere he had once seen a winged Mercury, and he wondered if Mercury felt as he felt when skimming over the earth.

His theory of running until he reached camp and the boys had one flaw in it: he lacked the endurance. Several times he stumbled, and finally he tottered, crumpled up, and fell. When he tried to rise, he failed. He must sit and rest, he decided, and next time he would merely walk and keep on going. As he sat and regained his breath, he noted that he was feeling quite warm and comfortable. He was not shivering, and it even seemed that a warm glow had come to his chest and trunk. And yet,

when he touched his nose or cheeks, there was no sensation. Running would not thaw them out. Nor would it thaw out his hands and feet. Then the thought came to him that the frozen portions of his body must be extending. He tried to keep this thought down, to forget it, to think of something else; he was aware of the panicky feeling that it caused, and he was afraid of the panic. But the thought asserted itself, and persisted, until it produced a vision of his body totally frozen. This was too much, and he made another wild run along the trail. Once he slowed down to a walk, but the thought of the freezing extending itself made him run again.

And all the time the dog ran with him, at his heels. When he fell down a second time, it curled its tail over its forefeet and sat in front of him, facing him, curiously eager and intent. The warmth and security of the animal angered him, and he cursed it till it flattened down its ears appeasingly. This time the shivering came more quickly upon the man. He was losing in his battle with the frost. It was creeping into his body from all sides. The thought of it drove him on, but he ran no more than a hundred feet, when he staggered and pitched headlong. It was his last panic. When he recovered his breath and control, he sat up and entertained in his mind the conception of meeting death with dignity. However, the conception did not come to him in such terms. His idea of it was that he had been making a fool of himself, running around like a chicken with its head cut off—such was the simile that occurred to him. Well, he was bound to freeze anyway, and he might as well take it decently. With this new-found peace of mind came the first glimmerings of drowsiness. A good idea, he thought, to sleep off to death. It was like taking an anesthetic. Freezing was not so bad as people thought. There were lots worse ways to die.

He pictured the boys finding his body next day. Suddenly he found himself with them, coming along the trail and looking for himself. And, still with them, he came around a turn in the trail and found himself lying in the snow. He did not belong with himself any more, for even then he was out of himself, standing with the boys looking at himself in the snow. It certainly was cold, was his thought. When he got back to the States, he could tell the folks what real cold was. He drifted on from this to a vision of the old-timer on Sulphur Creek. He could see him quite clearly, warm and comfortable, and smoking a pipe.

"You were right, old hoss; you were right," the man mumbled to the old-timer of Sulphur Creek.

Then the man drowsed off into what seemed to him the most comfortable and satisfying sleep he had ever known. The dog sat facing him and waiting. The brief day drew to a close in a long, slow twilight. There were no signs of a fire to be made, and, besides, never in the dog's experience had it known a man to sit like that in the snow and make no fire. As the twilight drew on, its eager yearning for the fire mastered it, and with a great lifting and shifting of forefeet, it whined softly, then flattened its ears down in anticipation of being chidden by the man. But the man remained silent. Later, the dog whined loudly. And still later it crept close to the man and caught the scent of death. This made the animal bristle and back away. A little longer it delayed, howling under the stars that leaped and danced and shone brightly in the cold sky. Then it turned and trotted up the trail in the direction of the camp it knew, where were the other food-providers and fire-providers.

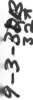

FOR DISCUSSION

1. Jack London viewed life as a struggle for survival against a cruel and indifferent nature. In this "survival of the fittest," who did London think was more fit to survive in the wilderness: the man or the dog? Why? Give quotes from the story to support your answer.

2. Early in "To Build a Fire," London points out that the man he is describing lacks several important character traits. What are they? In what way does the lack of the traits seem to make the man's fate inevitable?

3. "It certainly is cold," the man thinks several times during the story. We quickly learn that it is far colder than he realizes. How does the author make us *feel* cold? Give at least three details that impressed you most.

4. In a story, the point at which the outcome of the conflict is clear and the suspense is broken is called the *climax*. Where do you think the climax is in this story?

FOR COMPOSITION

• Describe an extremely *hot* setting, using details which make the heat as vivid as the cold in London's story.

Getting the red pony had been the biggest event in Jody's life so far. From Billy Buck, the hired hand, he would learn how to care for his pony. Billy knew everything about horses. Or did he?

THE GIFT

JOHN STEINBECK

SIX BOYS CAME over the hill half an hour early that afternoon, running hard, their heads down, their forearms working, their breath whistling. They swept by the house and cut across the stubble field to the barn. And then they stood self-consciously before the pony, and then they looked at Jody with eyes in which there was a new admiration and a new respect. Before today Jody had been a boy, dressed in overalls and a blue shirt—quieter than most, even suspected of being a little cowardly. And now he was different. Out of a thousand centuries they drew the ancient admiration of the footman for the horseman. They knew instinctively that a man on a horse is spiritually as well as physically bigger than a man on foot. They knew that Jody had been miraculously lifted out of equality with them, and had been placed over them. Gabilan put his head out of the stall and sniffed them.

"Why'n't you ride him?" the boys cried. "Why'n't you braid his tail with ribbons like in the fair?" "When you going to ride him?"

Jody's courage was up. He, too, felt the superiority of the horseman. "He's not old enough. Nobody can ride him for a long time. I'm going to train him on the long halter. Billy Buck is going to show me how."

"Well, can't we even lead him around a little?"

"He isn't even halter-broke," Jody said. He wanted to be completely alone when he took the pony out the first time. "Come and see the saddle."

They were speechless at the red morocco saddle, completely shocked out of comment. "It isn't much use in the brush," Jody explained. "It'll look pretty on him, though. Maybe I'll ride bareback when I go into the brush."

He let them feel the red saddle, and showed them the brass chain throat-latch on the bridle and the big brass buttons at each temple where the headstall and brow band crossed.

The whole thing was too wonderful. They had to go away after a little while, and each boy, in his mind, searched among his possessions for a bribe worthy of offering in return for a ride on the red pony when the time should come.

Jody was glad when they had gone. He took brush and currycomb from the wall, took down the barrier of the box stall, and stepped cautiously in. The pony's eyes glittered, and he edged around into kicking position. But Jody touched him on the shoulder and rubbed his high arched neck as he had always seen Billy Buck do, and he crooned, "So-o-o, boy," in a deep voice.

The pony gradually relaxed his tenseness. Jody curried and brushed until a pile of dead hair lay in the stall and until the pony's coat had taken on a deep red shine. Each time he finished he thought it might have been done better. He braided the mane into a dozen little pigtails, and he braided the forelock, and then he undid them and brushed the hair out straight again.

Jody did not hear his mother enter the barn. She was angry when she came, but when she looked in at the pony and at Jody working over him, she felt a curious pride rise up in her. "Have you forgot the woodbox?" she asked gently. "It's not far off from dark and there's not a stick of wood in the house, and the chickens aren't fed."

Jody quickly put up his tools. "I forgot, ma'am."

"Well, after this do your chores first. Then you won't forget. I expect you'll forget lots of things now if I don't keep an eye on you."

"Can I have carrots from the garden for him, ma'am?"

She had to think about that. "Oh—I guess so, if you only take the big tough ones."

"Carrots keep the coat good," he said, and again she felt the curious rush of pride.

Jody never waited for the triangle to get him out of bed after the coming of the pony. It became his habit to creep out of bed even before his mother was awake, to slip into his clothes and to go quietly down to the barn to see Gabilan. In the gray, quiet mornings when the land and the brush and the houses and the trees were silver-gray and black like a photograph negative, he stole toward the barn, past the sleeping stones and the sleeping cypress tree. The turkeys, roosting in the tree out of coyotes' reach, clicked drowsily. The fields glowed with a gray, frostlike light, and in the dew the tracks of rabbits and of field mice stood out sharply. The good dogs came stiffly out of their little houses, hackles up and deep growls in their throats. Then they caught Jody's scent, and their stiff tails rose up and waved a greeting— Doubletree Mutt, with the big thick tail, and Smasher, the incipient[1] shepherd—then went lazily back to their warm beds.

It was a strange time, and a mysterious journey, to Jody—an extension of a dream. When he first had the pony, he liked to torture himself during the trip by thinking Gabilan would not be in his stall and, worse, would never have been there. And he had other delicious little self-induced pains. He thought how the rats had gnawed ragged holes in the red saddle, and how the mice had nibbled Gabilan's tail until it was stringy and thin. He usually ran the last little way to the barn. He unlatched the rusty hasp of the barn door and stepped in, and no matter how quietly he opened the door, Gabilan was always looking at him over the barrier of the box stall and Gabilan whinnied softly and stamped his front foot, and his eyes had big sparks of red fire in them like oak-wood embers.

Sometimes, if the work horses were to be used that day, Jody found Billy Buck in the barn harnessing and currying. Billy stood with him and looked long at Gabilan and he told Jody a great many things about horses. He explained that they were terribly afraid for their feet, so that one must make a practice of lifting the legs and patting the hoofs and ankles to remove their terror. He told Jody how horses love conversation. He must talk to the pony all the time, and tell him the reasons for everything. Billy wasn't sure a horse could understand everything that was said to him, but it was impossible to say how much was understood. A horse never

[1] INCIPIENT: beginner.

kicked up a fuss if someone he liked explained things to him. Billy could give examples too. He had known, for instance, a horse nearly dead beat with fatigue to perk up when told it was only a little farther to his destination. And he had known a horse paralyzed with fright to come out of it when his rider told him what it was that was frightening him. While he talked in the mornings, Billy Buck cut twenty or thirty straws into neat three-inch lengths and stuck them into his hatband. Then, during the whole day, if he wanted to pick his teeth or merely to chew on something, he had only to reach up for one of them.

Jody listened carefully, for he knew and the whole country knew that Billy Buck was a fine hand with horses. Billy's own horse was a stringy cayuse with a hammer head, but he nearly always won the first prizes at the stock trials. Billy could rope a steer, take a double half-hitch about the horn with his riata, and dismount, and his horse would play the steer as an angler plays a fish, keeping a tight rope until the steer was down or beaten.

Every morning, after Jody had curried and brushed the pony, he let down the barrier of the stall, and Gabilan thrust past him and raced down the barn and into the corral. Around and around he galloped, and sometimes he jumped forward and landed on stiff legs. He stood quivering, stiff ears forward, eyes rolling so that the whites showed, pretending to be frightened. At last he walked, snorting, to the water trough and buried his nose in the water up to the nostrils. Jody was proud then, for he knew that was the way to judge a horse. Poor horses only touched their lips to the water, but a fine, spirited beast put his whole nose and mouth under, and only left room to breathe.

Then Jody stood and watched the pony, and he saw things he had never noticed about any other horse—the sleek, sliding flank muscles and the cords of the buttocks, which flexed like a closing fist, and the shine the sun put on the red coat. Having seen horses all his life, Jody had never looked at them very closely before. But now he noticed the moving ears which gave expression and even inflection[1] of expression to the face. The pony talked with his ears. You could tell exactly how he felt about everything by the way his ears pointed. Sometimes they were stiff and upright, and sometimes lax and sagging. They went back when he was angry or fearful, and forward when he was anxious and curious and pleased; and their exact position indicated which emotion he had.

Billy Buck kept his word. In the early fall the training began. First there was the halter-breaking, and that was the hardest because it was the first thing. Jody held a carrot and coaxed and promised and pulled on the rope. The pony set his feet like a burro when he felt the strain. But before long he learned. Jody walked all over the ranch leading him. Gradually he took to dropping the rope until the pony followed him unled wherever he went.

And then came the training on the long halter. That was slower work. Jody stood in the middle of a circle, holding the long halter. He clucked with his tongue and the pony started to walk in a big circle, held in by the long rope. He clucked again to make the pony trot, and again to make him gallop. Around and around Gabilan went, thundering and enjoying it immensely. Then he called, "Whoa," and the pony stopped. It was not long until Gabilan was perfect at it. But in many ways he was a bad pony. He bit Jody in the pants and stomped on Jody's feet. Now and then his ears went back and he aimed a tremendous kick at the boy. Every time he did

---

[1] INFLECTION: variation.

one of these bad things, Gabilan settled back and seemed to laugh to himself.

Billy Buck worked at the hair rope in the evenings before the fireplace. Jody collected tail hair in a bag, and he sat and watched Billy slowly constructing the rope, twisting a few hairs to make a string and rolling two strings together for a cord, and then braiding a number of cords to make the rope. Billy rolled the finished rope on the floor under his foot to make it round and hard.

The long-halter work rapidly approached perfection. Jody's father, watching the pony stop and start and trot and gallop, was a little bothered by it.

"He's getting to be almost a trick pony," he complained. "I don't like trick horses. It takes all the—dignity out of a horse to make him do tricks. Why, a trick horse is kind of like an actor—no dignity, no character of his own." And his father said, "I guess you better be getting him used to the saddle pretty soon."

Jody rushed for the harness room. For some time he had been riding the saddle on a sawhorse. He changed the stirrup length over and over, and could never get it just right. Sometimes, mounted on the saw-horse in the harness room, with collars and hames and tugs hung about him, Jody rode out beyond the room. He carried his rifle across the pommel. He saw the fields go flying by, and he heard the beat of the galloping hoofs.

It was a ticklish job, saddling the pony the first time. Gabilan hunched and reared and threw the saddle off before the cinch could be tightened. It had to be replaced again and again until at last the pony let it stay. And the cinching was difficult, too. Day by day Jody tightened the girth a little more until at last the pony didn't mind the saddle at all.

Then there was the bridle. Billy ex-plained how to use a stick of licorice for a bit until Gabilan was used to having something in his mouth. Billy explained, "Of course we could force-break him to everything, but he wouldn't be as good a horse if we did. He'd always be a little bit afraid, and he wouldn't mind because he wanted to."

The first time the pony wore the bridle he whipped his head about and worked his tongue against the bit until the blood oozed from the corners of his mouth. He tried to rub the headstall off on the manger. His ears pivoted about and his eyes turned red with fear and with general rambunctiousness. Jody rejoiced, for he knew that only a mean-souled horse does not resent training.

And Jody trembled when he thought of the time when he would first sit in the saddle. The pony would probably throw him off. There was no disgrace in that. The disgrace would come if he did not get up and mount again. Sometimes he dreamed that he lay in the dirt and cried and couldn't make himself mount again. The shame of the dream lasted until the middle of the day.

Gabilan was growing fast. Already he had lost the long-leggedness of the colt; his mane was getting longer and blacker. Under the constant currying and brushing his coat lay as smooth and gleaming as orange-red lacquer. Jody oiled the hoofs and kept them carefully trimmed so they would not crack.

The hair rope was nearly finished. Jody's father gave him an old pair of spurs and bent in the side bars and cut down the strap and took up the chainlets until they fitted. And then one day Carl Tiflin said, "The pony's growing faster than I thought. I guess you can ride him by Thanksgiving. Think you can stick on?"

"I don't know," Jody said shyly. Thanksgiving was only three weeks off.

He hoped it wouldn't rain, for rain would spot the red saddle.

Gabilan knew and liked Jody by now. He nickered when Jody came across the stubble field, and in the pasture he came running when his master whistled for him. There was always a carrot for him every time.

Billy Buck gave him riding instructions over and over. "Now when you get up there, just grab tight with your knees and keep your hands away from the saddle, and if you get throwed, don't let that stop you. No matter how good a man is, there's always some horse can pitch him. You just climb up again before he gets to feeling smart about it. Pretty soon, he won't throw you no more, and pretty soon he *can't* throw you no more. That's the way to do it."

"I hope it don't rain before," Jody said.

"Why not? Don't want to get throwed in the mud?"

That was partly it, and also he was afraid that in the flurry of bucking, Gabilan might slip and fall on him and break his leg or his hip. He had seen that happen to men before, had seen how they writhed on the ground like squashed bugs, and he was afraid of it.

He practiced on the sawhorse how he would hold the reins in his left hand and a hat in his right hand. If he kept his hands thus busy, he couldn't grab the horn if he felt himself going off. He didn't like to think of what would happen if he did grab the horn. Perhaps his father and Billy Buck would never speak to him again, they would be so ashamed. The news would get about and his mother would be ashamed too. And in the school yard—it was too awful to contemplate.

He began putting his weight in a stirrup when Gabilan was saddled, but he didn't throw his leg over the pony's back. That was forbidden until Thanksgiving.

Every afternoon he put the red saddle on the pony and cinched it tight. The pony was learning already to fill his stomach out unnaturally large while the cinching was going on, and then to let it down when the straps were fixed. Sometimes Jody led him up to the brush line and let him drink from the round green tub, and sometimes he led him up through the stubble field to the hilltop from which it was possible to see the white town of Salinas and the geometric fields of the great valley, and the oak trees clipped by the sheep. Now and then they broke through the brush and came to little cleared circles so hedged in that the world was gone and only the sky and the circle of brush were left from the old life. Gabilan liked these trips and showed it by keeping his head very high and by quivering his nostrils with interest. When the two came back from an expedition they smelled of the sweet sage they had forced through.

Time dragged on toward Thanksgiving, but winter came fast. The clouds swept down and hung all day over the land and brushed the hilltops, and the winds blew shrilly at night. All day the dry oak leaves drifted down from the trees until they covered the ground, and yet the trees were unchanged.

Jody had wished it might not rain before Thanksgiving, but it did. The brown earth turned dark and the trees glistened. The cut ends of the stubble turned black with mildew; the haystacks grayed from exposure to the damp, and on the roofs the moss, which had been all summer as gray as lizards, turned a brilliant yellow-green. During the week of rain, Jody kept the pony in the box stall out of the dampness, except for a little time after school when he took him out for exercise and to drink at the water trough in the upper corral. Not once did Gabilan get wet.

The wet weather continued until little new grass appeared. Jody walked to school dressed in a slicker and short rubber boots. At length one morning the sun came out brightly. Jody, at his work in the box stall, said to Billy Buck, "Maybe I'll leave Gabilan in the corral when I go to school today."

"Be good for him to be out in the sun," Billy assured him. "No animal likes to be cooped up too long. Your father and me are going back on the hill to clean the leaves out of the spring." Billy nodded and picked his teeth with one of his little straws.

"If the rain comes, though—" Jody suggested.

"Not likely to rain today. She's rained herself out." Billy pulled up his sleeves and snapped his arm bands. "If it comes on to rain—why, a little rain don't hurt a horse."

"Well, if it does come on to rain, you put him in, will you, Billy? I'm scared he might get cold so I couldn't ride him when the time comes."

"Oh sure! I'll watch out for him if we get back in time. But it won't rain today."

And so Jody, when he went to school, left Gabilan standing out in the corral.

Billy Buck wasn't wrong about many things. He couldn't be. But he was wrong about the weather that day, for a little after noon the clouds pushed over the hills and the rain began to pour down. Jody heard it start on the schoolhouse roof. He considered holding up one finger for permission to go to the outhouse and, once outside, running for home to put the pony in. Punishment would be prompt both at school and at home. He gave it up and took ease from Billy's assurance that rain couldn't hurt a horse. When school was finally out, he hurried home through the dark rain. The banks at the sides of the road spouted little jets of muddy water. The rain slanted and swirled under a cold and gusty wind. Jody dog-trotted home, slopping through the gravelly mud of the road.

From the top of the ridge he could see Gabilan standing miserably in the corral. The red coat was almost black, and streaked with water. He stood head down with his rump to the rain and wind. Jody arrived running and threw open the barn door and led the wet pony in by his forelock. Then he found a gunny sack and rubbed the soaked hair and rubbed the legs and ankles. Gabilan stood patiently, but he trembled in gusts like the wind.

When he had dried the pony as well as he could, Jody went up to the house and brought hot water down to the barn and soaked the grain in it. Gabilan was not very hungry. He nibbled at the hot mash, but he was not very much interested in it, and he still shivered now and then. A little steam rose from his damp back.

It was almost dark when Billy Buck and Carl Tiflin came home. "When the rain started we put up at Ben Herche's place, and the rain never let up all afternoon," Carl Tiflin explained. Jody looked reproachfully at Billy Buck and Billy felt guilty.

"You said it wouldn't rain," Jody accused him.

Billy looked away. "It's hard to tell, this time of year," he said, but his excuse was lame. He had no right to be fallible, and he knew it.

"The pony got wet, got soaked through."

"Did you dry him off?"

"I rubbed him with a sack and I gave him hot grain."

Billy nodded in agreement.

"Do you think he'll take cold, Billy?"

"A little rain never hurt anything," Billy assured him.

Jody's father joined the conversation then and lectured the boy a little. "A horse," he said, "isn't any lap-dog kind of thing." Carl Tiflin hated weakness and sickness, and he held a violent contempt for helplessness.

Jody's mother put a platter of steaks on the table and boiled potatoes and boiled squash, which clouded the room with their steam. They sat down to eat. Carl Tiflin still grumbled about weakness put into animals and men by too much coddling.

Billy Buck felt bad about his mistake. "Did you blanket him?" he asked.

"No. I couldn't find any blanket. I laid some sacks over his back."

"We'll go down and cover him up after we eat, then." Billy felt better about it then. When Jody's father had gone in to the fire and his mother was washing dishes, Billy found and lighted a lantern. He and Jody walked through the mud to the barn. The barn was dark and warm and sweet. The horses still munched their evening hay. "You hold the lantern!" Billy ordered. And he felt the pony's legs and tested the heat of the flanks. He put his cheek against the pony's gray muzzle and then he rolled up the eyelids to look at the eyeballs and he lifted the lips to see the gums, and he put his fingers inside the ears. "He don't seem so chipper," Billy said. "I'll give him a rubdown."

Then Billy found a sack and rubbed the pony's legs violently and he rubbed the chest and the withers. Gabilan was strangely spiritless. He submitted patiently to the rubbing. At last Billy brought an old cotton comforter from the saddle-room, and threw it over the pony's back and tied it at neck and chest with string.

"Now he'll be all right in the morning," Billy said.

Jody's mother looked up when he got back to the house. "You're late up from bed," she said. She held his chin in her hard hand and brushed the tangled hair out of his eyes and she said, "Don't worry about the pony. He'll be all right. Billy's as good as any horse doctor in the country."

Jody hadn't known she could see his worry. He pulled gently away from her and knelt down in front of the fireplace until it burned his stomach. He scorched himself through and then went in to bed, but it was a hard thing to go to sleep. He awakened after what seemed a long time. The room was dark but there was a grayness in the window like that which precedes the dawn. He got up and found his overalls and searched for the legs; and then the clock in the other room struck two. He laid his clothes down and got back into bed. It was broad daylight when he awakened again. For the first time he had slept through the ringing of the triangle. He leaped up, flung on his clothes, and went out of the door still buttoning his shirt. His mother looked after him for a moment and then went quietly back to her work. Her eyes were brooding and kind. Now and then her mouth smiled a little but without changing her eyes at all.

Jody ran on toward the barn. Halfway there he heard the sound he dreaded, the hollow, rasping cough of a horse. He broke into a sprint then. In the barn he found Billy Buck with the pony. Billy was rubbing its legs with his strong, thick hands. He looked up and smiled gaily. "He just took a little cold," Billy said. "We'll have him out of it in a couple of days."

Jody looked at the pony's face. The eyes were half closed and the lids thick and dry. In the eye corners a crust of hard mucus stuck. Gabilan's ears hung loosely sideways and his head was low. Jody put out his hand, but the pony did not move close to it. He coughed again and his whole body constricted with the effort. A little stream of thin fluid ran from his nostrils.

Jody looked back at Billy Buck. "He's awful sick, Billy."

"Just a little cold, like I said," Billy insisted. "You go get some breakfast and then go back to school. I'll take care of him."

"But you might have to do something else. You might leave him."

"No, I won't. I won't leave him at all. Tomorrow's Saturday. Then you can stay with him all day." Billy had failed again, and he felt badly about it. He had to cure the pony now.

Jody walked up to the house and took his place listlessly at the table. The eggs and bacon were cold and greasy, but he didn't notice it. He ate his usual amount. He didn't even ask to stay home from school. His mother pushed his hair back when she took his plate. "Billy'll take care of the pony," she assured him.

He moped through the whole day at school. He couldn't answer any questions or read any words. He couldn't even tell anyone the pony was sick, for that might make him sicker. And when school was finally out he started home in dread. He walked slowly and let the other boys leave him. He wished he might continue walking and never arrive at the ranch.

Billy was in the barn, as he had promised, and the pony was worse. His eyes were almost closed now, and his breath whistled shrilly past an obstruction in his nose. A film covered that part of the eyes that was visible at all. It was doubtful whether the pony could see any more. Now and then he snorted, to clear his nose, and by the action seemed to plug it tighter. Jody looked dispiritedly at the pony's coat. The hair lay rough and unkempt and seemed to have lost all of its old luster. Billy stood quietly beside the stall. Jody hated to ask, but he had to know.

"Billy, is he—is he going to get well?"

Billy put his fingers between the bars under the pony's jaw and felt about. "Feel here," he said, and he guided Jody's fingers to a large lump under the jaw. "When that gets bigger I'll open it up and then he'll get better."

Jody looked quickly away, for he had heard about that lump. "What is the matter with him?"

Billy didn't want to answer, but he had to. He couldn't be wrong three times. "Strangles," he said shortly, "but don't you worry about that. I'll pull him out of it. I've seen them get well when they were worse than Gabilan is. I'm going to steam him now. You can help."

"Yes," Jody said miserably. He followed Billy into the grain room and watched him make the steaming bag ready. It was a long canvas nose bag with straps to go over a horse's ears. Billy filled it one-third full of bran and then he added a couple of handfuls of dried hops. On top of the dry substance he poured a little carbolic acid and a little turpentine.

"I'll be mixing it all up while you run to the house for a kettle of boiling water," Billy said.

When Jody came back with the steaming kettle, Billy buckled the straps over Gabilan's head and fitted the bag tightly around his nose. Then through a little hole in the side of the bag he poured the boiling water on the mixture. The pony started away as a cloud of strong steam rose up, but then the soothing fumes crept through his nose and into his lungs, and the sharp steam began to clear out the nasal passages. He breathed loudly. His legs trembled in an ague, and his eyes closed against the biting cloud. Billy poured in more water and kept the steam rising for fifteen minutes. At last he set down the kettle and took the bag from Gabilan's nose. The pony looked better. He breathed freely, and his eyes were open wider than they had been.

"See how good it makes him feel," Billy

said. "Now we'll wrap him up in the blanket again. Maybe he'll be nearly well by morning."

"I'll stay with him tonight," Jody suggested.

"No. Don't you do it. I'll bring my blankets down here and put them in the hay. You can stay tomorrow and steam him if he needs it."

The evening was falling when they went to the house for their supper. Jody didn't even realize that someone else had fed the chickens and filled the woodbox. He walked up past the house to the dark brushline and took a drink of water from the tub. The spring water was so cold that it stung his mouth and drove a shiver through him. The sky above the hills was still light. He saw a hawk flying so high that it caught the sun on its breast and shone like a spark. Two blackbirds were driving him down the sky, glittering as they attacked their enemy. In the west, the clouds were moving in to rain again.

Jody's father didn't speak at all while the family ate supper, but after Billy Buck had taken his blankets and gone to sleep in the barn, Carl Tiflin built a high fire in the fireplace and told stories. He told about the wild man who ran naked through the country and had a tail and ears like a horse, and he told about the rabbit-cats of Moro Cojo that hopped into the trees for birds. He revived the famous Maxwell brothers, who found a vein of gold and hid the traces of it so carefully that they could never find it again.

Jody sat with his chin in his hands; his mouth worked nervously, and his father gradually became aware that he wasn't listening very carefully. "Isn't that funny?" he asked.

Jody laughed politely and said, "Yes, sir." His father was angry and hurt, then. He didn't tell any more stories. After a while, Jody took a lantern and went down to the barn. Billy Buck was asleep in the hay, and except that his breath rasped a little in his lungs, the pony seemed to be much better. Jody stayed a little while, running his fingers over the red rough coat, and then he took up the lantern and went back to the house. When he was in bed, his mother came into the room.

"Have you enough covers on? It's getting winter."

"Yes, ma'am."

"Well, get some rest tonight." She hesitated to go out, stood uncertainly. "The pony will be all right," she said.

Jody was tired. He went to sleep quickly and didn't awaken until dawn. The triangle sounded, and Billy Buck came up from the barn before Jody could get out of the house.

"How is he?" Jody demanded.

Billy always wolfed his breakfast. "Pretty good. I'm going to open that lump this morning. Then he'll be better maybe."

After breakfast Billy got out his best knife, one with a needle point. He whetted the shining blade a long time on a little carborundum stone. He tried the point and the blade again and again on his calloused thumb-ball, and at last he tried it on his upper lip.

On the way to the barn Jody noticed how the young grass was up and how the stubble was melting day by day into the new green crop of volunteer.[1] It was a cold, sunny morning.

As soon as he saw the pony, Jody knew he was worse. His eyes were closed and sealed shut with dried mucus. His head hung so low that his nose almost touched the straw of his bed. There was a little groan in each breath, a deep-seated, patient groan.

[1] VOLUNTEER: plants growing from seed that has sowed itself.

Billy lifted the weak head and made a quick slash with the knife. Jody saw the yellow pus run out. He held up the head while Billy swabbed out the wound with weak carbolic-acid salve.

"Now he'll feel better," Billy assured him. "That yellow poison is what makes him sick."

Jody looked unbelieving at Billy Buck. "He's awful sick."

Billy thought a long time what to say. He nearly tossed off a careless assurance, but he saved himself in time. "Yes, he's pretty sick," he said at last. "I've seen worse ones get well. If he doesn't get pneumonia, we'll pull him through. You stay with him. If he gets worse, you can come and get me."

For a long time after Billy went away, Jody stood beside the pony, stroking him behind the ears. The pony didn't flip his head the way he had done when he was well. The groaning in his breathing was becoming more hollow.

Doubletree Mutt looked into the barn, his big tail waving provocatively, and Jody was so incensed at his health that he found a hard black clod on the floor and deliberately threw it. Doubletree Mutt went yelping away to nurse a bruised paw.

In the middle of the morning, Billy Buck came back and made another steam bag. Jody watched to see whether the pony improved this time as he had before. His breathing eased a little, but he did not raise his head.

The Saturday dragged on. Late in the afternoon Jody went to the house and brought his bedding down and made up a place to sleep in the hay. He didn't ask permission. He knew from the way his mother looked at him that she would let him do almost anything. That night he left a lantern burning on a wire over the box stall. Billy had told him to rub the pony's legs every little while.

At nine o'clock the wind sprang up and howled around the barn. And in spite of his worry, Jody grew sleepy. He got into his blankets and went to sleep, but the breathy groans of the pony sounded in his dreams. And in his sleep he heard a crashing noise which went on and on until it awakened him. The wind was rushing through the barn. He sprang up and looked down the lane of stalls. The barn door had blown open, and the pony was gone.

He caught the lantern and ran outside into the gale, and he saw Gabilan weakly shambling away into the darkness, head down, legs working slowly and mechanically. When Jody ran up and caught him by the forelock, he allowed himself to be led back and put into his stall. His groans were louder, and a fierce whistling came from his nose. Jody didn't sleep any more then. The hissing of the pony's breath grew louder and sharper.

He was glad when Billy Buck came in at dawn. Billy looked for a time at the pony as though he had never seen him before. He felt the ears and flanks. "Jody," he said, "I've got to do something you won't want to see. You run up to the house for a while."

Jody grabbed him fiercely by the forearm. "You're not going to shoot him?"

Billy patted his hand. "No. I'm going to open a little hole in his windpipe so he can breathe. His nose is filled up. When he gets well, we'll put a little brass button in the hole for him to breathe through."

Jody couldn't have gone away if he had wanted to. It was awful to see the red hide cut, but infinitely more terrible to know it was being cut and not to see it. "I'll stay right here," he said bitterly. "You sure you got to?"

"Yes. I'm sure. If you stay, you can hold his head. If it doesn't make you sick, that is."

The fine knife came out again and was whetted again just as carefully as it had been the first time. Jody held the pony's head up and the throat taut, while Billy felt up and down for the right place. Jody sobbed once as the bright knife point disappeared into the throat. The pony plunged weakly away and then stood still, trembling violently. The blood ran thickly out and up the knife and across Billy's hand and into his shirtsleeve. The sure square hand sawed out a round hole in the flesh, and the breath came bursting out of the hole, throwing a fine spray of blood. With the rush of oxygen, the pony took a sudden strength. He lashed out with his hind feet and tried to rear, but Jody held his head down while Billy mopped the new wound with carbolic salve. It was a good job. The blood stopped flowing and the air puffed out the hole and sucked it in regularly with a little bubbling noise.

The rain brought in by the night wind began to fall on the barn roof. Then the triangle rang for breakfast. "You go up and eat while I wait," Billy said. "We've got to keep this hole from plugging up."

Jody walked slowly out of the barn. He was too dispirited to tell Billy how the barn door had blown open and let the pony out. He emerged into the wet gray morning and sloshed up to the house, taking a perverse[1] pleasure in splashing through all the puddles. His mother fed him and put dry clothes on. She didn't question him. She seemed to know he couldn't answer questions. But when he was ready to go back to the barn she brought him a pan of steaming meal. "Give him this," she said.

But Jody did not take the pan. He said, "He won't eat anything," and ran out of the house. At the barn, Billy showed him how to fix a ball of cotton on a stick, with which to swab out the breathing hole when it became clogged with mucus.

[1] PERVERSE: stubborn.

Jody's father walked into the barn and stood with them in front of the hall. At length he turned to the boy. "Hadn't you better come with me? I'm going to drive over the hill." Jody shook his head. "You better come on, out of this," his father insisted.

Billy turned on him angrily. "Let him alone. It's his pony, isn't it?"

Carl Tiflin walked away without saying another word. His feelings were badly hurt.

All morning Jody kept the wound open and the air passing in and out freely. At noon the pony lay wearily down on his side and stretched his nose out.

Billy came back. "If you're going to stay with him tonight, you better take a little nap," he said. Jody went absently out of the barn. The sky had cleared to a hard, thin blue. Everywhere the birds were busy with worms that had come to the damp surface of the ground.

Jody walked to the brush line and sat on the edge of the mossy tub. He looked down at the house and at the old bunkhouse and at the dark cypress tree. The place was familiar, but curiously changed. It wasn't itself any more, but a frame for things that were happening. A cold wind blew out of the east now, signifying that the rain was over for a little while. At his feet Jody could see the little arms of new weeds spreading out over the ground. In the mud about the spring were thousands of quail tracks.

Doubletree Mutt came sideways and embarrassed up through the vegetable patch, and Jody, remembering how he had thrown the clod, put his arm about the dog's neck and kissed him on his wide black nose. Doubletree Mutt sat still, as though he knew some solemn thing was happening. His big tail slapped the ground gravely. Jody pulled a swollen tick out of Mutt's neck and popped it dead between his thumbnails. It was a nasty thing. He washed his hands in the cold spring-water.

Except for the steady swish of the wind, the farm was very quiet. Jody knew his mother wouldn't mind if he didn't go in to eat his lunch. After a little while he went slowly back to the barn. Mutt crept into his own little house and whined softly to himself for a long time.

Billy Buck stood up from the box and surrendered the cotton swab. The pony still lay on his side and the wound in his throat bellowsed in and out. When Jody saw how dry and dead the hair looked, he knew at last that there was no hope for the pony. He had seen the dead hair before on dogs and on cows, and it was a sure sign. He sat heavily on the box and let down the barrier of the box stall. For a long time he kept his eyes on the moving wound, and at last he dozed, and the afternoon passed quickly. Just before dark his mother brought a deep dish of stew and left it for him and went away. Jody ate a little of it, and when it was dark, he set the lantern on the floor by the pony's head so he could watch the wound and keep it open. And he dozed again until the night chill awakened him. The wind was blowing fiercely, bringing the north cold with it. Jody brought a blanket from his bed in the hay and wrapped himself in it. Gabilan's breathing was quiet at last; the hole in his throat moved gently. The owls flew through the hayloft, shrieking and looking for mice. Jody put his hands down on his head and slept. In his sleep he was aware that the wind had increased. He heard it slamming about the barn.

It was daylight when he awakened. The barn door had swung open. The pony was gone. He sprang up and ran out into the morning light.

The pony's tracks were plain enough, dragging through the frostlike dew on the young grass, tired tracks with little lines between them where the hoofs had dragged. They headed for the brush line halfway up the ridge. Jody broke into a run and followed them. The sun shone on the sharp white quartz that stuck through the ground here and there. As he followed the plain trail, a shadow cut across in front of him. He looked up and saw a high circle of black buzzards, and the slowly revolving circle dropped lower and lower. The solemn birds soon disappeared over the ridge. Jody ran faster then, forced on by panic and rage. The trail entered the brush at last and followed a winding route among the tall sage bushes.

At the top of the ridge Jody was winded. He paused, puffing noisily. The blood pounded in his ears. Then he saw what he was looking for. Below, in one of the little clearings in the brush, lay the red pony. In the distance Jody could see the legs moving slowly and convulsively. And in a circle around him stood the buzzards, waiting for the moment of death they know so well.

Jody leaped forward and plunged down the hill. The wet ground muffled his steps and the brush hid him. When he arrived, it was all over. The first buzzard sat on the pony's head and its beak had just risen dripping with dark eye fluid. Jody plunged into the circle like a cat. The black brotherhood arose in a cloud, but the big one on the pony's head was too late. As it hopped along to take off, Jody caught its wing tip and pulled it down. It was nearly as big as he was. The free wing crashed into his face with the force of a club, but he hung on. The claws fastened on his leg and the wing elbows battered his head on either side. Jody groped blindly with his free hand. His fingers found the neck of the struggling bird. The red eyes looked into his face, calm and fearless and fierce; the naked head turned from side to side. Then the beak opened and vomited a stream of putrefied fluid. Jody brought up his knee and fell on the great bird. He held the neck to the ground with one hand while his other found a piece of sharp white quartz. The first blow broke the beak sideways and black blood spurted from the twisted, leathery mouth corners. He struck again and missed. The red fearless eyes still looked at him, impersonal and unafraid and detached. He struck again and again, until the buzzard lay dead, until its head was a red pulp. He was still beating the dead bird when Billy Buck pulled him off

and held him tightly to calm his shaking.

Carl Tiflin wiped the blood from the boy's face with a red bandana. Jody was limp and quiet now. His father moved the buzzard with his toe. "Jody," he explained, "the buzzard didn't kill the pony. Don't you know that?"

"I know it," Jody said wearily.

It was Billy Buck who was angry. He had lifted Jody in his arms, and had turned to carry him home. But he turned back on Carl Tiflin. " 'Course he knows it," Billy said furiously. "Can't you see how he'd feel about it?"

FOR DISCUSSION

1. Why did Jody attack the buzzard when he knew it had not killed his pony?

2. Why did Billy understand Jody's feelings at the end better than Jody's father did?

3. Explain the statement, "He [Billy] had no right to be fallible." What was Jody's opinion of Billy's skill with horses? Early in Gabilan's sickness Billy pretended to be very cheerful about the pony's progress. Later, when Jody said that Gabilan was very sick, Billy "nearly

tossed off a careless assurance, but he saved himself in time." Why did he finally tell Jody the truth?

FOR COMPOSITION

• Give as complete a character description of Jody as you can based on the evidence in the story. His classmates see him as "quieter than most, even suspected of being a little cowardly." Do his words, thoughts, and actions bear this out? Does he change during the story?

In Summary

FOR DISCUSSION

1. People must work out their relationships not only with other people, but with their own consciences as well. Who do you think is more successful in coming to terms with his conscience: Mark in "Sherrel" or Pete in "Sucker"?

2. Both Mark Twain in "Life on the Mississippi" and the barber in "Lather and Nothing Else" have to come to terms with a man of whom they are afraid. Do you think they are

both successful? How do you explain the difference in the solutions they chose?

3. Hal Borland in "High, Wide and Lonesome" and the trapper in "To Build a Fire" have different attitudes toward nature. How might Hal have helped the trapper in coming to terms with the northern wilderness?

4. Jody in "The Gift" and the narrator in "The Man He Killed" both have encounters with death. Does either of them arrive at an "agreement" with death or an explanation of its meaning?

OTHER THINGS TO DO

1. Three of the selections in this unit are part of longer works. Read one of the books—*High, Wide and Lonesome, Life on the Mississippi,* or *The Red Pony*—and explain to the class how the part that you read together fits into the whole.

2. From the stories in this unit, choose a scene in which two characters are in conflict and act out the dialogue between them. You will want to use the words given in the story, but you may add dialogue of your own so long as it is consistent with the character speaking. If little action is involved, you might tape record the scene rather than presenting it in person. Good scenes for this type of dramatization are

found in "Sucker," "Lather and Nothing Else," "Life on the Mississippi," and "The Gift."

3. Retell one of the stories in cartoon form. "To Build a Fire" or "The Gift," both of which involve a good deal of physical action, could be effectively told this way.

4. Write a short research paper on the history of Mississippi steamboats or of American Indians' struggles for control of their lands. Show how your information relates to Mark Twain's story or to Buffy Sainte-Marie's poem.

5. Tell about an experience of your own in which you came to terms with another person, with forces of nature or death, or with yourself. Compare what happened to you with what happened to at least one of the characters in this unit. Were the events similar? Did you react in similar ways?

The World of Words

SHERREL

When new words are formed by adding affixes (prefixes and suffixes) to existing words, stems, or roots, the process is called *derivation.* The narrator in "Sherrel" bitterly regrets the way he had treated his brother. He feels what is called "remorse." "Remorse" is derived from the Latin word *mordere,* meaning "to bite," by the addition of the prefix *re-,* meaning "again." What does *remorse* mean? Other words related to *remorse* are *morsel, mordant,* and *mordent.* How are they related, and what do they mean?

SUCKER

Although no two words ever mean exactly the same thing, some words have meanings

that are quite similar. Such words are called *synonyms.* In the story "Sucker," we could say that Sucker and Pete became *alienated, disaffected,* or *estranged.* The verbs *alienate, disaffect,* and *estrange* are synonyms. In what ways are their meanings similar? In what ways are they different? Which verb most accurately fits the action of the story?

HIGH, WIDE AND LONESOME

The study of the origins and histories of words is called *etymology.* The time-setting of "High, Wide and Lonesome" is the change of the season from winter to spring. Our names for the seasons—*spring, summer, fall* and *winter*—all go back to Old English. That is, they have been part of the language ever since

English became a separate and distinct language, sometime before the eighth century. *Spring* comes from Old English *springan,* which comes from an early root meaning "to move or jump." *Summer* comes from Old English *sumor,* which comes from an early root meaning "half-year." *Fall* comes from the Old English verb *feallen,* "to fall"—with fall meaning "season of leaf fall." *Winter* was also *winter* in Old English, going back to an early root meaning "wet." Thus winter indicates "season of wetness." The word *autumn,* however, comes from a different source. Where does *autumn* come from?

LATHER AND NOTHING ELSE

Many words in English can be traced back to the beginnings of the language in what we call Old English. But many other words were taken into English from other languages. We call these *borrowed words,* not that we intend to give them back. In "Lather and Nothing Else" there are many borrowed words, words such as *enemy, rejuvenate, sacrifice,* and *assassin. Enemy* came into English through Old French from the Latin word *inimicus* made up of *in-,* meaning "not," and *amicus,* meaning "friend." Thus an enemy is one who is not a friend. Where do the words *rejuvenate, sacrifice,* and *assassin* come from, and how do their meanings relate to their origins?

from LIFE ON THE MISSISSIPPI

1. The name *Mark Twain* is the pen name of Samuel Langhorne Clemens. That is, it is the name he used as a writer. As you learned from "Life on the Mississippi," the name *Mark Twain* is taken from the expression *mark twain,* or "by the mark of two fathoms," an expression used to describe the depth of navigable waters on the river. The name *Mark Twain* is also called a "pseudonym." The word *pseudonym* is a compound word made up of the Greek stems *pseudo-* and *-onym.* What do

these stems mean? What do they mean when put together? What does *pseudoscience* mean?

2. On page 32 Mark Twain describes Mr. Brown as follows: "He was a middle-aged, long, slim, bony, smooth-shaven, horse-faced, ignorant, stingy, malicious, snarling, fault-hunting, mote-magnifying tyrant." It is not easy to sustain such a string of adjectives each of which contributes something toward characterizing their object. Explain the meaning of each adjective and indicate what each tells us about Mr. Brown.

TO BUILD A FIRE

Jack London tells us that the trouble with the man in "To Build a Fire" was that "he was without imagination." London goes on to say: "He was quick and alert in the things of life, but only in the things, and not in the significances." What adjective, or adjectives, would accurately describe such a man? Can we call him *foolish, silly,* or *fatuous*? Or, using another set of *synonyms,* is he *stupid, obtuse,* or *dense*? Examine the meanings of these words and decide which of them describe the man in the story, keeping in mind London's description of him.

THE GIFT

In killing the buzzard, Jody is taking revenge for the loss of the pony on something that did not cause that loss. We would call this "vicarious" revenge. The word *vicarious* comes from the Latin word *vicarius,* meaning "substituting," which is derived from *vicis,* meaning "change" or "turn." Look up the meanings of *vicarious* to see how the word applies to Jody's experience. What other experiences could be called "vicarious"? Another word borrowed from Latin is *vicissitude.* How does this word relate to *vicarious*? What does *vicissitude* mean? Does it have any connection with Jody's experience? Explain.

Reader's Choice

The Adventures of Huckleberry Finn, *by Mark Twain.*

Escaping from his drunken father, Huck Finn joins forces with Jim, a runaway slave. As they float down the Mississippi on their raft they encounter cutthroats, con men, and two feuding families. Huck's most troublesome conflicts, however, are with his conscience: why can't he bring himself to do the right thing by turning Jim in to the authorities?

April Morning, *by Howard Fast.*

On an April morning in 1775, 15-year-old Adam Cooper sees his father killed by the British on Lexington Green. In the long day that follows Adam comes to harsh terms with the brutality of war and with the man he must become.

The Call of the Wild/White Fang, *by Jack London.*

"Kill or be killed, eat or be eaten, was the law." Both Buck and White Fang survive in the savage world of the Klondike by becoming more like wolves than dogs. Each dog, however, is torn between the call of the wild and the call of his love for one man. Two quite different endings make these an interesting pair of stories to read together and compare.

Death Be Not Proud, *by John Gunther.*

John Gunther, Jr. loved chemistry and music and sailing and talking. He was bursting with plans for college. But at sixteen he developed a brain tumor. His father tells of Johnny's courageous struggle with the affliction that finally killed him.

The Diary of a Young Girl, *by Anne Frank.*

In Hitler's Germany, to be a Jew was a crime punishable by imprisonment and death. Anne Frank and her family sought refuge in a small attic space that they shared with four other people. The diary that Anne kept during that time tells of her conflicts with her family, her falling in love, and her attempt to understand the forces that trapped her.

Durango Street, *by Frank Bonham.*

"Gang fighting . . . runaway . . . grand theft auto . . . ." Rufus Henry has an impressive record behind him as he leaves detention camp. His parole officer believes that Rufus can make a fresh start if he stays out of gangs. "But every boy at Pine Valley knew that the only way to stay alive in a big-city jungle was to join a fighting gang—before some other gang decided to use you for bayonet practice."

Jazz Country, *by Nat Hentoff.*

High-school senior Tom Curtis must choose between a college education and the unpredictable life of a jazz musician. More than anything else he wants to play trumpet, but professional jazzmen tell him, "Your life has been too easy for you to be making it as a jazz musician—and too white." As he struggles to be accepted by them he learns much about their problems as blacks—and about himself.

Lord of the Flies, *by William Golding.*

Cast away on an island without adults, a group of boys must work out their own rules. Will they follow Ralph, the democratic leader, or the warlike Jack? Golding's novel is both an exciting adventure story and a criticism of "civilized" human nature.

Marching to Freedom: The Life of Martin Luther King, Jr., *edited by Robert Bleiweiss.*

"You are as good as anyone else." Growing up in the shadow of prejudice, Martin remembered his parents' words and determined to work for justice for his people. Slowly he learned to return hate with the power of love. This biography presents not only the events of his life but an interpretation of his philosophy of nonviolence.

The Member of the Wedding, *by Carson McCullers.*

Frankie Addams, lonely and unhappy, takes comfort from the dream that she will go away with her brother and his bride after their wedding. Her being left behind is only one of the shocks and disappointments of being twelve years old. As "Frankie" changes to "F. Jasmine" and then to "Frances," she begins to sort out dreams from reality and to accept herself.

Mrs. Mike, *by Nancy and Benedict Freedman.*

Sixteen-year-old Kathy O'Fallon comes to northwest Canada from Boston to regain her health. There she meets and marries Sergeant Mike Flannigan of the Mounted Police and begins to share his dangerous and lonely life. When an epidemic nearly wipes out the children of their village, Kathy fears she has made the wrong choice.

The Old Man and the Sea, *by Ernest Hemingway.*

Santiago, an old Cuban fisherman, has gone eighty-four days without catching a fish. On the eighty-fifth day he hooks an enormous marlin who battles him for two days and nights. Alone in his boat, he matches his strength against the fish and the sea in a contest to the death.

A Separate Peace, *by John Knowles.*

Gene and Phineas are best friends during the early years of World War II. Handsome, daredevil Finny can believe no evil of anyone —certainly he can't believe Gene is jealous of him. In the "peace" of their boarding-school world Gene fights his hardest battle within himself: ". . . my war ended before I ever put on a uniform; I was on active duty all my time at school; I killed my enemy there."

The Sparrow's Fall, *by Fred Bosworth.*

Jacob Atook's tribe survives by hunting animals—but the missionary teaches of a God who loves even the little sparrows that fall. Jacob's marriage is to be arranged by the tribe —but he loves a girl who is promised to another. To follow his own beliefs may cost him his life. Pursued by the double threats of starvation and murder, he seeks his answers in a desperate hunt through the northern wilderness.

THE SHORT STORY

A SHORT STORY is a fictional account of events, brief enough to be read at a single sitting. But that definition gives only a hint of the pleasures that come from reading short stories.

We might look at the definition more closely. The events that make up a short story are called the *plot*. The plot tells what happened, but a plot is no more a short story than is a summary of an action the action itself. A summary of the details of an automobile accident would leave a lot out: feelings of the people involved, the looks of the place where the accident occurred, the sounds and sights that accompanied that unhappy event.

Those latter aspects—atmosphere, sounds, sights, smells—would be contained in the *setting* of a short story. A plot must unfold somewhere, and the somewhere is the setting. Of course a story with a weak plot may have a wonderful setting, so vivid that we imagine ourselves along the coast of France as we read, or in the jungles of the Amazon, or the snows of the Arctic. Such a story, despite weak action, would furnish its own kind of pleasure.

But going beyond simply plot and setting, stories introduce us to memorable *characters,* people we would not otherwise get to know. An Italian nobleman, an Indian leader, a soldier of the Civil War, and an English detective with an international reputation are among the people we encounter in the stories that follow, seeing life for a while from their *point of view,* or their friends', or that of the author who has created their world.

Finally we may extend into our own lives the general meanings of the specific stories in which such people figure. Indeed, such broad meanings, or *themes,* may be what cause some stories to remain with us long after details of plot and setting are forgotten.

Philip McFarland

THE ADVENTURE OF THE SPECKLED BAND

SIR ARTHUR CONAN DOYLE

ON GLANCING OVER my notes of the seventy-odd cases in which I have during the last eight years studied the methods of my friend Sherlock Holmes, I find none which presented more singular features than that which was associated with the well-known family of the Roylotts of Stoke Moran.[1] The events in question occurred in the early days of my association with Holmes, when we were sharing rooms as bachelors in Baker Street.

It was early in April in the year '83 that I woke one morning to find Sherlock Holmes standing, fully dressed, by the side of my bed. He was a late riser as a rule, and as the clock showed me that it was only a quarter past seven, I blinked up at him in some surprise, and perhaps just a little resentment, for I was myself regular in my habits.

"Very sorry to rouse you up, Watson," said he.

"What is it, then—a fire?" I asked.

"No; a client. It seems that a young lady has arrived in a considerable state of excitement, who insists upon seeing me. She is waiting now in the sitting room. Now, when young ladies wander about the metropolis at this hour of the morning, I presume that it is something very pressing

[1] STOKE MORAN: the Roylott estate.

which they have to communicate. Should it prove to be an interesting case, you would, I am sure, wish to follow it from the outset. I thought, at any rate, that I should give you the chance."

"My dear fellow, I would not miss it for anything."

I had no keener pleasure than in following Holmes in his professional investigations, and in admiring the rapid deductions, as swift as intuitions, and yet always founded on a logical basis, with which he unraveled the problems which were submitted to him. I rapidly threw on my clothes, and accompanied my friend down to the sitting room. A lady dressed in black and heavily veiled, who had been sitting in the window, rose as we entered.

"Good morning, madam," said Holmes, cheerily. "My name is Sherlock Holmes. This is my intimate friend and associate, Dr. Watson, before whom you can speak as freely as before myself. Ha! I am glad to see that my housekeeper, Mrs. Hudson, has had the good sense to light the fire. Pray draw up to it, and I shall order you a cup of hot coffee, for I observe that you are shivering."

"It is not cold which makes me shiver," said the woman, in a low voice, changing her seat as requested.

"What, then?"

"It is fear, Mr. Holmes. It is terror." She

had raised her veil; and we could see that she was indeed in a pitiable state of agitation, her face all drawn and gray, with restless, frightened eyes, like those of some hunted animal. Her features and her figure were those of a woman of thirty, but her hair was shot with premature gray, and her expression was weary and haggard. Sherlock Holmes ran her over with one of his quick, all-comprehensive glances.

"You must not fear," said he, soothingly. "We shall set matters right, I have no doubt. You have come in by train this morning, I see."

"You know me, then?"

"No, but I observe the second half of a return ticket in the palm of your left glove. You must have started early, and yet you had a good drive in a dogcart,[1] along heavy roads, before you reached the station."

The lady gave a violent start, and stared in bewilderment at my companion.

"There is no mystery, my dear madam," said he, smiling. "The left arm of your jacket is spattered with mud in no less than seven places. The marks are perfectly fresh. There is no vehicle save a dogcart which throws up mud in that way, and then only when you sit on the left-hand side of the driver."

"Whatever your reasons may be, you are perfectly correct," said she. "I started from home before six, reached the railway station of Leatherhead at twenty past, and came in by the first train to Waterloo. Sir, I can stand this strain no longer; I shall go mad if it continues. I have no one to turn to—none, save only one, who cares for me, and he, poor fellow, can be of little aid. I have heard of you, Mr. Holmes, from Mrs. Farintosh, whom you helped in the hour of her sore need. It was from her that I had your address. Oh, sir, do you not think that you could help me, too, and at least

[1] DOGCART: small open carriage.

throw a little light through the dense darkness which surrounds me? At present it is out of my power to reward you for your services, but in a month or six weeks I shall be married, with the control of my own income, and then at least you shall not find me ungrateful."

Holmes turned to his desk and drew out a small casebook, which he consulted.

"I can only say, madam, that I shall be happy to devote the same care to your case as I did to that of your friend. As to reward, my profession is its own reward; but you are at liberty to defray whatever expenses I may be put to, at the time which suits you best. And now I beg you will lay before us everything that may help us in forming an opinion upon the matter."

"My name is Helen Stoner," replied our visitor, "and I am living with my stepfather, who is the last survivor of one of the oldest Saxon families in England, the Roylotts of Stoke Moran, in Surrey."

Holmes nodded his head. "The name is familiar to me," said he.

"The family was at one time among the richest in England, and the estates extended many miles. In the last century, however, four successive heirs were of a dissolute and wasteful disposition, and the family ruin was eventually completed by a gambler in the days of the Regency. Nothing was left save a few acres of ground, and the two-hundred-year-old house, which is itself crushed under a heavy mortgage. The last squire dragged out his existence there, living the horrible life of an aristocratic pauper; but his only son, my stepfather, seeing that he must adapt himself to the new conditions, obtained an advance from a relative, which enabled him to take a medical degree, and went out to Calcutta, where, by his professional skill and his force of character, he established a large practice. In a fit of anger, however, caused by some robberies which had been perpetrated in the house, he beat his native butler to death, and narrowly escaped a capital sentence. As it was, he suffered a long term of imprisonment, and afterward returned to England a morose and disappointed man.

"When Dr. Roylott was in India, he married my mother, Mrs. Stoner, the young widow of Major General Stoner, of the Bengal Artillery. My sister Julia and I were twins, and we were only two years old at the time of my mother's remarriage. She had a considerable sum of money— not less than £1000[1] a year—and this she bequeathed to Dr. Roylott entirely while we resided with him, with a provision that a certain annual sum should be allowed to each of us in the event of our marriage. Shortly after our return to England my mother died—she was killed eight years ago in a railway accident. Dr. Roylott then abandoned his attempts to establish himself in practice in London, and took us to live with him in the old ancestral house at Stoke Moran. The money which my mother had left was enough for all our wants, and there seemed to be no obstacle to our happiness.

"But a terrible change came over our stepfather about this time. Instead of making friends and exchanging visits with our neighbors, who had at first been overjoyed to see a Roylott of Stoke Moran back in the old family seat, he shut himself up in his house, and seldom came out save to indulge in ferocious quarrels with whoever might cross his path. Violence of temper approaching to mania has been hereditary in the men of the family, and in my stepfather's case it had, I believe, been intensified by his long residence in the tropics. A series of disgraceful brawls took place, two of which ended in the police court, until at last he became the terror of the

[1] £1000: a thousand pounds. A pound is an English money unit.

village, and the folks would fly at his approach, for he is a man of immense strength and is absolutely uncontrollable in his anger.

"Last week he hurled the local blacksmith over a parapet into a stream, and it was only by paying over all the money which I could gather together that I was able to avert another public exposure. He had no friends at all save the wandering gypsies; and he would give these vagabonds leave to encamp upon the few acres of bramble-covered land which represent the family estate, and would accept in return the hospitality of their tents, wandering away with them sometimes for weeks on end. He has a passion also for Indian animals, which are sent over to him by a correspondent, and he has at this moment a cheetah and a baboon, which wander freely over his grounds, and are feared by the villagers almost as much as their master.

"You can imagine from what I say that my poor sister Julia and I had no great pleasure in our lives. No servant would stay with us, and for a long time we did all the work of the house. Julia was but thirty at the time of her death, and yet her hair had already begun to whiten, even as mine has."

"Your sister is dead, then?"

"She died just two years ago, and it is of her death that I wish to speak to you. You can understand that, living the life which I have described, we were little likely to see anyone of our own age and position. We had, however, an aunt, my mother's maiden sister, Miss Honoria Westphail, who lives near Harrow, and we were occasionally allowed to pay short visits at this lady's house. Julia went there at Christmas two years ago, and met there a major of marines, to whom she became engaged. My stepfather learned of the engagement when my sister returned, and offered no objection to the marriage; but within a fortnight of the day which had been fixed for the wedding, the terrible event occurred which has deprived me of my only companion."

Sherlock Holmes had been leaning back in his chair with his eyes closed and his head sunk in a cushion, but he half opened his lids now and glanced across at his visitor.

"Pray be precise as to details," said he.

"It is easy for me to be so, for every event of that dreadful time is seared into my memory. The manor house is, as I have already said, very old; and only one wing is now inhabited. The bedrooms in this wing are on the ground floor, the sitting rooms being in the central block of the buildings. Of these bedrooms the first is Dr. Roylott's, the second my sister's, and the third my own. There is no communication between them, but they all open out into the same corridor. Do I make myself plain?"

"Perfectly so."

"The windows of the three rooms are full length and open out upon the lawn. That fatal night Dr. Roylott had gone to his room early, though we knew that he had not retired to rest, for my sister was troubled by the smell of the strong Indian cigars which it was his custom to smoke. She left her room, therefore, and came into mine, where she sat for some time, chatting about her approaching wedding. At eleven o'clock she rose to leave me, but she paused at the door and looked back.

" 'Tell me, Helen,' said she, 'have you ever heard anyone whistle in the dead of the night?'

" 'Never,' said I.

" 'I suppose that you could not possibly whistle, yourself, in your sleep?'

" 'Certainly not. But why?'

" 'Because during the last few nights I have always, about three in the morning, heard a low, clear whistle. I am a light sleeper, and it has awakened me. I cannot tell where it came from—perhaps from the next room, perhaps from the lawn. I thought that I would just ask you whether you had heard it.'

" 'No, I have not. It must be those wretched gypsies in the plantation.'

" 'Very likely. And yet if it were on the lawn, I wonder that you did not hear it also.'

" 'Ah, but I sleep more heavily than you.'

" 'Well, it is of no great consequence, at any rate.' She smiled back at me and closed my door, and a few moments later I heard her key turn in the lock of her own door."

"Indeed," said Holmes. "Was it your custom always to lock yourselves in at night?"

"Always."

"And why?"

"I think that I mentioned to you that the doctor kept a cheetah and a baboon. We had no feeling of security unless our doors were locked."

"Quite so. Pray proceed with your statement."

"I could not sleep that night. A vague feeling of impending[1] misfortune impressed me. My sister and I, you will recollect, were twins, and you know how subtle are the links which bind two souls which are so closely allied. It was a wild night. The wind was howling outside, and the rain was beating and splashing against the windows. Suddenly, amid all the hubbub of the gale, there burst forth the wild scream of a terrified woman. I knew that it was my sister's voice. I sprang from my bed, wrapped a shawl around me, and rushed into the corridor. As I opened my door, I seemed to hear a low whistle, such as my sister described, and a few moments

---

[1] IMPENDING: due to happen soon.

later a clanging sound, as if a mass of metal had fallen.

"As I ran down the passage, my sister's door was unlocked, and revolved slowly upon its hinges. I stared at it horror-stricken, not knowing what was about to issue from it. By the light of the corridor lamp I saw my sister appear at the opening, her face blanched with terror, her hands groping for help, her whole figure swaying to and fro like that of a drunkard. I ran to her and threw my arms round her, but at that moment her knees seemed to give way and she fell to the ground. She writhed as one who is in terrible pain, and her limbs were dreadfully convulsed. At first I thought that she had not recognized me, but as I bent over her she suddenly shrieked out, in a voice which I shall never forget: 'Oh, my God! Helen! It was the band! The speckled band!' There was something else which she would fain have said, and she stabbed with her finger into the air in the direction of the doctor's room, but a fresh convulsion seized her and choked her words. I rushed out, calling loudly for my stepfather, and I met him hastening from his room in his dressing gown. When he reached my sister's side, she was unconscious, and though he poured brandy down her throat and sent for medical aid from the village, all efforts were in vain, for she slowly sank and died without having recovered her consciousness. Such was the dreadful end of my beloved sister."

"One moment," said Holmes; "are you sure about this whistle and metallic sound? Could you swear to it?"

"That was what the county coroner asked me at the inquiry. It is my strong impression that I heard it, and yet, among the crash of the gale and the creaking of an old house, I may possibly have been deceived."

"Was your sister dressed?"

"No, she was in her nightdress. In her right hand was found the charred stump of a match, and in her left a matchbox."

"Showing that she had struck a light and looked about her when the alarm took place. That is important. And what conclusions did the coroner come to?"

"He investigated the case with great care, for Dr. Roylott's conduct had long been notorious in the county, but he was unable to find any satisfactory cause of death. My evidence showed that the door had been fastened upon the inner side, and the windows were blocked by old-fashioned shutters with broad iron bars, which were secured every night. The walls were carefully sounded, and were shown to be quite solid all round, and the flooring was also thoroughly examined, with the same result. The chimney is wide, but is barred up by four large staples.[1] It is certain, therefore, that my sister was quite alone when she met her end. Besides, there were no marks of any violence upon her."

"How about poison?"

"The doctors examined her for it, but without success."

"What do you think that this unfortunate lady died of, then?"

"It is my belief that she died of pure fear and nervous shock, though what it was that frightened her I cannot imagine."

"Were gypsies in the plantation at the time?"

"Yes, there are nearly always some of them there."

"Ah, and what did you gather from this allusion to a band—a speckled band?"

"Sometimes I have thought that it was merely the wild talk of delirium, sometimes that it may have referred to some band of people, perhaps to these very gypsies in the plantation. I do not know whether the spotted handkerchiefs which so many of them wear over their heads

STAPLES: metal loops with pointed ends.

might have suggested the strange adjective she used."

Holmes shook his head like a man who is far from being satisfied.

"These are very deep waters," said he; "pray go on with your narrative."

"Two years have passed since then, and my life has been until lately lonelier than ever. A month ago, however, a dear friend whom I have known for many years, has done me the honor to ask my hand in marriage. His name is Armitage—Percy Armitage—the second son of Mr. Armitage, of Crane Water, near Reading. My stepfather has offered no opposition to the match, and we are to be married in the course of the spring. Two days ago some repairs were started in the west wing of the building, and my bedroom wall has been pierced, so that I have had to move into the chamber in which my twin sister died, and to sleep in the very bed in which she slept.

"Imagine my thrill of terror when last night, as I lay awake, thinking over her terrible fate, I suddenly heard in the silence of the night the low whistle which had been the herald of her own death. I sprang up and lit the lamp, but nothing was to be seen in the room. I was too shaken to go to bed again, however; so I dressed, and as soon as it was daylight I slipped down, got a dogcart at the Crown Inn, which is opposite, and drove to Leatherhead, from whence I have come on this morning with the one object of seeing you and asking your advice."

"You have done wisely," said my friend. "But have you told me all?"

"Yes, all."

"Miss Stoner, you have not. You are screening your stepfather."

"Why, what do you mean?"

For an answer Holmes pushed back the frill of black lace which fringed the hand that lay upon our visitor's knee. Five little livid spots, the marks of four fingers and a thumb, were printed upon the white wrist.

"You have been cruelly used," said Holmes.

The lady colored deeply and covered over her injured wrist. "He is a hard man," she said, "and perhaps he hardly knows his own strength."

There was a long silence, during which Holmes leaned his chin upon his hands and stared into the crackling fire.

"This is a very deep business," he said, at last.

"There are a thousand details which I should desire to know before I decide upon our course of action. Yet we have not a moment to lose. If we were to come to Stoke Moran today, would it be possible for us to see over these rooms without the knowledge of your stepfather?"

"As it happens, he spoke of coming into town today upon some most important business. It is probable that he will be away all day, and that there would be nothing to disturb you. We have a housekeeper now, but she is old and foolish, and I could easily get her out of the way."

"Excellent. You are not averse to this trip, Watson?"

"By no means."

"Then we shall both come. What are you going to do yourself?"

"I have one or two things which I would wish to do now that I am in town. But I shall return by the twelve o'clock train, so as to be there in time for your coming."

"And you may expect us early in the afternoon. I have some small business matters to attend to. Will you not wait and breakfast?"

"No, I must go. My heart is lightened already since I have confided my trouble to you. I shall look forward to seeing you again this afternoon." She dropped her thick black veil over her face and glided from the room.

"And what do you think of it all, Watson?" asked Holmes, after seeing her out.

"It seems to me to be a most dark and sinister business."

"Dark enough and sinister enough."

"Yet if the lady is correct in saying that the flooring and walls are sound, and that the door, window, and chimney are impassable, then her sister must have been undoubtedly alone when she met her mysterious end."

"What becomes, then, of these nocturnal whistles, and what of the very peculiar words of the dying woman?"

"I cannot think."

"When you combine the ideas of whistles at night, the presence of a band of gypsies who are on intimate terms with this old doctor, the fact that we have every reason to believe that the doctor has an interest in preventing his stepdaughter's marriage, the dying allusion to a band, and, finally, the fact that Miss Helen Stoner heard a metallic clang, which might have been caused by one of those metal bars which secured the shutters falling back into its place, I think that there is good ground to think that the mystery may be cleared along those lines."

"But what, then, did the gypsies do?"

"I cannot imagine."

"I see many objections to any such theory."

"And so do I. It is precisely for that reason that we are going to Stoke Moran this day. I want to see whether the objections are fatal, or if they may be explained away. But what in the name of the devil!"

The ejaculation had been drawn from my companion by the fact that our door had been suddenly dashed open, and that a huge man had framed himself in the aperture. His costume was a peculiar mixture of the professional and of the agricultural, having a black top hat, a long frock coat, and a pair of high gaiters,[1] with a hunting crop swinging in his hand. So tall was he that his hat actually brushed the crossbar of the doorway, and his breadth seemed to span it across from side to side. A large face, seared with a thousand wrinkles, burned yellow with the sun, and marked with every evil passion, was turned from one to the other of us, while his deep-set eyes, and his high, thin, fleshless nose, gave him somewhat the resemblance to a fierce old bird of prey.

"Which of you is Holmes?" asked this apparition.

"My name, sir; but you have advantage of me," said my companion quietly.

"I am Dr. Grimesby Roylott, of Stoke Moran."

"Indeed, Doctor," said Holmes blandly. "Pray take a seat."

"I will do nothing of the kind. My stepdaughter has been here. I have traced her. What has she been saying to you?"

"It is a little cold for the time of the year," said Holmes.

"What has she been saying to you?" screamed the old man, furiously.

"But I have heard that the crocuses promise well," continued my companion, imperturbably.

"Ha! You put me off, do you?" said our new visitor, taking a step forward and shaking his hunting crop. "I know you, you scoundrel! I have heard of you before. You are Holmes, the meddler."

My friend smiled.

"Holmes, the busybody!"

His smile broadened.

"Holmes, the Scotland Yard Jack-in-office!"[2]

---

[1] GAITERS: coverings worn over a shoe.

[2] SCOTLAND . . . OFFICE: impudent person from Scotland Yard, London's police headquarters. Holmes was not directly connected with Scotland Yard.

Holmes chuckled heartily. "Your conversation is most entertaining," said he. "When you go out, close the door, for there is a decided draft."

"I will go when I have said my say. Don't you dare meddle with my affairs. I know that Miss Stoner has been here. I traced her! I am a dangerous man to fall foul of! See here." He stepped forward, seized the poker, and bent it into a curve with his huge brown hands.

"See that you keep yourself out of my grip," he snarled; and hurling the twisted poker into the fireplace, he strode out of the room.

"He seems a very amiable person," said Holmes, laughing. "I am not quite so bulky, but if he had remained I might have shown him that my grip was not much more feeble than his own." As he spoke he picked up the steel poker, and with a sudden effort straightened it out again.

"Fancy his having the insolence to confound me with the official detective force! This incident gives zest to our investigation, however, and I only trust that our little friend will not suffer from her imprudence in allowing this brute to trace her. And now, Watson, we shall order breakfast, and afterward I shall walk down to Doctors' Commons, where I hope to get some data which may help us in this matter."

It was nearly one o'clock when Sherlock Holmes returned from his excursion. He held in his hand a sheet of blue paper, scrawled over with notes and figures.

"I have seen the will of the deceased wife," said he. "To determine its exact meaning, I have been obliged to work out the present prices of the investments with which it is concerned. The total income, which at the time of the wife's death was little short of £1100, is now, through the fall in agricultural prices, not more than £750. Each daughter can claim an income of £250, in case of marriage. It is evident, therefore, that if both girls had married, this beauty would have had a mere pittance, while even one of them would cripple him to a very serious extent. My morning's work has not been wasted, since it has proved that he has the very strongest motives for standing in the way of anything of the sort. And now, Watson, this is too serious for dawdling, especially as the old man is aware that we are interesting ourselves in his affairs; so if you are ready, we shall call a cab and drive to Waterloo. I should be very much obliged if you would slip your revolver into your pocket. An Eley's No. 2 is an excellent argument with gentlemen who can twist steel pokers into knots. That and a toothbrush are, I think, all that we need."

At Waterloo we were fortunate in catching a train for Leatherhead, where we hired a trap at the station inn, and drove for four or five miles through the lovely Surrey lanes. My companion sat in front of the trap, his arms folded, his hat pulled down over his eyes, and his chin sunk upon his breast, buried in the deepest thought. Suddenly, however, he started, tapped me on the shoulder, and pointed over the meadows.

"Look there!" said he.

A heavily timbered park stretched up in a gentle slope, thickening into a grove at the highest point. From amid the branches there jutted out the gray gables and high rooftree of a very old mansion.

"Stoke Moran?" said he.

"Yes, sir, that be the house of Dr. Grimesby Roylott," remarked the driver.

"There is some building going on there," said Holmes; "that is where we are going."

"There's the village," said the driver, pointing to a cluster of roofs some distance to the left; "but if you want to get to the house, you'll find it shorter to get over this stile, and so by the footpath over the fields. There it is where the lady is walking."

"And the lady, I fancy, is Miss Stoner," observed Holmes, shading his eyes. "Yes, I think we had better do as you suggest."

We got off, paid our fare, and the trap rattled back on its way to Leatherhead.

"I thought it as well," said Holmes, as we climbed the stile, "that this fellow should think we had come here as architects or on some definite business. It may stop his gossip. Good afternoon, Miss Stoner. You see that we have been as good as our word."

Our client of the morning had hurried forward to meet us with a face which spoke her joy. "I have been waiting so eagerly for you!" she cried, shaking hands with us warmly. "All has turned out splendidly. Dr. Roylott has gone to town, and it is unlikely that he will be back before evening."

"We have had the pleasure of making the doctor's acquaintance," said Holmes, and in a few words he sketched out what had occurred. Miss Stoner turned white to the lips as she listened.

"Good heavens!" she cried. "He has followed me, then."

"So it appears."

"He is so cunning that I never know when I am safe from him. What will he say when he returns?"

"He must guard himself, for he may find that there is someone more cunning than himself upon his track. You must lock yourself up from him tonight. If he is violent, we shall take you away to your aunt's at Harrow. Now, we must make the best use of our time, so kindly take us at once to the rooms which we are to examine."

The building was of gray, lichen-blotched stone, with a high central por-

tion, and two curving wings, like the claws of a crab, thrown out on each side. In one of these wings the windows were broken, and blocked with wooden boards, while the roof was partly caved in, a picture of ruin. The central portion was in little better repair, but the right-hand block was comparatively modern, and the blinds in the windows, with the blue smoke curling up from the chimneys, showed that this was where the family resided. Some scaffolding had been erected against the end wall, and the stonework had been broken into, but there were no signs of any workmen at the moment of our visit. Holmes walked slowly up and down the ill-trimmed lawn, and examined with deep attention the outsides of the windows.

"This, I take it, belongs to the room in which you used to sleep, the center one to your sister's, and the one next to the main building to Dr. Roylott's chamber?"

"Exactly so. But I am now sleeping in the middle one."

"Pending the alterations, as I understand. By the way, there does not seem to be any very pressing need for repairs at that end wall."

"There were none. I believe that it was an excuse to move me from my room."

"Ah! that is suggestive. Now, on the other side of this narrow wing runs the corridor from which these three rooms open. There are windows in it, of course?"

"Yes, but very small ones. Too narrow for anyone to pass through."

"As you both locked your doors at night, your rooms were unapproachable from that side. Now, would you have the kindness to go into your room and bar your shutters."

Miss Stoner did so, and Holmes, after a careful examination through the open window, endeavored in every way to force the shutter open, but without success. There was no slit through which a knife could be passed to raise the bar. Then with his lens he tested the hinges, but they were of solid iron, built firmly into the massive masonry. "Hum!" said he, scratching his chin in some perplexity. "My theory certainly presents some difficulties. No one could pass these shutters if they were bolted. Well, we shall see if the inside throws any light upon the matter."

A small side door led into the whitewashed corridor from which the three bedrooms opened. Holmes refused to examine the third chamber; so we passed at once to the second, that in which Miss Stoner was now sleeping, and in which her sister had met with her fate. It was a homely little room with a low ceiling and a gaping fireplace, after the fashion of old country houses. A brown chest of drawers stood in one corner, a narrow white-counterpaned bed in another, and a dressing table on the left-hand side of the window. These articles, with two small wickerwork chairs, made up all the furniture in the room, save for a square of Wilton carpet in the center. The baseboards and the paneling of the walls were of brown, worm-eaten oak, so old and discolored that it may have dated from the original building of the house. Holmes drew one of the chairs into a corner and sat silent, while his eyes traveled round and round and up and down, taking in every detail of the apartment.

"Where does that bell communicate with?" he asked, at last, pointing to a thick bell rope which hung down beside the bed, the tassel actually lying upon the pillow.

"It goes to the housekeeper's room."

"It looks newer than the other things."

"Yes, it was only put there a couple of years ago."

"Your sister asked for it, I suppose?"

"No, I never heard of her using it. We used always to get what we wanted for ourselves."

"Indeed, it seemed unnecessary to put so

nice a bell-pull there. You will excuse me for a few minutes while I satisfy myself as to this floor." He threw himself down upon his face with his lens in his hand, and crawled swiftly backward and forward, examining minutely the cracks between the boards. Then he did the same with the woodwork with which the chamber was paneled. At last he walked over to the bed, and spent some time in staring at it, and in running his eye up and down the wall. At last he took the bell rope in his hand and gave it a brisk tug.

"Why, it's a dummy," said he.

"Won't it ring?"

"No; it is not even attached to a wire. This is very interesting. You can see now that it is fastened to a hook just above where the little opening for the ventilator is."

"How very absurd! I never noticed that before."

"Very strange!" muttered Holmes, pulling at the rope. "There are one or two very singular points about this room. For example, what a fool a builder must be to open a ventilator into another room, when, with the same trouble, he might have communicated with the outside air!"

"That is also quite modern," said the lady.

"Done about the same time as the bell rope?" remarked Holmes.

"Yes, there were several little changes carried out about that time."

"They seem to have been of a most interesting character—dummy bell ropes, and ventilators which do not ventilate. With your permission, Miss Stoner, we shall now carry our researches into the inner apartment."

Dr. Grimesby Roylott's chamber was larger than that of his stepdaughter, but was as plainly furnished. A camp bed, a small wooden shelf full of books, mostly of a technical character, an armchair beside the bed, a plain wooden chair against the wall, a round table, and a large iron safe were the principal things which met the eye. Holmes walked slowly round and examined each and all of them with the keenest interest.

"What's in here?" he asked, tapping the safe.

"My stepfather's business papers, I think."

"Oh! you have been inside, then?"

"Only once, some years ago. I remember that it was full of papers."

"There isn't a cat in it, for example?"

"What a strange idea!"

"Well, look at this!" He took up a small saucer of milk which stood on the top of the safe.

"No; we don't keep a cat. But there is a cheetah and a baboon."

"Ah, yes; of course! Well, a cheetah is just a big cat, and yet a saucer of milk does not go very far in satisfying its wants, I dare say. There is one point which I should wish to determine." He squatted down in front of the wooden chair, and examined the seat of it with the greatest attention.

"Thank you. That is quite settled," said he, rising and putting his lens in his pocket.

"Hello! Here is something interesting!"

The object which had caught his eye was a small dog lash which lay on a corner of the bed. The lash, however, was curled upon itself, and tied so as to make a loop of whipcord.

"What do you make of that, Watson?"

"It's a common enough lash. But I don't know why it should be tied."

"That is not quite so common, is it? Ah, me! it's a wicked world, and when a clever man turns his brain to crime, it is the worst of all. I think that I have seen enough now, Miss Stoner, and with your permission we shall walk out upon the lawn."

I had never seen my friend's face so grim or his brow so dark as it was when we turned from the scene of this investigation. We had walked several times up and down the lawn, neither Miss Stoner nor myself liking to break in upon his thoughts before he roused himself from his reverie.

"It is very essential, Miss Stoner," said he, "that you should absolutely follow my advice in every respect."

"I shall most certainly do so."

"The matter is too serious for any hesitation. Your life may depend upon your compliance. Now, in the first place, both my friend and I must spend the night in your room."

Both Miss Stoner and I gazed at him in astonishment.

"Yes, it must be so. Let me explain. I believe that that is the village inn over there?"

"Yes, that is the Crown."

"Very good. Your windows would be visible from there?"

"Certainly."

"You must confine yourself to your room, on pretense of a headache, when your stepfather comes back. Then when you hear him retire for the night, you must open the shutters of your window, undo the hasp, put your lamp there as a signal to us, and then withdraw quietly with everything which you are likely to want into the room which you used to occupy. I have no doubt that, in spite of the repairs, you could manage there for one night."

"Oh, yes, easily."

"The rest you will leave in our hands."

"But what will you do?"

"We shall spend the night in your room, and we shall investigate the cause of this noise which has disturbed you."

"I believe, Mr. Holmes, that you have already made up your mind," said Miss Stoner.

"Perhaps I have."

"Then, for pity's sake, tell me what was

the cause of my sister's death."

"I should prefer to have clearer proofs before I speak."

"You can at least tell me whether my own thought is correct, and if she died from some sudden fright."

"No, I do not think so. I think that there was probably some more tangible cause. And now, Miss Stoner, we must leave you, for if Dr. Roylott returned and saw us, our journey would be in vain. Good-bye, and be brave, for if you will do what I have told you, you may rest assured that we shall soon drive away the dangers that threaten you."

Sherlock Holmes and I had no difficulty in engaging a bedroom and sitting room at the Crown Inn. They were on the upper floor, and from our window we could command a view of the avenue gate and of the inhabited wing of Stoke Moran. At dusk we saw Dr. Grimesby Roylott drive past, and a few minutes later we saw a sudden light spring up at the manor house as the lamp was lit in one of the sitting rooms.

"Do you know, Watson," said Holmes, as we sat together in the gathering darkness, "I have really some scruples as to taking you tonight. There is a distinct element of danger."

"Can I be of assistance?"

"Your presence might be invaluable."

"Then I shall certainly come."

"It is very kind of you."

"You speak of danger. You have evidently seen more in these rooms than was visible to me."

"No, but I fancy that I may have deduced a little more. I imagine that you saw all that I did."

"I saw nothing remarkable save the bell rope, and what purpose that could answer I confess is more than I can imagine."

"You saw the ventilator, too?"

"Yes, but I do not think that it is such a very unusual thing to have a small opening between two rooms. It was so small that a rat could hardly pass through."

"I knew that we should find a ventilator before ever we came to Stoke Moran."

"My dear Holmes!"

"Oh yes, I did. You remember in her statement she said that her sister could smell Dr. Roylott's cigar. Now, of course that suggested at once that there must be a communication between the two rooms. It could only be a small one, or it would have been remarked upon at the coroner's inquiry. I deduced a ventilator."

"But what harm can there be in that?"

"Well, there is at least a curious coincidence of dates. A ventilator is made, a cord is hung, and a lady who sleeps in the bed dies. Does not that strike you?"

"I cannot as yet see any connection."

"Did you observe anything very peculiar about that bed?"

"No."

"It was clamped to the floor. Did you ever see a bed fastened like that before?"

"I cannot say that I have."

"The lady could not move her bed. It must always be in the same relative position to the ventilator and to the rope—for so we may call it, since it was clearly never meant for a bell-pull."

"Holmes," I cried, "I seem to see dimly what you are hinting at! We are only just in time to prevent some subtle and horrible crime."

"Subtle enough and horrible enough. When a doctor does go wrong, he is the first of criminals. He has nerve and he has knowledge. This man strikes deep; but I think, Watson, that we shall be able to strike deeper still. But we shall have horrors enough before the night is over; for goodness' sake let us have a quiet pipe, and turn our minds for a few hours to something more cheerful."

About nine o'clock the lights at Stoke Moran were extinguished, and all was dark at the manor house. Two hours passed slowly away, and then, suddenly, just at the stroke of eleven, a single bright light shone out in front of us.

"That is our signal," said Holmes, springing to his feet; "it comes from the middle window."

As we passed out, he exchanged a few words with the landlord, explaining that we were going on a late visit to an acquaintance, and that it was possible that we might spend the night there. A moment later we were out on the dark road, a chill wind blowing in our faces, and one yellow light twinkling in front of us through the gloom to guide us on our somber errand.

There was little difficulty in entering the grounds, for unrepaired breaches gaped in the old park wall. Making our way among the trees, we reached the lawn, crossed it, and were about to enter through the window, when out from a clump of laurel bushes there darted what seemed to be a hideous and distorted child, who threw itself upon the grass with writhing limbs and then ran swiftly across the lawn into the darkness.

I whispered, "Did you see it?"

Holmes was for the moment as startled as I. His hand closed like a vise upon my wrist in his agitation. Then he broke into a low laugh, and put his lips to my ear.

"It is a nice household," he murmured. "That is the baboon."

I had forgotten the doctor's strange pets. There was a cheetah, too; perhaps we might find it upon our shoulders at any moment. I confess that I felt easier in my mind when, after following Holmes's example and slipping off my shoes, I found myself inside the bedroom. My companion noiselessly closed the shutters, moved the lamp onto the table, and cast his eyes round the room. All was as we had seen it in the daytime. Then creeping up to me

and making a trumpet of his hand, he whispered into my ear again so gently that it was all that I could do to distinguish the words:

"The least sound would be fatal to our plans."

I nodded to show that I had heard.

"We must sit without a light. He would see it through the ventilator."

I nodded again.

"Do not go asleep! Your very life may depend upon it. Have your pistol ready in case we should need it. I will sit on the side of the bed, and you in that chair."

I took out my revolver and laid it on the corner of the table.

Holmes had brought up a long, thin cane and this he placed upon the bed beside him. By it he laid the box of matches and the stump of a candle. Then he turned down the lamp, and we were left in darkness.

How shall I ever forget that dreadful vigil? I could not hear a sound, not even the drawing of a breath, and yet I knew that my companion sat open-eyed, within a few feet of me, in the same state of nervous tension in which I was myself. The shutters cut off the least ray of light, and we waited in absolute darkness. From outside came the occasional cry of a night bird, and once at our very window a long-drawn, catlike whine, which told us that the cheetah was indeed at liberty. Far away we could hear the deep tones of the parish clock, which boomed out every quarter of an hour. How long they seemed, those quarters! Twelve struck, and one and two and three, and still we sat, waiting for whatever might befall.

Suddenly there was the momentary gleam of a light up in the direction of the ventilator, which vanished immediately, but was succeeded by a strong smell of burning oil and heated metal. Someone in the next room had lit a dark lantern. I heard a sound of movement, and then all was silent, though the smell grew stronger. For half an hour I sat with straining ears. Then suddenly another sound became audible—a very gentle, soothing sound, like that of a small jet of steam escaping continually from a kettle. The instant that we heard it, Holmes sprang from the bed, struck a match, and lashed furiously with his cane at the bell-pull.

"You see it, Watson?" he yelled.

But I saw nothing. At the moment when Holmes struck the light I heard a low, clear whistle, but the sudden glare flashing into my weary eyes made it impossible for me to tell what it was at which my friend lashed so savagely. I could, however, see that his face was deadly pale, and filled with horror and loathing.

He had ceased to strike, and was gazing up at the ventilator, when suddenly there broke from the silence of the night the most horrible cry to which I have ever listened. It swelled up louder and louder, a hoarse yell of pain and fear and anger all mingled in the one dreadful shriek. They say that away down in the village, and even in the distant parsonage, that cry raised the sleepers from their beds. It struck cold to our hearts.

"What can it mean?" I gasped.

"It means that it is all over," Holmes answered. "And perhaps, after all, it is for the best. Take your pistol, and we will enter Dr. Roylott's room."

With a grave face he lit the lamp and led the way down the corridor. Twice he struck at the chamber door without any reply from within. Then he turned the handle and entered, I at his heels, with the cocked pistol in my hand.

It was a singular sight which met our eyes. On the table stood a dark lantern with the shutter half open, throwing a brilliant beam of light upon the iron safe, the door of which was ajar. Beside this table, on the wooden chair, sat Dr. Grimesby Roylott, clad in a long gray dressing gown, his bare ankles protruding beneath, and his feet thrust into red heelless Turkish slippers. Across his lap lay the short stock with the long lash which we had noticed during the day. His chin was cocked upward and his eyes were fixed in a dreadful, rigid stare at the corner of the ceiling. Round his brow he had a peculiar yellow band, with brownish speckles, which seemed to be bound tightly round his head. As we entered, he made neither sound nor motion.

"The band! the speckled band!" whispered Holmes.

I took a step forward. In an instant his strange headgear began to move, and there reared itself from among his hair the squat diamond-shaped head and puffed neck of a loathsome serpent.

"It is a swamp adder!" cried Holmes; "the deadliest snake in India. He has died within ten seconds of being bitten. In truth, the schemer falls into the pit which he digs for another. Let us thrust this creature back into its den, and we can then remove Miss Stoner to some place of shelter, and let the county police know what has happened."

As he spoke, he drew the dog whip swiftly from the dead man's lap, and throwing the noose round the reptile's neck, he drew it from its horrid perch and threw it into the iron safe, which he closed upon it.

Such are the true facts of the death of Dr. Grimesby Roylott, of Stoke Moran. It is not necessary that I should prolong a narrative which has already run to too great a length, by telling how we broke the sad news to the terrified girl, how we conveyed her by the morning train to the care of her good aunt at Harrow, of how the slow process of official inquiry came to the conclusion that the doctor met his fate while indiscreetly playing with a dangerous pet. The little which I had yet to learn of the case was told me by Sherlock Holmes as we traveled back next day.

"I had," said he, "come to an entirely erroneous conclusion, which shows, my dear Watson, how dangerous it always is to reason from insufficient data. The presence of the gypsies, and the use of the word *band*, which was used by the poor girl, no doubt to explain the appearance which she had caught a hurried glimpse of by the light of her match, were sufficient to put me upon an entirely wrong scent. I can only claim the merit that I instantly reconsidered my position when, however, it became clear to me that whatever danger threatened an occupant of the room could not come either from the window or the door.

"My attention was speedily drawn, as I have already remarked, to this ventilator, and to the bell rope which hung down to the bed. The discovery that this was a dummy, and that the bed was clamped to the floor, instantly gave rise to the suspicion that the rope was there as a bridge for something passing through the hole and coming to the bed. The idea of a snake instantly occurred to me, and when I coupled it with my knowledge that the doctor was furnished with a supply of creatures from India, I felt that I was probably on the right track. The idea of using a form of poison which could not possibly be discovered by any chemical test was just such a one as would occur to a clever and ruthless man who had had an Eastern training. The rapidity with which such a poison would take effect would also, from his point of view, be an advantage. It would be a sharp-eyed coroner, indeed, who could distinguish the two little dark punctures which would show where the poison fangs had done their work. Then I thought of the whistle. Of course he must recall the snake before the morning light revealed it to the victim. He had trained it, probably by the use of the milk which we saw, to return to him when summoned. He would put it through this ventilator at the hour that he thought best, with the certainty that it would crawl down the rope and land on the bed. It might or might not bite the occupant; perhaps she might escape every night for a week, but sooner or later she must fall a victim.

"I had come to these conclusions before ever I had entered his room. An inspection of his chair showed me that he had been in the habit of standing on it, which of course would be necessary in order that he should reach the ventilator. The sight of the safe, the saucer of milk, and the loop of whipcord was enough to finally dispel any doubts which may have remained. The metallic clang heard by Miss Stoner was obviously caused by her stepfather hastily closing the door of his safe upon its terrible occupant. Having once made up my mind, you know the steps which I took in order to put the matter to the proof. I heard the creature hiss, and I instantly lit the light and attacked it."

"With the result of driving it through the ventilator."

"And also with the result of causing it to turn upon its master at the other side. Some of the blows of my cane came home, and roused its snakish temper, so that it flew upon the first person it saw. In this way I am no doubt indirectly responsible for Dr. Grimesby Roylott's death, and I cannot say that it is likely to weigh very heavily upon my conscience."

FOR DISCUSSION

1. Why didn't Sherlock Holmes feel guilty about causing Dr. Roylott's death? Find a quotation in the story which shows Holmes's attitude about crime and punishment.

2. The *plot* of a story develops around a *conflict* which builds to a high point called the *climax*. The conflict in this story was between Helen Stoner and her stepfather, Dr. Roylott. Why did he oppose Helen's goal of marriage? What is the climax, or decisive turning point, in the conflict?

3. Following the climax is the *denouement*, the last part of the story in which the "loose ends" of the plot are tied up. This is especially important in a Sherlock Holmes story because it reveals Holmes's deductive method of solving a crime. How did his first conversation with Helen Stoner demonstrate this method? What was his original guess about the meaning of "the speckled band"? What clues caused him to abandon this deduction, made "from insufficient data," for the correct one?

On that evil, stormy night the hunters in the forest tracked a human prey.

THE INTERLOPERS

SAKI

IN A FOREST of mixed growth some-where on the eastern spurs of the Car-pathians[1] a man stood one winter night watching and listening, as though he waited for some beast of the woods to come within the range of his vision and, later, of his rifle. But the game for whose presence he kept so keen an outlook was none that figured in the sportsman's calen-dar as lawful and proper for the chase; Ulrich von Gradwitz patrolled the dark forest in quest of a human enemy.

The forest lands of Gradwitz were of wide extent and well stocked with game; the narrow strip of precipitous[2] woodland that lay on its outskirt was not remarkable for the game it harbored or the shooting it afforded, but it was the most jealously guarded of all its owner's territorial pos-sessions. A famous lawsuit in the days of his grandfather had wrested it from the illegal possession of a neighboring family of petty landowners; the dispossessed party had never acquiesced[3] in the judgment of the courts, and a long series of poaching affrays[4] and similar scandals had embit-tered the relationships between the families for three generations. The neighbor feud had grown into a personal one since Ulrich

had come to be head of his family; if there was a man in the world whom he detested and wished ill to, it was Georg Znaeym, the inheritor of the quarrel and the tireless game-snatcher and raider of the disputed border-forest.

The feud might, perhaps, have died down or been compromised if the personal ill will of the two men had not stood in the way: as boys they had thirsted for one another's blood, as men each prayed that misfortune might fall on the other; and this wind-scourged winter night Ulrich had banded together his foresters to watch the dark forest, not in quest of four-footed quarry, but to keep a lookout for the prowling thieves whom he suspected of being afoot from across the land boundary. The roebuck,[5] which usually kept in the sheltered hollows during a storm wind, were running like driven things tonight, and there was movement and unrest among the creatures that were wont to sleep through the dark hours. Assuredly there was a disturbing element in the forest, and Ulrich could guess the quarter from whence it came.

He strayed away by himself from the watchers whom he had placed in ambush on the crest of the hill, and wandered far down the steep slopes amid the wild tangle of undergrowth, peering through the tree trunks and listening through the whistling and skirling of the wind and the restless

[1] SPURS . . . CARPATHIANS: ridges of the mountain range between Poland and Czechoslovakia.
[2] PRECIPITOUS: steep.
[3] ACQUIESCED: agreed.
[4] POACHING AFFRAYS: fights while trespassing in order to steal game.

[5] ROEBUCK: a type of male deer.

From *The Short Stories of Saki* by H. H. Munro. Reprinted by permission of The Viking Press, Inc.

88

beating of the branches for sight or sound of the marauders. If only on this wild night, in this dark, lone spot, he might come across Georg Znaeym man to man, with none to witness—that was the wish that was uppermost in his thoughts.

And as he stepped round the trunk of a huge beech, he came face to face with the man he sought.

The two enemies stood glaring at one another for a long, silent moment. Each had a rifle in his hand; each had hate in his heart and murder uppermost in his mind. The chance had come to give full play to the passions of a lifetime. But a man who has been brought up under the code of a restraining civilization cannot easily nerve himself to shoot down his neighbor in cold blood and without word spoken, except for an offense against his hearth and honor. And before the moment of hesitation had given way to action, a deed of Nature's own violence overwhelmed them both.

A fierce shriek of the storm had been answered by a splitting crash over their heads, and ere they could leap aside, a mass of falling beech tree had thundered down on them. Ulrich von Gradwitz found himself stretched on the ground, one arm numb beneath him and the other held almost as helplessly in a tight tangle of forked branches, while both legs were pinned beneath the fallen mass. His heavy shooting boots had saved his feet from being crushed to pieces, but if his fractures were not as serious as they might have been, at least it was evident that he could not move from his present position till someone came to release him. The descending twigs had slashed the skin of his face, and he had to wink away some drops of blood from his eyelashes before he could take in a general view of the disaster. At his side, so near that under ordinary circumstances he could almost have touched him, lay Georg Znaeym, alive and strug-

gling but obviously as helplessly pinioned down as himself. All round them lay a thick-strewn wreckage of splintered branches and broken twigs.

Relief at being alive and exasperation at his captive plight brought a strange medley of pious thank-offerings and sharp curses to Ulrich's lips.

Georg, who was nearly blinded with the blood which trickled across his eyes, stopped his struggling for a moment to listen, and then gave a short, snarling laugh. "So you're not killed, as you ought to be, but you're caught anyway," he cried, "caught fast! Ho, what a jest—Ulrich von Gradwitz snarled in his stolen forest. There's real justice for you!" And he laughed again, mockingly and savagely.

"I'm caught in my own forest land," retorted Ulrich. "When my men come to release us, you will wish, perhaps, that you were in a better plight than caught poaching on a neighbor's land—shame on you!"

Georg was silent for a moment; then he answered quietly: "Are you sure that your men will find much to release? I have men, too, in the forest tonight, close behind me, and *they* will be here first and do the releasing. When they drag me out from under these branches, it won't need much clumsiness on their part to roll this mass of trunk right over on the top of you. Your men will find you dead under a fallen beech tree. For form's sake I shall send my condolences to your family."

"It is a useful hint," said Ulrich fiercely. "My men had orders to follow in ten minutes' time—seven of which must have gone by already—and when they get me out, I will remember the hint. Only, as you will have met your death poaching on my lands, I don't think I can decently send any message of condolence to your family."

"Good," snarled Georg, "good. We fight this quarrel out to the death, you and I and our foresters, with no cursed interlopers to come between us. Death and damnation to you, Ulrich von Gradwitz."

"The same to you, Georg Znaeym, forest-thief, game-snatcher."

Both men spoke with the bitterness of possible defeat before them, for each knew that it might be long before his men would seek him out or find him; it was a bare matter of chance which party would arrive first on the scene.

Both had now given up the useless struggle to free themselves from the mass of wood that held them down; Ulrich limited his endeavors to an effort to bring his one partially free arm near enough to his outer coat pocket to draw out his wine flask. Even when he had accomplished that operation, it was long before he could manage the unscrewing of the stopper or get any of the liquid down his throat. But what a heaven-sent draft it seemed! It was an open winter, and little snow had fallen as yet; hence the captives suffered less from the cold than might have been the case at that season of the year; nevertheless, the wine was warming and reviving to the wounded man, and he looked across with something like a throb of pity to where his enemy lay, just keeping the groans of pain and weariness from crossing his lips.

"Could you reach this flask if I threw it over to you?" asked Ulrich suddenly. "There is good wine in it, and one may as well be as comfortable as one can. Let us drink, even if tonight one of us dies."

"No, I can scarcely see anything, there is so much blood caked round my eyes," said Georg, "and in any case I don't drink wine with an enemy."

Ulrich was silent for a few minutes, and lay listening to the weary screeching of the wind. An idea was slowly forming and growing in his brain, an idea that gained strength every time that he looked across at the man who was fighting so grimly against pain and exhaustion. In the pain and languor that Ulrich himself was feeling, the old fierce hatred seemed to be dying down.

"Neighbor," he said presently, "do as you please if your men come first. It was a fair compact. But as for me, I've changed my mind. If my men are the first to come, you shall be the first to be helped, as though you were my guest. We have quarreled like devils all our lives over this stupid strip of forest, where the trees can't even stand upright in a breath of wind. Lying here tonight, thinking, I've come to think we've been rather fools; there are better things in life than getting the better of a boundary dispute. Neighbor, if you will help me to bury the old quarrel, I—I will ask you to be my friend."

Georg Znaeym was silent for so long that Ulrich thought perhaps he had fainted with the pain of his injuries. Then he spoke slowly and in jerks. "How the whole region would stare and gabble if we rode into the market square together. No one living can remember seeing a Znaeym and a von Gradwitz talking to one another in friendship. And what peace there would be among the forester folk if we ended our feud tonight. And if we chose to make peace among our people, there is none other to interfere, no interlopers from outside. You would come and keep the Sylvester night beneath my roof, and I would come and feast on some high day at your castle. I would never fire a shot on your land save when you invited me as a guest, and you should come and shoot with me down in the marshes where the wildfowl are. In all the countryside there are none that could hinder if we willed to make peace. I never thought to have wanted to do other than hate you all my life, but I think I have changed my mind about things too this last half hour. And you offered me your wine flask. Ulrich von Gradwitz, I will be your friend."

For a space both men were silent, turning over in their minds the wonderful changes that this dramatic reconciliation would bring about. In the cold, gloomy forest, with the wind tearing in fitful gusts through the naked branches and whistling round the tree trunks, they lay and waited for the help that would now bring release and succor to both parties. And each prayed a private prayer that his men might be the first to arrive, so that he might be the first to show honorable attention to the enemy that had become a friend.

Presently, as the wind dropped for a moment, Ulrich broke silence. "Let's shout for help," he said. "In this lull our voices may carry a little way."

"They won't carry far through the trees and undergrowth," said Georg, "but we can try. Together, then."

The two raised their voices in a prolonged hunting call.

"Together again," said Ulrich a few minutes later, after listening in vain for an answering hallo. "I heard something that time, I think," said Ulrich.

"I heard nothing but the pestilential wind," said Georg hoarsely.

There was silence again for some minutes, and then Ulrich gave a joyful cry. "I can see figures coming through the wood. They are following in the way I came down the hillside."

Both men raised their voices in as loud a shout as they could muster.

"They hear us! They've stopped. Now they see us. They're running down the hill towards us," cried Ulrich.

"How many of them are there?" asked Georg.

"I can't see distinctly," said Ulrich. "Nine or ten."

"Then they are yours," said Georg. "I had only seven out with me."

"They are making all the speed they can, brave lads," said Ulrich gladly.

"Are they your men?" asked Georg. "Are they your men?" he repeated impatiently, as Ulrich did not answer.

"No," said Ulrich with a laugh, the idiotic chattering laugh of a man unstrung with hideous fear.

"Who are they?" asked Georg quickly, straining his eyes to see what the other would gladly not have seen.

"Wolves."

FOR DISCUSSION

1. At first the main conflict in the story seems to be man against man; each man sees the other as his enemy. Who is the real enemy? What early clues are there to this hidden conflict?

2. The climax seems to come when Ulrich and Georg end their feud. Where is the climax of the larger feud? Why is there no denouement?

3. This story is *ironic* because it involves a contrast between what the characters expect to happen and what really happens. For example, what does Georg mean by "interlopers"? Who are the real interlopers in the forest? What other ironic contrasts can you point out?

"She had no evening clothes, no jewels, nothing. But she wanted only those things...."

THE NECKLACE
GUY DE MAUPASSANT

SHE WAS ONE OF those attractive pretty girls, born by a freak of fortune in a lower-middle-class family. She had no dowry, no expectations, no way of getting known, appreciated, loved and married by some wealthy gentleman of good family. And she allowed herself to be married to a junior clerk in the Ministry of Public Instruction.

She dressed plainly, having no money to spend on herself. But she was as unhappy as if she had known better days. Women have no sense of caste or breeding, their beauty, their grace, and their charm taking the place of birth and family. Their natural refinement, their instinctive delicacy and adaptability are their only passport to society, and these qualities enable daughters of the people to compete with ladies of gentle birth.

She always had a sense of frustration, feeling herself born for all the refinements and luxuries of life. She hated the bareness of her apartment, the shabbiness of the walls, the worn upholstery of the chairs, and the ugliness of the curtains. All these things, which another woman of her class would not even have noticed, were pain and grief to her. The sight of the little Breton maid doing her simple housework

aroused in her passionate regrets and hopeless dreams. She imagined hushed anterooms hung with oriental fabrics and lit by tall bronze candelabra, with two impressive footmen in knee breeches dozing in great armchairs, made drowsy by the heat of radiators. She imagined vast drawing rooms, upholstered in antique silk, splendid pieces of furniture littered with priceless curios, and dainty scented boudoirs, designed for teatime conversation with intimate friends and much sought-after society gentlemen, whose attentions every woman envies and desires.

When she sat down to dinner at the round table covered with a three-days-old cloth opposite her husband, who took the lid off the casserole with the delighted exclamation: "Ah! your good stew again! How lovely! It's the best dish in the world!" she was dreaming of luxurious dinners with gleaming silver and tapestries peopling the walls with classical figures and exotic birds in a fairy forest; she dreamed of exquisite dishes served on valuable china and whispered compliments listened to with a sphinxlike smile, while toying with the pink flesh of a trout or the wing of a hazel-hen.

She had no evening clothes, no jewels, nothing. But she wanted only those things; she felt that that was the kind of life for her. She so much longed to please, be envied, be fascinating and sought after.

She had a rich friend who had been with

GUY DE MAUPASSANT: pronounced gē də mō·pä-sän'.

"The Necklace" from *The Mountain Inn and Other Stories*, translated by H. N. P. Sloman. Reprinted by permission of Penguin Books Ltd.

her at a convent school, but she did not like going to see her now, the contrast was so painful when she went home. She spent whole days in tears; misery, regrets, hopeless longings caused her such bitter distress.

One evening her husband came home with a broad smile on his face and a large envelope in his hand: "Look!" he cried. "Here's something for you, dear!"

She tore open the envelope eagerly and pulled out a printed card with the words: "The Minister of Public Instruction and Mme. Georges Ramponneau request the honor of the company of M. and Mme. Loisel[1] at the Ministry on the evening of Monday, January 18th."

Instead of being delighted as her husband had hoped, she threw the invitation pettishly down on the table, murmuring: "What's the good of this to me?"

"But I thought you'd be pleased, dear! You never go out and this is an occasion, a great occasion. I had the greatest difficulty to get the invitation. Everybody wants one; it's very select and junior clerks don't often get asked. The whole official world will be there."

She looked at him crossly and declared impatiently: "What do you think I'm to wear?"

He hadn't thought of that and stuttered: "Why! the frock you wear for the theater. I think it's charming!"

He stopped in astonished bewilderment when he saw his wife was crying. Two great tears were running slowly down from the corners of her eyes to the corners of her mouth; he stammered: "What's the matter? What's the matter?"

But with a great effort she had controlled her disappointment and replied quietly, drying her wet cheeks: "Oh! Nothing! Only not having anything to wear I can't

go to the party. Pass on the invitation to some colleague whose wife is better dressed than I."

"Look here, Mathilde! How much would a suitable frock cost, something quite simple that would be useful on other occasions later on?"

She thought for a few seconds, doing a sum and also wondering how much she could ask for without inviting an immediate refusal and an outraged exclamation from the close-fisted clerk. At last with some hesitation she replied: "I don't know exactly but I think I could manage on four hundred francs."[2]

He went slightly pale, for this was just the amount he had put by to get a gun so that he could enjoy some shooting the following summer on the Nanterre plain with some friends who went out lark-shooting on Sundays. But he said: "Right! I'll give you four hundred francs, but try and get a really nice frock."

The date of the party was approaching and Mme. Loisel seemed depressed and worried, though her dress was ready. One evening her husband said to her: "What's the matter? The last three days you've not been yourself."

She replied: "It's rotten not to have a piece of jewelry, not a stone of any kind, to wear. I shall look poverty-stricken. I'd rather not go to the party."

He answered: "But you can wear some real flowers. That's very smart this year. For ten francs you could get two or three magnificent roses."

She was not impressed. "No, there's nothing more humiliating than to look poor in a crowd of wealthy women."

But her husband suddenly cried: "What a fool you are! Go to your friend, Mme. Forestier,[3] and ask her to lend you some of

---

[1] Loisel: lwä·zel′.

[2] francs: money units of France.
[3] Forestier: fô·re·styā′.

her jewelry. You know her well enough to do that."

She uttered a joyful cry: "That's a good idea! I'd never thought of it!"

Next day she went to her friend's house and explained her dilemma.

Mme. Forestier went to a glass-fronted wardrobe, took out a large casket, brought it over, opened it, and said to Mme. Loisel:

"Take what you like, my dear!"

First she looked at bracelets, then a pearl collar, then a Venetian cross in gold and stones, a lovely piece of work. She tried the various ornaments in front of the mirror, unable to make up her mind to take them off and put them back; she kept asking: "Haven't you got anything else?"

"Yes, go on looking; I don't know what you would like."

Suddenly she found a black satin case containing a magnificent diamond necklace, and she wanted it so desperately that her heart began to thump. Her hands were shaking as she picked it up. She put it round her throat over her high blouse and stood in ecstasy before her reflection in the glass. Then she asked hesitantly, her anxiety showing in her voice: "Could you lend me that, just that, nothing else?"

"But of course!"

She threw her arms round her friend's neck and kissed her wildly, and hurried home with her treasure.

The day of the party arrived. Mme. Loisel had a triumph. She was the prettiest woman in the room, elegant, graceful, smiling, in the seventh heaven of happiness. All the men looked at her, asked who she was, and wanted to be introduced. All the private secretaries wanted to dance with her. The Minister himself noticed her.

She danced with inspired abandon, intoxicated with delight, thinking of nothing in the triumph of her beauty and the glory of her success; she was wrapped in a cloud of happiness, the result of all the compliments, all the admiration, all these awakened desires, that wonderful success so dear to every woman's heart.

She left about four in the morning. Her husband had been dozing since midnight in a small, empty drawing room with three other gentlemen, whose wives were also enjoying themselves.

He threw over her shoulders the wraps he had brought for going home, her simple everyday coat, whose plainness clashed with the smartness of her ball dress. She was conscious of this and wanted to hurry away, so as not to be noticed by the ladies who were putting on expensive fur wraps.

Loisel tried to stop her: "Wait a minute! You'll catch cold outside. I'll call a cab."

But she would not listen and ran down the stairs. When they got into the street they could not find a cab and began to hunt for one, shouting to the drivers they saw passing in the distance. In despair they went down towards the Seine, shivering. At last, on the Embankment they found one of those old carriages that ply by night and are only seen in Paris after dark, as if ashamed of their shabbiness in the daytime. It took them back to their house in the Rue des Martyrs and they went sadly up to their apartment. For her this was the end; and he was remembering that he had got to be at the office at ten o'clock.

She took off the wraps she had put round her shoulders, standing in front of the glass to see herself once more in all her glory. But suddenly she uttered a cry; the diamond necklace was no longer round her neck. Her husband, already half undressed, asked: "What's the matter?"

She turned to him in a panic: "Mme. Forestier's necklace has gone!"

He stood up, dumfounded: "What? What do you mean? It's impossible!"

They searched in the folds of her dress,

in the folds of her cloak, in the pockets, everywhere; they could not find it. He asked: "Are you sure you had it on when you left the ball?"

"Yes, I fingered it in the hall at the Ministry."

"But, if you had lost it in the street, we should have heard it drop. It must be in the cab."

"Yes, it probably is. Did you take the number?"

"No! And you didn't notice it, I suppose?"

"No!"

They looked at each other, utterly crushed. Finally Loisel dressed again: "I'll go back along the way we walked and see if I can find it."

He went out and she remained in her evening dress, without the strength even to go to bed, collapsed on a chair, without a fire, her mind a blank.

Her husband returned about seven, having found nothing. He went to the police station, to the papers to offer a reward, to the cab companies, in fact anywhere that gave a flicker of hope.

She waited all day in the same state of dismay at this appalling catastrophe. Loisel came back in the evening, his face pale and lined; he had discovered nothing.

"You must write to your friend," he said, "and say you have broken the clasp of the necklace and are getting it mended. That will give us time to turn around."

So she wrote at his dictation. After a week they had lost all hope and Loisel, who had aged five years, declared: "We must do something about replacing it."

Next day they took the case which had contained the necklace to the jeweler whose name was in it. He looked up his books: "I did not sell the jewel, Madame; I must only have supplied the case."

They went from jeweler to jeweler, looking for a necklace like the other, trying to remember exactly what it was like, both of them sick with worry and anxiety.

At last in the Palais Royal they found a diamond necklace just like the one lost. Its price was forty thousand francs, but they could have it for thirty-six thousand.

So they asked the jeweler to keep it for three days. They made it a condition that he should take it back for thirty-four thousand if the first was found before the end of February.

Loisel had got eighteen thousand francs which his father had left him; he would borrow the rest.

He borrowed one thousand francs from one, five hundred from another, one hundred here, sixty there. He gave I.O.U.'s and notes of hand on ruinous terms, going to the loan sharks and moneylenders of every kind. He mortgaged the whole of the rest of his life, risked his signature on bills without knowing if he would ever be able to honor it; he was tormented with anxiety about the future, with the thought of the crushing poverty about to descend upon him and the prospect of physical privations and mental agony. Then he went and collected the necklace, putting down the thirty-six thousand francs on the jeweler's counter.

When Mme. Loisel took the necklace back to Mme. Forestier, the latter said rather coldly: "You ought to have brought it back sooner; I might have wanted it."

She did not open the case, as her friend had feared she might. If she had detected the replacement what would she have thought? What would she have said? Would she have considered her a thief?

Now Mme. Loisel learned to know the grim life of the very poor. However, she faced the position with heroic courage. This ghastly debt must be paid and she

Continued on page 107

IDEAS AND THE ARTS

As is true of many phrases, "point of view" has two quite different meanings. The simpler and basic meaning has to do with the purely physical character of perception, what we see with our eyes. In this sense, we all share pretty much the same point of view. People with normal powers of sight will see things in much the same way, as long as the observers occupy the same position. For an obvious example, if you look at the skyline of a city from a distance, a ten-story building will not seem very tall if the skyline also includes a twenty-story building and a thirty-story building. But if you stand at the foot of the ten-story building and look up, it will seem very high.

The other meaning of "point of view" is just the opposite. In this meaning everyone interprets the same thing in different ways. These ways may be quite close or quite far apart. For example, consider the different ways students can respond to the same teacher. One student may find the teacher pleasant, easy to understand and to work with. Another student might find this same teacher unpleasant, difficult to understand, and impossible to work with. Obviously each student has a different point of view toward the teacher. To distinguish this meaning of "point of view" from the meaning that refers to physical vision, we can use the word *orientation,* meaning "mental point of view."

Now let us suppose that all students in the class, except one, have much the same orientation toward the teacher that the first student has. In this situation we tend to think that the orientation of the majority is "true" or "right." And we may wonder why the small majority of one has a different orientation.

The answer may have nothing to do with the teacher at all. The teacher is what we call an "authority figure," someone who has the special right to control other people in a particular situation. The authority figure has the right to settle disagreements that arise in that situation. If we study the student who cannot get along with the teacher and observe his behavior in other situations, we might find that he always has a negative orientation whenever he meets an authority figure. We may find that he dislikes his football coach and his doctor, as well as the teacher. He may dislike anyone who has any right to control him. This dislike may have nothing to do with particular people, such as the teacher, but only with his orientation toward authority figures.

One of the most interesting things about orientation is the effect it may have on our perceptions, on our physical point of view. An experiment was once conducted on some sailors. The people conducting the experiment dressed an ordinary department-store mannequin of normal size in a naval officer's uniform. They then placed him in a kind of stage that was so lighted and arranged that ordinary eyesight could not tell whether the mannequin was leaning forward, leaning backward, or standing upright. Most sailors saw the mannequin as standing upright and as about the same size as themselves. A few sailors, however, saw him as larger than normal and leaning forward in a threatening manner. Something in the orientation of these sailors made them see it in this way. Their orientation clearly affected their perspective.

Each kind of point of view affects the other kind. What we see affects the way we feel and think. What we feel and think affects the way we see.

Morse Peckham

ART

A landscape painter has to be concerned with three different problems before he begins to paint. Each problem involves a question of point of view or orientation. First, the painter must decide on the physical point of view from which he wants to see the landscape as he paints it, or from which he wants to imagine what he sees, if he is inventing a landscape. Second, he must consider the ways of painting that are being used at the time he paints. These ways are called "conventions." A convention is simply something that everyone does; in this case it means a particular method or style of painting that is popular at the time. When a painter accepts and uses a convention (such as, for example, making his figures realistic or nonrealistic), he is accepting the point of view that it suggests. He must decide whether he wants to use this point of view or not. Third, he must consider his own particular orientation, or mental point of view. What is his attitude toward the landscape he is painting? What does he find important in it? What does he want to say about it?

John Constable's *Dedham Lock and Mill* may not appear unusual today, but when it first appeared it was regarded as revolutionary. Constable did not accept the convention of his time which assigned certain limited colors to certain objects. Constable felt that these conventions distorted our view of the natural world because they did not allow for the real colors of nature or for the actual light of the natural world. For this picture he chose a scene in a very quiet part of England, his own home country. He used the canal in order to reflect the light of the sky, and he used the buildings in order to contrast their color with the greens of the grass and trees. He wanted to paint a landscape that would show the world as it really is.

Joseph W. M. Turner lived in England about the same time as Constable, but he continued painting long after Constable was dead. His orientation led him to take a new and different point of view toward landscapes. In *Norham Castle, Sunrise,* for example, he is interested in light, and he only suggests the details of the landscape. He broke from the conventions of his time so sharply that most people were bewildered by his work. As a result he was not really understood and appreciated until after his death.

James McNeill Whistler, an American painter who lived after Constable and spent most of his life in England and France, had quite different interests. He also was discontented with the conventions of landscape painting in his day, conventions that for the most part had been established by Constable. The title of Whistler's painting, *Harmony in Blue and Silver: Trouville,* suggests what his orientation was. He was not really interested in landscape painting for its own sake, as was Constable. Just as, when he painted portraits, he was not interested in people for their own sakes. For Whistler, a landscape was an excuse to create color combinations and harmonies. Beauty as he conceived it was his chief interest, and his point of view led him to paint landscapes that would be a kind of visual music.

Vincent Van Gogh, a Dutch painter who lived after Whistler, had quite different interests. As *Road with Cypress and Stars* indicates, his greatest interest was his own personality. For a painter the most exciting part of painting is actually putting the paint on the canvas. In the past paint has been put on so that the brushstrokes would not be noticeable, unless one looked very closely at the picture. Van Gogh, however, made his brushstrokes so big and bold that they dominate the landscape. The landscape is an excuse for showing the brushstrokes and giving them their own meaning. For Van Gogh, who was a very emotional man, they meant his own emotional intensity and excitement.

The Flemish painter Joachim de Patinir lived about four hundred and fifty years ago, long before the preceding painters. He was interested in presenting landscapes for their own sake, but not in landscapes that actually existed. Although the subject of *St. Jerome in the Wilderness* is a religious subject, the saint is not the important part of the painting. In Patinir's day some men came to believe that they could understand the world through the use of human reason, without the aid of religion. This idea led Patinir to create a rational landscape. He wanted to show that the painter could comprehend all the important elements of his world in a single painting. The foreground, the middle, and the background are all in different colors. This differing reflects part of Patinir's desire to arrange the world as the human reason would comprehend it.

A hundred years later in China there lived a painter, Wang Chien, who painted according to the Chinese conventions of his day. If we compare this painting, *White Clouds over Hsiao and Hsiang* (after *Chao-Meng-fu*), with the others, we see that in spite of their differences the Europeans all used certain conventions. They all, for example, followed the laws of perspective, giving their figures the appearance of three dimensions. The Chinese painters did not use this convention. This is a constructed or invented landscape, like Patinir's, but its intention is different. The Chinese painter wanted to show the unity of man and nature, not the separation of reason from nature.

Morse Peckham

JOHN CONSTABLE (1776-1837) *DEDHAM LOCK AND MILL.* Victoria and Albert Museum, London.

JOSEPH MALLORD WILLIAM TURNER (1775-1851) *NORHAM CASTLE, SUNRISE.* The Tate Gallery, London.

JAMES ABBOTT McNEILL WHISTLER (1834-1903) *HARMONY IN BLUE AND SILVER: TROUVILLE.* Isabella Stewart Gardner Museum, Boston.

VINCENT VAN GOGH (1853-1890) *ROAD WITH CYPRESS AND STARS.* Kroller-Muller Museum, Otherlo, Holland.

JOACHIM DE PATINIR (c. 1475-1524) *ST. JEROME IN THE WILDERNESS.* Prado Museum, Madrid.

WANG CHIEN (1598-1677) *WHITE CLOUDS OVER HSIAO AND HSIANG.*
Smithsonian Institution, Freer Gallery of Art, Washington, D.C.

MUSIC

LUDWIG VAN BEETHOVEN:
SONATA #12, *Opus 26, First Movement*
[A number of recordings available]

Life would be very dull if we all had the same point of view toward everything. Differing points of view make life more interesting. They also bring to our attention things we might otherwise not notice. There are, for example, different points of view toward music and different points of view within music itself.

A major division can be made between what we call "classical" or "serious" music and what we call "semiclassical" or "popular" music. Serious music is that type which describes emotions and feelings of conflict, struggle, and disturbance, and also of power, triumph, and exaltation. Since we rarely succeed completely in everything we attempt, serious music is likely to reflect our sense of failure. Since popular music often deals with situations in which we do succeed, it is more likely to be concerned with success.

Attitudes toward music differ greatly. Some people, of course, find no importance in any kind of music. Some people find serious music extremely important. Others, of course, find great value in popular music and none in serious music. A final point of view is that we all need anything that tells us something about ourselves, including music.

Ideas about points of view are helpful for understanding music because music deals with points of view and changing points of view. A major difference between serious and popular music has to do with points of view. A piece of music will present many different points of view, often in quite rapid succession. A piece of popular music will usually present one point of view, or at most, two. Moreover, serious music will present different points of view toward the same musical material.

One device that makes music both serious and interesting is the variation of a theme. One way to create variation is to present a melody at the beginning of a composition and after that to alter it in different ways. Another way is to present the melody, restate it in different forms, and then repeat it in its original form. In some compositions two or more melodies are presented. Those melodies are then repeated. Then both melodies are changed or varied, sometimes separately and sometimes together. They are then repeated in their original form and sequence and are then varied again.

A widely used way of composing serious music is called "Theme and Variations." An example is the first movement of Beethoven's Sonata #12, *Opus 26.* In presenting the theme he lingers on his basic idea. He presents it once and then presents it again, with a few changes. Then he gives us a different section of his melody and finally returns to repeat his first interpretation. The form used here is known as the "a a b a" form. The theme is gentle, a little sad, perhaps, not at all energetic or ambitious.

The first variation introduces a little more energy and activity. The second variation is considerably more energetic. The first has broken rhythms, but the second has a very regular rhythm. Then there is a change. In the third variation a different point of view is presented. The original calm is made sad, disturbed, passionate. The fourth sounds rather questioning, as an attempt is made to break the original mood. The fifth variation turns the original mood into one of dancelike ease and gracefulness. It ends with a new melody returning us to the original mood.

Morse Peckham

would pay it. They got rid of the maid; they gave up the apartment and took an attic under the tiles. She did all the heavy work of the house as well as the hateful kitchen jobs. She washed up, ruining her pink nails on the coarse crockery and the bottoms of the saucepans. She washed the dirty linen and shirts and the kitchen cloths and dried them on a line. She carried the rubbish down to the street every morning and brought up the water, stopping on every floor to get her breath. And dressed as a woman of the people, she went to the fruiterer, the grocer and the butcher with her basket on her arm, bargaining in spite of their rudeness and fighting for every penny of her miserable pittance.

Every month some notes of hand had to be paid off and others renewed to gain time. Her husband worked in the evening keeping a tradesman's books and often at night he did copying at twenty-five centimes a page. This life went on for ten years.

After ten years they had paid everything back, including the interest and the accumulated compound interest.

Mme. Loisel now looked an old woman. She had become the strong, tough, coarse woman we find in the homes of the poor. Her hair was neglected, her skirt was askew, her hands were red, and her voice loud; she even scrubbed the floors. But sometimes, when her husband was at the office, she would sit down near the window and dream of that evening long ago, the ball at which she had been such a success.

What would have happened to her if she had not lost the necklace? Who can say? Life is such a strange thing with its changes and chances. Such a little thing can make or mar it!

One Sunday, when she had gone for a stroll in the Champs-Élysées as a change from the week's grind, she suddenly saw a lady taking a child for a walk. It was Mme. Forestier, still young, still beautiful, still attractive.

Mme. Loisel felt a wave of emotion. Should she speak to her? Yes, she would. Now that she had paid, she would tell her everything. Why not?

She went up to her: "Good morning, Jeanne!"

The other woman did not recognize her; surprised at being addressed in this familiar fashion by a common woman, she stammered: "But, Madame . . . I don't know you . . . there must be some mistake."

"No! I'm Mathilde Loisel!"

Her friend exclaimed: "Oh! Poor Mathilde, how you've changed!"

"Yes, I've had a pretty grim time since I saw you last, with lots of trouble—and it was all your fault!"

"My fault? What do you mean?"

"You remember that diamond necklace you lent me to go to the party at the Ministry?"

"Yes, what about it?"

"Well! I lost it!"

"What! But you brought it back to me."

"I brought you back another exactly like it; and for ten years we've been paying for it. You'll realize it hasn't been easy, for we had no money of our own. Well, now it's all over and I'm glad of it!"

Mme. Forestier had stopped: "You say you bought a diamond necklace to replace mine?"

"Yes! And you never spotted it, did you? They were as like as two peas."

And she smiled with simple proud pleasure.

Mme. Forestier, deeply moved, took both her hands: "Oh! my poor Mathilde! But mine was only paste, not worth more than five hundred francs at most!"

FOR DISCUSSION

1. Does the surprise ending in this story seem appropriate? Before answering, consider these questions: Did it make any difference at the ball that the necklace was paste? Would Mme. Loisel's life after the ball have been different if the necklace had been real? How does the paste necklace at the end of the story symbolize Mme. Loisel's values at the beginning of the story?

2. The main character in a story is called the *protagonist,* or hero. The protagonist's enemy or opponent is called the *antagonist.* Who is Mme. Loisel's antagonist? What is the conflict in this story? Where is the climax, the point beyond which there is no turning back in resolving the conflict?

FOR COMPOSITION

• Is Mme. Loisel's husband in any way responsible for what happens in this story? Write a brief composition in which you explain to what extent M. Loisel was or was not responsible. Use references from the story to support your arguments.

In a Greek myth Antaeus, giant son of the earth goddess Terra, forced all strangers to his country to wrestle to the death. No one could defeat him, for he rose with renewed strength every time he was thrown to his mother earth. Finally Hercules fought him successfully by holding him in the air and strangling him. Losing contact with the earth, Antaeus died. This story of a modern Antaeus suggests that the ancient myth still has relevance.

ANTAEUS
BORDEN DEAL

THIS WAS DURING the wartime, when lots of people were coming North for jobs in factories and war industries, when people moved around a lot more than they do now and sometimes kids were thrown into new groups and new lives that were completely different from anything they had ever known before. I remember this one kid; T. J. his name was, from somewhere down South, whose family moved into our building during that time. They'd come North with everything they owned piled into the back seat of an old-model sedan that you wouldn't expect could make the trip, with T. J. and his three younger sisters riding shakily atop the load of junk.

Our building was just like all the others there, with families crowded into a few rooms, and I guess there were twenty-five or thirty kids about my age in that one building. Of course, there were a few of us who formed a gang and ran together all the time after school, and I was the one who brought T. J. in and started the whole thing.

The building right next door to us was a factory where they made walking dolls.

From *Southwest Review*, Spring 1961; Southern Methodist University Press. Reprinted by permission of the author.

It was a low building with a flat, tarred roof that had a parapet all around it about head-high, and we'd found out a long time before that no one, not even the watchman, paid any attention to the roof because it was higher than any of the other buildings around. So my gang used the roof as a headquarters. We could get up there by crossing over to the fire escape from our own roof on a plank and then going on up. It was a secret place for us, where nobody else could go without our permission.

I remember the day I first took T. J. up there to meet the gang. He was a stocky, robust kid with a shock of white hair, nothing sissy about him except his voice—he talked different from any of us, and you noticed it right away. But I liked him anyway, so I told him to come on up.

We climbed up over the parapet and dropped down on the roof. The rest of the gang were already there.

"Hi," I said. I jerked my thumb at T. J. "He just moved into the building yesterday."

He just stood there, not scared or anything, just looking, like the first time you see somebody you're not sure you're going to like.

"Hi," Blackie said. "Where you from?"

"Marion County," T. J. said.

We laughed. "Marion County?" I said. "Where's that?"

He looked at me like I was a stranger, too. "It's in Alabama," he said, like I ought to know where it was.

"What's your name?" Charley said.

"T. J.," he said, looking back at him. He had pale blue eyes that looked washed-out, but he looked directly at Charley, waiting for his reaction. He'll be all right, I thought. No sissy in him . . . except that voice. Who ever talked like that?

"T. J.," Blackie said. "That's just initials. What's your real name? Nobody in the world has just initials."

"I do," he said. "And they're T. J. That's all the name I got."

His voice was resolute with the knowledge of his rightness, and for a moment no one had anything to say. T. J. looked around at the rooftop and down at the black tar under his feet. "Down yonder where I come from," he said, "we played out in the woods. Don't you-all have no woods around here?"

"Naw," Blackie said. "There's the park a few blocks over, but it's full of kids and cops and old women. You can't do a thing."

T. J. kept looking at the tar under his feet. "You mean you ain't got no fields to raise nothing in? No watermelons or nothing?"

"Naw," I said scornfully. "What do you want to grow something for? The folks can buy everything they need at the store."

He looked at me again with that strange, unknowing look. "In Marion County," he said, "I had my own acre of cotton and my own acre of corn. It was mine to plant ever' year."

He sounded like it was something to be proud of, and in some obscure way it made the rest of us angry. "Heck!" Blackie said. "Who'd want to have their own acre of cotton and corn?"

T. J. looked at him. "Well, you get part of the bale offen your acre," he said seriously. "And I fed my acre of corn to my calf."

We didn't really know what he was talking about, so we were more puzzled than angry; otherwise, I guess, we'd have chased him off the roof and wouldn't let him be part of our gang. But he was strange and different, and we were all attracted by his stolid sense of rightness and belonging, maybe by the strange softness of his voice contrasting our own tones of speech into harshness.

He moved his foot against the black tar. "We could make our own field right here," he said softly, thoughtfully. "Come spring we could raise us what we want to . . . watermelons and garden truck[1] and no telling what all."

"You'd have to be a good farmer to make these tar roofs grow any watermelons," I said. We all laughed.

But T. J. looked serious. "We could haul us some dirt up here," he said. "And spread it out even and water it, and before you know it, we'd have us a crop in here." He looked at us intently. "Wouldn't that be fun?"

"They wouldn't let us," Blackie said quickly.

"I thought you said this was you-all's roof," T. J. said to me. "That you-all could do anything you wanted up here."

"They've never bothered us," I said. I felt the idea beginning to catch fire in me. It was a big idea, and it took a while for it to sink in, but the more I thought about it, the better I liked it. "Say," I said to the gang, "he might have something there. Just make us a regular roof garden, with flowers and grass and trees and everything. And all ours, too," I said. "We wouldn't let anybody up here except the ones we wanted to."

[1] GARDEN TRUCK: vegetables grown for market.

"It'd take a while to grow trees," T. J. said quickly, but we weren't paying any attention to him. They were all talking about it suddenly, all excited with the idea after I'd put it in a way they could catch hold of it. Only rich people had roof gardens, we knew, and the idea of our own private domain excited them.

"We could bring it up in sacks and boxes," Blackie said. "We'd have to do it while the folks weren't paying any attention to us. We'd have to come up to the roof of our building and then cross over with it."

"Where could we get the dirt?" somebody said worriedly.

"Out of those vacant lots over close to school," Blackie said. "Nobody'd notice if we scraped it up."

I slapped T. J. on the shoulder. "Man, you had a wonderful idea," I said, and everybody grinned at him, remembering he had started it. "Our own private roof garden."

He grinned back. "It'll be ourn," he said. "All ourn." Then he looked thoughtful again. "Maybe I can lay my hands on some cotton seed, too. You think we could raise us some cotton?"

We'd started big projects before at one time or another, like any gang of kids, but they'd always petered out for lack of organization and direction. But this one didn't . . . somehow or other T. J. kept it going all through the winter months. He kept talking about the watermelons and the cotton we'd raise, come spring, and when even that wouldn't work, he'd switch around to my idea of flowers and grass and trees, though he was always honest enough to add that it'd take a while to get any trees started. He always had it on his

mind, and he'd mention it in school, getting them lined up to carry dirt that afternoon, saying in a casual way that he reckoned a few more weeks ought to see the job through.

Our little area of private earth grew slowly. T. J. was smart enough to start in one corner of the building, heaping up the carried earth two or three feet thick, so that we had an immediate result to look at, to contemplate with awe. Some of the evenings T. J. alone was carrying earth up to the building, the rest of the gang distracted by other enterprises or interests, but T. J. kept plugging along on his own, and eventually we'd all come back to him again, and then our own little acre would grow more rapidly.

He was careful about the kind of dirt he'd let us carry up there, and more than once he dumped a sandy load over the parapet into the areaway below because it wasn't good enough. He found out the kinds of earth in all the vacant lots for blocks around. He'd pick it up and feel it and smell it, frozen though it was sometimes, and then he'd say it was good growing soil or it wasn't worth anything and we'd have to go on somewhere else.

Thinking about it now, I don't see how he kept us at it. It was hard work, lugging paper sacks and boxes of dirt all the way up the stairs of our own building, keeping out of the way of the grownups so they wouldn't catch on to what we were doing. They probably wouldn't have cared, for they didn't pay much attention to us, but we wanted to keep it secret anyway. Then we had to go through the trap door to our roof, teeter over a plank to the fire escape, then climb two or three stories to the parapet and drop down onto the roof. All that for a small pile of earth that sometimes didn't seem worth the effort. But T. J. kept the vision bright within us, his words

shrewd and calculated toward the fulfillment of his dreams; and he worked harder than any of us. He seemed driven toward a goal that we couldn't see, a particular point in time that would be definitely marked by signs and wonders that only he could see.

The laborious earth just lay there during the cold months, inert and lifeless, the clods lumpy and cold under our feet when we walked over it. But one day it rained, and afterward there was a softness in the air and the earth was alive and giving again with moisture and warmth. That evening T. J. smelled the air, his nostrils dilating with the odor of the earth under his feet.

"It's spring," he said, and there was a gladness rising in his voice that filled us all with the same feeling. "It's mighty late for it, but it's spring. I'd just about decided it wasn't never gonna get here at all."

We were all sniffing at the air, too, trying to smell it the way that T. J. did, and I can still remember the sweet odor of the earth under our feet. It was the first time in my life that spring and spring earth had meant anything to me. I looked at T. J. then, knowing in a faint way the hunger within him through the toilsome winter months, knowing the dream that lay behind his plan. He was a new Antaeus, preparing his own bed of strength.

"Planting time," he said. "We'll have to find us some seed."

"What do we do?" Blackie said. "How do we do it?"

"First we'll have to break up the clods," T. J. said. "That won't be hard to do. Then we plant the seed, and after a while they come up. Then you got you a crop." He frowned. "But you ain't got it raised yet. You got to tend it and hoe it and take care of it, and all the time it's growing and growing while you're awake and while you're asleep. Then you lay it by when it's growed and let it ripen; and then you got you a crop."

"There's those wholesale seed houses over on Sixth," I said. "We could probably swipe some grass seed over there."

T. J. looked at the earth. "You-all seem mighty set on raising some grass," he said. "I ain't never put no effort into that. I spent all my life trying not to raise grass."

"But it's pretty," Blackie said. "We could play on it and take sunbaths on it. Like having our own lawn. Lots of people got lawns."

"Well," T. J. said. He looked at the rest of us, hesitant for the first time. He kept on looking at us for a moment. "I did have it in mind to raise some corn and vegetables. But we'll plant grass."

He was smart. He knew where to give in. And I don't suppose it made any difference to him really. He just wanted to grow something, even if it was grass.

"Of course," he said, "I do think we ought to plant a row of watermelons. They'd be mighty nice to eat while we was a-laying on that grass."

We all laughed. "All right," I said. "We'll plant us a row of watermelons."

Things went very quickly then. Perhaps half the roof was covered with the earth, the half that wasn't broken by ventilators, and we swiped pocketfuls of grass seed from the open bins in the wholesale seed house, mingling among the buyers on Saturdays and during the school lunch hour. T. J. showed us how to prepare the earth, breaking up the clods and smoothing it and sowing the grass seed. It looked rich and black now with moisture, receiving of the seed, and it seemed that the grass sprang up overnight, pale green in the early spring.

We couldn't keep from looking at it, unable to believe that we had created this delicate growth. We looked at T. J. with

understanding now, knowing the fulfillment of the plan he had carried alone within his mind. We had worked without full understanding of the task, but he had known all the time.

We found that we couldn't walk or play on the delicate blades, as we had expected to, but we didn't mind. It was enough just to look at it, to realize that it was the work of our own hands, and each evening the whole gang was there, trying to measure the growth that had been achieved that day.

One time a foot was placed on the plot of ground . . . one time only, Blackie stepping onto it with sudden bravado. Then he looked at the crushed blades, and there was shame in his face. He did not do it again. This was his grass, too, and not to be desecrated. No one said anything, for it was not necessary.

T. J. had reserved a small section for watermelons, and he was still trying to find some seed for it. The wholesale house didn't have any watermelon seed, and we didn't know where we could lay our hands on them. T. J. shaped the earth into mounds, ready to receive them, three mounds lying in a straight line along the edge of the grass plot.

We had just about decided that we'd have to buy the seed if we were to get them. It was a violation of our principles, but we were anxious to get the watermelons started. Somewhere or other, T. J. got his hands on a seed catalogue and brought it one evening to our roof garden.

"We can order them now," he said, showing us the catalogue. "Look!"

We all crowded around, looking at the fat, green watermelons pictured in full color on the pages. Some of them were split open, showing the red, tempting meat, making our mouths water.

"Now we got to scrape up some seed

money," T. J. said, looking at us. "I got a quarter. How much you-all got?"

We made up a couple of dollars between us, and T. J. nodded his head. "That'll be more than enough. Now we got to decide what kind to get. I think them Kleckley Sweets. What do you-all think?"

He was going into esoteric[1] matters beyond our reach. We hadn't even known there were different kinds of melons. So we just nodded our heads and agreed that yes, we thought the Kleckley Sweets too.

"I'll order them tonight," T. J. said. "We ought to have them in a few days."

Then an adult voice said behind us: "What are you boys doing up here?"

It startled us, for no one had ever come up here before, in all the time we had been using the roof of the factory. We jerked around and saw three men standing near the trap door at the other end of the roof. They weren't policemen, or night watchmen, but three men in plump business suits, looking at us. They walked toward us.

"What are you boys doing up here?" the one in the middle said again.

We stood still, guilt heavy among us, levied by the tone of voice, and looked at the three strangers.

The men stared at the grass flourishing behind us. "What's this?" the man said. "How did this get up here?"

"Sure is growing good, ain't it?" T. J. said conversationally. "We planted it."

The men kept looking at the grass as if they didn't believe it. It was a thick carpet over the earth now, a patch of deep greenness startling in the sterile industrial surroundings.

"Yes, sir," T. J. said proudly. "We toted that earth up here and planted that grass." He fluttered the seed catalogue. "And

[1] ESOTERIC: intended for or understood by only a small group.

we're just fixing to plant us some watermelon."

The man looked at him then, his eyes strange and faraway. "What do you mean, putting this on the roof of my building?" he said. "Do you want to go to jail?"

T. J. looked shaken. The rest of us were silent, frightened by the authority of his voice. We had grown up aware of adult authority, of policemen and night watchmen and teachers, and this man sounded like all the others. But it was a new thing to T. J.

"Well, you wan't using the roof," T. J. said. He paused a moment and added shrewdly, "So we just thought to pretty it up a little bit."

"And sag it so I'd have to rebuild it," the man said sharply. He turned away, saying to a man beside him, "See that all that junk is shoveled off by tomorrow."

"Yes, sir," the man said.

T. J. started forward. "You can't do that," he said. "We toted it up here, and it's our earth. We planted it and raised it and toted it up here."

The man stared at him coldly. "But it's my building," he said. "It's to be shoveled off tomorrow."

"It's our earth," T. J. said desperately. "You ain't got no right!"

The men walked on without listening and descended clumsily through the trap door. T. J. stood looking after them, his body tense with anger, until they had disappeared. They wouldn't even argue with him, wouldn't let him defend his earth-rights.

He turned to us. "We won't let 'em do it," he said fiercely. "We'll stay up here all day tomorrow and the day after that, and we won't let 'em do it."

We just looked at him. We knew that there was no stopping it. He saw it in our faces, and his face wavered for a moment before he gripped it into determination.

"They ain't got no right," he said. "It's our earth. It's our land. Can't nobody touch a man's own land."

We kept on looking at him, listening to the words but knowing that it was no use. The adult world had descended on us even in our richest dream, and we knew there was no calculating the adult world, no fighting it, no winning against it.

We started moving slowly toward the parapet and the fire escape, avoiding a last look at the green beauty of the earth that T. J. had planted for us . . . had planted deeply in our minds as well as in our experience. We filed slowly over the edge and down the steps to the plank, T. J. coming last, and all of us could feel the weight of his grief behind us.

"Wait a minute," he said suddenly, his voice harsh with the effort of calling. We stopped and turned, held by the tone of his voice, and looked up at him standing above us on the fire escape.

"We can't stop them?" he said, looking down at us, his face strange in the dusky light. "There ain't no way to stop 'em?"

"No," Blackie said with finality. "They own the building."

We stood still for a moment, looking up at T. J., caught into inaction by the decision working in his face. He stared back at us, and his face was pale and mean in the poor light, with a bald nakedness in his skin like cripples have sometimes.

"They ain't gonna touch my earth," he said fiercely. "They ain't gonna lay a hand on it! Come on."

He turned around and started up the fire escape again, almost running against the effort of climbing. We followed more slowly, not knowing what he intended. By the time we reached him, he had seized a board and thrust it into the soil, scooping it up and flinging it over the parapet into the areaway below. He straightened and looked us squarely in the face.

"They can't touch it," he said. "I won't let 'em lay a dirty hand on it!"

We saw it then. He stooped to his labor again and we followed, the gusts of his anger moving in frenzied labor among us as we scattered along the edge of earth, scooping it and throwing it over the parapet, destroying with anger the growth we had nurtured with such tender care. The soil carried so laboriously upward to the light and the sun cascaded swiftly into the dark areaway, the green blades of grass crumpled and twisted in the falling.

It took less time than you would think . . . the task of destruction is infinitely easier than that of creation. We stopped at the end, leaving only a scattering of loose soil, and when it was finally over, a stillness stood among the group and over the factory building. We looked down at the bare sterility of black tar, felt the harsh texture of it under the soles of our shoes, and the anger had gone out of us, leaving only a sore aching in our minds like over-stretched muscles.

T. J. stopped for a moment, his breathing slowing from anger and effort, caught into the same contemplation of destruction as all of us. He stooped slowly, finally, and picked up a lonely blade of grass left trampled under our feet and put it between his teeth, tasting it, sucking the greenness out of it into his mouth. Then he started walking toward the fire escape, moving before any of us were ready to move, and disappeared over the edge while we stared after him.

We followed him, but he was already halfway down to the ground, going on past the board where we crossed over, climbing down into the areaway. We saw the last section swing down with his weight, and then he stood on the concrete below us, looking at the small pile of anonymous earth scattered by our throwing. Then he walked across the place where we could see him and disappeared toward the street without glancing back, without looking up to see us watching him.

They did not find him for two weeks.

Then the Nashville police caught him just outside the Nashville freight yards. He was walking along the railroad track; still heading south, still heading home.

As for us, who had no remembered home to call us . . . none of us ever again climbed the escape-way to the roof.

FOR DISCUSSION

1. Why did T. J. destroy the garden and leave for home? What did he have in common with the Antaeus of Greek myth?

2. T. J. headed home, but the city boys had "no remembered home" to call them. How were their attitudes about their environment different from T. J.'s? Do you think T. J. made any permanent change in these attitudes?

FOR COMPOSITION

• What do you think is the theme (general meaning or lesson) of this story? Does it still apply now that most Americans live in cities, or does it make sense only for people brought up in the country?

To a science fiction writer like Ray Bradbury, there are cosmic mysteries even in a quiet picnic by the sea.

THE VACATION
RAY BRADBURY

IT WAS A DAY as fresh as grass growing up and clouds going over and butterflies coming down can make it. It was a day compounded from silences of bee and flower and ocean and land, which were not silences at all, but motions, stirs, flutters, risings, fallings, each in its own time and matchless rhythm. The land did not move, but moved. The sea was not still, yet was still. Paradox flowed into paradox, stillness mixed with stillness, sound with sound. The flowers vibrated and the bees fell in separate and small showers of golden rain on the clover. The seas of hill and the seas of ocean were divided, each from the other's motion, by a railroad track, empty, compounded of rust and iron marrow, a track on which, quite obviously, no train had run in many years. Thirty miles north it swirled on away to further mists of distance, thirty miles south it tunneled islands of cloud-shadow that changed their continental positions on the sides of far mountains as you watched.

Now, suddenly, the railroad track began to tremble.

A blackbird, standing on the rail, felt a rhythm grow faintly, miles away, like a heart beginning to beat.

The blackbird leaped up over the sea.

The rail continued to vibrate softly until, at long last, around a curve and along the shore came a small workman's handcar, its two-cylinder engine popping and spluttering in the great silence.

On top of this small four-wheeled car, on a double-sided bench facing in two directions and with a little surrey roof above for shade, sat a man, his wife and their small seven-year-old son. As the handcar traveled through lonely stretch after lonely stretch, the wind whipped their eyes and blew their hair, but they did not look back but only ahead. Sometimes they looked eagerly as a curve unwound itself, sometimes with great sadness, but always watchful, ready for the next scene.

As they hit a level straightaway, the machine engine gasped and stopped abruptly. In the now crushing silence, it seemed that the quiet of earth, sky and sea itself, by its friction, brought the car to a wheeling halt.

"Out of gas."

The man, sighing, reached for the extra can in the small storage bin and began to pour it into the tank.

His wife and son sat quietly looking at the sea, listening to the muted thunder, the whisper, the drawing back of huge tapestries of sand, gravel, green weed, and foam.

"Isn't the sea nice?" said the woman.

"I like it," said the boy.

"Shall we picnic here, while we're at it?"

The man focused some binoculars on

the green peninsula ahead.

"Might as well. The rails have rusted badly. There's a break ahead. We may have to wait while I set a few back in place."

"As many as there are," said the boy, "we'll have picnics!"

The woman tried to smile at this, then turned her grave attention to the man. "How far have we come today?"

"Not ninety miles." The man still peered through the glasses, squinting. "I don't like to go farther than that any one day, anyway. If you rush, there's no time to see. We'll reach Monterey day after tomorrow, Palo Alto the next day, if you want."

The woman removed her great shadowing straw hat, which had been tied over her golden hair with a bright yellow ribbon, and stood perspiring faintly, away from the machine. They had ridden so steadily on the shuddering rail car that the motion was sewn into their bodies. Now, with the stopping, they felt odd, on the verge of unraveling.

"Let's eat!"

The boy ran the wicker lunch basket down to the shore.

The boy and the woman were already seated by a spread tablecloth when the man came down to them, dressed in his business suit and vest and tie and hat as if he expected to meet someone along the way. As he dealt out the sandwiches and exhumed the pickles from their cool green Mason jars, he began to loosen his tie and unbutton his vest, always looking around as if he should be careful and ready to button up again.

"Are we all alone, Papa?" said the boy, eating.

"Yes."

"No one else, anywhere?"

"No one else."

"Were there people before?"

"Why do you keep asking that? It wasn't

that long ago. Just a few months. You remember."

"Almost. If I try hard, then I don't remember at all." The boy let a handful of sand fall through his fingers. "Were there as many people as there is sand here on the beach? What *happened* to them?"

"I don't know," the man said, and it was true.

They had wakened one morning and the world was empty. The neighbors' clothesline was still strung with blowing white wash, cars gleamed in front of other 7-A.M. cottages, but there were no farewells, the city did not hum with its mighty arterial traffics, phones did not alarm themselves, children did not wail in sunflower wildernesses.

Only the night before, he and his wife had been sitting on the front porch when the evening paper was delivered, and, not even daring to open the headlines out, he had said, "I wonder when He will get tired of us and just rub us all out?"

"It has gone pretty far," she said. "On and on. We're such fools, aren't we?"

"Wouldn't it be nice—" he lit his pipe and puffed it—"if we woke tomorrow and everyone in the world was gone and everything was starting over?" He sat smoking, the paper folded in his hand, his head resting back on the chair.

"If you could press a button right now and make it happen, would you?"

"I think I would," he said. "Nothing violent. Just have everyone vanish off the face of the earth. Just leave the land and the sea and the growing things, like flowers and grass and fruit trees. And the animals, of course, let them stay. Everything except man, who hunts when he isn't hungry, eats when full, and is mean when no one's bothered him."

"Naturally, we would be left." She smiled quietly.

"I'd like that," he mused. "All of time

ahead. The longest summer vacation in history. And us out for the longest picnic-basket lunch in memory. Just you, me, and Jim. No commuting. No keeping up with the Joneses. Not even a car. I'd like to find another way of traveling, an older way. Then, a hamper full of sandwiches, three bottles of pop, pick up supplies where you need them from empty grocery stores in empty towns, and summertime forever up ahead. . . ."

They sat a long while on the porch in silence, the newspaper folded between them.

At last she opened her mouth.

"Wouldn't we be *lonely?*" she said.

So that's how it was the morning of the new world. They had awakened to the soft sounds of an earth that was now no more than a meadow, and the cities of the earth sinking back into seas of saber-grass, marigold, marguerite and morning-glory. They had taken it with remarkable calm at first, perhaps because they had not liked the city for so many years, and had had so many friends who were not truly friends, and had lived a boxed and separate life of their own within a mechanical hive.

The husband arose and looked out the window and observed very calmly, as if it were a weather condition, "Everyone's gone," knowing this just by the sounds the city had ceased to make.

They took their time over breakfast, for the boy was still asleep, and then the husband sat back and said, "Now I must plan what to do."

"Do? Why . . . why, you'll go to work, of course."

"You still don't believe it, do you?" He laughed. "That I won't be rushing off each day at eight-ten, that Jim won't go to school again ever. School's out for all of us! No more pencils, no more books, no

more boss's sassy looks! We're let out, darling, and we'll never come back to the silly damn dull routines. Come on!"

And he had walked her through the still and empty city streets.

"They didn't die," he said. "They just . . . went away."

"What about the other cities?"

He went to an outdoor phone booth and dialed Chicago, then New York, then San Francisco.

Silence. Silence. Silence.

"That's it," he said, replacing the receiver.

"I feel guilty," she said. "Them gone and us here. And . . . I feel happy. Why? I *should* be unhappy."

"Should you? It's no tragedy. They weren't tortured or blasted or burned. They went easily and they didn't know. And now we owe nothing to no one. Our only responsibility is being happy. Thirty more years of happiness, wouldn't that be good?"

"But . . . then we must have more children!"

"To repopulate the world?" He shook his head slowly, calmly. "No. Let Jim be the last. After he's grown and gone let the horses and cows and ground squirrels and garden spiders have the world. They'll get on. And someday some other species that can combine a natural happiness with a natural curiosity will build cities that won't even look like cities to us, and survive. Right now, let's go pack a basket, wake Jim, and get going on that long thirty-year summer vacation. I'll beat you to the house!"

He took a sledge hammer from the small rail car, and while he worked alone for half an hour fixing the rusted rails into place the woman and the boy ran along the shore. They came back with dripping shells, a dozen or more, and some beautiful

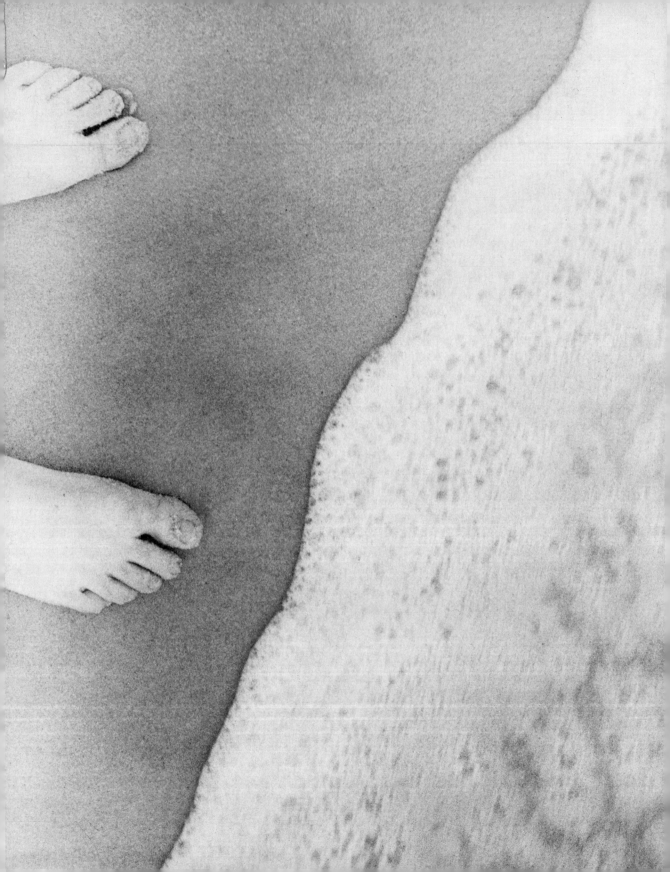

pink pebbles, and sat and the boy took school from the mother, doing homework on a pad with a pencil for a time, and then at high noon the man came down, his coat off, his tie thrown aside, and they drank orange pop, watching the bubbles surge up, glutting, inside the bottles. It was quiet. They listened to the sun tune the old iron rails. The smell of hot tar on the ties moved about them in the salt wind, as the husband tapped his atlas map lightly and gently.

"We'll go to Sacramento next month, May, then work up toward Seattle. Should make that by July first, July's a good month in Washington, then back down as the weather cools, to Yellowstone, a few miles a day, hunt here, fish there. . . ."

The boy, bored, moved away to throw sticks into the sea and wade out like a dog to retrieve them.

The man went on: "Winter in Tucson, then, part of the winter, moving toward Florida, up the coast in the spring, and maybe New York by June. Two years from now, Chicago in the summer. Winter, three years from now, what about Mexico City? Anywhere the rails lead us, anywhere at all, and if we come to an old offshoot rail line we don't know anything about, we'll just take it, go down it, to see where it goes. And some year we'll boat down the Mississippi, always wanted to do that. Enough to last us a lifetime. And that's just how long I want to take to do it all. . . ."

His voice faded. He started to fumble the map shut, but, before he could move, a bright thing fell through the air and hit the paper. It rolled off into the sand and made a wet lump.

His wife glanced at the wet place in the sand and then swiftly searched his face. His solemn eyes were too bright. And down one cheek was a track of wetness.

She gasped. She took his hand and held it, tight.

He clenched her hand very hard, his eyes shut now, and slowly he said, with difficulty, "Wouldn't it be nice if we went to sleep tonight and in the night, somehow, it all came back. All the foolishness, all the noise, all the hate, all the terrible things, all the nightmares, all the wicked people and stupid children, all the mess, all the smallness, all the confusion, all the hope, all the need, all the love. Wouldn't it be nice."

She waited and nodded her head once.

Then both of them started.

For standing between them, they knew not for how long, was their son, an empty pop bottle in one hand.

The boy's face was pale. With his free hand he reached out to touch his father's cheek, where the single tear had made its track.

"You," he said. "Oh, Dad, you. You haven't anyone to play with, *either*."

The wife started to speak.

The husband moved to take the boy's hand.

The boy jerked back. "Silly! Oh, silly! Silly fools! Oh, you dumb, dumb!" And, whirling, he rushed down to the ocean and stood there crying loudly.

The wife rose to follow, but the husband stopped her.

"No. Let him."

And then they both grew cold and quiet. For the boy, below on the shore, crying steadily, now was writing on a piece of paper and stuffing it in the pop bottle and ramming the tin cap back on and taking the bottle and giving it a great glittering heave up in the air and out into the tidal sea.

What, thought the wife, what did he write on the note? What's in the bottle?

The bottle moved out in the waves.

The boy stopped crying.

After a long while he walked up the shore, to stand looking at his parents. His face was neither bright nor dark, alive nor dead, ready nor resigned; it seemed a curious mixture that simply made do with time, weather and these people. They looked at him and beyond to the bay, where the bottle containing the scribbled note was almost out of sight now, shining in the waves.

Did he write what *we* wanted? thought the woman, did he write what he heard us just wish, just say?

Or did he write something for only himself, she wondered, that tomorrow he might wake and find himself alone in an empty world, no one around, no man, no woman, no father, no mother, no fool grownups with fool wishes, so he could trudge up to the railroad tracks and take the handcar motoring, a solitary boy, across the continental wilderness, on eternal voyages and picnics?

Is that what he wrote in the note?

Which?

She searched his colorless eyes, could not read the answer; dared not ask.

Gull shadows sailed over and kited their faces with sudden passing coolness.

"Time to go," someone said.

They loaded the wicker basket onto the rail car. The woman tied her large bonnet securely in place with its yellow ribbon, they set the boy's pail of shells on the floorboards, then the husband put on his tie, his vest, his coat, his hat, and they all sat on the benches of the car looking out at the sea where the bottled note was far out, blinking, on the horizon.

"Is asking enough?" said the boy. "Does wishing work?"

"Sometimes . . . *too* well."

"It depends on what you ask for."

The boy nodded, his eyes far away.

They looked back at where they had come from, and then ahead to where they were going.

"Good-bye, place," said the boy, and waved.

The car rolled down the rusty rails. The sound of it dwindled, faded. The man, the woman, the boy dwindled with it in distance, among the hills.

After they were gone, the rail trembled faintly for two minutes, and ceased. A flake of rust fell. A flower nodded.

The sea was very loud.

FOR DISCUSSION

1. What do you think Jim wished for in his note? Judging from the way the story made you feel, what would you have wished for in his place?

2. The story took place not in a gloomy forest or in a Martian cave, but on a sunny seashore. How did the author make this setting seem mysterious? Which of the five senses did he emphasize most?

3. Setting includes time as well as place. Do you think this story is set in the past, present, or future? Consider in your answer the description of the family's old life and their comments about the bad news in the newspaper.

FOR COMPOSITION

• Imagine that you are one of the people left on earth. Keep a diary for at least four days in which you record your changing reactions to what has happened, your descriptions of the setting, and your thoughts about the meaning of it all.

Sometimes a person's entire life is shaped by the time and place in which he is born. To be a Russian Jew in 1904 was to have very few chances for happiness.

THE STORY OF MY DOVECOT
ISAAC BABEL

To M. Gorky[1]

WHEN I WAS A kid I longed for a dovecot. Never in all my life have I wanted a thing more. But not till I was nine did Father promise the wherewithal to buy the wood to make one and three pairs of pigeons to stock it with. It was then 1904, and I was studying for the entrance exam to the preparatory class of the secondary school at Nikolayev in the Province of Kherson, where my people were at that time living. This province of course no longer exists, and our town has been incorporated in the Odessa Region.

I was only nine, and I was scared stiff of the exams. In both subjects, Russian language and arithmetic, I couldn't afford to get less than top marks. At our secondary school the *numerus clausus*[2] was stiff: a mere five percent. So that out of forty boys only two that were Jews could get into the preparatory class. The teachers used to put cunning questions to Jewish boys; no one else was asked such devilish questions. So when Father promised to buy the pigeons he demanded top marks with distinction in both subjects. He absolutely tortured me to death. I fell into a

state of permanent daydream, into an endless, despairing, childish reverie. I went to the exam deep in this dream, and nevertheless did better than everybody else.

I had a knack for book-learning. Even though they asked cunning questions, the teachers could not rob me of my intelligence and my avid memory. I was good at learning, and got top marks in both subjects. But then everything went wrong. Khariton Efrussi, the corn-dealer who exported wheat to Marseille, slipped someone a 500-rouble[3] bribe. My mark was changed from A to A−, and Efrussi Junior went to the secondary school instead of me. Father took it very badly. From the time I was six he had been cramming me with every scrap of learning he could, and that A− drove him to despair. He wanted to beat Efrussi up, or at least bribe two longshoremen to beat Efrussi up, but Mother talked him out of the idea, and I started studying for the second exam the following year, the one for the lowest class. Behind my back my people got the teacher to take me in one year through the preparatory and first-year courses simultaneously, and conscious of the family's despair, I got three whole books by heart. These were Smirnovsky's *Russian Grammar*, Yevtushevsky's *Problems*, and Putsykovich's *Manual of Early Russian History*. Children no longer cram from these

DOVECOT: small compartmented box for pigeons.
[1] M. GORKY: Maxim Gorky, Russian writer and revolutionary.
[2] NUMERUS CLAUSUS: closed number; quota.

[3] ROUBLE: money unit of the Soviet Union.

books, but I learned them by heart line upon line, and the following year in the Russian exam Karavayev gave me an unrivaled A+.

This Karavayev was a red-faced, irritable fellow, a graduate of Moscow University. He was hardly more than thirty. Crimson glowed in his manly cheeks as it does in the cheeks of peasant children. A wart sat perched on one cheek, and from it there sprouted a tuft of ash-colored cat's whiskers. At the exam, besides Karavayev, there was the Assistant Curator Pyatnitsky, who was reckoned a big noise in the school and throughout the province. When the Assistant Curator asked me about Peter the Great a feeling of complete oblivion came over me, an awareness that the end was near: an abyss seemed to yawn before me, an arid abyss lined with exultation and despair.

About Peter the Great I knew things by heart from Putsykovich's book and Pushkin's verses. Sobbing, I recited these verses, while the faces before me suddenly turned upside down, were shuffled as a pack of cards is shuffled. This card-shuffling went on, and meanwhile, shivering, jerking my back straight, galloping headlong, I was shouting Pushkin's stanzas at the top of my voice. On and on I yelled them, and no one broke into my crazy mouthings. Through a crimson blindness, through the sense of absolute freedom that had filled me, I was aware of nothing but Pyatnitsky's old face with its silver-touched beard bent toward me. He didn't interrupt me, and merely said to Karavayev, who was rejoicing for my sake and Pushkin's:

"What a people," the old man whispered, "those little Jews of yours! There's a devil in them!"

And when at last I could shout no more, he said:

"Very well, run along, my little friend."

I went out from the classroom into the corridor, and there, leaning against a wall that needed a coat of whitewash, I began to awake from my trance. About me Russian boys were playing, the school bell hung not far away above the stairs, the caretaker was snoozing on a chair with a broken seat. I looked at the caretaker, and gradually woke up. Boys were creeping toward me from all sides. They wanted to give me a jab, or perhaps just have a game, but Pyatnitsky suddenly loomed up in the corridor. As he passed me he halted for a moment, the frock coat flowing down his back in a slow heavy wave. I discerned embarrassment in that large, fleshy, upper-class back, and got closer to the old man.

"Children," he said to the boys, "don't touch this lad." And he laid a fat hand tenderly on my shoulder.

"My little friend," he went on, turning me towards him, "tell your father that you are admitted to the first class."

On his chest a great star flashed, and decorations jingled in his lapel. His great black uniformed body started to move away on its stiff legs. Hemmed in by the shadowy walls, moving between them as a barge moves through a deep canal, it disappeared in the doorway of the headmaster's study. The little servingman took in a tray of tea, clinking solemnly, and I ran home to the shop.

In the shop a peasant customer, tortured by doubt, sat scratching himself. When he saw me my father stopped trying to help the peasant make up his mind, and without a moment's hesitation believed everything I had to say. Calling to the assistant to start shutting up shop, he dashed out into Cathedral Street to buy me a school cap with a badge on it. My poor mother had her work cut out getting me away from the crazy fellow. She was pale at that moment, she was experiencing destiny. She kept smoothing me, and pushing me away as though she hated me. She said there was always a notice in the paper about those who had been admitted to the school, and that God would punish us, and that folk would laugh at us if we bought a school cap too soon. My mother was pale; she was experiencing destiny through my eyes. She looked at me with bitter compassion as one might look at a little cripple boy, because she alone knew what a family ours was for misfortunes.

All the men in our family were trusting by nature, and quick to ill-considered actions. We were unlucky in everything we undertook. My grandfather had been a rabbi somewhere in the Belaya Tserkov region. He had been thrown out for blasphemy, and for another forty years he lived noisily and sparsely, teaching foreign languages. In his eightieth year he started going off his head. My Uncle Leo, my father's brother, had studied at the Talmudic Academy in Volozhin. In 1892 he ran away to avoid doing military service, eloping with the daughter of someone serving in the commissariat in the Kiev military district. Uncle Leo took this woman to California, to Los Angeles, and there he abandoned her, and died in a house of ill fame among Negroes and Malays. After his death the American police sent us a heritage from Los Angeles, a large trunk bound with brown iron hoops. In this trunk there were dumbbells, locks of women's hair, uncle's talith, horsewhips with gilt handles, scented tea in boxes trimmed with imitation pearls. Of all the family there remained only crazy Uncle Simon-Wolf, who lived in Odessa, my father, and I. But my father had faith in people, and he used to put them off with the transports of first love. People could not forgive him for this, and used to play

him false. So my father believed that his life was guided by an evil fate, an inexplicable being that pursued him, a being in every respect unlike him. And so I alone of all our family was left to my mother. Like all Jews I was short, weakly, and had headaches from studying. My mother saw all this. She had never been dazzled by her husband's pauper pride, by his incomprehensible belief that our family would one day be richer and more powerful than all others on earth. She desired no success for us, was scared of buying a school jacket too soon, and all she would consent to was that I should have my photo taken.

On September 20, 1905, a list of those admitted to the first class was hung up at the school. In the list my name figured too. All our kith and kin kept going to look at this paper, and even Shoyl, my granduncle, went along. I loved that boastful old man, for he sold fish at the market. His fat hands were moist, covered with fish scales, and smelt of worlds chill and beautiful. Shoyl also differed from ordinary folk in the lying stories he used to tell about the Polish Rising of 1861. Years ago Shoyl had been a tavern-keeper at Skvira. He had seen Nicholas I's soldiers shooting Count Godlevski and other Polish insurgents. But perhaps he hadn't. *Now* I know that Shoyl was just an old ignoramus and a simple-minded liar, but his cock-and-bull stories I have never forgotten: they were good stories. Well now, even silly old Shoyl went along to the school to read the list with my name on it, and that evening he danced and pranced at our pauper ball.

My father got up the ball to celebrate my success, and asked all his pals—grain-dealers, real-estate brokers, and the traveling salesmen who sold agricultural machinery in our parts. These salesmen would sell a machine to anyone. Peasants and landowners went in fear of them: you couldn't break loose without buying something or other. Of all Jews, salesmen are the widest-awake and the jolliest. At our party they sang Hasidic songs consisting of three words only but which took an awful long time to sing, songs performed with endless comical intonations. The beauty of these intonations may only be recognized by those who have had the good fortune to spend Passover with the Hasidim or who have visited their noisy Volhynian synagogues. Besides the salesmen, old Lieberman who had taught me the Torah and ancient Hebrew honored us with his presence. In our circle he was known as Monsieur Lieberman. He drank more Bessarabian wine than he should have. The ends of the traditional silk tassels poked out from beneath his waistcoat, and in ancient Hebrew he proposed my health. In this toast the old man congratulated my parents and said that I had vanquished all my foes in single combat: I had vanquished the Russian boys with their fat cheeks, and I had vanquished the sons of our own vulgar parvenus.[1] So too in ancient times David King of Judah had overcome Goliath, and just as I had triumphed over Goliath, so too would our people by the strength of their intellect conquer the foes who had encircled us and were thirsting for our blood. Monsieur Lieberman started to weep as he said this, drank more wine as he wept, and shouted *"Vivat!"*[2] The guests formed a circle and danced an old-fashioned quadrille with him in the middle, just as at a wedding in a little Jewish town. Everyone was happy at our ball. Even Mother took a sip of vodka, though she neither liked the stuff nor understood how anyone else could—

[1] PARVENUS: people who have suddenly risen above their social and economic class without the background or qualifications for their new status.
[2] "VIVAT": roughly, "To life."

because of this she considered all Russians cracked, and just couldn't imagine how women managed with Russian husbands.

But our happy days came later. For Mother they came when of a morning, before I set off for school, she would start making me sandwiches; when we went shopping to buy my school things—pencil box, money box, satchel, new books in cardboard bindings, and exercise books in shiny covers. No one in the world has a keener feeling for new things than children have. Children shudder at the smell of newness as a dog does when it scents a hare, experiencing the madness which later, when we grow up, is called inspiration. And Mother acquired this pure and childish sense of the ownership of new things. It took us a whole month to get used to the pencil box, to the morning twilight as I drank my tea on the corner of the large, brightly lit table and packed my books in my satchel. It took us a month to grow accustomed to our happiness, and it was only after the first half-term that I remembered about the pigeons.

I had everything ready for them: one rouble fifty and a dovecot made from a box by Grandfather Shoyl, as we called him. The dovecot was painted brown. It had nests for twelve pairs of pigeons, carved strips on the roof, and a special grating that I had devised to facilitate the capture of strange birds. All was in readiness. On Sunday, October 20, I set out for the bird market, but unexpected obstacles arose in my path.

The events I am relating, that is to say my admission to the first class at the secondary school, occurred in the autumn of 1905. The Emperor Nicholas was then bestowing a constitution on the Russian people. Orators in shabby overcoats were clambering onto tall curbstones and haranguing the people. At night shots had been heard in the streets, and so Mother

didn't want me to go to the bird market. From early morning on October 20 the boys next door were flying a kite right by the police station, and our water carrier, abandoning all his buckets, was walking about the streets with a red face and brilliantined hair. Then we saw baker Kalistov's sons drag a leather vaulting-horse out into the street and start doing gym in the middle of the roadway. No one tried to stop them: Semernikov the policeman even kept inciting them to jump higher. Semernikov was girt with a silk belt his wife had made him, and his boots had been polished that day as they had never been polished before. Out of his customary uniform, the policeman frightened my mother more than anything else. Because of him she didn't want me to go out, but I sneaked out by the back way and ran to the bird market, which in our town was behind the station.

At the bird market Ivan Nikodimych, the pigeon-fancier, sat in his customary place. Apart from pigeons, he had rabbits for sale too, and a peacock. The peacock, spreading its tail, sat on a perch moving a passionless head from side to side. To its paw was tied a twisted cord, and the other end of the cord was caught beneath one leg of Ivan Nikodimych's wicker chair. The moment I got there I bought from the old man a pair of cherry-colored pigeons with luscious tousled tails, and a pair of crowned pigeons, and put them away in a bag on my chest under my shirt. After these purchases I had only forty copecks left, and for this price the old man was not prepared to let me have a male and female pigeon of the Kryukov breed. What I liked about Kryukov pigeons was their short, knobbly, good-natured beaks. Forty copecks was the proper price, but the fancier insisted on haggling, averting from me a yellow face scorched by the unsociable passions of bird-snarers. At the end of our bargaining, seeing that there were no other customers, Ivan Nikodimych beckoned me closer. All went as I wished, and all went badly.

Toward twelve o'clock, or perhaps a bit later, a man in felt boots passed across the square. He was stepping lightly on swollen feet, and in his worn-out face lively eyes glittered.

"Ivan Nikodimych," he said as he walked past the bird-fancier, "pack up your gear. In town the Jerusalem aristocrats are being granted a constitution. On Fish Street Grandfather Babel has been constitutioned to death."

He said this and walked lightly on between the cages like a barefoot ploughman walking along the edge of a field.

"They shouldn't," murmured Ivan Nikodimych in his wake. "They shouldn't!" he cried more sternly. He started collecting his rabbits and his peacock, and shoved the Kryukov pigeons at me for forty copecks. I hid them in my bosom and watched the people running away from the bird market. The peacock on Ivan Nikodimych's shoulder was last of all to depart. It sat there like the sun in a raw autumnal sky; it sat as July sits on a pink riverbank, a white-hot July in the long cool grass. No one was left in the market, and not far off shots were rattling. Then I ran to the station, cut across a square that had gone topsy-turvy, and flew down an empty lane of trampled yellow earth. At the end of the lane, in a little wheeled armchair, sat the legless Makarenko, who rode about town in his wheelchair selling cigarettes from a tray. The boys in our street used to buy smokes from him, children loved him, I dashed toward him down the lane.

"Makarenko," I gasped, panting from my run, and I stroked the legless one's shoulder, "have you seen Shoyl?"

The cripple did not reply. A light seemed to be shining through his coarse face built up of red fat, clenched fists, chunks of iron. He was fidgeting on his chair in his excitement, while his wife Kate, presenting a wadded behind, was sorting out some things scattered on the ground.

"How far have you counted?" asked the legless man, and moved his whole bulk away from the woman, as though aware in advance that her answer would be unbearable.

"Fourteen pair of leggings," said Kate, still bending over, "six undersheets. Now I'm a-counting the bonnets."

"Bonnets!" cried Makarenko, with a choking sound like a sob, "it's clear, Catherine, that God has picked on me, that I must answer for all. People are carting off whole rolls of cloth, people have everything they should, and we're stuck with bonnets."

And indeed a woman with a beautiful burning face ran past us down the lane. She was clutching an armful of fezzes in one arm and a piece of cloth in the other, and in a voice of joyful despair she was yelling for her children, who had strayed. A silk dress and a blue blouse fluttered after her as she flew, and she paid no attention to Makarenko who was rolling his chair in pursuit of her. The legless man couldn't catch up. His wheels clattered as he turned the handles for all he was worth.

"Little lady," he cried in a deafening voice, "where did you get that striped stuff?"

But the woman with the fluttering dress was gone. Round the corner to meet her leaped a rickety cart in which a peasant lad stood upright.

"Where've they all run to?" asked the lad, raising a red rein above the nags jerking in their collars.

"Everybody's on Cathedral Street," said Makarenko pleadingly, "everybody's there, sonny. Anything you happen to pick up, bring it along to me. I'll give you a good price."

The lad bent down over the front of the cart and whipped up his piebald nags.

Tossing their filthy croups like calves, the horses shot off at a gallop. The yellow lane was once more yellow and empty. Then the legless man turned his quenched eyes upon me.

"God's picked on me, I reckon," he said lifelessly, "I'm a son of man, I reckon."

And he stretched a hand spotted with leprosy toward me.

"What's that you've got in your sack?" he demanded, and took the bag that had been warming my heart.

With his fat hand the cripple fumbled among the tumbler pigeons and dragged to light a cherry-colored she-bird. Jerking back its feet, the bird lay still on his palm.

"Pigeons," said Makarenko, and squeaking his wheels he rode right up to me. "Damned pigeons," he repeated, and struck me on the cheek.

He dealt me a flying blow with the hand that was clutching the bird. Kate's wadded back seemed to turn upside down, and I fell to the ground in my new overcoat.

"Their spawn must be wiped out," said Kate, straightening up over the bonnets. "I can't a-bear their spawn, nor their stinking menfolk."

She said more things about our spawn, but I heard nothing of it. I lay on the ground, and the guts of the crushed bird trickled down from my temple. They flowed down my cheek, winding this way and that, splashing, blinding me. The tender pigeon-guts slid down over my forehead, and I closed my solitary unstopped-up eye so as not to see the world that spread out before me. This world was tiny, and it was awful. A stone lay just before my eyes, a little stone so chipped as to resemble the face of an old woman with a large jaw. A piece of string lay not far away, and a bunch of feathers that still breathed. My world was tiny, and it was awful. I closed my eyes so as not to see it, and pressed myself tight into the ground that lay beneath me in soothing dumbness. This trampled earth in no way resembled real life, waiting for exams in real life. Somewhere far away Woe rode across it on a great steed, but the noise of the hoofbeats grew weaker and died away, and silence, the bitter silence that sometimes overwhelms children in their sorrow, suddenly deleted the boundary between my body and the earth that was moving nowhither. The earth smelled of raw depths, of the tomb, of flowers. I smelled its smell and started crying, unafraid. I was walking along an unknown street set on either side with white boxes, walking in a getup of bloodstained feathers, alone between the pavements swept clean as on Sunday, weeping bitterly, fully and happily as I never wept again in all my life. Wires that had grown white hummed above my head, a watchdog trotted on in front, in the lane on one side a young peasant in a waistcoat was smashing a window frame in the house of Khariton Efrussi. He was smashing it with a wooden mallet, striking out with his whole body. Sighing, he smiled all around with the amiable grim of drunkenness, sweat, and spiritual power. The whole street was filled with a splitting, a snapping, the song of flying wood. The peasant's whole existence consisted in bending over, sweating, shouting queer words in some unknown, non-Russian language. He shouted the words and sang, shot out his blue eyes; till in the street there appeared a procession bearing the Cross and moving from the Municipal Building. Old men bore aloft the portrait of the neatly combed Tsar, banners with graveyard saints swayed above their heads, inflamed old women flew on in front. Seeing the procession, the peasant pressed his mallet to his chest and dashed off in pursuit of the banners, while I, waiting till the tail-end of the procession had passed, made my furtive way home. The house

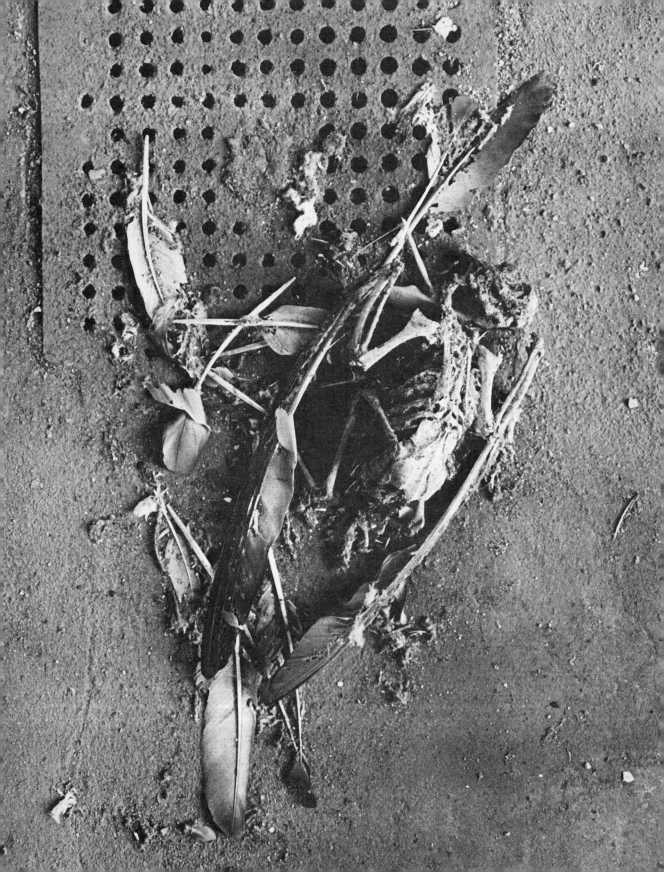

was empty. Its white doors were open, the grass by the dovecot had been trampled down. Only Kuzma was still in the yard. Kuzma the yardman was sitting in the shed laying out the dead Shoyl.

"The wind bears you about like an evil wood chip," said the old man when he saw me. "You've been away ages. And now look what they've done to Granddad."

Kuzma wheezed, turned away from me, and started pulling a fish out of a rent in Grandfather's trousers. Two pike perch had been stuck into Grandfather: one into the rent in his trousers, the other into his mouth. And while Grandfather was dead, one of the fish was still alive, and struggling.

"They've done Grandfather in, but nobody else," said Kuzma, tossing the fish to the cat. "He cursed them all good and proper, a wonderful damning and blasting it was. You might fetch a couple of pennies to put on his eyes."

But then, at ten years of age, I didn't know what need the dead had of pennies.

"Kuzma," I whispered, "save us."

And I went over to the yardman, hugged his crooked old back with its one shoulder higher than the other, and over this back I saw Grandfather. Shoyl lay in the sawdust, his chest squashed in, his beard twisted upwards, battered shoes on his bare feet. His feet, thrown wide apart, were dirty, lilac-colored, dead. Kuzma was fussing over him. He tied the dead man's jaws and kept glancing over the body to see what else he could do. He fussed as though over a newly purchased garment, and only cooled down when he had given the dead man's beard a good combing.

"He cursed the lot of 'em right and left," he said, smiling, and cast a loving look over the corpse. "If Tartars had crossed his path he'd have sent them packing, but Russians came, and their women with them, Rooski women. Russians just can't bring themselves to forgive; I know what Rooskis are."

The yardman spread some more sawdust beneath the body, threw off his carpenter's apron, and took me by the hand.

"Let's go to Father," he mumbled, squeezing my hand tighter and tighter. "Your father has been searching for you since morning, sure as fate you was dead."

And so with Kuzma I went to the house of the tax inspector, where my parents, escaping the pogrom, had sought refuge.

FOR DISCUSSION

1. Why was Isaac's pigeon crushed, his granduncle killed, and Jewish stores and homes looted? Before answering, consider the story's setting: Russia in the Revolution of 1905. In this case, time is as important as place in shaping the story.

2. Explain the different reactions to Isaac's success. Why did he shout as he finished the exam? Why did his father throw a party? Why did his mother worry?

3. Several times in the middle of describing a happy scene, the author inserted a comment such as, "unexpected obstacles arose in my path," or "All went as I wished, and all went badly." Why do you think the author included these hints of coming danger, or *foreshadowing?*

FOR COMPOSITION

• Why do you think the story is called "The Story of My Dovecot" when the dovecot plays such a small part in it? Use quotations from the story to support your answer.

The verger had his own ideas: "I think a lot of these young fellows waste a rare lot of time readin' when they might be doin' something useful."

THE VERGER

W. SOMERSET MAUGHAM

THERE HAD BEEN a christening that afternoon at St. Peter's, Neville Square, and Albert Edward Foreman still wore his verger's gown. He kept his new one, its folds as full and stiff as though it were made not of alpaca but of perennial bronze, for funerals and weddings (St. Peter's, Neville Square, was a church much favored by the fashionable for these ceremonies), and now he wore only his second best. He wore it with complacence, for it was the dignified symbol of his office, and without it (when he took it off to go home) he had the disconcerting sensation of being somewhat insufficiently clad. He took pains with it; he pressed it and ironed it himself. During the sixteen years he had been verger of this church he had had a succession of such gowns, but he had never been able to throw them away when they were worn out, and the complete series, neatly wrapped up in brown paper, lay in the bottom drawer of the wardrobe in his bedroom.

The verger busied himself quietly, replacing the painted wooden cover on the marble font, taking away a chair that had been brought for an infirm old lady, and waited for the vicar to have finished in the vestry so that he could tidy up in there and go home. Presently he saw him walk across the chancel, genuflect in front of the high altar and come down the aisle; but he still wore his cassock.

"What's he 'anging about for?" the verger said to himself. "Don't 'e know I want my tea?"

The vicar had been but recently appointed, a red-faced energetic man in the early forties, and Albert Edward still regretted his predecessor, a clergyman of the old school who preached leisurely sermons in a silvery voice and dined out a great deal with his more aristocratic parishioners. He liked things in church to be just so, but he never fussed; he was not like this new man who wanted to have his finger in every pie. But Albert Edward was tolerant. St. Peter's was in a very good neighborhood and the parishioners were a very nice class of people. The new vicar had come from the East End and he couldn't be expected to fall in all at once with the discreet ways of his fashionable congregation.

"All this 'ustle," said Albert Edward. "But give 'im time, he'll learn."

When the vicar had walked down the aisle so far that he could address the verger without raising his voice more than was becoming in a place of worship, he stopped.

"Foreman, will you come into the vestry for a minute. I have something to say to you."

"Very good, sir."

VERGER: A verger takes care of the church interior and serves as the clergyman's attendant during ceremonies.

The vicar waited for him to come up and they walked up the church together.

"A very nice christening, I thought, sir. Funny 'ow the baby stopped cryin' the moment you took him."

"I've noticed they very often do," said the vicar, with a little smile. "After all, I've had a good deal of practice with them."

It was a source of subdued pride to him that he could nearly always quiet a whimpering infant by the manner in which he held it, and he was not unconscious of the amused admiration with which mothers and nurses watched him settle the baby in the crook of his surpliced arm. The verger knew that it pleased him to be complimented on his talent.

The vicar preceded Albert Edward into the vestry. Albert Edward was a trifle surprised to find the two churchwardens there. He had not seen them come in. They gave him pleasant nods.

"Good afternoon, my lord. Good afternoon, sir," he said to one after the other.

They were elderly men, both of them, and they had been churchwardens almost as long as Albert Edward had been verger. They were sitting now at a handsome refectory table that the old vicar had brought many years before from Italy, and the vicar sat down in the vacant chair between them. Albert Edward faced them, the table between him and them, and wondered with slight uneasiness what was the matter. He remembered still the occasion on which the organist had got into trouble and the bother they all had had to hush things up. In a church like St. Peter's, Neville Square, they couldn't afford a scandal. On the vicar's red face was a look of resolute benignity, but the others bore an expression that was slightly troubled.

"He's been naggin' them, he 'as," said the verger to himself. "He's jockeyed them into doin' something, but they don't 'alf like it. That's what it is, you mark my words."

But his thoughts did not appear on Albert Edward's clean-cut and distinguished features. He stood in a respectful but not obsequious attitude. He had been in service before he was appointed to his ecclesiastical office, but only in very good houses, and his deportment was irreproachable. Starting as a page boy in the household of a merchant prince, he had risen by due degrees from the position of fourth to first footman; for a year he had been single-handed butler to a widowed peeress and, till the vacancy occurred at St. Peter's, butler with two men under him in the house of a retired ambassador. He was tall, spare, grave and dignified. He looked, if not like a duke, at least like an actor of the old school who specialized in dukes' parts. He had tact, firmness and self-assurance. His character was unimpeachable.

The vicar began briskly.

"Foreman, we've got something rather unpleasant to say to you. You've been here a great many years, and I think his lordship and the general agree with me that you've fulfilled the duties of your office to the satisfaction of everybody concerned."

The two churchwardens nodded.

"But a most extraordinary circumstance came to my knowledge the other day, and I felt it my duty to impart it to the churchwardens. I discovered to my astonishment that you could neither read nor write."

The verger's face betrayed no sign of embarrassment.

"The last vicar knew that, sir," he replied. "He said it didn't make no difference. He always said there was a great deal too much education in the world for 'is taste."

"It's the most amazing thing I ever heard," cried the general. "Do you mean to say that you've been verger of this church for sixteen years and never learned to read or write?"

"I went into service when I was twelve, sir. The cook in the first place tried to teach me once, but I didn't seem to 'ave the knack for it, and then what with one thing and another I never seemed to 'ave the time. I've never really found the want of it. I think a lot of these young fellows waste a rare lot of time readin' when they might be doin' something useful."

"But don't you want to know the news?" said the other churchwarden. "Don't you ever want to write a letter?"

"No, me lord, I seem to manage very well without. And of late years now they've all these pictures in the papers, I get to know what's goin' on pretty well. Me wife's quite a scholar, and if I want to write a letter she writes it for me. It's not as if I was a bettin' man."

The two churchwardens gave the vicar a troubled glance and then looked down at the table.

"Well, Foreman, I've talked the matter over with these gentlemen, and they quite agree with me that the situation is impossible. At a church like St. Peter's, Neville Square, we cannot have a verger who can neither read nor write."

Albert Edward's thin, sallow face reddened and he moved uneasily on his feet, but he made no reply.

"Understand me, Foreman, I have no complaint to make against you. You do your work quite satisfactorily; I have the highest opinion both of your character and of your capacity; but we haven't the right to take the risk of some accident that might happen owing to your lamentable ignorance. It's a matter of prudence as well as of principle."

"But couldn't you learn, Foreman?" asked the general.

"No, sir, I'm afraid I couldn't, not now.

You see, I'm not as young as I was, and if I couldn't seem able to get the letters in me 'ead when I was a nipper,[1] I don't think there's much chance of it now."

"We don't want to be harsh with you, Foreman," said the vicar. "But the church-wardens and I have quite made up our minds. We'll give you three months, and if at the end of that time you cannot read and write, I'm afraid you'll have to go."

Albert Edward had never liked the new vicar. He'd said from the beginning that they'd made a mistake when they gave him St. Peter's. He wasn't the type of man they wanted with a classy congregation like that. And now he straightened himself a little. He knew his value and he wasn't going to allow himself to be put upon.

"I'm very sorry, sir; I'm afraid it's no good. I'm too old a dog to learn new tricks. I've lived a good many years without knowin' 'ow to read and write, and without wishin' to praise myself—self-praise is no recommendation—I don't mind sayin' I've done my duty in that state of life in which it 'as pleased a merciful providence to place me, and if I *could* learn now I don't know as I'd want to."

"In that case, Foreman, I'm afraid you must go."

"Yes, sir, I quite understand. I shall be 'appy to 'and in my resignation as soon as you've found somebody to take my place."

But when Albert Edward with his usual politeness had closed the church door behind the vicar and the two churchwardens, he could not sustain the air of unruffled dignity with which he had borne the blow inflicted upon him, and his lips quivered. He walked slowly back to the vestry and hung up on its proper peg his verger's gown. He sighed as he thought of all the grand funerals and smart weddings it had seen. He tidied everything up, put on his coat, and hat in hand walked down the

[1] NIPPER: little boy.

aisle. He locked the church door behind him.

He strolled across the square, but deep in his sad thoughts, he did not take the street that led him home, where a nice strong cup of tea awaited him; he took the wrong turning. He walked slowly along. His heart was heavy. He did not know what he should do with himself. He did not fancy the notion of going back to domestic service; after being his own master for so many years—for the vicar and churchwardens could say what they liked; it was he that had run St. Peter's, Neville Square—he could scarcely demean himself by accepting a situation. He had saved a tidy sum, but not enough to live on without doing something, and life seemed to cost more every year. He had never thought to be troubled with such questions. The vergers of St. Peter's, like the popes of Rome, were there for life. He had often thought of the pleasant reference the vicar would make, in his sermon at evensong the first Sunday after his death, to the long and faithful service and the exemplary character of their late verger Albert Edward Foreman. He sighed deeply.

Albert Edward was a nonsmoker and a total abstainer, but with a certain latitude; that is to say, he liked a glass of beer with his dinner, and when he was tired he enjoyed a cigarette. It occurred to him now that one would comfort him, and since he did not carry them, he looked about him for a shop where he could buy a packet of Gold Flakes. He did not at once see one and walked on a little. It was a long street, with all sorts of shops in it, but there was not a single one where you could buy cigarettes.

"That's strange," said Albert Edward.

To make sure he walked right up the street again. No, there was no doubt about it. He stopped and looked reflectively up and down.

"I can't be the only man as walks along this street and wants a fag," he said. "I shouldn't wonder but what a fellow might do very well with a little shop here. Tobacco and sweets, you know."

He gave a sudden start.

"That's an idea," he said. "Strange 'ow things come to you when you least expect it."

He turned, walked home, and had his tea.

"You're very silent this afternoon, Albert," his wife remarked.

"I'm thinkin'," he said.

He considered the matter from every point of view, and next day he went along the street and by good luck found a little shop to let that looked as though it would exactly suit him. Twenty-four hours later he had taken it, and when a month after that he left St. Peter's, Neville Square, forever, Albert Edward Foreman set up in business as a tobacconist and newsagent. His wife said it was a dreadful comedown after being verger of St. Peter's, but he answered that you had to move with the times, the church wasn't what it was, and enceforward he was going to render unto Caesar what was Caesar's.[1] Albert Edward did very well. He did so well that in a year or so it struck him that he might take a second shop and put a manager in. He looked for another long street that hadn't got a tobacconist in it, and when he found it, and a shop to let, took it and stocked it. This was a success too. Then it occurred to him that if he could run two he could run half a dozen, so he began walking about London, and whenever he found a long street that had no tobacconist and a shop to let, he took it. In the course of ten years he had acquired no less than ten shops, and he was making money hand over fist. He went round to all of them himself every Monday, collected the week's

---

[1] RENDER . . . CAESAR'S: an allusion to the New Testament parable (Matthew 22:15–21).

takings, and took them to the bank.

One morning when he was there paying in a bundle of notes and a heavy bag of silver, the cashier told him that the manager would like to see him. He was shown into an office and the manager shook hands with him.

"Mr. Foreman, I wanted to have a talk to you about the money you've got on deposit with us. D'you know exactly how much it is?"

"Not within a pound or two, sir; but I've got a pretty rough idea."

"Apart from what you paid in this morning, it's a little over thirty thousand pounds. That's a very large sum to have on deposit, and I should have thought you'd do better to invest it."

"I wouldn't want to take no risk, sir. I know it's safe in the bank."

"You needn't have the least anxiety. We'll make you out a list of absolutely gilt-edged securities. They'll bring you in a better rate of interest than we can possibly afford to give you."

A troubled look settled on Mr. Foreman's distinguished face.

"I've never 'ad anything to do with stocks and shares, and I'd 'ave to leave it all in your 'ands," he said.

The manager smiled.

"We'll do everything. All you'll have to do next time you come in is just to sign the transfers."

"I could do that all right," said Albert uncertainly. "But 'ow should I know what I was signin'?"

"I suppose you can read," said the manager a trifle sharply.

Mr. Foreman gave him a disarming smile.

"Well, sir, that's just it. I can't. I know it sounds funny like, but there it is; I can't read or write, only me name, an' I only learnt to do that when I went into business."

The manager was so surprised that he jumped up from his chair.

"That's the most extraordinary thing I ever heard."

"You see, it's like this, sir: I never 'ad the opportunity until it was too late, and then some'ow I wouldn't. I got obstinate like."

The manager stared at him as though he were a prehistoric monster.

"And do you mean to say that you've built up this important business and amassed a fortune of thirty thousand pounds without being able to read or write? Man, what would you be now if you had been able to?"

"I can tell you that, sir," said Mr. Foreman, a little smile on his still aristocratic features. "I'd be verger of St. Peter's, Neville Square."

FOR DISCUSSION

1. The major characters in a story are often called "round" because they have many different sides to their personalities. Like real people, they are often complicated and unpredictable. What are some of the sides of his personality that Foreman reveals in his attitudes toward his gown, the new vicar, and his dismissal? Do any of these aspects of his personality seem inconsistent with each other?

2. Minor characters in a story are usually "flat"; that is, only one side of their personality is developed. Often they are types rather than individuals. What side do we see of the old vicar, the new vicar, the bank manager, and Mrs. Foreman?

The fierce Nez Percé Indians who had held off thousands of soldiers were coming to his town! The boy was wild with excitement.

JACOB
JACK SCHAEFER

THOSE MOCCASINS? Mine. Though I never wore them. Had them on just once to see if they fitted. They did. A bit tight but I could get them on.

Don't touch them. The leather's old and dry and the stitching rotted. Ought to be. They've been hanging there a long time. Look close and you can see the craftsmanship. The best. They're Nez Percé[1] moccasins. Notice the design worked into the leather. It's faint now but you can make it out. Don't know how they did that but the Nez Percé could really work leather. A professor who studied such things told me once that design means they're for a chief. For his ceremonial appearances, sort of his dress-up footwear. Said only a chief could use that design. But it's there. Right there on those moccasins.

Yes. They're small. Boy-size. That's because I was a boy then. But they're a chief's moccasins all the same. Kept them down the years because I'm proud of them. And because they mind me of a man. He had a red skin. Copper would be closer the color. A muddy copper. And I only saw him once. But he was a man.

That was a long way from here. A long way. In years and in miles. I was ten then, maybe eleven, maybe twelve, in that neigh-

borhood. I disremember exactly. Best I can do is place it in the late seventies. Funny how definite things like dates and places slip away and other stray things, like the way you felt at certain times and how your first wild strawberries tasted, can remain clear and sharp in your mind. We were living, my folks and my older brother and myself, in a little town in eastern Montana. Not much of a place. Just a small settlement on the railroad that wouldn't have amounted to anything except that it had a stretch of double track where a train going one direction could pull off to let one going the other get past. My father was a switchman. Looked after track and handled the west-end switch. That was why we were there.

The Indian smell was still in the air in those days. People around here and nowadays wouldn't know what that means. It was a knowing and a remembering that not so far away were still real, live free-footed fighting Indians that might take to raiding again. They were pegged on treaty lands and supposed to stay there. But they were always hot over one thing or another, settlers gnawing into their hunting grounds or agents pinching their rations or maybe the government forgetting to keep up treaty payments. You never knew when they might get to figuring they'd been pushed far enough and would start council fires up in the hills and come sudden and silent out of the back trails, making trouble. It was only a year or two since the Custer affair

[1] NEZ PERCÉ: pronounced něz′pûrs′.

on the Little Big Horn southwest of where we were. No one with any experience in those things expected the treaty that ended that business to hold long.

Don't take me wrong. We didn't look for Indians behind bushes and sit around shivering at night worrying about attacks. The nearest reservation was a fair jump away, and if trouble started we'd know about it long before it reached us, if it ever did. Matter of fact, it never did. I grew up in that territory and never once was mixed in any Indian trouble past an argument over the price of a blanket. Never even saw any fighting Indians except this once I'm telling about and then they weren't fighting any more. It was just a smell in the air, the notion there might be trouble any time. Indians were quite a topic when I was a boy and the talk of an evening chewed it plenty.

Expect I heard as much of it as any of the boys around our settlement. Maybe more. My father had been in the midst of the Sioux outbreak in Minnesota in the early sixties. He'd seen things that could harden a man. They settled his mind on the subject. "Only good Indian," he'd say, "is a dead one." Yes. That's not just a saying out of the storybooks. There were men who really said it. And believed it. My father was one. Said it and believed it and said it so often I'd not be stretching the truth past shape to figure he averaged it couple times a week, and so naturally we boys believed it too, hearing it all the time. I'll not argue with anyone wants to believe it even today. I'm only telling you what happened to me.

Hearing that kind of talk, we boys around the settlement had our idea what Indians were like. I can speak for myself, anyway. The Indians I saw sometimes passing through on a train or loafing around a town the few times I was in one with the folks didn't count. They were tame ones.

They were scrawny mostly, and they hung around where white people were and traded some and begged liquor when they couldn't buy it. They weren't dangerous or even interesting. They didn't matter more'n mules or dogs or anything like that cluttering the landscape. It was the wild ones filled my mind, the fighting kind that lived the way they always had and went on the warpath, and made the government send out troops and sign treaties with them. Can't recall exactly what I thought they looked like, but they were big and fierce and dangerous and they liked to burn out homesteaders' cabins and tie people to wagon wheels and roast them alive over slow fires, and it took a brave man to go hunting them and look at them down the sights of his gun.

Days I felt full of ginger I'd plan to grow up quick and be an Indian fighter. Late afternoon, before evening chores, I'd scout the countryside with the stick I used for a gun and when I'd spot a spray of red sumac poking out of a brush clump, I'd belly it in the grass and creep to good cover and poke my gun through and draw my bead. I'd pull on the twig knob that was my trigger and watch careful, and sometimes I'd have to fire again and then I'd sit up and cut another notch on the stick. I had my private name for that. Making good Indians, I called it.

What's that got to do with those moccasins? Not much I guess. But I'm telling this my way. It's all part of what I remember when I sit back and study those moccasins a spell.

The year I'm talking about was a quiet one with the Sioux but there was some Indian trouble all right, along in the fall and a ways away, over in the Nez Percé country in Idaho. It started simple enough like those things often did. There was this band lived in a valley, maybe seven hundred of them all told, counting the squaws and young ones. Biggest safe estimate I heard was three hundred braves—fighting men, I mean. Can't remember the name of the valley, though I should. My brother settled there. But I can recall the name of the chief. That sticks. Always will. Not the Indian of it because that was a fancy mouthful. What it meant. Mountain Elk. Not that exactly. Big-Deer-That-Walks-the-High-Places. Mountain Elk is close enough. But people didn't call him that. Most Indians had a short name got tagged to them somehow and were called by it. His was Jacob. Sounded funny first time I heard it but not after I'd been hearing it a while.

As I say, this trouble started simple enough. We heard about it from the telegraph operator at the settlement who took his meals at our place. He picked up information relaying stuff through his key. News of all kinds and even military reports. Seems settlers began closing in around Jacob's valley and right soon began looking at the land there. Had water, which was important in that country. Some of them pushed in and Jacob and his boys pushed them back out. So complaints were being made and more people wanted to move in, and talk went around that land like that was too good for Indians anyway because they didn't use it right, the way white men would, and when there was enough steam up, a government man went in to see Jacob. Suggested the band would be better off living in some outside reservation. Get regular rations and have an agent to look after them. No, Jacob said, he and his were doing all right. Had been for quite a spell and expected to keep on doing the same. Sent his thanks to the Great White Chief for thinking about him but he wasn't needing any help. So after a while the pressure was stronger and another government man went in. Offered to buy the land and move the band in style to a reservation. No, said Jacob, he and his children—he called

them all his children though he wasn't much past thirty himself—he and his children liked their land and weren't interested in selling. Their fathers had given up land too much in the past and been forced to keep wandering and had found this place when no one wanted it, and it was good and they had stayed there. Most of them then living had been born there and they wanted to die there too, and that was that.

Well, the pressure went on building and there were ruckuses here and yonder around the valley when some more settlers tried moving in and a bunch of young braves got out of hand and killed a few. So another government man went in, this time with a soldier escort. He didn't bother with arguing or bargaining. He told Jacob the Great White Chief had issued a decree and this was that the whole tribe was to be moved by such and such a date. If they went peaceable, transportation would be provided and good rations. If they kept on being stubborn, soldiers would come and make them move and that would be a bad business all around. Yes, said Jacob, that would be a bad business but it wouldn't be his doing. He and his children wouldn't have made the storm but they would stand up to it if it came. He had spoken and that was that.

So the days went along toward the date set, which was in the fall I'm telling about. Jacob and his band hadn't made any preparations for leaving, and the officer in charge of this whole operation thought Jacob was bluffing and he'd just call that bluff. He sent about four hundred soldiers under some colonel into the valley the week before the moving was supposed to happen, and Jacob and the others, the whole lot of them, just faded away from their village and off into the mountains behind the valley. The colonel sent scouting parties after them but couldn't make contact. He didn't know what to do in that situation so he set up camp there in the valley to wait and got real peeved when some of Jacob's Nez Percés slipped down out of the mountains one night and stampeded his stock. Finally he had his new orders and on the supposed moving day he carried them out. He put his men to destroying the village and they wiped it level to the ground, and the next morning early there was sharp fighting along his upper picket lines[1] and he lost quite a few men before he could jump his troops into the field in decent force.

That was the beginning. The government wanted to open the valley for homesteading but couldn't without taking care of Jacob first. The colonel tried. He chased Jacob and his band into the mountains and thought overtaking them would be easy, with the squaws and young ones slowing Jacob down, but Jacob had hidden them off somewhere and was traveling light with his braves. He led this colonel a fast run through rough country and caught him off watch a few times and whittled away at his troops every odd chance till this colonel had to turn back, not being outfitted for a real campaign. When he—that'd be this colonel—got back, he found Jacob had beat him there and made things mighty unpleasant for those left holding the camp before slipping away again. About this time the government realized what it was up against and recalled the colonel—and maybe whoever was his boss—and assigned a general, a brigadier, to the job and began mounting a real expedition.

We heard plenty about what happened after that, not just from the telegraph operator but from my brother, who was busting the seams of his breeches those days and wanting to strike out for himself, and signed with the freighting company that got the contract carting supplies for the troops. He didn't see any of the fighting but he was close to it several times and he wrote home what was happening. Once a week he'd promised to write and did pretty well at it. He'd send his letters along to be posted whenever any of the wagons were heading back, and my mother would read them out to my father and me when they arrived. Remember best the fat one came after he reached the first camp and saw Jacob's valley. Took him two chunks of paper both sides to tell about it. Couldn't say enough about the thick green grass and the stream tumbling into a small lake and running quiet out again, and the good trees stepping up the far slopes and the mountains climbing on to the end of time all around. Made a man want to put his feet down firm on the ground and look out steady like the standing trees and stretch tall. Expect that's why my brother quit his job soon as the trouble was over and drove his own stakes there.

Yes, I know. I'm still a long way from those moccasins. I'm over in Idaho in Jacob's valley. But I get to remembering, and then I get to forgetting maybe you're not interested in all the sidelines of what I started to tell you. I'll try to move it faster.

As I was saying, the government outfitted a real expedition to go after Jacob. A brigadier general and something like a thousand men. There's no point telling all that happened, except that this expedition didn't accomplish much more than that first colonel and his men did. They chased Jacob farther and almost penned him a few times and killed a lot of braves and got wind of where his women and their kids were hidden, and forced him to move them farther into the mountains, with them getting out just in time, not being able to carry much with them. But that wasn't catching Jacob and stopping him and his braves from carrying on their hop-skip-and-jump

[1] PICKET LINES: groups of soldiers detached from the main troop in order to warn the others of enemy attacks.

war against all whites in general and these troops in particular. Then a second general went in, and about a thousand more soldiers with them, and they had hard fighting off and on over a couple hundred miles and more, and the days drove on into deep winter and Jacob was licked. Not by the government and its soldiers and their guns. By the winter. He and his braves, what was left of them, had kept two generals and up to two thousand troops busy for four months fighting through parts of three states, and then the winter licked him. He came to the second general under truce in what remained of his chief's rig and took off his headdress and laid it on the ground and spoke. His children were scattered in the mountains, he said, and the cold bit sharp and they had few blankets and no food. Several of the small ones had been found frozen to death. From the moment the sun passed overhead that day he would fight no more. If he was given time to search for his children and bring them together, he would lead them wherever the Great White Chief wished.

There. I'm closer to those moccasins now, even though I'm still way over in Idaho. No. Think it was in western Montana where Jacob surrendered to that second general. Well, the government decided to ship these Nez Percés to the Dump, which was what people called the Indian Territory, where they chucked all the tribes whose lands weren't just cut down but were taken away altogether. That meant Jacob and his children, all that was left of them, about three hundred counting the squaws and kids, would be loaded on a special train and sent along the railroad that ran through our settlement. These Nez Percé Indians would be passing within a stone's throw of our house and we would have a chance to see them at least through the windows and maybe, if there was need

for switching, the train would stop and we would have a good look.

Wonder if you can scratch up any real notion what that meant to us boys around the settlement. To me maybe most of all. These weren't tame Indians. These were wild ones. Fighting Indians. About the fightingest Indians on record. Sure, the Sioux wiped out Custer. But there were a lot more Sioux than soldiers in that scuffle. These Nez Percés had held their own mighty well against a big chunk of the whole United States Army of those days. They were so outnumbered it had got past being even a joke. Any way you figured, it had been about one brave to six or seven soldiers, and those braves hadn't been well armed at the start and had to pick up guns and ammunition as they went along, from soldiers they killed. Some of them were still using arrows at the finish. I'm not being funny when I tell you they kept getting bigger and fiercer in my mind all the time I was hearing about that long running fight in the mountains. It was notches for Nez Percés I was cutting on my stick now, and the way I felt about them even doing that took nerve.

The day came the train was to pass through—sometime late afternoon was the first report—and all of us settlement boys stayed near the telegraph shack waiting. It was cold, though there wasn't much snow around. We'd sneaked into the shack, where there was a stove, till the operator was peeved at our chattering and shooed us out, and I expect I did more than my share of the chattering because in a way these were my Indians because my brother was connected with the expedition that caught them. Don't think the other boys liked how I strutted about that. Well, anyway, the sun went down and we all had to scatter home for supper and the train hadn't come. Afterwards some of us slipped back to the shack and waited some more while the operator cussed at having to stick around waiting for word, and one by one we were yanked away when our fathers came looking for us, and still the train hadn't come.

It was some time past midnight and I'd finally got to sleep, when I popped up in bed at a hammering on the door. I looked into the kitchen. Father was there in his nightshirt, opening the outside door, and the operator was on the step, cussing some more that he'd had word the train was coming, would get there in half an hour, and they'd have to switch it and hold it till the westbound night freight went past. Father added his own cussing and pulled on his pants and boots and heavy jacket and lit his lantern. By time he'd done that, I had my things on too. My mother was up then and objecting, but my father thought some and shushed her. "Fool kid," he said, "excited about Indians all the time. Do him good to see what thieving, smelly things they are." So I went with him. The late moon was up and we could see our way easy, and I stayed in the shack with the operator, and my father went off to set his signal and tend his switch. Certain enough, in about twenty minutes the train came along and swung onto the second line of track and stopped.

The telegraph operator stepped out and started talking to a brakeman. I was scared stiff. I stood in the shack doorway and looked at the train and I was shaking inside like I had some kind of fever. It wasn't much of a train. Just an engine and little fuel car and four old coaches. No caboose. Most trains had cabooses in those days because they carried a lot of brakemen. Had to have them to wrangle the hand brakes. Expect the brakeman the operator was talking to was the only one this train had. Expect that was why it was so late. I mean the railroad wasn't wasting any good

equipment and any extra men on this train, and it was being shoved along slow, when and as how, between other trains.

I stood there, shaking inside, and the engine was wheezing some and the engineer and fireman were moving slow and tired around it, fussing with an oilcan and a tin of grease. That was the only sign of life I could see along the whole train. What light there was in the coaches—only one lantern lit in each—wasn't any stronger than the moonlight outside, and that made the windows blanklike and I couldn't see through them. Except for the wheezing engine, that train was a tired and sleeping or dead thing on the track. Then I saw someone step down from the first coach and stretch and move into the moonlight. He was a soldier, a captain, and he looked tired and sleepy and disgusted with himself and the whole world. He pulled a cigar from a pocket and leaned against the side of the coach, lighting the cigar and blowing out smoke in a slow puff. Seeing him so lazy and casual, I stopped shaking and moved into the open and closer to the coach and shifted around, trying to find an angle that would stop the light reflection on the windows and let me see in. Then I stopped still.

The captain was looking at me. "Why does everybody want to gawk at them? Even kids." He took a long drag on his cigar and blew a pair of fat smoke rings. "You must want to bad," he said. "Up so late. Go on in, take a look." I stared at him, scared now two ways. I was scared to go in where those Indians were and scared not to, after he'd said I could and just about ordered I should. "Go ahead," he said. "They don't eat boys. Only girls. Only at lunchtime." And sudden I knew he was just making a tired joke, and it would be all right and I went up the steps to the front platform and peered in.

Indians. Fighting Indians. The fighting

Nez Percés, who had led United States soldiers a bloody chase through the mountains of three states. The big and fierce redmen who had fought many times their own number of better-armed soldiers to a frequent standstill in the high passes. And they weren't big and they weren't fierce at all. They were huddled figures on the coach seats, two to a seat down the twin rows, braves and squaws and young ones alike, all dusty and tired and hunched together at the shoulders in drowsy silence or sprawled apart over the windowsills and seat-arms in sleep. In the dim light they looked exactly like the tame Indians I'd seen, and they seemed to shrink and shrivel even more as I looked at them and there was no room in me for any emotion but disappointment, and when I noticed the soldiers sleeping in the first seats close to me, I sniffed to myself at the silly notion any guards might be needed on that train. There wasn't the slightest hint of danger anywhere around. Being on that train was no different from being off it except that it was being on a stopped train and not being outside on the ground. It didn't even take any particular nerve to do what I did when I started walking down the aisle.

The only way I know to describe it is that I was in a sort of trance of disappointment and I wanted to see everything and I went straight down the aisle looking all around me. And those Indians acted like I wasn't there at all. Those that were awake. Each of them had his eyes fixed somewhere, maybe out a window or at the floor or just at some point ahead, and didn't move them. They knew I was there. I could tell that. A feeling. A little crawling on my skin. But they wouldn't look at me. They were somehow off away in a place all their own and they weren't going to let me come near getting in there with them or let me know they even saw me outside of it. Except one. He was a young one, a boy like me only a couple years younger, and he was scrooged down against a sleeping brave—maybe his father—and his small eyes, solid black in the dim light, looked at me, and his head turned slow to keep them on me as I went past and I could sense them on me as I went on till the back of the seat shut them off.

Still in that funny trance I went into the next coach and through it and to the third coach and on to the last. Each was the same. Soldiers slumped in sleep and the huddled figures of the Indians in different pairings and sprawled positions, but the effect the same, and then at the end of the last car I saw him. He had a seat to himself and the headdress with its red-tipped feathers hung from the rack above the seat. He was asleep with an arm along the windowsill, his head resting on it. I stopped and stared at him, and the low light from the lantern near the end of the coach shone on the coppery texture of his face and the bare skin of his chest where it showed through the fallen-apart folds of the blanket wrapped around him. I stared at him and I felt cheated and empty inside. Even Jacob wasn't big or fierce. He wasn't as big as my father. He was short. Maybe broad and rather thick in the body but not much, even that way. And his face was quiet and—well, the only word I can ever think of is "peaceful."

I stared at him and then I started a little because he wasn't sleeping. One eyelid had twitched a bit. All at once I knew he was just pretending. He was pretending to be asleep so he wouldn't have to be so aware of the stares of anyone coming aboard to gawk at him. And sudden I felt ashamed and I hurried to the back platform to leave the train, and in the shadows there I stumbled over a sleeping soldier and heard him rousing himself as I scrambled down the steps.

That started what happened afterwards.

Except I'm really to blame for it all. Mean to say it probably wouldn't have happened if I hadn't been hurrying and wakened that soldier. He didn't know I was there. He was too full of sleep at first and didn't know what had awakened him. While I stayed in the dark shadow by the coach, afraid to go out into the moonlight, he stood up and stretched and came down the steps without noticing me and went around the end of the train toward the wider shadow on the other side, and as he went I saw him pulling a bottle out of a pocket.

I felt safe again and started away and turned to look back, and the light was just right for me to see some movement inside through the window by the last seat. Jacob was standing up. All kinds of wild notions poured through my mind and I couldn't move and then he was emerging through the rear door onto the platform and I wasn't exactly scared because I wasn't conscious of feeling anything at all except that I couldn't move. Time seemed to hang there motionless around me. Then I realized he wasn't doing anything and wasn't going to do anything. He wasn't even aware of me, or if he was, I was without meaning for him and he had seen me and dismissed me. He was standing quiet by the rear railing, and his blanket was left inside and the cold night air was blowing against his bare chest above his leather breeches but he didn't appear to notice that. He was looking back along the double iron line of the track toward the tiny point of light that was my father's lantern by the west switch. He stood there, still and quiet, and I stayed where I was and watched him, and he did not move and stood there looking far along the westward track; and that was what we were doing, Jacob and I, when the soldier came back around the end of the train.

Thinking about it later, I couldn't blame that soldier too much. Maybe had orders to keep the Indians in their seats or not let them on the rear platform or something like that. Probably was worried about drinking on duty and not wanting to be caught letting anything slip with the tang plain on his breath. Could be, too, he'd taken on more than he could handle right. Anyway he was surprised and mad when he saw Jacob standing there. He reached first and pulled some object off the platform floor and when he had it I could see it was his rifle. Then he jumped up the steps and started prodding Jacob with the rifle barrel toward the door. Jacob looked at him once and away and turned slow and started to move, and the soldier must have thought Jacob moved too slow because he swung the gun around to use the stock end like a club and smack Jacob on the back. I couldn't see exactly what happened then because the scuffle was too sudden and quick, but there was a blur of movement and the soldier came tumbling off the platform to the ground near me and the gun landed beside him. He was so mad he tripped all over himself getting to his feet and scrabbling for the gun, and he whipped it up and hip-aimed it at Jacob and tried to fire it, and the breech mechanism jammed some way and he clawed at it to make it work.

And Jacob stood there on the platform, still and quiet again, looking down at the soldier, with bare breast broadside to the gun. I could see his eyes bright and black in the moonlight and the shining on the coppery firmness of his face and he did not move, and of a sudden I realized he was waiting. He was waiting for the bullet. He was expecting it and waiting for it and he would not move.

And I jumped forward and grabbed the rifle barrel and pulled hard on it. "No," I shouted. "Not like that."

And the soldier stumbled and fell against me and both of us went down and someone was yelling at us; and when I managed to get to my feet I saw it was the captain, and the soldier was up too, standing stiff and awkward at attention. "Bloody Indian," the soldier said. "Trying to get away."

The captain looked up and saw Jacob standing there and jerked a bit with recognizing who it was.

"He was not," I said. "He was just standing there."

The captain looked at the soldier and shook his head slow. "You'd have shot that one." The captain shook his head again like he was disgusted and tired of everything and maybe even of living. "What's the use," he said. He flipped a thumb at the soldier. "Pick up your gun and get on forward." The soldier hurried off and the captain looked at Jacob and Jacob looked down at him, still and quiet and not moving a muscle. "There's fools of every color," the captain said, and Jacob's eyes brightened a little as if he understood, and I expect he did because I'd heard he could speak English when he wanted to. The captain wiped a hand across his face. "Stand on that damned platform as long as you want," he said. He remembered he had a cigar in his other hand and looked at it and it was out and he threw it on the ground and swung around and went toward the front of the train again, and I wanted to follow him but I couldn't because now Jacob was looking at me.

He looked down at me what seemed a long time and then he motioned at me, and I could tell he wanted me to step out further into the moonlight. I did and he leaned forward to peer at me. He reached a hand out toward me, palm flat and down, and said something in his own language and for a moment I was there with him in the world that was different and beyond my own everyday world, and then he swung away and stepped to stand by the rear railing again and I knew I was outside again, outside of his mind and put away and no more to him than any other object around.

He was alone there, looking far down the track, and it sank slow and deep in me that he was looking far past the tiny light point of my father's lantern, far on where the lone track ran straight along the slow-rising reaches of distance into the horizon that led past the longest vision at last to the great climbing mountains. He was looking back along the iron trail that was taking him and his children away from a valley that would make a man want to put his feet firm on the earth and stretch tall, and was taking them to an unknown place where they would not be themselves any longer but only some among many of many tribes and tongues and all dependent on the bounty of a forgetful government. It wasn't an Indian I was seeing there any more. It was a man. It wasn't Jacob, the tamed chief that even foolish kids could gawk at. It was Mountain Elk, the Big-Deer-That-Walks-the-High-Places, and he was big, really big, and he was one meant to walk the high places.

He stood there looking down the track and the westbound night freight came rumbling out of the east and strained past, and he stood there watching it go westward along the track; and his train began to move, creeping eastward slow and feeling forward, and I watched it go and long as I could see him he was standing there, still and quiet, looking straight out along the back trail.

Well. I've taken you to where I was headed. It's only a hop now to those moccasins. I tried to tell the other boys about it the next day, and likely boasted and strutted in the telling, and they wouldn't believe me. Oh, they'd believe I saw the Indians all right. Had to. The telegraph operator backed my saying I was there. Even that I went aboard. But they wouldn't believe the rest. And because they wouldn't believe me, I had to keep pounding it at them, telling it over and over. Expect I was getting to be mighty unpopular.

But Jacob saved me, even though I never saw him again. There was a day a bunch of us boys were playing some game or other back of the telegraph shack and sudden we realized someone had come up from somewhere and was watching us. An Indian. Seemed to be just an ordinary, everyday sort of tame Indian. But he was looking us over intent and careful, and he picked me and came straight to me. He put out a hand, palm flat and down, and said something to me in his Indian talk and pointed off to the east and south and back again to me, and reached inside the old blanket he had fastened around him with a belt, and took out a dirty cloth-wrapped package and laid it at my feet and went away and faded out of sight around the shack. When I unrolled that package, there were those moccasins.

Funny thing. I never wanted to go around telling my story to the other boys again. Didn't need to. Whether they believed or not wasn't important any more. I had those moccasins. In a way they made me one of Jacob's children. Remembering that has helped me sometimes in tough spots.

FOR DISCUSSION

1. There is an old Indian saying: "Never judge a man until you have walked a mile in his moccasins." In what sense did the narrator stand in Jacob's moccasins even before he received the gift?

2. Jacob's name was Big-Deer-That-Walks-the-High-Places. But by the whites, he was called only Jacob. Why? The boy who tells the story was brought up with stereotypes, or oversimplified ideas, of what Indians were like: dirty thieves or fierce warriors. What happened to make him say, "It wasn't an Indian I was seeing there any more. It was a man"?

3. Jacob was not tall, or fierce, or old. What qualities enabled him to lead his people? Show how the conflict over the valley and the scene on the train demonstrate these qualities.

FOR COMPOSITION

• In this story we see Jacob only through the eyes of others, yet we learn much about what he must have felt. Imagine that you are Jacob standing at the rear of the train. Write what goes through your mind as you think back on what is past and look ahead to the reservation where your "children" are being taken.

His purse-snatching career ended abruptly when Roger met Mrs. Luella Bates Washington Jones.

THANK YOU, M'AM
LANGSTON HUGHES

SHE WAS A LARGE woman with a large purse that had everything in it but a hammer and nails. It had a long strap, and she carried it slung across her shoulder. It was about eleven o'clock at night, dark, and she was walking alone, when a boy ran up behind her and tried to snatch her purse. The strap broke with the sudden single tug the boy gave it from behind. But the boy's weight and the weight of the purse combined caused him to lose his balance. Instead of taking off full blast as he had hoped, the boy fell on his back on the sidewalk, and his legs flew up. The large woman simply turned around and kicked him right square in his blue-jeaned sitter. Then she reached down, picked the boy up by his shirt front, and shook him until his teeth rattled.

After that the woman said, "Pick up my pocketbook, boy, and give it here."

She still held him tightly. But she bent down enough to permit him to stoop and pick up her purse. Then she said, "Now ain't you ashamed of yourself?"

Firmly gripped by his shirt front, the boy said, "Yes'm."

The woman said, "What did you want to do it for?"

The boy said, "I didn't aim to."

She said, "You a lie!"

By that time two or three people passed,

stopped, turned to look, and some stood watching.

"If I turn you loose, will you run?" asked the woman.

"Yes'm," said the boy.

"Then I won't turn you loose," said the woman. She did not release him.

"Lady, I'm sorry," whispered the boy.

"Um-hum! Your face is dirty. I got a great mind to wash your face for you. Ain't you got nobody home to tell you to wash your face?"

"No'm," said the boy.

"Then it will get washed this evening," said the large woman, starting up the street, dragging the frightened boy behind her.

He looked as if he were fourteen or fifteen, frail and willow-wild, in tennis shoes and blue jeans.

The woman said, "You ought to be my son. I would teach you right from wrong. Least I can do right now is to wash your face. Are you hungry?"

"No'm," said the being-dragged boy. "I just want you to turn me loose."

"Was I bothering *you* when I turned that corner?" asked the woman.

"No'm."

"But you put yourself in contact with *me*," said the woman. "If you think that that contact is not going to last a while, you got another thought coming. When I get through with you, sir, you are going to remember Mrs. Luella Bates Washington Jones."

Sweat popped out on the boy's face, and he began to struggle. Mrs. Jones stopped, jerked him around in front of her, put a half nelson about his neck, and continued to drag him up the street. When she got to her door, she dragged the boy inside, down a hall, and into a large kitchenette-furnished room at the rear of the house. She switched on the light and left the door open. The boy could hear other roomers laughing and talking in the large house. Some of their doors were open, too, so he knew he and the woman were not alone. The woman still had him by the neck in the middle of her room.

She said, "What is your name?"

"Roger," answered the boy.

"Then, Roger, you go to that sink and wash your face," said the woman, where-upon she turned him loose—at last. Roger looked at the door—looked at the woman —looked at the door—*and went to the sink.*

"Let the water run until it gets warm," she said. "Here's a clean towel."

"You gonna take me to jail?" asked the boy, bending over the sink.

"Not with that face, I would not take you nowhere," said the woman. "Here I am trying to get home to cook me a bite to eat, and you snatch my pocketbook! Maybe you ain't been to your supper either, late as it be. Have you?"

"There's nobody home at my house," said the boy.

"Then we'll eat," said the woman. "I believe you're hungry—or been hungry—to try to snatch my pocketbook!"

"I want a pair of blue suede shoes," said the boy.

"Well, you didn't have to snatch *my* pocketbook to get some suede shoes," said Mrs. Luella Bates Washington Jones. "You could of asked me."

"M'am?"

The water dripping from his face, the boy looked at her. There was a long pause. A very long pause. After he had dried his face, and not knowing what else to do, dried it again, the boy turned around, wondering what next. The door was open. He could make a dash for it down the hall. He could run, run, run, *run!*

The woman was sitting on the daybed.

After a while she said, "I were young once, and I wanted things I could not get."

There was another long pause. The boy's mouth opened. Then he frowned, not knowing he frowned.

The woman said, "Um-hum! You thought I was going to say *but*, didn't you? You thought I was going to say *but I didn't snatch people's pocketbooks.* Well, I wasn't going to say that." Pause. Silence. "I have done things, too, which I would not tell you, son—neither tell God, if He didn't already know. Everybody's got something in common. So you set down while I fix us something to eat. You might run that comb through your hair so you will look presentable."

In another corner of the room behind a screen was a gas plate and an icebox. Mrs. Jones got up and went behind the screen. The woman did not watch the boy to see if he was going to run now, nor did she watch her purse, which she left behind her on the daybed. But the boy took care to sit on the far side of the room, away from the purse, where he thought she could easily see him out of the corner of her eye if she wanted to. He did not trust the woman *not* to trust him. And he did not want to be mistrusted now.

"Do you need somebody to go to the store," asked the boy, "maybe to get some milk or something?"

"Don't believe I do," said the woman, "unless you just want sweet milk your-self. I was going to make cocoa out of this canned milk I got here."

"That will be fine," said the boy.

She heated some lima beans and ham she had in the icebox, made the cocoa, and set the table. The woman did not ask the boy anything about where he lived, or his folks, or anything else that would embarrass him. Instead, as they ate, she told him about her job in a hotel beauty shop that stayed open late, what the work was like, and how all kinds of women came in and out, blondes, redheads, and Spanish. Then she cut him a half of her ten-cent cake.

"Eat some more, son," she said.

When they were finished eating, she got up and said, "Now here, take this ten dollars and buy yourself some blue suede shoes. And next time, do not make the mistake of latching onto *my* pocketbook *nor nobody else's*—because shoes got by devilish ways will burn your feet. I got to get my rest now. But from here on in, son, I hope you will behave yourself."

She led him down the hall to the front door and opened it. "Good night! Behave yourself, boy!" she said, looking out into the street as he went down the steps.

The boy wanted to say something other than, "Thank you, m'am," to Mrs. Luella Bates Washington Jones, but although his lips moved, he couldn't even say that as he turned at the foot of the barren stoop and looked up at the large woman in the door. Then she shut the door.

FOR DISCUSSION

1. If Mrs. Jones had been only tough or only kind to Roger, she could not have reached him as she did. Find passages in the story where she was both tough and kind at the same time. Why was this effective?

2. What did Mrs. Jones show about herself by not saying, "but I didn't steal pocketbooks"?

3. Twice Roger could have fled and didn't. Why didn't he leave when Mrs. Jones first released him? Were his reasons for staying the same the second time, when Mrs. Jones was cooking?

FOR COMPOSITION

• Roger wanted to say, "Thank you, m'am" as he left but he couldn't say anything. If you were Roger, what would you have said? Using the words you think Roger might, write a note to Mrs. Jones expressing your thanks.

PETER TWO
IRWIN SHAW

IT WAS SATURDAY night and people were killing each other by the hour on the small screen. Policemen were shot in the line of duty, gangsters were thrown off roofs, and an elderly lady was slowly poisoned for her pearls, and her murderer brought to justice by a cigarette company after a long series of discussions in the office of a private detective. Brave, unarmed actors leaped at villains holding forty-fives, and ingénues[1] were saved from death by the knife by the quick thinking of various handsome and intrepid young men.

Peter sat in the big chair in front of the screen, his feet up over the arm, eating grapes. His mother wasn't home, so he ate the seeds and all as he stared critically at the violence before him. When his mother was around, the fear of appendicitis hung in the air and she watched carefully to see that each seed was neatly extracted and placed in an ashtray. Too, if she were home, there would be irritated little lectures on the quality of television entertainment for the young, and quick-tempered fiddling with the dials to find something that was vaguely defined as educational. Alone, daringly awake at eleven o'clock, Peter ground the seeds between his teeth, enjoying the impolite noise and the solitude and freedom of the empty house. During the television commercials Peter closed his eyes and imagined himself hurling bottles at large unshaven men with pistols and walking slowly up dark stairways toward the door behind which everyone knew the Boss was waiting, the bulge of his shoulder holster unmistakable under the cloth of his pencil-striped flannel jacket.

Peter was thirteen years old. In his class there were three other boys with the same given name, and the history teacher, who thought he was a funny man, called them Peter One, Peter Two (now eating grapes, seeds and all), Peter Three, and Peter the Great. Peter the Great was, of course, the smallest boy in the class. He weighed only sixty-two pounds, and he wore glasses, and in games he was always the last one to be chosen. The class always laughed when the history teacher called out "Peter the Great," and Peter Two laughed with them, but he didn't think it was so awfully funny.

He had done something pretty good for Peter the Great two weeks ago, and now they were what you might call friends. All the Peters were what you might call friends, on account of that comedian of a history teacher. They weren't *real* friends, but they had something together, something the other boys didn't have. They didn't like it, but they had it, and it made them responsible for each other. So two weeks ago, when Charley Blaisdell, who weighed a hundred and twenty, took Peter the Great's

[1] INGÉNUES (ăn·zhā·nü′): innocent girls or young women.

cap at recess and started horsing around with it, and Peter the Great looked as if he was going to cry, he, Peter Two, grabbed the cap and gave it back and faced Blaisdell. Of course, there was a fight, and Peter thought it was going to be his third defeat of the term, but a wonderful thing happened. In the middle of the fight, just when Peter was hoping one of the teachers would show up (they sure showed up plenty of times when you didn't need them), Blaisdell let a hard one go. Peter ducked and Blaisdell hit him on the head and broke his arm. You could tell right off he broke his arm, because he fell to the ground yelling, and his arm just hung like a piece of string. Walters, the gym teacher, finally showed up and carried Blaisdell off, yelling all the time, and Peter the Great came up and said admiringly, "Boy, one thing you have to admit, you sure have a hard head."

Blaisdell was out of class two days, and he still had his arm in the sling, and every time he was excused from writing on the blackboard because he had a broken arm, Peter got a nice warm feeling all over. Peter the Great hung around him all the time, doing things for him and buying him sodas, because Peter the Great's parents were divorced and gave him all the money he wanted, to make up to him. And that was O.K.

But the best thing was the feeling he'd had since the fight. It was like what the people on the television must feel after they'd gone into a room full of enemies and come out with the girl or with the papers or with the suspect, leaving corpses and desolation behind them. Blaisdell weighed a hundred and twenty pounds but that hadn't stopped Peter any more than the fact that the spies all had two guns apiece ever stopped the F.B.I. men on the screen. They saw what they had to do and they went in and did it, that was all. Peter

couldn't phrase it for himself, but for the first time in his life he had a conscious feeling of confidence and pride in himself.

"Let them come," he muttered obscurely, munching grape seeds and watching the television set through narrowed eyes, "just let them come."

He was going to be a dangerous man, he felt, when he grew up, but one to whom the weak and the unjustly hunted could safely turn. He was sure he was going to be six feet tall, because his father was six feet tall, and all his uncles, and that would help. But he would have to develop his arms. They were just too thin. After all, you couldn't depend on people breaking their bones on your head every time. He had been doing push-ups each morning and night for the past month. He could only do five and a half at a time so far, but he was going to keep at it until he had arms like steel bars. Arms like that really could mean the difference between life and death later on, when you had to dive under the gun and disarm somebody. You had to have quick reflexes, too, of course, and be able to feint to one side with your eyes before the crucial moment. And, most important of all, no matter what the odds, you had to be fearless. One moment of hesitation and it was a case for the morgue. But now, after the battle of Peter the Great's cap, he didn't worry about that part of it, the fearless part. From now on, it would just be a question of technique.

Comedians began to appear all over the dial, laughing with a lot of teeth, and Peter went into the kitchen and got another bunch of grapes and two tangerines from the refrigerator. He didn't put on the light in the kitchen and it was funny how mysterious a kitchen could be near midnight when nobody else was home, and there was only the beam of the light from the open refrigerator, casting shadows from the milk bottles onto the linoleum. Until recently he hadn't liked the dark too much and he always turned on lights wherever he went, but you had to practice being fearless, just like anything else.

He ate the two tangerines standing in the dark in the kitchen, just for practice. He ate the seeds, too, to show his mother. Then he went back into the living room, carrying the grapes.

The comedians were still on and still laughing. He fiddled with the dial, but they were wearing funny hats and laughing and telling jokes about the. income tax on all the channels. If his mother hadn't made him promise to go to sleep by ten o'clock, he'd have turned off the set and gone to bed. He decided not to waste his time and got down on the floor and began to do push-ups, trying to be sure to keep his knees straight. He was up to four and slowing down when he heard the scream. He stopped in the middle of a push-up and waited, just to make sure. The scream came again. It was a woman and it was real loud. He looked up at the television set. There was a man there talking about floor wax, a man with a mustache and a lot of teeth, and it was a cinch *he* wasn't doing any screaming.

The next time the scream came there was moaning and talking at the end of it, and the sound of fists beating on the front door. Peter got up and turned off the television, just to be sure the sounds he was hearing weren't somehow being broadcast.

The beating on the door began again and a woman's voice cried "Please, please, *please* . . ." and there was no doubt about it any more.

Peter looked around him at the empty room. Three lamps were lit and the room was nice and bright and the light was re-flected on the grapes and off the glass of the picture of the boats on Cape Cod that his Aunt Martha painted the year she was up there. The television set stood in the corner, like a big blind eye now that the light was out. The cushions of the soft chair he had been sitting in to watch the programs were pushed in and he knew his mother would come and plump them out before she went to sleep, and the whole room looked like a place in which it was impossible to hear a woman screaming at midnight and beating on the door with her fists and yelling, "Please, please, *please*. . . ."

The woman at the door yelled "Murder, murder, he's killing me!" and for the first time Peter was sorry his parents had gone out that night.

"Open the door!" the woman yelled. "Please, *please* open the door!" You could tell she wasn't saying please just to be polite by now.

Peter looked nervously around him. The room, with all its lights, seemed strange, and there were shadows behind everything. Then the woman yelled again, just noise this time. Either a person is fearless, Peter thought coldly, or he isn't fearless. He started walking slowly toward the front door. There was a long mirror in the foyer and he got a good look at himself. His arms looked very thin.

The woman began hammering once more on the front door and Peter looked at it closely. It was a big steel door, but it was shaking minutely, as though somebody with a machine was working on it. For the first time he heard another voice. It was a man's voice, only it didn't sound quite like a man's voice. It sounded like an animal in a cave, growling and deciding to do something unreasonable. In all the scenes of threat and violence on the television set, Peter had never heard anything at all like it. He moved slowly toward the door, feel-ing the way he had felt when he had the flu, remembering how thin his arms looked in the mirror, regretting that he had de-cided to be fearless.

"Oh, God!" the woman yelled, "Oh, God, don't do it!"

Then there was some more hammering

and the low, animal sound of the beast in the cave that you never heard over the air, and he threw the door open.

Mrs. Chalmers was there in the vestibule, on her knees, facing him, and behind her Mr. Chalmers was standing, leaning against the wall, with the door to his own apartment open behind him. Mr. Chalmers was making that funny sound and he had a gun in his hand and he was pointing it at Mrs. Chalmers.

The vestibule was small and it had what Peter's mother called Early American wallpaper and a brass light fixture. There were only the two doors opening on the vestibule, and the Chalmers had a mat in front of theirs with "Welcome" written on it. The Chalmers were in their mid-thirties, and Peter's mother always said about them, "One thing about our neighbors, they *are* quiet." She also said that Mrs. Chalmers put a lot of money on her back.

Mrs. Chalmers was kind of fat and her hair was pretty blonde and her complexion was soft and pink and she always looked as though she had been in the beauty parlor all afternoon. She always said "My, you're getting to be a big boy" to Peter when she met him in the elevator, in a soft voice, as though she was just about to laugh. She must have said that fifty times by now. She had a good, strong smell of perfume on her all the time, too.

Mr. Chalmers wore pince-nez[1] glasses most of the time and he was getting bald and he worked late at his office a good many evenings of the week. When he met Peter in the elevator he would say, "It's getting colder," or "It's getting warmer," and that was all, so Peter had no opinion about him, except that he looked like the principal of a school.

But now Mrs. Chalmers was on her knees in the vestibule and her dress was torn and she was crying and there were

black streaks on her cheeks and she didn't look as though she'd just come from the beauty parlor. And Mr. Chalmers wasn't wearing a jacket and he didn't have his glasses on and what hair he had was mussed all over his head and he was leaning against the Early American wallpaper making this animal noise, and he had a big, heavy pistol in his hand and he was pointing it right at Mrs. Chalmers.

"Let me in!" Mrs. Chalmers yelled, still on her knees. "You've got to let me in. He's going to kill me. *Please!*"

"Mrs. Chalmers . . ." Peter began. His voice sounded as though he were trying to talk under water, and it was very hard to say the "s" at the end of her name. He put out his hands uncertainly in front of him, as though he expected somebody to throw him something.

"Get inside, you," Mr. Chalmers said.

Peter looked at Mr. Chalmers. He was only five feet away and without his glasses he was squinting. Peter feinted with his eyes, or at least later in his life he thought he had feinted with his eyes. Mr. Chalmers didn't do anything. He just stood there, with the pistol pointed, somehow, it seemed to Peter, at both Mrs. Chalmers and himself at the same time. Five feet was a long distance, a long, long distance.

"Good night," Peter said, and he closed the door.

There was a single sob on the other side of the door and that was all.

Peter went in and put the uneaten grapes back in the refrigerator, flicking on the light as he went into the kitchen and leaving it on when he went out. Then he went back to the living room and got the stems from the first bunch of grapes and threw them into the fireplace, because otherwise his mother would notice and look for the seeds and not see them and give him four tablespoons of milk of magnesia the next day.

Then, leaving the lights on in the living

---

[1] PINCE-NEZ (păns′ nā′): eyeglasses that are clipped to the bridge of the nose.

room, although he knew what his mother would say about that when she got home, he went into his room and quickly got into bed. He waited for the sound of shots. There were two or three noises that might have been shots, but in the city it was hard to tell.

He was still awake when his parents came home. He heard his mother's voice, and he knew from the sound she was complaining about the lights in the living room and kitchen, but he pretended to be sleeping when she came into his room to look at him. He didn't want to start in with his mother about the Chalmers, because then she'd ask when it had happened and she'd want to know what he was doing up at twelve o'clock.

He kept listening for shots for a long time, and he got hot and damp under the covers and then freezing cold. He heard several sharp, ambiguous noises in the quiet night, but nothing that you could be sure about, and after a while he fell asleep.

In the morning, Peter got out of bed early, dressed quickly, and went silently out of the apartment without waking his parents. The vestibule looked just the way it always did, with the brass lamp and the flowered wallpaper and the Chalmers' door-mat with "Welcome" on it. There were no bodies and no blood. Sometimes when Mrs. Chalmers had been standing there waiting for the elevator, you could smell her perfume for a long time after. But now there was no smell of perfume, just the dusty, apartment-house usual smell. Peter stared at the Chalmers' door nervously

while waiting for the elevator to come up, but it didn't open and no sound came from within.

Sam, the man who ran the elevator and who didn't like him, anyway, only grunted when Peter got into the elevator, and Peter decided not to ask him any questions. He went out into the chilly, bright Sunday-morning street, half expecting to see the morgue wagon in front of the door, or at least two or three prowl cars. But there was only a sleepy woman in slacks airing a boxer and a man with his collar turned up hurrying up from the corner with the newspapers under his arm.

Peter went across the street and looked up to the sixth floor, at the windows of the Chalmers' apartment. The Venetian blinds were pulled shut in every room and all the windows were closed.

A policeman walked down the other side of the street, heavy, blue and purposeful, and for a moment Peter felt close to arrest. But the policeman continued on toward the avenue and turned the corner and disappeared and Peter said to himself, They never know anything.

He walked up and down the street, first on one side, then on the other, waiting, although it was hard to know what he was waiting for. He saw a hand come out through the blinds in his parents' room and slam the window shut, and he knew he ought to get upstairs quickly with a good excuse for being out, but he couldn't face them this morning, and he would invent an excuse later. Maybe he would even say he had gone to the museum, although he doubted that his mother would swallow that. Some excuse. Later.

Then, after he had been patrolling the street for almost two hours, and just as he was coming up to the entrance of his building, the door opened and Mr. and Mrs. Chalmers came out. He had on his pince-nez and a dark-gray hat, and Mrs. Chal-

mers had on her fur coat and a red hat with feathers on it. Mr. Chalmers was holding the door open politely for his wife, and she looked, as she came out the door, as though she had just come from the beauty parlor.

It was too late to turn back or avoid them, and Peter just stood still, five feet from the entrance.

"Good morning," Mr. Chalmers said as he took his wife's arm and they started walking past Peter.

"Good morning, Peter," said Mrs. Chalmers in her soft voice, smiling at him. "Isn't it a nice day today?"

"Good morning," Peter said, and he was surprised that it came out and sounded like good morning.

The Chalmers walked down the street toward Madison Avenue, two married people, arm in arm, going to church or to a big hotel for Sunday breakfast. Peter watched them, ashamed. He was ashamed of Mrs. Chalmers for looking the way she did the night before, down on her knees, and yelling like that and being so afraid. He was ashamed of Mr. Chalmers for making the noise that was not like the noise of a human being, and for threatening to shoot Mrs. Chalmers and not doing it. And he was ashamed of himself because he had been fearless when he opened the door, but had not been fearless ten seconds later, with Mr. Chalmers five feet away with the gun. He was ashamed of himself for not taking Mrs. Chalmers into the apartment, ashamed because he was not lying now with a bullet in his heart. But most of all he was ashamed because they had all said good morning to each other and the Chalmers were walking quietly together, arm in arm, in the windy sunlight, toward Madison Avenue.

It was nearly eleven o'clock when Peter got back to the apartment, but his parents had gone back to sleep. There was a pretty good program on at eleven, about counter-spies in Asia, and he turned it on automatically, while eating an orange. It was pretty exciting, but then there was a part in which an Oriental held a ticking bomb in his hand in a roomful of Americans, and Peter could tell what was coming. The hero, who was fearless and who came from California, was beginning to feint with his eyes, and Peter reached over and turned the set off. It closed down with a shivering, collapsing pattern. Blinking a little, Peter watched the blind screen for a moment.

Ah, he thought in sudden, permanent disbelief, after the night in which he had faced the incomprehensible, shameless, weaponed grownup world and had failed to disarm it, ah, they can have that; that's for kids.

FOR DISCUSSION

1. Why would Peter be fascinated with violent television shows one day, and the next day think, "that's for kids"? Do you think the events of the story make this change in him believable?

2. How do you explain the change in the Chalmers from Saturday night to Sunday morning? Is this change believable? Why did Peter feel ashamed for Mr. and Mrs. Chalmers?

3. The story is called "Peter Two," but the three Peters at school have nothing to do with the fight between Mr. and Mrs. Chalmers. What is the main conflict that ties together the two parts of the story (school and apartment house)?

FOR COMPOSITION

• A character is best revealed through his actions, especially action in a crisis. What does the crisis with Mr. and Mrs. Chalmers reveal about Peter? Is this consistent with what the story showed about him earlier? Find clues at the beginning of the story that prepare the reader for Peter's reaction to Mr. Chalmers's gun.

Clutching his toy sword, the child went adventuring—into a real battle.

CHICKAMAUGA
AMBROSE BIERCE

ONE SUNNY AUTUMN afternoon a child strayed away from its rude home in a small field and entered a forest unobserved. It was happy in a new sense of freedom from control, happy in the opportunity of exploration and adventure; for this child's spirit, in bodies of its ancestors, had for many thousands of years been trained to memorable feats of discovery and conquest—victories in battles whose critical moments were centuries, whose victors' camps were cities of hewn stone. From the cradle of its race it had conquered its way through two continents, and passing a great sea, had penetrated a third, there to be born to war and dominion as a heritage.

The child was a boy aged about six years, the son of a poor planter. In his younger manhood the father had been a soldier, had fought against naked savages, and followed the flag of his country into the capital of a civilized race to the far South. In the peaceful life of a planter the warrior-fire survived; once kindled, it is never extinguished. The man loved military books and pictures, and the boy had understood enough to make himself a wooden sword, though even the eye of his father would hardly have known it for what it was. This weapon he now bore bravely, as became the son of an heroic race, and pausing now and again in the sunny spaces of the forest assumed, with some exaggeration, the postures of aggression and defense that he had been taught by the engraver's art. Made reckless by the ease with which he over-came invisible foes attempting to stay his advance, he committed the common enough military error of pushing the pursuit to a dangerous extreme, until he found himself upon the margin of a wide but shallow brook, whose rapid waters barred his direct advance against the flying foe that had crossed with illogical ease. But the intrepid victor was not to be baffled; the spirit of the race which had passed the great sea burned unconquerable in that small breast and would not be denied. Finding a place where some boulders in the bed of the stream lay but a step or a leap apart, he made his way across and fell again upon the rear-guard of his imaginary foe, putting all to the sword.

Now that the battle had been won, prudence required that he withdraw to his base of operations. Alas! like many a mightier conquerer, and like one, the mightiest, he could not

> "curb the lust for war,
> Nor learn that tempted Fate will leave the
>   loftiest star."

Advancing from the bank of the creek he suddenly found himself confronted with a new and more formidable enemy: in the path that he was following sat, bolt upright, with ears erect and paws suspended before it, a rabbit! With a startled cry the child turned and fled, he knew not in what direction, calling with inarticulate cries for his mother, weeping, stumbling, his tender skin cruelly torn by brambles, his little heart beating hard with terror—breathless, blind with tears—lost in the forest! Then, for more than an hour, he wandered with erring feet through the tangled undergrowth, till at last, overcome by fatigue, he lay down in a narrow space between two rocks, within a few yards of the stream, and still grasping his toy sword, no longer a weapon but a companion, sobbed himself to sleep. The wood birds sang merrily above his head; the squirrels, whisking their bravery of tail, ran barking from tree to tree, unconscious of the pity of it, and somewhere far away was a strange, muffled thunder, as if the partridges were drumming in celebration of nature's victory over the son of her immemorial enslavers. And back at the little plantation, where white men and black were hastily searching the fields and hedges in alarm, a mother's heart was breaking for her missing child.

Hours passed, and then the little sleeper rose to his feet. The chill of the evening was in his limbs, the fear of the gloom in his heart. But he had rested, and he no longer wept. With some blind instinct which impelled to action he struggled through the undergrowth about him and came to a more open ground—on his right the brook, to the left a gentle acclivity studded with infrequent trees; over all, the gathering gloom of twilight. A thin, ghostly mist rose along the water. It frightened and repelled him; instead of recrossing, in the direction whence he had come, he turned his back upon it, and went forward toward the dark enclosing wood. Suddenly he saw before him a strange moving object which he took to be some large animal—a dog, a pig—he could not name it; perhaps it was a bear. He had seen pictures of bears, but knew of nothing to their discredit and had vaguely wished to meet one. But something in form or movement of this object—something in the awkwardness of its approach—told him that it was not a bear, and

curiosity was stayed by fear. He stood still, and as it came slowly on gained courage every moment, for he saw that at least it had not the long, menacing ears of the rabbit. Possibly his impressionable mind was half conscious of something familiar in its shambling, awkward gait. Before it had approached near enough to resolve his doubts, he saw that it was followed by another and another. To right and to left were many more; the whole open space about him was alive with them—all moving toward the brook.

They were men. They crept upon their hands and knees. They used their hands only, dragging their legs. They used their knees only, their arms hanging idle at their sides. They strove to rise to their feet, but fell prone in the attempt. They did nothing naturally, and nothing alike, save only to advance foot by foot in the same direction. Singly, in pairs and in little groups, they came on through the gloom, some halting now and again while others crept slowly past them, then resuming their movement. They came by dozens and by hundreds; as far on either hand as one could see in the deepening gloom they extended, and the black wood behind them appeared to be inexhaustible. The very ground seemed in motion toward the creek. Occasionally one who had paused did not again go on, but lay motionless. He was dead. Some, pausing, made strange gestures with their hands, erected their arms and lowered them again, clasped their heads; spread their palms upward, as men are sometimes seen to do in public prayer.

Not all of this did the child note; it is what would have been noted by an elder observer; he saw little but that these were men, yet crept like babes. Being men, they were not terrible, though unfamiliarly clad. He moved among them freely, going from one to another and peering into their faces with childish curiosity. All their faces were singularly white and many were streaked and gouted with red. Something in this— something too, perhaps, in their grotesque attitudes and movements—reminded him of the painted clown whom he had seen last summer in the circus, and he laughed as he watched them. But on and ever on they crept, these maimed and bleeding men, as heedless as he of the dramatic contrast between his laughter and their own ghastly gravity. To him it was a merry spectacle. He had seen his father's Negroes creep upon their hands and knees for his amuse-ment—had ridden them so, "making be-lieve" they were his horses. He now ap-proached one of these crawling figures from behind and with an agile movement mounted it astride. The man sank upon his breast, recovered, flung the small boy fiercely to the ground as an unbroken colt might have done, then turned upon him a face that lacked a lower jaw—from the upper teeth to the throat was a great red gap fringed with hanging shreds of flesh and splinters of bone. The unnatural promi-nence of nose, the absence of chin, the fierce eyes, gave this man the appearance of a great bird of prey crimsoned in throat and breast by the blood of its quarry. The man rose to his knees, the child to his feet. The man shook his fist at the child; the child, terrified at last, ran to a tree near by, got upon the farther side of it, and took a more serious view of the situation. And so the clumsy multitude dragged itself slowly and painfully along in hideous pantomime —moved forward down the slope like a swarm of great black beetles, with never a sound of going—in silence profound, abso-lute.

Instead of darkening, the haunted land-scape began to brighten. Through the belt of trees beyond the brook shone a strange red light, the trunks and branches of the trees making a black lacework against it. It struck the creeping figures and gave them monstrous shadows, which caricatured their movements on the lit grass. It fell upon their faces, touching their whiteness with a ruddy tinge, accentuating the stains with which so many of them were freaked and maculated. It sparkled on buttons and bits of metal in their clothing. Instinctively the child turned toward the growing splen-dor and moved down the slope with his horrible companions; in a few moments had passed the foremost of the throng— not much of a feat, considering his advan-tages. He placed himself in the lead, his wooden sword still in hand, and solemnly directed the march, conforming his pace to theirs and occasionally turning as if to see that his forces did not straggle. Surely such a leader never before had such a following.

Scattered about upon the ground now slowly narrowing by the encroachment of this awful march to water were certain articles to which, in the leader's mind, were coupled no significant associations: an occa-sional blanket, tightly rolled lengthwise, doubled and the ends bound together with a string; a heavy knapsack here, and there a broken rifle—such things, in short, as are found in the rear of retreating troops, the "spoor" of men flying from their hunt-ers. Everywhere near the creek, which here had a margin of lowland, the earth was trodden into mud by the feet of men and horses. An observer of better experience in the use of his eyes would have noticed that these footprints pointed in both direc-tions; the ground had been twice passed over—in advance and in retreat. A few hours before, these deperate, stricken men, with their more fortunate and now distant comrades, had penetrated the forest in thousands. Their successive battalions, breaking into swarms and reforming in lines, had passed the child on every side— had almost trodden on him as he slept. The rustle and murmur of their march had not awakened him. Almost within a stone's throw of where he lay they had fought a battle; but all unheard by him were the roar of the musketry, the shock of the cannon, "the thunder of the captains and the shouting." He had slept through it all, grasping his little wooden sword with perhaps a tighter clutch in unconscious sympathy with his martial environment, but as heedless of the grandeur of the struggle as the dead who had died to make the glory.

The fire beyond the belt of woods on the farther side of the creek, reflected to earth from the canopy of its own smoke, was now suffusing the whole landscape. It transformed the sinuous line of mist to the vapor of gold. The water gleamed with dashes of red, and red, too, were many of the stones protruding above the surface. But that was blood; the less desperately wounded had stained them in crossing. On them, too, the child now crossed with eager steps; he was going to the fire. As he stood upon the farther bank he turned about to look at the companions of his march. The advance was arriving at the creek. The stronger had already drawn themselves to the brink and plunged their faces into the flood. Three or four who lay without motion appeared to have no heads. At this the child's eyes expanded with wonder; even his hospitable understanding could not accept a phenomenon implying such vitality as that. After slaking their thirst these men had not had the strength to back away from the water, nor to keep their heads above it. They were drowned. In rear of these, the open spaces of the forest showed the leader as many formless figures of his grim command as at first; but not nearly so many were in motion. He waved his cap for their encouragement and smilingly pointed with his weapon in the direction of the guiding light—a pillar of fire to this strange exodus.

Confident of the fidelity of his forces, he now entered the belt of woods, passed through it easily in the red illumination, climbed a fence, ran across a field, turning now and again to coquet with his responsive shadow, and so approached the blazing ruin of a dwelling. Desolation everywhere. In all the wide glare not a living thing was visible. He cared nothing for that; the spectacle pleased, and he danced with glee in imitation of the wavering flames. He ran about, collecting fuel, but every object that he found was too heavy for him to cast in from the distance to which the heat limited his approach. In despair he flung in his sword—a surrender to the superior forces of nature. His military career was at an end.

Shifting his position, his eyes fell upon some outbuildings which had an oddly familiar appearance, as if he had dreamed of them. He stood considering them with wonder, when suddenly the entire plantation, with its enclosing forest, seemed to turn as if upon a pivot. His little world swung half around; the points of the compass were reversed. He recognized the blazing building as his own home!

For a moment he stood stupefied by the power of the revelation, then ran with stumbling feet, making a half-circuit of the ruin. There, conspicuous in the light of the conflagration, lay the dead body of a woman—the white face turned upward, the hands thrown out and clutched full of grass, the clothing deranged, the long dark hair in tangles and full of clotted blood. The greater part of the forehead was torn away, and from the jagged hole the brain protruded, overflowing the temple, a frothy mass of gray, crowned with clusters of crimson bubbles—the work of a shell.

The child moved his little hands, making wild, uncertain gestures. He uttered a series of inarticulate and indescribable cries—something between the chattering of an ape and the gobbling of a turkey—a startling, soulless, unholy sound, the language of a devil. The child was a deaf-mute.

Then he stood motionless, with quivering lips, looking down upon the wreck.

FOR DISCUSSION

1. How does the child's being a deaf-mute help to explain the story?

2. Chickamauga, Georgia, was the scene of a Civil War battle. Usually a battle is described through the eyes of a soldier, or from an historian's more distant point of view. Why do you think Bierce chose to describe the scene as a deaf-mute child would have understood it? Is the scene more or less horrible from the child's point of view than it would be from a soldier's?

3. The contrast between what the reader knows and what a character doesn't know is called *dramatic irony*. One humorous example from the story is the child's hope that the strange object is a bear rather than a terrifying rabbit. What other examples of dramatic irony can you find? Is their effect humorous or not?

FOR COMPOSITION

• Retell the story or some part of the story from a different point of view—the child's mother, a farmhand, a retreating soldier, an enemy soldier, a newspaper reporter. Because the child is a deaf-mute, his story had to be told by an *omniscient observer,* someone outside the story who knows everything. You may either use this device of an observer or pretend to be a character in the scene describing it in his own words.

"The fact that his landlady appeared to be slightly off her rocker didn't worry Billy in the least. After all, she was harmless—there was no question about that."

THE LANDLADY

ROALD DAHL

BILLY WEAVER had traveled down from London on the slow afternoon train, with a change at Bristol on the way, and by the time he got to Bath it was about nine o'clock in the evening and the moon was coming up out of a clear starry sky over the houses opposite the station entrance. But the air was deadly cold and the wind was like a flat blade of ice on his cheeks.

"Excuse me," he said, "but is there a fairly cheap hotel not too far away from here?"

"Try The Bell and Dragon," the porter answered, pointing down the road. "They might take you in. It's about a quarter of a mile along on the other side."

Billy thanked him and picked up his suitcase and set out to walk the quarter-mile to The Bell and Dragon. He had never been to Bath before. He didn't know anyone who lived there. But Mr. Greenslade at the Head Office in London had told him it was a splendid town. "Find your own lodgings," he had said, "and then go along and report to the Branch Manager as soon as you've got yourself settled."

Billy was seventeen years old. He was wearing a new navy blue overcoat, a new brown trilby hat, and a new brown suit, and he was feeling fine. He walked briskly down the street. He was trying to do everything briskly these days. Briskness, he had decided, was *the* one common characteristic of all successful businessmen. The big shots up at Head Office were absolutely fantastically brisk all the time. They were amazing.

There were no shops on this wide street that he was walking along, only a line of tall houses on each side, all of them identical. They had porches and pillars and four or five steps going up to their front doors, and it was obvious that once upon a time they had been very swanky residences. But now, even in the darkness, he could see that the paint was peeling from the woodwork on their doors and windows, and that the handsome white façades[1] were cracked and blotchy from neglect.

Suddenly, in a downstairs window that was brilliantly illuminated by a street lamp not six yards away, Billy caught sight of a printed notice propped up against the glass in one of the upper panes. It said BED AND BREAKFAST. There was a vase of pussy willows, tall and beautiful, standing just underneath the notice.

He stopped walking. He moved a bit closer. Green curtains (some sort of velvety material) were hanging down on either side of the window. The pussy willows looked wonderful beside them. He went right up and peered through the glass into the room, and the first thing he saw was a bright fire burning in the hearth. On the carpet in front of the fire, a pretty little dachshund was curled up asleep with its nose tucked

[1] FAÇADES (fə·säds'): the faces or fronts of buildings.

into its belly. The room itself, so far as he could see in the half-darkness, was filled with pleasant furniture. There was a baby-grand piano and a big sofa and several plump armchairs; and in one corner he spotted a large parrot in a cage. Animals were usually a good sign in a place like this, Billy told himself; and all in all, it looked to him as though it would be a pretty decent house to stay in. Certainly it would be more comfortable than The Bell and Dragon.

On the other hand, a pub would be more congenial than a boarding house. There would be beer and darts in the evenings, and lots of people to talk to, and it would probably be a good bit cheaper, too. He had stayed a couple of nights in a pub once before and he had liked it. He had never stayed in any boarding houses, and, to be perfectly honest, he was a tiny bit frightened of them. The name itself conjured up images of watery cabbage, rapacious landladies, and a powerful smell of kippers in the living room.

After dithering about like this in the cold for two or three minutes, Billy decided that he would walk on and take a look at The Bell and Dragon before making up his mind. He turned to go.

And now a queer thing happened to him. He was in the act of stepping back and turning away from the window when all at once his eye was caught and held in the most peculiar manner by the small notice that was there. BED AND BREAKFAST, it said.

BED AND BREAKFAST, BED AND BREAKFAST, BED AND BREAKFAST. Each word was like a large black eye staring at him through the glass, holding him, compelling him, forcing him to stay where he was and not to walk away from that house, and the next thing he knew, he was actually moving across from the window to the front door of the house, climbing the steps that led up to it, and reaching for the bell.

He pressed the bell. Far away in a back room he heard it ringing, and then *at once* —it must have been at once because he hadn't even had time to take his finger from the bell button—the door swung open and a woman was standing there.

Normally you ring the bell and you have at least a half-minute's wait before the door opens. But this dame was like a jack-in-the-box. He pressed the bell—and out she popped! It made him jump.

She was about forty-five or fifty years old, and the moment she saw him, she gave him a warm welcoming smile.

"*Please* come in," she said pleasantly. She stepped aside, holding the door wide open, and Billy found himself automatically starting forward into the house. The compulsion or, more accurately, the desire to follow after her into that house was extraordinarily strong.

"I saw the notice in the window," he said, holding himself back.

"Yes, I know."

"I was wondering about a room."

"It's *all* ready for you, my dear," she said. She had a round pink face and very gentle blue eyes.

"I was on my way to The Bell and Dragon," Billy told her. "But the notice in your window just happened to catch my eye."

"My dear boy," she said, "why don't you come in out of the cold?"

"How much do you charge?"

"Five and sixpence[1] a night, including breakfast."

It was fantastically cheap. It was less than half of what he had been willing to pay.

"If that is too much," she added, "then perhaps I can reduce it just a tiny bit. Do you desire an egg for breakfast? Eggs are expensive at the moment. It would be sixpence less without the egg."

"Five and sixpence is fine," he answered. "I should like very much to stay here."

"I knew you would. Do come in."

She seemed terribly nice. She looked exactly like the mother of one's best school friend welcoming one into the house to stay for the Christmas holidays. Billy took off his hat, and stepped over the threshold.

"Just hang it there," she said, "and let me help you with your coat."

There were no other hats or coats in the hall. There were no umbrellas, no walking sticks—nothing.

"We have it *all* to ourselves," she said, smiling at him over her shoulder as she led the way upstairs. "You see, it isn't very often I have the pleasure of taking a visitor into my little nest."

The old girl was slightly dotty, Billy told himself. But at five and sixpence a night, who gives a damn about that? "I should've thought you'd be simply swamped with applicants," he said politely.

"Oh, I am, my dear, I am, of course I am. But the trouble is that I'm inclined to be just a teeny weeny bit choosy and particular—if you see what I mean."

"Ah, yes."

"But I'm always ready. Everything is always ready day and night in this house just on the off chance that an acceptable young gentleman will come along. And it is

[1] FIVE AND SIXPENCE: about seventy-six cents.

such a pleasure, my dear, such a very great pleasure when now and again I open the door and I see someone standing there who is just *exactly* right." She was halfway up the stairs, and she paused with one hand on the stair rail, turning her head and smiling down at him with pale lips. "Like you," she added, and her blue eyes traveled slowly all the way down the length of Billy's body, to his feet, and then up again.

On the second-floor landing she said to him, "This floor is mine."

They climbed up a second flight. "And this one is *all* yours," she said. "Here's your room. I do hope you'll like it." She took him into a small but charming front bedroom, switching on the light as she went in.

"The morning sun comes right in the window, Mr. Perkins. It *is* Mr. Perkins, isn't it?"

"No," he said. "It's Weaver."

"Mr. Weaver. How nice. I've put a water bottle between the sheets to air them out, Mr. Weaver. It's such a comfort to have a hot water bottle in a strange bed with clean sheets, don't you agree? And you may light the gas fire at any time if you feel chilly."

"Thank you," Billy said. "Thank you ever so much." He noticed the the bedspread had been taken off the bed, and that the bedclothes had been neatly turned back on one side, all ready for someone to get in.

"I'm so glad you appeared," she said, looking earnestly into his face. "I was beginning to get worried."

"That's all right," Billy answered brightly. "You mustn't worry about me." He put his suitcase on the chair and started to open it.

"And what about supper, my dear? Did you manage to get anything to eat before you came here?"

"I'm not a bit hungry, thank you," he said. "I think I'll just go to bed as soon as possible because tomorrow I've got to get up rather early and report to the office."

"Very well, then. I'll leave you now so that you can unpack. But before you go to bed, would you be kind enough to pop into the sitting room on the ground floor and sign the book? Everyone has to do that because it's the law of the land, and we don't want to go breaking any laws at *this* stage in the proceedings, do we?" She gave him a little wave of the hand and went quickly out of the room and closed the door.

Now, the fact that his landlady appeared to be slightly off her rocker didn't worry Billy in the least. After all, she was not only harmless—there was no question about that—but she was also quite obviously a kind and generous soul. He guessed that she had probably lost a son in the war, or something like that, and had never gotten over it.

So a few minutes later, after unpacking his suitcase and washing his hands, he trotted downstairs to the ground floor and entered the living room. His landlady wasn't there, but the fire was glowing in the hearth, and the little dachshund was still sleeping soundly in front of it. The room was wonderfully warm and cozy. I'm a lucky fellow, he thought, rubbing his hands. This is a bit of all right.

He found the guest book lying open on the piano, so he took out his pen and wrote down his name and address. There were only two other entries above his on the page, and, as one always does with guest books, he started to read them. One was a Christopher Mulholland from Cardiff. The other was Gregory W. Temple from Bristol.

That's funny, he thought suddenly.

Christopher Mulholland. It rings a bell.

Now where on earth had he heard that rather unusual name before?

Was he a boy at school? No. Was it one of his sister's numerous young men, perhaps, or a friend of his father's? No, no, it wasn't any of those. He glanced down again at the book.

> *Christopher Mulholland*
> *231 Cathedral Road, Cardiff*
>
> *Gregory W. Temple*
> *27 Sycamore Drive, Bristol*

As a matter of fact, now he came to think of it, he wasn't at all sure that the second name didn't have almost as much of a familiar ring about it as the first.

"Gregory Temple?" he said aloud, searching his memory. "Christopher Mulholland? . . ."

"Such charming boys," a voice behind him answered, and he turned and saw his landlady sailing into the room with a large silver tea tray in her hands. She was holding it well out in front of her, and rather high up, as though the tray were a pair of reins on a frisky horse.

"They sound somehow familiar," he said.

"They do? How interesting."

"I'm almost positive I've heard those names before somewhere. Isn't that queer? Maybe it was in the newspapers. They weren't famous in any way, were they? I mean famous cricketers or footballers or something like that?"

"Famous," she said, setting the tea tray down on the low table in front of the sofa. "Oh no, I don't think they were famous. But they were extraordinarily handsome, both of them, I can promise you that. They were tall and young and handsome, my dear, just exactly like you."

Once more, Billy glanced down at the book. "Look here," he said, noticing the dates. "This last entry is over two years old."

"It is?"

"Yes, indeed. And Christopher Mulholland's is nearly a year before that—more than *three years* ago."

"Dear me," she said, shaking her head and heaving a dainty little sigh. "I would never have thought it. How time does fly away from us all, doesn't it, Mr. Wilkins?"

"It's Weaver," Billy said. "W-e-a-v-e-r."

"Oh, of course it is!" she cried, sitting down on the sofa. "How silly of me. I do apologize. In one ear and out the other, that's me, Mr. Weaver."

"You know something?" Billy said. "Something that's really quite extraordinary about all this?"

"No, dear, I don't."

"Well, you see—both of these names, Mulholland and Temple, I not only seem to remember each one of them separately, so to speak, but somehow or other, in some peculiar way, they both appear to be sort of connected together as well. As though they were both famous for the same sort of thing, if you see what I mean—like . . . well . . . like Dempsey and Tunney, for example, or Churchill and Roosevelt."

"How amusing," she said. "But come over here now, dear, and sit down beside me on the sofa and I'll give you a nice cup of tea and a ginger biscuit before you go to bed."

"You really shouldn't bother," Billy said. "I didn't mean you to do anything like that." He stood by the piano, watching her as she fussed about with the cups and saucers. He noticed that she had small, white, quickly moving hands, and red fingernails.

"I'm almost positive it was in the newspapers I saw them," Billy said. "I'll think of it in a second. I'm sure I will."

There is nothing more tantalizing than a

thing like this which lingers just outside the borders of one's memory. He hated to give up.

"Now wait a minute," he said. "Wait just a minute. Mulholland . . . Christopher Mulholland . . . wasn't *that* the name of the Eton schoolboy who was on a walking tour through the West Country, and then all of a sudden. . . ."

"Milk?" she said. "And sugar?"

"Yes, please. And then all of a sudden. . . ."

"Eton schoolboy?" she said. "Oh no, my dear, that can't possibly be right because *my* Mr. Mulholland was certainly not an Eton schoolboy when he came to me. He was a Cambridge undergraduate. Come over here now and sit next to me and warm yourself in front of this lovely fire. Come on. Your tea's all ready for you." She patted the empty place beside her on the sofa, and she sat there smiling at Billy and waiting for him to come over.

He crossed the room slowly, and sat down on the edge of the sofa. She placed his teacup on the table in front of him.

"*There* we are," she said. "How nice and cosy this is, isn't it?"

Billy started sipping his tea. She did the same. For half a minute or so, neither of them spoke. Billy knew that she was looking at him. Her body was half turned toward him, and he could feel her eyes resting on his face, watching him over the rim of her teacup. Now and again, he caught a whiff of a peculiar smell that seemed to emanate directly from her person. It was not in the least unpleasant, and it reminded him—well, he wasn't quite sure what it reminded him of. Pickled walnuts? New leather? Or was it the corridors of a hospital?

"Mr. Mulholland was a great one for his tea," she said at length. "Never in my life have I seen anyone drink as much tea

as dear, sweet Mr. Mulholland."

"I suppose he left fairly recently," Billy said. He was still puzzling his head about the two names. He was positive now that he had seen them in the newspapers—in the headlines.

"Left?" she said, arching her brows. "But my dear boy, he never left. He's still here. Mr. Temple is also here. They're on the fourth floor, both of them together."

Billy set down his cup slowly on the table, and stared at his landlady. She smiled back at him, and then she put out one of her white hands and patted them comfortingly on the knee. "How old are you, my dear?" she asked.

"Seventeen."

"Seventeen!" she cried. "Oh, it's the perfect age! Mr. Mulholland was also seventeen. But I think he was a trifle shorter than you are, in fact I'm sure he was, and his teeth weren't *quite* so white. You have the most beautiful teeth, Mr. Weaver, did you know that?"

"They're not as good as they look," Billy said. "They've got simply masses of fillings in them at the back."

"Mr. Temple, of course, was a little older," she said, ignoring his remark. "He was actually twenty-eight. And yet I never would have guessed it if he hadn't told me, never in my whole life. There wasn't a *blemish* on his body."

"A what?" Billy said.

"His skin was *just* like a baby's."

There was a pause. Billy picked up his teacup and took another sip of his tea, then he set it down again gently in its saucer. He waited for her to say something else, but she seemed to have lapsed into another of her silences. He sat there staring straight ahead of him into the far corner of the room, biting his lower lip.

"That parrot," he said at last. "You know something? It had me completely fooled when I first saw it through the window from the street. I could have sworn it was alive."

"Alas, no longer."

"It's most terribly clever the way it's been done," he said. "It doesn't look in the least bit dead. Who did it?"

"I did."

"*You* did?"

"Of course," she said. "And have you met my little Basil as well?" She nodded toward the dachshund curled up so comfortably in front of the fire. Billy looked at it. And suddenly, he realized that this animal had all the time been just as silent and motionless as the parrot. He put out a hand and touched it gently on the top of its back. The back was hard and cold, and when he pushed the hair to one side with his fingers, he could see the skin underneath, grayish-black and dry and perfectly preserved.

"Good gracious me," he said. "How absolutely fascinating." He turned away from the dog and stared with deep admiration at the little woman beside him on the sofa. "It must be most awfully difficult to do a thing like that."

"Not in the least," she said. "I stuff *all* my little pets myself when they pass away. Will you have another cup of tea?"

"No, thank you," Billy said. The tea tasted faintly of bitter almonds, and he didn't care for it.

"You did sign the book, didn't you?"

"Oh, yes."

"That's good. Because later on, if I happen to forget what you were called, then I can always come down here and look it up. I still do that almost every day with Mr. Mulholland and Mr. . . . Mr. . . . ."

"Temple," Billy said. "Gregory Temple. Excuse my asking, but haven't there been *any* other guests here except them in the last two or three years?"

Holding her teacup high in one hand, inclining her head slightly to the left, she looked up at him out of the corners of her eyes and gave him another gentle little smile.

"No, my dear," she said. "Only you."

FOR DISCUSSION

1. This story ends abruptly. Why isn't it necessary for the author to tell you what is going to happen?

2. This story also is told from the point of view of a character who doesn't understand what is happening to him. At what point did you begin to appreciate the dramatic irony of it; that is, at what point did you realize that the main character was walking into a trap?

3. Does it seem plausible that Billy would be unaware to the very end what his landlady had planned for him? What indications were there at the beginning of the story that he might be easily fooled? At what points did he come close to realizing what was going on?

FOR COMPOSITION

• Imagine that a few days after the story ends the police come to investigate Billy's disappearance. Write the dialogue that might take place between them and the landlady. Be careful to make her character and her style of speaking consistent with what is shown in the story.

"No one attacks me without being punished." For one member of the Montresor family, this motto became an obsession. The man who had insulted him must suffer horribly in revenge.

THE CASK OF AMONTILLADO
EDGAR ALLAN POE

THE THOUSAND INJURIES of Fortunato I had borne as I best could; but when he ventured upon insult, I vowed revenge. You, who so well know the nature of my soul, will not suppose, however, that I gave utterance to a threat. At length I would be avenged; this was a point definitely settled —but the very definitiveness with which it was resolved precluded the idea of risk. I must not only punish but punish with impunity. A wrong is unredressed when retribution overtakes its redresser. It is equally unredressed when the avenger fails to make himself felt as such to him who has done the wrong.

It must be understood that neither by word nor deed had I given Fortunato cause to doubt my good will. I continued, as was my wont, to smile in his face, and he did not perceive that my smile *now* was at the thought of his immolation.

He had a weak point—this Fortunato— although in other regards he was a man to be respected and even feared. He prided himself on his connoisseurship in wine. Few Italians have the true virtuoso spirit. For the most part their enthusiasm is adopted to suit the time and opportunity, to practice imposture upon the British and Austrian millionaires. In painting and gemmary[1] Fortunato, like his countrymen, was a quack—but in the matter of old wines

he was sincere. In this respect I did not differ from him materially: I was skillful in the Italian vintages myself, and bought largely whenever I could.

It was about dusk, one evening during the supreme madness of the carnival season, that I encountered my friend. He accosted me with excessive warmth, for he had been drinking much. The man wore motley. He had on a tight-fitting parti-striped dress, and his head was surmounted by the conical cap and bells. I was so pleased to see him that I thought I should never have done wringing his hand.

I said to him, "My dear Fortunato, you are luckily met. How remarkably well you are looking today. But I have received a pipe[2] of what passes for Amontillado and I have my doubts."

"How?" said he. "Amontillado? A pipe? Impossible! And in the middle of the carnival!"

"I have my doubts," I replied; "and I was silly enough to pay the full Amontillado price without consulting you in the matter. You were not to be found, and I was fearful of losing a bargain."

"Amontillado!"

"I have my doubts."

"Amontillado!"

"And I must satisfy them."

"Amontillado!"

"As you are engaged, I am on my way to

AMONTILLADO (ə·mŏn′tə·lä′dō): a Spanish wine.
[1] GEMMARY: the art of cutting stones.
[2] PIPE: large cask for wines.

Luchesi. If anyone has a critical turn, it is he. He will tell me—"

"Luchesi cannot tell Amontillado from sherry."

"And yet some fools will have it that his taste is a match for your own."

"Come, let us go."

"Whither?"

"To your vaults."

"My friend, no; I will not impose upon your good nature. I perceive you have an engagement. Luchesi—"

"I have no engagement—come."

"My friend, no. It is not the engagement, but the severe cold with which I perceive you are afflicted. The vaults are insufferably damp. They are incrusted with niter."[1]

"Let us go, nevertheless. The cold is merely nothing. Amontillado! You have been imposed upon. And as for Luchesi, he cannot distinguish sherry from Amontillado."

Thus speaking, Fortunato possessed himself of my arm. Putting on a mask of black silk and drawing a roquelaure closely about my person, I suffered him to hurry me to my palazzo.

There were no attendants at home; they had absconded to make merry in honor of the time. I had told them that I should not return until the morning, and had given them explicit orders not to stir from the house. These orders were sufficient, I well knew, to insure their immediate disappearance, one and all, as soon as my back was turned.

I took from their sconces two flambeaux,[2] and giving one to Fortunato, bowed him through several suites of rooms to the archway that led into the vaults. I passed down a long and winding staircase, requesting him to be cautious as he followed. We came at length to the foot of the descent, and stood together upon the damp ground of the catacombs[3] of the Montresors.

The gait of my friend was unsteady, and the bells upon his cap jingled as he strode.

"The pipe," he said.

"It is farther on," said I; "but observe the white webwork which gleams from these cavern walls."

He turned towards me, and looked into my eyes with two filmy orbs that distilled the rheum of intoxication.[4]

"Niter?" he asked at length.

"Niter," I replied. "How long have you had that cough?"

"Ugh! ugh! ugh!—ugh! ugh! ugh!—ugh! ugh! ugh!—ugh! ugh! ugh!—ugh! ugh! ugh!"

My poor friend found it impossible to reply for many minutes.

"It is nothing," he said at last.

"Come," I said with decision, "we will go back; your health is precious. You are rich, respected, admired, beloved; you are happy, as once I was. You are a man to be missed. For me it is no matter. We will go back; you will be ill, and I cannot be responsible. Besides, there is Luchesi—"

"Enough," he said, "the cough is a mere nothing: it will not kill me. I shall not die of a cough."

"True—true," I replied; "and, indeed, I had no intention of alarming you unnecessarily—but you should use all proper caution. A draught of this Medoc will defend us from the damps."

Here I knocked off the neck of a bottle which I drew from a long row of its fellows that lay upon the mold.

"Drink," I said, presenting him the wine.

He raised it to his lips with a leer. He paused and nodded to me familiarly, while his bells jingled.

"I drink," he said, "to the buried that repose around us."

---

[1] NITER: potassium nitrate, which forms on the damp walls of caves.
[2] TOOK . . . FLAMBEAUX: took from their holders two torches.

[3] CATACOMBS: underground burial passages.
[4] TWO . . . INTOXICATION: two glazed eyes from which fell tears of drunkenness.

"And I to your long life."

He again took my arm, and we proceeded.

"These vaults," he said, "are extensive."

"The Montresors," I replied, "were a great and numerous family."

"I forget your arms."

"A huge human foot d'or,[1] in a field azure; the foot crushes a serpent rampant[2] whose fangs are imbedded in the heel."

"And the motto?"

"Nemo me impune lacessit."[3]

"Good!" he said.

The wine sparkled in his eyes, and the bells jingled. My own fancy grew warm with the Medoc. We had passed through long walls of piled bones, with casks and puncheons[4] intermingling, into the inmost recesses of the catacombs. I paused again, and this time I made bold to seize Fortunato by an arm above the elbow.

"The niter!" I said; "see, it increases. It hangs like moss upon the vaults. We are below the river's bed. The drops of moisture trickle among the bones. Come, we will go back ere it is too late. Your cough—"

"It is nothing," he said; "let us go on. But first, another draught of the Medoc."

I broke and reached him a flagon of De Grâve. He emptied it at a breath. His eyes flashed with a fierce light. He laughed and threw the bottle upwards with a gesticulation I did not understand.

I looked at him in surprise. He repeated the movement—a grotesque one.

"You do not comprehend?" he said.

"Not I," I replied.

"Then you are not of the brotherhood."

"How?"

"You are not of the masons."

"Yes, yes," I said; "yes, yes."

"You? Impossible! A mason?"

"A mason," I replied.

"A sign," he said, "a sign."

"It is this," I answered, producing from beneath the folds of my roquelaure a trowel.

"You jest," he exclaimed, recoiling a few paces. "But let us proceed to the Amontillado."

"Be it so," I said, replacing the tool beneath the cloak, and again offering him my arm. He leaned upon it heavily. We continued our route in search of the Amontillado. We passed through a range of low arches, descended, passed on, and descending again, arrived at a deep crypt, in which the foulness of the air caused our flambeaux rather to glow than flame.

At the most remote end of the crypt there appeared another less spacious. Its walls had been lined with human remains, piled to the vault overhead, in the fashion of the great catacombs of Paris. Three sides of this interior crypt were still ornamented in this manner. From the fourth side the bones had been thrown down and lay promiscuously upon the earth, forming at one point a mound of some size. Within the wall thus exposed by the displacing of the bones, we perceived a still interior crypt or recess, in depth about four feet, in width three, in height six or seven. It seemed to have been constructed for no especial use within itself, but formed merely the interval between two of the colossal supports of the roof of the catacombs, and was backed by one of their circumscribing walls of solid granite.

It was in vain that Fortunato, uplifting his dull torch, endeavored to pry into the depth of the recess. Its termination the feeble light did not enable us to see.

"Proceed," I said; "herein is the Amontillado. As for Luchesi—"

"He is an ignoramus," interrupted my friend as he stepped unsteadily forward, while I followed immediately at his heels.

[1] D'OR: of gold.
[2] RAMPANT: in a position to strike.
[3] "NEMO . . . LACESSIT": "No one strikes me with impunity."
[4] PUNCHEONS: type of wine cask.

In an instant he had reached the extremity of the niche, and finding his progress arrested by the rock, stood stupidly bewildered. A moment more and I had fettered him to the granite. In its surface were two iron staples, distant from each other about two feet, horizontally. From one of these depended a short chain, from the other a padlock. Throwing the links about his waist, it was but the work of a few seconds to secure it. He was too much astounded to resist. Withdrawing the key, I stepped back from the recess.

"Pass your hand," I said, "over the wall; you cannot help feeling the niter. Indeed, it is very damp. Once more let me implore you to return. No? Then I must positively leave you. But I must first render you all the little attentions in my power."

"The Amontillado!" ejaculated my friend, not yet recovered from his astonishment.

"True," I replied; "the Amontillado."

As I said these words, I busied myself among the pile of bones of which I have before spoken. Throwing them aside, I soon uncovered a quantity of building stone and mortar. With these materials and with the aid of my trowel, I began vigorously to wall up the entrance of the niche.

I had scarcely laid the first tier of the masonry when I discovered that the intoxication of Fortunato had in a great measure worn off. The earliest indication I had of this was a low moaning cry from the depth of the recess. It was not the cry of a drunken man. There was then a long and obstinate silence. I laid the second tier, and the third, and the fourth; and then I heard the furious vibrations of the chain. The noise lasted for several minutes, during which, that I might hearken to it with the more satisfaction, I ceased my labors and sat down upon the bones. When at last the clanking had subsided, I resumed the trowel, and finished without interruption the fifth, the sixth, and the seventh tier. The wall was now nearly upon a level with my breast. I again paused, and holding the flambeaux over the mason work, threw a few feeble rays upon the figure within.

A succession of loud and shrill screams, bursting suddenly from the throat of the chained form, seemed to thrust me violently back. For a brief moment I hesitated —I trembled. Unsheathing my rapier, I began to grope with it about the recess; but the thought of an instant reassured me. I placed my hand upon the solid fabric of the catacombs, and felt satisfied. I reapproached the wall. I replied to the yells of him who clamored. I re-echoed—I aided —I surpassed them in volume and in strength. I did this, and the clamorer grew still.

It was now midnight, and my task was drawing to a close. I had completed the eighth, the ninth, and the tenth tier. I had finished a portion of the last and the eleventh; there remained but a single stone to be fitted and plastered in. I struggled with its weight; I placed it partially in its destined position.

But now there came from out the niche a low laugh that erected the hairs upon my head. It was succeeded by a sad voice, which I had difficulty in recognizing as that of the noble Fortunato. The voice said—

"Ha! ha! ha!—he! he! he!—a very good joke, indeed—an excellent jest. We will have many a rich laugh about it at the palazzo—he! he! he!—over our wine—he! he! he!"

"The Amontillado!" I said.

"He! he! he!—he! he! he!—yes, the Amontillado. But is it not getting late? Will not they be awaiting us at the palazzo —the Lady Fortunato and the rest? Let us be gone."

"Yes," I said, "let us be gone."

"For the love of God, Montresor!"

"Yes," I said, "for the love of God!"

But to these words I hearkened in vain for a reply. I grew impatient. I called aloud—

"Fortunato!"

No answer. I called again—

"Fortunato!"

No answer still. I thrust a torch through the remaining aperture and let it fall within. There came forth in return only a jingling of the bells. My heart grew sick—on account of the dampness of the catacombs. I hastened to make an end of my labor. I forced the last stone into its position; I plastered it up. Against the new masonry I re-erected the old rampart of bones. For the half of a century no mortal has disturbed them. *In pace requiescat!*[1]

[1] IN PACE REQUIESCAT!: May he rest in peace!

FOR DISCUSSION

1. Does Montresor's vengeance meet his two requirements for success (p. 171)? Is there any evidence that he feels regret for what he has done?

2. The story is told from the point of view of the murderer, rather than the victim. How do we know what the victim feels? What is the first clue that he is uneasy?

3. Often it is difficult to know what the narrator of a story is like because he presents the best side of himself. In the first paragraph of the story Montresor assumes that his listener will sympathize with his plan. Do you? What is your impression of Montresor as a person? At what point in the story did you form this impression?

4. What details in the story impressed you as most horrible? What would have been lost if Montresor had locked Fortunato into a dungeon cell rather than walling him into the catacombs?

FOR COMPOSITION

• What would be the effect of telling this story from Fortunato's point of view rather than Montresor's? In what ways would the story be more or less horrible? Why do you think Poe chose the point of view he did?

Civil war is perhaps the most terrible of conflicts because it turns families against each other and sets citizens to destroying their own country. Ireland in 1920 was divided between Free Staters, who supported the self-rule of a southern Ireland still loyal to Britain, and Republicans, who wanted a united Ireland independent of Britain. Dublin, capital of the Free State, was the scene of bitter fighting.

THE SNIPER

LIAM O'FLAHERTY

THE LONG JUNE twilight faded into night. Dublin lay enveloped in darkness but for the dim light of the moon that shone through fleecy clouds, casting a pale light as of approaching dawn over the streets and the dark waters of the Liffey. Around the beleaguered Four Courts the heavy guns roared. Here and there through the city machine guns and rifles broke the silence of the night spasmodically, like dogs barking on lone farms. Republicans and Free Staters were waging civil war.

On a rooftop near O'Connell Bridge a Republican sniper lay watching. Beside him lay his rifle, and over his shoulders were slung a pair of field glasses. His face was the face of a student—thin and ascetic—but his eyes had the cold gleam of the fanatic. They were deep and thoughtful, the eyes of a man who is used to look at death.

He was eating a sandwich hungrily. He had eaten nothing since morning. He had been too excited to eat. He finished the sandwich, and taking a flask of whiskey from his pocket, he took a short draught. Then he returned the flask to his pocket. He paused for a moment, considering whether he should risk a smoke. It was

"The Sniper," from *Spring Sowing* by Liam O'Flaherty. Reprinted by permission of Harcourt Brace Jovanovich, Inc., and Jonathan Cape Limited.

dangerous. The flash might be seen in the darkness, and there were enemies watching. He decided to take the risk. Placing a cigarette between his lips, he struck a match, inhaled the smoke hurriedly, and put out the light. Almost immediately, a bullet flattened itself against the parapet of the roof. The sniper took another whiff and put out the cigarette. Then he swore softly and crawled away to the left.

Cautiously he raised himself and peered over the parapet. There was a flash, and a bullet whizzed over his head. He dropped immediately. He had seen the flash. It came from the opposite side of the street.

He rolled over the roof to a chimney stack in the rear and slowly drew himself up behind it until his eyes were level with the top of the parapet. There was nothing to be seen—just the dim outline of the opposite housetop against the blue sky. His enemy was under cover.

Just then an armored car came across the bridge and advanced slowly up the street. It stopped on the opposite side of the street fifty yards ahead. The sniper could hear the dull panting of the motor. His heart beat faster. It was an enemy car. He wanted to fire, but he knew it was useless. His bullets would never pierce the steel that covered the gray monster.

Then round the corner of a side street came an old woman, her head covered by a tattered shawl. She began to talk to the man in the turret of the car. She was pointing to the roof where the sniper lay. An informer.

The turret opened. A man's head and shoulders appeared, looking toward the sniper. The sniper raised his rifle and fired. The head fell heavily on the turret wall. The woman darted toward the side street. The sniper fired again. The woman whirled round and fell with a shriek into the gutter.

Suddenly from the opposite roof a shot rang out, and the sniper dropped his rifle with a curse. The rifle clattered to the roof. The sniper thought the noise would wake the dead. He stopped to pick the rifle up. He couldn't lift it. His forearm was dead. He muttered, "I'm hit."

Dropping flat onto the roof, he crawled back to the parapet. With his left hand he felt the injured right forearm. The blood was oozing through the sleeve of his coat. There was no pain—just a deadened sensation, as if the arm had been cut off.

Quickly he drew his knife from his pocket, opened it on the breastwork of the parapet, and ripped open the sleeve. There was a small hole where the bullet had entered. On the other side there was no hole. The bullet had lodged in the bone. It must have fractured it. He bent the arm below the wound. The arm bent back easily. He ground his teeth to overcome the pain.

Then, taking out his field dressing, he ripped open the packet with his knife. He broke the neck of the iodine bottle and let the bitter fluid drip into the wound. A paroxysm of pain swept through him. He placed the cotton wadding over the wound and wrapped the dressing over it. He tied the end with his teeth. Then he lay still against the parapet, and closing his eyes, he made an effort of will to overcome the pain.

In the street beneath all was still. The armored car had retired speedily over the bridge, with the machine gunner's head hanging lifeless over the turret. The woman's corpse lay still in the gutter.

The sniper lay for a long time nursing his wounded arm and planning escape. Morning must not find him wounded on the roof. The enemy on the opposite roof covered his escape. He must kill that enemy, and he could not use his rifle. He had only a revolver to do it. Then he thought of a plan.

Taking off his cap, he placed it over the muzzle of his rifle. Then he pushed the rifle slowly upwards over the parapet until the cap was visible from the opposite side of the street. Almost immediately there was a report, and a bullet pierced the center of the cap. The sniper slanted the rifle forward. The cap slipped down into the street. Then, catching the rifle in the middle, the sniper dropped his left hand over the roof and let it hang, lifelessly. After a few moments he let the rifle drop to the street. Then he sank to the roof, dragging his hand with him.

Crawling quickly to the left, he peered up at the corner of the roof. His ruse[1] had succeeded. The other sniper, seeing the cap and rifle fall, thought that he had killed his man. He was now standing before a row of chimney pots, looking across, with his head clearly silhouetted against the western sky.

The Republican sniper smiled and lifted his revolver above the edge of the parapet. The distance was about fifty yards—a hard shot in the dim light—and his right arm was paining him like a thousand devils. He took a steady aim. His hand trembled with eagerness. Pressing his lips together, he took a deep breath through his nostrils and fired. He was almost deafened with the report, and his arm shook with the recoil.

[1] RUSE: action meant to confuse or mislead.

Then, when the smoke cleared, he peered across and uttered a cry of joy. His enemy had been hit. He was reeling over the parapet in his death agony. He struggled to keep his feet, but he was slowly falling forward as if in a dream. The rifle fell from his grasp, hit the parapet, fell over, bounded off the pole of a barber's shop beneath, and then cluttered onto the pavement.

Then the dying man on the roof crumpled up and fell forward. The body turned over and over in space and hit the ground with a dull thud. Then it lay still.

The sniper looked at his enemy falling, and he shuddered. The lust of battle died in him. He became bitten by remorse. The sweat stood out in beads on his forehead. Weakened by his wound and the long summer day of fasting and watching on the roof, he revolted from the sight of the shattered mass of his dead enemy. His teeth chattered. He began to gibber to himself, cursing the war, cursing himself, cursing everybody.

He looked at the smoking revolver in his hand, and with an oath he hurled it to the roof at his feet. The revolver went off with the concussion, and the bullet whizzed past the sniper's head. He was frightened back to his senses by the shock. His nerves steadied. The cloud of fear scattered from his mind, and he laughed.

Taking the whiskey flask from his pocket, he emptied it at a draught. He felt reckless under the influence of the spirits. He decided to leave the roof and look for his company commander to report. Everywhere around was quiet. There was not much danger in going through the streets. He picked up his revolver and put it in his pocket. Then he crawled down through the skylight to the house underneath.

When the sniper reached the laneway on the street level, he felt a sudden curiosity as to the identity of the enemy sniper whom he had killed. He decided that he was a good shot whoever he was. He wondered if he knew him. Perhaps he had been in his own company before the split in the army. He decided to risk going over to have a look at him. He peered around the corner into O'Connell Street. In the upper part of the street there was heavy firing, but around here all was quiet.

The sniper darted across the street. A machine gun tore up the ground around him with a hail of bullets, but he escaped. He threw himself face downwards beside the corpse. The machine gun stopped.

Then the sniper turned over the dead body and looked into his brother's face.

FOR DISCUSSION

1. What details from the setting of this story make it plausible that the sniper could shoot his own brother without intending to?

2. The *theme*, or meaning of a story, must apply not only to the particular events of a story, but to life in general. What meaning does "brother" have besides "male child of the same parents"? Using this larger definition, what do you think is the theme of "The Sniper"?

3. What do the sniper's actions reveal about the kind of person he is? What does his attitude about war seem to be? What causes him to reverse that attitude momentarily?

FOR COMPOSITION

• What do you think is the sniper's reaction to the discovery that he had killed his brother? Write your answer either in the form of a *postlude* (a continuation of the story, like another chapter) or a *postscript* (an explanation added to the end of the story). Be sure to indicate whether there is any change in his feelings about war and killing.

"I was lying there ... planning to kill Anvil—and the thought of it had a sweetness like summer fruit."

THE WHITE CIRCLE
JOHN BELL CLAYTON

AS SOON AS I saw Anvil squatting up in the tree like some hateful creature that belonged in trees, I knew I had to take a beating, and I knew the kind of beating it would be. But still I had to let it be that way, because this went beyond any matter of courage or shame.

The tree was *mine*. I want no doubt about that. It was a seedling that grew out of the slaty bank beside the dry creek-mark across the road from the house, and the thirteen small apples it had borne that year were the thirteen most beautiful things on this beautiful earth.

The day I was twelve Father took me up to the barn to look at the colts—Saturn, Jupiter, Devil, and Moonkissed, the whiteface. Father took a cigar out of his vest pocket and put one foot on the bottom plank of the fence and leaned both elbows on the top of the fence, and his face looked quiet and pleased and proud, and I liked the way he looked, because it was as if he had a little joke or surprise that would turn out nice for me.

"Tucker," Father said presently, "I am not unaware of the momentousness of this day. Now there are four of the finest colts in Augusta County; if there are four any finer anywhere in Virginia, I don't know where you'd find them unless Arthur Hancock over in Albemarle would have them."

Father took one elbow off the fence and looked at me. "Now do you suppose," he asked, in that fine, free, good humor, "that if I were to offer you a little token to commemorate this occasion you could make a choice?"

"Yes, sir," I said.

"Which one?" Father asked. "Devil? He's wild."

"No, sir," I said. "I would like to have the apple tree below the gate."

Father looked at me for at least a minute. You would have to understand his pride in his colts to understand the way he looked. But at twelve how could I express how *I* felt? My setting such store in having the tree as my own had something to do with the coloring of the apples as they hung among the green leaves; it had something also to do with their ripening, not in autumn when the world was full of apples, but in midsummer when you *wanted* them; but it had more to do with a way of life that had come down through the generations. I would have given one of the apples to Janie. I would have made of it a ceremony. While I would not have said the words, because at twelve you have no such words, I would have handed over the apple with something like this in mind: "Janie, I want to give you this apple. It came from my tree. The tree stands on my father's land. Before my father had the land, it belonged to his father, and before that it belonged to my great-grandfather.

It's the English family land. It's almost sacred. My possession of this tree forges of me a link in this owning ancestry that must go back clear beyond Moses and all the old Bible folks."

Father looked at me for that slow, peculiar minute in our lives. "All right, son," he said. "The tree is yours in fee simple to bargain, sell, and convey or to keep and nurture and eventually hand down to your heirs or assigns forever unto eternity. You have a touch of poetry in your soul and that fierce, proud love of the land in your heart; when you grow up, I hope you don't drink too much."

I didn't know what he meant by that, but the tree was mine, and now there perched Anvil, callously munching one of my thirteen apples and stowing the rest inside his ragged shirt until it bulged out in ugly lumps. I knew the apples pressed cold against his hateful belly, and to me the coldness was a sickening evil.

I picked a rock up out of the dust of the road and tore across the creek bed and said, "All right, Anvil—climb down!"

Anvil's milky eyes batted at me under the strangely fair eyebrows. There was not much expression on his face. "Yaannh!" he said. "You stuck-up little priss, you hit me with that rock. You just do!"

"Anvil," I said again, "climb down. They're my apples."

Anvil quit munching for a minute and grinned at me. "You want an apple? I'll give you one. Yaannh!" He suddenly cocked back his right arm and cracked me on the temple with the half-eaten apple.

I let go with the rock, and it hit a limb with a dull chub sound, and Anvil said, "You're fixin' to git it—you're real-ly fixin' to git it."

"I'll shake you down," I said. "I'll shake you clear down."

"Clear down?" Anvil chortled. "Where

do you think I'm at? Up on top of Walker Mountain? It wouldn't hurt none if I was to fall out of this runty bush on my head."

I grabbed one of his bare feet and pulled backwards, and down Anvil came amidst a flutter of broken twigs and leaves. We both hit the ground. I hopped up, and Anvil arose with a faintly vexed expression.

He hooked a leg in back of my knees and shoved a paw against my chin. I went down in the slate. He got down and pinioned my arms with his knees. I tried to kick him in the back of the head but could only flail my feet helplessly in the air.

"You might as well quit kickin'," he said.

He took one of my apples from his shirt and began eating it, almost absent-mindedly.

"You dirty filthy stinkin' sow," I said.

He snorted. "I couldn't be a sow, but you take that back."

"I wish you were fryin' in the middle of hell right this minute."

"Take back the stinkin' part," Anvil said thoughtfully. "I don't stink."

He pressed his knees down harder, pinching and squeezing the flesh of my arms.

I sobbed, "I take back the stinkin' part."

"That's better," Anvil said.

He ran a finger back into his jaw to dislodge a fragment of apple from his teeth. For a moment he examined the fragment and then wiped it on my cheek.

"I'm goin' to tell Father," I said desperately.

" 'Father,' " Anvil said with falsetto mimicry. " 'Father.' Say 'Old Man.' You think your old man is some stuff on a stick, don't you? You think he don't walk on the ground, don't you? You think you and your whole stuck-up family don't walk on the ground. Say 'Old Man.' Shut up your blubberin'. Say 'Old Man.' "

"Old Man. I wish you were dead."

"Yaannh!" Anvil said. "Stop blubberin'.

Now call me Uncle Anvil.' Say 'Uncle Sweetie Peetie Tweetie Beg-Your-Pardon Uncle Anvil.' Say it!"

He caught my hair in his hands and wallowed my head against the ground until I said every bitter word of it. Three times.

Anvil tossed away a spent, maltreated core that had been my apple. He gave my head one final thump upon the ground and said "Yaannh!" again in a satisfied way.

He released me and got up. I lay there with my face muscles twitching in outrage.

Anvil looked down at me. "Stop blubberin'," he commanded.

"I'm not cryin'," I said.

I was lying there with a towering, homicidal detestation, planning to kill Anvil —and the thought of it had a sweetness like summer fruit.

There were times when I had no desire to kill Anvil. I remember the day his father showed up at the school. He was a dirty, half-crazy, itinerant knickknack peddler. He had a club, and he told the principal he was going to beat the meanness out of Anvil or beat him to death. Anvil scudded under a desk and lay there trembling and whimpering until the principal finally drove the ragged old man away. I had no hatred for Anvil then.

But another day, just for the sheer filthy meanness of it, he crawled through a classroom window after school hours and befouled the floor. And the number of times he pushed over smaller boys, just to see them hit the packed hard earth of the schoolyard and to watch the fright on their faces as they ran away, was more than I could count.

And still another day he walked up to me as I leaned against the warmth of the schoolhack shed in the sunlight, feeling the nice warmth of the weather-beaten boards.

"They hate me," he said dismally. "They hate me because my old man's crazy."

As I looked at Anvil, I felt that in the background I was seeing that demented, bitter father trudging his lonely, vicious way through the world.

"They don't hate you," I lied. "Anyway, I don't hate you." That was true. At that moment I didn't hate him. "How about comin' home and stayin' all night with me?"

So after school Anvil went along with me—and threw rocks at me all the way home.

Now I had for him no soft feeling of any kind. I planned—practically—his extinction as he stood there before me commanding me to cease the blubbering out of my heart.

"Shut up now," Anvil said. "I never hurt you. Stop blubberin'."

"I'm not cryin'," I said.

"You're still mad, though." He looked at me appraisingly.

"No, I'm not," I lied. "I'm not even mad. I was a little bit mad, but not now."

"Well, whattaya look so funny around the mouth and eyes for?"

"I don't know. Let's go up to the barn and play."

"Play whut?" Anvil looked at me truculently.[1] He didn't know whether to be suspicious or flattered. "I'm gettin' too big to play. To play much, anyway," he added undecidedly. "I might play a little bit if it ain't some sissy game."

"We'll play anything," I said eagerly.

"All right," he said. "Race you to the barn. You start."

I started running toward the wire fence, and at the third step he stuck his foot between my legs and I fell forward on my face.

"Yaannh!" he croaked. "That'll learn you."

"Learn me what?" I asked as I got up. "Learn me what?" It seemed important to

[1] TRUCULENTLY: in a savage, cruel way.

know that. Maybe it would make some difference in what I planned to do to Anvil.
It seemed very important to know what it
was that Anvil wanted to, and never could,
teach me and the world.

"It'll just learn you," he said doggedly.
"Go ahead; I won't trip you any more."

So we climbed the wire fence and raced
across the burned field the hogs ranged in.

We squeezed through the heavy sliding
doors onto the barn floor, and the first
thing that caught Anvil's eye was the irregular circle that Father had painted there.
He wanted to know what it was and I said
"Nothing," because I wasn't yet quite
ready, and Anvil forgot about it for the
moment and wanted to play jumping from
the barn floor out to the top of the fresh
rick of golden straw.

I said, "No. Who wants to do that, anyway?"

"I do," said Anvil. "Jump, you puke. Go
ahead and jump!"

I didn't want to jump. The barn had been
built on a hill. In front the ground came
up level with the barn floor, but in back
the floor was even with the top of the
straw rick, with four wide, terrible yawning feet between.

I said, "Nawh, there's nothin' to jump-
in'."

"Oh, there ain't, hanh!" said Anvil,
"Well, try it—"

He gave me a shove, and I went out into
terrifying space. He leaped after and upon
me, and we hit the pillowy side of the
straw rick and tumbled to the ground in a
smothering slide.

"That's no fun," I said, getting up and
brushing the chaff from my face and hair.

Anvil himself had lost interest in it by
now and was idly munching another of my
apples.

"I know somethin'," I said. "I know a
good game. Come on, I'll show you."

Anvil stung me on the leg with the apple

as I raced through the door of the cutting
room. When we reached the barn floor, his
eyes again fell on the peculiar white circle.
"That's to play prisoner's base with," I
said. "That's the base."

"That's a funny-lookin' base," he said
suspiciously. "I never saw any base that
looked like that."

I could feel my muscles tensing, but I
wasn't particularly excited. I didn't trust
myself to look up toward the roof where
the big mechanical hayfork hung suspended from the long metal track that ran
back over the steaming mows of alfalfa
and red clover. The fork had vicious sharp
prongs that had never descended to the
floor except on one occasion Anvil knew
nothing about.

I think Father had been drinking the
day he bought the hayfork in Staunton.
It was an unwieldy involved contraption of
ropes, triggers, and pulleys which took
four men to operate. A man came out to
install the fork, and for several days he
climbed up and down ladders, bolting the
track in place and arranging the various
gadgets. Finally, when he said it was ready,
Father had a load of hay pulled into the
barn and called the men in from the fields
to watch and assist in the demonstration.

I don't remember the details. I just remember that something went very badly
wrong. The fork suddenly plunged down
with a peculiar ripping noise and embedded
itself in the back of one of the work horses.
Father said very little. He simply painted
the big white circle on the barn floor, had
the fork hauled back up to the top, and
fastened the trigger around the rung of a
stationary ladder eight feet off the floor,
where no one could inadvertently pull it.

Then he said quietly, "I don't ever want
anyone ever to touch this trip rope or to
have occasion to step inside this circle."

So that was why I didn't now look up
toward the fork.

"I don't want to play no sissy prisoner's base," Anvil said. "Let's find a nest of young pigeons."

"All right," I lied. "I know where there's a nest. But one game of prisoner's base first."

"You don't know where there's any pigeon nest," Anvil said. "You wouldn't have the nerve to throw them up against the barn if you did."

"Yes, I would too," I protested. "Now let's play one game of prisoner's base. Get in the circle and shut your eyes and start countin'."

"Oh, all right," Anvil agreed wearily. "Let's get it over with and find the pigeons. Ten, ten, double ten, forty-five—"

"Right in the middle of the circle," I told him. "And count slow. How'm I goin' to hide if you count that way?"

Anvil now counted more slowly. "Five, ten, fifteen—"

I gave Anvil one last vindictive look and sprang up the stationary ladder and swung out on the trip rope of the unpredictable hayfork with all my puny might.

The fork's whizzing descent was accompanied by that peculiar ripping noise. Anvil must have jumped instinctively. The fork missed him by several feet.

For a moment Anvil stood absolutely still. He turned around and saw the fork, still shimmering from its impact with the floor. His face became exactly the pale green of the carbide we burned in our acetylene lighting plant at the house. Then he looked at me, at the expression of my face, and his Adam's apple bobbed queerly up and down, and a little stream of water trickled down his right trouser leg and over his bare foot.

"You tried to kill me," he said thickly.

He did not come toward me. Instead, he sat down. He shook his head sickly. After a few sullen, bewildered moments he reached into his shirt and began hauling out my apples one by one.

"You can have your stinkin' old apples," he said. "You'd do that for a few dried-up little apples. Your old man owns everything in sight. I ain't got nothin'. Go ahead and keep your stinkin' old apples."

He got to his feet and slowly walked out of the door.

Since swinging off the trip rope I had neither moved nor spoken. For a moment more I stood motionless and voiceless, and then I ran over and grabbed up the nine apples that were left and called, "Anvil! Anvil!" He continued across the field without even pausing.

I yelled, "Anvil! Wait, I'll give them to you."

Anvil climbed the fence without looking back and set off down the road toward the store. Every few steps he kicked his wet trouser leg.

Three sparrows flew out of the door in a dusty, chattering spiral. Then there was only the image of the hayfork shimmering and terrible in the great and growing and accusing silence and emptiness of the barn.

FOR DISCUSSION

1. Not many fights between twelve-year-olds end with one boy trying to kill the other. What is it in Anvil's personality and in Tucker's feelings about the apple tree that drive Tucker to this extreme?

2. Tucker, who has a "touch of poetry" in his soul and "a fierce, proud love of the land" in his heart, sees himself as a good person being attacked by mean, evil Anvil for no reason. Does Anvil agree in the way he sees himself and Tucker? How do the two boys' fathers influence the way they feel about themselves and about one another?

3. Which of the following seems to you a good statement of the theme of this story? Could more than one apply? Try writing the theme in your own words.

    a) "It is preoccupation with possession, more than anything else that prevents men from living freely and nobly." Bertrand Russell

    b) "Revenge, at first though sweet, bitter ere long back on itself recoils." John Milton

    c) "Years of love have been forgot in the hatred of a minute." Edgar Allan Poe

    d) "Folks never understand the folks they hate." James Russell Lowell

    e) "Pride goeth before destruction, and a haughty spirit before a fall." Proverbs

FOR COMPOSITION

• Both boys in this story commit crimes, Tucker a large one, Anvil many small ones. Which boy is more to blame? Find as many arguments as you can to support your answer, then debate the question with classmates who made the other choice.

"The earth seemed to be moving, locusts crawling everywhere; she could not see the lands at all, so thick was the swarm."

A MILD ATTACK OF LOCUSTS
DORIS LESSING

THE RAINS THAT year were good; they were coming nicely just as the crops needed them—or so Margaret gathered when the men said they were not too bad. She never had an opinion of her own on matters like the weather, because even to know about what seems a simple thing like the weather needs experience. Which Margaret had not got. The men were Richard her husband, and old Stephen, Richard's father, a farmer from way back; and these two might argue for hours whether the rains were ruinous or just ordinarily exasperating. Margaret had been on the farm three years. She still did not understand how they did not go bankrupt altogether, when the men never had a good word for the weather, or the soil, or the government. But she was getting to learn the language. Farmers' language. And they neither went bankrupt nor got very rich. They jogged along doing comfortably.

Their crop was maize.[1] Their farm was three thousand acres on the ridges that rise up toward the Zambesi escarpment—high, dry windswept country, cold and dusty in winter, but now, in the wet season, steamy with the heat rising in wet soft waves off miles of green foliage. Beautiful it was, with the sky blue and brilliant halls of air, and the bright green folds and hollows of

[1] MAIZE: corn.

country beneath, and the mountains lying sharp and bare twenty miles off across the rivers. The sky made her eyes ache; she was not used to it. One does not look so much at the sky in the city she came from. So that evening when Richard said: "The government is sending out warnings that locusts are expected, coming down from the breeding grounds up North," her instinct was to look about her at the trees. Insects—swarms of them—horrible! But Richard and the old man had raised their eyes and were looking up over the mountain. "We haven't had locusts in seven years," they said. "They go in cycles, locusts do." And then: "There goes our crop for this season!"

But they went on with the work of the farm just as usual until one day they were coming up the road to the homestead for the midday break, when old Stephen stopped, raised his finger and pointed: "Look, look, there they are!"

Out ran Margaret to join them, looking at the hills. Out came the servants from the kitchen. They all stood and gazed. Over the rocky levels of the mountain was a streak of rust-colored air. Locusts. There they came.

At once Richard shouted at the cookboy. Old Stephen yelled at the houseboy. The cookboy ran to beat the old ploughshare hanging from a tree branch, which was used to summon the laborers at moments of crisis. The houseboy ran off to the store to collect tin cans, any old bit of metal. The farm was ringing with the clamor of the gong; and they could see the laborers come pouring out of the compound, pointing at the hills and shouting excitedly. Soon they had all come up to the house, and Richard and old Stephen were giving them orders—Hurry, hurry, hurry.

And off they ran again, the two white men with them, and in a few minutes Margaret could see the smoke of fires rising from all around the farmlands. Piles of wood and grass had been prepared there. There were seven patches of bared soil, yellow and oxblood color and pink, where the new mealies were just showing, making a film of bright green; and around each drifted up thick clouds of smoke. They were throwing wet leaves on to the fires now, to make it acrid and black. Margaret was watching the hills. Now there was a long, low cloud advancing, rust-color still, swelling forward and out as she looked. The telephone was ringing. Neighbors— quick, quick, there come the locusts. Old Smith had had his crop eaten to the ground. Quick, get your fires started. For of course, while every farmer hoped the locusts would overlook his farm and go on to the next, it was only fair to warn each other; one must play fair. Everywhere, fifty miles over the countryside, the smoke was rising from myriads[1] of fires. Margaret answered the telephone calls, and between calls she stood watching the locusts. The air was darkening. A strange darkness, for the sun was blazing—it was like the darkness of a veldt[2] fire, when the air gets thick with smoke. The sunlight comes down distorted, a thick, hot orange. Oppressive it was, too, with the heaviness of a storm. The locusts were coming fast. Now half the sky was darkened. Behind the reddish veils in front,

[1] MYRIADS: large, indefinite numbers.
[2] VELDT (fĕlt): open grazing area in southern Africa.

which were the advance guards of the swarm, the main swarm showed in dense black cloud, reaching almost to the sun itself.

Margaret was wondering what she could do to help. She did not know. Then up came old Stephen from the lands. "We're finished, Margaret, finished! Those beggars can eat every leaf and blade off the farm in half an hour! And it is only early afternoon—if we can make enough smoke, make enough noise till the sun goes down, they'll settle somewhere else perhaps. . . ." And then: "Get the kettle going. It's thirsty work, this."

So Margaret went to the kitchen, and stoked up the fire, and boiled the water. Now, on the tin roof of the kitchen she could hear the thuds and bangs of falling locusts, or a scratching slither as one skidded down. Here were the first of them. From down on the lands came the beating and banging and clanging of a hundred gasoline cans and bits of metal. Stephen impatiently waited while one gasoline can was filled with tea, hot, sweet and orange-colored, and the other with water. In the meantime, he told Margaret about how twenty years back he was eaten out, made bankrupt, by the locust armies. And then, still talking, he hoisted up the gasoline cans, one in each hand, by the wood pieces set cornerwise across each, and jogged off down to the road to the thirsty laborers. By now the locusts were falling like hail on to the roof of the kitchen. It sounded like a heavy storm. Margaret looked out and saw the air dark with a crisscross of the insects, and she set her teeth and ran out into it—what the men could do, she could. Overhead the air was thick, locusts everywhere. The locusts were flopping against her, and she brushed them off, heavy red-brown creatures, looking at her with their beady old-men's eyes while they clung with hard, serrated legs. She held her breath

with disgust and ran through into the house. There it was even more like being in a heavy storm. The iron roof was reverberating, and the clamor of iron from the lands was like thunder. Looking out, all the trees were queer and still, clotted with insects, their boughs weighed to the ground. The earth seemed to be moving, locusts crawling everywhere, she could not see the lands at all, so thick was the swarm. Toward the mountains it was like looking into driving rain—even as she watched, the sun was blotted out with a fresh onrush of them. It was a half-night, a perverted blackness. Then came a sharp crack from the bush—a branch had snapped off. Then another. A tree down the slope leaned over and settled heavily to the ground. Through the hail of insects a man came running. More tea, more water was needed. She supplied them. She kept the fires stoked and filled cans with liquid, and then it was four in the afternoon, and the locusts had been pouring across overhead for a couple of hours. Up came old Stephen again, crunching locusts underfoot with every step, locusts clinging all over him; he was cursing and swearing, banging with his old hat at the air. At the doorway he stopped briefly, hastily pulling at the clinging insects and throwing them off, then he plunged into the locust-free living room.

"All the crops finished. Nothing left," he said.

But the gongs were still beating, the men still shouting, and Margaret asked: "Why do you go on with it, then?"

"The main swarm isn't settling. They are heavy with eggs. They are looking for a place to settle and lay. If we can stop the main body settling on our farm, that's everything. If they get a chance to lay their eggs, we are going to have everything eaten flat with hoppers later on." He picked a stray locust off his shirt and split it down with his thumbnail—it was clotted inside with eggs. "Imagine that multiplied by millions. You ever seen a hopper swarm on the march? Well, you're lucky."

Margaret thought an adult swarm was bad enough. Outside now the light on the earth was a pale, thin yellow, clotted with moving shadows; the clouds of moving insects thickened and lightened like driving rain. Old Stephen said, "They've got the wind behind them, that's something."

"Is it very bad?" asked Margaret fearfully, and the old man said emphatically: "We're finished. This swarm may pass over, but once they've started, they'll be coming down from the North now one after another. And then there are the hoppers—it might go on for two or three years."

Margaret sat down helplessly, and thought: Well, if it's the end, it's the end. What now? We'll all three have to go back to town. . . . But at this, she took a quick look at Stephen, the old man who had farmed forty years in this country, been bankrupt twice, and she knew nothing would make him go and become a clerk in the city. Yet her heart ached for him, he looked so tired, the worry lines deep from nose to mouth. Poor old man. . . . He had lifted up a locust that had got itself somehow into his pocket, holding it in the air by one leg. "You've got the strength of a steel spring in those legs of yours," he was telling the locust, good-humoredly. Then, although he had been fighting locusts, squashing locusts, yelling at locusts, sweeping them in great mounds into the fires to burn for the last three hours, nevertheless he took this one to the door and carefully threw it out to join its fellows, as if he would rather not harm a hair of its head. This comforted Margaret; all at once she felt irrationally cheered. She remembered it was not the first time in the last three years the man had announced their final and irremediable ruin.

"Get me a drink, lass," he then said, and she set the bottle of whiskey by him.

In the meantime, out in the pelting storm of insects, her husband was banging the gong, feeding the fires with leaves, the insects clinging to him all over—she shuddered. "How can you bear to let them touch you?" she asked. He looked at her, disapproving. She felt suitably humble—just as she had when he had first taken a good look at her city self, hair waved and golden, nails red and pointed. Now she was a proper farmer's wife, in sensible shoes and a solid skirt. She might even get to letting locusts settle on her—in time.

Having tossed back a whiskey or two, old Stephen went back into the battle, wading now through glistening brown waves of locusts.

Five o'clock. The sun would set in an hour. Then the swarm would settle. It was as thick overhead as ever. The trees were ragged mounts of glistening brown.

Margaret began to cry. It was all so hopeless—if it wasn't a bad season, it was locusts; if it wasn't locusts, it was armyworm or veldt fires. Always something. The rustling of the locust armies was like a big forest in the storm; their settling on the roof was like the beating of the rain; the ground was invisible in a sleek, brown, surging tide—it was like being drowned in locusts, submerged by the loathsome brown flood. It seemed as if the roof might sink in under the weight of them, as if the door might give in under their pressure and these rooms fill with them—and it was getting so dark . . . she looked up. The air was thinner; gaps of blue showed in the dark, moving clouds. The blue spaces were cold and thin—the sun must be setting. Through the fog of insects she saw figures approaching. First old Stephen, marching bravely along, then her husband, drawn and haggard with weariness. Behind them the servants. All were crawling all over

with insects. The sound of the gongs had stopped. She could hear nothing but the ceaseless rustle of a myriad wings.

The two men slapped off the insects and came in.

"Well," said Richard, kissing her on the cheek, "the main swarm has gone over."

"For the Lord's sake," said Margaret angrily, still half-crying, "what's here is bad enough, isn't it?" For although the evening air was no longer black and thick, but a clear blue, with a pattern of insects whizzing this way and that across it, everything else—trees, buildings, bushes, earth, was gone under the moving brown masses.

"If it doesn't rain in the night and keep them here—if it doesn't rain and weight them down with water, they'll be off in the morning at sunrise."

"We're bound to have some hoppers. But not the main swarm—that's something."

Margaret roused herself, wiped her eyes, pretended she had not been crying, and fetched them some supper, for the servants were too exhausted to move. She sent them down to the compound to rest.

She served the supper and sat listening. There is not one maize plant left, she heard. Not one. The men would get the planters out the moment the locusts had gone. They must start all over again.

But what's the use of that, Margaret wondered, if the whole farm was going to be crawling with hoppers? But she listened while they discussed the new government pamphlet that said how to defeat the hoppers. You must have men out all the time, moving over the farm to watch for movement in the grass. When you find a patch of hoppers, small lively black things, like crickets, then you dig trenches around the patch or spray them with poison from pumps supplied by the government. The government wanted them to cooperate in a world plan for eliminating this plague forever. You should attack locusts at the source. Hoppers, in short. The men were talking as if they were planning a war, and

Margaret listened, amazed.

In the night it was quiet; no sign of the settled armies outside, except sometimes a branch snapped, or a tree could be heard crashing down.

Margaret slept badly in the bed beside Richard, who was sleeping like the dead, exhausted with the afternoon's fight. In the morning she woke to yellow sunshine lying across the bed—clear sunshine, with an occasional blotch of shadow moving over it. She went to the window. Old Stephen was ahead of her. There he stood outside, gazing down over the bush. And she gazed, astounded—and entranced, much against her will. For it looked as if every tree, every bush, all the earth, were lit with pale flames. The locusts were fanning their wings to free them of the night dews. There was a shimmer of red-tinged gold light everywhere.

She went out to join the old man, stepping carefully among the insects. They stood and watched. Overhead the sky was blue, blue and clear.

"Pretty," said old Stephen, with satisfaction.

Well, thought Margaret, we may be ruined, we may be bankrupt, but not everyone has seen an army of locusts fanning their wings at dawn.

Over the slopes, in the distance, a faint red smear showed in the sky, thickened and spread. "There they go," said old Stephen. "There goes the main army, off south."

And now from the trees, from the earth all round them, the locusts were taking wing. They were like small aircraft, maneuvering for the take-off, trying their wings to see if they were dry enough. Off they went. A reddish brown steam was rising off the miles of bush, off the lands, the earth. Again the sunlight darkened.

And as the clotted branches lifted, the weight on them lightening, there was nothing but the black spines of branches, trees. No green left, nothing. All morning they watched, the three of them, as the brown crust thinned and broke and dissolved, flying up to mass with the main army, now a brownish-red smear in the southern sky. The lands which had been filmed with green, the new tender mealie plants, were stark and bare. All the trees stripped. A devastated landscape. No green, no green anywhere.

By midday the reddish cloud had gone. Only an occasional locust flopped down. On the ground were the corpses and the wounded. The African laborers were sweeping these up with branches and collecting them in tins.

"Ever eaten sun-dried locust?" asked old Stephen. "That time twenty years ago, when I went broke, I lived on mealie meal and dried locusts for three months. They aren't bad at all—rather like smoked fish, if you come to think of it."

But Margaret preferred not even to think of it.

After the midday meal the men went off to the lands. Everything was to be replanted. With a bit of luck another swarm would not come traveling down just this way. But they hoped it would rain very soon, to spring some new grass, because the cattle would die otherwise—there was not a blade of grass left on the farm. As for Margaret, she was trying to get used to the idea of three or four years of locusts. Locusts were going to be like bad weather, from now on, always imminent. She felt like a survivor after war—if this devastated and mangled countryside was not ruin, well, what then was ruin?

But the men ate their supper with good appetites.

"It could have been worse," was what they said. "It could be much worse."

FOR DISCUSSION

1. Why do you think this story is told from the point of view of Margaret, a city girl? How do her feelings about the locusts differ from the feelings of her husband and father-in-law?

2. Why is Margaret cheered when old Stephen sets the locust outside and later when they see the locusts at dawn?

FOR COMPOSITION

• What do you think is the theme of this story? First show how it applies to the specific details of the story, then how it might apply to life in general. What can people who will never even see a locust learn from "A Mild Attack of Locusts"?

His name meant "Gawaine the Boldhearted," but he whimpered with fear at the thought of slaying a dragon.

THE FIFTY-FIRST DRAGON

HEYWOOD BROUN

OF ALL THE PUPILS at the knight school Gawaine le Coeur-Hardy[1] was among the least promising. He was tall and sturdy, but his instructors soon discovered that he lacked spirit. He would hide in the woods when the jousting class was called, although his companions and members of the faculty sought to appeal to his better nature by shouting to him to come out and break his neck like a man. Even when they told him that the lances were padded, the horses no more than ponies, and the field unusually soft for late autumn, Gawaine refused to grow enthusiastic. The Headmaster and the Assistant Professor of Pleasance[2] were discussing the case one spring afternoon, and the Assistant Professor could see no remedy but expulsion.

"No," said the Headmaster, as he looked out at the purple hills which ringed the school, "I think I'll train him to slay dragons."

"He might be killed," objected the Assistant Professor.

"So he might," replied the Headmaster brightly; "but," he added more soberly, "we must consider the greater good. We are responsible for the formation of this lad's character."

"Are the dragons particularly bad this year?" interrupted the Assistant Professor.

This was characteristic. He always seemed restive when the head of the school began to talk ethics and the ideals of the institution.

"I've never known them worse," replied the Headmaster. "Up in the hills to the south last week they killed a number of peasants, two cows, and a prize pig. And if this dry spell holds, there's no telling when they may start a forest fire simply by breathing around indiscriminately."

"Would any refund on the tuition fee be necessary in case of an accident to young Coeur-Hardy?"

"No," the principal answered judicially; "that's all covered in the contract. But as a matter of fact he won't be killed. Before I send him up in the hills, I'm going to give him a magic word."

"That's a good idea," said the Professor. "Sometimes they work wonders."

From that day on Gawaine specialized in dragons. His course included both theory and practice. In the morning there were long lectures on the history, anatomy, manners, and customs of dragons. Gawaine did not distinguish himself in these studies. He had a marvelously versatile gift for forgetting things. In the afternoon he showed to better advantage, for then he would go down to the South Meadow and practice with a battle-ax. In this exercise he was truly impressive, for he had enormous strength as well as speed and grace. He even developed a deceptive display of ferocity. Old alumni say that it was a thrill-

[1] GAWAINE LE COEUR-HARDY (gə·wān′ lə ker′ är·dê′): Gawaine the Boldhearted.
[2] PLEASANCE: Recreation.

ing sight to see Gawaine charging across the field toward the dummy paper dragon which had been set up for his practice. As he ran he would brandish his ax and shout, "A murrain[1] on thee!" or some other vivid bit of campus slang. It never took him more than one stroke to behead the dummy dragon.

Gradually his task was made more difficult. Paper gave way to papier-mâché[2] and finally to wood, but even the toughest of these dummy dragons had no terrors for Gawaine. One sweep of the ax always did the business. There were those who said that when the practice was protracted until dusk and the dragons threw long, fantastic shadows across the meadow, Gawaine did not charge so impetuously nor shout so loudly. It is possible there was malice in this charge. At any rate, the Headmaster decided by the end of June that it was time for the test. Only the night before, a dragon had come close to the school grounds and had eaten some of the lettuce from the garden. The faculty decided that Gawaine was ready. They gave him a diploma and a new battle-ax, and the Headmaster summoned him to a private conference.

"Sit down," said the Headmaster. "Have a cigarette."

Gawaine hesitated.

"Oh, I know it's against the rules," said the Headmaster; "but after all, you have received your preliminary degree. You are no longer a boy. You are a man. Tomorrow you will go out into the world, the great world of achievement."

Gawaine took a cigarette. The Headmaster offered him a match, but he produced one of his own and began to puff away with a dexterity which quite amazed the principal.

[1] MURRAIN (mûr′ ĭn): plague.
[2] PAPIER-MÂCHÉ (pa·pyā′ mä·shā′): hard substance of paper pulp mixed with glue.

"Here you have learned the theories of life," continued the Headmaster, resuming the thread of his discourse; "but after all, life is not a matter of theories. Life is a matter of facts. It calls on the young and the old alike to face these facts, even though they are hard and sometimes unpleasant. Your problem, for example, is to slay dragons."

"They say that those dragons down in the south wood are five hundred feet long," ventured Gawaine timorously.

"Stuff and nonsense!" said the Headmaster. "The curate saw one last week from the top of Arthur's Hill. The dragon was sunning himself down in the valley. The curate didn't have an opportunity to look at him very long because he felt it was his duty to hurry back to make a report to me. He said the monster—or shall I say, the big lizard?—wasn't an inch over two hundred feet. But the size has nothing at all to do with it. You'll find the big ones even easier than the little ones. They're far slower on their feet and less aggressive, I'm told. Besides, before you go I'm going to equip you in such fashion that you need have no fear of all the dragons in the world."

"I'd like an enchanted cap," said Gawaine.

"What's that?" asked the Headmaster testily.

"A cap to make me disappear," explained Gawaine.

The Headmaster laughed indulgently. "You mustn't believe all those old wives' stories," he said. "There isn't any such thing. A cap to make you disappear, indeed! What would you do with it? You haven't even appeared yet. Why, my boy, you could walk from here to London, and nobody would so much as look at you. You're nobody. You couldn't be more invisible than that."

Gawaine seemed dangerously close to a

relapse into his old habit of whimpering. The Headmaster reassured him: "Don't worry; I'll give you something much better than an enchanted cap. I'm going to give you a magic word. All you have to do is to repeat this magic charm once and no dragon can possibly harm a hair of your head. You can cut off his head at your leisure."

He took a heavy book from the shelf behind his desk and began to run through it. "Sometimes," he said, "the charm is a whole phrase or even a sentence. I might, for instance, give you 'To make the'—No, that might not do. I think a single word would be best for dragons."

"A short word," suggested Gawaine.

"It can't be too short or it wouldn't be potent. There isn't so much hurry as all that. Here's a splendid magic word: 'Rumplesnitz.' Do you think you can learn that?"

Gawaine tried and in an hour or so he seemed to have the word well in hand. Again and again he interrupted the lesson to inquire, "And if I say 'Rumplesnitz' the dragon can't possibly hurt me?" And always the Headmaster replied, "If you only say 'Rumplesnitz,' you are perfectly safe."

Toward morning Gawaine seemed resigned to his career. At daybreak the Headmaster saw him to the edge of the forest and pointed him to the direction in which he should proceed. About a mile away to the southwest a cloud of steam hovered over an open meadow in the woods, and the Headmaster assured Gawaine that under the steam he would find a dragon. Gawaine went forward slowly. He wondered whether it would be best to approach the dragon on the run, as he did in his practice in the South Meadow, or to walk slowly toward him, shouting "Rumplesnitz" all the way.

The problem was decided for him. No sooner had he come to the fringe of the meadow than the dragon spied him and began to charge. It was a large dragon, and yet it seemed decidedly aggressive in spite of the Headmaster's statement to the contrary. As the dragon charged, it released huge clouds of hissing steam through its nostrils. It was almost as if a gigantic teapot had gone mad. The dragon came forward so fast, and Gawaine was so frightened, that he had time to say "Rumplesnitz" only once. As he said it he swung his battle-ax, and off popped the head of the dragon. Gawaine had to admit that it was even easier to kill a real dragon than a wooden one, if only you said "Rumplesnitz."

Gawaine brought the ears home and a small section of the tail. His schoolmates and the faculty made much of him, but the Headmaster wisely kept him from being spoiled by insisting that he go on with his work. Every clear day Gawaine rose at dawn and went out to kill dragons. The Headmaster kept him at home when it rained, because he said the woods were damp and unhealthy at such times and that he didn't want the boy to run needless risks. Few good days passed in which Gawaine failed to get a dragon. On one particularly fortunate day he killed three, a husband and wife and a visiting relative. Gradually he developed a technique. Pupils who sometimes watched him from the hilltops a long way off said that he often allowed the dragon to come within a few feet before he said "Rumplesnitz." He came to say it with a mocking sneer. Occasionally he did stunts. Once when an excursion party from London was watching him he went into action with his right hand tied behind his back. The dragon's head came off just as easily.

As Gawaine's record of killings mounted higher, the Headmaster found it impossible to keep him completely in hand. He fell into the habit of stealing out at night and engaging in long drinking bouts at the village tavern. It was after such a debauch that he rose a little before dawn one fine August morning and started out after his fiftieth dragon. His head was heavy and his mind sluggish. He was heavy in other respects as well, for he had adopted the somewhat vulgar practice of wearing his medals, ribbons and all, when he went out dragon hunting. The decorations began on his chest and ran all the way down to his abdomen. They must have weighed at least eight pounds.

Gawaine found a dragon in the same meadow where he killed the first one. It was a fair-sized dragon, but evidently an old one. Its face was wrinkled and Gawaine thought he had never seen so hideous a countenance. Much to the lad's disgust the monster refused to charge, and Gawaine was obliged to walk toward him. He whistled as he went. The dragon regarded him hopelessly but craftily. Of course it had heard of Gawaine. Even when the lad raised his battle-ax, the dragon made no move. It knew that there was no salvation in the quickest thrust of the head, for it had been informed that this hunter was protected by an enchantment. It merely waited, hoping something would turn up.

Gawaine raised the battle-ax and suddenly lowered it again. He had grown very pale, and he trembled violently.

The dragon suspected a trick. "What's the matter?" it asked, with false solicitude.

"I've forgotten the magic word," stammered Gawaine.

"What a pity!" said the dragon. "So that was the secret. It doesn't seem quite sporting to me, all this magic stuff, you know. Not cricket, as we used to say when I was a little dragon; but after all, that's a matter of opinion."

Gawaine was so helpless with terror that the dragon's confidence rose immeasurably and it could not resist the temptation to show off a bit.

"Could I possibly be of any assistance?" it asked. "What's the first letter of the magic word?"

"It begins with an 'R,'" said Gawaine weakly.

"Let's see," mused the dragon, "that doesn't tell us much, does it? What sort of a word is this? Is it an epithet, do you think?"

Gawaine shook his head.

"Well, then," said the dragon, "we'd better get down to business. Will you surrender?"

With the suggestion of a compromise Gawaine mustered up enough courage to speak.

"What will you do if I surrender?" he asked.

"Why, I'll eat you," said the dragon.

"And if I don't surrender?"

"I'll eat you just the same."

"Then it doesn't mean any difference, does it?" moaned Gawaine.

"It does to me," said the dragon with a smile. "I'd rather you didn't surrender. You'd taste much better if you didn't."

The dragon waited for a long time for Gawaine to ask "Why?" but the boy was too frightened to speak. At last the dragon had to give the explanation without his cue line. "You see," he said, "if you don't surrender you'll taste better because you'll die game."

This was an old and ancient trick of the dragon's. By means of some such quip he was accustomed to paralyze his victims with laughter and then to destroy them. Gawaine was sufficiently paralyzed as it was, but laughter had no part in his helplessness. With the last word of the joke the dragon drew back his head and struck. In that second there flashed into the mind of Gawaine the magic word of "Rumple-

snitz," but there was no time to say it. There was time only to strike, and without a word Gawaine met the onrush of the dragon with a full swing. He put all his back and shoulders into it. The impact was terrific, and the head of the dragon flew almost a hundred yards and landed in a thicket.

Gawaine did not remain frightened very long after the death of the dragon. His mood was one of wonder. He was enormously puzzled. He cut off the ears of the monster almost in a trance. Again and again he thought to himself, "I didn't say 'Rumplesnitz'!" He was sure of that, and yet there was no question that he had killed the dragon. In fact, he had never killed one so utterly. Never before had he driven a head for anything like the same distance. Twenty-five yards was perhaps his best previous record. All the way back to the knight school he kept rumbling about in his mind, seeking an explanation for what had occurred. He went to the Headmaster immediately, and after closing the door, told him what had happened. "I didn't say 'Rumplesnitz,'" he explained with great earnestness.

The Headmaster laughed. "I'm glad you've found out," he said. "It makes you ever so much more of a hero. Don't you see that? Now you know that it was you who killed all these dragons, and not that foolish little word 'Rumplesnitz.'"

Gawaine frowned. "Then it wasn't a magic word, after all?" he asked.

"Of course not," said the Headmaster; "you ought to be too old for such foolishness. There isn't any such thing as a magic word."

"But you told me it was magic," protested Gawaine. "You said it was magic, and now you say it isn't."

"It wasn't magic in a literal sense," answered the Headmaster, "but it was much more wonderful than that. The word gave you confidence. It took away your fears. If I hadn't told you that, you might have been killed the very first time. It was your battle-ax did the trick."

Gawaine surprised the Headmaster by his attitude. He was obviously distressed by the explanation. He interrupted a long philosophic and ethical discourse by the Headmaster with, "If I hadn't of hit 'em all mighty hard and fast, any one of 'em might have crushed me like a, like a—" He fumbled for a word.

"Egg shell," suggested the Headmaster.

"Like a egg shell," assented Gawaine and he said it many times. All through the evening meal people who sat near him heard him muttering, "Like a egg shell, like a egg shell."

The next day was clear, but Gawaine did not get up at dawn. Indeed, it was almost noon when the Headmaster found him cowering in bed, with the clothes pulled over his head. The principal called the Assistant Professor of Pleasance, and together they dragged the boy toward the forest.

"He'll be all right as soon as he gets a couple more dragons under his belt," explained the Headmaster.

The Assistant Professor of Pleasance agreed. "It would be a shame to stop such a fine run," he said. "Why, counting that one yesterday, he's killed fifty dragons."

They pushed the boy into a thicket above which hung a meager cloud of steam. It was obviously quite a small dragon. But Gawaine did not come back that night or the next. In fact, he never came back. Some weeks afterwards, brave spirits from the school explored the thicket, but they could find nothing to remind them of Gawaine except the metal parts of his medals. Even the ribbons had been devoured.

The Headmaster and the Assistant Professor of Pleasance agreed that it would be just as well not to tell the school how Gawaine had achieved his record and still less how he came to die. They held that it might have a bad effect on school spirit. Accordingly, Gawaine has lived in the memory of the school as its greatest hero. No visitor succeeds in leaving the building today without seeing a great shield which hangs on the wall of the dining hall. Fifty pairs of dragons' ears are mounted upon the shield, and underneath in gilt letters is "Gawaine le Coeur-Hardy," followed by the simple inscription, "He killed fifty dragons." The record has never been equaled.

FOR DISCUSSION

1. Learning that he, not the magic word, has slain the dragons should increase Gawaine's self-confidence. Why does it have just the opposite effect?

2. " 'I'm glad you've found out,' " the Headmaster said. " 'It makes you ever so much more of a hero.' " Do you think Gawaine is heroic in fearlessly slaying the fifty dragons? Would he have been more or less heroic in slaying the fifty-first?

3. The author uses irony in this story for humorous effect. For example, when the Headmaster keeps Gawaine home from his dragon slaying on rainy days to avoid "needless risks," the contrast between the great danger from dragons and the slight danger from damp weather is humorous. What other examples can you find?

FOR COMPOSITION

• Although this is a humorous story, it contains a serious lesson. Suggest some modern situations in which the theme of "The Fifty-first Dragon" could apply. What are the twentieth-century equivalents of dragons and magic words?

In Summary

1. Suppose you were asked to reorganize this unit by adding one more story to each section. Choose one story from each of the five pairs below, explaining why you think it would be the better choice:

    a. Plot: "Thank You, M'am" or "The Cask of Amontillado"

    b. Setting: "Jacob" or "Peter Two"

    c. Character: "The Speckled Band" or "Antaeus"

    d. Point of View: "The story of My Dovecot" or "The Vacation"

    e. Theme: "The Interlopers" or "The Landlady"

2. Several of the stories in this unit have ironic surprise endings: "The Necklace," "The Interlopers," "The Verger," "Chickamauga," and "The Sniper." Which one surprised you most? Which one do you think is most effective in emphasizing the theme of the story? Is there any ending you should like to see changed?

3. Looking back over the whole short story unit, which character stands out in your mind as most unusual? Which one do you think is most lifelike and realistic? You may have to skim one or two stories a second time to explain your choices.

4. Discuss any of the characters in this unit as he would be seen by a character from another story. For example, what would Sherlock Holmes think of Montresor and his plan? How would T.J. in "Antaeus" feel about Tucker in "The White Circle"? What would Margaret in "A Mild Attack of Locusts" have to say about Mathilde in "The Necklace"? What would Jacob's reaction be if he read "Peter Two"?

5. Several of the stories you have read involve characters faced with defeat, among them "Jacob," "Antaeus," "The Verger," "The Story of My Dovecot," and "A Mild Attack of Locusts." What meaning do these authors find in the experience of defeat? Do the stories all have similar themes, or are they different?

OTHER THINGS TO DO

1. Summarize several of the stories in this unit by telling them in the form of "telegrams" (15 words) or "night letters" (100 words).

2. Illustrate the setting from one or two of the stories in which the setting is important. Try to show the atmosphere of the story by your illustration: is it peaceful? frightening? gloomy?

3. Choose one of the questions "For Discussion" to discuss with no more than five other students gathered around a tape recorder. Perhaps one student could act as moderator. If several groups do this you may want to listen to each others' tapes, or you may give the tape to your teacher for evaluation.

4. Choose a passage from one of the stories to read orally into a tape recorder. Vary your voice to show different characters speaking and to emphasize suspense or emotion. You may have to do it over several times before you are ready to play it for the class.

5. Report an event or describe a photograph as they might be seen from two opposite points of view. The facts must stay the same, but you may change the *connotations*, or emotional overtones, of the words used to describe them. For example, the word "slim" implies a positive connotation, while "skinny" implies a negative one. A student who has failed a test might (negatively) call his teacher "a mean old grouch who likes to fail kids." His principal might see (positively) "a mature teacher who controls his classes well and maintains high standards."

6. Choose any television show, movie, or novel to compare with at least one of the stories in this unit. Analyze them both in terms of character, theme, setting, and other terms learned in this unit.

7. Write a new ending for any of the stories in this unit. If it is a serious story, you might enjoy writing a humorous ending.

The World of Words

THE ADVENTURE OF THE SPECKLED BAND

Dr. Watson speaks of his admiration for Sherlock Holmes's "rapid *deductions*" which are, he says, "as swift as *intuitions*." There is some question about Watson's use of the word *deduction*, according to the way we use the word today. As we use the word, it refers to a form of reasoning from statements (called "premises") that we regard as true. Thus we might say: "All fish can swim. This creature is a fish. Therefore, this creature can swim." In this form of reasoning, the conclusion follows necessarily from the stated premises. Since this is not what Holmes did, the word *deduction* does not fit his actions. The word *induction* is more appropriate here. Induction, or inductive reasoning, leads to a conclusion about all members of a class of objects by examining enough members of the class to make the conclusion convincing. Using this form of reasoning, we would examine the habits of a number of fish, and if each of these could swim, we would make the conclusion that all fish can swim. Since neither word fits Holmes's methods exactly, it might be best just to say that he worked by merely examining whatever evidence was before him. But Watson also suggests that Holmes worked by *intuition*. What is meant by the word *intuition*? Can the word be applied to Holmes's methods of working?

THE INTERLOPERS

The word *interloper* is an interesting compound of *inter* from Latin, meaning "between" or "among," and *loper* from Dutch, meaning "running." The Dutch word *loper* and the English word *leaping* are what are called *cognates*. That is, they are words in different languages that go back to the same source. *Loper* is from an older Dutch word *loopen*, meaning "to run." *Leaping* is from an Old English word *hleapan*, also meaning "to run." And both go back to an earlier common root. What other English words would you guess come from *loper*?

THE NECKLACE

The word *vain* can be applied to various situations in "The Necklace." Like most words, *vain* has more than one meaning so that when it is used one must look at the *context* (the words surrounding it) in order to determine its meaning. Explain the meaning of *vain* in each of the following sentences. Consult a dictionary if necessary. (1) "Mme. Loisel was *vain* about her appearance." (2) "Loisel made a *vain* attempt to find the necklace." A related word is *vanity*. Write two separate sentences using *vanity* with two separate meanings.

ANTAEUS

Like Antaeus, T. J. was a man of the earth. Here are five *synonyms*. They are used as adjectives that are similar in that each indicates a relationship to earth, but they do not indicate exactly the same relationship— *earthly, terrestrial, worldly, mundane, earthy*. Examine the meaning of each adjective and explain how these meanings differ.

THE VACATION

We sometimes think that if we know the source, or *etymology*, of a word we will be able to grasp its meaning. This is not always so, because the meanings of words often drift and change so that the meaning of a word is often quite different from its original meaning. The word *gentle*, for example, originally meant "born of a noble family." The word *vacation* comes from the Latin word *vacare*, meaning "to be empty." Other words from the same source are *vacant, vacate, vacuum*. What does the word *vacation* mean today? As used in the title of Bradbury's story, is there anything that suggests the origin of the word?

THE STORY OF MY DOVECOT

1. A *euphemism* is an inoffensive word or phrase that is used in place of one that might be offensive or unpleasant. In Babel's story we read that the narrator's grandfather "started going off his head." And later we read "They've done Grandfather in." The first phrase refers to insanity and the second refers to killing. Since we find both insanity and killing unpleasant, we try to avoid words that refer directly to them. Thus instead of the word *insane,* we might say "off his head," and instead of *kill,* we might say "done him in." What other euphemisms can you think of for these situations? The words *dead* and *death* are other words we try to avoid. What euphemisms do we use in place of them? What other euphemisms are used to avoid offensive or unpleasant words?

2. In the last sentence of the story we find the word *pogrom.* It is a *borrowed word.* From what language? How is the word *pogrom* put together and what does it mean?

THE VERGER

All languages consist of a variety of *dialects.* Dialects differ according to location and cultural level. Albert Edward Foreman's reveals his lack of education. He speaks with what is called a "cockney" or lower class London accent. To enable the reader to understand Foreman, Maugham does not make his speech much different from standard English, but there are differences in his speech that mark it as a dialect. Examine Foreman's speeches and point out these differences. Two British slang words that Foreman might well have used are "bloke" and "rum." What do these words mean?

JACOB

"These moccasins?" Schaefer's story begins. The word moccasin is one of the many *borrowed words* from the various languages of the Indians of North America. Indian words were used for many plants and animals that settlers found in America, such as *squash, hominy, succotash, chipmunk, raccoon, woodchuck.* The names of many states are taken from Indian words, such as *Alabama, Arkansas, Kentucky, Massachusetts, Missouri.* The names

of rivers, such as *Mississippi, Niagara, Potomac, Juniata,* and *Susquehanna,* also come from Indian words, as does the name of a lake in Massachusetts called *Chargoggagoggmanchaugagoggchaubunagungamaugg.* Translated, this means, "You fish your side of the lake, we'll fish our side, and nobody fishes in the middle." By the way, where does the word *Indian* come from? Why were the natives of America called "Indians"?

THANK YOU, M'AM

Sometimes words that refer to one specific object gradually come to refer to a wide range of objects. This process is called *generalization.* In Hughes's story, Mrs. Jones takes some food from the "icebox." The word *icebox* originally referred to a chest or box in which ice was put to keep food cool. When refrigerators came into use, cooled by electricity or gas, the name *icebox* was extended to cover them. The word is still used in this way. One particular kind of refrigerator was called "Frigidaire." This was a trade name, but it was often used to refer to any kind of refrigerator. Then there is *Kodak,* the name of a particular make of hand camera that is widely used as the name for all similar cameras. The word *gift* is another example of generalization. In Old English it referred to a dowry, a wedding gift from the bride's parents. It gradually came to refer to all kinds of gifts. What other examples of generalization can you think of?

PETER TWO

Peter decides that the action he has been watching on television is unreal, that it does not correspond to events in the real world. Various words, or *synonyms,* share the meaning of "unreal," but they differ in the attitude they express toward what is unreal. What meanings do you associate with the following words: *artificial, synthetic, simulated, spurious, specious, counterfeit?* How do these meanings differ? What different attitudes are expressed by these words? For example, what is the difference between saying that something is "artificial" and saying that it is "counterfeit"?

CHICKAMAUGA

An *allusion* is a reference to a person, place, thing, or event that a reader might be expected to recognize. Allusions are quite indirect so that the reader must be aware or he will miss them. They are a way of extending our use of language, for through a brief reference a writer can express much more than he actually states. For example, if we say that a man has "Lincolnesque" features, we have, through an allusion to Abraham Lincoln, created a picture that a reader can fill in for himself. The title of Bierce's story is an allusion to an especially bloody battle of the American Civil War. There is another allusion on page 162 where the boy points toward the fire in the woods—"in the direction of the guiding light—a pillar of fire to this strange exodus." The last phrase here—*a pillar of fire to this strange exodus*—is an allusion to the story in the Book of *Exodus* in the Old Testament where Moses leads the Israelites through a wilderness after their escape from Egypt. To guide them on their way God provides "a pillar of cloud by day" and "a pillar of fire by night." For a reader who knows both stories, this allusion emphasizes the hopelessness of the situation in Bierce's story. See if you can identify allusions in your own language or in the language of others.

THE LANDLADY

Roald Dahl's story is full of clues to guide the reader. The word *clue* is itself somewhat of a mystery in that what it means here has little apparent connection with its original meaning. It is an example of what is called *transfer of meaning*. *Clue* (or, as it is also spelled, *clew*) originally meant "a ball" or "globular mass," and it still has the meaning "a ball of yarn or thread." It also refers to a specific ball of thread, the one that was used to guide Theseus, an ancient Greek hero, out of a labyrinth in which he had been placed. Details of this situation can be found in the story of Theseus in Greek mythology. The point here is that a labyrinth is a series of confusing passages from which it is difficult to escape.

Theseus was able to release thread from the ball as he entered the labyrinth. Thus the thread provided him the *clue* he needed to escape. The word *clue*, then, in addition to its original meaning, took on the additional meaning that it now holds. How would you state that meaning?

THE CASK OF AMONTILLADO

Montresor says that he wants to "redress" a wrong that has been done to him, and he speaks of himself as an "avenger." But are these words appropriate for what Montresor does? Does he seek *redress* or *revenge*? Is he an *avenger* or a *revenger*? Examine carefully the meanings of the verbs *avenge, redress,* and *revenge,* as well as the nouns derived from them. Then decide which words are most appropriate for the action Montresor takes. Explain your choice or choices.

THE SNIPER

The literal meaning of a word, the meaning you find in a dictionary, is called its "*denotation*." But part of the meaning of a word comes from the feelings the word arouses in us. For example, the words *house* and *home* have much the same denotation, but *home* has *connotations* that *house* does not have. *Home* arouses feelings within us, feelings that depend on our experiences with our family as well as with the place we live. The eyes of the sniper, we are told "had the cold gleam of the fanatic." The words *fanatic, enthusiast, extremist* all denote someone who is strongly devoted to some cause or activity. The words have much the same denotation, but their connotations are different. Examine the meanings of these words and explain their differences in both denotation and connotation. Which has the most favorable connotation? Which has the least favorable?

THE WHITE CIRCLE

Many of our most useful, everyday words have been in English since English became a separate language. They are *native* words.

Many other words have been borrowed from other languages. Many words have been borrowed from Latin, and these often appear more formal, less ordinary, than the words from Old English. For example, the word *dog* is from Old English; the word *canine* is from Latin. Both kinds of words are useful, and often there is no suitable substitute for the borrowed one. "The White Circle" contains many words that have been borrowed from Latin. Some of these are *momentousness, commemorate, homicidal, itinerant, vicious, extinction, truculently.* Look up the meanings of these words and see if you can replace them with more common, everyday words.

A MILD ATTACK OF LOCUSTS

When two or more words come into a language from the same source but by different routes they are called *doublets.* The word *locust* came into English through French from the Latin word *locusta,* meaning "locust" or "shell-fish." The word *lobster* came directly into Old English from the same Latin word, *locusta.* It may seem strange that *locust* and *lobster* come from the same source. If you consider what locusts and lobsters are like, do you see any reasons that would connect them with the same original name?

THE FIFTY-FIRST DRAGON

1. Beginning with the Latin word *draco,* meaning "serpent" or "dragon," a number of words have come into English. Some of these are *dragoon, pendragon, rankle,* and *tarragon.* By doing some detective work, using clues from a dictionary, explain how these words have come into English from *draco.*

2. One of Gawaine's major problems had to do with the word *confidence.* Some synonyms of confidence are *assurance* and *aplomb.* What differences do you find among these three words? Which of them can be applied to Gawaine? Is the word *arrogant* an appropriate word to describe Gawaine? Why or why not?

Reader's Choice

Best Short Stories, *Eric Berger, ed.*

Each of these stories can be read in a few minutes. Some are only a page long, but they fit a large package of humor and suspense into a small space. Like many of the stories in this unit, they end with a surprise twist.

Chilling Stories from Rod Serling's Twilight Zone, *adapted by Walter B. Gibson.*

In the twilight zone between this dimension and the next, anything can happen: a murderer is captured through ESP, a traveler in time is helpless to prevent Lincoln's assassination, and a U-boat captain sails a foggy sea forever as punishment for his cruelty during World War II. These stories of the supernatural are taken from the television series of the same name.

Great Stories of Sherlock Holmes, *by Sir Arthur Conan Doyle.*

Sherlock Holmes and his assistant, Dr. Watson, are at their most brilliant in these fast-moving stories of crime. The reader has many opportunities to test his crime-solving skills.

Great Tales of Action and Adventure, *George Bennett, ed.*

There are no dull moments in this collection of suspense-filled stories. Among the contents are mystery stories, tales of man against nature, an Arthur C. Clarke science fiction story, and a suicide attempt.

Great Tales of Horror, *by Edgar Allan Poe.*

The beating of a dead man's heart beneath the floor . . . a woman buried alive . . . a dungeon equipped with rats underfoot and a razor-sharp pendulum overhead—these are some of the frightening details from this collection of Poe's masterpieces of horror.

In the Midst of Life, *by Ambrose Bierce.*

Before his disappearance in Mexico in 1913, Ambrose Bierce came to be called "Bitter Bierce." This collection of his short stories helps to explain that name. His acid humor is quite evident in these stories of soldiers and civilians.

Kiss Kiss, *by Roald Dahl.*

British author Roald Dahl has written many stories, several of which are based on his experiences in the Royal Air Force. But whether or not they are based on fact, Dahl's stories have an unusual twist that never fails to catch the reader's attention.

The Lottery, *by Shirley Jackson.*

Shirley Jackson's stories deal not with supernatural horrors, but with everyday ones of prejudice, intolerance, and insensitivity. In the title story a town stones to death one of its citizens only because it is a tradition that must be followed. Other stories in this collection are lighter and some are humorous.

Ten Modern American Short Stories, *David A. Sohn, ed.*

Most of these stories are about students. In "A Turn with the Sun" by John Knowles, a new boy in school struggles for recognition by the social elite. A high-school boy in "A Sense of Shelter," by John Updike, tries to tell a girl that he loves her. Other stories offer humor, sadness, and adventure.

The Martian Chronicles, *by Ray Bradbury.*

Mr. Bradbury has been called one of the best science fiction writers. He lives up to that title in this chronicle of Earthmen on Mars from the years 1999 to 2026, during which they attempt to build a new civilization.

POETRY

HOW DOES POETRY differ from prose? The difference is not that one uses plain "prosy" words and the other fancy "poetic" words. Language could hardly be more simple than this:

> Whose woods these are I think I know.
> His house is in the village though;
> He will not see me stopping here
> To watch his woods fill up with snow.

Thirty words in all, and not a one of them difficult; in fact, all but two are words of one syllable. So what makes those four lines poetry, whereas the words surrounding them here are prose?

For one thing, the sound they make, arranged as they are, is special. In this case, every other syllable is stressed: *woods, are, think, know,* and so on to the end. Prose doesn't set up such rhythms, and consequently prose is generally less pleasing to the ear.

Yet there are poems that do not have stresses falling as regularly as do the stresses in those four lines. Nor do they have rhyme, as those lines do: *know* rhyming with *though* and *snow.* Neither the American Indian poems nor the poems by Carl Sandburg that follow make use of rhyme or regular stresses; yet we regard them as poetry. Why?

Mostly it is a matter of the way they use language. The words in a poem are charged with meaning. In the fourth line quoted above, for instance, consider "fill up." To fill up a pitcher of milk is prose; to fill woods up with snow is poetry—a way of speaking that we recognize as unusual and even magical, though we may do so less with our minds than with our hearts.

Philip McFarland

Sound

The poet listens carefully to the sounds of words and, like a musician, he arranges them according to melody and rhythm. Listen for the music in these poems.

JAZZ FANTASIA
CARL SANDBURG

Drum on your drums, batter on your banjos, sob on the long cool winding saxophones. Go to it, O jazzmen.

Sling your knuckles on the bottoms of the happy tin pans, let your trombones ooze, and go husha-husha-hush with the slippery sandpaper.

Moan like an autumn wind high in the lonesome treetops, moan soft like you wanted somebody terrible, cry like a racing car slipping away from a motorcycle-cop bang-bang! you jazzmen, bang altogether drums, traps, banjos, horns, tin cans—make two people fight on the top of a stairway and scratch each other's eyes in a clinch tumbling down the stairs.

Can the rough stuff. . . . Now a Mississippi steamboat pushes up the night river with a hoo-hoo-hoo-oo . . . and the green lanterns calling to the high soft white stars . . . a red moon rides on the humps of the low river hills. . . . Go to it, O jazzmen.

FOR DISCUSSION

1. "Jazz Fantasia" has neither rhyme nor a regular pattern of rhythm. How can you tell it is poetry?

2. When words imitate the sound they stand for, the effect is called *onomatopoeia*. Some examples are "buzz," "swish," and "cuckoo." What examples of onomatopoeic words can you find from the poem?

3. Although a line like "sling your knuckles on the bottoms of the happy tin pans" does not imitate sounds exactly, it strongly suggests the quick sharp rhythm of knuckles on pie plates. What tempo, volume, and mood are suggested in other lines? At what points does the music change suddenly?

FOR COMPOSITION

• Go to any place where there are many sounds (repairmen, birds, traffic, water, etc.). Describe what you hear, making up your own onomatopoeic words as needed. You may write your description in prose, or like "Jazz Fantasia," in *free verse:* poetry without a regular pattern of rhyme or rhythm.

A grocery list is not usually considered poetry. But the next two poems are lists of groceries and merchandise—words chosen for their exotic sounds and arranged with an ear for their rhythm.

JAMAICA MARKET
AGNES MAXWELL-HALL

Honey, pepper, leaf-green limes,
Pagan fruit whose names are rhymes,
Mangoes, breadfruit, ginger roots,
Granadillas, bamboo shoots,
Cho-cho, ackees, tangerines,   5
Lemons, purple Congo beans,
Sugar, okras, kola nuts,
Citrons, hairy cocoanuts,
Fish, tobacco, native hats,
Gold bananas, woven mats,   10
Plantains, wild thyme, pallid leeks,
Pigeons with their scarlet beaks,
Oranges and saffron yams,
Baskets, ruby guava jams,
Turtles, goat skins, cinnamon,   15
Allspice, conch shells, golden rum.
Black skins, babel—and the sun
That burns all colors into one.

FOR COMPOSITION

1. Mark the stressed and unstressed syllables of the poem. (For example, Jack and Jill went up the hill / to fetch a pail of water.) This pattern of stressed sounds in poetry is called *meter*. A combination of one accented (stressed) and one or more unaccented syllables is called a *foot*. The first line has four feet. Is the meter the same throughout the poem? Does it move quickly or slowly? What sounds from a tropical open-air market do you think it might be imitating?

2. What besides the rhythm makes "Jamaica Market" a poem rather than a random list of items? Does the poet seem to notice the appearance of the goods for sale, or only their names?

CARGOES

JOHN MASEFIELD

Quinquereme* of Nineveh* from distant Ophir*
Rowing home to haven in sunny Palestine,
With a cargo of ivory,
And apes and peacocks,
Sandalwood, cedarwood, and sweet white wine.   5

Stately Spanish galleon coming from the Isthmus,
Dipping through the tropics by the palm-green shores,
With a cargo of diamonds,
Emeralds, amethysts,
Topazes, and cinnamon, and gold moidores.*   10

Dirty British coaster with a salt-caked smokestack
Butting through the Channel in the mad March days,
With a cargo of Tyne coal,
Road-rail, pig-lead,
Firewood, ironware, and cheap tin trays.   15

---

¹ QUINQUEREME (kwin'kwǝ·rēm'): ancient ship having five rows of oars. NINEVEH (nin'ǝ·vǝ): ancient city on the Tigris River, in Asia Minor. OPHIR (ō'fer): ancient country rich in gold. ¹⁰ MOIDORES (moi·dōrz'): former Portuguese coins made of gold.

FOR DISCUSSION

1. Read "Cargoes" aloud, listening carefully. In which parts did your voice glide smoothly from word to word? In which part were you forced to stop abruptly between words? How do the differences in sound reflect the differences among the types of boats and their cargoes?

2. *Alliteration* is the repetition of the same sound at the beginning of two or more words in a line. "*Home* to *haven*" is one example.

What other examples can you find in this poem?

FOR COMPOSITION

• Choose a group of related words whose sounds you like and arrange them so they go well together. They do not have to rhyme or make sense unless you want them to. Some possibilities for long and unusual words are flowers, animals, towns and rivers, medicines, and foods. If you know another language, combine words from it with English ones.

NIGHT JOURNEY
THEODORE ROETHKE

Now as the train bears west,
Its rhythm rocks the earth,
And from my Pullman berth
I stare into the night
While others take their rest.　　　5
Bridges of iron lace,
A suddenness of trees,
A lap of mountain mist
All cross my line of sight,
Then a bleak wasted place,　　　10
And a lake below my knees.
Full on my neck I feel
The straining at a curve;
My muscles move with steel,
I wake in every nerve.　　　15
I watch a beacon swing
From dark to blazing bright;
We thunder through ravines
And gullies washed with light.
Beyond the mountain pass　　　20
Mist deepens on the pane;
We rush into a rain
That rattles double glass.

"Night Journey," copyright 1940 by Theodore Roethke, from *The Collected Poems of Theodore Roethke*. Reprinted by permission of Doubleday & Company, Inc.

Wheels shake the roadbed stone,
The pistons jerk and shove,   25
I stay up half the night
To see the land I love.

FOR DISCUSSION

1. How does the rhythm of the poem suggest a train trip? (Rhythm includes not only meter, but alliteration, onomatopoeia, pauses, harshness or softness of words—anything that is part of the sound of the poem.)

2. "A suddenness of trees" suggests the way sights seem to flash past a train window. A plane, of course, is high above trees, and a car often travels more slowly or at a greater distance from the landscape. What other lines from the poem describe sights and feelings that make train travel different from other means of transportation?

FOR COMPOSITION

• List some of the sights, sounds, and feelings of a trip by plane, boat, car, bicycle, skis, or foot (hiking, climbing, or running). You might make the list more vivid by using comparisons such as "bridges of *iron lace*" or "We *thunder* through ravines." If you have time, try arranging your impressions into a poem.

THE RAVEN

EDGAR ALLAN POE

Once upon a midnight dreary, while I pondered, weak and weary,
Over many a quaint and curious volume of forgotten lore—
While I nodded, nearly napping, suddenly there came a tapping,
As of someone gently rapping, rapping at my chamber door.
" 'Tis some visitor," I muttered, "tapping at my chamber door—   5
   Only this and nothing more."

Ah, distinctly I remember it was in the bleak December,
And each separate dying ember wrought its ghost upon the floor.
Eagerly I wished the morrow; vainly I had sought to borrow
From my books surcease of sorrow—sorrow for the lost Lenore,   10
For the rare and radiant maiden whom the angels name Lenore—
   Nameless *here* for evermore.

And the silken, sad, uncertain rustling of each purple curtain
Thrilled me, filled me with fantastic terrors never felt before;
So that now, to still the beating of my heart, I stood repeating,   15
" 'Tis some visitor entreating entrance at my chamber door,
Some late visitor entreating entrance at my chamber door—
   This it is and nothing more."

Presently my soul grew stronger; hesitating then no longer,
"Sir," said I, "or Madam, truly your forgiveness I implore,   20
But the fact is I was napping, and so gently you came rapping,
And so faintly you came tapping, tapping at my chamber door,
That I scarce was sure I heard you"—here I opened wide the door—
   Darkness there and nothing more.

Deep into that darkness peering, long I stood there wondering, fearing,   25
Doubting, dreaming dreams no mortal ever dared to dream before;
But the silence was unbroken, and the stillness gave no token,
And the only word there spoken was the whispered word, "Lenore?"
This I whispered, and an echo murmured back the word, "Lenore!"
   Merely this and nothing more.   30

Back into the chamber turning, all my soul within me burning,
Soon again I heard a tapping somewhat louder than before.
"Surely," said I, "surely that is something at my window lattice;
Let me see, then, what thereat is, and this mystery explore;
Let my heart be still a moment and this mystery explore—   35
   'Tis the wind and nothing more!"

Open here I flung the shutter, when, with many a flirt and flutter,
In there stepped a stately Raven of the saintly days of yore;
Not the least obeisance* made he; not a minute stopped or stayed he;
But, with mien* of lord or lady, perched above my chamber door,   40
Perched upon a bust of Pallas* just above my chamber door—
   Perched, and sat, and nothing more.

Then this ebony bird beguiling my sad fancy into smiling,
By the grave and stern decorum of the countenance it wore,
"Though thy crest be shorn and shaven, thou," I said, "art sure no craven;*   45
Ghastly grim and ancient Raven wandering from the Nightly shore,
Tell me what thy lordly name is on the Night's Plutonian* shore!"
   Quoth the Raven ,"Nevermore."

Much I marveled this ungainly fowl to hear discourse so plainly,
Though its answer little meaning, little relevancy bore;   50
For we cannot help agreeing that no living human being
Ever yet was blessed with seeing bird above his chamber door,
Bird or beast upon the sculptured bust above his chamber door,
   With such name as "Nevermore."

But the Raven, sitting lonely on the placid bust, spoke only   55
That one word, as if his soul in that one word he did outpour.
Nothing further then he uttered—not a feather then he fluttered—
Till I scarcely more than muttered, "Other friends have flown before;
On the morrow *he* will leave me, as my hopes have flown before."
   Then the bird said, "Nevermore."   60

Startled at the stillness broken by reply so aptly spoken,
"Doubtless," said I, "what it utters is its only stock and store
Caught from some unhappy master whom unmerciful Disaster
Followed fast and followed faster till his songs one burden bore,
Till the dirges* of his hope that melancholy burden bore   65
   Of 'Never—nevermore.' "

But the Raven still beguiling all my fancy into smiling,
Straight I wheeled a cushioned seat in front of bird and bust and door;
Then, upon the velvet sinking, I betook myself to linking
Fancy unto fancy, thinking what this ominous bird of yore—   70
What this grim, ungainly, ghastly, gaunt, and ominous bird of yore—
   Meant in croaking, "Nevermore."

---

[39] OBEISANCE (ō·bā′səns): deep bow.   [40] MIEN (mēn): air, manner.   [41] PAL-
LAS: Pallas Athena, Greek goddess of wisdom.   [45] CREST . . . CRAVEN: A
raven has no crest. The speaker is suggesting that the bird resembles a
person who has been humiliated for cowardice, although he really is no
coward.   [47] PLUTONIAN: hellish. In Greek mythology Pluto ruled the world
of the dead.   [65] DIRGES: funeral songs.

This I sat engaged in guessing, but no syllable expressing
To the fowl whose fiery eyes now burned into my bosom's core;
This and more I sat divining, with my head at ease reclining   75
On the cushion's velvet lining that the lamplight gloated o'er,
But whose velvet-violet lining with the lamplight gloating o'er,
   She shall press, ah, nevermore!

Then, methought, the air grew denser, perfumed from an unseen censer*
Swung by seraphim* whose footfalls tinkled on the tufted floor.   80
"Wretch," I cried, "thy God hath lent thee, by these angels he hath sent thee*
Respite,* respite and nepenthe* from thy memories of Lenore;
Quaff,* oh quaff this kind nepenthe and forget this lost Lenore!"
   Quoth the Raven, "Nevermore."

"Prophet!" said I, "thing of evil! Prophet still, if bird or devil,   85
Whether Tempter sent, or whether tempest tossed thee here ashore,
Desolate yet all undaunted, on this desert land enchanted,
On this home by Horror haunted; tell me truly, I implore,
Is there—*is* there balm in Gilead?*—tell me—tell me, I implore!"
   Quoth the Raven, "Nevermore."   90

"Prophet!" said I, "thing of evil! Prophet still, if bird or devil!
By that Heaven that bends above us—by that God we both adore—
Tell this soul with sorrow laden if, within the distant Aidenn,*
It shall clasp a sainted maiden whom the angels name Lenore,
Clasp a rare and radiant maiden whom the angels name Lenore."   95
   Quoth the Raven, "Nevermore."

"Be that word our sign of parting, bird or fiend!" I shrieked, upstarting.
"Get thee back into the tempest and the Night's Plutonian shore!
Leave no black plume as a token of that lie thy soul hath spoken!
Leave me loneliness unbroken! Quit the bust above my door!   100
Take thy beak from out my heart, and take thy form from off my door!"
   Quoth the Raven, "Nevermore."

---

79 CENSER: container for burning incense.   80 SERAPHIM: angels.   81 WRETCH
. . . SENT THEE: Here the speaker begins talking to himself, saying that he
ought to lose himself in the God-given dreams of the seraphim, forgetting
Lenore.   82 RESPITE (res'pət): temporary relief.   NEPENTHE (nə·pen'thē): in
ancient times, a medicine used to lessen suffering.   83 QUAFF: drink deeply.
89 BALM IN GILEAD: a reference to the biblical lament "Is there no balm in
Gilead?" meaning "Is there no relief from sufferings?" Balm is a healing
ointment, and Gilead was a part of ancient Israel.   93 AIDENN: heaven.

FOR DISCUSSION

1. Which is more impressive in this poem, *what* the poet says or *how* he says it?

2. This is an excellent poem for reading aloud because of its strong use of rhythm, rhyme, and repetition. Diagram the meter of the poem. Then diagram the rhyme scheme: "weary" would be *a,* "lore" *b,* "tapping" *c,* and "door" *b* again. What rhyme is repeated throughout the poem? Are there any other rhymes besides those at the ends of lines?

3. The repeated "nevermore" builds a mood of melancholy hopelessness. What are some other words from the poem that contribute to this mood?

FOR COMPOSITION

• A bird sitting above the door repeating one word endlessly is an unlikely subject for eighteen verses of poetry. What significance does the raven have for the narrator? At first he is amused at the raven; later he curses the bird as a "fiend" and "demon." Show how this change in attitude comes about.

HOUSE SONG TO THE EAST
TRADITIONAL NAVAHO SONG

Far in the east, far below, there a house was made;
    Delightful house.
God of Dawn, there his house was made;
    Delightful house.
The Dawn, there his house was made;   5
    Delightful house.
White Corn, there its house was made;
    Delightful house.
Soft possessions, for them a house was made;
    Delightful house.   10
Water in plenty, surrounding, for it a house was made;
    Delightful house.
Corn pollen, for it a house was made;
    Delightful house.
The ancients make their presence delightful;   15
    Delightful house.

Before me, may it be delightful.
Behind me, may it be delightful.
Around me, may it be delightful.
Below me, may it be delightful.   20
Above me, may it be delightful.
All [universally], may it be delightful.

From *Navaho Houses,* the 17th Annual Report of the Bureau of American Ethnology.
Reprinted by permission of the Smithsonian Institution. (1895).

FROM

THE PEOPLE, YES
CARL SANDBURG

What did Hiamovi, the red man, Chief of
    the Cheyennes, have?
To a great chief at Washington and to a
    chief of peoples across the waters,
    Hiamovi spoke: 5
"There are birds of many colors—red, blue,
    green, yellow,
Yet it is all one bird.
There are horses of many colors—brown,
    black, yellow, white,   10
Yet it is all one horse.
So cattle, so all living things, animals,
    flowers, trees.
So men in this land, where once were only
    Indians, are now men of many colors—   15
    white, black, yellow, red.
Yet all one people.
That this should come to pass was in the
    heart of the Great Mystery.
It is right thus—and everywhere there   20
    shall be peace."
Thus Hiamovi, out of a tarnished and weather-
    worn heart of old gold, out of a living
    dawn gold.

Image

While some poems are like music, others are more like paintings; they create pictures in the reader's mind. Words that appeal to the sense of sight or to any of the other senses are called *images*. Often a poet creates an image by comparing two things which are not usually considered alike. These implied comparisons, or *figurative language*, help to show familiar things in a new light.

THE PRODUCE DISTRICT
THOM GUNN

After the businesses had moved, before
The wrecking started
For the high-rise blocks:
An interim:
Whoever walked along these streets   5
Found it was shared with him
Only by pigeons, single or in flocks.

Where each night trucks had waited
By warehouse and worn ramp
With oranges or celery to unload,   10
Now it was smell of must, rot, fungus, damp.
The crumbling and decay accelerated,
Old mattresses and boards in heaps
Losing their colors with their shapes,
The smaller things   15
Blending the humus, on the road.
And silence—no, small creaks,
Small patterings,
While now, above, the thump and whirr of wings.
The pigeons, gray on gray,   20
In greater number
Than ever here before
Pecked round the rotting lumber,
Perched on the roofs and walls,

Or wheeled between the faded signs   25
And broken ornamental scrolls.
I watched the work of spiders, rats, and rain,
And turning onto Front Street found
I was not there alone.
He stood unmoving on the littered ground   30
In bright scrubbed denims
An airgun loosely in his hands
Staring at something overhead.

Shooting pigeons. I looked at his lined face,
Hard, ruddy, any age,   35
Cracking into a smile.
Short graying hair. He shrugged and said,
What's there to do on Sundays,
Sooner do this than booze.

I stood beside him while   40
He aimed at a parapet some forty-five yards off.
A bang. One pigeon as the others rose
A lump of fluff
Dropped from among them lightly to the street.
Cool air, high fog, and underfoot   45
Through soft mould, shapes felt like uneven root
Ridging a forest floor.
The place losing itself, lost now, unnamed,
Birds wheeling back, with a low threshing sound.
He aimed   50
And then once more
I heard the gun repeat
Its accurate answer to the wilderness,
Echoing it and making it complete.
The maple shoots pushed upwards through the ground.   55

FOR DISCUSSION

1. Which images in the poem appeal to the sense of smell? of hearing? of touch? From those that appeal to the sense of sight, which ones can you see in your mind most clearly?

2. "The Produce District" is filled with images of destruction and decay. Which ones do you think are most effective in building the mood of the poem?

Even the shape of a poem can help to create an image.

BEAUTIFUL
E. E. CUMMINGS

Beautiful

is the
unmea
ning
of(sil   5

ently)fal

ling(e
ver
yw
here)s   10

Now

FOR DISCUSSION

• Write out Cummings's poem in a regular sentence. Why did he write it as he did? These questions may help you:

   a. How do your eyes move as you read the poem? What does that have to do with its subject?

   b. Why is "falling" spaced as it is?

   c. Why is "everywhere" spaced over four lines?

   d. What is the double meaning of the last two lines?

From *95 Poems,* © 1958 by E. E. Cummings. Reprinted by permission of Harcourt Brace Jovanovich, Inc.

THE RANCHER

KEITH WILSON

Hard old gray eyes, no pity
in him after years branding cattle—
a cruel man with cows & men

he drove both hard & once
when he was 70 tried to kill   5
a young puncher for smiling at his

old wife, sat down & cried in fury
because his grown sons took his
ivoryhandled .45 away, held

his head in his arms & didn't   10
ever come back to the dance.
After awhile his wife went slowly

out into the clear night
saying how late it is getting
now isn't it? without   15

pity for his eyes, him showing
nothing the next morning
barking at the hands to get

popping, the sun already up,
coffee on the fire & him   20
stifflegged, hard pot hanging

over the saddlehorn, he led
fall's last drive
across the hazy range.

FOR DISCUSSION

• A short story might take many pages to show what this poem suggests in a much smaller space. One form of "shorthand" the poet uses is vivid images. Which images show the rancher's pride? his humiliation? his toughness?

SONG OF THE SKY LOOM

TRADITIONAL TEWA SONG

O our Mother the Earth, O our Father the Sky,
Your children are we, and with tired backs
We bring you the gifts that you love.
Then weave for us a garment of brightness;
May the warp be the white light of morning,   5
May the weft be the red light of evening,
May the fringes be the falling rain,
May the border be the standing rainbow.
Thus weave for us a garment of brightness
That we may walk fittingly where birds sing,   10
That we may walk fittingly where grass is green,
O our Mother the Earth, O our Father the Sky!

FOR DISCUSSION

• "Song of the Sky Loom" is a religious song of the Tewa Indians, who depended on rain from the sky for their food supply. Why do you think they compare the sky to a blanket loom rather than to the ocean or to a herd of sheep? How does each part of the blanket correspond to part of the sky?

FOR COMPOSITION

• Figurative language may take the form of a metaphor (implied comparison) or simile (stated comparison using "like" or "as"). "Song of the Sky Loom" is a metaphor. If it were written, "The Sky is *like* a loom on which a bright garment is woven," or "The sky is *as* beautiful *as* a bright garment," then it would be a simile. Find a picture or photograph that interests you and describe it by writing as many similes and metaphors as you can think of.

From *Songs of the Tewa* by Herbert Joseph Spinden. Copyright 1933 by Herbert Joseph Spinden. Published under the auspices of the Exposition of Indian Tribal Arts, Inc.

SALE TODAY

PHYLLIS McGINLEY

What syrup, what unusual sweet,
   Sticky and sharp and strong,
Wafting its poison through the street,
   Has lured this buzzing throng
That swarms along the counters there
   Where bargain bait is dangled—
Clustered like flies in honeyed snare,
   Shrill, cross, and well entangled?

FOR DISCUSSION

• What metaphor does the poet use to describe the shoppers? What attitude toward the shoppers and the sale is suggested by the metaphor?

"Sale Today" from the book *A Pocketful of Wry*, by Phyllis McGinley. Copyright © 1940 by Phyllis McGinley. Reprinted by permission of Hawthorne Books, 70 Fifth Ave., N.Y., N.Y.

A PATCH OF OLD SNOW
ROBERT FROST

There's a patch of old snow in a corner,
    That I should have guessed
Was a blow-away paper the rain
    Had brought to rest.

It is speckled with grime as if
    Small print overspread it,
The news of a day I've forgotten—
    If I ever read it.

FOR DISCUSSION

• What attitude about "the news of the day"

does Frost's metaphor imply? Consider every detail of the snow image: old, grimy, melting.

THREE JET PLANES
MAY SWENSON

Three jet planes skip above the roofs
    through a tri-square of blue
    tattooed by TV crossbars
    that lean in cryptic concert in their wake.

Like skaters on a lake   5
    combined into perfect arrowhead up there
    they sever space with bloodless speed
    and are gone without a clue

but a tiny bead the eye can scarcely find
leaving behind   10
where they first burst into blue
the invisible boiling wind of sound

As horsemen used to do
As horsemen used to gallop through
    a hamlet on hunting morn   15
    and heads and arms were thrust
    through windows
    leaving behind them the torn
    shriek of the hound
    and their wrestling dust   20

Above the roofs three jet planes
    leave their hoofs of violence on naive ground.

FOR DISCUSSION
• A figure of speech which gives human characteristics to something not human is called *personification*. The jet planes are personified in two similes: *"like* skaters on a lake" and *"As* horsemen used to do." How are the planes similar to skaters and horsemen?

FOR COMPOSITION
• Personify several nonhuman things or ideas.

Your personification may take the form of a simile ("The stream laughed like a happy child") or a metaphor ("The laughing stream danced over the rocks.") Some subjects you might choose are: the wind, the ocean, rain, an old car, an abandoned house, a flock of geese, war, prejudice, music, spring.

CORNER
RALPH POMEROY

The cop slumps alertly on his motorcycle,
Supported by one leg like a leather stork.
His glance accuses me of loitering.
I can see his eyes moving like a fish
In the green depths of his green goggles.   5

His ease is fake. I can tell.
My ease is fake. And he can tell.
The fingers armored by his gloves
Splay and clench, itching to change something.

As if he were my enemy or my death,   10
I just standing there watching.
I spit out my gum which has gone stale.
I knock out a new cigarette—
Which is my bravery.
It is all imperceptible: 15
The way I shift my weight,
The way he creaks in his saddle.

The traffic is specific though constant.
The sun surrounds me, divides the street between us.
His crash helmet is whiter in the shade.   20
It is like a bull ring as they say it is just before the fighting.
I cannot back down. I am there.

Everything holds me back.
I am in danger of disappearing into the sunny dust.
My levis bake and my T shirt sweats.   25

My cigarette makes my eyes burn.
But I don't dare drop it.

Who made him my enemy?
Prince of coolness. King of fear.
Why do I lean here waiting?   30
Why does he lounge there watching?

I am becoming sunlight.
My hair is on fire. My boots run like tar.
I am hung-up by the bright air.

Something breaks through all of a sudden,   35
And he blasts off, quick as a craver,
Smug in his power; watching me watch.

FOR DISCUSSION

1. What images does the narrator use to describe the cop? How do they reveal his attitude toward his "enemy"? Is he completely sure of his attitude?

2. Which image did you find most effective in building the feeling of tension between the two characters?

IDEAS AND THE ARTS

A famous English writer once said that it is more civilized to enjoy the shadow of a blade of grass upon a stone than to be overwhelmed by the spectacle of Niagara Falls. This observation raises an interesting question: Why do we tend to think that something large must be of great value? We often say, "the bigger the better," and this seems to make sense until we apply it to a real example. We might ask, "Is a large but imperfect flower better than a small but perfect one?" or "Is a large but imperfect novel better than a small but perfect short story?" These are questions that can be answered equally well with "yes" or "no." In other words, they cannot be answered at all. When we come upon questions like these, we should try not to answer them but to discover why they are asked and what they signify.

Nothing in the world is valuable in itself. Whatever is valuable is so only because human beings say it is valuable. Value is not a quality like redness or coldness that all people with normal nervous systems will agree on. It is, instead, a quality that people attribute or give to things. And the most common way of showing that something man-made is valuable is to make it big. The palaces of kings have always been made large to show how valuable the king or the kingdom is. Churches are often the largest buildings in towns to express the value of religion. And business corporations often build vast headquarters, larger than they need, to show the value of the corporation.

It is, of course, not logical to say that what is large is also valuable, but then human beings are not always logical. When the English writer said that the shadow of a blade of grass upon a stone is more valuable than Niagara Falls, he was objecting to the faulty logic that connects largeness with value.

The shadow of a blade of grass upon a stone is what we call an "image." It is just the opposite of a "spectacle," such as Niagara Falls or the skyline of a mountain range. A spectacle includes innumerable details, so many that we cannot see them all. A spectacle is too big for us to grasp and comprehend. It is wider than our field of vision or our field of understanding.

An image is just the opposite. From the infinite details of the world it presents just one detail. That detail is isolated, and because of that isolation we can examine it without becoming confused and distracted by other details. We can concentrate our attention upon it with all the powers of our observation. Because of that isolation and concentration, we can see an image clearly and understand it. We can find meaning in it, and by finding meaning in it we give it value. For these reasons, poets and painters often concentrate the whole meaning of poems and paintings in an image. That concentrated meaning has more power than it would have if it were spread over a large work.

Morse Peckham

ART

Many painters like to paint spectacles, huge canvases or wall murals, often crowded with details. Other painters are like lyric poets. These painters like to concentrate on single images to make them intense and valuable. They prefer to work on small canvases, with few details. Still others create small or middle-sized pictures in which all kinds of details are tucked away in relatively unimportant parts of the picture.

Tom Wesselmann is a contemporary American painter. His *Still-Life No. 34* is part of a very long tradition. A still life is a picture of ordinary, everyday objects. A common subject is flowers, but various kinds of foods are also popular. Some painters use dishes, teapots, and vases. Here Wesselmann has made the Coca-Cola bottle the most important element in his composition. Nothing could be more commonplace, except most of the other things he has included. He has made the bottle interesting by echoing all of its shapes and curves elsewhere in the picture, and by so doing he has given it value.

Jan Vermeer was a Dutch painter of the seventeenth century. He painted small pictures, usually of interiors. He gave them life and intensity through his use of light. He would concentrate on a particular image, although he also used other images within each painting. Thus his paintings contain numerous images that can be looked at and enjoyed in their own right. The first image here is from *Girl with Wine Glass and Two Gentlemen.* It is of a window that is made of pieces of old glass set in new glass. This gives Vermeer a chance not only to paint two kinds of glass but also to paint light coming through the glass.

The next is from *The Artist in His Studio.* You can see the top of the painter's easel in the lower right hand corner of this detail. Here Vermeer has concentrated on two things. First, the brass chandelier gives him a chance to paint reflected light. These bits of reflected light give life and sparkle to the whole painting. On the wall is a map of the Low Countries, now Holland and Belgium, and of a bit of Northern France. The map is made with the west at the top. This map allows him to include someone else's creation in his own. He makes the map another kind of picture by using its folds and bulges to bring out the play of light and shadow.

The third detail from Vermeer is found in his *Lady Seated at the Virginal.* Musical instruments are often used in still lifes because painters have felt a relationship between color, light, and shape in painting and rhythm, harmony, and melody in music. Here Vermeer has painted the end of the pianolike virginal and a viola da gamba, the ancestor of the modern cello. The color of the wood, the glow of its polish, the geometry of the strings, and the body of the viola are here the subjects of his concentration.

Francisco de Zurbarán was a Spanish painter who lived sometime before Vermeer. He painted this picture when the still life was just coming into prominence. Before this, as with Vermeer, the single, glowing image was part of a larger picture. The still-life painters took these details from larger paintings and began to use them as subjects for separate paintings. Here Zurbarán has arranged some vases and a metal bowl and several plates so that the light came from the left. Then he was able to concentrate on the charm of their shapes and colors brought out by the cross-light.

William Harnett was an American painter who worked in the last part of the nineteenth century. He painted a special kind of still life, known as *trompe-l'oeil* painting, which means "fool the eye" painting.

After the Hunt is a good example. The painting is so realistic that from a little distance you are not quite sure whether it is a painting or a collection of real objects. In this kind of painting, the painter himself seems to be eliminated. The viewer becomes interested in the objects themselves, the way they are put together and the abstract design they make. Harnett, the painter, is probably more interested in the composition of curves, lines and shapes than he is in the objects themselves. Yet like all painters who are interested in the image, he likes to paint things that have great emotional meaning for us. But we are often not aware of these meanings until we see them isolated by a fine painter.

Morse Peckham

TOM WESSELMANN (born 1931) *STILL-LIFE NO. 34.* Collection of Mr. and Mrs. Jack W. Glenn, Laguna Beach, California.

JAN VERMEER (1632-1675) *GIRL WITH WINE GLASS AND TWO GENTLEMEN* (detail). Herzog Anton Ulrich-Museum, Brunswick, Germany.

236

Photo: Art Reference Bureau

JAN VERMEER (1632-1675) *THE ARTIST IN HIS STUDIO* (detail). Kunsthistorisches Museum, Vienna.

JAN VERMEER (1632-1675) *LADY SEATED AT THE VIRGINAL* (detail). National Gallery, London.

FRANCISCO DE ZURBARÁN (1598-1664) *STILL-LIFE.* Prado Museum, Madrid.

WILLIAM HARNETT (1848-1892) *AFTER THE HUNT.* California Palace of the Legion of Honor, San Francisco.

MUSIC

CLAUDE DEBUSSY:
IBÉRIA
[A number of recordings available]

Poetry and painting often isolate bits and pieces of the world in what we call "images." This isolation leads us to concentrate on single details, making these details more intense and meaningful. Music can do the same thing by presenting bits and pieces of the aural world, the world that comes to us through our sense of hearing.

The special sound of an instrument is called its "timbre" (tăm′bər), one of the basic elements of music. When two instruments are played together, they can produce a timbre that no single instrument can produce. Another element is rhythm. Composers often write whole pieces or short passages which concentrate the listener's attention on the rhythm. Rhythm is the regular repetition of a sound. A third element is volume, the loudness or softness with which music is played. With a full symphony orchestra the range of volume is enormous. The composer can use a single instrument playing very softly, or he can call for all the instruments, perhaps a hundred or so, to play all at the same time as loudly as they can. Sudden contrasts between loudness and softness can make us concentrate on volume for its own sake. A fourth element is speed. A great many notes played in a very short time give a sense of speed. A composer can make us concentrate on the element of speed by contrasting very fast passages with very slow ones. A fifth element is pitch: whether the musical sound is what we call "high" or "low." Sixth, and finally, there is the element of melody. Melody, very simply, is a sequence of musical sounds in constantly changing pitch. A composer concentrates attention on melody by repeating it.

French composer Claude Debussy was intensely interested in the sound of music as something interesting and exciting in its own right. He liked to select single elements of music and to concentrate attention on them. Thus his music is highly imagistic. An excellent example is found in his work for orchestra called *Ibéria,* a name for Spain. The work is in three parts: Part I is called "Along the Streets and Alleys"; Part II, "The Perfumes of the Night"; Part III, "The Morning of a Holiday." To give the feeling of Spain he uses Spanish melodies and rhythms. But he is not trying to write Spanish music. Nor is he trying to create musical pictures. What he is trying to do is to create musical sounds that will have the same effect on a listener as actual sights might on a visitor to Spain. He is using aural imagery.

A tourist in a strange country is constantly attracted by bits and pieces of his surroundings. Not being used to the country, he is struck by individual images. To recreate the impressions of a visitor, Debussy does not create massive sounds. He almost never uses the whole orchestra at once. Instead, he will isolate a rhythm and play with it. Or he will pick out a brief melody and repeat it two or three times. Or he will select a single instrument and concentrate on it, just as a tourist in a crowded marketplace might pick out one image for his concentration. Occasionally he uses sounds one might actually hear. At the end of Part II and at the beginning of Part III we hear the church bells of a religious holiday. We hear trumpets that suggest a procession. At the same time we hear an exciting rhythm that suggests the excitement of the crowds.

Morse Peckham

In this poem and the one following, two children live in imaginary worlds unknown to their parents.

THE DREAMER
WILLIAM CHILDRESS

He spent his childhood hours in a den
of rushes, watching the gray rain braille
the surface of the river. Concealed
from the outside world, nestled within,
he was safe from parents, God, and eyes   5
that looked upon him accusingly,
as though to say: Even at your age,
you could do better. His camouflage
was scant, but it served, and at evening,
when fireflies burned holes into heaven,   10
he took the path homeward in the dark,
a small Noah, leaving his safe ark.

FOR DISCUSSION

1. What images of safety does the poet use to describe the child's feeling for his hiding place?

2. What dangers could a small child have to hide from? Are they real or imagined? Does the poet say?

THE CENTAUR

MAY SWENSON

The summer that I was ten—
Can it be there was only one
summer that I was ten? It must

have been a long one then—
each day I'd go out to choose   5
a fresh horse from my stable

which was a willow grove
down by the old canal.
I'd go on my two bare feet.

But when, with my brother's jack-knife,   10
I had cut me a long limber horse
with a good thick knob for a head,

and peeled him slick and clean
except a few leaves for the tail.
and cinched my brother's belt   15

around his head for a rein,
I'd straddle and canter him fast
up the grass bank to the path,

trot along in the lovely dust
that talcumed over his hoofs,   20
hiding my toes, and turning

his feet to swift half-moons.
The willow knob with the strap
jouncing between my thighs

was the pommel* and yet the poll*   25
of my nickering pony's head.
My head and my neck were mine,

²⁵ POMMEL: upper front part of a saddle.   ²⁵ POLL: top of the head.

yet they were shaped like a horse.
My hair flopped to the side
like the mane of a horse in the wind.   30

My forelock* swung in my eyes,
my neck arched and I snorted.
I shied and skittered and reared,

stopped and raised my knees,
pawed at the ground and quivered.   35
My teeth bared as we wheeled

and swished through the dust again.
I was the horse and the rider,
and the leather I slapped to his rump

spanked my own behind.   40
Doubled, my two hoofs beat
a gallop along the bank,

the wind twanged in my mane,
my mouth squared to the bit.
And yet I sat on my steed   45

quiet, negligent riding,
my toes standing the stirrups,
my thighs hugging his ribs.

At a walk we drew up to the porch.
I tethered* him to a paling.   50
Dismounting, I smoothed my skirt

and entered the dusky hall.
My feet on the clean linoleum
left ghostly toes in the hall.

Where have you been? said my mother.   55
Been riding, I said from the sink,
and filled me a glass of water.

What's that in your pocket? she said.
Just my knife. It weighted my pocket
and stretched my dress awry.   60

---

31 forelock: lock of hair that grows or falls on the forehead.   50 tethered:
tied loosely in order to permit some freedom of movement.

Go tie back your hair, said my mother,
and *Why is your mouth all green?*
*Rob Roy, he pulled some clover
as we crossed the field,* I told her.

FOR DISCUSSION

• There seems to be a contradiction in this poem. Who is the horse? Who is the rider? This kind of apparent contradiction is called a *paradox.* The poet emphasizes it in lines like "the leather I slapped to his rump spanked my own behind." Where else is it emphasized? What does this show about a child's imagination?

FOR COMPOSITION

• Choose some memory from your younger days and share it with the class: a hiding place, a game, a fear, a pet, a friendship. You may tell it in prose or in free verse—either way, include some figurative language. (You may want to reread "The Dreamer" and "The Centaur" before you begin.)

BEACH ALONG L STREET
CHIANG YEE

Sea and sky are one color without horizon.
A lonely seagull repeatedly examines me
Asking suddenly who is more leisurely.
"Well, either you or me," echoed I.

A strong wind, and the seagull can no longer stand.
He has to ride the wind and go
Up and up, floating in the air.
How is it better than my freedom?

FOR DISCUSSION

• A seagull soaring usually suggests freedom. What is the unexpected answer to the question in the last line?

Reprinted from *The Silent Traveller in Boston.* Written and illustrated by Chiang Yee. By permission of W. W. Norton & Company, Inc. Copyright © 1959 by W. W. Norton & Company, Inc.

Mood

The poems in this section are less concerned with showing you a scene or experience than they are with sharing the poet's thoughts and feelings. These passing thoughts and feelings make up a mood: sorrow, joy, weariness, reverence. Short, personal poems which communicate emotion or mood are called *lyric poems*. In ancient Greece such poems were accompanied by a harplike instrument called a lyre.

A LOON I THOUGHT IT WAS
TRADITIONAL CHIPPEWA SONG

A loon I thought it was,
But it was my love's splashing oar.
To Sault Ste. Marie he has departed,
My love has gone on before me,
Never again can I see him.
A loon I thought it was,
But it was my love's splashing oar.

From *The American Indians and Their Music* by Frances Densmore. Johnson Reprint Corporation.

THE CRAZY WOMAN
GWENDOLYN BROOKS

I shall not sing a May song.
A May song should be gay.
I'll wait until November
And sing a song of gray.

I'll wait until November.　　　5
That is the time for me.
I'll go out in the frosty dark
And sing most terribly.

And all the little people
Will stare at me and say,　　　10
"That is the Crazy Woman
Who would not sing in May."

DUST OF SNOW
ROBERT FROST

The way a crow
Shook down on me
The dust of snow
From a hemlock tree

Has given my heart
A change of mood
And saved some part
Of a day I had rued.*

8 RUED: regretted.

LOVELIEST OF TREES

A. E. HOUSMAN

Loveliest of trees, the cherry now
Is hung with bloom along the bough,
And stands about the woodland ride
Wearing white for Eastertide.

Now, of my threescore years and ten,   5
Twenty will not come again,
And take from seventy springs a score,
It only leaves me fifty more.

And since to look at things in bloom
Fifty springs are little room,   10
About the woodlands I will go
To see the cherry hung with snow.

FOR DISCUSSION
• What mood is communicated by each of these four poems? What image from nature is used to express the mood in each one?

LAMENT OF A MAN FOR HIS SON

TRADITIONAL INDIAN SONG

Son, my son!

I will go up to the mountain
And there I will light a fire
To the feet of my son's spirit,
And there will I lament him;   5
Saying,
O my son,
What is my life to me, now you are departed!

Son, my son,
In the deep earth   10
We softly laid thee in a Chief's robe,
In a warrior's gear.
Surely there,
In the spirit land
Thy deeds attend thee!   15
Surely,
The corn comes to the ear again!

But I, here,
I am the stalk that the seed-gatherers
Descrying empty, afar, left standing.   20
Son, my son!
What is my life to me, now you are departed!

FOR DISCUSSION

1. How are the father's feelings emphasized by the repeated lyrics?

2. Explain the metaphors, "Surely, the corn comes to the ear again!" and "I am the (empty) stalk that the seed-gatherers . . . left standing." In the midst of his sorrow, what other emotion does the father feel?

THOSE WINTER SUNDAYS

ROBERT HAYDEN

Sundays too my father got up early
and put his clothes on in the blueblack cold,
then with cracked hands that ached
from labor in the weekday weather made
banked fires blaze. No one ever thanked him.   5

I'd wake and hear the cold splintering, breaking.
When the rooms were warm, he'd call,
and slowly I would rise and dress,
fearing the chronic angers of that house,

Speaking indifferently to him,   10
who had driven out the cold
and polished my good shoes as well.
What did I know, what did I know
of love's austere and lonely offices?

FOR DISCUSSION

• "Offices" as used in this poem may mean an act performed for another or a religious service. It comes from a Latin word meaning performance of duty. "Austere" means stern, strict, or plain. What kind of man was the father? How did the narrator feel about his father when he was a boy? How have his feelings changed as he tells the poem? What emotion is suggested by the repetition of "What did I know"?

TRAVELING THROUGH THE DARK
WILLIAM STAFFORD

Traveling through the dark I found a deer
dead on the edge of the Wilson River road.
It is usually best to roll them into the canyon:
that road is narrow; to swerve might make more dead.

By glow of the tail-light I stumbled back of the car   5
and stood by the heap, a doe, a recent killing;
she had stiffened already, almost cold.
I dragged her off; she was large in the belly.

My fingers touching her side brought me the reason—
her side was warm; her fawn lay there waiting,   10
alive, still, never to be born.
Beside that mountain road I hesitated.

The car aimed ahead its lowered parking lights;
under the hood purred the steady engine.
I stood in the glare of the warm exhaust turning red;   15
around our group I could hear the wilderness listen.

I thought hard for us all—my only swerving—,
then pushed her over the edge into the river.

FOR DISCUSSION

1. The first stanza is unemotional, matter-of-fact. What is the logical thing to do with the deer?

2. How are the next three stanzas different in feeling from the first? What sense does the poet appeal to? Why does he hesitate before pushing the deer over?

3. What thoughts and emotions are suggested in the last stanza? Who are "us all"?

FOR COMPOSITION

• Choose one of the preceding poems in this section on "Mood." Explain the mood of the poem, then tell of some experience of your own when you had similar thoughts and feelings. Compare your experience with that described in the poem.

STOPPING BY WOODS ON A SNOWY EVENING
ROBERT FROST

Whose woods these are I think I know.
His house is in the village though;
He will not see me stopping here
To watch his woods fill up with snow.

My little horse must think it queer   5
To stop without a farmhouse near
Between the woods and frozen lake
The darkest evening of the year.

He gives his harness bells a shake
To ask if there is some mistake.   10
The only other sound's the sweep
Of easy wind and downy flake.

The woods are lovely, dark and deep,
But I have promises to keep,
And miles to go before I sleep,   15
And miles to go before I sleep.

FOR DISCUSSION

1. Why does the speaker stop by the woods? (His reason is apparently one that neither his horse nor the owner of the woods would understand.)

2. What are his feelings about the woods and about the "promises" toward which he is driving?

3. How does the repetition of the last line add to the mood of the poem?

THEIR LONELY BETTERS

W. H. AUDEN

As I listened from a beach-chair in the shade
To all the noises that my garden made,
It seemed to me only proper that words
Should be withheld from vegetables and birds.

A robin with no Christian name ran through   5
The Robin-Anthem which was all it knew,
And rustling flowers for some third party waited
To say which pairs, if any, should get mated.

No one of them was capable of lying,
There was not one which knew that it was dying   10
Or could have with a rhythm or a rhyme
Assumed responsibility for time.

Let them leave language to their lonely betters
Who count some days and long for certain letters;
We, too, make noises when we laugh or weep,   15
Words are for those with promises to keep.

FOR DISCUSSION

1. Auden's poem and Frost's end with the same phrase. How is the contrast between man and nature (animals) in this poem similar to that in "Stopping by Woods on a Snowy Evening"?

2. Stanza two suggests some ways that human beings are the "betters" of plants and animals: they have individual identities (a "Christian name" is a person's first name, which sets him apart from other members of his family) and they can make choices (the flowers must wait for a "third party," wind or a bee, to be mated). In stanza three, however, "better" seems to be ironic. In what ways are human beings not better?

3. *Language* is the key to the difference between human beings and other forms of life.

Without language, birds and flowers can't notice time or know they are dying or hope for letters. How do these differences make people "lonely"?

FOR COMPOSITION

• Poets often, through personification, use language such as "the lonely breeze crying through the trees" or "happy crickets fiddling away." "Stopping by Woods on a Snowy Evening" and "Their Lonely Betters," on the other hand emphasize that human emotions are not from nature. In what ways does having a *language* (spoken or written) make a human being different from being a plant or animal? Begin with the differences suggested in the poems and see how much further you can explore the idea.

Irony

In the short space of a poem a writer can make dramatic ironic contrasts—between what is expected and what really happens, between what is said and what is meant, between the way things are and the way they ought to be . . . .

THOSE TWO BOYS
FRANKLIN P. ADAMS

When Bill was a lad he was terribly bad.
    He worried his parents a lot;
He'd lie and he'd swear and pull little girls' hair;
    His boyhood was naught but a blot.

At play and in school he would fracture each rule—   5
    In mischief from autumn to spring;
And the villagers knew when to manhood he grew
    He would never amount to a thing.

When Jim was a child he was not very wild;
    He was known as a good little boy;   10
He was honest and bright and the teacher's delight—
    To his mother and father a joy.

All the neighbors were sure that his virtue'd endure,
    That his life would be free of a spot;
They were certain that Jim had a great head on him   15
    And that Jim would amount to a lot.

And Jim grew to manhood and honor and fame
    And bears a good name;
While Bill is shut up in a dark prison cell—
    You never can tell.   20

FOR DISCUSSION

1. What is there ironic about this poem?

2. How does the change in meter in the last stanza set it off from the rest of the poem? Why do you think the poet did this?

From *Tobogganing on Parnassus* by Franklin P. Adams, copyright 1911 by Doubleday & Company, Inc. Reprinted by permission of the publisher.

JOHN AND JANE

THOMAS HARDY

He sees the world as a boisterous place
Where all things bear a laughing face,
And humorous scenes go hourly on,
    Does John.

They find the world a pleasant place   5
Where all is ecstasy and grace,
Where a light has risen that cannot wane,
    Do John and Jane.

They see as a palace their cottage-place,
Containing a pearl of the human race,   10
A hero, maybe, hereafter styled,
    Do John and Jane with a baby-child.

They rate the world as a gruesome place,
Where fair looks fade to a skull's grimace—
As a pilgrimage they would fain get done—   15
    Do John and Jane with their worthless son.

FOR DISCUSSION

1. What stage in life does each of the four stanzas represent?

2. How is the last stanza an ironic contrast to the other three?

3. How is this poem similar to "Those Two Boys"?

WHEN I HEARD THE LEARN'D ASTRONOMER
WALT WHITMAN

When I heard the learn'd astronomer,
When the proofs, the figures, were ranged in columns before me,
When I was shown the charts and diagrams, to add, divide, and measure them,
When I sitting heard the astronomer where he lectured with much applause in
      the lecture room,
How soon unaccountable I became tired and sick,
Till rising and gliding out I wandered off by myself,
In the mystical moist night-air, and from time to time
Looked up in perfect silence at the stars.

FOR DISCUSSION

1. The astronomer is presumably talking about stars. Why doesn't the word "stars" appear until the end of the poem? Why is it ironic that the poet leaves the lecture room for the reason he does?

2. What two ways of looking at nature are being contrasted?

FOR COMPOSITION

• How is the language of the last four lines different from those of the first four? How does this difference reflect the difference between the views of the astronomer and the poet, and the change in the poet's feelings as he leaves the lecture?

A MAN SAID TO THE UNIVERSE

STEPHEN CRANE

A man said to the universe:
"Sir, I exist!"
"However," replied the universe,
"The fact has not created in me
A sense of obligation."

FOR DISCUSSION

1. What attitude about himself does the man reveal in his remark?

2. What reply do you think the man expected? How was it different from what he got?

I MET A SEER

STEPHEN CRANE

I met a seer.
He held in his hands
The book of wisdom.
"Sir," I addressed him,
"Let me read."   5
"Child —" he began.
"Sir," I said,
"Think not that I am a child,
For already I know much
Of that which you hold.   10
Aye, much."

He smiled.
Then he opened the book
And held it before me—
Strange that I should have grown so suddenly blind.   15

FOR DISCUSSION

1. What is the speaker's attitude about himself?

2. Why is the last line ironic? In what sense is the speaker blind?

In the 1930s Puerto Rico suffered serious economic difficulties. Some Puerto Ricans blamed the United States and called for independence; others hoped to cure their island's problems by making her a state. Lloréns Torres, a Puerto Rican poet, was interested in the plight of the jíbaro, or peasant.

JÍBARO

LUIS LLORÉNS TORRES

A *jíbaro* came to San Juan
And a bunch of Yankee-lovers
Came upon him in the park
Hoping to win him over.
They told him about Uncle Sam,
About Wilson and E. Root,*
About liberty, and the vote,
About the dollar, and about habeas corpus,
And the *jíbaro* answered: Mmmmm.

[6] E. ROOT: Elihu Root, American government official and winner of the Nobel Peace Prize.

FOR DISCUSSION

1. What tone of voice is suggested for the Yankee-lovers' speech? In what tone of voice do you think the *jíbaro* answers, "Mmmmm"?

2. The Yankee-lovers speak of ideals. By contrast, what is the *jíbaro* probably thinking?

From *Poet in the Fortress* by Thomas Aitken, Jr. Copyright 1964 by Thomas Aitken, Jr. Reprinted by permission of The American Library, Inc., New York.

FROM

SONNETS FROM CHINA
SONNET XV
W. H. AUDEN

As evening fell the day's oppression lifted;
Far peaks came into focus; it had rained:
Across wide lawns and cultured flowers drifted
The conversation of the highly trained.

Two gardeners watched them pass and priced their shoes: 5
A chauffeur waited, reading in the drive,
For them to finish their exchange of views;
It seemed a picture of the private life.

Far off, no matter what good they intended,
The armies waited for a verbal error   10
With all the instruments for causing pain:

And on the issue of their charm depended
A land laid waste, with all its young men slain,
Its women weeping, and its towns in terror.

FOR DISCUSSION

1. What details from the first two stanzas emphasize the wealthy and refined atmosphere of the embassy?

2. After the line, "It seemed a picture of the private life," the poem suddenly changes. What is the hidden significance of the conversations at the embassy?

FOR COMPOSITION

• Explain, in prose, the irony that Auden sees in embassy life. Does he find it amusing? outrageous? tragic? Refer to the poem until you have made its meaning clear; then you may expand his theme with details of your own.

APOSTROPHE TO MAN

EDNA ST. VINCENT MILLAY

(on reflecting that the world is ready to go to war again)

Detestable race, continue to expunge yourself, die out.
Breed faster, crowd, encroach, sing hymns, build bombing airplanes;
Make speeches, unveil statues, issue bonds, parade;
Convert again into explosives the bewildered ammonia and
    the distracted cellulose;
Convert again into putrescent* matter drawing flies   5
The hopeful bodies of the young; exhort,
Pray, pull long faces, be earnest, be all but overcome,
    be photographed;
Confer, perfect your formulae, commercialize
Bacteria harmful to human tissue,
Put death on the market;   10
Breed, crowd, encroach, expand, expunge yourself, die out,
Homo called *sapiens.*

APOSTROPHE: speech directed to person not present; rhetorical speech.
5 PUTRESCENT: rotting.

FOR DISCUSSION

1. What does *Homo sapiens* mean? What is the ironic meaning of *"Homo* called *sapiens"*?

2. What is the speaker's attitude toward the human race? Is the poem meant to be taken literally, or is there a contrast between what the poet says and what she means?

3. What is the effect of placing "sings hymns" next to "build bombing airplanes" and "be all but overcome" next to "be photographed"?

FOR COMPOSITION

• To say that Edna St. Vincent Millay was opposed to war would not do justice to this poem. What is it about mankind that drove her to fury and despair? In her view, what weaknesses in human nature are the causes of war?

From *Collected Poems,* Harper & Row. Copyright 1934, 1962 by Edna St. Vincent Millay and Norma Millay Ellis.

Theme

Sometimes the main purpose of a poem is to teach a lesson. A poet may use a single image or event to suggest a much larger meaning. This meaning is called the theme.

Archy, the speaker in this poem, is a poet reincarnated in the form of a cockroach. He writes by hurling himself at the keys of a typewriter. This explains the strange form of the poem: Archy can't make capital letters, and he doesn't want to waste his strength on punctuation.

THE LESSON OF THE MOTH
DON MARQUIS

i was talking to a moth
the other evening
he was trying to break into
an electric light bulb
and fry himself on the wires   5

why do you fellows
pull this stunt i asked him
because it is the conventional
thing for moths or why
if that had been an uncovered   10
candle instead of an electric
light bulb you would
now be a small unsightly cinder
have you no sense
plenty of it he answered   15
but at times we get tired
of using it
we get bored with the routine
and crave beauty
and excitement   20
fire is beautiful
and we know that if we get

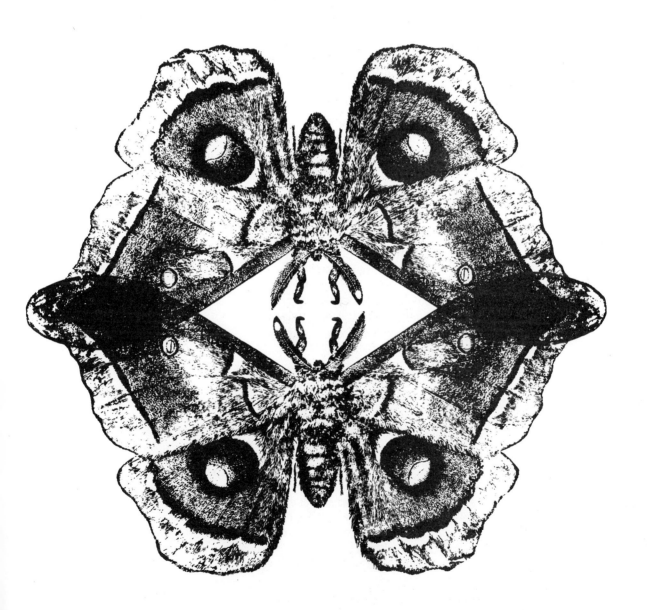

too close it will kill us
but what does that matter
it is better to be happy
for a moment   25
and be burned up with beauty
than to live a long time
and be bored all the while
so we wad all our life up   30
into one little roll
and then we shoot the roll
that is what life is for
it is better to be a part of beauty
for one instant and then cease to   35
exist than to exist forever
and never be a part of beauty
our attitude toward life
is come easy go easy
we are like human beings   40
used to be before they became
too civilized to enjoy themselves

and before i could argue him
out of his philosophy
he went and immolated himself   45
on a patent cigar lighter
i do not agree with him
myself i would rather have
half the happiness and twice
the longevity   50

but at the same time i wish
there was something i wanted
as badly as he wanted to fry himself
                                        archy

FOR DISCUSSION

1. What philosophy of life is represented by the moth's throwing himself at the fire? Do any human beings live that way, or are they all too "civilized?"

2. What is Archy's feeling about the moth's way of life? Do you agree with him?

FOR COMPOSITION

• How should the first part of the poem be read? Re-write it through line 15, adding punctuation to indicate who is speaking and where sentences and questions begin and end.

IN PLACE OF A CURSE

JOHN CIARDI

At the next vacancy for God, if I am elected,
I shall forgive last the delicately wounded
who, having been slugged no harder than anyone else,
never got up again, neither to fight back,
nor to finger their jaws in painful admiration.   5

They who are wholly broken, and they in whom
mercy is understanding, I shall embrace at once
and lead to pillows in heaven. But they who are
the meek by trade, baiting the best of their betters
with extortions of a mock-helplessness   10

I shall take last to love, and never wholly.
Let them all into Heaven—I abolish Hell—
but let it be read over them as they enter:
"Beware the calculations of the meek, who gambled nothing,
gave nothing, and could never receive enough."   15

FOR DISCUSSION

1. Christ's Sermon on the Mount included the words, "Blessed are the meek: for they shall inherit the earth" (Matthew 5:5). What did he mean by "meek"? Does Ciardi mean the same thing by "the meek by trade"?

2. Ciardi would not bless "the meek by trade." What punishment would he substitute "in place of a curse"?

From *39 Poems* by John Ciardi. Copyright 1959 by Rutgers, The State University. Reprinted by permission of the author.

GRASS-TOPS
WITTER BYNNER

What bird are you in the grass-tops?
Your poise is enough of an answer,
With your wing-tips like up-curving fingers
Of the slow-moving hands of a dancer . . .

And what is so nameless as beauty,
Which poets, who give it a name,
Are only unnaming forever?—
Content, though it go, that it came.

FOR DISCUSSION

• What image does the poet develop in the first stanza? What universal theme does he find in this picture of a single bird? Restate the second stanza in your own words.

OUTDISTANCED
LARRY RUBIN

This man of canes is in my way, snailing
Over three-quarters the girth of the sidewalk—
A wrinkled road-hog menacing
The speed of youth. I'll jet past
That wooden gentleman, with flashing
Countenance and polite excuses, the way
The sun outstrips the stars. Should
Grandfathers turn to lumber above their graves?
I'll pass him now; I'll look. He has my face.

FOR DISCUSSION

1. What is the young man's attitude toward the old man? How does the last sentence reverse this attitude?

2. What is the irony of the title of the poem? State the poem's theme in your own words.

THE EAGLE'S SONG
TRADITIONAL INDIAN SONG

Said the Eagle:
    I was astonished
    When I heard that there was death.

    My home, alas,
    Must I leave it!   5
    All beholding summits,
    Shall I see thee no more!

    North I went,
    Leaning on the wind;
    Through the forest resounded   10
    The cry of the hunted doe.

    East I went,
    Through the hot dawning;
    There was the smell of death in my nostrils.

    South I went, seeking   15
    The place where there is no death.
    Weeping I heard
    The voice of women
    Wailing for their children.

    West I went,   20
    On the world encompassing water;
    Death's trail was before me.

    People, O people,
    Needs be that we must die!

    Therefore let us make   25
    Songs together.
    With a twine of songs to bind us
    To the middle Heaven,
    The white way of souls.

The American Rhythm. Copyright renewed 1950 by Harry P. Mera, Kenneth M. Chapman and Mary C. Wheelwright. Copyright renewed 1958 by Kenneth M. Chapman and Mary C. Wheelwright. Reprinted by permission of the publisher, Houghton Mifflin Company.

There we shall be at rest, 30
With our songs
We shall roam no more!

FOR DISCUSSION

• What does the eagle find in his search for "the place where there is no death"? What answer does he offer to people who "needs must die"?

FOR COMPOSITION

• Both "Outdistanced" and "The Eagle's Song" use concrete images to suggest abstract themes of life and death. What images from each poem reflect the poet's culture and environment (white city, Indian wilderness)? Which images in each are universal—that is, which ones would be meaningful to people of all cultures? How are the themes of the two poems similar?

A FATHER SEES A SON NEARING MANHOOD

CARL SANDBURG

A father sees a son nearing manhood.
What shall he tell that son?
"Life is hard; be steel; be a rock."
And this might stand him for the storms
and serve him for humdrum and monotony   5
and guide him amid sudden betrayals
and tighten him for slack moments.
"Life is a soft loam; be gentle; go easy."
And this too might serve him.
Brutes have been gentled where lashes failed.   10
The growth of a frail flower in a path up
has sometimes shattered and split a rock.
A tough will counts. So does desire.
So does a rich soft wanting.
Without rich wanting nothing arrives.   15
Tell him too much money has killed men
and left them dead years before burial:
the quest of lucre beyond a few easy needs
has twisted good enough men
sometimes into dry thwarted worms.   20
Tell him time as a stuff can be wasted.
Tell him to be a fool every so often
and to have no shame over having been a fool
yet learning something out of every folly
hoping to repeat none of the cheap follies   25
thus arriving at intimate understanding
of a world numbering many fools.
Tell him to be alone often and get at himself
and above all tell himself no lies about himself,
whatever the white lies and protective fronts   30
he may use amongst other people.
Tell him solitude is creative if he is strong
and the final decisions are made in silent rooms.
Tell him to be different from other people
if it comes natural and easy being different.   35
Let him have lazy days seeking his deeper motives.
Let him seek deep for where he is a born natural.

From *The People, Yes* by Carl Sandburg, copyright 1936 by Harcourt Brace Jovanovich, Inc.; renewed 1964 by Carl Sandburg. Reprinted by permission of the publisher.

278

Then he may understand Shakespeare
and the Wright brothers, Pasteur, Pavlov,
Michael Faraday and free imaginations   40
bringing changes into a world resenting change.
He will be lonely enough
to have time for the work
he knows as his own.

FOR DISCUSSION

1. Why could it be good advice either to be hard or to be soft?

2. Why would a father advise his son to be a fool, to be alone, and to be lazy?

3. Of all the advice a father might give, which does Carl Sandburg think is most important? What clues are there in the structure of the poem that this is the most important?

LIES

YEVGENY YEVTUSHENKO

Telling lies to the young is wrong.
Proving to them that lies are true is wrong.
Telling them that God's in his heaven
and all's well with the world is wrong.
The young know what you mean. The young are people.   5
Tell them the difficulties can't be counted,
and let them see not only what will be
but see with clarity these present times.
Say obstacles exist they must encounter
sorrow happens, hardship happens.   10
The hell with it. Who never knew
the price of happiness will not be happy.
Forgive no error you recognize,
it will repeat itself, increase,
and afterwards our pupils   15
will not forgive in us what we forgave.

"Lies" by Yevgeny Yevtushenko, translated by Robin Milner-Gulland and Peter Levi, S. J. Reprinted by permission of Penguin Books Ltd.

FOR DISCUSSION

1. Why shouldn't the young be told that "God's in his heaven, and all's well with the world"? Why does Yevtushenko think that this is a lie?

2. Explain what is meant by "Who never knew the price of happiness will not be

happy." Do you agree with the poet?

FOR COMPOSITION

• Both Sandburg and Yevtushenko speak of the importance of lies in conversations between the generations. Are their ideas about lies similar? In what ways are their ideas similar or different? Whose advice do you prefer?

In Summary

1. What poem would you choose as your favorite from this unit? Do you like it because of its sound, images, mood, or theme—or for some other reason? Would you have chosen the same poem a year ago?

2. Which do you find more effective in presenting a theme, poetry or prose? Compare a poem and a story with similar themes, such as "The Sniper" and "Outdistanced" or "Jacob" and the selection from "The People, Yes" or "The Story of My Dovecot" and "Apostrophe to Man." What advantages and disadvantages does each form offer?

3. Much of the poetry in this unit is written in free verse. What evidence can you find that these poems were not just written in some haphazard way? If a poet is not working within the limits of rhyme scheme and meter, what other elements of rhythm must he consider? Find at least two poems which show careful attention to rhythm in spite of being written in free verse.

4. *Satire* is writing which ridicules the foolishness or evil of man's behavior. Which poems in this unit would you consider satirical? What aspects of human behavior do they attack?

5. Some of the poems from this unit that are concerned with death are "The Raven," "The Produce District," "Lament of a Man for His Son," "Sonnet XV," "The Lesson of the Moth," and "The Eagle's Song." Can you find any two that are similar in image, mood, tone, or theme?

OTHER THINGS TO DO

1. Choose one or more poems to read orally to the class. Those in the section on "Sound" are good, or you might choose a narrative poem (one that tells a story). If you have a group of three or more, arrange the poem for choral reading: girl's solo, boy's solo, duet, chorus, etc. The more combinations and changes of voices you have, the more effective your presentation will be. Whether you perform "live" or on a tape recorder, allow plenty of time for rehearsals.

2. Make a collection of figurative language from your reading, from everyday conversations, and from television. Cut out those you find in magazines and newspapers. You will find as many figures of speech in advertisements as in any book of poetry!

3. Bind a collection of poems into a book and illustrate it with drawings or photographs. The book might include poems written by yourself or your classmates, or it might just be poems that you especially like. Don't overlook sources like *The Poetry of Rock* (Reader's Choice).

4. Choose one poet who interests you and learn more about him. Read as many of his poems as you can. Prepare a report for the class explaining how his life related to his work, and how his poetry developed. Learn at least one of his poems; that is, memorize it as you try to understand every part of it.

5. Write a *parody* of a familiar poet. "Parody" means imitation of an author's style; a parody of Poe, for example, would include alliteration, repetition, a strong rhythm and long, emotional words. An easy way to start is to change the words of a single poem. Parody is often humorous because a frivolous subject is treated in serious style or vice versa, as in

> Once upon a lunchtime greasy, while I
> pondered, pale and queasy
> Over many a foul and festering hotplate
> of forgotten store . . .

Mad magazine is a good source of other examples. You will also find a thesaurus and a rhyming dictionary helpful.

Reader's Choice

The Birds and Beasts Were There, *selected by William Cole.*

Every animal imaginable is presented in this collection of almost 300 poems. Some are humorous, some sad—many are surprising. Poets from this anthology included in Cole's volume are John Ciardi, E. E. Cummings, Roald Dahl, Robert Frost, Thomas Hardy, Don Marquis, Edna St. Vincent Millay, and Theodore Roethke.

Collected Sonnets, *by Edna St. Vincent Millay.*

This volume contains more than 150 sonnets, selected by Miss Millay herself from her complete works. This is an intriguing and thought-provoking volume.

Complete Poems of Robert Frost, *by Robert Frost.*

The simple and eloquent voice of one of America's best-known poets is heard in this collection which contains beautiful examples of Frost's wit and wisdom.

Fifty Poems, *by E. E. Cummings.*

If you enjoyed unpuzzling "Beautiful," you might like to read more of Cummings's poems. His unusual use of language gives new meaning to words, syllables, and even single letters. A reader who takes the time to think about them can find in his poems many surprises and much beauty.

The Panther and the Lash, *by Langston Hughes.*

Often referred to as America's "Black poet laureate" Langston Hughes enjoyed a career that spanned many years. This volume contains many poems written in his later years and becomes even more significant when compared with the poems of Mr. Hughes's early years.

Poems to Solve, *by May Swenson.*

Often deceptively simple, these poems give the reader much to pause and reflect about. Miss Swenson's unique style and immense talent make her one of the most widely read of today's poets.

Poems of Stephen Crane, *selected by Gerald D. McDonald.*

If "A Man Said to the Universe" and "I Met a Seer" made you think, you might want to read some more of Stephen Crane's poems. Often bitterly ironic, they express his fierce sense of justice and hatred of cruelty. Those in this collection are about love, war, God, and the search for truth.

The Poetry of Rock, *edited by Richard Goldstein.*

Richard Goldstein, rock music critic, has collected the lyrics of the rock songs from 1952–1968 that he feels can best stand alone as poetry. The book begins with a short history of rock and its development "from the bargain basement of American culture . . . into a full-fledged art form."

Reflections on a Gift of Watermelon Pickle, *edited by Stephen Dunning, Edward Lueders, and Hugh Smith.*

Reading this collection of modern verse is a sheer delight. Here one finds the most provocative poems by the best contemporary poets. The simple format of the volume belies the complexities of the poetry found here.

Shrieks at Midnight—Macabre Poems Eerie and Humorous, *selected by Sara and John E. Brewton.*

Ghosts, ghouls, corpses, and cannibals meet in this amusing collection of verse. Lewis Carroll, Edward Lear, Ogden Nash, Hilaire Belloc and other well-known humorous poets are included, but some of the best poems are anonymous: epitaphs, old ballads, and atrocious puns. Mixed with humor is irony.

DRAMA

THE TWO PLAYS that follow come from worlds and times far in the past, but their meanings belong very much to the present. One is a play written about 1595, in the England of Queen Elizabeth I. It tells of the love for each other, many years earlier, of a boy and a girl in the Italian city of Verona. There were reasons, which seemed sound to their elders, why those two young people should not have allowed their love to grow, and the tension of the play comes from seeing the different attitudes of youth and age, then as now, in conflict. Now, as then, people fall in love against the advice or wishes of others. As long as they continue to do so, *Romeo and Juliet* will matter.

The second play goes even further back into time, back five centuries before the birth of Christ, to ancient Greece. Twenty-four hundred years have passed since the citizens of Athens first saw a performance of Sophocles' great play *Antigone* (an·tĭg′ə·nē), and yet that play too remains as timely as ever it could have been in all those ages past.

Antigone is less about love than loyalty. It acknowledges that each of us is a part of several larger wholes: a member of a family, of a school, of a town or city, of a nation, of the human race. That being so, where does our loyalty first of all lie? Usually the answer is relatively simple. If we saw a bear attacking a man, few of us would hesitate to help the man if we could; our loyalty would instinctively be to a fellow human being.

But what if loyalty to our family, say, dictates one course of conduct, and loyalty to the nation another course, directly opposed to the first? That is the question, enduring and perhaps finally unanswerable, that lies at the heart of *Antigone*.

Philip McFarland

The story of young lovers who are separated, and finally destroyed, by the hatred between their two families is as old as third-century Greece and as modern as West Side Story. Shakespeare's audience was already familiar with variations of the story when Romeo and Juliet *was first presented. The play owes its popularity to the poetic force of the language with which Shakespeare made the old plot new and to his genius for bringing characters to life on the stage. Although it is set in fourteenth-century Italy,* Romeo and Juliet *could happen in any time and place.*

ROMEO AND JULIET
WILLIAM SHAKESPEARE

CHARACTERS

ESCALUS, *Prince of Verona*
PARIS, *a young count, kinsman to the Prince*
MONTAGUE } *heads of two houses feuding*
CAPULET } *with each other*
ROMEO, *son to Montague*
MERCUTIO, *kinsman to the Prince and friend to Romeo*
BENVOLIO, *nephew to Montague and cousin to Romeo*
TYBALT, *nephew to Lady Capulet*
FRIAR LAURENCE }
FRIAR JOHN } *Franciscan priests*
BALTHASAR, *servant to Romeo*
ABRAHAM, *servant to Montague*

SAMPSON }
GREGORY } *servants of Capulet*
PETER, *servant to Juliet's nurse*
AN APOTHECARY
THREE MUSICIANS
AN OFFICER
LADY MONTAGUE, *wife to Montague*
LADY CAPULET, *wife to Capulet*
JULIET, *daughter to Capulet*
NURSE *to Juliet*
SPEAKER *of the Prologue*
Citizens of Verona, Gentlemen and Gentlewomen of both houses, Maskers, Torchbearers, Pages, Guards, Watchmen, Servants, and Attendants

SCENE: *Verona; Mantua*

[*Enter Speaker.*]

SPEAKER.   Two households, both alike in dignity,
   In fair Verona, where we lay our scene,
From ancient grudge break to new mutiny,
   Where civil blood makes civil hands unclean.
From forth the fatal loins of these two foes
   A pair of star-crossed lovers take their life;
Whose misadventured piteous overthrows

DIGNITY: rank

MUTINY: violence

5

STAR-CROSSED: ill-fated

286

Doth with their death bury their parents' strife.
The fearful passage of their death-marked love,
    And the continuance of their parents' rage,   10
Which, but their children's end, naught could remove,
    Is now the two hours' traffic of our stage;
The which if you with patient ears attend,
What here shall miss, our toil shall strive to mend.

BUT: except for

[*Exit.*]

ACT I

SCENE I.   *Verona. A public place.*

[*Enter Sampson and Gregory, of the house of Capulet, with swords and bucklers.*]

SAMPSON.   Gregory, on my word, we'll not carry coals.
GREGORY.   No, for then we should be colliers.*
SAMPSON.   I mean, an we be in choler, we'll draw.
GREGORY.   Aye, while you live, draw your neck out of
collar.*   5
SAMPSON.   I strike quickly, being moved.
GREGORY.   But thou art not quickly moved to strike.
SAMPSON.   A dog of the house of Montague moves me.
GREGORY.   To move is to stir, and to be valiant is to
stand. Therefore, if thou art moved, thou run'st away.   10
SAMPSON.   A dog of that house shall move me to stand.
I will take the wall* of any man or maid of Montague's.
GREGORY.   That shows thee a weak slave; for the weak-
est goes to the wall. . . .* Draw thy tool! Here comes
two of the house of Montagues.   15

AN: if

MOVED: angered

TOOL: sword

[*Enter two other servingmen, Abraham and Balthasar.*]

SAMPSON.   My naked weapon is out. Quarrel! I will back
thee.
GREGORY.   How? Turn thy back and run?
SAMPSON.   Fear me not.
GREGORY.   No, marry; I fear thee!   20
SAMPSON.   Let us take the law of our sides;* let them
begin.

MARRY: indeed

1-2 WE'LL . . . COLLIERS: Sampson says, "We'll take no insults [carry coals]," to which Gregory teasingly replies, "No, for then we should be coal dealers [colliers]."   3-5 CHOLER . . . COLLAR: Again, Gregory deliberately mistakes choler (anger) for collar (hangman's noose).
12 TAKE THE WALL: prove to be better.   14 TO THE WALL: pushed to the rear.   21 TAKE . . . SIDES: "keep ourselves in the right."

GREGORY.   I will frown as I pass by, and let them take it
as they list.   LIST: please

SAMPSON.   Nay, as they dare. I will bite my thumb* at   25
them, which is disgrace to them if they bear it.

ABRAHAM.   Do you bite your thumb at us, sir?

SAMPSON.   I do bite my thumb, sir.

ABRAHAM.   Do you bite your thumb at us, sir?

SAMPSON.   [*Aside to Gregory*] Is the law of our side, if   30
I say aye?

GREGORY.   [*Aside to Sampson*] No.

SAMPSON.   No, sir, I do not bite my thumb at you, sir;
but I bite my thumb, sir.

GREGORY.   Do you quarrel, sir?   35

ABRAHAM.   Quarrel, sir? No, sir.

SAMPSON.   But if you do, sir, I am for you. I serve as
good a man as you.

ABRAHAM.   No better.

SAMPSON.   Well, sir.   40

.[*Enter Benvolio.*]

GREGORY.   Say "better"; here comes one of my master's
kinsmen.

SAMPSON.   Yes, better, sir.

ABRAHAM.   You lie.

SAMPSON.   Draw, if you be men. Gregory, remember thy   45
swashing blow.

[*They fight.*]

BENVOLIO.   Part, fools!
Put up your swords. You know not what you do.

[*He pushes their swords aside.*]
[*Enter Tybalt.*]

TYBALT.   What, art thou drawn among these heartless   HEARTLESS HINDS: cowardly ser-
hinds? Turn thee, Benvolio! Look upon thy death.   50   vants

BENVOLIO.   I do but keep the peace. Put up thy sword,
Or manage it to part these men with me.

TYBALT.   What, drawn, and talk of peace? I hate the
word
As I hate hell, all Montagues, and thee.
Have at thee, coward!   55

[*They fight.*]
[*Enter an Officer, and three or four Citizens with clubs or
partisans.*]

25 BITE MY THUMB: an insulting gesture.

OFFICER.   Clubs, bills, and partisans! Strike! Beat them
down!

CITIZENS.   Down with the Capulets! Down with the
Montagues!

[*Enter Capulet and Lady Capulet.*]

CAPULET.   What noise is this? Give me my long sword, ho! 60

LADY CAPULET.   A crutch, a crutch! Why call you for a
sword?

CAPULET.   My sword, I say! Old Montague is come
And flourishes his blade in spite of me.

SPITE: defiance

[*Enter Montague and Lady Montague.*]

MONTAGUE.   Thou villain Capulet!—Hold me not; let me   65
go.

LADY MONTAGUE.   Thou shalt not stir one foot to seek a
foe.

[*Enter Prince Escalus, with his Attendants.*]

PRINCE.   Rebellious subjects, enemies to peace,
Profaners of this neighbor-stainèd steel—   70
Will they not hear? What, ho! You men, you beasts,
That quench the fire of your pernicious rage
With purple fountains issuing from your veins!
On pain of torture, from those bloody hands
Throw your mistempered* weapons to the ground   75
And hear the sentence of your movèd prince.
Three civil brawls, bred of an airy word*
By thee, old Capulet, and Montague,
Have thrice disturbed the quiet of our streets
And made Verona's ancient citizens   80
Cast by their grave beseeming ornaments
To wield old partisans, in hands as old,
Cankered with peace, to part your cankered hate.
If ever you disturb our streets again,
Your lives shall pay the forfeit of the peace.   85
For this time all the rest depart away.
You, Capulet, shall go along with me;
And, Montague, come you this afternoon,
To know our farther pleasure in this case,
To old Freetown, our common judgment place.   90
Once more, on pain of death, all men depart.

[*Exeunt all but Montague, Lady Montague, and Benvolio.*]

⁷⁵ MISTEMPERED: used in anger.   ⁷⁷ BRED . . . WORD: started by a trivial
insult.

MONTAGUE.   Who set this ancient quarrel new abroach?*
 Speak, nephew, were you by when it began?
BENVOLIO.   Here were the servants of your adversary,
 And yours, close fighting ere I did approach.   95
 I drew to part them. In the instant came
 The fiery Tybalt, with his sword prepared;
 Which, as he breathed defiance to my ears,
 He swung about his head and cut the winds,
 Who, nothing hurt withal, hissed him in scorn.   100   WITHAL: nevertheless
 While we were interchanging thrusts and blows,
 Came more and more, and fought on part and part,
 Till the Prince came, who parted either part.
LADY MONTAGUE.   O, where is Romeo? Saw you him
 today? Right glad I am he was not at this fray.   105
BENVOLIO.   Madam, an hour before the worshiped sun
 Peered forth the golden window of the east,
 A troubled mind drave me to walk abroad;
 Where, underneath the grove of sycamore
 That westward rooteth from the city's side,   110
 So early walking did I see your son.
 Towards him I made, but he was ware of me   WARE: aware
 And stole into the covert of the wood.
 I, measuring his affections by my own,
 Which then most sought where most might not be
    found,*   115
 Being one too many by my weary self,
 Pursued my humor not pursuing his,*
 And gladly shunned who gladly fled from me.
MONTAGUE.   Many a morning hath he there been seen,
 With tears augmenting the fresh morning's dew,   120
 Adding to clouds more clouds with his deep sighs;
 But all so soon as the all-cheering sun
 Should in the farthest east begin to draw
 The shady curtains from Aurora's* bed,
 Away from light steals home my heavy son   125   HEAVY: sorrowing
 And private in his chamber pens himself,
 Shuts up his windows, locks fair daylight out,
 And makes himself an artificial night.
 Black and portentous must this humor prove   HUMOR: mood
 Unless good counsel may the cause remove.   130
BENVOLIO.   My noble uncle, do you know the cause?
MONTAGUE.   I neither know it nor can learn of him.

---

92 SET . . . ABROACH: reopened this old feud. 115 MOST SOUGHT . . .
FOUND: most wanted solitude. 117 PURSUED . . . HIS: "acted according
to my own mood in not questioning him about his." 124 AURORA'S:
Aurora was the Roman goddess of the dawn.

BENVOLIO. Have you importuned him by any means?

IMPORTUNED: questioned

MONTAGUE. Both by myself and many other friends;
  But he, his own affections' counselor,   135
  Is to himself—I will not say how true—
  But to himself so secret and so close,
  So far from sounding and discovery,

SOUNDING: understanding

  As is the bud bit with an envious worm
  Ere he can spread his sweet leaves to the air   140
  Or dedicate his beauty to the sun.
  Could we but learn from whence his sorrows grow,
  We would as willingly give cure as know.*

[Enter Romeo.]

BENVOLIO. See, where he comes! So please you step aside;
  I'll know his grievance, or be much denied.   145
MONTAGUE. I would thou wert so happy by thy stay
  To hear true shrift. Come, madam, let's away.

SHRIFT: confession

[Exeunt Montague and Lady Montague.]

BENVOLIO. Good morrow, cousin.
ROMEO.   Is the day so young?
BENVOLIO. But new struck nine.
ROMEO.   Ay me! Sad hours seem long.
  Was that my father that went hence so fast?   150
BENVOLIO. It was. What sadness lengthens Romeo's
    hours?
ROMEO. Not having that which, having, makes them
    short.*
BENVOLIO. In love?
ROMEO. Out.
BENVOLIO. Of love?   155
ROMEO. Out of her favor where I am in love.
BENVOLIO. Alas that Love, so gentle in his view,
  Should be so tyrannous and rough in proof!
ROMEO. Alas that Love, whose view is muffled still,
  Should, without eyes, see pathways to his will!*   160
  Where shall we dine? O me! What fray was here?
  Yet tell me not, for I have heard it all.
  Here's much to do with hate, but more with love.
  Why then, O brawling love! O loving hate!
  O anything, of nothing first create!   165
  O heavy lightness! Serious vanity!

143 GIVE . . . KNOW: "cure his sorrows as know their cause." 152 WHICH . . . SHORT: "which, if I had it, would shorten them." 159–160 ALAS . . . WILL: "Alas, that Cupid, who is always blindfolded, should nevertheless find ways to make us fall in love."

Misshapen chaos of well-seeming forms!
Feather of lead, bright smoke, cold fire, sick health!
Still-waking sleep, that is not what it is!
This love feel I, that feel no love in this.*   170
Dost thou not laugh?
BENVOLIO.   No, coz, I rather weep.   coz: cousin
ROMEO.   Good heart, at what?
BENVOLIO.   At thy good heart's oppression.
ROMEO.   Why, such is love's transgression.
Griefs of mine own lie heavy in my breast,
Which thou wilt propagate, to have it prest   175
With more of thine. This love that thou hast shown
Doth add more grief to too much of mine own.
Love is a smoke made with the fume of sighs;
Being purged, a fire sparkling in lovers' eyes;   PURGED: cleared away
Being vexed, a sea nourished with lovers' tears.   180
What is it else? A madness most discreet,
A choking gall, and a preserving sweet.   GALL: bitter drink
Farewell, my coz.
BENVOLIO.   Soft! I will go along.   SOFT: wait
An if you leave me so, you do me wrong.
ROMEO.   Tut! I have left myself; I am not here.   185
This is not Romeo; he's some other where.
BENVOLIO.   Tell me in sadness,* who is that you love?
ROMEO.   What, shall I groan and tell thee?
BENVOLIO.   Groan? Why, no;
But sadly tell me who.
ROMEO.   Bid a sick man in sadness make his will.   190
Ah, word ill urged to one that is so ill!
In sadness, cousin, I do love a woman.
BENVOLIO.   I aimed so near when I supposed you loved.
ROMEO.   A right good markman! And she's fair I love.
BENVOLIO.   A right fair mark, fair coz, is soonest hit.   195
ROMEO.   Well, in that hit you miss. She'll not be hit
With Cupid's arrow. She hath Dian's wit,*
And, in strong proof of chastity well armed,
From Love's weak childish bow she lives unharmed.
She will not stay the siege of loving terms,   200   STAY: endure
Nor bide* th' encounter of assailing eyes,
Nor ope her lap to saint-seducing gold.
O, she is rich in beauty; only poor

[170] THIS . . . THIS: "I feel these effects of love, but find no pleasure in them." [187] SADNESS: seriousness. In the following lines Romeo and Benvolio pun on the two meanings of sadness: grief and seriousness. [197] DIAN'S WIT: the wisdom of Diana, Roman goddess of the moon, who scorned men.

That, when she dies, with beauty dies her store.
BENVOLIO. Then she hath sworn that she will still live   STILL: always
    chaste?   205
ROMEO. She hath, and in that sparing make huge waste;
    For beauty, starved with her severity,
    Cuts beauty off from all posterity.
    She is too fair, too wise, wisely too fair,
    To merit bliss by making me despair.   210   BLISS: heaven
    She hath forsworn to love, and in that vow   FORSWORN: sworn not
    Do I live dead that live to tell it now.
BENVOLIO. Be ruled by me; forget to think of her.
ROMEO. O, teach me how I should forget to think.
BENEVOLIO. By giving liberty unto thine eyes.   215
    Examine other beauties.
ROMEO.   'Tis the way
    To call hers, exquisite, in question more.*
    These happy masks that kiss fair ladies' brows,
    Being black, puts us in mind they hide the fair.
    He that is strucken blind cannot forget   220
    The precious treasure of his eyesight lost.
    Show me a mistress that is passing fair,
    What doth her beauty serve but as a note   NOTE: reminder
    Where I may read who passed that passing fair?
    Farewell! Thou canst not teach me to forget.   225
BENVOLIO. I'll pay that doctrine, or else die in debt.*

    [*Exeunt.*]

216-217 'TIS . . . MORE: "Comparisons would only convince me further of her exquisite beauty." 226 I'LL . . . DEBT: "I'll teach you that lesson or die trying."

FOR DISCUSSION

1. How does the first scene show the depth of hatred between the families of Montague and Capulet? Do we learn the cause of the conflict?

2. What differences are there in the attitudes of Benvolio, Tybalt, Romeo, Montague, and Capulet toward the old feud?

3. The typical melancholy lover, in Shakespeare's time as well as now, was supposed to lose his appetite, sleep poorly, and wander about sighing sadly. Romeo exhibits all these symptoms, and more. What is the cause of his unhappiness? What cure does Benvolio suggest?

4. In contrast to their servants' vulgar prose speech, the noble characters speak in *blank verse* (unrhymed lines of five feet each). Read a few lines of each aloud—can you hear the difference? (In longer passages you can see as well that prose lines do not all begin with capital letters.) Listen for this difference throughout the play.

SCENE II. *Verona. A street.*

[*Enter Capulet, Paris, and a Servant.*]

CAPULET.   But Montague is bound as well as I,
  In penalty alike; and 'tis not hard, I think,
  For men so old as we to keep the peace.
PARIS.   Of honorable reckoning are you both,   RECKONING: reputation
  And pity 'tis you lived at odds so long.   5
  But now, my lord, what say you to my suit?
CAPULET.   But saying o'er what I have said before.
  My child is yet a stranger in the world,
  She hath not seen the change of fourteen years.
  Let two more summers wither in their pride   10
  Ere we may think her ripe to be a bride.
PARIS.   Younger than she are happy mothers made.
CAPULET.   And too soon marred are those so early made.
  Earth hath swallowed all my hopes but she;*
  She is the hopeful lady of my earth.   15
  But woo her, gentle Paris, get her heart;
  My will to her consent is but a part.
  An she agree, within her scope of choice
  Lies my consent and fair according voice.
  This night I hold an old accustomed feast,   20
  Whereto I have invited many a guest,
  Such as I love; and you among the store
  One more, most welcome, makes my number more.
  At my poor house look to behold this night
  Earth-treading stars* that make dark heaven light.   25
  Such comfort as do lusty young men feel
  When well-appareled April on the heel
  Of limping Winter treads, even such delight
  Among fresh female buds shall you this night
  Inherit at my house. Hear all, all see,   30
  And like her most whose merit most shall be;
  Which, on more view of many, mine, being one,
  May stand in number, though in reckoning none.
  Come, go with me.
  [*To Servant, giving him a paper*] Go, sirrah, trudge
      about
  Through fair Verona; find those persons out   35
  Whose names are written there, and to them say
  My house and welcome on their pleasure stay.   STAY: wait

[*Exeunt Capulet and Paris.*]

14 EARTH . . . SHE: "All my other children are buried." 25 EARTH-
TREADING STARS: beautiful women.

SERVANT.   Find them out whose names are written here?
It is written that the shoemaker should meddle with
his yard and the tailor with his last, the fisher with his   40
pencil and the painter with his nets;* but I am sent to
find those persons whose names are here writ, and can
never find what names the writing person hath here
writ. I must to the learned. In good time.

SERVANT: FIND: understand

[*Enter Benvolio and Romeo.*]

BENVOLIO.   Tut, man, one fire burns out another's burning,   45
    One pain is lessened by another's anguish;
Turn giddy, and be holp by backward turning;
    One desperate grief cures with another's languish.
Take thou some new infection to thy eye,
And the rank poison of the old will die.   50

HOLP: helped
LANGUISH: suffering

ROMEO.   Your plantain leaf* is excellent for that.
BENVOLIO.   For what, I pray thee?
ROMEO.   For your broken shin.
BENVOLIO.   Why, Romeo, art thou mad?
ROMEO.   Not mad, but bound more than a madman is;
    Shut up in prison, kept without my food,   55
    Whipped and tormented and—God-den, good fellow.
SERVANT.   God gi' go-den.* I pray, sir, can you read?
ROMEO.   Aye, mine own fortune in my misery.
SERVANT.   Perhaps you have learned it without book.
    But, I pray, can you read anything you see?   60
ROMEO.   Aye, if I know the letters and the language.
SERVANT.   Ye say honestly. Rest you merry!*
ROMEO.   Stay, fellow; I can read. [*He reads.*]
    "Signior Martino and his wife and daughters; County
Anselme and his beauteous sisters; the lady widow of   65
Vitruvio; Signior Placentio and his lovely nieces; Mer-
cutio and his brother Valentine; mine uncle Capulet,
his wife and daughters; my fair niece Rosaline; Livia;
Signior Valentio and his cousin Tybalt; Lucio and the
lively Helena."   70
A fair assembly. Whither should they come?

COUNTY: count

SERVANT.   Up.
ROMEO.   Whither? To supper?

---

[41] NETS: The servant means that people should stick to the things they
know best, but he gets his workmen and tools mixed up. [51] PLANTAIN
LEAF: Plantain leaves were considered a cure for both infection and
bruises. Romeo is making fun of Benvolio's advice. [56-57] GOD-DEN . . .
GOD GI' GOD-DEN: shortened forms of "Good evening" and "God give
you a good evening." [62] REST YOU MERRY: "God keep you merry," a
farewell salutation. Thinking that Romeo means he cannot read, the
servant prepares to depart.

SERVANT.   To our house.

ROMEO.   Whose house?   75

SERVANT.   My master's.

ROMEO.   Indeed I should have asked you that before.

SERVANT.   Now, I'll tell you without asking. My master
   is the great rich Capulet; and if you be not of the
   house of Montagues, I pray come and crush a cup of   80
   wine. Rest you merry!

   [*Exit.*]

BENVOLIO.   At this same ancient feast of Capulet's
   Sups the fair Rosaline whom thou so loves;
   With all the admirèd beauties of Verona.
   Go thither, and with unattainted eye   85   UNATTAINTED: unprejudiced
   Compare her face with some that I shall show,
   And I will make thee think thy swan a crow.

ROMEO.   When the devout religion of mine eye
       Maintains such falsehood, then turn tears to fires;
   And these, who, often drowned, could never die,   90
       Transparent heretics, be burnt for liars!
   One fairer than my love? The all-seeing sun
   Ne'er saw her match since first the world begun.

BENVOLIO.   Tut! You saw her fair, none else being by,
   Herself poised with herself in either eye;   95   POISED: compared
   But in that crystal scales let there be weighed
   Your lady's love against some other maid
   That I will show you shining at this feast,
   And she shall scant show well that now seems best.

ROMEO.   I'll go along, no such sight to be shown,   100
   But to rejoice in splendor of mine own.*

   [*Exeunt.*]

101 SPLENDOR . . . OWN: "the beauty of my own love [Rosaline]."

FOR DISCUSSION

1. Paris wishes Capulet's permission to marry
his daughter Juliet. What does Capulet answer? What feeling for his daughter does he
reveal in this scene?

2. Besides adding humor, how does the incident with the illiterate servant contribute to
the plot of the story?

SCENE III. *A room in Capulet's house.*

[*Enter Lady Capulet and Nurse.*]

LADY CAPULET.   Nurse, where's my daughter? Call her
    forth to me.
NURSE.   Now . . . I bade her come. What, lamb! What,
    ladybird! God forbid! Where's this girl? What, Juliet!

[*Enter Juliet.*]

JULIET.   How now! Who calls?
NURSE.   Your mother.
JULIET.   Madam, I am here.   5
    What is your will?
LADY CAPULET.   This is the matter—Nurse, give leave
    awhile;
    We must talk in secret—Nurse, come back again.
    I have remembered me; thou 's hear our counsel.   THOU 's: thou shalt
    Thou know'st my daughter's of a pretty age.   10
NURSE.   Faith, I can tell her age unto an hour.
LADY CAPULET.   She's not fourteen.
NURSE.   I'll lay fourteen of my teeth—
    And yet, to my teen be it spoken, I have but four   TEEN: sorrow
    She's not fourteen. How long is it now
    To Lammastide?   LAMMASTIDE: August 1, a holy
LADY CAPULET.   A fortnight and odd days.   15   day
NURSE.   Even or odd, of all days in the year,
    Come Lammas Eve at night shall she be fourteen.
    Susan and she—God rest all Christian souls!—
    Were of an age. Well, Susan is with God;
    She was too good for me. But, as I said,   20
    On Lammas Eve at night shall she be fourteen;
    That shall she, marry; I remember it well.
    'Tis since the earthquake now eleven years;
    And she was weaned—I never shall forget it—
    For then she could stand high-lone; nay, by the rood,   25   ROOD: cross
    She could have run and waddled all about;
    For even the day before, she broke her brow;
    And then my husband—God be with his soul!—
    'A was a merry man—took up the child.   'A: he
    "Yea," quoth he, "dost thou fall upon thy face?   30
    Thou will fall backward when thou hast more wit;
    Wilt thou not, Jule?" and, by my holidam,
    The pretty wretch left crying and said, "Aye."
    To see, now, how a jest shall come about!
    I warrant, an I should live a thousand years,   35

I never should forget it. "Wilt thou not, Jule?" quoth he;
And, pretty fool, it stinted and said, "Aye." STINTED: stopped
LADY CAPULET. Enough of this. I pray thee hold thy
 peace. . . .
NURSE. Peace, I have done. God mark thee to His grace!
Thou wast the prettiest babe that e'er I nursed. 40
An I might live to see thee married once,
I have my wish.
LADY CAPULET. Marry, that "marry" is the very theme MARRY: indeed
I came to talk of. Tell me, daughter Juliet,
How stands your dispositions to be married? 45
JULIET. It is an honor that I dream not of.
NURSE. An honor?
LADY CAPULET. Well, think of marriage now. Younger
 than you,
Here in Verona, ladies of esteem,
Are made already mothers. By my count, 50
I was your mother much upon these years
That you are now a maid. Thus then in brief:
The valiant Paris seeks you for his love.
NURSE. A man, young lady! Lady, such a man
As all the world—why, he's a man of wax.* 55
LADY CAPULET. Verona's summer hath not such a flower.
NURSE. Nay, he's a flower; in faith, a very flower.
LADY CAPULET. What say you? Can you love the gentle-
 man?
This night you shall behold him at our feast.
Read o'er the volume of young Paris' face, 60
And find delight writ there with beauty's pen;
Examine every married lineament,*
And see how one another lends content;*
And what obscured in this fair volume lies
Find written in the margent of his eyes. 65
This precious book of love, this unbound lover,
To beautify him only lacks a cover.
The fish lives in the sea, and 'tis much pride
For fair without the fair within to hide.
That book in many's eyes doth share the glory, 70
That in gold clasps locks in the golden story;
So shall you share all that he doth possess,
By having him, making yourself no less.
NURSE. No less? Nay, bigger! Women grow by men.

[55] MAN OF WAX: a model in wax; perfect. [62] MARRIED LINEAMENT: well-matched feature. [63] ONE . . . CONTENT: "One feature enhances another."

LADY CAPULET.   Speak briefly, can you like of* Paris' love? 75
JULIET.   I'll look to like, if looking liking move;*
   But no more deep will I endart mine eye
   Than your consent gives strength to make it fly.

[*Enter Servant.*]

SERVANT.   Madam, the guests are come, supper served
   up, you called, my young lady asked for, the nurse 80
   cursed in the pantry, and everything in extremity. I
   must hence to wait; I beseech you follow straight.

                                                STRAIGHT: immediately

[*Exit.*]

LADY CAPULET.   We follow thee. Juliet, the County stays.
NURSE.   Go, girl, seek happy nights to happy days.

[*Exeunt.*]

---

75 LIKE OF: be agreeable to.   76 I'LL . . . MOVE: "I'll try to like him, if
mere looking can produce affection."

FOR DISCUSSION

1. Contrast Lady Capulet's and the Nurse's attitudes toward Paris's marriage proposal with the attitude shown by Capulet in Scene ii.

2. One of Lady Capulet's arguments for marriage is that she gave birth to Juliet when she was about the age that Juliet is now. What age is Lady Capulet now? How can you explain the fact that she and her husband are referred to elsewhere in the play as "old"?

3. Lady Capulet compares Paris to a fine book. Explain the parts of this complicated metaphor: What is the writing? the margin? the cover?

4. How does Juliet seem to feel about marrying Paris?

Scene iv.   *A street.*

[Enter Romeo, Mercutio, Benvolio, with five or six other Maskers; Torchbearers.]

ROMEO.   What, shall this speech be spoke for our excuse?*
  Or shall we on without apology?

BENVOLIO.   The date is out of such prolixity.*
  We'll have no Cupid hookwinked with a scarf,   HOODWINKED: blindfolded
  Bearing a Tartar's painted bow of lath,*   5
  Scaring the ladies like a crowkeeper;*
  Nor no without-book prologue,* faintly spoke
  After the prompter, for our entrance;
  But let them measure us by what they will,   MEASURE: judge
  We'll measure them a measure* and be gone.   10

ROMEO.   Give me a torch. I am not for this ambling.
  Being but heavy, I will bear the light.

MERCUTIO.   Nay, gentle Romeo, we must have you dance.

ROMEO.   Not I, believe me. You have dancing shoes
  With nimble soles; I have a soul of lead   15
  So stakes me to the ground I cannot move.

MERCUTIO.   You are a lover; borrow Cupid's wings
  And soar with them above a common bound.   BOUND: limit

ROMEO. I am too sore enpiercèd with his shaft
  To soar with his light feathers, and so bound   20
  I cannot bound a pitch above dull woe.   PITCH: distance
  Under love's heavy burden do I sink.

MERCUTIO.   And, to sink in it, should you burden love—
  Too great oppression for a tender thing.

ROMEO.   Is love a tender thing? It is too rough,   25
  Too rude, too boisterous, and it pricks like thorn.

MERCUTIO.   If love be rough with you, be rough with love;
  Give me a case to put my visage in. *[Puts on a mask.]*   VISAGE: mask
  A visor for a visor! What care I
  What curious eye doth quote deformities?*   30
  Here are the beetle brows shall blush for me.   BLUSH: be ugly

BENVOLIO.   Come, knock and enter; and no sooner in,
  But every man betake him to his legs.*

ROMEO.   A torch for me; let wantons light of heart
  Tickle the senseless rushes with their heels,   35   RUSHES: floor covering

---

[1] SHALL . . . EXCUSE: "Shall we deliver this speech to introduce ourselves?"   [3] DATE . . . PROLIXITY: "Such wordiness is old-fashioned."   [5] TARTAR'S . . . LATH: a painted wooden bow, curved like a Cupid's bow.   [6] CROWKEEPER: boy dressed as a scarecrow.   [7] WITHOUT-BOOK PROLOGUE: memorized speech.   [10] MEASURE THEM A MEASURE: dance a dance with them.   [30] WHAT . . . DEFORMITIES: "What do I care who sees my ugliness?"   [33] BETAKE . . . LEGS: start dancing.

For I am proverbed with a grandsire phrase:*
I'll be a candleholder and look on.
The game was ne'er so fair, and I am done.*

CANDLEHOLDER: bystander

MERCUTIO.   Tut, dun's the mouse, the constable's own
    word.
If thou art Dun, we'll draw thee from the mire*   40
Or, save your reverence, love, wherein thou stickest
Up to the ears. Come, we burn daylight, ho!

BURN DAYLIGHT: waste time

ROMEO.   Nay, that's not so.
MERCUTIO.   I mean, sir, in delay
  We waste our lights in vain, like lights by day.
Take our good meaning, for our judgment sits   45
  Five times in that ere once in our five wits.
ROMEO.   And we mean well in going to this masque,
  But 'tis no wit to go.
MERCUTIO.   Why, may one ask?
ROMEO.   I dreamt a dream tonight.

TONIGHT: last night

MERCUTIO.   And so did I.
ROMEO.   Well, what was yours?
MERCUTIO.   That dreamers often lie.   50
ROMEO.   In bed asleep, while they do dream things true.
MERCUTIO.   O, then I see Queen Mab* hath been with
    you.
She is the fairies' midwife, and she comes
In shape no bigger than an agate stone
On the forefinger of an alderman,   55
Drawn with a team of little atomies

ATOMIES: tiny creatures

Over men's noses as they lie asleep.
Her wagon spokes made of long spinners' legs,

SPINNERS': spiders'

The cover, of the wings of grasshoppers;
Her traces,* of the smallest spider web;   60
Her collars, of the moonshine's watery beams;
Her whip, of cricket's bone; the lash, of film;
Her wagoner, a small gray-coated gnat,
Not half so big as a round little worm
Pricked from the lazy finger of a maid;   65
Her chariot is an empty hazelnut
Made by the joiner squirrel or old grub,

JOINER: carpenter

Time out o' mind the fairies' coachmakers.
And in this state she gallops night by night

STATE: grand style

---

36 PROVERBED . . . PHRASE: advised by an old saying.   38 I AM DONE: "I'll
give up dancing."   40 DUN . . . MIRE: Dun was a common name for a
horse; "Dun's in the mire," a game whose object was to carry a log
from a room. (Mercutio's lighthearted wordplay is an attempt to
raise Romeo's spirits.)   52 QUEEN MAB: Celtic queen of the fairies.
60 TRACES: straps by which a wagon is pulled.

Through lovers' brains, and then they dream of love;   70
On courtiers' knees, that dream on curtsies straight;
O'er lawyers' fingers, who straight dream on fees;
O'er ladies' lips, who straight on kisses dream,
Which oft the angry Mab with blisters plagues,
Because their breath with sweetmeats tainted are.   75
Sometimes she gallops o'er a courtier's nose,
And then dreams he of smelling out a suit;*
And sometime comes she with a tithe-pig's tail
Tickling a parson's nose as 'a lies asleep,
Then he dreams of another benefice.   80   BENEFICE: income
Sometimes she driveth o'er a soldier's neck,
And then dreams he of cutting foreign throats,
Of breaches, ambuscadoes, Spanish blades,   AMBUSCADOES: ambushes
Of healths five fathom deep; and then anon   ANON: immediately
Drums in his ear, at which he starts and wakes,   85
And being thus frighted, swears a prayer or two
And sleeps again. This is that very Mab
That plats the manes of horses in the night,   PLATS: braids
And bakes the elflocks* in foul sluttish hairs,
Which, once untangled, much misfortune bodes.   90
This is the hag, when maids lie on their backs,
That presses them and learns them first to bear,
Making them women of good carriage.
This is she—
ROMEO.   Peace, peace, Mercutio, peace!
Thou talk'st of nothing.
MERCUTIO.   True, I talk of dreams,   95
Which are the children of an idle brain,
Begot of nothing but vain fantasy,
Which is as thin of substance as the air,
And more inconstant than the wind, who woos
Even now the frozen bosom of the north,   100
And, being angered, puffs away from thence,
Turning his face to the dew-dropping south.*
BENVOLIO.   This wind you talk of blows us from our-
     selves.
Supper is done, and we shall come too late.
ROMEO.   I fear, too early; for my mind misgives   105   MISGIVES: dreads
Some consequence yet hanging in the stars*
Shall bitterly begin his fearful date
With this night's revels, and expire the term   EXPIRE: end

---

[77] SUIT: someone who may be willing to buy the courtier's influence.
[89] ELFLOCKS: snarled hair, said to be the work of elves.   [102] DEW-DROP-
PING SOUTH: the wet south wind.   [106] HANGING IN THE STARS: destined.

Of a despisèd life, closed in my breast
By some vile forfeit of untimely death.   110
But He that hath the steerage of my course
Direct my sail! On, lusty gentlemen!
BENVOLIO.   Strike, drum.

[*They march about the stage and Exeunt.*]

FOR DISCUSSION

• As the friends approach Capulet's party in their costumes, Benvolio is anxious to be on time for the dancing and Mercutio is in a teasing, talkative mood. Why doesn't Romeo share their good spirits?

SCENE v.   *A hall in Capulet's house.*

[*Enter Musicians, and Servingmen with napkins.*]

FIRST SERVINGMAN.   Where's Potpan, that he helps not to
take away? He shift a trencher! He scrape a trencher!   TRENCHER: wooden plate
SECOND SERVINGMAN.   When good manners shall lie all in
one or two men's hands, and they unwashed too, 'tis
a foul thing.   5
FIRST SERVINGMAN.   Away with the joint-stools, remove
the court cupboard, look to the plate. Good thou, save
me a piece of marchpane; and, as thou loves me, let the   MARCHPANE: a candy
porter let in Susan Grindstone and Nell. Anthony and
Potpan!   10
SECOND SERVINGMAN.   Aye, boy, ready.
FIRST SERVINGMAN.   You are looked for and called for,
asked for and sought for in the great chamber.
THIRD SERVINGMAN.   We cannot be here and there too.
Cheerly, boys! Be brisk awhile, and the longer liver   15
take all.

[*Exeunt.*]
[*Enter Capulet, Lady Capulet, Juliet, Tybalt, and others of
his house, meeting the guests.*]

CAPULET.   Welcome, gentlemen! Ladies that have their
toes
Unplagued with corns will walk a bout with you.
Ah, my mistresses, which of you all
Will now deny to dance? She that makes dainty,*   20
She, I'll swear, hath corns. Am I come near ye now?

20 MAKES DAINTY: appears reluctant.

Welcome, gentlemen! I have seen the day
That I have worn a visor and could tell
A whispering tale in a fair lady's ear,
Such as would please; 'tis gone, 'tis gone, 'tis gone.   25
You are welcome, gentlemen! Come, musicians, play.

[*Music plays, and they dance.*]

A hall,* a hall! Give room! And foot it, girls.
More light, you knaves; and turn the tables up,
And quench the fire, the room is grown too hot.
Ah, sirrah, this unlooked-for sport* comes well.   30
Nay, sit, nay, sit, good cousin Capulet.
For you and I are past our dancing days.
How long is 't now since last yourself and I
Were in a mask?
SECOND CAPULET.   By'r Lady, thirty years.
CAPULET.   What, man! 'Tis not so much, 'tis not so
          much.   35
  Tis since the nuptial of Lucentio,
Come Pentecost as quickly as it will,
Some five-and-twenty years; and then we masked.
SECOND CAPULET.   'Tis more, 'tis more. His son is elder, sir;
His son is thirty.
CAPULET.   Will you tell me that?   40
His son was but a ward two years ago.   WARD: minor
ROMEO.   [*To a Servingman*] What lady's that which
          doth enrich the hand
Of yonder knight?
SERVINGMAN.   I know not, sir.
ROMEO.   O, she doth teach the torches to burn bright!   45
It seems she hangs upon the cheek of night
As a rich jewel in an Ethiop's ear;
Beauty too rich for use, for earth too dear!
So shows a snowy dove trooping with crows,
As yonder lady o'er her fellows shows.   50
The measure done, I'll watch her place of stand,
And, touching hers, make blessèd my rude hand.   RUDE: rough
Did my heart love till now? Forswear it, sight!   FORSWEAR: deny
For I ne'er saw true beauty till this night.
TYBALT.   This, by his voice, should be a Montague.   55
Fetch me my rapier, boy. What, dares the slave
Come hither, covered with an antic face,*
To fleer and scorn at our solemnity?   FLEER: mock

---

²⁷ A HALL: "Stand back [for the dancers]."   ³⁰ UNLOOKED-FOR SPORT:
The maskers were not expected.   ⁵⁷ ANTIC FACE: grotesque mask.

Now, by the stock and honor of my kin,
To strike him dead I hold it not a sin.   60
CAPULET. Why, how now, kinsman? Wherefore storm
   you so?
TYBALT. Uncle, this is a Montague, our foe,
   A villain that is hither come in spite   IN SPITE: insolently
   To scorn at our solemnity this night.
CAPULET. Young Romeo is it?
TYBALT.   'Tis he, that villain Romeo.   65
CAPULET. Content thee, gently coz, let him alone.
   'A bears him like a portly gentleman;
   And, to say truth, Verona brags of him
   To be a virtuous and well-governed youth.
   I would not for the wealth of all this town   70
   Here in my house do him disparagement.   DISPARAGEMENT: insult
   Therefore be patient; take no note of him.
   It is my will, the which if thou respect,
   Show a fair presence and put off these frowns,
   An ill-beseeming semblance for a feast.   75   SEMBLANCE: appearance
TYBALT. It fits when such a villain is a guest.
   I'll not endure him.
CAPULET.   He shall be endured.
   What, goodman* boy! I say he shall. Go to!
   Am I the master here, or you? Go to!
   You'll not endure him! God shall mend my soul!   80
   You'll make a mutiny among my guests!
   You will set cock-a-hoop!* You'll be the man!
TYBALT. Why, uncle, 'tis a shame.
CAPULET.   Go to, go to!
   You are a saucy boy. Is 't so, indeed?
   This trick may chance to scathe you; I know what.   85   SCATHE: harm
   You must contrary me! Marry, 'tis time—
   Well said, my hearts!—You are a princox; go!   PRINCOX: impudent youth
   Be quiet, or—More light, more light!—For shame!
   I'll make you quiet—What, cheerly, my hearts!
TYBALT. Patience perforce with willful choler meeting   90
   Makes my flesh tremble in their different greeting.
   I will withdraw. But this intrusion shall,
   Now seeming sweet, convert to bitt'rest gall.

   [*Exit.*]

ROMEO. [*To Juliet*] If I profane with my unworthiest
   hand

_____

78 GOODMAN: term for a man of lower rank than a gentleman.   82 SET
COCK-A-HOOP: start trouble.

This holy shrine, the gentle fine is this: 95
My lips, two blushing pilgrims, ready stand
    To smooth that rough touch with a tender kiss.*
JULIET.   Good pilgrim, you do wrong your hand too
        much,
    Which mannerly devotion shows in this;
For saints have hands that pilgrims' hands do touch,   100
    And palm to palm is holy palmers' kiss.*
ROMEO.   Have not saints lips, and holy palmers too?
JULIET.   Aye, pilgrim, lips that they must use in prayer.
ROMEO.   O, then, dear saint, let lips do what hands do;
    They pray, grant thou, lest faith turn to despair.   105
JULIET.   Saints do not move, though grant for prayers'
        sake.
ROMEO.   Then move not while my prayer's effect I take.*
    Thus from my lips, by thine, my sin is purged.

[*Kisses her.*]

94–97 IF . . . KISS: After taking Juliet's hand, Romeo kisses it gently to
apologize for his bold gesture. Praising her, he compares himself to a
pilgrim at the shrine of his saint.   100–101 FOR . . . KISS: Juliet suggests
that a handclasp is the usual palmer's, or pilgrim's, kiss.   106–107 SAINTS
. . . TAKE: Juliet still resists, on the grounds that saints cannot act, or
"move"; they only answer prayers. Romeo counters by telling her not
to "move," while he answers his own prayer.

JULIET.   Then have my lips the sin that they have took.

ROMEO.   Sin from my lips? O trespass sweetly urged!   110
  Give me my sin again.

  [*Kisses her.*]

JULIET.   You kiss by the book.   BY THE BOOK: by formal rules

NURSE.   Madam, your mother craves a word with you.

ROMEO.   What is her mother?

NURSE.   Marry, bachelor,
  Her mother is the lady of the house,
  And a good lady, and a wise and virtuous.   115
  I nursed her daughter that you talked withal;   WITHAL: with
  I tell you, he that can lay hold of her
  Shall have the chinks.   CHINKS: money

ROMEO.   Is she a Capulet?
  O dear account! My life is my foe's debt.*

BENVOLIO.   Away, be gone; the sport is at the best.   120

ROMEO.   Aye, so I fear; the more is my unrest.

CAPULET.   Nay, gentlemen, prepare not to be gone;
  We have a trifling foolish banquet towards.   TOWARDS: to come
  Is it e'en so? Why then, I thank you all;
  I thank you, honest gentlemen. Good night.   125
  More torches here! Come on then, let's to bed.
  Ah, sirrah, by my fay, it waxes late;   FAY: faith
  I'll to my rest.

  [*Exeunt all but Juliet and Nurse.*]

JULIET.   Come hither, Nurse. What is yond gentleman?

NURSE.   The son and heir of old Tiberio.   130

JULIET.   What's he that now is going out of door?

NURSE.   Marry, that, I think, be young Petruchio.

JULIET.   What's he that follows here, that would not
  dance?

NURSE.   I know not.

JULIET.   Go ask his name. [*Aside*] If he be marrièd,   135
  My grave is like to be my wedding bed.

NURSE.   His name is Romeo, and a Montague;
  The only son of your great enemy.

JULIET.   My only love, sprung from my only hate!
  Too early seen unknown, and known too late!   140
  Prodigious birth of love it is to me   PRODIGIOUS: monstrous
  That I must love a loathèd enemy.

NURSE.   What's this? What's this?

---

119 O . . . DEBT: "Oh costly exchange, since my life now belongs to my
enemy [Juliet]."

JULIET.   A rhyme I learnt even now
  Of one I danced withal.
NURSE.   Anon, anon!
  Come, let's away; the strangers all are gone.   145

  [*Exeunt.*]

FOR DISCUSSION

1. Another conflict between Montague and Capulet erupts in this scene. Who starts it? What does Capulet do to keep the peace? How do you explain his reasonableness here when he was so anxious for a fight in the first scene?

2. The first words between Romeo and Juliet are in the form of a sonnet, in which he is seen as a pilgrim and she as the object of his religious devotion. Although their mood is playful, the religious comparison emphasizes the seriousness of their love. What other indications are there that both Romeo and Juliet have fallen desperately in love?

ACT II

PROLOGUE

  [*Enter Speaker.*]

SPEAKER.   Now old Desire doth in his deathbed lie,
      And young Affection gapes to be his heir;   GAPES: longs
    That fair for which love groaned for and would die,   FAIR: Rosaline
      With tender Juliet matched, is now not fair.
    Now Romeo is beloved and loves again,   5
      Alike bewitched by the charm of looks;
    But to his foe supposed he must complain,   COMPLAIN: pay court
      And she steal love's sweet bait from fearful hooks.
    Being held a foe, he may not have access
      To breathe such vows as lovers use to swear;   10   USE TO: usually
    And she as much in love, her means much less
      To meet her new belovèd anywhere;
    But passion lends them power, time means, to meet,
    Temp'ring extremities with extreme sweet.

  [*Exit.*]

  SCENE I.   *A lane by the wall of Capulet's orchard.*

  [*Enter Romeo, alone.*]

ROMEO.   Can I go forward when my heart is here?

Turn back, dull earth, and find thy center out.*

[*He climbs the wall and leaps down within the orchard.*]
[*Enter Benvolio with Mercutio.*]

BENVOLIO.   Romeo! My cousin Romeo!
MERCUTIO.   He is wise
   And, on my life, hath stolen him home to bed.
BENVOLIO.   He ran this way and leapt this orchard wall.   5
   Call, good Mercutio.
MERCUTIO.   Nay, I'll conjure too.
   Romeo! Humors! Madman! Passion! Lover!
   Appear thou in the likeness of a sigh!
   Speak but one rhyme, and I am satisfied;
   Cry but "Ay me" pronounce but "love" and "dove";   10   GOSSIP: close friend
   Speak to my gossip Venus one fair word,
   One nickname for her purblind son and heir,   PURBLIND: entirely blind
   Young Abraham Cupid, he that shot so true
   When King Cophetua loved the beggar maid!*
   He heareth not, he stirreth not, he moveth not;   15
   The ape is dead, and I must conjure him.
   I conjure thee by Rosaline's bright eyes,
   By her high forehead and her scarlet lip . . .
   That in thy likeness thou appear to us!
BENVOLIO.   An if he hear thee, thou wilt anger him.   20
MERCUTIO.   This cannot anger him; 'twould anger him
   To raise a spirit in his mistress' circle,*
   Of some strange nature, letting it there stand
   Till she had laid it and conjured it down.
   That were some spite; my invocation   25   SPITE: vexation
   Is fair and honest; in his mistress' name,
   I conjure only but to raise up him.
BENVOLIO.   Come, he hath hid himself among these trees
   To be consorted with the humorous night.   HUMOROUS: damp
   Blind is his love and best befits the dark.   30
MERCUTIO.   If Love be blind, Love cannot hit the
          mark. . . .
   Romeo, good night; I'll to my truckle bed;*
   This field bed is too cold for me to sleep.
   Come, shall we go?
BENVOLIO.   Go then, for 'tis in vain
   To seek him here that means not to be found.   35

[*Exeunt Benvolio and Mercutio.*]

2 TURN . . . OUT: "Turn back, dull flesh [he is speaking to himself], and
find your heart [Juliet]."   14 WHEN . . . BEGGAR MAID: Mercutio refers
to a ballad of the time.   22 CIRCLE: the magic circle in which conjurers
(wizards) performed.   32 TRUCKLE BED: trundle bed (a child's bed).

FOR DISCUSSION

• Benvolio and Mercutio still think that Romeo believes himself in love with Rosaline. What difference is there in the way each treats his friend's infatuation?

SCENE II.   *Capulet's orchard.*

ROMEO.   [*Coming forward*] He jests at scars that never
        felt a wound.

[*Juliet appears above at her window.*]

But, soft! What light through yonder window breaks?
It is the east, and Juliet is the sun.
Arise, fair sun, and kill the envious moon,
Who is already sick and pale with grief   5
That thou, her maid,* art far more fair than she.
Be not her maid, since she is envious;
Her vestal livery is but sick and green,
And none but fools do wear it; cast it off.
It is my lady, O, it is my love!   10
O, that she knew she were!
She speaks, yet she says nothing. What of that?
Her eye discourses; I will answer it.   DISCOURSES: speaks
I am too bold; 'tis not to me she speaks.
Two of the fairest stars in all the heaven,   15
Having some business, do entreat her eyes
To twinkle in their spheres till they return.
What if her eyes were there, they in her head?   THEY: the stars
The brightness of her cheek would shame those stars
As daylight doth a lamp; her eyes in heaven   20
Would through the airy region stream so bright
That birds would sing and think it were not night.
See how she leans her cheek upon her hand!
O, that I were a glove upon that hand,
That I might touch that cheek!
JULIET.   Ay me!
ROMEO.   [*Aside*]   She speaks.   25
O, speak again, bright angel! For thou art
As glorious to this night, being o'er my head,
As is a wingèd messenger of heaven
Unto the white upturnèd wond'ring eyes
Of mortals that fall back to gaze on him   30
When he bestrides the lazy-pacing clouds

⁶ HER MAID: In ancient times unmarried girls were supposed to be under
the protection of Diana, goddess of the moon.

And sails upon the bosom of the air.

JULIET.   O Romeo, Romeo! Wherefore art thou Romeo?
Deny thy father and refuse thy name;
Or, if thou wilt not, be but sworn my love   35
And I'll no longer be a Capulet.

ROMEO.   [*Aside*] Shall I hear more, or shall I speak at
this?

JULIET.   'Tis but thy name that is my enemy;
Thou art thyself, though not a Montague.*
What's Montague? It is nor hand, nor foot,   40
Nor arm, nor face, nor any other part
Belonging to a man. O, be some other name!
What's in a name? That which we call a rose
By any other word would smell as sweet;
So Romeo would, were he not Romeo called,   45
Retain that dear perfection which he owes   OWES: owns
Without that title. Romeo, doff thy name;
And for thy name, which is no part of thee,
Take all myself.

ROMEO.   [*To Juliet*] I take thee at thy word.   50
Call me but "Love," and I'll be new baptized;
Henceforth I never will be Romeo.

JULIET.   What man art thou, that, thus bescreened in
night,
So stumblest on my counsel?   COUNSEL: private thoughts

ROMEO.   By a name
I know not how to tell thee who I am.   55
My name, dear saint, is hateful to myself
Because it is an enemy to thee.
Had I it written, I would tear the word.

JULIET.   My ears have yet not drunk a hundred words
Of thy tongue's uttering, yet I know the sound.   60
Art thou not Romeo, and a Montague?

ROMEO.   Neither, fair maid, if either thee dislike.

JULIET.   How cam'st thou hither, tell me, and wherefore?
The orchard walls are high and hard to climb,
And the place death, considering who thou art,   65
If any of my kinsmen find thee here.

ROMEO.   With love's light wings did I o'erperch these   O'ERPERCH: fly over
walls;
For stony limits cannot hold love out,
And what love can do, that dares love attempt.
Therefore thy kinsmen are no stop to me.   70

---

³⁹ THOU . . . MONTAGUE: "You would be yourself, even if you were not
a Montague."

JULIET.   If they do see thee, they will murder thee.
ROMEO.   Alack, there lies more peril in thine eye
    Than twenty of their swords! Look thou but sweet,
    And I am proof against their enmity.*
JULIET.   I would not for the world they saw thee here.   75
ROMEO.   I have night's cloak to hide me from their eyes;
    And but thou love me, let them find me here.
    My life were better ended by their hate
    Than death proroguèd, wanting of thy love.   PROROGUÈD: postponed
JULIET.   By whose direction found'st thou out this place?   80
ROMEO.   By Love, that first did prompt me to inquire.
    He lent me counsel, and I lent him eyes.
    I am no pilot, yet wert thou as far
    As that vast shore washed with the farthest sea,
    I should adventure for such merchandise.   85
JULIET.   Thou know'st the mask of night is on my face;
    Else would a maiden blush bepaint my cheek
    For that which thou hast heard me speak tonight.
    Fain would I dwell on form; fain, fain deny   FAIN: gladly
    What I have spoke; but farewell compliment!   90   COMPLIMENT: formalities
    Dost thou love me? I know thou wilt say "Aye,"
    And I will take thy word. Yet, if thou swear'st,
    Thou mayst prove false. At lovers' perjuries,
    They say, Jove* laughs. O gentle Romeo,
    If thou dost love, pronounce it faithfully;   95
    Or if thou think'st I am too quickly won,
    I'll frown and be perverse and say thee nay
    So thou wilt woo; but else, not for the world.
    In truth, fair Montague, I am too fond,   FOND: foolish
    And therefore thou mayst think my 'havior light;   100
    But trust me, gentleman, I'll prove more true
    Than those that have more cunning to be strange.   STRANGE: reserved
    I should have been more strange, I must confess,
    But that thou overheard'st, ere I was ware,
    My truelove's passion. Therefore pardon me,   105
    And not impute this yielding to light love,
    Which the dark night hath so discoverèd.   DISCOVERÈD: revealed
ROMEO.   Lady, by yonder blessèd moon I vow,
    That tips with silver all these fruit-tree tops—
JULIET.   O, swear not by the moon, the inconstant moon   110
    That monthly changes in her circled orb,
    Lest that thy love prove likewise variable.
ROMEO.   What shall I swear by?

73–74 LOOK . . . ENMITY: "If you will look favorably on me, I shall be
armored against their hatred." 94 JOVE: Jupiter, chief of the Roman
gods.

JULIET.   Do not swear at all;
  Or if thou wilt, swear by thy gracious self,
  Which is the god of my idolatry,   115   IDOLATRY: worship
  And I'll believe thee.
ROMEO.   If my heart's dear love—
JULIET.   Well, do not swear. Although I joy in thee,
  I have no joy of this contract tonight.
  It is too rash, too unadvised, too sudden,
  Too like the lightning, which doth cease to be   120
  Ere one can say it lightens. Sweet, good night.
  This bud of love, by summer's rip'ning breath,
  May prove a beauteous flow'r when next we meet.
  Good night, good night! As sweet repose and rest
  Come to thy heart as that within my breast!   125
ROMEO.   O, wilt thou leave me so unsatisfied?
JULIET.   What satisfaction canst thou have tonight?
ROMEO.   The exchange of thy love's faithful vow for
    mine.
JULIET.   I gave thee mine before thou didst request it;
  And yet I would it were to give again.   130
ROMEO.   Wouldst thou withdraw it? For what purpose,
    love?
JULIET.   But to be frank and give it thee again.   FRANK: generous
  And yet I wish but for the thing I have.
  My bounty is as boundless as the sea,   BOUNTY: generosity
  My love as deep; the more I give to thee,   135
  The more I have, for both are infinite.

  [*The Nurse calls from within the house.*]

  I hear some noise within. Dear love, adieu!
  Anon, good Nurse! Sweet Montague, be true.
  Stay but a little; I will come again.

  [*Exit.*]

ROMEO.   O blessèd, blessèd night! I am afeard,   140
  Being in night, all this is but a dream,
  Too flattering-sweet to be substantial.

  [*Re-enter Juliet.*]

JULIET.   Three words, dear Romeo, and good night
    indeed.
  If that thy bent of love be honorable,   BENT: intention
  Thy purpose marriage, send me word tomorrow,   145
  By one that I'll procure to come to thee,
  Where and what time thou wilt perform the rite;
  And all my fortunes at thy foot I'll lay

And follow thee, my lord, throughout the world.

NURSE. [*Within*] Madam! 150

JULIET. I come anon. [*To Romeo*] But if thou meanest
not well, I do beseech thee—

NURSE. [*Within*] Madam!

JULIET.   By and by I come.
    [*To Romeo*] To cease thy strife and leave me to my   STRIFE: endeavors
        grief.
    Tomorrow will I send.

ROMEO.   So thrive my soul—   155

JULIET.   A thousand times good night!

    [*Exit.*]

ROMEO.   A thousand times the worse, to want thy light.
    Love goes toward love as schoolboys from their books,
    But love from love, toward school with heavy looks.

    [*Juliet enters once again.*]

JULIET.   Hist! Romeo, hist! O for a falconer's voice   160
    To lure this tassel-gentle* back again!
    Bondage is hoarse and may not speak aloud;*
    Else would I tear the cave where Echo lies,
    And make her airy tongue more hoarse than mine
    With repetition of my Romeo's name.*   165

ROMEO.   It is my soul that calls upon my name.
    How silver-sweet sound lovers' tongues by night,
    Like softest music to attending ears!   ATTENDING: attentive

JULIET.   Romeo!

ROMEO.   My sweet?

JULIET.   What o'clock tomorrow
    Shall I send to thee?

ROMEO.   By the hour of nine.   170

JULIET.   I will not fail. 'Tis twenty year till then.
    I have forgot why I did call thee back.

ROMEO.   Let me stand here till thou remember it.

JULIET.   I shall forget, to have thee still stand there,
    Rememb'ring how I love thy company.   175

ROMEO.   And I'll still stay, to have thee still forget,
    Forgetting any other home but this.

JULIET.   'Tis almost morning. I would have thee gone—
    And yet no farther than a wanton's bird,   WANTON'S: careless child's
    That lets it hop a little from her hand,   180
    Like a poor prisoner in his twisted gyves,   GYVES: bonds

---

[161] TASSEL-GENTLE: male falcon. [162] BONDAGE . . . ALOUD: "I am under
my parents' supervision and cannot speak loudly for fear of being
overheard." [164-165] MAKE . . . NAME: "make the nymph Echo hoarser
than I with echoing my cries for you."

And with a silk thread plucks it back again,
So loving-jealous of his liberty.
ROMEO.   I would I were thy bird.
JULIET.   Sweet, so would I.
Yet I should kill thee with much cherishing.   185
Good night, good night! Parting is such sweet sorrow
That I shall say good night till it be morrow.

[*Exit.*]

ROMEO.   Sleep dwell upon thine eyes, peace in thy
    breast!
Would I were sleep and peace, so sweet to rest!
Hence will I to my ghostly father's* cell,   190   DEAR HAP: good fortune
His help to crave and my dear hap to tell.

[*Exit.*]

190 GHOSTLY FATHER'S: father confessor's (Friar Laurence's).

FOR DISCUSSION

1. Why is Romeo silent when Juliet first appears? What finally causes him to speak?

2. When Romeo first saw Juliet he called her brighter than torchlight. In this scene he compares her to the sun, whose beauty makes the moon envious. What other images of *light* are there in this scene? What purpose do they serve besides emphasizing Juliet's beauty?

3. Paraphrase (restate in your own words) Juliet's speech beginning " 'Tis but thy name that is my enemy" (line 38).

4. Just as Romeo's language is more romantic than Juliet's direct speech, her thinking is more practical than his. What three things does she fear? What plan does she propose?

SCENE III.   *Friar Laurence's room.*

[*Enter Friar Laurence alone, carrying a basket of herbs and other plants.*]

FRIAR.   The gray-eyed morn smiles on the frowning
    night,
Check'ring the eastern clouds with streaks of light;
And fleckèd darkness like a drunkard reels
From forth day's path and Titan's fiery wheels.*
Now, ere the sun advance his burning eye   5
The day to cheer and night's dank dew to dry,
I must upfill this osier cage of ours   OSIER CAGE: wicker basket
With baleful weeds and precious-juicèd flowers. . . .   BALEFUL: poisonous
O, mickle is the powerful grace that lies   MICKLE: great
In plants, herbs, stones, and their true qualities;   10

4 TITAN'S FIERY WHEELS: the wheels on the sun's gold chariot.

For nought so vile that on the earth doth live
But to the earth some special good doth give;
Nor aught so good but, strained from that fair use,
Revolts from true birth, stumbling on abuse.
Virtue itself turns vice, being misapplied,   15
And vice sometime's by action dignified.

[*Enter Romeo, unseen by Friar Laurence.*]

Within the infant rind of this weak flower
Poison hath residence and medicine power;
For this, being smelt, with that part cheers each part;*
Being tasted, slays all senses with the heart.   20
Two such opposèd kings encamp them still
In man as well as herbs—grace and rude will;
And where the worser is predominant,
Full soon the canker death eats up that plant.   CANKER: worm
ROMEO.   Good morrow, Father.
FRIAR.   *Benedicite!*   25   BENEDICITE: God bless you
What early tongue so sweet saluteth me?
Young son, it argues a distemperèd head
So soon to bid good morrow to thy bed.
Care keeps his watch in every old man's eye,
And where care lodges, sleep will never lie;   30
But where unbruisèd youth with unstuffed brain   UNSTUFFED: untroubled
Doth couch his limbs, there golden sleep doth reign.
Therefore thy earliness doth me assure
Thou art up-roused with some distemp'rature;
Or if not so, then here I hit it right: 35
Our Romeo hath not been in bed tonight.
ROMEO.   That last is true; the sweeter rest was mine.
FRIAR.   God pardon sin! Wast thou with Rosaline?
ROMEO.   With Rosaline, my ghostly Father? No.
I have forgot that name and that name's woe.   40
FRIAR.   That's my good son; but where hast thou been
        then?
ROMEO.   I'll tell thee ere thou ask it me again.
I have been feasting with mine enemy,
Where on a sudden one hath wounded me
That's by me wounded. Both our remedies   45
Within thy help and holy physic lies.   PHYSIC: healing
I bear no hatred, blessèd man, for, lo,
My intercession likewise steads my foe.   STEADS: aids
FRIAR.   Be plain, good son, and homely in thy drift;*

---

19 THIS . . . PART: "This flower, when smelled, revives every part of the
body."   49 HOMELY . . . DRIFT: "plain in your language."

Riddling confession finds but riddling shrift.*   50

ROMEO.   Then plainly know my heart's dear love is set

On the fair daughter of rich Capulet.

As mine on hers, so hers is set on mine,

And all combined, save what thou must combine   SAVE: except for

By holy marriage. When and where and how   55

We met, we wooed, and made exchange of vow,

I'll tell thee as we pass; but this I pray,

That thou consent to marry us today.

FRIAR.   Holy Saint Francis! What a change is here!

Is Rosaline, that thou didst love so dear,   60

So soon forsaken? Young men's love then lies

Not truly in their hearts, but in their eyes.

Jesu Maria! What a deal of brine

Hath washed thy sallow cheeks for Rosaline!

How much salt water thrown away in waste   65

To season love, that of it doth not taste!

The sun not yet thy sighs from heaven clears,

Thy old groans yet ring in mine ancient ears.

Lo, here upon thy cheek the stain doth sit

Of an old tear that is not washed off yet.   70

If e'er thou wast thyself, and these woes thine,

Thou and these woes were all for Rosaline.

And art thou changed? Pronounce this sentence then:

Women may fall when there's no strength in men.*

ROMEO.   Thou chid'st me oft for loving Rosaline.   75   CHID'ST: scolded

FRIAR.   For doting, not for loving, pupil mine.

ROMEO.   And bad'st me bury love.   BAD'ST: bid

FRIAR.   Not in a grave

To lay one in, another out to have.

ROMEO.   I pray thee chide me not. Her I love now

Doth grace for grace and love for love allow.   80   GRACE: favor

The other did not so.

FRIAR.   O, she knew well

Thy love did read by rote, that could not spell.*

But come, young waverer, come, go with me.

In one respect I'll thy assistant be;

For this alliance may so happy prove   85

To turn your households' rancor to pure love.

ROMEO.   O, let us hence; I stand on sudden haste.

FRIAR.   Wisely and slow; they stumble that run fast.

 [*Exeunt.*]

⁵⁰ RIDDLING . . . SHRIFT: "A deceptive confession cannot earn true forgiveness."   ⁷⁴ WOMEN . . . MEN: "Women may be fickle if men are not
faithful."   ⁸² THY . . . SPELL: "You recited the words of love without
really meaning them."

FOR DISCUSSION

1. Friar Laurence begins this scene with a *soliloquy,* a speech addressed directly to the audience rather than to another character. This technique was commonly used by playwrights of Shakespeare's time to reveal a character's private thoughts. What moral does the Friar find in the healing and poisonous powers of plants?

2. Assuming that Romeo has spent the night with Rosaline, the Friar is astonished to learn that he wants to marry Juliet instead. The new love seems to him a "doting" (foolish infatuation) like the old. What evidence does Romeo offer that his love for Juliet is different? Why does the Friar agree to help even though he thinks Romeo is acting in haste and knows that both families will be opposed to the marriage?

SCENE IV. *A street.*

[Enter Benvolio and Mercutio.]

MERCUTIO.   Where the devil should this Romeo be?
Came he not home tonight?
BENVOLIO.   Not to his father's. I spoke with his man.
MERCUTIO.   Why, that same pale hard-hearted wench, that Rosaline,
Torments him so that he will sure run mad.   5
BENVOLIO.   Tybalt, the kinsman to old Capulet,
Hath sent a letter to his father's house.
MERCUTIO.   A challenge, on my life.
BENVOLIO.   Romeo will answer it.
MERCUTIO.   Any man that can write may answer a letter.   10
BENVOLIO.   Nay, he will answer the letter's master, how he dares, being dared.
MERCUTIO.   Alas, poor Romeo! He is already dead: stabbed with a white wench's black eye; run through the ear with a love song; the very pin of his heart cleft   15
with the blind bow-boy's butt-shaft; and is he a man to encounter Tybalt?

BUTT-SHAFT: arrow

BENVOLIO.   Why, what is Tybalt?
MERCUTIO.   More than Prince of Cats.* O, he's the courageous captain of compliments.* He fights as you   20
sing pricksong—keeps time, distance, and proportion; he rests his minim rests, one, two, and the third in your bosom! The very butcher of a silk button, a duelist, a duelist! A gentleman of the very first house, of the first and second cause. Ah, the immortal   25
passado! The *punto reverso!* The hay!*

PRICKSONG: written music

¹⁹ PRINCE OF CATS: a play on Tybalt's name, which is similar to "Tybert," the cat in a medieval fable. ²⁰ CAPTAIN OF COMPLIMENTS: master of the fine points of dueling. ²⁵⁻²⁶ THE FIRST . . . HAY: dueling terms describing the various maneuvers.

BENVOLIO.   The what?

MERCUTIO.   The pox of such antic, lisping, affecting fantasticoes—these new tuners of accent! "By Jesu, a very good blade! A very tall man . . . !" Why, is not 30 this a lamentable thing, grandsire, that we should be thus afflicted with these strange flies, these fashion-mongers, these pardon-me's, who stand so much on the new form that they cannot sit at ease on the old bench? O, their bones, their bones! 35

FANTASTICOES: foolishmen

[*Enter Romeo.*]

BENVOLIO.   Here comes Romeo, here comes Romeo.

MERCUTIO.   Without his roe,* like a dried herring. O flesh, flesh, how art thou fishified! Now is he for the numbers that Petrarch* flowed in. Laura, to his lady, was a kitchen wench—marry, she had a better love to 40 be-rhyme her; Dido* a dowdy; Cleopatra a gypsy; Helen and Hero hildings and harlots;* Thisbe* a gray eye or so, but not to the purpose. Signior Romeo, *bon jour!* There's a French salutation to your French slop. You gave us the counterfeit fairly last night. 45

NUMBERS: verses

HELEN: Helen of Troy

FRENCH SLOP: loose-fitting breeches

ROMEO.   Good morrow to you both. What counterfeit did I give you?

MERCUTIO.   The slip, sir, the slip. Can you not conceive?

CONCEIVE: understand

ROMEO.   Pardon, good Mercutio. My business was great, and in such a case as mine a man may strain courtesy. 50

MERCUTIO.   That's as much as to say, such a case as yours constrains a man to bow in the hams.

CASE: physical state

ROMEO.   Meaning, to curtsy.

MERCUTIO.   Thou hast most kindly hit it.

ROMEO.   A most courteous exposition. 55

MERCUTIO.   Nay, I am the very pink of courtesy.

PINK: perfect example

ROMEO.   Pink for flower.

MERCUTIO.   Right.

ROMEO.   Why, then is my pump well-flowered.*

MERCUTIO.   Sure wit! Follow me this jest now till thou 60 hast worn out thy pump, that, when the single sole of

---

[37] WITHOUT HIS ROE: looking thin and feeble. Mercutio is also playing on the sound of his name: lacking the "Ro," only a sigh—"me-o"—remains. [39] PETRARCH: Italian poet, who composed love sonnets to Laura. [41] DIDO: in Roman legend, the Queen of Carthage, who committed suicide when abandoned by Aeneas. [42] HERO . . . HARLOTS: In Greek legend, Hero was a priestess loved by Leander. Here, Hero and Helen of Troy are referred to as good-for-nothings. [42] THISBE: heroine of a story similar to that of Romeo and Juliet. [59] THEN . . . WELL-FLOWERED: Since *pink* is a kind of *flower*, Romeo's shoe, which is pinked (decorated) can be said to be flowered (a pun on *floored*).

it is worn, the jest may remain, after the wearing,
solely singular.

ROMEO. O single-soled jest, solely singular for the
singleness!*   65

MERCUTIO. Come between us, good Benvolio; my wits
faint.

ROMEO. Switch and spurs, switch and spurs; or I'll cry
a match.*

MERCUTIO. Nay, if our wits run the wild-goose chase, I 70
am done; for thou hast more of the wild goose in one
of thy wits than, I am sure, I have in my whole five.
Was I with you there for the goose?

ROMEO. Thou wast never with me for anything when
thou wast not there for the goose.   75

MERCUTIO. I will bite thee by the ear for that jest.

ROMEO. Nay, good goose, bite not.

MERCUTIO. Thy wit is a very bitter sweeting; it is a most
sharp sauce.

ROMEO. And is it not, then, well served in to a sweet 80
goose?

MERCUTIO. O, here's a wit of cheveril, that stretches
from an inch narrow to an ell broad!

ROMEO. I stretch it out for that word "broad," which
added to the goose, proves thee far and wide a broad 85
goose.

MERCUTIO. Why, is not this better now than groaning
for love? Now art thou sociable, now art thou
Romeo. . . .

BENVOLIO. Stop there, stop there! . . .   90

ROMEO. Here's goodly gear!

[*Enter Nurse and her servant Peter.*]

A sail, a sail!

MERCUTIO. Two, two; a shirt and a smock.*

NURSE. Peter!

PETER. Anon!   95

NURSE. My fan, Peter.

MERCUTIO. Good Peter, to hide her face; for her fan's
the fairer face. . . .

NURSE. . . . Gentlemen, can any of you tell me where I
may find the young Romeo?   100

ROMEO. I can tell you; but young Romeo will be older

SOLELY SINGULAR: all alone

SWEETING: kind of apple

CHEVERIL: stretchable leather
ELL BROAD: forty-five inches

BROAD: obvious

GEAR: stuff

64–65 SINGLE-SOLED . . . SINGLENESS: "weak joke, unique only for its
feebleness." 68–69 SWITCH . . . MATCH: "Urge on your wits, or I'll claim
a victory in this battle of wits." 93 SHIRT . . . SMOCK: a man and a
woman.

when you have found him than he was when you
sought him. I am the youngest of that name, for fault
of a worse.

NURSE. You say well.   105

MERCUTIO. Yea, is the worst well? Very well took, i'
faith; wisely, wisely.   TOOK: understood

NURSE. If you be he, sir, I desire some confidence with
you. . . .   CONFIDENCE: conference

MERCUTIO. Romeo, will you come to your father's?   110
We'll to dinner thither.

ROMEO. I will follow you.

MERCUTIO. Farewell, ancient lady. Farewell, [*singing*]
"lady, lady, lady."

[*Exeunt Mercutio, Benvolio.*]

NURSE. I pray you, sir, what saucy merchant was this   115
that was so full of his ropery?   ROPERY: mischief

ROMEO. A gentleman, Nurse, that loves to hear himself
talk and will speak more in a minute than he will stand
to in a month.

NURSE. An 'a speak anything against me, I'll take him   120
down, an 'a were lustier than he is, and twenty such
Jacks; and if I cannot, I'll find those that shall. . . .   JACKS: knaves
Scurvy knave! Pray you, sir, a word: and, as I told you,
my young lady bid me inquire you out. What she bid
me say, I will keep to myself. But first let me tell ye, if 125
ye should lead her into a fool's paradise, as they say, it
were a very gross kind of behavior, as they say; for
the gentlewoman is young, and therefore, if you
should deal double with her, truly it were an ill thing
to be offered to any gentlewoman, and very weak   130   WEAK: ungentlemanly
dealing.

ROMEO. Nurse, commend me* to thy lady and mistress.
I protest unto thee—

NURSE. Good heart, and i' faith, I will tell her as much.
Lord, Lord, she will be a joyful woman.   135

ROMEO. What wilt thou tell her, Nurse? Thou dost not
mark me.   MARK: pay attention to

NURSE. I will tell her, sir, that you do protest; which, as
I take it, is a gentlemanlike offer.

ROMEO. Bid her devise   140
Some means to come to shrift this afternoon;
And there she shall at Friar Laurence' cell
Be shrived and married. Here is for thy pains. SHRIVED: purified

---

[132] COMMEND ME: "give my respects."

NURSE. No, truly, sir; not a penny.

ROMEO. Go to; I say you shall.   145

NURSE. This afternoon, sir? Well, she shall be there.

ROMEO. And stay, good Nurse: behind the abbey wall
Within this hour my man shall be with thee
And bring thee cords made like a tackled stair,   STAIR: rope ladder
Which to the high topgallant of my joy   150   TOPGALLANT: peak
Must be my convoy in the secret night.
Farewell. Be trusty, and I'll quit thy pains.   QUIT: reward
Farewell. Commend me to thy mistress.

NURSE. Now God in heaven bless thee! Hark you, sir.

ROMEO. What say'st thou, my dear Nurse?   155

NURSE. Is your man secret? Did you ne'er hear say,
"Two may keep counsel, putting one away?"

ROMEO. I warrant thee my man's as true as steel.

NURSE. Well, sir, my mistress is the sweetest lady. Lord,
Lord! When 'twas a little prating thing—O, there is a 160   PRATING: babbling
nobleman in town, one Paris, that would fain lay knife
aboard; but she, good soul, had as lief see a toad, a   LIEF: willingly
very toad, as see him. I anger her sometimes, and tell
her that Paris is the properer man; but, I'll warrant
you, when I say so, she looks as pale as any clout in 165   CLOUT: cloth
the versal world. Doth not rosemary and Romeo begin   VERSAL WORLD: universe
both with a letter?

ROMEO. Aye, Nurse; what of that? Both with an *R*.

NURSE. Ah, mocker! That's the dog's name. *R* is for the
—No; I know it begins with some other letter; and 170
she hath the prettiest sententious of it, of you and   SENTENTIOUS: brief sayings
rosemary, that it would do you good to hear it.

ROMEO. Commend me to thy lady.

NURSE. Aye, a thousand times. [*Romeo leaves*] Peter!

PETER. Anon!   175

NURSE. Before, and apace.   APACE: quickly

[*Exit after Peter.*]

FOR DISCUSSION

• This scene is intended mostly for humorous effect—Romeo and Mercutio exchange witticisms and Mercutio insults the Nurse, who is attempting to be elegant—but it also contains two serious developments. What is the probable nature of the letter from Tybalt? What arrangements does Romeo make for his marriage to Juliet?

SCENE V. *Capulet's orchard.*

[*Enter Juliet.*]

JULIET.   The clock struck nine when I did send the Nurse;
In half an hour she promised to return.
Perchance she cannot meet him. That's not so.
O, she is lame! Love's heralds should be thoughts
Which ten times faster glide than the sun's beams,   5
Driving back shadows over lowering hills.

    LOWERING: darkening

Therefore do nimble-pinioned* doves draw Love,
And therefore hath the wind-swift Cupid wings.
Now is the sun upon the highmost hill
Of this day's journey, and from nine till twelve   10
Is three long hours; yet she is not come.
Had she affections and warm youthful blood,
She would be as swift in motion as a ball;
My words would bandy her to my sweet love,

    BANDY: toss

And his to me.   15
But old folks, marry, feign as they were dead—

    FEIGN AS: appear as if

Unwieldy, slow, heavy and pale as lead.

[*Enter Nurse and Peter.*]

O God, she comes! O honey Nurse, what news?
Hast thou met with him? Send thy man away.
NURSE.   Peter, stay at the gate.   [*Exit Peter.*]   20
JULIET.   Now, good sweet Nurse—O Lord, why look'st
    thou sad?
Though news be sad, yet tell them merrily;
If good, thou sham'st the music of sweet news
By playing it to me with so sour a face.
NURSE.   I am aweary, give me leave awhile.   25
Fie, how my bones ache! What a jaunce have I had!

    JAUNCE: tiring trip

JULIET.   I would thou hadst my bones, and I thy news.
Nay, come, I pray thee, speak; good, good Nurse, speak.
NURSE.   Jesu, what haste! Can you not stay awhile?
Do you not see that I am out of breath?   30
JULIET.   How art thou out of breath when thou hast
    breath
To say to me that thou art out of breath?
The excuse that thou dost make in this delay
Is longer than the tale thou dost excuse.
Is thy news good or bad? Answer to that.   35

---

7 NIMBLE-PINIONED: swift-winged. The chariot of Venus, Roman goddess
of love, was thought to be drawn by doves.

Say either, and I'll stay the circumstance.
Let me be satisfied: is 't good or bad?
NURSE.   Well, you have made a simple choice; you know   SIMPLE: foolish
not how to choose a man. Romeo? No, not he. Though
his face be better than any man's, yet his leg excels   40
all men's; and for a hand and a foot, and a body,
though they be not to be talked on, yet they are past
compare. He is not the flower of courtesy, but, I'll
warrant him, as gentle as a lamb. Go thy ways, wench;
serve God. What, have you dined at home?   45
JULIET.   No, no! But all this did I know before.
What says he of our marriage? What of that?
NURSE.   Lord, how my head aches! What a head have I!
It beats as it would fall in twenty pieces.
My back o' t'other side—O, my back, my back!   50
Beshrew your heart for sending me about   BESHREW: curse
To catch my death with jauncing up and down!
JULIET.   I' faith, I am sorry that thou art not well.
Sweet, sweet, sweet Nurse, tell me, what says my love?
NURSE.   Your love says, like an honest gentleman, and a   55
courteous, and a kind, and a handsome, and, I warrant,
a virtuous—Where is your mother?
JULIET.   Where is my mother! Why, she is within;
Where should she be? How oddly thou repliest:
"Your love says, like an honest gentleman,   60
'Where is your mother?'"
NURSE.   O God's Lady dear!
Are you so hot? Marry come up, I trow.   HOT: angry
Is this the poultice for my aching bones?
Henceforward do your messages yourself.
JULIET.   Here's such a coil! Come, what says Romeo?   65   COIL: turmoil
NURSE.   Have you got leave to go to shrift today?
JULIET.   I have.
NURSE.   Then hie you hence to Friar Laurence' cell;   HIE: hurry
There stays a husband to make you a wife.
Now comes the wanton blood up in your cheeks;   70
They'll be in scarlet straight at any news.
Hie you to church; I must another way,
To fetch a ladder, by the which your love
Must climb a bird's nest soon when it is dark.
I am the drudge, and toil in your delight,   75
But you shall bear the burden soon at night.
Go; I'll to dinner; hie you to the cell.
JULIET.   Hie to high fortune! Honest Nurse, farewell.

[*Exeunt.*]

SCENE VI.   *Friar Laurence's cell.*

[*Enter Friar Laurence and Romeo.*]

FRIAR.   So smile the heavens upon this holy act
That after hours with sorrow chide us not!
ROMEO.   Amen, amen! But come what sorrow can,
It cannot countervail the exchange of joy   COUNTERVAIL: outweigh
That one short minute gives me in her sight.   5
Do thou but close our hands with holy words,
Then love-devouring Death do what he dare—
It is enough I may but call her mine.
FRIAR.   These violent delights have violent ends
And in their triumph die, like fire and powder,   10
Which, as they kiss, consume. The sweetest honey
Is loathsome in his own deliciousness
And in the taste confounds the appetite.   CONFOUNDS: destroys
Therefore love moderately; long love doth so;
Too swift arrives as tardy as too slow.   15

[*Enter Juliet.*]

Here comes the lady. O, so light a foot
Will ne'er wear out the everlasting flint.*
A lover may bestride the gossamer   GOSSAMER: cobweb
That idles in the wanton summer air,   WANTON: playful
And yet not fall; so light is vanity.   20

JULIET.   Good even to my ghostly confessor.
FRIAR.   Romeo shall thank thee, daughter, for us both.
JULIET.   As much to him, else is his thanks too much.
ROMEO.   Ah, Juliet, if the measure of thy joy
Be heaped like mine, and that thy skill be more   25   THAT: if
To blazon it, then sweeten with thy breath   BLAZON: describe
This neighbor air, and let rich music's tongue
Unfold the imagined happiness that both
Receive in either by this dear encounter.
JULIET.   Conceit, more rich in matter than in words,   30   CONCEIT: imagination
Brags of his substance, not of ornament.
They are but beggars that can count their worth;
But my true love is grown to such excess
I cannot sum up sum of half my wealth.
FRIAR.   Come, come with me, and we will make short   35
        work;
For, by your leaves, you shall not stay alone
Till Holy Church incorporate two in one.

   [*Exeunt.*]

17 WILL NE'ER . . . FLINT: "Juliet's footsteps are lighter even than drops
of water, which themselves can wear away rocks."

FOR DISCUSSION

1. What danger does Friar Laurence see in this hasty marriage? What is Romeo's response to his warning? Is there any evidence that the Friar has a plan for solving the difficulties that the marriage will create?

2. Do you think the Friar should have agreed to marry Romeo and Juliet at once? What might he have encouraged them to do instead? Does the marriage seem likely to bring peace between the feuding families, or to divide them further?

ACT III

SCENE I.　*The public square.*

[Enter Mercutio, Benvolio, and a Page.]

BENVOLIO.　I pray thee, good Mercutio, let's retire.
The day is hot, the Capulets are abroad,
And, if we meet, we shall not 'scape a brawl,
For now, these hot days, is the mad blood stirring.

MERCUTIO.　Thou art like one of these fellows that, when　5
he enters the confines of a tavern, claps me his sword
upon the table and says, "God send me no need of
thee!" and by the operation of the second cup draws
him on the drawer,* when indeed there is no need.

BENVOLIO.　Am I like such a fellow?　10

MERCUTIO.　Come, come, thou art as hot a Jack in thy
mood as any in Italy; and as soon moved to be moody,　MOODY: angry
and as soon moody to be moved.*

BENVOLIO.　And what to?

MERCUTIO.　Nay, an there were two such, we should　15
have none shortly, for one would kill the other. Thou!
Why, thou wilt quarrel with a man that hath a hair
more or a hair less in his beard than thou hast. Thou
wilt quarrel with a man for cracking nuts, having no
other reason but because thou hast hazel eyes. What　20
eye but such an eye would spy out such a quarrel?
Thy head is as full of quarrels as an egg is full of meat;
and yet thy head hath been beaten as addle as an egg
for quarreling. Thou hast quarreled with a man for
coughing in the street, because he hath wakened thy　25
dog that hath lain asleep in the sun. Didst thou not fall
out with a tailor for wearing his new doublet before　DOUBLET: jacket
Easter? With another for tying his new shoes with old
riband? And yet thou wilt tutor me from quarreling!　RIBAND: ribbon

BENVOLIO.　An I were so apt to quarrel as thou art, any　30
man should buy the fee simple of my life for an hour
and a quarter.*

MERCUTIO.　The fee simple? O simple!

[Enter Tybalt, and others of the Capulet family.]

8–9 DRAWS . . . DRAWER: draws his sword against the waiter.
12–13 MOODY TO BE MOVED: short-tempered.　30–32 AN I . . . QUARTER: "If
I were as quarrelsome as you, I'd trade my chances of a longer life for
a certain hour and a quarter."

BENVOLIO.   By my head, here come the Capulets.

MERCUTIO.   By my heel, I care not.   35

TYBALT.   Follow me close, for I will speak to them.
Gentlemen, good den; a word with one of you.

MERCUTIO.   And but one word with one of us? Couple it
with something; make it a word and a blow.

TYBALT.   You shall find me apt enough to that, sir, an   40   OCCASION: reason
you will give me occasion.

MERCUTIO.   Could you not take some occasion without
giving?

TYBALT.   Mercutio, thou consortest with Romeo—

MERCUTIO.   Consort! What, dost thou make us min-   45
strels? An thou make minstrels of us, look to hear
nothing but discords.* Here's my fiddlestick; here's
that shall make you dance. 'Zounds, consort!

BENVOLIO.   We talk here in the public haunt of men.
Either withdraw unto some private place,   50
Or reason coldly of your grievances,
Or else depart. Here all eyes gaze on us.

MERCUTIO.   Men's eyes were made to look, and let them
gaze. I will not budge for no man's pleasure, I.

[*Enter Romeo.*]

TYBALT.   Well, peace be with you, sir. Here comes my
man.   55

MERCUTIO.   But I'll be hanged, sir, if he wear your livery.   LIVERY: servant's uniform
Marry, go before to field, he'll be your follower;
Your worship in that sense may call him man.

TYBALT.   Romeo, the love I bear thee can afford
No better term than this: thou art a villain.   60

ROMEO.   Tybalt, the reason that I have to love thee
Doth much excuse the appertaining rage
To such a greeting.* Villain am I none.
Therefore farewell. I see thou know'st me not.

TYBALT.   Boy, this shall not excuse the injuries   65
That thou hast done me; therefore turn and draw.

ROMEO.   I do protest, I never injured thee,
But love thee better than thou canst devise   DEVISE: imagine
Till thou shalt know the reason of my love;
And so, good Capulet, which name I tender   70   TENDER: value
As dearly as mine own—be satisfied.

45–47 CONSORT . . . DISCORDS: a quibble on the two meanings of *consort*—"to associate with," as Tybalt uses it, and "to make music."
62–63 DOTH . . . GREETING: "cools the anger that would usually follow
such a greeting."

MERCUTIO.   O calm, dishonorable, vile submission!
  *Alla stoccata** carries it away.   [*He draws his sword.*]
  Tybalt, you ratcatcher,* will you walk?
TYBALT.   What wouldst thou have with me?   75
MERCUTIO.   Good King of Cats, nothing but one of your
  nine lives. That I mean to make bold withal, and, as
  you shall use me hereafter, dry-beat the rest of the   DRY-BEAT: bruise
  eight. Will you pluck your sword out of his pilcher   PILCHER: scabbard
  by the ears? Make haste, lest mine be about your ears   80
  ere it be out.
TYBALT.   I am for you.   [*He draws his sword.*]
ROMEO.   Gentle Mercutio, put thy rapier up.
MERCUTIO.   Come, sir, your *passado!*   [*They fight.*]   PASSADO: lunge
ROMEO.   Draw, Benvolio; beat down their weapons.   85
  Gentlemen, for shame, forbear this outrage!
  Tybalt, Mercutio, the Prince expressly hath
  Forbid this bandying in Verona streets.
  Hold, Tybalt! Good Mercutio!

[73] *Alla stoccata:* a fencing term in reference to Tybalt's skill. Mercutio
thinks Romeo is afraid.   [74] RATCATCHER: a cat. This is another play on
Tybalt's name, which is similar to that of a cat in a medieval tale.

[*Tybalt under Romeo's arm stabs Mercutio, and flees with the other Capulets.*]

MERCUTIO.   I am hurt.
  A plague o' both houses! I am sped.   90   SPED: done for
  Is he gone, and hath nothing?   NOTHING: no wounds
BENVOLIO.   What, are thou hurt?
MERCUTIO.   Aye, aye, a scratch, a scratch. Marry, 'tis
    enough.
  Where is my Page? Go, villain, fetch a surgeon.

  [*Exit Page.*]

ROMEO.   Courage, man. The hurt cannot be much.
MERCUTIO.   No, 'tis not so deep as a well, nor so wide as   95
    a church door; but 'tis enough, 'twill serve. Ask for me
    tomorrow, and you shall find me a grave* man. I am
    peppered, I warrant, for this world. A plague o' both   PEPPERED: finished
    your houses! 'Zounds, a dog, a rat, a mouse, a cat, to
    scratch a man to death! A braggart, a rogue, a villain, 100
    that fights by the book of arithmetic! Why the devil
    came you between us? I was hurt under your arm.
ROMEO.   I thought all for the best.
MERCUTIO.   Help me into some house, Benvolio,
  Or I shall faint. A plague o' both your houses!   105
  They have made worms' meat of me. I have it,
  And soundly too. Your houses!

  [*Exeunt Mercutio and Benvolio.*]

ROMEO.   This gentleman, the Prince's near ally,   ALLY: relative
  My very friend, hath got this mortal hurt
  In my behalf; my reputation stained   110
  With Tybalt's slander—Tybalt, that an hour
  Hath been my cousin! O sweet Juliet,
  Thy beauty hath made me effeminate
  And in my temper softened valor's steel!

  [*Re-enter Benvolio.*]

BENVOLIO.   O Romeo, Romeo, brave Mercutio's dead!   115
  That gallant spirit hath aspired the clouds,
  Which too untimely here did scorn the earth.   ASPIRED: risen to
ROMEO.   This day's black fate on moe days doth depend;   MOE: more
  This but begins the woe others must end.
BENVOLIO.   Here comes the furious Tybalt back again.   120

  [*Re-enter Tybalt.*]

---

[97] GRAVE: a pun, meaning both "serious" and "burial place."

ROMEO.   Alive in triumph, and Mercutio slain!
  Away to heaven, respective lenity,   LENITY: mercy
  And fire-eyed fury be my conduct now!
  Now Tybalt, take the "villain" back again
  That late thou gav'st me; for Mercutio's soul   125
  Is but a little way above our heads,
  Staying for thine to keep him company.
  Either thou or I, or both, must go with him.
TYBALT.   Thou, wretched boy, that didst consort him here,
  Shalt with him hence.
ROMEO.   This shall determine that.   130

  [*They fight. Tybalt falls, dead.*]

BENVOLIO.   Romeo, away, be gone!
  The citizens are up, and Tybalt slain.
  Stand not amazed. The Prince will doom thee death
  If thou art taken. Hence, be gone, away!
ROMEO.   O, I am fortune's fool!   FOOL: plaything
BENVOLIO.   Why dost thou stay?   135

  [*Exit Romeo.*]

  [*Enter Citizens.*]

CITIZEN.   Which way ran he that killed Mercutio?
  Tybalt, that murderer, which way ran he?
BENVOLIO.   There lies that Tybalt.
CITIZEN.   Up, sir, go with me.
  I charge thee in the Prince's name obey.

  [*Enter Prince, Montague, Capulet, their Wives, and all.*]

PRINCE.   Where are the vile beginners of this fray?   140
BENVOLIO.   O noble Prince, I can discover all   DISCOVER: reveal
  The unlucky manage of this fatal brawl.   MANAGE: conduct
  There lies the man, slain by young Romeo,
  That slew thy kinsman, brave Mercutio.
LADY CAPULET.   Tybalt, my cousin! O my brother's child! 145
  O Prince! O cousin! Husband! O, the blood is spilt
  Of my dear kinsman! Prince, as thou art true,
  For blood of ours shed blood of Montague.
  O cousin, cousin!
PRINCE.   Benvolio, who began this bloody fray?   150
BENVOLIO.   Tybalt, here slain, whom Romeo's hand did
      slay.
  Romeo, that spoke him fair, bid him bethink   FAIR: courteously
  How nice the quarrel was, and urged withal   NICE: trifling
  Your high displeasure. All this—utterèd

With gentle breath, calm look, knees humbly bowed— 155
Could not take truce with the unruly spleen   UNRULY SPLEEN: bad temper
Of Tybalt deaf to peace, but that he tilts
With piercing steel at bold Mercutio's breast;
Who, all as hot, turns deadly point to point,
And, with a martial scorn, with one hand beats   160
Cold death aside and with the other sends
It back to Tybalt, whose dexterity
Retorts it. Romeo, he cries aloud,   RETORTS: returns
"Hold, friends! Friends, part!" And swifter than his
    tongue,
His agile arm beats down their fatal points,   165
And 'twixt them rushes; underneath whose arm
An envious thrust from Tybalt hit the life   ENVIOUS: malicious
Of stout Mercutio, and then Tybalt fled;
But by and by comes back to Romeo,
Who had but newly entertained revenge,   170
And to 't they go like lightning, for ere I
Could draw to part them, was stout Tybalt slain;
And, as he fell, did Romeo turn and fly.
This is the truth, or let Benvolio die.
LADY CAPULET.   He is a kinsman to the Montague;   175
   Affection makes him false, he speaks not true.
   Some twenty of them fought in this black strife,
   And all those twenty could but kill one life.
   I beg for justice, which thou, Prince, must give.
   Romeo slew Tybalt; Romeo must not live.   190
PRINCE.   Romeo slew him; he slew Mercutio.
   Who now the price of his dear blood doth owe?
MONTAGUE.   Not Romeo, Prince; he was Mercutio's friend.
   His fault concludes but what the law should end:
   The life of Tybalt.*
PRINCE.   And for that offense   185
   Immediately we do exile him hence.
   I have an interest in your hate's proceeding,
   My blood for your rude brawls doth lie a-bleeding;
   But I'll amerce you with so strong a fine   AMERCE: punish
   That you shall all repent the loss of mine.   190
   I will be deaf to pleading and excuses;
   Nor tears nor prayers shall purchase out abuses.*
   Therefore use none. Let Romeo hence in haste,
   Else, when he's found, that hour is his last.

184–185 HIS . . . TYBALT: "Romeo's only crime was that he carried out
the sentence against Tybalt that the law would have ordered anyway—
namely, his death." 192 PURCHASE OUT ABUSES: buy forgiveness for
crimes.

Bear hence this body and attend our will.   195
Mercy but murders, pardoning those that kill.

[*Exit with others.*]

FOR DISCUSSION

1. What reason does Tybalt have for challenging Romeo to fight? Why does Romeo try to avoid the conflict?

2. How are Mercutio's dying words typical of his character throughout the play?

3. Romeo finally duels with Tybalt in spite of the prince's warning and his own reluctance to harm Juliet's kinsman. Why does he feel forced to kill Tybalt? Do you think he acted wisely, or did he have another choice?

SCENE II.   *Capulet's orchard.*

[*Enter Juliet alone.*]

JULIET.   Gallop apace, you fiery-footed steeds,*
Towards Phoebus' lodging! Such a wagoner
As Phaëton* would whip you to the west
And bring in cloudy night immediately.
Spread thy close curtain, love-performing night,   5
That runaway's eyes may wink, and Romeo   RUNAWAY'S: sun's
Leap to these arms untalked of and unseen.
Lovers can see to do their amorous rites
By their own beauties; or, if love be blind,
It best agrees with night. Come, civil night,   10
Thou sober-suited matron all in black. . . .
Hood my unmanned blood, bating in my cheeks,
With thy black mantle till strange love grow bold,*
Think true love acted simple modesty.
Come, night; come, Romeo; come, thou day in night;   15
For thou wilt lie upon the wings of night
Whiter than new snow upon a raven's back.
Come, gentle night; come, loving, black-browed night;
Give me my Romeo; and, when he shall die,
Take him and cut him out in little stars,   20
And he will make the face of heaven so fine
That all the world will be in love with night
And pay no worship to the garish sun.

---

¹ FIERY-FOOTED STEEDS: in Roman mythology horses that drew the chariot of Phoebus, the sun god.   ³ PHAËTON: Phoebus' son, who was inexperienced in driving the chariot and let the horses run away with him. ¹²⁻¹³ HOOD . . . BOLD: Juliet asks night to mask her embarrassment until she becomes used to Romeo's presence.

O, I have bought the mansion of a love,
But not possessed it; and, though I am sold, 25
Not yet enjoyed. So tedious is this day
As is the night before some festival
To an impatient child that hath new robes
And may not wear them. O, here comes my Nurse,

[*Enter Nurse, with a ladder made of cords.*]

And she brings news; and every tongue that speaks 30
But Romeo's name speaks heavenly eloquence.
Now, Nurse, what news? What hast thou there, the
    cords
That Romeo bid thee fetch?
NURSE.   Aye, aye, the cords.
JULIET.   Ay me! What news? Why dost thou wring thy
    hands?
NURSE.   Ah, welladay! He's dead, he's dead, he's dead! 35   WELLADAY: alas
  We are undone, lady, we are undone!
  Alack the day! He's gone, he's killed, he's dead!
JULIET.   Can heaven be so envious?
NURSE.   Romeo can,
  Though heaven cannot. O Romeo, Romeo!
  Who ever would have thought it? Romeo! 40
JULIET.   What devil art thou, that dost torment me thus?
  This torture should be roared in dismal hell.
  Hath Romeo slain himself? Say thou but aye,
  And that bare vowel *I* shall poison more
  Than the death-darting eye of cockatrice.* 45
  I am not I, if there be such an aye,
  Or those eyes shut that makes thee answer aye.
  If he be slain, say aye; or if not, no.
  Brief sounds determine of my weal or woe.   WEAL: well-being
NURSE.   I saw the wound, I saw it with mine eyes— 50
  God save the mark!*—here on his manly breast.
  A piteous corse, a bloody piteous corse!   CORSE: corpse
  Pale, pale as ashes, all bedaubed in blood,
  All in gore-blood. I swounded at the sight.   SWOUNDED: swooned
JULIET.   O, break, my heart! Poor bankrout, break at   BANKROUT: bankrupt
    once! 55
  To prison, eyes, ne'er look on liberty!
  Vile earth, to earth resign;* end motion here;
  And thou and Romeo press one heavy bier!   BIER: coffin with its stand
NURSE.   O Tybalt, Tybalt, the best friend I had!

45 COCKATRICE: fabulous serpent that could kill with a glance. 51 GOD
SAVE THE MARK: an exclamation used to avert bad luck when discussing
a disastrous thing. 57 VILE . . . RESIGN: "Miserable body, surrender
yourself to death."

O courteous Tybalt! Honest gentleman!   60
That ever I should live to see thee dead!
JULIET.   What storm is this that blows so contrary?
  Is Romeo slaughtered, and is Tybalt dead?
  My dearest cousin, and my dearer lord?
  Then, dreadful trumpet, sound the general doom!   65
  For who is living, if those two are gone?
NURSE.   Tybalt is gone, and Romeo banishèd;
  Romeo that killed him, he is banishèd.
JULIET.   O God! Did Romeo's hand shed Tybalt's blood?
NURSE.   It did, it did; alas the day, it did!   70
JULIET.   O serpent heart, hid with a flowering face!
  Did ever dragon keep so fair a cave?
  Beautiful tyrant! Fiend angelical!
  Dove-feathered raven! Wolvish-ravening lamb!
  Despisèd substance of divinest show!   75
  Just opposite to what thou justly seem'st,
  A damnèd saint, an honorable villain!
  O nature, what hadst thou to do in hell,
  When thou didst bower the spirit of a fiend   BOWER: shelter
  In mortal paradise of such sweet flesh?   80
  Was ever book containing such vile matter
  So fairly bound? O, that deceit should dwell
  In such a gorgeous palace!
NURSE.   There's no trust,
  No faith, no honesty in men; all perjured,
  All forsworn, all naught, all dissemblers.   85   DISSEMBLERS: impostors
  Ah, where's my man? Give me some *aqua vitae.*   AQUA VITAE: brandy
  These griefs, these woes, these sorrows make me old.
  Shame come to Romeo!
JULIET.   Blistered be thy tongue
  For such a wish! He was not born to shame.
  Upon his brow shame is ashamed to sit;   90
  For 'tis a throne where honor may be crowned
  Sole monarch of the universal earth.
  O, what a beast was I to chide at him!
NURSE.   Will you speak well of him that killed your
    cousin?
JULIET.   Shall I speak ill of him that is my husband?   95
  Ah, poor my lord, what tongue shall smooth thy name
  When I, thy three-hours wife, have mangled it?
  But wherefore, villain, didst thou kill my cousin?
  That villain cousin would have killed my husband.
  Back, foolish tears, back to your native spring;   100
  Your tributary drops belong to woe,   TRIBUTARY: donated

Continued on page 346

IDEAS AND THE ARTS

A martyr is someone who sacrifices himself for something in which he believes. He may even sacrifice his own life. Whatever form his sacrifice takes, we refer to it as "martyrdom." If we approve of the martyr's cause, we will admire him and may even seek to imitate him, at least to some extent. If we do not approve of his cause, we may regard him as foolish. Either way, however, we will find him interesting.

We can see martyrdom more clearly if we try to understand what produces martyrs. In considering Shakespeare's *Romeo and Juliet,* we can say that Juliet is a martyr to the ideal of love, or we can say that she is a martyr to the ideal of family loyalty. In Sophocles' *Antigone,* Antigone can be regarded as a martyr to political power, or as a martyr to the traditions that one is responsible for the proper burial of members of one's family. The fact that we can describe the martyrdom of each figure in two different ways gives us some insight into what produces martyrs. The martyr is caught in a conflict between two ideals that cannot be reconciled. These ideals can also be called "social values."

Social values can be explained as instructions about how to act that we learn from our society. One example of a social value is that we should always tell the truth. That is what we are taught when we are children. As we get older, however, we are also taught that in certain situations it is proper not to tell the truth. We are taught the value of "white lies," and we justify white lies by appealing to what we call "higher values." One justification for white lies is the value that we should not hurt people's feelings, at least not when we can

avoid it without creating other problems. Here, then, we have two strong social values: 1) that we should always tell the truth, and 2) that we should not hurt people's feelings. Since these two values can conflict, we are also instructed about situations in which one value should give way to another. Sometimes the more important value is truth, and sometimes the more important value is kindness. As long as we can follow these instructions, we can usually find ways to avoid conflict.

There are, however, other situations for which our society has given us no special instructions. When conflict arises in these situations, we must use our best judgment. We must do what seems best to us without relying on what anyone else might think. In such situations we become concerned with who and what we are. We become individuals. When we are caught between conflicting values and do not know which to choose, although we must choose, we begin to feel our own identities as human beings. Individuality, then, emerges from value conflict.

It is this emergence of the individual that makes martyrs interesting. Juliet is a good example. She is just an ordinary well-to-do girl of the Italian aristocracy, until she has to choose between conflicting values. Or she is just an ordinary girl in love, until she has to choose. Before she has to choose, she merely represents the value of family loyalty or the value of love. But when she has to choose, she becomes an individual. She becomes interesting for herself, not for the values she represents. This is why we have a grudging admiration for all martyrs, even when we do not admire the values they have chosen. They may be wrong in their choice, but they have become distinct individuals.

Morse Peckham

336

ART

We say that martyrs are individuals who die for a cause, or who accept suffering rather than give up something they believe in. They are martyrs not simply because they hold a certain belief or value. They have had to choose between conflicting values, and in making their choice they become distinct individuals. It is perhaps more correct to say that they are martyrs because of their individuality and uniqueness.

In the early days of Christianity, when Christians were being persecuted by the Roman emperors, there were a great many martyrs. In Alexandria there was once a persecution of Christians so intense that most of them fled from the city. Apollonia, however, stayed in the city and continued to preach the Christian beliefs and to convert pagans. She was arrested and was offered the chance to reject her Christian belief and to worship pagan gods. She refused, and as punishment her teeth were torn out and she was cast on a fire and burned to death. Piero della Francesca, a great Italian painter of the fifteenth century, shows her holding a pair of dental pincers, a symbol of her martyrdom. The painting might have been commissioned by a guild of dentists, because she is regarded as their patron saint. Della Francesca shows Apollonia's powerful will and her determination not to surrender her religious beliefs.

Quite a different kind of martyr was Mary Magdalen. She appears in the New Testament, and we are told that Jesus cast devils out of her. Today we would say that he freed her from wicked impulses. She came to be identified with an unnamed woman, a repentant sinner, who washed Jesus' feet, dried them with her hair, and anointed them with precious ointment. According to her later legend she was cast adrift at sea and landed in France. There she spent the rest of her life in tears of repentance, with her food provided by angels. Georges de la Tour, in his *Mary Magdalen,* painted in France in the seventeenth century, shows her meditating on her martyrdom to repentance. She holds a skull, the sign of death that comes to all men, and she gazes at the box which held the ointment with which she anointed Jesus' feet.

St. Cecilia is the patron saint of musicians. She was a Christian who refused to worship pagan gods, and she was executed for her refusal. We are told that she was strengthened in her devotion to Christianity and in her resistance to hostile forces because she could hear the singing of angels. She could play all musical instruments, and according to her legend, she invented the organ. She was a Christian martyr, but she was also a martyr to her music and to art. Artists have always loved to paint her, perhaps because they find a common interest in her career. A lifetime of devotion to one's art is often a social and economic martyrdom. The nineteenth-century English painter John William Waterhouse, in his *St. Cecilia,* presents her as a medieval painter might have imagined her, though he would not have painted her like this. She has been reading the music in a massbook and has been transported into a vision of angelic music.

Girodet, an early nineteenth-century French artist, presents another different kind of martyr. Atala was an Indian girl from Florida who appeared in a novel of the time. She dies rather than marry the man she loves because she had vowed to her mother that she would never yield to any man. Girodet's painting, *The Entombment of Atala,* shows her on her deathbed, and it also shows Choctas, the man she loves, and a priest. The priest is supposed to be a missionary. Atala is a martyr to the conflict between what she owed her mother and what she owes to a husband. Faced with an impossible choice, she finds the solution in death.

Ophelia, in Shakespeare's play *Hamlet,* faces a somewhat similar conflict. She loves Hamlet, but her father has told her to have nothing to do with him. When Hamlet accidentally murders her father, she is caught in a conflict between her love and her family loyalty. As sometimes happens with people who are faced with a difficult choice, she loses her individuality instead of gaining it. That is, she loses her sanity and is accidentally drowned while gathering flowers. John Everett Millais, an English painter of the mid-nineteenth century, shows her as she floats down the stream, singing, but incapable of rescuing herself. She is surrounded by the flowers she speaks of in her mad scene in the play.

The story of Apollo and Daphne comes from Greek mythology. Daphne is quite a different kind of martyr from Ophelia, but she is a little like Atala. She was a nymph, the daughter of a river. She was, therefore, an immortal being although she was not really a goddess. She was a follower of Artemis, the goddess of the hunt and of virginity. Apollo, the god of the sun and of poetry, fell in love with her and pursued her. She fled from him, but he almost caught her. At the last moment she prayed to the goddess of the earth to save her from Apollo, and she was changed into a laurel. For this reason the laurel has been regarded as sacred to Apollo. The painter Pollaiuolo presents Daphne and Apollo in Renaissance costume. In the background is the valley of the Arno river, near Florence where the picture was painted.

Morse Peckham

PIERO DELLA FRANCESCA OR ASSISTANT (late 15th century) *SAINT APOLLONIA.* National Gallery of Art, Washington, D.C.

GEORGES DE LA TOUR (c. 1590-1652) *MARY MAGDALEN.* Musée du Louvre.

340

Photo: Telarci-Giraudon

JOHN WILLIAM WATERHOUSE (1849-1917) *SAINT CECILIA*. Maas Gallery, London.

ANNE-LOUIS GIRODET DE ROUCY-TRIOSON (1767-1824) *THE ENTOMBMENT OF ATALA.* Musée du Louvre.

JOHN EVERETT MILLAIS (1829-1896) *OPHELIA*. The Tate Gallery, London.

ANTONIO DEL POLLAIUOLO (c. 1432-1498) *APOLLO AND DAPHNE.* National Gallery, London.

MUSIC

GEORGE FREDERICK HANDEL:
THE MESSIAH, *Sections 38–42*
[A number of recordings available]

We do not know when music began to be used in church services, but it was probably within two or three hundred years after the beginning of Christianity. Early church music was not very elaborate. Eventually very complex music came to be used, particularly when composers began to write music for special religious occasions or for occasions with religious significance.

An enormous amount of music has been written for use in religious services. But there is another kind of religious music: that which came into being because people were interested in understanding their religion outside of churches. This interest is known as the secular interest in religion. Composers have responded to this interest by writing about religious subjects intended for secular performances.

Some people believe we are born with a capacity for religious feeling, just as we are born with a capacity to learn language. Yet, although we have the capacity to learn language, we still have to learn what it means and how to use it. The same thing is true of religion. Even if we are born with religious feelings, we still have to learn what these feelings mean and how to use them. For this reason, music cannot directly express religious emotions. Thus, if a composer wants to write religious music, he must tell us that it is religious music, and this he usually does by setting religious words to his music. A long musical work that uses religious words is called an "oratorio." Frequently the words are taken from the Bible and set to music for orchestra, chorus, and soloists.

One of the most famous oratorios is the *Messiah* by Handel. The subject is Jesus Christ. In the book of Isaiah in the Old Testament there are prophecies that God would send the Jews a great leader known as the Messiah. Christians believe that Jesus was that Messiah, but Jews do not. The idea that Jesus was that Messiah is found in the New Testament. For this reason the words to the *Messiah* are taken from both the Old and New Testaments.

Jesus was martyred because of His belief that He was the Son of God, and that God had sent Him into the world to redeem mankind from sin. Only a few followers shared this belief with Him. The rest of His society was convinced that this belief was false and dangerous. The triumph of Christianity after the crucifixion reflects the immense emotional power created by martyrdom for a belief. All Christians who were later martyred for their beliefs felt that they were repeating the martyrdom of Jesus.

Handel's *Messiah* consists of fifty-two separate pieces of music, arranged in three parts. Part I tells of the coming of Christ; Part II tells of His initial rejection and ultimate acceptance as the Messiah; Part III tells of man's redemption from sin and Jesus' ascension to Heaven. Toward the end of Part II a bass voice sings of how the nations and the kings of earth were united against the Messiah (No. 38). A chorus urges man to break these bonds and to reject their power (No. 39). A tenor sings of how the Lord will scorn His enemies and destroy their power (Nos. 40 and 41). The chorus now sings the great and famous "Hallelujah." The words here all come from the last book of the New Testament, Revelation. The chorus sings of the victory of Christ and the conversion of all people to believe in Him.

Morse Peckham

Which you, mistaking, offer up to joy.
My husband lives, that Tybalt would have slain;
And Tybalt's dead, that would have slain my husband.
All this is comfort; wherefore weep I then?   105
Some word there was, worser than Tybalt's death,
That murdered me. I would forget it fain;   FAIN: gladly
But O, it presses to my memory
Like damnèd guilty deeds to sinners' minds:
"Tybalt is dead, and Romeo—banishèd."   110
That "banishèd," that one word "banishèd,"
Hath slain ten thousand Tybalts. Tybalt's death
Was woe enough, if it had ended there;
Or, if sour woe delights in fellowship
And needly will be ranked with other griefs,   115
Why followed not, when she said "Tybalt's dead,"
Thy father, or thy mother, nay, or both,
Which modern lamentation might have moved?   MODERN: ordinary
But with a rearward following Tybalt's death,
"Romeo is banishèd"—to speak that word   120
Is father, mother, Tybalt, Romeo, Juliet,
All slain, all dead. "Romeo is banishèd!"
There is no end, no limit, measure, bound,
In that word's death; no words can that woe sound.
Where is my father and my mother, Nurse?   125
NURSE.   Weeping and wailing over Tybalt's corse.
Will you go to them? I will bring you thither.
JULIET.   Wash they his wounds with tears? Mine shall
       be spent,
When theirs are dry, for Romeo's banishment.
Take up those cords. Poor ropes, you are beguiled,   130   BEGUILED: cheated
Both you and I, for Romeo is exiled.
He made you for a highway to my bed;
But I, a maid, die maiden-widowèd.
NURSE.   Hie to your chamber. I'll find Romeo
To comfort you. I wot well where he is.   135
Hark ye, your Romeo will be here at night.
I'll to him; he is hid at Laurence' cell.
JULIET.   O, find him! Give this ring to my true knight
And bid him come to take his last farewell.

[*Exit with Nurse.*]

FOR DISCUSSION

• What conflict is created for Juliet by the news that Tybalt is dead and Romeo banished? Which emotion does she feel most strongly in the end?

SCENE III. *Friar Laurence's cell.*

[*Enter Friar Laurence.*]

FRIAR.   Romeo, come forth; come forth, thou fearful
   man.
Affliction is enamored of thy parts,*
And thou art wedded to calamity.

[*Enter Romeo.*]

ROMEO.   Father, what news? What is the Prince's doom?
What sorrow craves acquaintance at my hand   5
That I yet know not?
FRIAR.   Too familiar
Is my dear son with such sour company.
I bring thee tidings of the Prince's doom.
ROMEO.   What less than doomsday is the Prince's doom?   DOOMSDAY: death
FRIAR.   A gentler judgment vanished from his lips: 10   VANISHED: issued
Not body's death, but body's banishment.
ROMEO.   Ha, banishment? Be merciful, say "death";
For exile hath more terror in his look,
Much more than death. Do not say "banishment"!
FRIAR.   Here from Verona art thou banishèd.   15
Be patient, for the world is broad and wide.
ROMEO.   There is no world without Verona walls,   WITHOUT: outside
But purgatory, torture, hell itself.
Hence banishèd is banished from the world,
And world's exile is death; then "banishèd"   20
Is death mistermed. Calling death "banishment,"
Thou cut'st my head off with a golden ax
And smil'st upon the stroke that murders me.
FRIAR.   O deadly sin! O rude unthankfulness!
Thy fault our law calls death; but the kind Prince,   25
Taking thy part, hath rushed aside the law,
And turned that black word "death" to "banishment."
This is dear mercy, and thou seest it not.   DEAR: rare
ROMEO.   'Tis torture, and not mercy. Heaven is here,
Where Juliet lives; and every cat and dog   30
And little mouse, every unworthy thing,
Live here in heaven and may look on her;
But Romeo may not. More validity,   VALIDITY: worth
More honorable state, more courtship lives
In carrion flies than Romeo. They may seize   35

—————

2 ENAMORED . . . PARTS: "in love with your character."

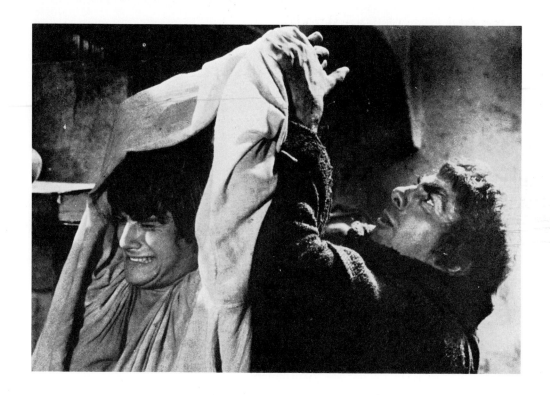

On the white wonder of dear Juliet's hand
And steal immortal blessing from her lips,
Who, even in pure and vestal modesty,
Still blush, as thinking their own kisses sin;
But Romeo may not, he is banishèd.   40
This may flies do, when I from this must fly;
They are free men, but I am banishèd.
And sayest thou yet that exile is not death?
Hadst thou no poison mixed, no sharp-ground knife,
No sudden mean of death, though ne'er so mean,*   45
But "banishèd" to kill me?—"banishèd"?
O Friar, the damnèd use that word in hell;
Howling attends it. How hast thou the heart,
Being a divine, a ghostly confessor,
A sin-absolver, and my friend professed,   50
To mangle me with that word "banishèd"?
FRIAR.   Thou fond mad man, hear me a little speak.   FOND: foolish
ROMEO.   O, thou wilt speak again of banishment.
FRAIR.   I'll give thee armor to keep off that word;
Adversity's sweet milk, philosophy,   55

45 No . . . MEAN: "no quick method of dying, even though it be a
lowly one."

To comfort thee, though thou art banishèd.

ROMEO.   Yet "banishèd"? Hang up philosophy!   YET: still
  Unless philosophy can make a Juliet,
  Displant a town, reverse a prince's doom,
  It helps not, it prevails not. Talk no more.   60

FRIAR.   O, then I see that madmen have no ears.

ROMEO.   How should they, when that wise men have
    no eyes?

FRIAR.   Let me dispute with thee of thy estate.   ESTATE: situation

ROMEO.   Thou canst not speak of that thou dost not feel.
  Wert thou as young as I, Juliet thy love,   65
  An hour but married, Tybalt murderèd,
  Doting like me, and like me banishèd,
  Then mightst thou speak, then mightst thou tear thy
    hair
  And fall upon the ground, as I do now,
  Taking the measure of an unmade grave.   70

[*Knocking within.*]

FRAIR.   Arise, one knocks. Good Romeo, hide thyself.

ROMEO.   Not I; unless the breath of heartsick groans
  Mistlike infold me from the search of eyes.

[*Knock.*]

FRIAR.   Hark, how they knock! Who's there? Romeo,
    arise;
  Thou wilt be taken—Stay awhile!—Stand up!   75

[*Knock.*]

  Run to my study.—By and by!—God's will,   BY AND BY: at once
  What simpleness is this!—I come, I come!   [*Knock.*]   SIMPLENESS: silliness
  Who knocks so hard? Whence come you? What's your
    will?

[*Enter Nurse.*]

NURSE.   Let me come in, and you shall know my errand.
  I come from Lady Juliet.

FRIAR.   Welcome then.   80

NURSE.   O holy Friar, O, tell me, holy Friar,
  Where is my lady's lord, where's Romeo?

FRIAR.   There on the ground, with his own tears made
    drunk.

NURSE.   O, he is even in my mistress' case,
  Just in her case! O woeful sympathy!   85
  Piteous predicament! Even so lies she,
  Blubb'ring and weeping, weeping and blubb'ring.

Stand up, stand up! Stand, an you be a man.
For Juliet's sake, for her sake, rise and stand!
Why should you fall into so deep an O?   90   O: state of grief
ROMEO.   [*Rises*] Nurse!
NURSE.   Ah sir, ah sir! Death's the end of all.
ROMEO.   Spak'st thou of Juliet? How is it with her?
Doth not she think me an old murderer,
Now I have stained the childhood of our joy   95
With blood removed but little from her own?
Where is she? And how doth she? And what says
My concealed lady to our canceled love?   CONCEALED LADY: secret wife
NURSE.   O, she says nothing, sir, but weeps and weeps;
And now falls on her bed, and then starts up,   100
And Tybalt calls;* and then on Romeo cries,
And then down falls again.
ROMEO.   As if that name,
Shot from the deadly level of a gun,
Did murder her, as that name's cursèd hand
Murdered her kinsman. O, tell me, Friar, tell me,   105
In what vile part of this anatomy
Doth my name lodge? Tell me, that I may sack
The hateful mansion.

[*He offers to stab himself, but the Nurse snatches the
dagger away.*]

FRIAR.   Hold thy desperate hand!
Art thou a man? Thy form cries out thou art;
Thy tears are womanish, thy wild acts denote   110
The unreasonable fury of a beast.
Unseemly woman in a seeming man,
And ill-beseeming beast in seeming both.
Thou hast amazed me! By my holy order,
I thought thy disposition better tempered.   115
Hast thou slain Tybalt? Wilt thou slay thyself,
And slay thy lady that in thy life lives,
By doing damnèd hate upon thyself?
Why rail'st thou on thy birth, the heaven, and earth?   RAIL'ST: denounce
Since birth and heaven and earth, all three do meet   120
In thee at once, which thou at once wouldst lose.
Fie, fie, thou sham'st thy shape, thy love, thy wit;   WIT: intellect
Which, like a usurer, abound'st in all,
And usest none in that true use indeed
Which should bedeck thy shape, thy love, thy wit.*   125

---

[101] TYBALT CALLS: "and cries Tybalt's name."   [123-125] WHICH . . . WIT:
"Like a moneylender [usurer] who refuses to lend his money and earn
interest, you do not use your natural endowments for your own good."

Thy noble shape is but a form of wax,
Digressing from the valor of a man;
Thy dear love sworn but hollow perjury,
Killing that love which thou hast vowed to cherish;
Thy wit, that ornament to shape and love,   130
Misshapen in the conduct of them both,
Like powder in a skilless soldier's flask,
Is set afire by thine own ignorance,
And thou dismembered with thine own defense*
What, rouse thee, man! Thy Juliet is alive,   135
For whose dear sake thou wast but lately dead.   HAPPY: fortunate
There art thou happy. Tybalt would kill thee,
But thou slew'st Tybalt. There art thou happy.
The law that threatened death becomes thy friend
And turns it to exile. There art thou happy.   140
A pack of blessings light upon thy back;
Happiness courts thee in her best array;
But, like a misbehaved and sullen wench,
Thou pout'st upon thy fortune and thy love.
Take heed, take heed, for such die miserable.   145
Go get thee to thy love, as was decreed,
Ascend her chamber; hence, and comfort her.
But look thou stay not till the watch be set;*
For then thou canst not pass to Mantua,
Where thou shalt live till we can find a time   150
To blaze your marriage, reconcile your friends,   BLAZE: announce
Beg pardon of the Prince, and call thee back
With twenty hundred thousand times more joy
Than thou went'st forth in lamentation.
Go before, Nurse. Commend me to thy lady,   155
And bid her hasten all the house to bed—
Which heavy sorrow makes them apt unto.
Romeo is coming.
NURSE.   O Lord, I could have stayed here all the night
To hear good counsel. O, what learning is!   160
My lord, I'll tell my lady you will come.
ROMEO.   Do so, and bid my sweet prepare to chide.
NURSE.   Here, sir, a ring she bid me give you, sir.
Hie you, make haste, for it grows very late.
ROMEO.   How well my comfort is revived by this!   165

[*Exit the Nurse.*]

130–134 THY WIT . . . DEFENSE: "Because you are carried away by your
emotions, your intellect, which should be used to defend yourself and
your love, destroys them instead."   148 LOOK . . . SET: "Be sure to leave
before the guards are posted at the gates of the city."

FRIAR.   Go hence; good night; and here stands all your
        state:*
    Either be gone before the watch be set,
    Or by the break of day disguised from hence.
    Sojourn in Mantua. I'll find out your man,
    And he shall signify from time to time   170
    Every good hap to you that chances here.   HAP: fortune
    Give me thy hand. 'Tis late. Farewell; good night.
ROMEO.   But that a joy past joy calls out on me,
    It were a grief, so brief to part with thee.
    Farewell.   175

    [*Exeunt.*]

166 HERE . . . STATE: "This is your entire situation."

FOR DISCUSSION

1. Compare Romeo's reaction to the news of his banishment with Juliet's. Whose emotions are more violent, his or hers? Whose are more believable? Whose are more in keeping with earlier actions and mood?

2. Why does Romeo reject the "armor" of philosophy offered by Friar Laurence? When Romeo attempts suicide the Friar accuses him of not really caring for Juliet. Explain his reasoning. What hope does the Friar offer at the end of the scene? Which do you think is more comfort to Romeo, this hope or the prospect of seeing Juliet again?

SCENE IV.   *A room in Capulet's house.*

[*Enter Capulet, Lady Capulet, and Paris.*]

CAPULET.   Things have fallen out, sir, so unluckily   FALLEN OUT: happened
    That we have had no time to move our daughter.   MOVE: persuade
    Look you, she loved her kinsman Tybalt dearly,
    And so did I. Well, we were born to die.
    'Tis very late; she'll not come down tonight.   5
    I promise you, but for your company,
    I would have been abed an hour ago.
PARIS.   These times of woe afford no times to woo.
    Madam, good night. Commend me to your daughter.
LADY CAPULET.   I will, and know her mind early tomor-
        row.   10
    Tonight she's mewed up to her heaviness.*
CAPULET.   Sir Paris, I will make a desperate tender
    Of my child's love. I think she will be ruled
    In all respects by me; nay, more, I doubt it not.
    Wife, go you to her ere you go to bed;   15
    Acquaint her here of my son Paris' love
    And bid her—mark you me?—on Wednesday next—

11 MEWED . . . HEAVINESS: "confined with her grief."

But soft! What day is this?

PARIS.   Monday, my lord.

CAPULET.   Monday! Ha, ha! Well, Wednesday is too
    soon.

O' Thursday let it be. O' Thursday, tell her,   20
She shall be married to this noble earl.
Will you be ready? Do you like this haste?
We'll keep no great ado—a friend or two;
For hark you, Tybalt being slain so late,
It may be thought we held him carelessly,   25
Being our kinsman, if we revel much.
Therefore we'll have some half a dozen friends,
And there an end. But what say you to Thursday?

PARIS.   My lord, I would that Thursday were tomorrow.

CAPULET.   Well, get you gone. O' Thursday be it then.   30
    [*To his wife*] Go you to Juliet ere you go to bed;
    Prepare her, wife, against this wedding day.   AGAINST: for
    [*To Paris*] Farewell, my lord. [*To his servants*] Light
        to my chamber, ho!
    Afore me, it is so very late
    That we may call it early by and by.   35
    Good Night.

    [*Exeunt.*]

SCENE v.   *Capulet's orchard.*

[*Enter Romeo and Juliet on her balcony.*]

JULIET.   Wilt thou be gone? It is not yet near day.
    It was the nightingale, and not the lark,*
    That pierced the fearful hollow of thine ear.   FEARFUL: frightened
    Nightly she sings on yond pomegranate tree.
    Believe me, love, it was the nightingale.   5

ROMEO.   It was the lark, the herald of the morn—
    No nightingale. Look, love, what envious streaks
    Do lace the sev'ring clouds in yonder east.
    Night's candles are burnt out, and jocund day   NIGHT'S CANDLES: stars
    Stands tiptoe on the misty mountaintops.   10
    I must be gone and live, or stay and die.

JULIET.   Yond light is not daylight; I know it, I.
    It is some meteor that the sun exhales
    To be to thee this night a torchbearer,
    And light thee on thy way to Mantua.   15

---

² NIGHTINGALE . . . LARK: The lovers are debating whether dawn is
breaking; for the nightingale sings during the night, the lark at daybreak.

Therefore stay yet; thou need'st not to be gone.
ROMEO.   Let me be ta'en, let me be put to death.
   I am content, so thou wilt have it so.
   I'll say yon gray is not the morning's eye;
   'Tis but the pale reflex of Cynthia's brow;*   20
   Nor that is not the lark whose notes do beat
   The vaulty heaven so high above our heads.
   I have more care to stay than will to go.   CARE: desire
   Come, death, and welcome! Juliet wills it so.
   How is't, my soul? Let's talk; it is not day.   25
JULIET.   It is, it is! Hie hence, be gone, away!
   It is the lark that sings so out of tune,
   Straining harsh discords and unpleasing sharps.   SHARPS: high notes
   Some say the lark makes sweet division;   DIVISION: melody
   This doth not so, for she divideth us.   30
   Some say the lark and loathèd toad change eyes;*
   O, now I would they had changed voices too,
   Since arm from arm that voice doth us affray,   AFFRAY: frighten
   Hunting thee hence with hunt's-up* to the day.
   O, now be gone! More light and light it grows.   35
ROMEO.   More light and light; more dark and dark our
       woes.

   [*Enter Nurse.*]

NURSE.   Madam!
JULIET.   Nurse?
NURSE.   Your lady mother is coming to your chamber.
   The day is broke; be wary, look about.   [*Exit.*]   40
JULIET.   Then, window, let day in, and let life out.
ROMEO.   Farewell, farewell! One kiss, and I'll descend.

   [*He climbs down from the balcony to the orchard.*]

JULIET.   Art thou gone so? Love, lord, aye husband,
       friend?
   I must hear from thee every day in the hour,
   For in a minute there are many days.   45
   O, by this count I shall be much in years
   Ere I again behold my Romeo!
ROMEO.   Farewell!
   I will omit no opportunity
   That may convey my greetings, love, to thee.
JULIET.   O, think'st thou we shall ever meet again?   50
ROMEO.   I doubt it not, and all these woes shall serve

---

20 REFLEX . . . BROW: reflection of the moon. The moon goddess Diana
was sometimes called Cynthia.   31 LARK . . . EYES: "The sweetly singing
lark should have the croaking toad's beautiful eyes, instead of its own
dull ones."   34 HUNT'S-UP: song to waken hunters.

For sweet discourses in our times to come.
JULIET.   O God, I have an ill-divining soul!
    Methinks I see thee, now thou art below,
    As one dead in the bottom of a tomb.   55
    Either my eyesight fails, or thou look'st pale.
ROMEO.   And trust me, love, in my eye so do you.
    Dry sorrow drinks our blood.* Adieu, adieu!   [*Exit.*]
JULIET.   O Fortune, Fortune! all men call thee fickle.
    If thou art fickle, what dost thou with him*   60
    That is renowned for faith? Be fickle, Fortune,
    For then, I hope, thou wilt not keep him long
    But send him back.

    [*Enter Lady Capulet.*]

LADY CAPULET.   Ho, daughter! Are you up?
JULIET.   Who is 't that calls? It is my lady mother.   65
    Is she not down so late, or up so early?
    What unaccustomed cause procures her hither?   PROCURES: brings
LADY CAPULET.   Why, how now, Juliet?
JULIET.   Madam, I am not well.
LADY CAPULET.   Evermore weeping for your cousin's
    death?
    What, wilt thou wash him from his grave with tears?   70
    And if thou couldst, thou couldst not make him live.
    Therefore have done. Some grief shows much of love,
    But much of grief shows still some want of wit.
JULIET.   Yet let me weep for such a feeling loss.
LADY CAPULET.   So shall you feel the loss, but not the
    friend   75
    Which you weep for.
JULIET.   Feeling so the loss,
    I cannot choose but ever weep the friend.
LADY CAPULET.   Well, girl, thou weep'st not so much for
    his death
    As that the villain lives which slaughtered him.
JULIET.   What villain, madam?
LADY CAPULET.   That same villain Romeo.   80
JULIET.   [*Aside*] Villain and he be many miles asunder.   ASUNDER: apart
    [*To her mother*] God pardon him! I do, with all my
    heart;
    And yet no man like he doth grieve my heart.
LADY CAPULET.   That is because the traitor murderer
    lives.
JULIET.   Aye, madam, from the reach of these my hands.   85

58 DRY . . . BLOOD: Elizabethans believed that sorrow dried up the blood.
60 WHAT . . . HIM: "Why do you have anything to do with him?"

Would none but I might venge my cousin's death!

LADY CAPULET.   We will have vengeance for it, fear thou
        not.

Then weep no more. I'll send to one in Mantua,

Where that same banished runagate doth live,   RUNAGATE: fugitive

Shall give him such an unaccustomed dram   90   DRAM: poisonous drink

That he shall soon keep Tybalt company;

And then, I hope, thou wilt be satisfied.

JULIET.   Indeed, I never shall be satisfied

With Romeo till I behold him—dead*—

Is my poor heart so for a kinsman vexed.   95

Madam, if you could find out but a man

To bear a poison, I would temper it   TEMPER: mix

That Romeo should, upon receipt thereof,

Soon sleep in quiet. O, how my heart abhors

To hear him named and cannot come to him   100

To wreak the love I bore my cousin Tybalt   WREAK: avenge

Upon his body that hath slaughtered him!

LADY CAPULET.   Find thou the means, and I'll find such
        a man.

But now I'll tell thee joyful tidings, girl.

JULIET.   And joy comes well in such a needy time.   105

What are they, I beseech your ladyship?

LADY CAPULET.   Well, well, thou hast a careful father,   CAREFUL: considerate
        child;

One who, to put thee from thy heaviness,

Hath sorted out a sudden day of joy

That thou expects not nor I looked not for.   110

JULIET.   Madam, in happy time, what day is that?

LADY CAPULET.   Marry, my child, early next Thursday
        morn

The gallant, young, and noble gentleman,

The County Paris, at Saint Peter's Church,

Shall happily make thee there a joyful bride.   115

JULIET.   Now by Saint Peter's Church, and Peter too,

He shall not make me there a joyful bride!

I wonder at this haste, that I must wed

Ere he that should be husband comes to woo.

I pray you tell my lord and father, madam,   120

I will not marry yet; and when I do, I swear

It shall be Romeo, whom you know I hate,

Rather than Paris. These are news indeed!

---

94 DEAD: Read this as the last word of line 94 and the first word of line
95. In this scene Juliet carefully chooses her words to avoid revealing
her true feelings to her mother without denying her love for Romeo.

LADY CAPULET.   Here comes your father. Tell him so
      yourself,
  And see how he will take it at your hands.   125

[*Enter Capulet and Nurse.*]

CAPULET.   When the sun sets the air doth drizzle dew,
  But for the sunset of my brother's son
  It rains downright.
  How now! A conduit, girl? What, still in tears?   CONDUIT: fountain
  Evermore show'ring? In one little body   130
  Thou counterfeits a bark, a sea, a wind: BARK: boat
  For still thy eyes, which I may call the sea,
  Do ebb and flow with tears; the bark thy body is,
  Sailing in this salt flood; the winds, thy sighs,
  Who, raging with thy tears and they with them,   135
  Without a sudden calm will overset
  Thy tempest-tossèd body. How now, wife?
  Have you delivered to her our decree?
LADY CAPULET.   Aye, sir; but she will none, she gives
      you thanks.*
  I would the fool were married to her grave!   140
CAPULET.   Soft! Take me with you, take me with you,
      wife.
  How! Will she none? Doth she not give us thanks?
  Is she not proud? Doth she not count her blest,
  Unworthy as she is, that we have wrought
  So worthy a gentleman to be her bride?   145   BRIDE: bridegroom
JULIET.   Not proud you have, but thankful that you have.
  Proud can I never be of what I hate,
  But thankful even for hate that is meant love.
CAPULET.   How how, how how, chop-logic? What is this?   CHOP-LOGIC: quibbler
  "Proud" and "I thank you" and "I thank you not"—   150
  And yet "not proud." Mistress minion, you,   MINION: spoiled pet
  Thank me no thankings nor proud me no prouds,
  But fettle your fine joints 'gainst Thursday next
  To go with Paris to Saint Peter's Church,
  Or I will drag thee on a hurdle thither.   155
  Out, you green-sickness carrion! Out, you baggage!
  You tallow-face!
LADY CAPULET.   [*To her husband*] Fie, fie! What, are
      you mad?
JULIET.   Good father, I beseech you on my knees,
  Hear me with patience but to speak a word.   160
CAPULET.   Hang thee, young baggage! Disobedient
      wretch!
139 SHE WILL . . . THANKS: "She will have none of it, thank you."

I tell thee what: get thee to church o' Thursday
Or never after look me in the face.
Speak not, reply not, do not answer me!
My fingers itch. Wife, we scarce thought us blest   165
That God had lent us but this only child;
But now I see this one is one too much,
And that we have a curse in having her.
Out on her, hilding!   HILDING: wretch
NURSE.   God in heaven bless her!
   You are to blame, my lord, to rate her so.   170   RATE: abuse
CAPULET.   And why, my lady Wisdom? Hold your
      tongue,
   Good Prudence. Smatter with your gossips, go!   SMATTER: chatter
NURSE.   I speak no treason.
CAPULET.   O, God ye god den.
NURSE.   May not one speak?
CAPULET.   Peace, you mumbling fool!
   Utter your gravity o'er a gossip's bowl,   175
   For here we need it not.
LADY CAPULET.   You are too hot.
CAPULET.   God's bread! It makes me mad.
   Day, night, hour, tide, time, work, play,
   Alone, in company, still my care hath been
   To have her matched; and having now provided   180
   A gentleman of noble parentage,
   Of fair demesnes, youthful, and nobly trained,   DEMESNES: possessions
   Stuffed, as they say, with honorable parts,
   Proportioned as one's thought would wish a man—
   And then to have a wretched puling fool,   185   PULING: whining
   A whining mammet, in her fortune's tender,*   MAMMET: doll
   To answer, "I'll not wed, I cannot love,
   I am too young, I pray you pardon me"!
   But, an you will not wed, I'll pardon you!*
   Graze where you will, you shall not house with me.   190
   Look to 't, think on 't; I do not use to jest.
   Thursday is near; lay hand on heart, advise.   ADVISE: consider
   An you be mine, I'll give you to my friend;
   An you be not, hang, beg, starve, die in the streets;
   For, by my soul, I'll ne'er acknowledge thee,   195
   Nor what is mine shall never do thee good.
   Trust to 't, bethink you. I'll not be forsworn.   [*Exit.*]   FORSWORN: denied
JULIET.   Is there no pity sitting in the clouds
   That sees into the bottom of my grief?
   O sweet my mother, cast me not away!   200

186 IN HER FORTUNE'S TENDER: "when she is offered good fortune."
189 I'LL PARDON YOU: "I'll turn you out of my house."

Delay this marriage for a month, a week;
Or if you do not, make the bridal bed
In that dim monument where Tybalt lies.

LADY CAPULET.   Talk not to me, for I'll not speak a word.
   Do as thou wilt, for I have done with thee.   205

   [*Exit.*]

JULIET.   O God! O Nurse, how shall this be prevented?
   My husband is on earth, my faith in heaven.*
   How shall that faith return again to earth
   Unless that husband send it me from heaven
   By leaving earth? Comfort me, counsel me!   210
   Alack, alack, that heaven should practice stratagems
   Upon so soft a subject as myself!
   What say'st thou? Hast thou not a word of joy?
   Some comfort, Nurse.

NURSE.   Faith, here it is.
   Romeo is banished, and all the world to nothing*   215   CHALLENGE: reclaim
   That he dares ne'er come back to challenge you;
   Or if he do, it needs must be by stealth.
   Then, since the case so stands as now it doth,
   I think it best you married with the County.
   O, he's a lovely gentleman!   220
   Romeo's a dishclout to him. An eagle, madam,   DISHCLOUT: dishcloth
   Hath not so green, so quick, so fair an eye
   As Paris hath. Beshrew my very heart,
   I think you are happy in this second match,
   For it excels your first; or if it did not,   225
   Your first is dead; or 'twere as good he were
   As living here and you no use of him.

JULIET.   Speak'st thou from thy heart?

NURSE.   And from my soul too, else beshrew them both.

JULIET.   Amen!   230

NURSE.   What?

JULIET.   Well, thou hast comforted me marvelous much.
   Go in; and tell my lady I am gone,
   Having displeased my father, to Laurence' cell,
   To make confession and to be absolved.   235

NURSE.   Marry, I will; and this is wisely done.

   [*Exit.*]

JULIET.   Ancient damnation!* O most wicked fiend!
   Is it more sin to wish me thus forsworn,*

---

[207] MY FAITH IN HEAVEN: "My marriage vow is registered in heaven."
[215] ALL . . . NOTHING: the odds are very good.   [237] ANCIENT DAMNATION:
"You old devil."   [238] FORSWORN: guilty of breaking her marriage vow.

Or to dispraise my lord with that same tongue
Which she hath praised him with above compare   240
So many thousand times? Go, counselor!
Thou and my bosom henceforth shall be twain.*
I'll to the Friar to know his remedy.
If all else fail, myself have power to die.

[*Exit.*]

²⁴² THOU . . . TWAIN: "I shall confide in you no longer."

FOR DISCUSSION

1. Earlier Capulet seemed an understanding father, concerned that Juliet not marry too soon, nor against her will. Now, without her consent, he promises her to Paris in less than a week and threatens to throw her out of the house for her "ingratitude." What is his excuse for this sudden haste? Do you think his actions would have seemed reasonable by the standards of the time? Do they seem reasonable to you?

2. The dramatic irony in Scene v builds with each mention of Romeo and Paris, of death and weddings. Show how almost every one of Juliet's speeches in the first part of this scene has a different meaning for her and for the audience than it has for her mother.

3. Bitterly disappointed by her mother's rejection and her Nurse's advice to forget Romeo and marry Paris, Juliet must face her problem alone. What action does she take? How has she changed since Act I, Scene iii?

4. Act III is full of contrasts between life and death, love and hate, night and day, youth and age, impulsiveness and reasonableness. Point out several examples and discuss the effect of such contrasts on the audience. Why did Shakespeare deliberately place opposites together?

ACT IV

SCENE I. *Friar Laurence's cell.*

[*Enter Friar Laurence and Paris.*]

FRIAR.   On Thursday, sir? The time is very short.
PARIS.   My father Capulet will have it so,
  And I am nothing slow to slack his haste.*
FRIAR.   You say you do not know the lady's mind.
  Uneven is the course; I like it not.   5
PARIS.   Immoderately she weeps for Tybalt's death,
  And therefore have I little talked of love,
  For Venus smiles not in a house of tears.
  Now, sir, her father counts it dangerous
  That she do give her sorrow so much sway;*   10
  And in his wisdom hastes our marriage
  To stop the inundation of her tears,
  Which, too much minded by herself alone,
  May be put from her by society.*
  Now do you know the reason of this haste.   15
FRIAR.   [*Aside*] I would I knew not why it should be
      slowed.
  [*To Paris*] Look, sir, here comes the lady toward my
      cell.

[*Enter Juliet.*]

PARIS.   Happily met, my lady and my wife!
JULIET.   That may be, sir, when I may be a wife.
PARIS.   That "may be" must be, love, on Thursday next.   20
JULIET.   What must be shall be.
FRIAR.   That's a certain text.   CERTAIN TEXT: truth
PARIS.   Come you to make confession to this father?
JULIET.   To answer that, I should confess to you.
PARIS.   Do not deny to him that you love me.
JULIET.   I will confess to you that I love him.   25
PARIS.   So will ye, I am sure, that you love me.
JULIET.   If I do so, it will be of more price,
  Being spoke behind your back, than to your face.
PARIS.   Poor soul, thy face is much abused with tears.
JULIET.   The tears have got small victory by that,   30
  For it was bad enough before their spite.*

---

³ I . . . HASTE: "I am not reluctant to marry and thus will not hold him
back." ¹⁰ THAT . . . SWAY: "that she allows her sorrow to overwhelm
her." ¹³⁻¹⁴ WHICH . . . SOCIETY: "Alone, she is absorbed by her sorrow; the company of a husband may help her forget it." ³¹ BEFORE
THEIR SPITE: before they (the tears) did their damage.

PARIS.   Thou wrong'st it, more than tears, with that
      report.
JULIET.   That is no slander, sir, which is a truth;
   And what I spake, I spake it to my face.
PARIS.   Thy face is mine, and thou hast slandered it.   35
JULIET.   It may be so, for it is not mine own.
   Are you at leisure, holy Father, now,
   Or shall I come to you at evening Mass?
FRIAR.   My leisure serves me, pensive daughter, now.   PENSIVE: sorrowful
   My lord, we must entreat the time alone.*   40
PARIS. God shield I should disturb devotion!*
   Juliet, on Thursday early will I rouse ye.
   Till then, adieu, and keep this holy kiss.   [*Exit.*]
JULIET.   O, shut the door, and when thou hast done so,
   Come weep with me, past hope, past care, past help!   45
FRIAR.   O Juliet, I already know thy grief;
   It strains me past the compass of my wits.
   I hear thou must, and nothing may prorogue it,   PROROGUE: postpone
   On Thursday next be married to this County.
JULIET.   Tell me not, Friar, that thou hearest of this,   50
   Unless thou tell me how I may prevent it.
   If in thy wisdom thou canst give no help,
   Do thou but call my resolution wise,
   And with this knife I'll help it presently.   PRESENTLY: at once
   God joined my heart and Romeo's, thou our hands;   55
   And ere this hand, by thee to Romeo's sealed,
   Shall be the label to another deed,
   Or my true heart with treacherous revolt
   Turn to another, this shall slay them both.
   Therefore, out of thy long-experienced time,   60
   Give me some present counsel; or, behold,
   'Twixt my extremes and me this bloody knife   EXTREMES: suffering
   Shall play the umpire, arbitrating that
   Which the commission of thy years and art   COMMISSION: authority
   Could to no issue of true honor bring.   65   ISSUE: solution
   Be not so long to speak. I long to die
   If what thou speak'st speak not of remedy.
FRIAR.   Hold, daughter! I do spy a kind of hope,
   Which craves as desperate an execution
   As that is desperate which we would prevent.   70
   If, rather than to marry County Paris,
   Thou hast the strength of will to slay thyself,
   Then is it likely thou wilt undertake
   A thing like death to chide away this shame,

[40] ENTREAT . . . ALONE: ask to be left alone.   [41] GOD . . . DEVOTION:
"God forbid that I should interfere with your prayers."

That cop'st with death himself to scape from it;   75   cop'st: bargains
And, if thou dar'st, I'll give thee remedy.
JULIET.   O, bid me leap, rather than marry Paris,
From off the battlements of any tower,
Or walk in thievish ways, or bid me lurk
Where serpents are; chain me with roaring bears,   80
Or hide me nightly in a charnel house,*
O'ercovered quite with dead men's rattling bones,
With reeky shanks and yellow chapless skulls;   CHAPLESS: jawless
Or bid me go into a new-made grave
And hide me with a dead man in his shroud—   85
Things that, to hear them told, have made me trem-
    ble—
And I will do it without fear or doubt,
To live an unstained wife to my sweet love.
FRIAR.   Hold, then. Go home, be merry, give consent
To marry Paris. Wednesday is tomorrow.   90
Tomorrow night look that thou lie alone;
Let not the Nurse lie with thee in thy chamber.
Take thou this vial, being then in bed,
And this distillèd liquor drink thou off;
When presently through all thy veins shall run   95
A cold and drowsy humor, for no pulse   HUMOR: fluid
Shall keep his native progress, but surcease;
No warmth, no breath, shall testify thou livest;
The roses in thy lips and cheeks shall fade
To paly ashes, thy eyes' windows fall   100   WINDOWS: lids
Like death when he shuts up the day of life;
Each part, deprived of supple government,   GOVERNMENT: motion
Shall, stiff and stark and cold, appear like death:
And in this borrowed likeness of shrunk death:
Thou shalt continue two and forty hours,   105
And then awake as from a pleasant sleep.
Now, when the bridegroom in the morning comes
To rouse thee from thy bed, there art thou dead.
Then, as the manner of our country is,
In thy best robes uncovered on the bier   110
Thou shalt be borne to that same ancient vault
Where all the kindred of the Capulets lie.
In the meantime, against thou shalt awake,   AGAINST: before
Shall Romeo by my letters know our drift;   DRIFT: intention
And hither shall he come; and he and I   115
Will watch thy waking, and that very night
Shall Romeo bear thee hence to Mantua.

⁸¹ CHARNEL HOUSE: vault where bones from old graves were stored.

And this shall free thee from this present shame,
If no inconstant toy nor womanish fear   INCONSTANT TOY: whim
  Abate thy valor in the acting it.   120
JULIET.   Give me, give me! O, tell not me of fear!
FRIAR.   Hold; get you gone, be strong and prosperous
  In this resolve. I'll send a friar with speed
  To Mantua, with my letters to thy lord.
JULIET.   Love give me strength! And strength shall help
      afford.   125
  Farewell, dear Father!   *[Exit with Friar.]*

FOR DISCUSSION

• What plan does Friar Laurence offer to save Juliet from marriage to Paris? What chance do you think this plan has of succeeding? Why does such a desperate measure seem necessary?

SCENE II.   *Hall in Capulet's house.*

[Enter Capulet, Lady Capulet, Nurse, and two or three servants.]

CAPULET.   So many guests invite as here are writ.

[Exit a servingman.]

Sirrah, go hire me twenty cunning cooks.   CUNNING: expert
SERVINGMAN.   You shall have none ill, sir; for I'll try if   ILL: unskillful
  they can lick their fingers.
CAPULET.   How canst thou try them so?   5
SERVINGMAN.   Marry, sir, 'tis an ill cook that cannot lick
  his own fingers;* therefore he that cannot lick his
  fingers goes not with me.
CAPULET.   Go, begone.   *[Exit servingman.]*
  We shall be much unfurnished for this time.   10   UNFURNISHED: lacking provisions
  What, is my daughter gone to Friar Laurence?
NURSE.   Aye, forsooth.   FORSOOTH: indeed
CAPULET.   Well, he may chance to do some good on her.
  A peevish self-willed harlotry it is.*

[Enter Juliet.]

NURSE.   See where she comes from shrift with merry   SHRIFT: confession
      look.   15
CAPULET.   How now, my headstrong! Where have you
      been gadding?

⁶⁻⁷ CANNOT . . . FINGERS: cannot eat his own cooking. ¹⁴ A PEEVISH . . .
IS: "She is a silly, good-for-nothing girl."

JULIET.   Where I have learnt me to repent the sin
    Of disobedient opposition
    To you and your behests, and am enjoined   ENJOINED: directed
    By holy Laurence to fall prostrate here,   20
    And beg your pardon. Pardon, I beseech you!
    Henceforward I am ever ruled by you.
CAPULET.   Send for the County. Go tell him of this.
    I'll have this knot knit up tomorrow morning.
JULIET.   I met the youthful lord at Laurence' cell   25
    And gave him what becomèd love I might,   BECOMÈD: proper
    Not stepping o'er the bounds of modesty.
CAPULET.   Why, I am glad on 't. This is well. Stand up.
    This is as 't should be. Let me see the County.
    Aye, marry, go, I say, and fetch him hither.   30
    Now, afore God! This reverend holy Friar,
    All our whole city is much bound to him.   BOUND: obligated
JULIET. Nurse, will you go with me into my closet   CLOSET: private room
    To help me sort such needful ornaments
    As you think fit to furnish me tomorrow?   35
LADY CAPULET.   No, not till Thursday. There is time
    enough.
CAPULET.   Go, Nurse, go with her. We'll to church
    tomorrow.

    [*Exeunt Juliet and Nurse.*]

LADY CAPULET.   We shall be short in our provision.   PROVISION: preparation
    'Tis now near night.
CAPULET.   Tush, I will stir about,
    And all things shall be well, I warrant thee, wife.   40
    Go thou to Juliet, help to deck up her.   DECK UP: dress
    I'll not to bed tonight; let me alone.
    I'll play the housewife for this once. What, ho!
    They are all forth. Well, I will walk myself
    To County Paris, to prepare up him   45
    Against tomorrow. My heart is wondrous light,   AGAINST: for
    Since this same wayward girl is so reclaimed.

    [*Exeunt.*]

SCENE III.   *Juliet's chamber.*

[*Enter Juliet and Nurse.*]

JULIET.   Aye, those attires are best; but, gentle Nurse,
    I pray thee leave me to myself tonight;
    For I have need of many orisons   ORISONS: prayers
    To move the heavens to smile upon my state,

Which, well thou know'st, is cross and full of sin. 5 CROSS: unnatural

[Enter Lady Capulet.]

LADY CAPULET.   What, are you busy, ho? Need you my
    help?
JULIET.   No, madam; we have culled such necessaries CULLED: chosen
    As are behoveful for our state tomorrow. BEHOVEFUL: necessary
    So please you, let me now be left alone,
    And let the Nurse this night sit up with you; 10
    For I am sure you have your hands full all,
    In this so sudden business.
LADY CAPULET.   Good night.
    Get thee to bed, and rest; for thou hast need.

[Exeunt Lady Capulet and Nurse.]

JULIET.   Farewell! God knows when we shall meet again.
    I have a faint cold fear thrills through my veins 15
    That almost freezes up the heat of life.
    I'll call them back again to comfort me.
    Nurse!—What should she do here?
    My dismal scene I needs must act alone.
    Come, vial. 20
    What if this mixture do not work at all?
    Shall I be married then tomorrow morning?
    No, no; this shall forbid it. Lie thou there.

[Laying down her dagger.]

What if it be a poison which the Friar
Subtly hath ministered to have me dead, 25 MINISTERED: supplied
Lest in this marriage he should be dishonored
Because he married me before to Romeo?
I fear it is; and yet methinks it should not,
For he hath still been tried a holy man. TRIED: proved
How if, when I am laid into the tomb, 30
I wake before the time that Romeo
Come to redeem me? There's a fearful point!
Shall I not then be stifled in the vault,
To whose foul mouth no healthsome air breathes in,
And there die strangled ere my Romeo comes? 35
Or, if I live, is it not very like
The horrible conceit of death and night, CONCEIT: image
Together with the terror of the place—
As in a vault, an ancient receptacle
Where for this many hundred years the bones 40
Of all my buried ancestors are packed;

Where bloody Tybalt, yet but green in earth,*
Lies fest'ring in his shroud; where, as they say,
At some hours in the night spirits resort—
Alack, alack, is it not like that I,　　　　　　　　45
So early waking, what with loathsome smells,
And shrieks like mandrakes'* torn out of the earth,
That living mortals, hearing them, run mad—
O, if I wake, shall I not be distraught,
Environèd with all these hideous fears,　　　　　　50
And madly play with my forefathers' joints,
And pluck the mangled Tybalt from his shroud,
And, in this rage, with some great kinsman's bone
As with a club dash out my desperate brains?
O, look! Methinks I see my cousin's ghost　　　　55　　　　SPIT: impale
Seeking out Romeo, that did spit his body
Upon a rapier's point. Stay, Tybalt, stay!
Romeo, I come! This do I drink to thee.

[*She drinks the potion and falls upon her bed.*]

⁴² GREEN IN EARTH: newly buried.　⁴⁷ MANDRAKES: plants whose forked
root resembles the human body. When uprooted, they were believed
to shriek, driving the hearer mad.

FOR DISCUSSION

• Before she drinks the potion, Juliet is filled with horrible imaginings. What four things does she fear might happen to her? What does it show about her character that she drinks the potion in spite of these dangers? Was there any evidence earlier in the play that she had this much courage? Do you think it is, in fact, a courageous act?

SCENE IV.　*Hall in Capulet's house.*

[*Enter Lady Capulet and Nurse.*]

LADY CAPULET.　Hold, take these keys and fetch more
　　　spices, Nurse.
NURSE.　They call for dates and quinces in the pastry.　　　　PASTRY: bakery room

[*Enter Capulet.*]

CAPULET.　Come, stir, stir, stir! The second cock hath
　　　crowed,
The curfew bell hath rung, 'tis three o'clock.
Look to the baked meats, good Angelica;　　　　　　5　　　ANGELICA: Lady Capulet
Spare not for cost.
NURSE.　　　　　　Go, you cotquean, go,　　　　　　COTQUEAN: male houseworker

Get you to bed. Faith, you'll be sick tomorrow
For this night's watching.
CAPULET.   No, not a whit! What! I have watched ere now
All night for lesser cause, and ne'er been sick.   10
LADY CAPULET.   Aye, you have been a mouse-hunt in
    your time;

MOUSE-HUNT: nighthawk

But I will watch you from such watching now.

[*Exeunt Lady Capulet and Nurse.*]

CAPULET.   A jealous hood, a jealous hood!

JEALOUS HOOD: jealous woman

[*Enter three or four Servingmen with spits and logs and
baskets.*]

                                Now, fellow,
What's there?
FIRST SERVINGMAN.   Things for the cook, sir; but I know
not what.   15
CAPULET.   Make haste, make haste.

[*Exit First Servingman.*]

Sirrah, fetch drier logs.
Call Peter; he will show thee where they are.
SECOND SERVINGMAN.   I have a head, sir, that will find
    out logs,
And never trouble Peter for the matter.   20
CAPULET.   Mass, and well said; ha!
Thou shalt be loggerhead.   [*Exit Second Servingman.*]

LOGGERHEAD: blockhead

Good faith, 'tis day.
The County will be here with music straight,
For so he said he would. I hear him near.   25

[*Music is heard within.*]

Nurse! Wife! What, ho! What, Nurse, I say!

[*Enter Nurse.*]

Go waken Juliet; go and trim her up.
I'll go and chat with Paris. Hie, make haste,
Make haste. The bridegroom he is come already.
Make haste, I say.   [*Exit.*]

SCENE v.   *Juliet's chamber.*

[*Enter the Nurse.*]

NURSE.   Mistress! What, mistress! Juliet! Fast, I warrant
    her, she.

FAST: fast asleep

Why, lamb! Why, lady! Fie, you slugabed.
Why, love, I say! Madam! Sweetheart! Why, bride!
What, not a word? You take your pennyworths now;
Sleep for a week; for the next night, I warrant,   5
The County Paris hath set up his rest
That you shall rest but little. God forgive me!
Marry, and amen, how sound is she asleep!
I needs must wake her. Madam, madam, madam!
Aye, let the County take you in your bed;   10
He'll fright you up, i' faith. Will it not be?

[*Draws aside the curtains.*]

What, dressed, and in your clothes, and down again?   DOWN: back in bed
I must needs wake you. Lady! Lady! Lady!
Alas, alas! Help, help! My lady's dead!
O welladay that ever I was born!   15
Some *aqua vitae*, ho! My lord! My lady!

[*Enter Lady Capulet.*]

LADY CAPULET.   What noise is here?
NURSE.   O lamentable day!
LADY CAPULET.   What is the matter?
NURSE.   Look, look! O heavy day!   HEAVY: unhappy
LADY CAPULET.   O me, O me! My child, my only life!
  Revive, look up, or I will die with thee!   20
  Help, help! Call help.

[*Enter Capulet.*]

CAPULET.   For shame, bring Juliet forth; her lord is come.
NURSE.   She's dead, deceased; she's dead; alack the day!
LADY CAPULET.   Alack the day, she's dead, she's dead,
     she's dead!
CAPULET.   Ha! Let me see her. Out alas! She's cold;   25
  Her blood is settled, and her joints are stiff;
  Life and these lips have long been separated.
  Death lies on her like an untimely frost
  Upon the sweetest flower of all the field.
NURSE.   O lamentable day!
LADY CAPULET.   O woeful time!   30
CAPULET.   Death, that hath ta'en her hence to make me
     wail,
  Ties up my tongue and will not let me speak.

[*Enter Friar Laurence and Paris, with Musicians.*]

FRIAR.   Come, is the bride ready to go to church?

CAPULET.   Ready to go, but never to return.
 O son!...   35
 Death is my son-in-law, Death is my heir;
 My daughter he hath wedded. I will die
 And leave him all. Life, living, all is Death's.   LIVING: property
PARIS.   Have I thought long to see this morning's face,
 And doth it give me such a sight as this?   40
LADY CAPULET.   Accursed, unhappy, wretched, hateful
     day!
 Most miserable hour that e'er time saw
 In lasting labor of his pilgrimage!*
 But one, poor one—one poor and loving child—
 But one thing to rejoice and solace in,   45
 And cruel Death hath catched it from my sight!
NURSE.   O woe! O woeful, woeful, woeful day!
 Most lamentable day, most woeful day
 That ever ever I did yet behold!
 O day! O day! O day! O hateful day!   50
 Never was seen so black a day as this.
 O woeful day! O woeful day!
PARIS.   Beguiled, divorcèd, wrongèd, spited, slain!
 Most detestable Death, by thee beguiled,
 By cruel, cruel thee quite overthrown.   55
 O love! O life! Not life, but love in death!
CAPULET.   Despised, distressèd, hated, martyred, killed!
 Uncomfortable time, why cam'st thou now   UNCOMFORTABLE: distressing
 To murder, murder our solemnity?
 O child! O child! My soul, and not my child!   60
 Dead art thou! Alack, my child is dead,
 And with my child my joys are burièd.
FRIAR.   Peace, ho, for shame! Confusion's cure lives not   CONFUSION'S: disaster's
 In these confusions. Heaven and yourself
 Had part in this fair maid; now heaven hath all,   65
 And all the better is it for the maid.
 Your part in her you could not keep from death,
 But heaven keeps his part in eternal life.
 The most you sought was her promotion,
 For 'twas your heaven she should be advanced;   70
 And weep ye now, seeing she is advanced
 Above the clouds, as high as heaven itself?
 O, in this love, you love your child so ill
 That you run mad, seeing that she is well.   WELL: in heaven
 She's not well married that lives married long,   75
 But she's best married that dies married young.
 Dry up your tears and stick your rosemary

43 IN ... PILGRIMAGE: "during the unceasing troubles of his journey."

On this fair corse; and, as the custom is,
In all her best array bear her to church;
For though fond nature bids us all lament, 80
Yet nature's tears are reason's merriment.* NATURE'S: sentimentality's
CAPULET.   All things that we ordainèd festival
Turn from their office to black funeral;*
Our instruments to melancholy bells,
Our wedding cheer to a sad burial feast; 85 CHEER: food
Our solemn hymns to sullen dirges change,
Our bridal flowers serve for a buried corse,
And all things change them to the contrary.
FRIAR.   Sir, go you in; and, madam, go with him;
And go, Sir Paris. Everyone prepare 90
To follow this fair corse unto her grave.
The heavens do lour upon you for some ill; LOUR: frown
Move them no more by crossing their high will. CROSSING: opposing

[*Exeunt casting rosemary on her and shutting the curtains.
The Nurse and Musicians remain.*]

FIRST MUSICIAN.   Faith, we may put up our pipes and be
gone.
NURSE.   Honest good fellows, ah, put up, put up; 95
For well you know this is a pitiful case.   [*Exit.*]
FIRST MUSICIAN.   Aye, by my troth, the case may be
amended.

[*Enter Peter.*]

PETER.   Musicians, O, musicians, "Heart's ease,"
"Heart's ease"! O, and you will have me live, play
"Heart's ease." 100
FIRST MUSICIAN.   Why "Heart's ease"?
PETER.   O, musicians, because my heart itself plays "My
heart is full of woe." O, play me some merry dump to DUMP: sad song
comfort me.
FIRST MUSICIAN.   Not a dump we; 'tis no time to play 105
now.
PETER.   You will not then?
FIRST MUSICIAN.   No.
PETER.   I will then give it you soundly.
FIRST MUSICIAN.   What will you give us? 110
PETER.   No money, on my faith, but the gleek. I will give GLEEK: gibe
you the minstrel.*

<hr>

81 NATURE'S . . . MERRIMENT: "What our natural feelings cause us to
mourn, our reason tells us to rejoice in."   82–83 ALL . . . FUNERAL: "Let
all that we planned for the wedding be altered to suit a funeral."
111–112 GIVE . . . MINSTREL: "insult you by calling you 'minstrel'."

FIRST MUSICIAN.   Then will I give you the serving-
creature.

PETER.   Then will I lay the serving-creature's dagger on   115
your pate. I will carry no crotchets. I'll *re* you, I'll *fa*   PATE: head
you. Do you note me?

FIRST MUSICIAN.   An you *re* us and *fa* us, you note us.

SECOND MUSICIAN.   Pray you put up your dagger, and
put out your wit.   120   PUT OUT: exhibit

PETER.   Then have at you with my wit! I will dry-beat
you with an iron wit, and put up my iron dagger.
Answer me like men:

> "When griping grief the heart doth wound,
>   And doleful dumps the mind oppress,   125
> Then music with her silver sound"—

Why "silver sound"? Why "music with her silver
sound"? What say you, Simon Catling?*

FIRST MUSICIAN.   Marry, sir, because silver hath a sweet
sound.   130

PETER.   Pretty! What say you, Hugh Rebeck?*

SECOND MUSICIAN.   I say "silver sound" because musicians sound for silver.

PETER.   Pretty too! What say you, James Soundpost?*

THIRD MUSICIAN.   Faith, I know not what to say.   135

PETER.   O, I cry you mercy,* you are the singer; I will
say for you. It is "music with her silver sound" because musicians have no gold for sounding:

> "Then music with her silver sound
> With speedy help doth lend redress."   140

[*Exit.*]

FIRST MUSICIAN.   What a pestilent knave is this same!   PESTILENT: bothersome

SECOND MUSICIAN.   Hang him, Jack! Come, we'll in here,
tarry for the mourners, and stay dinner.

[*Exit with others.*]

---

128 CATLING: a lute string made of catgut. Peter gives the musicians
names appropriate to their professions.   131 REBECK: a fiddle with three
strings.   134 SOUNDPOST: post that supports the bridge of a stringed
instrument.   136 CRY YOU MERCY: beg your pardon.

FOR DISCUSSION

1. The Capulets believe Juliet to be dead. How do they react to the news of her death? What causes them to react in this manner?

2. In the course of the play, Juliet is torn by many conflicts. Some are external, caused by people or forces outside herself; others are internal, struggles within herself that she must resolve with her own decisions. What conflicts does she experience in relation to Romeo, her family, the Nurse, and Friar Laurence? Is each of these primarily internal or external? Which of them do you think is the main conflict of the play?

ACT V

SCENE I. *Mantua. A street.*

[*Enter Romeo.*]

ROMEO.   If I may trust the flattering truth of sleep,
My dreams presage some joyful news at hand.
My bosom's lord sits lightly in his throne,
And all this day an unaccustomed spirit
Lifts me above the ground with cheerful thoughts.   5
I dreamt my lady came and found me dead—
Strange dream that gives a dead man leave to think!—
And breathed such life with kisses in my lips
That I revived and was an emperor.
Ah me! How sweet is love itself possessed,   10
When but love's shadows are so rich in joy!*

[*Enter Romeo's servant, Balthasar.*]

News from Verona! How now, Balthasar?
Dost thou not bring me letters from the Friar?
How doth my lady? Is my father well?
How fares my Juliet? That I ask again,   15
For nothing can be ill if she be well.
BALTHASAR.   Then she is well, and nothing can be ill.
Her body sleeps in Capel's monument,
And her immortal part with angels lives.
I saw her laid low in her kindred's vault   20
And presently took post to tell it you.
O, pardon me for bringing these ill news,
Since you did leave it for my office, sir.
ROMEO.   Is it even so? Then I defy you, stars!
Thou know'st my lodging. Get me ink and paper   25
And hire post-horses. I will hence tonight.
BALTHASAR.   I do beseech you, sir, have patience.

PRESAGE: foresee
BOSOM'S LORD: heart

LEAVE: permission

WELL: in heaven
MONUMENT: tomb

TOOK POST: rode fast

OFFICE: duty

10–11 How. . . JOY: "How sweet the reality of love must be, when the thought of it is so joyful."

Your looks are pale and wild and do import   IMPORT: signify
  Some misadventure.
ROMEO.   Tush, thou art deceived.
  Leave me and do the thing I bid thee do.   30
  Hast thou no letters to me from the Friar?
BALTHASAR.   No, my good lord.
ROMEO.   No matter; get thee gone
  And hire those horses. I'll be with thee straight.

  [*Exit Balthasar.*]

  Well, Juliet, I will lie with thee tonight.
  Let's see for means. O mischief, thou art swift   35
  To enter in the thoughts of desperate men!
  I do remember an apothecary—   APOTHECARY: druggist
  And hereabouts 'a dwells—which late I noted
  In tattered weeds, with overwhelming brows,   WEEDS: clothing
  Culling of simples.* Meager were his looks;   40
  Sharp misery had worn him to the bones;
  And in his needy shop a tortoise hung,
  An alligator stuffed, and other skins
  Of ill-shaped fishes; and about his shelves
  A beggarly account of empty boxes,   45
  Green earthen pots, bladders, and musty seeds,
  Remnants of packthread, and old cakes of roses
  Were thinly scatterèd, to make up a show.
  Noting this penury, to myself I said,   PENURY: poverty
  "An if a man did need a poison now   50
  Whose sale is present death in Mantua,
  Here lives a caitiff wretch would sell it him."   CAITIFF: miserable
  O, this same thought did but forerun my need,
  And this same needy man must sell it me.
  As I remember, this should be the house.   55
  Being holiday, the beggar's shop is shut.
  What, ho! Apothecary!

  [*Enter Apothecary.*]

APOTHECARY.   Who calls so loud?
ROMEO.   Come hither, man. I see that thou art poor.
  Hold, there is forty ducats. Let me have
  A dram of poison, such soon-speeding gear   60
  As will disperse itself through all the veins
  That the life-weary taker may fall dead,
  And that the trunk may be discharged of breath
  As violently as hasty powder fired
  Doth hurry from the fatal cannon's womb.   65
40 CULLING . . . SIMPLES: selecting medicinal plants.

APOTHECARY.   Such mortal drugs I have, but Mantua's law
  Is death to any he that utters them.   UTTERS: distributes
ROMEO.   Art thou so bare and full of wretchedness
  And fear'st to die? Famine is in thy cheeks,
  Need and oppression starveth in thy eyes,   70
  Contempt and beggary hangs upon thy back.
  The world is not thy friend, nor the world's law;
  The world affords no law to make thee rich.
  Then be not poor, but break it and take this.   THIS: the money
APOTHECARY.   My poverty but not my will consents.   75
ROMEO.   I pay thy poverty and not thy will.
APOTHECARY.   Put this in any liquid thing you will
  And drink it off, and if you had the strength
  Of twenty men, it would dispatch you straight.
ROMEO.   There is thy gold—worse poison to men's souls,   80
  Doing more murder in this loathsome world,
  Than these poor compounds that thou mayst not sell.
  I sell thee poison; thou hast sold me none.
  Farewell! Buy food and get thyself in flesh.
  Come, cordial and not poison, go with me   85   CORDIAL: reviving drink
  To Juliet's grave; for there must I use thee.

  [*Exeunt.*]

FOR DISCUSSION

• In his response to the news of Juliet's death Romeo seems to be a different person from the Romeo reacting to the sentence of banishment. How do you account for the change in him?

SCENE II.   *Friar Laurence's cell.*

[*Enter Friar John.*]

JOHN.   Holy Franciscan Friar! Brother, ho!

[*Enter Friar Laurence.*]

LAURENCE.   This same should be the voice of Friar John.
  Welcome from Mantua! What says Romeo?
  Or, if his mind be writ, give me his letter.
JOHN.   Going to find a barefoot brother out—   5
  One of our order, to associate me   ASSOCIATE: help
  Here in this city visiting the sick—
  And finding him, the searchers of the town,   SEARCHERS: health officials
  Suspecting that we both were in a house
  Where the infectious pestilence did reign,   10

Sealed up the doors, and would not let us forth,
So that my speed to Mantua there was stayed.*
LAURENCE.   Who bare my letter, then, to Romeo?
JOHN.   I could not send it—here it is again—
Nor get a messenger to bring it thee,   15
So fearful were they of infection.
LAURENCE.   Unhappy fortune! By my brotherhood,
The letter was not nice but full of charge
Of dear import,* and the neglecting it
May do much danger. Friar John, go hence;   20
Get me an iron crow and bring it straight   CROW: crowbar
Unto my cell.   CELL: room
JOHN.   Brother, I'll go and bring it thee.

[*Exit.*]

LAURENCE.   Now must I go to the monument alone.
Within this three hours will fair Juliet wake.
She will beshrew me much that Romeo   25   BESHREW: blame
Hath had no notice of these accidents,   ACCIDENTS: incidents
But I will write again to Mantua,
And keep her at my cell till Romeo come.
Poor living corse, closed in a dead man's tomb!   [*Exit.*]

SCENE III.   *A churchyard. In it a tomb belonging to the Capulets.*

[*Enter Paris and his Page with flowers and scented water.*]

PARIS.   Give me thy torch, boy. Hence, and stand aloof.
Yet put it out, for I would not be seen.
Under yond yew tree lay thee all along,*
Holding thine ear close to the hollow ground.
So shall no foot upon the churchyard tread,   5
Being loose, unfirm, with digging up of graves,
But thou shalt hear it. Whistle then to me,
As signal that thou hear'st something approach.
Give me those flowers. Do as I bid thee, go.
PAGE.   [*Aside*] I am almost afraid to stand alone   10
Here in the churchyard; yet I will adventure.

[*Moves back among the gravestones.*]

PARIS.   Sweet flower, with flowers thy bridal bed I
                strew—

---

¹² SO . . . STAYED: "so that I never got to Mantua." ¹⁸⁻¹⁹ THE . . .
IMPORT: "The letter was full of matters of great importance."
³ LAY . . . ALONG: stretch out full-length.

O woe! Thy canopy is dust and stones—
Which with sweet water nightly I will dew,   SWEET: scented
   Or, wanting that, with tears distilled by moans.   15
The obsequies that I for thee will keep   OBSEQUIES: funeral rites
Nightly shall be to strew thy grave and weep.

[*The Page whistles.*]

The boy gives warning something doth approach.
What cursèd foot wanders this way tonight
To cross my obsequies and true love's rite?   20
What, with a torch? Muffle me, night, awhile.   MUFFLE: hide

[*Paris moves back into the darkness.*]

[*Enter Romeo, and Balthasar with a torch, a mattock, and a crowbar.*]

ROMEO.   Give me that mattock and the wrenching iron.
  Hold, take this letter. Early in the morning
  See thou deliver it to my lord and father.
  Give me the light. Upon thy life I charge thee,   25
  Whate'er thou hear'st or seest, stand all aloof
  And do not interrupt me in my course.
  Why I descend into this bed of death
  Is partly to behold my lady's face,
  But chiefly to take thence from her dead finger   30
  A precious ring, a ring that I must use
  In dear employment.* Therefore hence, be gone.
  But if thou, jealous, dost return to pry   JEALOUS: curious
  In what I farther shall intend to do,
  By heaven, I will tear thee joint by joint   35
  And strew this hungry churchyard with thy limbs.
  The time and my intents are savage-wild,
  More fierce and more inexorable far
  Than empty tigers or the roaring sea.
BALTHASAR.   I will be gone, sir, and not trouble ye.   40
ROMEO.   So shalt thou show me friendship. Take thou
    that.

[*Handing him money.*]

Live, and be prosperous, and farewell, good fellow.
BALTHASAR.   [*Aside*] For all this same, I'll hide me
    hereabout.
  His looks I fear, and his intents I doubt.

[*He moves behind the gravestones.*]

ROMEO.   Thou detestable maw, thou womb of death,   45   MAW: stomach
³² DEAR EMPLOYMENT: important business.

Gorged with the dearest morsel of the earth,
Thus I enforce thy rotten jaws to open,
And in despite I'll cram thee with more food!

IN DESPITE: spitefully

[*Romeo opens the tomb.*]

PARIS.   This is that banished haughty Montague
    That murdered my love's cousin, with which grief   50
    It is supposed the fair creature died;
    And here is come to do some villainous shame
    To the dead bodies. I will apprehend him.
    Stop thy unhallowèd toil, vile Montague!
    Can vengeance be pursued further than death?   55
    Condemnèd villain, I do apprehend thee.
    Obey, and go with me; for thou must die.
ROMEO.   I must indeed, and therefore came I hither.
    Good gentle youth, tempt not a desperate man.
    Fly hence and leave me. Think upon these gone;   60
    Let them affright thee. I beseech thee, youth,
    Put not another sin upon my head
    By urging me to fury. O, be gone!
    By heaven, I love thee better than myself,
    For I come hither armed against myself.   65
    Stay not, be gone. Live, and hereafter say
    A madman's mercy bid thee run away.
PARIS.   I do defy thy conjurations.

CONJURATIONS: solemn appeals

    And apprehend thee for a felon here.
ROMEO.   Wilt thou provoke me? Then have at thee, boy!   70

[*They fight.*]

PAGE.   O Lord, they fight! I will go call the watch.   [*Exit.*]
PARIS.   O, I am slain! [*Paris falls.*] If thou be merciful,
    Open the tomb, lay me with Juliet.   [*He dies.*]
ROMEO.   In faith, I will. Let me peruse this face.
    Mercutio's kinsman, noble County Paris!   75
    What said my man when my betossèd soul
    Did not attend him as we rode? I think
    He told me Paris should have married Juliet.
    Said he not so? Or did I dream it so?
    Or am I mad, hearing him talk of Juliet,   80
    To think it was so? O, give me thy hand,
    One writ with me in sour misfortune's book!
    I'll bury thee in a triumphant grave.
    A grave? O, no, a lantern, slaughtered youth,

LANTERN: windowed tower

    For here lies Juliet, and her beauty makes   85
    This vault a feasting presence full of light.
    Death, lie thou there, by a dead man interred.

[*He places Paris in the tomb.*]

How oft when men are at the point of death
Have they been merry—which their keepers call
A lightning before death. O, how may I   90
Call this a lightning? O my love! My wife!
Death, that hath sucked the honey of thy breath,
Hath had no power yet upon thy beauty.
Thou art not conquered. Beauty's ensign yet   ENSIGN: flag
Is crimson in thy lips and in thy cheeks,   95
And Death's pale flag is not advancèd there.
Tybalt, liest thou there in thy bloody sheet?
O, what more favor can I do to thee
Than with that hand that cut thy youth in twain
To sunder his that was thine enemy?   100   SUNDER: sever
Forgive me, cousin! Ah, dear Juliet,
Why art thou yet so fair? Shall I believe
That unsubstantial Death is amorous,
And that the lean abhorrèd monster keeps
Thee here in dark to be his paramour?   105
For fear of that I still will stay with thee
And never from this palace of dim night
Depart again. Here, here will I remain
With worms that are thy chambermaids. O, here
Will I set up my everlasting rest   110
And shake the yoke of inauspicious stars
From this world-wearied flesh. Eyes, look your last!
Arms, take your last embrace! And, lips, O you
The doors of breath, seal with a righteous kiss
A dateless bargain to engrossing Death!*   115
Come, bitter conduct; come, unsavory guide!
Thou desperate pilot, now at once run on   PILOT: Romeo
The dashing rocks thy seasick weary bark!
Here's to my love! [*He drinks the poison.*] O true
    Apothecary!
Thy drugs are quick. Thus with a kiss I die.   120

[*He kisses Juliet and dies.*]

[*Enter Friar Laurence, with lantern, crowbar and spade.*]

FRIAR.   Saint Francis be my speed! How oft tonight
Have my old feet stumbled at graves! Who's there?
BALTHASAR.   Here's one, a friend, and one that knows
    you well.
FRIAR.   Bliss be upon you! Tell me, good my friend,

---

115 A . . . DEATH: "an everlasting contract with greedy Death."

What torch is yond that vainly lends his light   125
To grubs and eyeless skulls? As I discern,   GRUBS: insect larvae
It burneth in the Capels' monument.
BALTHASAR.   It doth so, holy sir; and there's my master,
One that you love.
FRIAR.   Who is it?
BALTHASAR.   Romeo.
FRIAR.   How long hath he been there?
BALTHASAR.   Full half an hour.   130
FRIAR.   Go with me to the vault.
BALTHASAR.   I dare not, sir.
My master knows not but I am gone hence,
And fearfully did menace me with death
If I did stay to look on his intents.
FRIAR.   Stay then; I'll go alone. Fear comes upon me.   135
O, much I fear some ill unthrifty thing.   UNTHRIFTY: unlucky
BALTHASAR.   As I did sleep under this yew tree here,
I dreamt my master and another fought,
And that my master slew him.
FRIAR.   Romeo!
Alack, alack, what blood is this which stains   140
The stony entrance of this sepulcher?
What mean these masterless and gory swords
To lie discolored by this place of peace?

[*Enters the tomb.*]

Romeo! O, pale! Who else? What, Paris too?
And steeped in blood? Ah, what an unkind hour   145
Is guilty of this lamentable chance!
The lady stirs.   [*Juliet rises.*]
JULIET.   O comfortable Friar! Where is my lord?   COMFORTABLE: comforting
I do remember well where I should be,
And there I am. Where is my Romeo?   150
FRIAR.   I hear some noise. Lady, come from that nest
Of death, contagion, and unnatural sleep.
A greater power than we can contradict
Hath thwarted our intents. Come, come away.
Thy husband in thy bosom there lies dead;   155
And Paris too. Come, I'll dispose of thee
Among a sisterhood of holy nuns.
Stay not to question, for the watch is coming.
Come, go, good Juliet. I dare no longer stay.
JULIET.   Go, get thee hence, for I will not away.   160

[*Exit Friar.*]

What's here? A cup, closed in my truelove's hand?
Poison, I see, hath been his timeless end.   TIMELESS: untimely
O churl! Drunk all, and left no friendly drop
To help me after? I will kiss thy lips;
Haply some poison yet doth hang on them   165
To make me die with a restorative.   [*Kisses him.*]   RESTORATIVE: reviving drink
Thy lips are warm!

[*Enter several Watchmen, with Paris's Page.*]

FIRST WATCHMAN.   Lead, boy. Which way?
JULIET.   Yea, noise? Then I'll be brief. O happy dagger!

[*Snatches Romeo's dagger.*]

This is thy sheath; there rust, and let me die.   170

[*She stabs herself and falls.*]

PAGE.   This is the place. There, where the torch doth
    burn.
FIRST WATCHMAN.   The ground is bloody. Search about
    the churchyard.
Go, some of you; whoe'er you find attach.   ATTACH: arrest

[*Exeunt some of the Watchmen.*]

Pitiful sight! Here lies the County slain;

And Juliet bleeding, warm, and newly dead,   175
Who here hath lain this two days burièd.
Go, tell the Prince; run to the Capulets;
Raise up the Montagues; some others search.

[*Exeunt others of the Watchmen.*]

We see the ground whereon these woes do lie,
But the true ground of all these piteous woes   180
We cannot without circumstance descry.*

[*Re-enter some of the Watchmen with Balthasar.*]

SECOND WATCHMAN. Here's Romeo's man. We found
    him in the churchyard.
FIRST WATCHMAN. Hold him in safety till the Prince
    come hither.

[*Enter Friar Laurence and another Watchman.*]

THIRD WATCHMAN. Here is a friar that trembles, sighs
      and weeps.
We took this mattock and this spade from him   185
As he was coming from this churchyard's side.
FIRST WATCHMAN. A great suspicion!* Stay the friar too.

[*Enter the Prince and Attendants.*]

PRINCE. What misadventure is so early up
    That calls our person from our morning rest?

[*Enter Capulet, Lady Capulet, and curious Citizens.*]

CAPULET. What should it be, that they so shriek abroad? 190
LADY CAPULET. O, the people in the street cry "Romeo,"
    Some "Juliet," and some "Paris"; and all run
    With open outcry toward our monument.
PRINCE. What fear is this which startles in our ears?
FIRST WATCHMAN. Sovereign, here lies the County Paris
      slain;   195
And Romeo dead; and Juliet, dead before,
Warm and new killed.
PRINCE. Search, seek, and know how this foul murder
    comes.
FIRST WATCHMAN. Here is a friar, and slaughtered
      Romeo's man,
With instruments upon them fit to open   200
These dead men's tombs.

180–181 BUT . . . DESCRY: "But we will not know what really caused their deaths until we have more details."   187 A GREAT SUSPICION: "very suspicious."

CAPULET.   O heavens! O wife, look how our daughter
        bleeds!
    This dagger hath mista'en, for, lo, his house   HOUSE: scabbard
    Is empty on the back of Montague,
    And it mis-sheathèd in my daughter's bosom!   205
LADY CAPULET.   O me! This sight of death is as a bell
    That warns my old age to a sepulcher.

[*Enter Montague and other Citizens.*]

PRINCE.   Come, Montague; for thou art early up
    To see thy son and heir more early down.
MONTAGUE.   Alas, my liege, my wife is dead tonight!   210   LIEGE: lord
    Grief of my son's exile hath stopped her breath.
    What further woe conspires against mine age?
PRINCE.   Look, and thou shalt see.
MONTAGUE.   [*Seeing Romeo's body*] O thou untaught!
        What manners is in this,
    To press before thy father to a grave?   215
PRINCE.   Seal up the mouth of outrage for a while,
    Till we can clear these ambiguities*
    And know their spring, their head, their true descent;
    And then will I be general of your woes
    And lead you even to death.* Meantime forbear,   220
    And let mischance be slave to patience.
    Bring forth the parties of suspicion.
FRIAR.   I am the greatest, able to do least,
    Yet most suspected, as the time and place
    Doth make against me, of this direful murder;   225
    And here I stand, both to impeach and purge
    Myself condemnèd and myself excused.
PRINCE.   Then say at once what thou dost know in this.
FRIAR.   I will be brief, for my short date of breath
    Is not so long as is a tedious tale.   230
    Romeo, there dead, was husband to that Juliet;
    And she, there dead, that Romeo's faithful wife.
    I married them; and their stolen marriage day
    Was Tybalt's doomsday, whose untimely death
    Banished the new-made bridegroom from this city;   235
    For whom, and not for Tybalt, Juliet pined.
    You, to remove that siege of grief from her,
    Betrothed and would have married her perforce   PERFORCE: forcibly
    To County Paris. Then comes she to me

---

²¹⁶⁻²¹⁷ SEAL . . . AMBIGUITIES: "Cease your cries of grief until we can
clear up these mysteries." ("Seal up the mouth of outrage" may also
refer to the closing of the burial vault.) ²¹⁹⁻²²⁰ AND . . . DEATH: "I
will then be the chief mourner, even to being the first to die of grief."

And with wild looks bid me devise some mean   240
To rid her from this second marriage,
Or in my cell there would she kill herself.
Then gave I her, so tutored by my art,
A sleeping potion, which so took effect
As I intended, for it wrought on her   245   WROUGHT: worked
The form of death. Meantime I writ to Romeo
That he should hither come as this dire night   AS: on
To help to take her from her borrowed grave,
Being the time the potion's force should cease.
But he which bore my letter, Friar John,   250
Was stayed by accident, and yesternight
Returned my letter back. Then all alone
At the prefixèd hour of her waking
Came I to take her from her kindred's vault,
Meaning to keep her closely at my cell   255   CLOSELY: secretly
Till I conveniently could send to Romeo.
But when I came, some minute ere the time
Of her awakening, here untimely lay
The noble Paris and true Romeo dead.
She wakes, and I entreated her come forth   260
And bear this work of heaven with patience.
But then a noise did scare me from the tomb,
And she, too desperate, would not go with me,
But, as it seems, did violence on herself.
All this I know, and to the marriage   265
Her Nurse is privy; and if aught in this   PRIVY: in on the secret
Miscarried by my fault, let my old life
Be sacrificed some hour before his time
Unto the rigor of severest law.
PRINCE.   We still have known thee for a holy man.   270
    Where's Romeo's man? What can he say to this?
BALTHASAR.   I brought my master news of Juliet's death;
    And then in post he came from Mantua   IN POST: in haste
    To this same place, to this same monument.
    This letter he early bid me give his father,   275
    And threatened me with death, going in the vault,
    If I departed not and left him there.
PRINCE.   Give me the letter; I will look on it.
    Where is the County's Page, that raised the watch?
    Sirrah, what made your master* in this place?   280
PAGE.   He came with flowers to strew his lady's grave;
    And bid me stand aloof, and so I did.
    Anon comes one with light to ope the tomb,

<hr>

[280] WHAT . . . MASTER: "What was Paris doing?"

And by and by my master drew on him;
And then I ran away to call the watch.   285
PRINCE.   This letter doth make good the Friar's words,   MAKE GOOD: verify
Their course of love, the tidings of her death.
And here he writes that he did buy a poison
Of a poor 'pothecary, and therewithal
Came to this vault to die and lie with Juliet.   290
Where be these enemies? Capulet! Montague!
See what a scourge is laid upon your hate,   SCOURGE: punishment
That Heaven finds means to kill your joys with love.   JOYS: children
And I, for winking at your discords too
Have lost a brace of kinsmen. All are punished.   295
CAPULET.   O brother Montague, give me thy hand.
This is my daughter's jointure, for no more   JOINTURE: dowry
Can I demand.
MONTAGUE.   But I can give thee more;
For I will raise her statue in pure gold,
That whiles Verona by that name is known,   300
There shall no figure at such rate be set   RATE: value
As that of true and faithful Juliet.
CAPULET.   As rich shall Romeo's by his lady's lie,
Poor sacrifices of our enmity!
PRINCE.   A glooming peace this morning with it brings. 305
    The sun, for sorrow, will not show his head.
Go hence, to have more talk of these sad things;
    Some shall be pardoned, and some punishèd,
For never was a story of more woe
Than this of Juliet and her Romeo.   310

[*Exeunt all.*]

FOR DISCUSSION

1. How does it happen that Romeo kills Paris? What irony does Romeo see in this?

2. The love story of Romeo and Juliet ends with their deaths. Why does the play go on so much longer? What is the purpose of the Friar's long summary of what has happened? Why is it appropriate for Prince Escalus to speak the last words of the play?

THE PLAY AS A WHOLE

1. How do the following people regard Romeo and Juliet's love: Mercutio, the Capulets, Friar Laurence, the Nurse? Show how their attitudes leave the lovers more and more isolated as the play progresses.

2. In one scene the Nurse acts as a willing messenger between Romeo and Juliet and speaks highly of Romeo; in another, she dismisses Romeo as a "dishcloth" compared to Paris. How do you explain these changes of heart? Is she motivated primarily by sympathy for Juliet, or by something else? What function does she serve in the play as a whole?

3. Shakespeare often used dramatic irony to heighten suspense or create humor. One situation involving dramatic irony occurs when Lady Capulet discusses their "enemy" Romeo with Juliet, not knowing he is her daughter's husband. Find other examples from III, i; IV, i; and V, iii. What is the effect of the irony in each case?

4. There is much talk in the play of misfortune and the stars that govern men's lives. Can the tragic ending be blamed on bad luck, or did the lovers create their own fate? Of the following, which are the result of deliberate choices by Romeo or Juliet, and which are the result of accident or coincidence:

a. Romeo's presence at the Capulets' ball
b. Romeo's overhearing Juliet's declaration of love
c. their speedy, secret marriage
d. the deaths of Mercutio and Tybalt; Romeo's banishment
e. Juliet's "death in life"
f. Romeo's failure to receive the Friar's message
g. the death of Paris
h. the deaths of Romeo and Juliet

FOR COMPOSITION

1. Both Romeo and Juliet are changed in important ways by the events of the play. Contrast their characters in Act I with the Romeo and Juliet of Act V. What do you think are the most important turning points in these changes? (You may wish to trace the changes in just one of the characters in more detail.)

2. What theme of the play is stated by Friar Laurence in his discussion of plants and men (II, iii)? How does he restate the theme at the end of Act II, and how is it emphasized again by the conclusion of the play?

3. The Prince ends the play promising that "some shall be pardoned, and some punished." If you had to be the judge, who would be pardoned, and who—if anyone—would be punished for the lovers' deaths?

Written in the fifth century B.C., *Antigone is one of a trilogy of Greek plays about the family of Oedipus, ruler of Thebes. After Oedipus' death his son Eteocles became king. Polynices, his other son, led an expedition against Thebes to seize the throne, and in the ensuing battle the two brothers killed each other. Creon, the new king, buried Eteocles with honor but ordered that anyone who buried Polynices would be killed. To be left to rot was a dreadful fate for an ancient Greek, for it was believed that the souls of unburied bodies could not go safely into Hades.*

ANTIGONE
SOPHOCLES

CHARACTERS

ISMENE (ĭs·mē′nē) ⎫
ANTIGONE ⎬ *daughters of Oedipus*
CREON (krē′on), *King of Thebes*
HAEMON (hē′man), *son of Creon*
TEIRESIAS (tī·rē′sĭ·əs), *a blind prophet*
A SENTRY

A MESSENGER
EURYDICE (ū·rĭd′ə·sē), *wife of Creon*
CHORUS of *Theban elders*
King's attendants
Queen's attendants
A boy leading Teiresias
Soldiers

SCENE. *Before the Palace at Thebes*

[*Enter Ismene from the central door of the Palace. Antigone follows, anxious and urgent; she closes the door carefully, and comes to join her sister.*]

ANTIGONE.   O sister! Ismene dear, dear sister Ismene!
    You know how heavy the hand of God is upon us;
    How we who are left must suffer for our father,
        Oedipus.
    There is no pain, no sorrow, no suffering, no dishonor
    We have not shared together, you and I.   5
    And now there is something more. Have you heard
        this order,
    The latest order that the King has proclaimed to the
        city?
    Have you heard how our dearest are being treated like
        enemies?

Antigone from *Sophocles: The Theban Plays*, translated by E. F. Watling. Copyright © E. F. Watling, 1947. Reprinted by permission of Penguin Books Ltd.

ISMENE.   I have heard nothing about any of those we
      love,
  Neither good nor evil—not, I mean, since the death   10
  Of our two brothers, both fallen in a day.
  The Argive army,* I hear, was withdrawn last night.
  I know no more to make me sad or glad.
ANTIGONE.   I thought you did not. That's why I brought
      you out here,
  Where we shan't be heard, to tell you something alone. 15
ISMENE.   What is it, Antigone? Black news, I can see
  already.
ANTIGONE.   O Ismene, what do you think? Our two dear
      brothers . . .
  Creon has given funeral honors to one,
  And not to the other; nothing but shame and ignominy.
  Eteocles* has been buried, they tell me, in state,   20
  With all honorable observances due to the dead.
  But Polynices,* just as unhappily fallen—the order
  Says he is not to be buried, not to be mourned;
  To be left unburied, unwept, a feast of flesh
  For keen-eyed carrion birds. The noble Creon!   25
  It is against you and me he has made this order.
  Yes, against me. And soon he will be here himself
  To make it plain to those that have not heard it,
  And to enforce it. This is no idle threat;
  The punishment for disobedience is death by stoning. 30
  So now you know. And now is the time to show
  Whether or not you are worthy of your high blood.
ISMENE.   My poor Antigone, if this is really true,
  What more can *I* do, or undo, to help you?
ANTIGONE.   *Will* you help me? Will you do something
  with me? Will you?   35
ISMENE.   Help you do what, Antigone? What do you
  mean?
ANTIGONE.   Would you help me lift the body . . . you
  and me?
ISMENE.   You cannot mean . . . to bury him? Against
  the order?
ANTIGONE. Is he not my brother, and yours, whether you
      like it
  Or not? *I* shall never desert him, never.   40
ISMENE.   How could you dare, when Creon has expressly
  forbidden it?
ANTIGONE.   He has no right to keep me from my own.

---

12 ARGIVE ARMY: this army, from Argos in Greece, attacked Thebes.
20 ETEOCLES: (ē·tē′ō·klēz).   **22** POLYNICES: (pŏl·ĭ·nī′sēz).

ISMENE. O sister, sister, do you forget how our father
    Perished in shame and misery, his awful sin
    Self-proved, blinded by his own self-mutilation?   45
    And then his mother, his wife—for she was both—
    Destroyed herself in a noose of her own making.
    And now our brothers, both in a single day
    Fallen in an awful exaction of death for death,
    Blood for blood, each slain by the other's hand.   50
    Now we two left; and what will be the end of us,
    If we transgress the law and defy our king?
    O think, Antigone; we are women; it is not for us
    To fight against men; our rulers are stronger than we,
    And we must obey in this, or in worse than this.   55
    May the dead forgive me, I can do no other
    But as I am commanded; to do more is madness.
ANTIGONE. No; then I will not ask you for your help.
    Nor would I thank you for it, if you gave it.
    Go your own way; I will bury my brother;   60
    And if I die for it, what happiness!
    Convicted of reverence—I shall be content
    To lie beside a brother whom I love.

We have only a little time to please the living,
But all eternity to love the dead.   65
There I shall lie for ever. Live, if you will;
Live, and defy the holiest laws of heaven.
ISMENE.   I do not defy them; but I cannot act
Against the State. I am not strong enough.
ANTIGONE.   Let that be your excuse, then. I will go   70
And heap a mound of earth over my brother.
ISMENE.   I fear for you, Antigone; I fear—
ANTIGONE.   You need not fear for me. Fear for yourself.
ISMENE.   At least be secret. Do not breathe a word.
I'll not betray your secret.   75
ANTIGONE.   Publish it
To all the world! Else I shall hate you more.
ISMENE.   Your heart burns! Mine is frozen at the thought.
ANTIGONE.   I know my duty, where true duty lies.
ISMENE.   If you can do it; but you're bound to fail.   80
ANTIGONE.   When I have *tried* and failed, I shall have
failed.
ISMENE.   No sense in starting on a hopeless task.
ANTIGONE.   Oh, I shall hate you if you talk like that!
And *he* will hate you, rightly. Leave me alone
With my own madness. There is no punishment   85
Can rob me of my honorable death.
ISMENE.   Go then, if you are determined, to your folly.
But remember that those who love you . . . love you
still.

[*Ismene goes into the Palace. Antigone leaves the stage by
a side exit.*]

FOR DISCUSSION

• Why does Antigone insist upon burying Polynices in spite of Creon's order? What reasons does Ismene give for not helping her?

[*Enter the Chorus of Theban elders.*]

CHORUS.   Hail the sun! the brightest of all that ever
Dawned on the City of Seven Gates, City of Thebes!   90
Hail the golden dawn over Dirce's river*
Rising to speed the flight of the white invaders
        Homeward in full retreat!
    The army of Polynices was gathered against us,
In angry dispute his voice was lifted against us,   95
Like ravening bird of prey he swooped around us
With white wings flashing, with flying plumes,
        With armed hosts ranked in thousands.
    At the threshold of seven gates in a circle of blood
His swords stood round us, his jaws were opened
        against us;   100
But before he could taste our blood, or consume us
        with fire,
He fled, fled with the roar of the dragon behind him
        And thunder of war in his ears.
    The Father of Heaven abhors the proud tongue's
        boasting;
He marked the oncoming torrent, the flashing stream   105
Of their golden harness, the clash of their battle gear;
He heard the invader cry Victory over our ramparts,
        And smote him with fire to the ground.
    Down to the ground from the crest of his hurricane
        onslaught
He swung, with the fiery brands of his hate brought
        low: 110
Each and all to their doom of destruction appointed
        By the god that fighteth for us.
    Seven invaders at seven gates seven defenders
Spoiled of their bronze for a tribute to Zeus; save two
Luckless brothers in one fight matched together   115
        And in one death laid low.
    Great is the victory, great be the joy
In the city of Thebes, the city of chariots.
Now is the time to fill the temples
With glad thanksgiving for warfare ended;   120
Shake the ground with the night-long dances,
Bacchus* afoot and delight abounding.
    But see, the King comes here,
Creon, the son of Menoeceus,

91 DIRCE'S RIVER: Dirce, wife of a former ruler of Thebes, was murdered and her body thrown into a stream that afterward was named for her.   122 BACCHUS (băk'əs): Greek god of wine.

Whom the gods have appointed for us   125
In our recent change of fortune.
What matter is it, I wonder,
That has led him to call us together
By his special proclamation?

[*The central door is opened, and Creon enters.*]

CREON.   My councillors: now that the gods have brought
            our city   130
Safe through a storm of trouble to tranquillity,
I have called you especially out of all my people
To conference together, knowing that you
Were loyal subjects when King Laius* reigned,
And when King Oedipus so wisely ruled us,   135
And again, upon his death, faithfully served
His sons, till they in turn fell—both slayers, both slain,
Both stained with brother-blood, dead in a day—
And I, their next of kin, inherited
The throne and kingdom which I now possess.   140
    No other touchstone can test the heart of a man,
The temper of his mind and spirit, till he be tried
In the practice of authority and rule.
For my part, I have always held the view,
And hold it still, that a king whose lips are sealed   145
By fear, unwilling to seek advice, is damned.
And no less damned is he who puts a friend
Above his country; I have no good word for him.
As God above is my witness, who sees all,
When I see any danger threatening my people,   150
Whatever it may be, I shall declare it.
No man who is his country's enemy
Shall call himself my friend. Of this I am sure—
Our country is our life; only when she
Rides safely, have we any friends at all.   155
Such is my policy for our common weal.
    In pursuance of this, I have made a proclamation
Concerning the sons of Oedipus, as follows:
Eteocles, who fell fighting in defense of the city,
Fighting gallantly, is to be honored with burial   160
And with all the rites due to the noble dead.
The other—you know whom I mean—his brother
        Polynices,
Who came back from exile intending to burn and
        destroy
His fatherland and the gods of his fatherland,
_____
134 KING LAIUS (lā′əs): father of Oedipus and former king of Thebes.

To drink the blood of his kin, to make them slaves— 165
He is to have no grave, no burial,
No mourning from anyone; it is forbidden.
He is to be left unburied, left to be eaten
By dogs and vultures, a horror for all to see.
I am determined that never, if I can help it, 170
Shall evil triumph over good. Alive
Or dead, the faithful servant of his country
Shall be rewarded.
CHORUS.   Creon, son of Menoeceus,
You have given your judgment for the friend and for
the enemy. 175
As for those that are dead, so for us who remain.
Your will is law.
CREON.   See then that it be kept.
CHORUS.   My lord, some younger would be fitter for
that task.
CREON.   Watchers are already set over the corpse. 180
CHORUS.   What other duty then remains for us?
CREON.   Not to connive at any disobedience.
CHORUS.   If there were any so mad as to ask for death—
CREON.   Ay, that is the penalty. There is always someone
Ready to be lured to ruin by hope of gain. 185

[*He turns to go. A Sentry enters from the side of the stage.
Creon pauses at the Palace door.*]

SENTRY.   My lord: if I am out of breath, it is not from
haste.
I have not been running. On the contrary, many a time
I stopped to think and loitered on the way,
Saying to myself "Why hurry to your doom,
Poor fool?" and then I said "Hurry, you fool. 190
If Creon hears this from another man,
Your head's as good as off." So here I am,
As quick as my unwilling haste could bring me;
In no great hurry, in fact. So now I am here . . .
But I'll tell my story . . . though it may be nothing after
all. 195
And whatever I have to suffer, it can't be more
Than what God wills, so I cling to that for my comfort.
CREON.   Good heavens, man, whatever is the matter?
SENTRY.   To speak of myself first—I never did it, sir;
Nor saw who did; no one can punish me for that. 200
CREON.   You tell your story with a deal of artful precau-
tion.
It's evidently something strange.

SENTRY. It is.
　　So strange, it's very difficult to tell.
CREON. Well, out with it, and let's be done with you. 205
SENTRY. It's this, sir. The corpse . . . someone has just
　　Buried it and gone. Dry dust over the body
　　They scattered, in the manner of holy burial.
CREON. What! Who dared to do it?
SENTRY. I don't know, sir.   210
　　There was no sign of a pick, no scratch of a shovel;
　　The ground was hard and dry—no trace of a wheel;
　　Whoever it was has left no clues behind him.
　　When the sentry on the first watch showed it us,
　　We were amazed. The corpse was covered from sight— 215
　　Not with a proper grave—just a layer of earth—
　　As it might be, the act of some pious passer-by.
　　There were no tracks of an animal either, a dog
　　Or anything that might have come and mauled the
　　　　body.
　　Of course we all started pitching in to each other,   220
　　Accusing each other, and might have come to blows,
　　With no one to stop us; for anyone might have done it,
　　But it couldn't be proved against him, and all denied it.
　　We were all ready to take hot iron in hand
　　And go through fire and swear by God and heaven   225
　　We hadn't done it, nor knew of anyone
　　That could have thought of doing it, much less done it.
　　　　Well, we could make nothing of it. Then one of our men
　　Said something that made all our blood run cold—
　　Something we could neither refuse to do, nor do,   230
　　But at our own risk. What he said was "This
　　Must be reported to the King; we can't conceal it."
　　So it was agreed. We drew lots for it, and I,
　　Such is my luck, was chosen. So here I am,
　　As much against my will as yours, I'm sure;   235
　　A bringer of bad news expects no welcome.
CHORUS. My lord, I fear—I feared it from the first—
　　That this may prove to be an act of the gods.
CREON. Enough of that! Or I shall lose my patience.
　　Don't talk like an old fool, old though you be.   240
　　Blasphemy, to say the gods could give a thought
　　To carrion flesh! Held him in high esteem,
　　I suppose, and buried him like a benefactor—
　　A man who came to burn their temples down,
　　Ransack their holy shrines, their land, their laws?   245
　　Is that the sort of man you think gods love?
　　Not they. No. There's a party of malcontents
　　In the city, rebels against my word and law,

Shakers of heads in secret, impatient of rule;
They are the people, I see it well enough,   250
Who have bribed their instruments to do this thing.
Money! Money's the curse of man, none greater.
That's what wrecks cities, banishes men from home,
Tempts and deludes the most well-meaning soul,
Pointing out the way to infamy and shame.   255
Well, they shall pay for their success.

[*To the Sentry*]

See to it!
See to it, you! Upon my oath, I swear,
As Zeus is my god above: either you find
The perpetrator of this burial   260
And bring him here into my sight, or death—
No, not your mere death shall pay the reckoning,
But, for a living lesson against such infamy,
You shall be racked and tortured till you tell
The whole truth of this outrage; so you may learn   265
To seek your gain where gain is yours to get,
Not try to grasp it everywhere. In wickedness
You'll find more loss than profit.
SENTRY.   May I say more?
CREON.   No more; each word you say but stings me more. 270
SENTRY.   Stings in your ears, sir, or in your deeper
    feelings?
CREON.   Don't bandy words, fellow, about my feelings.
SENTRY.   Though I offend your ears, sir, it is not I
    But he that's guilty that offends your soul.
CREON.   Oh, born to argue, were you?   275
SENTRY.   Maybe so;
    But still not guilty in this business.
CREON.   Doubly so, if you have sold your soul for money.
SENTRY.   To think that thinking men should think so
    wrongly!
CREON.   Think what you will. But if you fail to find   280
    The doer of this deed, you'll learn one thing:
    Ill-gotten gain brings no one any good.

[*He goes into the Palace.*]

SENTRY.   Well, heaven send they find him. But whether
        or no,
    They'll not find me again, that's sure. Once free,
    Who never thought to see another day,   285
    I'll thank my lucky stars, and keep away.

[*Exit.*]

CHORUS. Wonders are many on earth, and the greatest
     of these
Is man, who rides the ocean and takes his way
Through the deeps, through wind-swept valleys of
     perilous seas
      That surge and sway.   290
     He is master of ageless Earth, to his own will bending
The immortal mother of gods by the sweat of his brow,
As year succeeds to year, with toil unending
      Of mule and plough.
     He is lord of all things living; birds of the air,   295
Beasts of the field, all creatures of sea and land
He taketh, cunning to capture and ensnare
      With sleight of hand;
     Hunting the savage beast from the upland rocks,
Taming the mountain monarch in his lair,   300
Teaching the wild horse and the roaming ox
      His yoke to bear.
     The use of language, the wind-swift motion of brain
He learnt; found out the laws of living together
In cities, building him shelter against the rain   305
      And wintry weather.
     There is nothing beyond his power. His subtlety
Meeteth all chance, all danger conquereth.
For every ill he hath found its remedy,
      Save only death.   310
     O wondrous subtlety of man, that draws
To good or evil ways! Great honor is given
And power to him who upholdeth his country's laws
      And the justice of heaven.
     But he that, too rashly daring, walks in sin   315
In solitary pride to his life's end.
At door of mine shall never enter in
      To call me friend.

[*Severally, seeing some persons approach from a distance*]

O gods! A wonder to see!
Surely it cannot be—   320
It is no other—
Antigone!
Unhappy maid—
Unhappy Oedipus' daughter; it is she they bring.
Can she have rashly disobeyed   325
The order of our King?

[*Enter the Sentry, bringing Antigone guarded by two more soldiers.*]

SENTRY.   We've got her. Here's the woman that did the deed.
We found her in the act of burying him. Where's the King?
CHORUS.   He is just coming out of the palace now.

[*Enter Creon.*]

CREON.   What's this? What am I just in time to see?   330
SENTRY.   My lord, an oath's a very dangerous thing,
Second thoughts may prove us liars. Not long since
I swore I wouldn't trust myself again
To face your threats; you gave me a drubbing the first time.
But there's no pleasure like an unexpected pleasure,   335
Not by a long way. And so I've come again,
Though against my solemn oath. And I've brought this lady,
Who's been caught in the act of setting that grave in order.
And no casting lots for it this time—the prize is mine
And no one else's. So take her; judge and convict her.   340
I'm free, I hope, and quit of the horrible business.
CREON.   How did you find her? Where have you brought her from?
SENTRY.   She was burying the man with her own hands, and that's the truth.
CREON.   Are you in your senses? Do you know what you are saying?
SENTRY.   I saw her myself, burying the body of the man   345

Whom you said not to bury. Don't I speak plain?
CREON.   How did she come to be seen and taken in the
    act?
SENTRY.   It was this way.
    After I got back to the place,
    With all your threats and curses ringing in my ears,   350
    We swept off all the earth that covered the body,
    And left it a sodden naked corpse again;
    Then sat up on the hill, on the windward side,
    Keeping clear of the stench of him, as far as we could;
    All of us keeping each other up to the mark,   355
    With pretty sharp speaking, not to be caught napping
        this time.
    So this went on some hours, till the flaming sun
    Was high in the top of the sky, and the heat was
        blazing.
    Suddenly a storm of dust, like a plague from heaven,
    Swept over the ground, stripping the trees stark bare,   360
    Filling the sky; you had to shut your eyes
    To stand against it. When at last it stopped,
    There was the girl, screaming like an angry bird,
    When it finds its nest left empty and little ones gone.
    Just like that she screamed, seeing the body   365
    Naked, crying and cursing the ones that had done it.
    Then she picks up the dry earth in her hands,
    And pouring out of a fine bronze urn she's brought
    She makes her offering three times to the dead.
    Soon as we saw it, down we came and caught her.   370
    She wasn't at all frightened. And so we charged her
    With what she'd done before, and this. She admitted it,
    I'm glad to say—though sorry too, in a way.
    It's good to save your own skin, but a pity
    To have to see another get into trouble,   375
    Whom you've no grudge against. However, I can't say
    I've ever valued anyone else's life
    More than my own, and that's the honest truth.
CREON [*to Antigone*].   Well, what do you say—you,
        hiding your head there:
    Do you admit, or do you deny the deed?   380
ANTIGONE.   I do admit it. I do not deny it.
CREON [*to the Sentry*].   You—you may go. You are dis-
        charged from blame.

    [*Exit Sentry.*]

    Now tell me, in as few words as you can,
    Did you know the order forbidding such an act?

ANTIGONE.   I knew it, naturally. It was plain enough.   385
CREON.   And yet you dared to contravene it?
ANTIGONE.   Yes.
  That order did not come from God. Justice,
  That dwells with the gods below, knows no such law.
  I did not think your edicts strong enough   390
  To overrule the unwritten unalterable laws
  Of God and heaven, you being only a man.
  They are not of yesterday or today, but everlasting,
  Though where they came from, none of us can tell.
  Guilty of their transgression before God   395
  I cannot be, for any man on earth.
  I knew that I should have to die, of course,
  With or without your order. If it be soon,
  So much the better. Living in daily torment
  As I do, who would not be glad to die?   400
  This punishment will not be any pain.
  Only if I had let my mother's son
  Lie there unburied, then I could not have borne it.
  This I can bear. Does that seem foolish to you?
  Or is it you that are foolish to judge me so?   405
CHORUS.   She shows her father's stubborn spirit: foolish
  Not to give way when everything's against her.
CREON.   Ah, but you'll see. The over-obstinate spirit
  Is soonest broken; as the strongest iron will snap
  If over-tempered in the fire to brittleness.   410
  A little halter is enough to break
  The wildest horse. Proud thoughts do not sit well
  Upon subordinates. This girl's proud spirit
  Was first in evidence when she broke the law;
  And now, to add insult to her injury,   415
  She gloats over her deed. But, as I live,
  She shall not flout my orders with impunity.
  My sister's child—ay, were she even nearer,
  Nearest and dearest, she should not escape
  Full punishment—she, and her sister too,   420
  Her partner, doubtless, in this burying.
    Let her be fetched! She was in the house just now;
  I saw her, hardly in her right mind either.
  Often the thoughts of those who plan dark deeds
  Betray themselves before the deed is done.   425
  The criminal who being caught still tries
  To make a fair excuse, is damned indeed.
ANTIGONE.   Now you have caught, will you do more than
  kill me?

CREON.   No, nothing more; that is all I could wish.
ANTIGONE.   Why then delay? There is nothing that you
    can say   430
  That I should wish to hear, as nothing I say
  Can weigh with you. I have given my brother burial.
  What greater honor could I wish? All these
  Would say that what I did was honorable,
  But fear locks up their lips. To speak and act   435
  Just as he likes is a king's prerogative.
CREON.   You are wrong. None of my subjects thinks as
  you do.
ANTIGONE.   Yes, sir, they do; but dare not tell you so.
CREON.   And you are not only alone, but unashamed.
ANTIGONE.   There is no shame in honoring my brother.   440
CREON.   Was not his enemy, who died with him, your
  brother?
ANTIGONE.   Yes, both were brothers, both of the same
  parents.
CREON.   You honor one, and so insult the other.
ANTIGONE.   He that is dead will not accuse me of that.
CREON.   He will, if you honor him no more than the
  traitor.   445
ANTIGONE.   It was not a slave, but his brother, that died
  with him.
CREON.   Attacking his country, while the other defended
  it.
ANTIGONE.   Even so, we have a duty to the dead.
CREON.   Not to give equal honor to good and bad.
ANTIGONE.   Who knows? In the country of the dead that
  may be the law.   450
CREON.   An enemy can't be a friend, even when dead.
ANTIGONE.   My way is to share my love, not share my
  hate.
CREON.   Go then, and share your love among the dead.
  We'll have no woman's law here, while I live.

[*Enter Ismene from the Palace.*]

CHORUS.   Here comes Ismene, weeping   455
  In sisterly sorrow; a darkened brow,
  Flushed face, and the fair cheek marred
  With flooding rain.
CREON.   You crawling viper! Lurking in my house
  To suck my blood! Two traitors unbeknown   460
  Plotting against my throne. Do you admit
  To a share in this burying, or deny all knowledge?

ISMENE.   I did it—yes—if she will let me say so.
I am as much to blame as she is.
ANTIGONE.   No.   465
That is not just. You would not lend a hand
And I refused your help in what I did.
ISMENE.   But I am not ashamed to stand beside you
Now in your hour of trial, Antigone.
ANTIGONE.   Whose was the deed, Death and the dead are
witness.   470
I love no friend whose love is only words.
ISMENE.   O sister, sister, let me share your death,
Share in the tribute of honor to him that is dead.
ANTIGONE.   You shall not die with me. You shall not
claim
That which you would not touch. One death is enough. 475
ISMENE.   How can I bear to live, if you must die?
ANTIGONE.   Ask Creon. Is not he the one you care for?
ISMENE.   You do yourself no good to taunt me so.
ANTIGONE.   Indeed no: even my jests are bitter pains.
ISMENE.   But how, O tell me, how can I still help you?   480
ANTIGONE.   Help yourself. I shall not stand in your way.
ISMENE.   For pity, Antigone—can I not die with you?
ANTIGONE.   You chose; life was your choice, when mine
was death.
ISMENE.   Although I warned you that it would be so.
ANTIGONE.   Your way seemed right to some, to others
mine.   485
ISMENE.   But now both in the wrong, and both con-
demned.
ANTIGONE.   No, no. You live. My heart was long since
dead,
So it was right for me to help the dead.
CREON.   I do believe the creatures both are mad;
One lately crazed, the other from her birth.   490
ISMENE.   Is it not likely, sir? The strongest mind
Cannot but break under misfortune's blows.
CREON.   Yours did, when you threw in your lot with hers.
ISMENE.   How could I wish to live without my sister?
CREON.   You have no sister. Count her dead already.   495
ISMENE.   You could not take her—kill your own son's
bride?
CREON.   Oh, there are other fields for him to plough.
ISMENE.   No truer troth was ever made than theirs.

FOR DISCUSSION

1. Because Greek plays rarely changed from one scene to another, much of the most exciting action had to take place offstage. How is Antigone's discovery of her brother's body vividly presented in spite of this handicap?

2. What is Antigone's attitude as she faces Creon's wrath? To what higher law than his does she appeal?

3. Whose side does the Chorus take in this conflict? With whom do you sympathize, Creon or Antigone? Why?

4. Why does Antigone reject Ismene's offer to die with her?

CREON.   No son of mine shall wed so vile a creature.

ANTIGONE.   O Haemon, can your father spite you so?   500

CREON.   You and your paramour, I hate you both.

CHORUS.   Sir, would you take her from your own son's
  arms?

CREON.   Not I, but death shall take her.

CHORUS.   Be it so.
  Her death, it seems, is certain.   505

CREON.   Certain it is.
  No more delay. Take them, and keep them within—
  The proper place for women. None so brave
  As not to look for some way of escape
  When they see life stand face to face with death.   510

[*The women are taken away.*]

CHORUS.   Happy are they who know not the taste of evil.
  From a house that heaven hath shaken
  The curse departs not
  But falls upon all of the blood,
  Like the restless surge of the sea when the dark storm
    drives   515
  The black sand hurled from the deeps
  And the Thracian gales boom down
  On the echoing shore.
    In life and in death is the house of Labdacus*
      stricken.
  Generation to generation,   520
  With no atonement,
  It is scourged by the wrath of a god.
  And now for the dead dust's sake is the light of
    promise,
  The tree's last root, crushed out
  By pride of heart and the sin   525
  Of presumptuous tongue.
    For what presumption of man can match thy power.

519 LABDACUS: Oedipus' grandfather.

O Zeus, that art not subject to sleep or time
Or age, living for ever in bright Olympus?
Tomorrow and for all time to come,   530
As in the past,
This law is immutable:
For mortals greatly to live is greatly to suffer.
   Roving ambition helps many a man to good,
And many it falsely lures to light desires,   535
Till failure trips them unawares, and they fall
On the fire that consumes them. Well was it said,
Evil seems good
To him who is doomed to suffer;
And short is the time before that suffering comes.   540
   But here comes Haemon,
Your youngest son.
Does he come to speak his sorrow
For the doom of his promised bride,
The loss of his marriage hopes?   545
CREON.   We shall know it soon, and need no prophet to
     tell us.

[*Enter Haemon.*]

Son, you have heard, I think, our final judgment
On your late betrothed. No angry words, I hope?
Still friends, in spite of everything, my son?
HAEMON.   I am your son, sir; by your wise decisions   550
     My life is ruled, and them I shall always obey.
     I cannot value any marriage-tie
     Above your own good guidance.
CREON.   Rightly said.
     You father's will should have your heart's first place. 555
     Only for this do fathers pray for sons
     Obedient, loyal, ready to strike down
     Their fathers' foes, and love their fathers' friends.
     To be the father of unprofitable sons
     Is to be the father of sorrows, a laughing-stock   560
     To all one's enemies. Do not be fooled, my son,
     By lust and the wiles of a woman. You'll have bought
     Cold comfort if your wife's a worthless one.
     No wound strikes deeper than love that is turned to
        hate.
     This girl's an enemy; away with her,   565
     And let her go and find a mate in Hades.
     Once having caught her in a flagrant act—
     The one and only traitor in our State—

I cannot make myself a traitor too;
So she must die. Well may she pray to Zeus,   570
The God of Family Love. How, if I tolerate
A traitor at home, shall I rule those abroad?
   He that is a righteous master of his house
Will be a righteous statesman. To transgress
Or twist the law to one's own pleasure, presume   575
To order where one should obey, is sinful,
And I will have none of it.
He whom the State appoints must be obeyed
To the smallest matter, be it right—or wrong.
And he that rules his household, without a doubt,   580
Will make the wisest king, or, for that matter,
The staunchest subject. He will be the man
You can depend on in the storm of war,
The faithfullest comrade in the day of battle.
There is no more deadly peril than disobedience;   585
States are devoured by it, homes laid in ruins,
Armies defeated, victory turned to rout.
While simple obedience saves the lives of hundreds
Of honest folk. Therefore, I hold to the law,
And will never betray it—least of all for a woman.   590
Better be beaten, if need be, by a man,
Than let a woman get the better of us.
CHORUS.   To me, as far as an old man can tell,
It seems your Majesty has spoken well.
HAEMON.   Father, man's wisdom is the gift of heaven,   595
The greatest gift of all. I neither am
Nor wish to be clever enough to prove you wrong,
Though all men might not think the same as you do.
Nevertheless, I have to be your watchdog,
To know what others say and what they do,   600
And what they find to praise and what to blame.
Your frown is a sufficient silencer
Of any word that is not for your ears.
But *I* hear whispers spoken in the dark;
On every side I hear voices of pity   605
For this poor girl, doomed to the cruelest death,
And most unjust, that ever woman suffered
For an honorable action—burying a brother
Who was killed in battle, rather than leave him naked
For dogs to maul and carrion birds to peck at.   610
Has she not rather earned a crown of gold?—
Such is the secret talk about the town.
   Father, there is nothing I can prize above
Your happiness and well-being. What greater good

Can any son desire? Can any father 615
Desire more from his son? Therefore I say,
Let not your first thought be your only thought.
Think if there cannot be some other way.
Surely, to think your own the only wisdom,
And yours the only word, the only will, 620
Betrays a shallow spirit, an empty heart.
It is no weakness for the wisest man
To learn when he is wrong, know when to yield.
So, on the margin of a flooded river
Trees bending to the torrent live unbroken, 625
While those that strain against it are snapped off.
A sailor has to tack and slacken sheets
Before the gale, or find himself capsized.
    So, Father, pause, and put aside your anger.
I think, for what my young opinion's worth, 630
That, good as it is to have infallible wisdom,
Since this is rarely found, the next best thing
Is to be willing to listen to wise advice.

CHORUS.   There is something to be said, my lord, for his
        point of view,
And for yours as well; there is much to be said on both
        sides. 635

CREON.   Indeed! Am I to take lessons at my time of life
From a fellow of his age?

HAEMON.   No lesson you need be ashamed of.
It isn't a question of age, but of right and wrong.

CREON.   Would you call it right to admire an act of disobedience? 640

HAEMON.   Not if the act were also dishonorable.

CREON.   And was not this woman's action dishonorable?

HAEMON.   The people of Thebes think not.

CREON.   The people of Thebes!
Since when do I take my orders from the people of
        Thebes? 645

HAEMON.   Isn't that rather a childish thing to say?

CREON.   No. I am king, and responsible only to myself.

HAEMON.   A one-man state? What sort of a state is that?

CREON.   Why, does not every state belong to its ruler?

HAEMON.   You'd be an excellent king—on a desert island. 650

CREON.   Of course, if you're on the woman's side—

HAEMON.   No, no—
Unless you're the woman. It's you I'm fighting for.

CREON.   What, villain, when every word you speak is
against me?

HAEMON.   Only because I know you are wrong, wrong. 655

CREON. Wrong? To respect my own authority?
HAEMON. What sort of respect tramples on all that is holy?
CREON. Despicable coward! No more will than a woman!
HAEMON. I have nothing to be ashamed of.
CREON. Yet you plead her cause. 660
HAEMON. No, *yours*, and mine, and that of the gods of the dead.
CREON. You'll never marry her this side of death.
HAEMON. Then, if she dies, she does not die alone.
CREON. Is that a threat, you impudent—
HAEMON. Is it a threat 665
To try to argue against wrong-headedness?
CREON. You'll learn what wrong-headedness is, my friend, to your cost.
HAEMON. O Father, I could call you mad, were you not my father.
CREON. Don't toady me, boy; keep that for your lady-love.
HAEMON. You mean to have the last word, then? 670
CREON. I do.
And what is more, by all the gods in heaven,
I'll make you sorry for your impudence.

[*Calling to those within*]

Bring out that she-devil, and let her die
Now, with her bridegroom by to see it done! 675
HAEMON. That sight I'll never see. Nor from this hour
Shall you see me again. Let those that will
Be witness of your wickedness and folly.

[*Exit.*]

CHORUS. He is gone, my lord, in very passionate haste.
And who shall say what a young man's wrath may do? 680
CREON. Let him go! Let him do! Let him rage as never man raged,
He shall not save those women from their doom.
CHORUS. You mean, then, sire, to put them both to death?
CREON. No, not the one whose hand was innocent.
CHORUS. And to what death do you condemn the other? 685
CREON. I'll have her taken to a desert place
Where no man ever walked, and there walled up
Inside a cave, alive, with food enough
To acquit ourselves of the blood-guiltiness
That else would lie upon our commonwealth. 690

There she may pray to Death, the god she loves,
And ask release from death; or learn at last
What hope there is for those who worship death.

[*Exit.*]

CHORUS.   Where is the equal of Love?
　Where is the battle he cannot win,   695
　The power he cannot outmatch?
　In the farthest corners of earth, in the midst of the sea,
　He is there; he is here
　In the bloom of a fair face
　Lying in wait;   700
　And the grip of his madness
　Spares not god or man,
　　Marring the righteous man,
　Driving his soul into mazes of sin
　And strife, dividing a house.   705
　For the light that burns in the eyes of a bride of desire
　Is a fire that consumes.
　At the side of the great gods
　Aphrodite* immortal
　Works her will upon all.   710

[*The doors are opened and Antigone enters, guarded.*]

But here is a sight beyond all bearing,
At which my eyes cannot but weep;
Antigone forth faring
To her bridal-bower of endless sleep.

ANTIGONE.   You see me, countrymen, on my last journey, 715
　Taking my last leave of the light of day;
　Going to my rest, where death shall take me
　Alive across the silent river.
　No wedding-day; no marriage-music;
　Death will be all my bridal dower.   720
CHORUS.   But glory and praise go with you, lady,
　To your resting-place. You go with your beauty
　Unmarred by the hand of consuming sickness,
　Untouched by the sword, living and free,
　As none other that ever died before you.   725
ANTIGONE.   The daughter of Tantalus, a Phrygian maid,*
　Was doomed to a piteous death on the rock
　Of Sipylus, which embraced and imprisoned her,
　Merciless as the ivy; rain and snow

709 APHRODITE (ăf·rə·dī′tē): Greek goddess of love and beauty.
726 MAID: Niobe (nī′ō·bē), her extreme pride in her children caused the
children to be slain. Niobe was then turned into a pillar of stone on
Mt. Sipylus.

Beat down upon her, mingled with her tears,   730
As she wasted and died. Such was her story,
And such is the sleep that I shall go to.
CHORUS.   She was a goddess of immortal birth,
And we are mortals; the greater the glory,
To share the fate of a god-born maiden,   735
A living death, but a name undying.
ANTIGONE.   Mockery, mockery! By the gods of our
      fathers,
Must you make me a laughing-stock while I yet live?
O lordly sons of my city! O Thebes!
Your valleys of rivers, your chariots and horses!   740
No friend to weep at my banishment
To a rock-hewn chamber of endless durance,
In a strange cold tomb alone to linger
Lost between life and death for ever.
CHORUS.   My child, you have gone your way   745
To the outermost limit of daring
And have stumbled against Law enthroned.
This is the expiation
You must make for the sin of your father.
ANTIGONE.   My father—the thought that sears my soul— 750
The unending burden of the house of Labdacus.
Monstrous marriage of mother and son . . .
My father . . . my parents . . . O hideous shame!
Whom now I follow, unwed, curse-ridden,
Doomed to this death by the ill-starred marriage   755
That marred my brother's life.
CHORUS.   An act of homage is good in itself, my daughter;
But authority cannot afford to connive at disobedience.
You are the victim of your own self-will.
ANTIGONE.   And must go the way that lies before me.   760
No funeral hymn; no marriage-music;
No sun from this day forth, no light,
No friend to weep at my departing.

FOR DISCUSSION

1. At first it seems incredible that Haemon can speak with such calm obedience to his father, who has just ordered his future wife executed. When does it become clear that he is just pretending in order to win Creon's support? What arguments does he offer against killing Antigone? How do Creon's replies finally drive him to reveal his true feelings?

2. What punishment does Creon plan for Antigone?

3. Why does the "comfort" offered by the Chorus make Antigone angry? What two causes do they blame for her fate?

[*Enter Creon.*]

CREON.   Weeping and wailing at the door of death!
There'd be no end of it, if it had force   765
To buy death off. Away with her at once,
And close her up in her rock-vaulted tomb.
Leave her and let her die, if die she must,
Or live within her dungeon. Though on earth
Her life is ended from this day, her blood   770
Will not be on our hands.
ANTIGONE.   So to my grave,
My bridal-bower, my everlasting prison,
I go, to join those many of my kinsmen
Who dwell in the mansions of Persephone,*   775
Last and unhappiest, before my time.
Yet I believe my father will be there
To welcome me, my mother greet me gladly,
And you, my brother, gladly see me come.
Each one of you my hands have laid to rest,   780
Pouring the due libations on your graves.
It was by this service to your dear body, Polynices,
I earned the punishment which now I suffer,
Though all good people know it was for your honor.
    O but I would not have done the forbidden thing   785
For any husband or for any son.
For why? I could have had another husband
And by him other sons, if one were lost;
But, father and mother lost, where would I get
Another brother? For thus preferring you,   790
My brother, Creon condemns me and hales me away,
Never a bride, never a mother, unfriended,
Condemned alive to solitary death.
What law of heaven have I transgressed? What god
Can save me now? What help or hope have I,   795
In whom devotion is deemed sacrilege?
If this is God's will, I shall learn my lesson
In death; but if my enemies are wrong,
I wish them no worse punishment than mine.
CHORUS.   Still the same tempest in the heart   800
Torments her soul with angry gusts.
CREON.   The more cause then have they that guard her
To hasten their work; or they too suffer.

---

775 PERSEPHONE (pər·sĕf'ə·nē): the wife of Pluto and queen of the dead
and the underworld.

CHORUS.   Alas, that word had the sound of death.
CREON.   Indeed there is no more to hope for.   805
ANTIGONE.   Gods of our fathers, my city, my home,
Rulers of Thebes! Time stays no longer.
Last daughter of your royal house
Go I, *his* prisoner, because I honored
Those things to which honor truly belongs.   810

[*Antigone is led away.*]

CHORUS.   Such was the fate, my child, of Danae*
Locked in a brazen bower,
A prison secret as a tomb,
Where was no day.
Daughter of kings, her royal womb   815
Garnered the golden shower
Of life from Zeus. So strong is Destiny,
No wealth, no armory, no tower,
No ship that rides the angry sea
Her mastering hand can stay.   820
And Dryas' son,* the proud Edonian king,
Pined in a stony cell
At Dionysus' bidding pent
To cool his fire
Till, all his full-blown passion spent,   825
He came to know right well
What god his ribald tongue was challenging
When he would break the fiery spell
Of the wild Maenads' revelling
And vex the Muses' choir.   830
It was upon the side
Of Bosporus, where the Black Rocks stand
By Thracian Salmydessus over the twin tide,
That Thracian Ares laughed to see
How Phineus' angry wife most bloodily   835
Blinded his two sons' eyes that mutely cried
For vengeance; crazed with jealousy
The woman smote them with the weaving-needle in
her hand.
Forlorn they wept away
Their sad step-childhood's misery   840
Predestined from their mother's ill-starred marriage-
day.

---

811 DANAE (dān′ə·ē): imprisoned by her father when he learned that
she would someday have a son who would grow up and kill him.
821 DRYAS′ SON: Lykurgus who, refusing to recognize the divinity of
Dionysus, was driven insane as punishment.

She was of old Erechtheid blood,
Cave-dwelling daughter of the North-wind God;
On rocky steeps, as mountain ponies play,
The wild winds nursèd her maidenhood.   845
On her, my child, the gray Fates laid hard hands, as
    upon thee.

[*Enter Teiresias, the blind prophet, led by a boy.*]

TEIRESIAS.   Gentlemen of Thebes, we greet you, my com-
    panion and I,
Who share one pair of eyes on our journeys together—
For the blind man goes where his leader tells him to.
CREON.   You are welcome, father Teiresias. What's your
    news?   850
TEIRESIAS.   Ay, news you shall have; and advice, if you
    can heed it.
CREON.   There was never a time when I failed to heed it,
    father.
TEIRESIAS.   And thereby have so far steered a steady
    course.
CREON.   And gladly acknowledge the debt we owe to
    you.
TEIRESIAS.   Then mark me now; for you stand on a
    razor's edge.   855
CREON.   Indeed? Grave words from your lips, good
    priest. Say on.
TEIRESIAS.   I will; and show you all that my skill reveals.
At my seat of divination, where I sit
These many years to read the signs of heaven,
An unfamiliar sound came to my ears   860
Of birds in vicious combat, savage cries
In strange outlandish language, and the whirr
Of flapping wings; from which I well could picture
The gruesome warfare of their deadly talons.
Full of foreboding then I made the test   865
Of sacrifice upon the altar fire.
There was no answering flame; only rank juice
Oozed from the flesh and dripped among the ashes,
Smouldering and sputtering; the gall vanished in a puff,
And the fat ran down and left the haunches bare.   870
Thus (through the eyes of my young acolyte,
Who sees for me, that I may see for others)
I read the signs of failure in my quest.
    And why? The blight upon us is *your* doing.
The blood that stains our altars and our shrines,   875
The blood that dogs and vultures have licked up,

It is none other than the blood of Oedipus
Spilled from the veins of his ill-fated son.
Our fires, our sacrifices, and our prayers
The gods abominate. How should the birds   880
Give any other than ill-omened voices,
Gorged with the dregs of blood that man has shed?

Mark this, my son: all men fall into sin.
But sinning, he is not for ever lost
Hapless and helpless, who can make amends   885
And has not set his face against repentance.
Only a fool is governed by self-will.
    Pay to the dead his due. Wound not the fallen.
It is no glory to kill and kill again.
My words are for your good, as is my will,   890
And should be acceptable, being for your good.
CREON.   You take me for your target, reverend sir,
   Like all the rest. I know your art of old,
   And how you make me your commodity
   To trade and traffic in for your advancement.   895
   Trade as you will; but all the silver of Sardis
   And all the gold of India will not buy
   A tomb for yonder traitor. No. Let the eagles
   Carry his carcass up to the throne of Zeus;
   Even that would not be sacrilege enough   900
   To frighten me from my determination
   Not to allow this burial. No man's act
   Has power enough to pollute the goodness of God.
   But great and terrible is the fall, Teiresias,
   Of mortal men who seek their own advantage   905
   By uttering evil in the guise of good.
TEIRESIAS.   Ah, is there any wisdom in the world?
CREON.   Why, what is the meaning of that wide-flung
   taunt?
TEIRESIAS.   What prize outweighs the priceless worth of
   prudence?
CREON.   Ay, what indeed? What mischief matches the
   lack of it?   910
TEIRESIAS.   And there you speak of your own symptom,
   sir.
CREON.   I am loth to pick a quarrel with you, priest.
TEIRESIAS. You do so, calling my divination false.
CREON. I say all prophets seek their own advantage.
TEIRESIAS.   All kings, say I, seek gain unrighteously.   915
CREON.   Do you forget to whom you say it?
TEIRESIAS.   No.
   Our king and benefactor, by my guidance.
CREON.   Clever you may be, but not therefore honest.
TEIRESIAS.   Must I reveal my yet unspoken mind?   920
CREON.   Reveal all; but expect no gain from it.
TEIRESIAS.   Does that still seem to you my motive, then?
CREON.   Nor is my will for sale, sir, in your market.

TEIRESIAS.   Then hear this. Ere the chariot of the sun
    Has rounded once or twice his wheeling way,   925
    You shall have given a son of your own loins
    To death, in payment for death—two debts to pay:
    One for the life that you have sent to death,
    The life you have abominably entombed;
    One for the dead still lying above ground   930
    Unburied, unhonored, unblest by the gods below.
    You cannot alter this. The gods themselves
    Cannot undo it. It follows of necessity
    From what you have done. Even now the avenging
        Furies,
    The hunters of Hell that follow and destroy,   935
    Are lying in wait for you, and will have their prey,
    When the evil you have worked for others falls on
        you.
    Do I speak this for my gain? The time shall come,
    And soon, when your house will be filled with the
        lamentation
    Of men and of women; and every neighboring city   940
    Will be goaded to fury against you, for upon them
    Too the pollution falls when the dogs and vultures
    Bring the defilement of blood to their hearths and
        altars.
      I have done. You pricked me, and these shafts of
        wrath
    Will find their mark in your heart. You cannot escape   945
    The sting of their sharpness.
    Lead me home, my boy.
    Let us leave him to vent his anger on younger ears,
    Or school his mind and tongue to a milder mood
    Than that which now possesses him.   950
    Lead on.

  [*Exit.*]

CHORUS.
    He has gone, my lord. He has prophesied terrible
        things.
    And for my part, I that was young and now am old
    Have never known his prophecies proved false.
CREON.   It is true enough; and my heart is torn in two.   955
    It is hard to give way, and hard to stand and abide
    The coming of the curse. Both ways are hard.
CHORUS.   If you would be advised, my good lord
    Creon—

CREON.   What must I do? Tell me, and I will do it.

CHORUS.   Release the woman from her rocky prison.   960
    Set up a tomb for him that lies unburied.

CREON.   Is it your wish that I consent to this?

CHORUS. It is, and quickly. The gods do not delay
    The stroke of their swift vengeance on the sinner.

CREON.   It is hard, but I must do it. Well I know   965
    There is no armor against necessity.

CHORUS. Go. Let your own hand do it, and no other.

CREON.   I will go this instant.
    Slaves there! One and all.
    Bring spades and mattocks out on the hill!   970
    My mind is made; 'twas I imprisoned her,
    And I will set her free. Now I believe
    It is by the laws of heaven that man must live.

    [*Exit.*]

CHORUS.   O Thou whose name is many,*
    Son of the Thunderer, dear child of his Cadmean
        bride,   975
    Whose hand is mighty
    In Italia,
    In the hospitable valley
    Of Eleusis,
    And in Thebes,   980
    The mother-city of thy worshipers,
    Where sweet Ismenus gently watereth
    The soil whence sprang the harvest of the dragon's
        teeth;*
    Where torches on the crested mountains gleam,
    And by Castalia's stream   985
    The nymph-train in thy dance rejoices,
    When from the ivy-tangled glens
    Of Nysa and from vine-clad plains
    Thou comest to Thebes where the immortal voices
    Sing thy glad strains.   990
    Thebes, where thou lovest most to be,
    With her, thy mother, the fire-stricken one,*
    Sickens for need of thee.

---

973 O THOU WHOSE NAME IS MANY: The reference here and in succeeding lines is to Dionysus and to rites held in honor of him.   983 DRAGON'S TEETH: Cadmus, founder of Thebes, planted dragon's teeth from which grew men to help him build the city.   992 FIRE-STRICKEN ONE: Dionysus' mother Semele was granted one wish by Zeus. She wished to see Zeus but the brightness and splendor of his appearance caused her death.

Healer of all her ills;
Come swiftly o'er the high Parnassian hills,   995
Come o'er the sighing sea.
   The stars, whose breath is fire, delight
To dance for thee; the echoing night
Shall with thy praises ring.
Zeus-born, appear! With Thyiads reveling   1000
Come, bountiful
Iacchus, King!

[*Enter a Messenger, from the side of the stage.*]

MESSENGER.   Hear, men of Cadmus' city, hear and attend,
  Men of the house of Amphion,* people of Thebes!
  What is the life of man? A thing not fixed   1005
  For good or evil, fashioned for praise or blame.
  Chance raises a man to the heights, chance casts him
      down,
  And none can fortell what will be from what is.
  Creon was once an enviable man;
  He saved his country from her enemies,   1010
  Assumed the sovereign power, and bore it well,
  The honored father of a royal house.
  Now all is lost; for life without life's joys
  Is living death; and such a life is his.
  Riches and rank and show of majesty   1015
  And state, where no joy is, are empty, vain
  And unsubstantial shadows, of no weight
  To be compared with happiness of heart.
CHORUS.   What is your news? Disaster in the royal
  house?
MESSENGER.   Death; and the guilt of it on living heads.   1020
CHORUS.   Who dead? And by what hand?
MESSENGER.   Haemon is dead,
  Slain by his own—
CHORUS.   His father?
MESSENGER.   His own hand.   1025
  His father's act it was that drove him to it.
CHORUS.   Then all has happened as the prophet said.
MESSENGER.   What's next to do, your worships will
  decide.

[*The Palace door opens.*]

CHORUS.   Here comes the Queen, Eurydice. Poor soul,

1004 AMPHION: husband of Niobe.

It may be she has heard about her son.   1030

[Enter Eurydice, attended by women.]

EURYDICE.   My friends, I heard something of what you
          were saying
As I came to the door. I was on my way to prayer
At the temple of Pallas, and had barely turned the
          latch
When I caught your talk of some near calamity.
I was sick with fear and reeled in the arms of my
          women.   1035
But tell me what is the matter; what have you heard?
I am not unacquainted with grief,* and I can bear it.
MESSENGER.   Madam, it was I that saw it, and will tell
          you all.
To try to make it any lighter now
Would be to prove myself a liar. Truth   1040
Is always best.
It was thus. I attended your husband,
The King, to the edge of the field where lay the body
Of Polynices, in pitiable state, mauled by the dogs.
We prayed for him to the Goddess of the Roads,* and
          to Pluto,   1045
That they might have mercy upon him. We washed the
          remains
In holy water, and on a fire of fresh-cut branches
We burned all that was left of him, and raised
Over his ashes a mound of his native earth.
That done, we turned toward the deep rock-chamber   1050
Of the maid that was married with death.
Before we reached it,
One that stood near the accursed place had heard
Loud cries of anguish, and came to tell King Creon.
As he approached, came strange uncertain sounds   1055
Of lamentation, and he cried aloud:
"Unhappy wretch! Is my foreboding true?
Is this the most sorrowful journey that ever I went?
My son's voice greets me. Go, some of you, quickly
Through the passage where the stones are thrown
          apart,   1060
Into the mouth of the cave, and see if it be
My son, my own son Haemon that I hear.

1037 I AM NOT . . . GRIEF: Eurydice's other son was killed at the beginning of the war.   1045 GODDESS OF THE ROADS: Hecate (hĕk′ə·tē) with
Persephone, referred to as queen of Hades.

If not, I am the sport of gods."
We went
And looked, as bidden by our anxious master.   1065
There in the furthest corner of the cave
We saw her hanging by the neck. The rope
Was of the woven linen of her dress.
And, with his arms about her, there stood he
Lamenting his lost bride, his luckless love,   1070
His father's cruelty.
When Creon saw them,
Into the cave he went, moaning piteously.
"O my unhappy boy," he cried again,
"What have you done? What madness brings you here 1075
To your destruction? Come away, my son,
My son, I do beseech you, come away!"
His son looked at him with one angry stare,
Spat in his face, and then without a word
Drew sword and struck out. But his father fled   1080
Unscathed. Whereon the poor demented boy
Leaned on his sword and thrust it deeply home
In his own side, and while his life ebbed out
Embraced the maid in loose-enfolding arms,
His spurting blood staining her pale cheeks red.   1085

[*Eurydice goes quickly back into the Palace.*]

Two bodies lie together, wedded in death,
Their bridal sleep a witness to the world
How great calamity can come to man
Through man's perversity.
CHORUS.   But what is this?   1090
The Queen has turned and gone without a word.
MESSENGER.   Yes. It is strange. The best that I can hope
Is that she would not sorrow for her son
Before us all, but vents her grief in private
Among her women. She is too wise, I think,   1095
To take a false step rashly.
CHORUS.   It may be.
Yet there is danger in unnatural silence
No less than in excess of lamentation.
MESSENGER.   I will go in and see, whether in truth   1100
There is some fatal purpose in her grief.
Such silence, as you say, may well be dangerous.

[*He goes in.*]

[*Enter Attendants preceding the King.*]

CHORUS.   The King comes here.
   What the tongue scarce dares to tell
   Must now be known   1105
   By the burden that proves too well
   The guilt, no other man's
   But his alone.

[*Enter Creon with the body of Haemon.*]

CREON.   The sin, the sin of the erring soul
   Drives hard unto death.   1110
   Behold the slayer, the slain,
   The father, the son.
   O the curse of my stubborn will!
   Son, newly cut off in the newness of youth,
   Dead for my fault, not yours.   1115
CHORUS.   Alas, too late you have seen the truth.
CREON.   I learn in my sorrow. Upon my head
   God has delivered this heavy punishment,
   Has struck me down in the ways of wickedness,
   And trod my gladness under foot.   1120
   Such is the bitter affliction of mortal man.

[*Enter the Messenger from the Palace.*]

MESSENGER.   Sir, you have this and more than this to
       bear.
   Within there's more to know, more to your pain.
CREON.   What more? What pain can overtop this pain?
MESSENGER.   She is dead—your wife, the mother of him
       that is dead—   1125
   The death-wound fresh in her heart. Alas, poor lady!
CREON.   Insatiable Death, wilt thou destroy me yet?
   What say you, teller of evil?
   I am already dead,
   And is there more?   1130
   Blood upon blood?
   More death? My wife?

[*The central doors open, revealing the body of Eurydice.*]

CHORUS.   Look then, and see; nothing is hidden now.
CREON.   O second horror!
   What fate awaits me now?   1135
   My child here in my arms . . . and there, the other . . .
   The son . . . the mother . . .
MESSENGER.   There at the altar with the whetted knife
   She stood, and as the darkness dimmed her eyes

Called on the dead, her elder son and this, 1140
And with her dying breath cursed you, their slayer.
CREON.   O horrible . . .
Is there no sword for me,
To end this misery?
MESSENGER.   Indeed you bear the burden of two deaths. 1145
It was her dying word.
CREON.   And her last act?
MESSENGER.   Hearing her son was dead, with her own
hand
She drove the sharp sword home into her heart.
CREON.   There is no man can bear this guilt but I. 1150
It is true, I killed him.
Lead me away, away. I live no longer.
CHORUS.   'Twere best, if anything is best in evil times.
What's soonest done, is best, when all is ill.
CREON.   Come, my last hour and fairest, 1155
My only happiness . . . come soon.
Let me not see another day.
Away . . . away . . .
CHORUS.   The future is not to be known; our present care
Is with the present; the rest is in other hands. 1160
CREON.   I ask no more than I have asked.
CHORUS.   Ask nothing.
What is to be, no mortal can escape.
CREON.   I am nothing. I have no life.
Lead me away . . . 1165
That have killed unwittingly
My son, my wife.
I know not where I should turn,
Where to look for help.
My hands have done amiss, my head is bowed 1170
With fate too heavy for me.

[*Exit.*]

CHORUS.   Of happiness the crown
And chiefest part
Is wisdom, and to hold
The gods in awe. 1175
This is the law
That, seeing the stricken heart
Of pride brought down,
We learn when we are old.

[*Exeunt.*]

FOR DISCUSSION

1. At one point Antigone seems to doubt the rightness of her act. What reason does she offer for valuing her brother above a husband or a son? Are you impressed by this argument?

2. What disaster does Teiresias prophesy for Creon? Why is it ironic that the prophet is blind while Creon can see?

3. Why do you think Creon finally gives in so suddenly?

4. Creon leaves the palace intending to right the wrongs he has done. Why does he fail? How does Teirsesias' terrible prophecy come true?

THE PLAY AS A WHOLE

1. Sophocles raises a particular conflict, between Antigone and Creon, into a universal one (that is, one which may be found in all times and places). What ideas about law, justice, loyalty, and obedience are symbolized by Creon and Antigone? We do not live in an absolute monarchy now, and girls are not sentenced to death for trying to bury their brothers. Can you still see how the play is relevant to modern times? Choose one modern conflict similar to the one in *Antigone* and show how the play relates to it. If Sophocles were writing now, how would he treat the conflict? What would the ending be?

2. What seems to be the main cause of Antigone's and Creon's misfortune? At various points in the play many possible causes are suggested: bad luck (fate), a family curse by which children suffer for their parents' wrongs, the will of the gods, or the individual's own choice. Do the characters seem cursed by one of the first three possibilities, or do they seem to choose their own fates? You may find quotes from the play to support your answer, but concentrate on what *happens,* as it shows Sophocles' interpretation of the legend.

FOR COMPOSITION

• What do you think is the theme of the play? Often in Greek plays the Chorus explain the theme, but in *Antigone* they are inconsistent, sometimes blaming Antigone, sometimes Creon. Which of the two is more to blame? What are we supposed to learn from their sufferings? Remember that the theme should apply to the whole play and to life in general.

In Summary

FOR DISCUSSION

1. Both *Romeo and Juliet* and *Antigone* are tragedies; that is, they involve people in high places defeated by overwhelming forces. Often the forces that destroy are faults within the characters themselves. Although a tragic play ends unhappily, the main characters learn and grow through their suffering; the audience feels not only pity for their destruction, but also admiration for the nobility with which they face it. Who do you think is the main tragic figure in *Antigone*, Antigone or Creon?

2. Unlike a sad movie or soap opera which offer only "a good cry," a tragic play is supposed to teach its audience to fear the forces which destroy human life. What are the destructive forces in each of the plays? Are they faults within the main characters or are they external?

3. In which play does man seem to have more control over his own destiny, *Romeo and Juliet* or *Antigone*? Consider the part that chance or fate plays in the plot of each. Could the tragic ending of either play have been avoided if the characters had acted differently, or were they doomed to destruction no matter what they did?

4. Compare and contrast the two pairs of lovers. In what ways do they represent different ideas of romantic love? Remember that the plays were written over 2000 years apart.

5. *Romeo and Juliet* is full of action, while most of the action in *Antigone* takes place offstage. Which type of drama do you prefer, Greek or Elizabethan? Which of these scenes might be more effective if it were changed from offstage to onstage or vice versa:
   a. the discovery of Juliet's "death"
   b. the deaths of Romeo and Juliet
   c. Antigone's burial of Polynices
   d. the deaths of Antigone and Haemon

6. In what way are the opinions of the Nurse in *Romeo and Juliet* similar to those of the Chorus in *Antigone*? Did you find yourself agreeing or disagreeing with them? On what basis do they seem to make their judgments?

OTHER THINGS TO DO

1. If there is a professional or university theater near you, watch for productions of Greek or Shakespearean dramas or other plays that a high school audience would enjoy. Your teacher can help you decide which ones might be too difficult. Read the play together in advance, then go to see it as a class. You might ask the director or some of the actors to discuss the production with you afterward; they are usually pleased to talk to student groups if given some advance notice.

2. Choose a scene from one of the unit plays or one of the plays in "Reader's Choice" to read to the class. If it is one they have not read, give some background information about the characters who are speaking. Rehearse with a tape recorder until you feel that you and the other readers are making the meaning of every line clear. If you are doing a scene from *Romeo and Juliet* you might find it helpful to compare your performance with a recording of professional actors doing the same scene.

3. Divide the class into small groups and have each group choose a scene to *improvise* (act without a script). Scenes can be chosen from real life (a parent-child conflict, for example), from the news, or from myths and Bible stories. Another possibility is to choose a scene, such as Antigone's imprisonment, which is mentioned in the play but not shown.

After the actors have tried the scene once as they think it might have happened, the group may suggest changes and try it again. When they are satisfied with the results they should write out the dialogue with stage directions. Some groups or individuals may want to expand this activity into the writing of a one-act play.

4. Write a research paper on the Greek and Elizabethan stage, audience, or actors and costuming. Show how the differences between them affected the types of plays written in those times. Why, for example, did Shakespeare include so many fight scenes and other physical action? If you are researching the stage, you might build models of the two types of stage; if costumes, you might draw charts of typical clothing from the two periods.

5. Before he wrote *Romeo and Juliet*, Shakespeare used the same story in *A Midsummer Night's Dream*. There it appears as a play within a play. Read the appropriate section (Act V, Scene i) and compare it with *Romeo and Juliet*.

The World of Words

ROMEO AND JULIET

1. *Romeo and Juliet* was written in the 1590s. Since that time, of course, English has changed a great deal. Not only is Shakespeare's language difficult because of its subtlety, it also presents some difficulties to us because of the playwright's use of words now *obsolete* or *archaic*. Archaic words are those that were once current but are now "old-fashioned" and used only for effect. *Yon* to mean "that" or "those" (as in "yon fair hills") and *enow* for "enough" are examples. Give the meanings of the following archaic words. (Remember, they are words that were current in Shakespeare's day, and when used now—to create a sense of antiquity in a poem, for instance—would have the same meaning now as then.) *"Aye,* while you live . . . (I, i, 4); "nothing hurt *withal"* (I, i, 100); "Go, *sirrah"* (I, ii, 34); "by my *fay"* (I, v, 127); *"Alack,* there lies more peril . . ." (II, ii, 72); *"Fain* would I dwell on form . . ." (II, ii, 89); *"Anon,* good Nurse!" (II, ii, 138); "I *trow"* (II, v, 62); "Ah, *welladay!"* (III, ii, 35); "I *wot* well where he is" (III, ii, 135); *"Hie,* hence . . ." (III, v, 26).

2. By contrast to archaic words, *obsolete* words are words no longer used (if at all) in the sense in which they once were. *Fond* in Shakespeare's day meant "foolish," "idiotic," as in "Thou fond mad man . . ." (III, iii, 52).

That sense of the word is now obsolete, replaced by other meanings in the same way that weapons or machines become obsolete. The following examples of obsolete diction are among those that occur in *Romeo and Juliet*. What did the italicized words mean in Shakespeare's day? What do they mean now? "One desperate grief cures with another's *languish"* (I, ii, 48); "How stands your *disposition* to be married?" (I, iii, 45); "An ill-beseeming *semblance* for a feast" (I, v, 75); "grace and *rude* will" (II, iii, 22); *"Conceit,* more rich in matter than in words" (II, vi, 30); "which name I *tender*/As dearly as mine own" (III, i, 71–72); "How *nice* the quarrel was" (III, i, 153); "I'll help it *presently"* (IV, i, 54); "A cold and drowsy *humor"* (IV, i, 96); "he hath still been *tried* a holy man" (IV, iii, 29); "he that *utters* them" (V, i, 67); "these *accidents"* (V, ii, 26).

ANTIGONE

1. Using the language effectively is in part a matter of precision, and precision often comes from knowing which of several possible words most accurately says what you want to say. In *Antigone*, Polynices is referred to as a *corpse* (line 206). Would *body* be an adequate substitution: Polynices' *body?* Would *cadaver?* Would *remains?* Would *carcass?* Where appropriate, explain why the substitution would be less effective than the original word.

2. Man's wisdom, according to Haemon, is the gift of heaven (l. 599). Is *wisdom* the same as *intelligence*? If not, how do they differ? How does *wisdom* differ from *prudence*? From *knowledge*?

3. Creon speaks of Ismene as innocent (l. 688). In that sense, he means she is not guilty of a crime, but we use *innocent* more broadly sometimes to refer to a childlike state. What are the differences in meaning of *innocent, naive, ignorant, simple, ingenuous, unsophisticated,* and *guileless*?

Reader's Choice

Lost in the Stars, *by Maxwell Anderson.*

This dramatic adaptation of Alan Paton's *Cry, the Beloved Country* explores the racial tensions seething below the surface of South Africa. A black minister comes to Johannesburg seeking his missing son, only to find that the boy is accused of murdering one of the whites who had tried to break through the apartheid color line.

A Man for All Seasons, *by Robert Bolt.*

When King Henry VIII of England named his friend Sir Thomas More Lord Chancellor of England, he hardly expected to have the favor repaid with disobedience. But Thomas could not support Henry's plan to make himself head of the English Church. Declaring himself "the king's good servant, but God's first," Sir Thomas faced Henry's wrath and the threat of death for treason.

Romanoff and Juliet, *by Peter Ustinov.*

In this untragic modern version of Shakespeare's story, the lovers are an American girl and a Russian Communist boy who meet in a neutral European country. To complicate matters further, both Igor Romanoff and Juliet Monkworth already are engaged, and Juliet's fiancé suddenly arrives on the scene.

The Trial of the Catonsville Nine, *by Daniel Berrigan.*

Based on the real-life trial of a group of clergymen and other pacifists who burned draft files in protest against the Vietnam war, this play raises the same question as *Antigone:* Whom should man obey when human law seems to contradict divine law?

West Side Story, *by Arthur Laurents.*

This popular Broadway musical closely follows the plot of *Romeo and Juliet,* only the Capulets and Montagues have become Sharks and Jets, rival street gangs fighting in the streets of New York. Maria, a Puerto Rican girl, and Tony, a Polish boy, are drawn together in spite of the hatred between their friends and families. Even if the play is not available to you, you should enjoy listening to the album—as in many musicals, most of the story is told in the songs.

My Sweet Charlie, *by David Westheimer.*

Two outcasts from society, one white, one black, both seek refuge in an abandoned summer house. Gradually their suspicions and prejudices give way to a growing respect for one another, but their friendship is doomed by the realities of life outside their hiding place.

THE GENERATIONS

THE BOY OF TWELVE vows when he grows up not to make the same mistakes rearing his son that his father is making with him. The girl of fourteen is sure she will never forget how it feels to be that age, and when she grows older will look upon others at that stage of their lives—fourteen then as she once was—with understanding and tolerance.

But we don't remember as much as we think we will. Sometimes maybe, if we find something specific to call the past back—letters, an old photograph—and pause and think hard, we might be able to put the grown man or woman once more into the feelings of youth. Most of the time, though, adults go about their business with their own distractions and preoccupations to blur and even erase those memories they had meant to keep in focus forever.

If the older generation tends to forget how it feels to be young (some forget more than others, of course), likewise many among the younger generation are unable to imagine what it must be like to be old. The differences are so profound. Not only physical differences of energy and zest, but other differences too: on the one hand, of innocence and idealism, of impatience and inexperience and little responsibility; and on the other, of awareness and skepticism and obligations and the burdens of habit. No wonder such contrasting outlooks exist between young and old. Perhaps what is astonishing is not that the generations are sometimes at odds; the wonder is that they get along as well as they do.

These selections examine some of the differences between the viewpoints of youth and age. In doing so, they bridge the years, letting the young know what it is to be old, and the old remember what it was to be young.

Philip McFarland

What protection does a small boy have against an angry father?

THUS I REFUTE BEELZY

JOHN COLLIER

"THERE GOES THE tea bell," said Mrs. Carter. "I hope Simon hears it."

They looked out from the window of the drawing room. The long garden, agreeably neglected, ended in a waste plot. Here a little summerhouse was passing close by beauty on its way to complete decay. This was Simon's retreat. It was almost completely screened by the tangled branches of the apple tree and the pear tree, planted too close together, as they always are in the suburbs. They caught a glimpse of him now and then, as he strutted up and down, mouthing and gesticulating, performing all the solemn mumbo-jumbo of small boys who spend long afternoons at the forgotten ends of long gardens.

"There he is, bless him!" said Betty.

"Playing his game," said Mrs. Carter. "He won't play with the other children any more. And if I go down there—the temper! And comes in tired out!"

"He doesn't have his sleep in the afternoons?" asked Betty.

"You know what Big Simon's ideas are," said Mrs. Carter. " 'Let him choose for himself,' he says. That's what he chooses, and he comes in as white as a sheet."

"Look! He's heard the bell," said Betty. The expression was justified, though the bell had ceased ringing a full minute ago. Small Simon stopped in his parade exactly as if its tinny dingle had at that moment reached his ear. They watched him perform certain ritual sweeps and scratchings

with his little stick, and come lagging over the hot and flaggy grass toward the house.

Mrs. Carter led the way down to the playroom, or garden room, which was also the tea room for hot days. It had been the huge scullery[1] of this tall Georgian house. Now the walls were cream-washed, there was coarse blue net in the windows, canvas-covered armchairs on the stone floor, and a reproduction of Van Gogh's *Sunflowers* over the mantelpiece.

Small Simon came drifting in, and accorded Betty a perfunctory greeting. His face was an almost perfect triangle, pointed at the chin, and he was paler than he should have been. "The little elf-child!" cried Betty.

Simon looked at her. "No," said he.

At that moment the door opened, and Mr. Carter came in, rubbing his hands. He was a dentist, and washed them before and after everything he did. "You!" said his wife. "Home already!"

"Not unwelcome, I hope," said Mr. Carter, nodding to Betty. "Two people canceled their appointments; I decided to come home. I said, I hope I am not unwelcome."

"Silly!" said his wife. "Of course not."

"Small Simon seems doubtful," continued Mr. Carter. "Small Simon, are you sorry to see me at tea with you?"

"No, Daddy."

"No, what?"

"No, Big Simon."

"That's right. Big Simon and Small Si-

[1] SCULLERY: room attached to the kitchen for dishwashing and other chores.

mon. That sounds more like friends, doesn't it? At one time little boys had to call their father 'sir.' If they forgot—a good spanking. On the bottom, Small Simon! On the bottom!" said Mr. Carter, washing his hands once more with his invisible soap and water.

The little boy turned crimson with shame or rage.

"But now, you see," said Betty, to help, "you can call your father whatever you like."

"And what," asked Mr. Carter, "has Small Simon been doing this afternoon? While Big Simon has been at work."

"Nothing," muttered his son.

"Then you have been bored," said Mr. Carter. "Learn from experience, Small Simon. Tomorrow, do something amusing, and you will not be bored. I want him to learn from experience, Betty. That is my way, the new way."

"I have learned," said the boy, speaking like an old, tired man, as little boys so often do.

"It would hardly seem so," said Mr. Carter, "if you sit on your behind all the afternoon, doing nothing. Had *my* father caught me doing nothing, I should not have sat very comfortably."

"He played," said Mrs. Carter.

"A bit," said the boy, shifting on his chair.

"Too much," said Mrs. Carter. "He comes in all nervy and dazed. He ought to have his rest."

"He is six," said her husband. "He is a reasonable being. He must choose for himself. But what game is this, Small Simon, that is worth getting nervy and dazed over? There are very few games as good as all that."

"It's nothing," said the boy.

"Oh come," said his father. "We are friends, are we not? You can tell me. I was a Small Simon once, just like you, and played the same games you play. Of course

there were no airplanes in those days. With whom do you play this fine game? Come on, we must all answer civil questions, or the world would never go round. With whom do you play?"

"Mr. Beelzy," said the boy, unable to resist.

"Mr. Beelzy?" said his father, raising his eyebrows inquiringly at his wife.

"It's a game he makes up," said she.

"Not makes up!" cried the boy. "Fool!"

"That is telling stories," said his mother. "And rude as well. We had better talk of something different."

"No wonder he is rude," said Mr. Carter, "if you say he tells lies, and then insist on changing the subject. He tells you his fantasy: you implant a guilt feeling. What can you expect? A defense mechanism. Then you get a real lie."

"Like in *These Three*," said Betty. "Only different, of course. *She* was an unblushing little liar."[1]

"I would have made her blush," said Mr. Carter, "in the proper part of her anatomy. But Small Simon is in the fantasy stage. Are you not, Small Simon? You just make things up."

"No, I don't," said the boy.

"You do," said his father. "And because you do, it is not too late to reason with you. There is no harm in a fantasy, old chap. There is no harm in a bit of make-believe. Only you have to know the difference between day dreams and real things, or your brain will never grow. It will never be the brain of a Big Simon. So come on. Let us hear about this Mr. Beelzy of yours. Come on. What is he like?"

"He isn't like anything," said the boy.

"Like nothing on earth?" said his father. "That's a terrible fellow."

---

[1] SHE...LIAR: a reference to Lillian Hellman's play, *The Children's Hour*, in which a little girl's lies cause the dismissal of two teachers. *These Three* is a movie adaptation of the play.

"I'm not frightened of him," said the child, smiling. "Not a bit."

"I should hope not," said his father. "If you were, you would be frightening yourself. I am always telling people, older people than you are, that they are just frightening themselves. Is he a funny man? Is he a giant?"

"Sometimes he is," said the little boy.

"Sometimes one thing, sometimes another," said his father. "Sounds pretty vague. Why can't you tell us just what he's like?"

"I love him," said the small boy. "He loves me."

"That's a big word," said Mr. Carter. "That might be better kept for real things, like Big Simon and Small Simon."

"He is real," said the boy, passionately. "He's not a fool. He's real."

"Listen," said his father. "When you go down the garden there's nobody there. Is there?"

"No," said the boy.

"Then you think of him, inside your head, and he comes."

"No," said Small Simon. "I have to make marks. On the ground. With my stick."

"That doesn't matter."

"Yes, it does."

"Small Simon, you are being obstinate,"[1] said Mr. Carter. "I am trying to explain something to you. I have been longer in the world than you have, so naturally I am older and wiser. I am explaining that Mr. Beelzy is a fantasy of yours. Do you hear? Do you understand?"

"Yes, Daddy."

"He is a game. He is a let's-pretend."

The little boy looked down at his plate, smiling resignedly.

"I hope you are listening to me," said his father. "All you have to do is to say, 'I have been playing a game of let's-pretend.

With someone I make up, called Mr. Beelzy.' Then no one will say you tell lies, and you will know the difference between dreams and reality. Mr. Beelzy is a day-dream."

The little boy still stared at his plate.

"He is sometimes there and sometimes not there," pursued Mr. Carter. "Sometimes he's like one thing, sometimes another. You can't really see him. Not as you see me. I am real. You can't touch him. You can touch me. I can touch you." Mr. Carter stretched out his big, white, dentist's hand, and took his little son by the nape of the neck. He stopped speaking for a moment and tightened his hand. The little boy sank his head still lower.

"Now you know the difference," said Mr. Carter, "between a pretend and a real thing. You and I are one thing; he is another. Which is the pretend? Come on. Answer me. What is the pretend?"

"Big Simon and Small Simon," said the little boy.

"Don't!" cried Betty, and at once put her hand over her mouth, for why should a visitor cry "Don't!" when a father is explaining things in a scientific and modern way? Besides, it annoys the father.

"Well, my boy," said Mr. Carter, "I have said you must be allowed to learn from experience. Go upstairs. Right up to your room. You shall learn whether it is better to reason, or to be perverse and obstinate. Go up. I shall follow you."

"You are not going to beat the child?" cried Mrs. Carter.

"No," said the little boy. "Mr. Beelzy won't let him."

"Go on up with you!" shouted his father.

Small Simon stopped at the door. "He said he wouldn't let anyone hurt me," he whimpered. "He said he'd come like a lion, with wings on, and eat them up."

"You'll learn how real he is!" shouted his father after him. "If you can't learn it

[1] OBSTINATE: stubborn.

at one end, you shall learn it at the other. I'll have your breeches down. I shall finish my cup of tea first, however," said he to the two women.

Neither of them spoke. Mr. Carter finished his tea, and unhurriedly left the room, washing his hands with his invisible soap and water.

Mrs. Carter said nothing. Betty could think of nothing to say. She wanted to be talking for she was afraid of what they might hear.

Suddenly it came. It seemed to tear the air apart. She cried, "What was that? He's hurt him." She sprang out of her chair, her silly eyes flashing behind her glasses. "I'm going up there!" she cried, trembling.

"Yes, let us go up," said Mrs. Carter. "Let us go up. That was not Small Simon."

It was on the second-floor landing that they found the shoe, with the man's foot still in it, like that last morsel of a mouse which sometimes falls unnoticed from the side of the jaws of the cat.

FOR DISCUSSION

1. Is this a story with a "happy ending"? Why or why not?

2. Mr. Carter prides himself on being a "modern" father who is a friend to his son rather than a disciplinarian. Does he seem to have a good relationship with his son? How do his words and actions reveal that he is not as modern as he would like to think?

3. Why do you think children sometimes invent imaginary playmates? Did you suspect before the ending that Mr. Beelzy might be more than a figment of Simon's imagination?

What details does the author use to convince us that he is real?

FOR COMPOSITION

• Small Simon apparently spent long hours in conversation with Mr. Beelzy in the summerhouse. What do you suppose they talked about? Write a page or two of dialogue between them. If you think Mr. Beelzy wouldn't have been audible to an observer, try writing Simon's monologue with pauses during which he listens to his friend. You will have to show in Simon's answers what Mr. Beelzy probably said.

No one at the game booed "so loud as Mr. Whalen, who often talked long and seriously to Marvin about sportsmanship."

THE HERO

MARGARET JACKSON

MR. WHALEN CAME into the kitchen by the back door and closed it softly behind him. He looked anxiously at his wife.

"Is Marv in?" he asked.

"He's resting," she whispered. Mr. Whalen nodded. He tiptoed through the dining room and went into the front hall as quiet as a mouse, and hung his hat and coat away. But he could not resist peeking into the darkened living room. A fire burned on the hearth, and on the couch lay a boy, or young man, who looked, at first glance, as though he were at least seven feet tall. He had a throw pulled up around his neck, and his stocking feet stuck out from the cuffs of his corduroy trousers over the end of the sofa.

"Dad?" a husky young voice said.

"Yes. Did I waken you? I'm sorry."

"I wasn't sleeping. I'm just resting."

Mr. Whalen went over to the couch and looked down at the long figure with deep concern.

"How do you feel?" he asked tenderly.

"Swell, Dad. I feel fine. I feel as though I'm going to be lucky tonight."

"That's fine! That's wonderful!" said his father fervently.

"What time is it, Dad?"

"Quarter to six."

"About time for me to get up and have my supper. Is it ready? I ought to stretch a bit."

"You lie still now, Marv. I'll see about your supper."

Mr. Whalen hurried back into the kitchen.

"He's awake," he informed his wife. "Is his supper ready?"

"In a minute, dear. I'm just making his tea."

Mr. Whalen went back into the living room with his anxious, bustling air.

The young man was up from the couch. He had turned on the light in a table lamp. He was putting on his shoes. He looked very young, not more than sixteen. His hair was thick as taffy and about the same color. He was thin, with a nose a little too big, and with clear blue eyes and a pleasant mouth and chin. He was not especially handsome, except to his father, who thought him the finest-looking boy in the whole wide world. The boy looked up a little shyly and smiled, and somehow his father's opinion was justified.

"I couldn't hit a thing in short practice yesterday," Marvin said. "That means I'll be hot tonight. Red hot!"

"I hope so. I certainly hope so."

"You're going to the game, aren't you, Dad? You and Mother?"

It was a superfluous question. Wild horses couldn't have kept Mr. Whalen from the evening event.

Marvin rose from his chair. He went up

and up and up. Six feet four in his stocking feet, a hundred and seventy-six pounds, and sixteen years of age. Marvin flexed his muscles, crouched a little, and made a twisting leap into the air, one arm going up over his head in a swinging circle, his hand brushing the ceiling. He landed lightly as a cat. His father watched him, appearing neither astonished nor amused. There was nothing but the most profound respect and admiration in Mr. Whalen's eyes.

"We've been timing that pivot. Mr. Leach had two guards on me yesterday and they couldn't hold me, but I couldn't hit. Well, Dad, let's eat. I ought to be getting up to the gym."

They went into the kitchen, where the supper was laid on a clean cloth at a small round table. There was steak and potatoes and salad and chocolate cake for his parents, toast and tea and coddled eggs for the boy.

"I don't think you ought to put the cake out where Marv can see it, when he can't have any," fussed Mr. Whalen.

Marvin grinned. "It's okay, Dad. I don't mind. I'll eat some when I get home."

"Did you take your shower? Dry yourself good?"

"Sure, Dad. Of course."

"Was the doctor at school today? This was the day he was to check the team, wasn't it?"

"Yes. He was there. I'm okay. The arch supports Mr. Leach sent for came. You know, my left foot's been getting a little flat. Doc thought I ought to have something while I'm still growing."

"It's a good thing. Have you got them here?"

"Yes. I'll get them."

"No. Just tell me where they are. I'll look at them."

"In my room. In my gym shoes."

Mr. Whalen wasn't eating a bite of sup-

per. It just gave him indigestion to eat on game nights. He got too excited. He couldn't stand it. The boy was eating calmly. He ate four coddled eggs. He ate six pieces of toast. He drank four cups of tea with lemon and sugar. In the boy's room Mr. Whalen checked the things in his bag—the white woolen socks, the clean folded towel, the shoes with their arch supports, and the like. The insets looked all right, his father thought. The fine, heavy satin playing suits would be packed in the box in which they came from the dry cleaner's, to keep them from getting wrinkled before the game.

There, alone in Marvin's room, with Marvin's ties hanging on his dresser, with his windbreaker thrown down in a chair and his high school books on the table, Mr. Whalen felt a little ill. He pressed his hand over his heart. He mustn't show his anxiety, he thought. The boy was calm. He felt lucky. Mustn't break that feeling. Mr. Whalen went back into the kitchen with an air of cheer, a plump, middle-aged man with a retreating hairline and kind, anxious, brown eyes. Mr. Whalen was a few inches shorter than his wife. But he had never regretted marrying a tall woman. Look at his boy!

Marv was looking at the funnies in the evening paper. Mr. Whalen resisted the temptation to look at the kitchen clock. The boy would know when to go. He took the front part of the paper and sat down and tried to put his mind on the news. Mrs. Whalen quietly washed the supper dishes. Marvin finished the funnies in the local paper and handed it to his father. Mr. Whalen took it and read the news that Hilltown High was to play Sunset High, of Stone City, at the local gym that evening. The Stone City team hadn't lost a game. They were grooming for the state championship. Mr. Whalen felt weak. He hoped Marvin hadn't read this. Indignation grew in the father, as he read on down the column, that the odds were against the local team. How dare Mr. Minton print such nonsense for the boys to read—to discourage them? It was outrageous. Mr. Whalen would certainly give the editor a piece of his mind. Perhaps Marvin had read it and believed it! Everything was so important—the psychology wasn't good.

Marvin had finished the funnies in the city paper, and he put it down and rose. He said a little ruefully, "I'm still hungry, but I can't eat more now."

"I'll have something ready for you when you get home," his mother said.

Marvin went into his room and came back in his windbreaker, his hair combed smoothly on his head.

"I'll see you at the gym," he said. "Sit where you always do, will you, Dad?"

"Yes. Yes. We'll be there."

"Okay. I'll be seeing you."

"Don't you want me to take you down in the car?"

"No. Thanks, Dad, but no. It'll do me good to run down there. It won't take me but a minute."

A shrill whistle sounded from the street.

"There's Johnny." Marvin left at once.

Mr. Whalen looked at his watch. "Better hurry, Mother. The first game starts at seven. We won't get our regular seats if we're late."

"I'm not going to the gym at half-past six," said Mrs. Whalen definitely. "We'll be there in time, and no one will take our seats. If you don't calm down, you are going to have a stroke at one of these games."

"I'm perfectly calm," said Mr. Whalen indignantly; "I'm as calm as—as calm as a June day. That's how calm I am. You know I'm not of a nervous temperament. Just because I want to get to the game on time, you say I am excited. You're as up in the air as I am."

"I am not," said Mrs. Whalen. She sat down at the cleared table and looked at the advertisements in the paper. Mr. Whalen looked at his watch again. He fidgeted.

"You can go ahead, if you like," she said. "I'll come alone."

"No, no," he protested, "I'll wait for you. Do you think we had better take the car? I put it up, but I can get it out again."

"We'll walk," she said. "It will do you good—quiet your nerves."

"I'm not nervous," he almost shouted. Then he subsided again, muttered a little, pretended to read the paper, checked his watch against the kitchen clock to see if it had stopped.

"If we're going to walk . . ." he said in a minute.

Mrs. Whalen looked at him with pity. He couldn't help it, she knew. She folded the papers and put them away, took off her white apron, smoothed her hair, and went to get her wraps. Mr. Whalen was at the front door, his overcoat on, his hat in his hand. She deliberately puttered, getting the cat off the piano and putting him out of doors, locking the kitchen door, turning out lights, hunting for her gloves. Mr. Whalen was almost frantic by the time she joined him on the front porch. They went down the walk together, and when they reached the sidewalk they met neighbors also bound for the gym.

"How's Marv?" asked the man next door. "Is he all right?"

"Marv's fine, just fine. He couldn't be better."

"Boy, oh, boy," said the other enthusiastically, "would I like to see the boys whip Stone City! It would be worth a million dollars—a cool million. Stone City thinks no one can beat them. We'd burn the town down."

"Oh, this game doesn't matter so much," said Mr. Whalen depreciatingly. "The team is working toward the tournaments. Be a shame to show all their stuff tonight."

"Well, we'll see. We'll see."

They went ahead. At the next corner they met other friends.

"How's Marv? How's the big boy?"

"He's fine. He's all right." Mr. Whalen's chest expansion increased. Cars were parked all along the sidewalk before the group of township school buildings—the grade school and the high school, with the fine brick gymnasium between them. The walks were crowded now, for the whole town, except those in wheelchairs or just born, went to the games, and this was an important game with Hilltown's hereditary foe. Mr. Whalen grew very anxious about their seats. If Marvin looked around for them and didn't find them. . . . He hurried his wife a little. They went into the outer hall of the gymnasium. The school principal was standing there talking to the coach, Mr. Leach. Mr. Whalen's heart plummeted. Had anything gone wrong? Had something happened to Marvin? He looked at them anxiously, but they spoke in normal tones.

"Good evening, Mrs. Whalen. Good evening, Tom."

Several small boys were running up and down the stairs, and the school principal turned and spoke to them severely. The Whalens had to make room for a young married couple, he carrying a small baby, she holding the hand of a little boy. Then they reached the window where the typing teacher was tearing off ticket stubs. Mr. Whalen paid his half dollar and they went inside the iron bar and up the steps to the gym proper.

The gymnasium wasn't half full. The bleachers which rose on either side of the shining, sacred floor with its cabalistic[1] markings were spotted with people. The Hilltown eighth grade was playing the Sugar Ridge eighth grade. The boys scrambled, fell down, got up, and threw the

[1] CABALISTIC: secretive and mysterious.

ball, panted and heaved and struggled on the floor. A basketball flew about. A group of smaller children were seated in a tight knot, and two little girls whose only ambition in life was to become high school cheerleaders led a piercing yell:

> Hit 'em high,
>   Hit 'em low;
> Come on, eighth grade,
>   Let's go!

The voices of the junior high were almost piping. Mr. Whalen remembered how he had suffered when Marvin was in the eighth grade and they had to go to the games at six o'clock to watch him play. The junior-high games were very abbreviated, with six-minute quarters, which was all the state athletic association would let them play. Marvin had been five feet ten at thirteen, but too thin. He had put on a little weight in proportion to his height since then, but his father thought he should be heavier. The present eighth-grade team could not compare with Marvin's, Mr. Whalen decided.

But the boys did try hard. They were winning. The gun sounded, the junior high went to pieces with wild cheering, and the teams trotted off the floor, panting, sweating, happy.

Almost at once another group came on in secondhand white wool tops and the old blue satin trunks from last year. This was the second team. The boys were pretty good. They practiced, throwing the ball from far out, running in under the basket, passing to one another. Mr. and Mrs. Whalen had found their regular seats unoccupied, halfway between the third and fourth uprights which supported the lofty gymnasium ceiling. Mr. Whalen sat down a little weakly and wiped his forehead. Mrs. Whalen began at once to visit with a friend sitting behind her, but Mr. Whalen could not hear what anyone said.

The Stone City reserves came out on the floor to warm up. They looked like first-string men.

Mr. Leach was talking to the timekeeper. He was a good coach—a mighty good coach. They were lucky to keep him here at Hilltown. The luckiest thing that had ever happened to the town was when Mr. Leach had married a Hilltown girl who didn't want to move away. They'd never have been able to hold him otherwise. It meant so much to the boys to have a decent, kindly man to coach them. Some of the high school coaches felt that their teams had to win, no matter how. It would be very bad to have his boy under such an influence, thought Mr. Whalen, who simply could not bear to see the team defeated, and who was always first to yell "Thief!" and "Robber!"

The officials came out in their green shirts, and Mr. Whalen almost had heart failure. There was that tall, thin man who had fouled Marvin every time he had moved in the tournaments last year. He was always against Hilltown. He had been so unfair that Mr. Leach had complained about him to the state association. The only time Mr. Leach had ever done such a thing. Oh, this was awful. Mr. Whalen twisted his hat in his hands. The other official he had seen often. He was fair—very fair. Sugar Ridge had complained about him for favoring Hilltown, but Mr. Whalen thought him an excellent referee.

The gymnasium was filling fast now. All the high school students—two hundred of them—were packed in the cheering section. The junior high was swallowed up, lost. The cheering section looked as though not one more could get into it, and yet youngsters kept climbing up, squeezing in. The rest of the space was filled with townspeople, from toddlers in snow suits to gray-bearded dodderers. On the opposite side of the gymnasium, the visiting fans were filling their seats. Big crowd from Stone City. Businessmen and quarrymen and stone carvers and their wives and children. They must feel confident of winning, Mr. Whalen thought. Their cheerleaders were out on the floor. Where were Hilltown's? Ah, there they were—Beth and Mary. Hilltown's cheerleaders were extremely pretty, dressed in blue satin slacks with white satin shirts, the word "Yell" in blue letters over their shoulders—a true gilding of the lily. Mary was Marvin's girl. She was the prettiest girl in town. And she had personality, too, and vigor.

Now the two girls leaped into position, spun their hands, spread out their arms, catapulted their bodies into the air in perfect synchronization, and the breathless cheering section came out in a long roll.

Hello, Stone City,
Hello, Stone City,
Hilltown says,
Hello-o-o-o!

Not to be outdone, the Stone City leaders, in crimson-and-gold uniforms, returned the compliment:

Hello, Hilltown . . .

and the sound came nicely across the big gym. Mr. Whalen got a hard knot in his throat, and the bright lights and colors of the gymnasium swam in a mist. He couldn't help it. They were so young. Their voices were so young!

The whistle blew. The reserves were at it.

Mr. Whalen closed his eyes and sat still. It would be so long; the cheering wouldn't really start, the evening wouldn't begin until the team came out. He remembered when Marvin was born. He had been tall then—twenty-two inches. Mr. Whalen prayed, his lips moving a little, that Marvin wouldn't get hurt tonight. Suppose he had a heart attack and fell dead, like that boy at Capital City years ago. Suppose he got knocked against one of the steel uprights and hurt his head—damaged his brain? Suppose he got his knee injured? Mr. Whalen opened his eyes. He must not think of those things. He had promised his wife he would not worry so. He felt her hand, light but firm, on his arm.

"Here are the Lanes," she said.

Mr. Whalen spoke to them. Johnny's parents crowded in behind the Whalens. Johnny's father's hand fell on Mr. Whalen's shoulder.

"How's Marv tonight?"

"Fine, fine. How's Johnny?"

"Couldn't be better. I believe the boys are going to take them."

The two fathers looked at each other and away. Mr. Whalen felt a little better.

"How's business?" asked Johnny's father, and they talked about business a moment or two, but they were not interested.

There was a crisis of some kind on the floor. Several players were down in a pile. Someone was hurt. Mr. Whalen bit the edge of his felt hat. The boy was up now. The Stone City coach was out on the floor, but the boy shook his head. He was all right. The game was resumed.

At last it was over. The reserves had won. Mr. Whalen thought that was a bad omen. The eighth grade had won. The reserves had won. No, it was too much. The big team would lose. If the others had lost, he would have considered that a bad omen too. Every omen was bad to Mr. Whalen at this stage. The floor was empty. The high school band played "Indiana," and "Onward, Hilltown," and everyone stood up and sang.

There was a breathless pause, and then a crashing cheer hit the ceiling of the big gym and bounced back. The Team was out. Out there on the floor in their blue satin suits, with jackets over their white tops, warming up, throwing the ball deftly about. What caused the change? Mr. Whalen never knew, but everything was quick now, almost professional in tone and quality. Self-confidence, authority, had come into the gymnasium. Ten or twelve boys out there warming up. But there was really only one boy on the floor for Mr. Whalen, a tall, thin, fair boy with limber legs still faintly brown from summer swimming. Mr. Whalen did not even attempt to tear his eyes from Marvin.

The Stone City team came out. Mr. Whalen looked away from Marvin for a moment to study them. Two or three of them were as tall as Marvin, maybe taller. He felt indignant. They must be seniors, all of them. Or five-year men. He studied the boys. He liked to see if he could pick out the first-string men from the lot. He could almost always do it—not by their skill or their height, but by their faces. That little fellow with the pug nose—he was a first-string man. And the two big ones—the other tall man Mr. Whalen discarded correctly. And the boy with the thick chest. What it was, he wasn't sure—some carelessness, some ease that marked the first-string men. The others were always a little self-conscious, a little too eager.

The referee blew the whistle. The substitutes left the floor, carrying extra jackets. The boy with the pug nose came forward for Stone City. So he was captain? Mr. Whalen felt gratified in his judgment. Marvin came forward for his team. He was captain too. There was a Number 1 in blue on the sleeveless white satin shirt he wore. The referee talked to them. The boys took their positions, the umpire his along the edge of the floor. The cheering section roared:

> We may be rough,
> We may be tough,
> But we're the team
> That's got the stuff!
> Fight! Fight! Fight!

Mary turned a complete somersault, her lithe young body going over backward, her heels in the air, then hitting the floor to bounce her straight up in a spread eagle. Her pretty mouth was open in a square. The rooting swelled. The substitutes sat down with their coaches. Marvin stood back out of the center ring until the referee, ball in hand, waved him in. The ball went into the air as the whistle blew, and the game was on.

Marvin got the tip-off straight to Johnny. Marv ran down into the corner, where he circled to confuse his guard. Johnny brought the ball down over the line, faked a pass and drew out Marvin's guard, bounced the ball to Perk, who carried it almost to the foul line and passed to Marvin, who threw the ball into the basket. Stone City leaped outside, threw the ball in, a long pass. Perk leaped for it, but missed. The tall Stone City forward dribbled, dodging skillfully. The guards were smothering him, but he pivoted, flung the ball over his head and into the basket. A basket each in the first minute of play!

Mr. Whalen had stopped breathing. He was in a state of suspended animation. The game was very fast—too fast. Stone City scored a second and a third time. Marvin called time out. Someone threw a wet towel from the bench, and it slid along the floor. The boys wiped their faces with it, threw it back. They whispered together. The referee blew the whistle. Yes, they were going to try the new trick play they had been practicing. It worked. Marvin's pivot was wonderful. The score was four to six.

Marvin played with a happy romping abandon. He was skillful, deft, acute. But he was also gay. The youngsters screamed his name. Mr. Whalen saw Mary's rapt, adoring look. Marvin romped down the floor like a young colt.

At the end of the quarter, the score was fourteen to ten in Stone City's favor. At the end of the half, it was still in Stone City's favor, but only fourteen to thirteen. Stone City didn't score in the second quarter.

Mr. Whalen felt a deep disquietude. He had been watching the tall center on the other team, the pivot man. He had thick, black, curly hair and black eyes. Mr. Whalen thought he looked tough. He had fouled Marvin twice in the first half. That is, he had been called for two fouls, but he had fouled him oftener. Mr. Whalen was sure he had tripped Marvin that time Marvin fell on the floor and cracked his elbow. Marvin had jumped up again at once. The Stone City center was a dirty player and ought to be taken off the floor. The school band was playing, but Mr. Whalen couldn't hear it. He was very upset. If the referees were going to let Stone City foul Hilltown and get away with it. . . . He felt hot under the collar. He felt desperate.

"Why don't you go out and smoke?" his wife asked. Mr. Whalen folded his overcoat to mark his place and went out of the gym. He smoked two cigarettes as fast as he could. He would stay out here. The stars were cool and calm above his head. The night air was fresh. He couldn't stand it in the gymnasium. He would wait here until the game was over. If Marvin was hurt, he wouldn't see it. He resolved this firmly. But when the whistle blew and he heard the burst of cheering, he rushed back into the gymnasium like a man going to a fire.

The second half had begun. Again the big center fouled Marvin. Marvin got two free throws and made both good.

Fifteen to fourteen now! The crowd went wild. The game got very fast again. Mr. Whalen watched Marvin and his opponent like a hawk. There! It happened.

Mr. Whalen was on his feet, yelling, "Watch him! Watch him!"

Continued on page 450

IDEAS AND THE ARTS

All over the world generations are in conflict. There is conflict between young people and adults and between middle-aged adults and older adults. It does not seem to matter what political system a country has. Generation conflict is found in communist countries as well as in capitalist countries. Nor does the economic development of a country seem to make much difference. Generation conflict is found in economically backward countries as well as in the most economically advanced countries.

No doubt there always has been some conflict of generations. Young people always want to experiment, to find out what they are made of and what they are good for. They believe they must try all forms and possibilities of life. To the adult, such behavior often appears aimless and purposeless. But for the young it is the only way they can find out which of the various purposes in life is good for them. If they cannot accept the experience of others, they must find out for themselves. Their search involves many risks, including the risk of failure, but they believe that they must take risks to discover what they are made of. These risks are often painful to an adult who has learned what he believes he can and cannot do and sees no point of further testing. He often forgets, however, that he cannot transfer his experience to someone else. These differences have always been with us.

There has also always been conflict between middle-aged adults and older adults. The middle-aged want the world arranged so that it will be satisfactory to those who are at the height of their capabilities. The older adults prefer a world arranged to make things easier for those whose capabilities have begun to fail.

It may also be true that we are more aware of such conflicts today simply because of the rapid spread of news. Conflict of any kind always attracts attention and is reported in the news.

Nevertheless, something new is happening that makes the world a different place from what it was and increases the possibilities of generation conflict. What is new is the rapidity of what we call "culture change." The word *culture* here refers to all the patterns of behavior that are shared by a particular community or society. It refers to the ways in which particular groups of people live. An example of culture change is the invention of the automobile. The automobile made it easier for people to have new experiences; new experiences change the ways people live.

But more important than any single invention is the increasing rate of inventions and the increasing rate of culture change. Changes in the ways in which information is distributed is a good example. One hundred and fifty years ago mechanical printing presses took the place of hand-powered presses. Fifty years ago radio was introduced. Twenty-five years ago television came on the scene. Within the past ten years computers have become commonplace. What all this means is that the rate at which information is gathered and distributed has become faster and faster.

Within the twentieth century the rate of culture change has rapidly increased. And all of these changes affect relations between generations. Young people adapt to change more rapidly than adults, and the differences in behavior that result increase the possibilities of conflict. Although there is always generation conflict, that conflict is intensified by rapid change.

Morse Peckham

440

There has always been conflict between what adults want out of life and what young people want. And adults are very often sure that they know what the young *ought* to want out of life, while the young are equally certain that they must find out for themselves.

The theme of the first picture, *The Sacrifice of Isaac,* by Caravaggio, is the sacrifice of youth to the interests of age. The story is found in the Old Testament, in the book of Genesis. Abraham had no children for many years, but finally a son was born to him, whom he named Isaac. To test Abraham's faith and devotion, the Lord ordered Abraham to go on a a journey to a mountain top and there to sacrifice the life of his only son to the Lord. Without hesitation, Abraham followed the Lord's instructions, but just as he was about to kill his son, an angel of the Lord told him not to do so, for he had proved his faith and devotion. Then Abraham saw a ram caught in the thicket, and he sacrificed the ram instead. Caravaggio has caught the dramatic moment of this story. The artist employs great realism in depicting strong emotion and resistance on the face of Isaac.

In Holland during the seventeenth century lived a very great painter named Rembrandt van Rijn. His greatness came from his compassion for all men, for young and old, for weak and strong, for both parties in any conflict. No one has painted with greater feeling the conflict of generations.

The second painting is Rembrandt's *The Reconciliation of David and Absalom.* The story of David and Absalom, from the Old Testament, is the story of a son who rebels against his father, is forgiven and again rebels, and is eventually killed by his father's supporters. David was King in Israel and had full power to judge and punish. Absalom felt that David should have punished another son, Amnon, Absalom's half brother, for a crime. So Absalom had Amnon killed and then fled for his own safety. David was persuaded to let Absalom come back to the court, but he refused to see him for two years. Finally, by a trick, Absalom won his way into David's presence, knelt before him, and was embraced and forgiven. This is the moment Rembrandt has chosen. Part of the emotional power of the picture comes from the knowledge that Absalom will rebel again and be killed and that David will mourn his death deeply.

The third painting is Rubens's *The Prodigal Son.* The story behind this painting comes from the New Testament, from the book of Luke. A younger son demanded of his father his share of what he would inherit at his father's death. When he received his inheritance, he went away and wasted it. (To be prodigal is to be wasteful.) To make a living he worked as a servant keeping pigs. In despair he returned and asked his father to take him back as a servant. But his father received him as his son and held a great feast to celebrate his return. This painting shows the son returning on his knees. The parents look at him with suspicion. This is the climactic moment before he is forgiven.

The next two paintings present two versions of three ages, or generations, of man. The first, called *The Three Ages,* might be the work of Giorgione, a Venetian painter of the early sixteenth century, or of Bellini, an older man who came under Giorgione's influence. If Bellini painted the picture, this would give it further interest, as an example of how the old can renew themselves by taking on the interest of younger people. The youth in the center is hardly more than a boy. He is looking doubtfully at a letter or document that he does not understand. The mature man on the right is explaining the document, as he should. The old man on the left is looking away, out of the picture, toward the viewer. He appears to be no longer interested in the affairs of life, and is perhaps saying farewell.

Old Age, Adolescence and Infancy is another version of the three ages of man, painted by Salvador Dali, the twentieth-century Spanish painter. This strange painting is at once a landscape with figures and at the same time three heads. Each head illustrates the appearance of the three ages, while each landscape suggests the interests of the three stages of life. Each part of the painting, then, is simultaneously a portrait of each age and a vision of the interests of each.

Edgar Degas, a late-nineteenth century French artist, painted *Degas' Father Listening to Pagans Playing the Guitar.* The painting is not just a portrait of the two men we see. It is in the tradition of paintings about the ages of man. The young man at the left is full of the vigor and pride of youth. The older man at the right is bent with age. The young man looks forward. The older man's gaze is inward and meditative, while the music on the piano forms a kind of halo around his head. He is already partially separated from the world.

Morse Peckham

MICHELANGELO MERISI DA CARAVAGGIO (1573-1610) *THE SACRIFICE OF ISAAC.* Uffizi Gallery, Florence.

REMBRANDT VAN RIJN (1606-1669) *THE RECONCILIATION OF DAVID AND ABSALOM.* Hermitage, Leningrad.

PETER PAUL RUBENS (1577-1640) *THE PRODIGAL SON.* Musée Royal des Beaux-Arts, Antwerp.

SCHOOL OF GIORGIONE (early 16th century) *THE THREE AGES OF MAN.* Pitti Palace, Florence.

SALVADOR DALI (born 1904) *OLD AGE, ADOLESCENCE AND INFANCY.* Collection of Reynolds A. Morse, Cleveland.

EDGAR DEGAS (1834-1917) *DEGAS' FATHER LISTENING TO PAGANS PLAYING THE GUITAR*. Museum of Fine Arts, Boston.

MUSIC

LUDWIG VAN BEETHOVEN:
SYMPHONY #5
[A number of recordings available]

Conflict between generations can arise from several causes. One cause is that the interests of youth are different from those of age. The young want to explore life, to test it and themselves. They want to know if they are strong enough and intelligent enough to face courageously the difficulties of human experience. They want to find ways to make life better for themselves and others.

Older people quite often have different interests. They may have achieved what they term success, or they may have accepted what they term failure. Either way, they have probably defined the limits of what they can expect from life and what life can expect from them. Whether content or not, they have quite often settled down to living within the limits they have decided to accept.

Conflict between generations may occur when new beliefs are aired and old traditions questioned. Since new beliefs present new possibilities, the young are usually interested in them. Youth's elders are far less interested in new beliefs. With great effort they have come to certain conclusions about the possibilities of the human existence, and they do not want those conclusions disturbed.

These reasons for conflict cannot be expressed directly in music. Music informs us only about feelings and emotions inside us. To express a specific kind of conflict, such as that between generations, a composer must use words. Music, however, can expess the *feelings* of conflict better than words can. And whatever in the outside world causes feelings of conflict, those feelings are always the same.

Sometimes we can study the kind of world a composer lived in and say that he wrote music about emotional conflict because society was experiencing a particular kind of conflict at that time. Beethoven wrote a great deal of music filled with conflict because he was living at a time when one particular new belief was coming to the fore. That belief was that the value of a man is determined not by the social position into which he was born, but by the value of his achievements.

Beethoven's *Symphony #5* is a musical drama about conflict. The first movement presents the conflict. The second movement retreats from the conflict in order to consider what life would be like without that conflict. The third movement summons the energy to renew the conflict. The fourth movement releases that energy and triumphs over the conflict.

Beethoven himself said that the famous four opening notes of the first movement expressed Fate. The word *fate* expresses the feeling that we cannot control our lives, and that we cannot get out of life what we want. These downward moving four notes are repeated many times. Then another theme moves upward. It presents the possibility that the depressing message of the first four-note theme is wrong. Now there is a struggle between the two themes. The second theme fails in its efforts to overcome, but something has been gained. At the very end, the four notes move upward instead of downward. This upward movement expresses the determination to continue the conflict. The surrender to fate has been overcome by the determination to struggle against fate.

Morse Peckham

The Stone City center had driven his elbow into Marvin's stomach. Marvin was doubled up. Marvin was down on the floor. A groan went up from the bleachers. Mr. Whalen started out on the floor. Something held him. He looked around blindly. His wife had a firm grip on his coattails. She gave him a smart yank and pulled him unexpectedly down on the bench beside her.

"He doesn't want you on the floor," she said fiercely.

Mr. Whalen was very angry, but he controlled himself. He sat still. Marvin was up again. Mary led a cheer for him. Marvin was all right. He got two more free throws. Now Hilltown was three points ahead. Marvin was fouled again, got two more free throws and missed them both. He was hurt! He never missed free throws—well, hardly ever. What was the matter with the referee? Was he crazy? Was he bribed? Mr. Whalen groaned.

Stone City took time out, and in the last minute of the third quarter they made three quick baskets. It put them ahead again, three points. A foul was called on Marvin —for pushing.

"Why, he never did at all!" yelled Mr. Whalen. "He couldn't stop fast enough— that's not a foul! Just give them the ball, boys! Don't try to touch it!"

"Will you hush?" demanded his wife.

The Stone City forward made one of the two throws allowed. It was the quarter.

The game was tied three times in the last quarter. With five minutes to play, the big center fouled Marvin again. His last personal. He was out of the game. The Hilltown crowd booed him. None so loud as Mr. Whalen, who often talked long and seriously to Marvin about sportsmanship.

Then Marvin got hot. He couldn't miss. Everyone on the team fed him the ball, and he could throw it from anywhere and it went, plop, right into the basket. Marvin pivoted. His height, his spring, carried him away from his guards. Marvin pranced. His long legs carried him where he would. He threw the ball over his head and from impossible angles. Once he was knocked down on the floor, and he threw from there and made the basket. His joy, his perfection, his luck, caused the crowd to burst into continuous wild cheering. Stone City took time out. They ran in substitutes, but they couldn't stop Marvin. Perk would recover the ball; he and Johnny fed it skillfully to Marvin, and Marvin laid it in. The gun went off with Hilltown twelve points ahead.

Mr. Whalen was a wreck. He could hardly stand up. Mrs. Whalen took his arm and half supported him toward the stairs that led down to the school grounds. The Stone City fans were angry. A big, broad-shouldered man with fierce black eyes complained in a loud, quarrelsome voice:

"That skinny kid—that Whalen boy— he fouled my boy! Who cares? But when my boy protects himself, what happens? They put him off the floor. They put my Guido out, so Hilltown wins. I get my hands on that tall monkey and I'll fix him."

"Be careful. That's my son you're talking about." The strength had returned to Mr. Whalen. He was strong as a lion. Mrs. Whalen pulled at his arm, but he jerked away. He turned on the crowded stairs. "Before you do anything to Marvin," he said, his voice loud and high, "you'd better do something to me. Your son fouled repeatedly."

"That's a lie!" yelled the other, and Mr. Whalen hit him. He hit him right in the stomach as hard as he could punch him. Instantly there was a melee. Johnny's father was punching somebody, and for a moment the crowd heaved and milled on the stairs. Someone screamed. Something like a bolt of lightning hit Mr. Whalen in the eye, and he struck back.

Friends were pulling him away. The town marshal shouldered good-naturedly between the combatants. The big man was in the grip of others from Stone City, who dragged him back up the stairs. Mr. Whalen struggled with his captors, fellow townsmen, who sympathized with him but had no intention of letting him fight. Johnny's mother and Marvin's mother hustled their men out into the cold night air.

"Really!" the high school principal was saying anxiously. "Really, we mustn't have any trouble. The boys don't fight. If we could just keep the fathers away from the games! Really, Mrs. Whalen, this won't do."

"I've got a good notion to take a poke at him too," said Mr. Whalen, who was clear above himself.

In the kitchen, Mr. Whalen looked in a small mirror at his reflection. He felt wonderful. He felt marvelous. He was going to have a black eye. He grabbed his wife and kissed her soundly.

"They beat them!" he said. "They beat Stone City!"

"You old fool!" cried Mrs. Whalen. "I declare I'd be ashamed of Marvin if he acted like that. You and Johnny's father—fighting like hoodlums."

"I don't care!" said Mr. Whalen. "I'm glad I hit him. Teach him a lesson. I feel great. I'm hungry. Make some coffee, Mother."

Marvin wouldn't be in for an hour. He would have a date with Mary at the soda parlor, to which the whole high school would repair. They heard the siren blowing, they looked out of the window and saw the reflection of the bonfire on the courthouse lawn. They heard the fire engine. The team was having a ride on the fire engine. Mr. Whalen stood on his front porch and cheered. The town was wild with joy. Not a citizen that wasn't up in the air tonight.

At last Marvin came in. He was cheerful, practical.

"Did you really have a fight, Dad? Someone told me you popped Guido's father. . . . Boy, are you going to have a shiner!" Marvin was greatly amused. He examined his father's eye, recommended an ice pack.

"I want it to get black," said Mr. Whalen stubbornly.

"We sure fixed Guido," said Marvin, and laughed.

"Did you have a fight?" asked his father eagerly.

"Heck, no! I'm going to get him a date with Betty. He noticed her. He's coming up next Sunday. Their team went downtown for sodas because Guido wanted to meet Betty. I wasn't sore at him. I only mean he was easy to handle. I saw right away that I could make him foul me, give me extra shots, get him off the floor. It's very easy to do with a big clumsy guy like that."

Mr. Whalen fingered his swelling eye and watched Marvin eat two hot ham sandwiches and a big slab of chocolate cake and drink a quart of milk. Marvin had already had a soda.

"You must sleep late in the morning," Mr. Whalen said. "Maybe you got too tired tonight. Now, don't eat too much cake."

Mr. Whalen's eye hurt. Mrs. Whalen got him to bed and put a cold compress on it.

"Old ninny," she murmured, and stooped and kissed him. Mr. Whalen sighed. He was exhausted. He was getting too old to play basketball, he thought confusedly.

FOR DISCUSSION

1. Explain the irony of the last sentence. How is "He was getting too old to play basketball" more than a careless mistake?

2. Who is the "hero" referred to in the title, Mr. Whalen or Marv?

3. The author contrasts Mr. Whalen's attitudes about the game with Marv's. How do they differ in their approach to: preparations for the game, the importance of winning, the "dirty player" Guido? What theme is developed through these contrasts?

4. Could a story like "The Hero" be written about a mother and daughter? Since girls' sports don't carry much glory in most parts of the country, what are some areas in which a mother might try to find satisfaction through her daughter's success?

FOR COMPOSITION

• How much interest should parents take in their high school sons' and daughters' activities? What effect does Mr. Whalen's over-interest seem to have on his son and wife? How would you feel if you were his son? Which do you think is more harmful, a parent who tries to live through his children or one who takes little interest in what they do?

ALL THE YEARS OF HER LIFE

MORLEY CALLAGHAN

THEY WERE CLOSING the drugstore, and Alfred Higgins, who had just taken off his white jacket, was putting on his coat and getting ready to go home. The little gray-haired man, Sam Carr, who owned the drugstore, was bending down behind the cash register, and when Alfred Higgins passed him, he looked up and said softly, "Just a moment, Alfred. One moment before you go."

The soft, confident, quiet way in which Sam Carr spoke made Alfred start to button his coat nervously. He felt sure his face was white. Sam Carr usually said, "Good night," brusquely, without looking up. In the six months he had been working in the drugstore Alfred had never heard his employer speak softly like that. His heart began to beat so loud it was hard for him to get his breath. "What is it, Mr. Carr?" he asked.

"Maybe you'd be good enough to take a few things out of your pocket and leave them here before you go," Sam Carr said.

"What things? What are you talking about?"

"You've got a compact and a lipstick and at least two tubes of toothpaste in your pockets, Alfred."

"What do you mean? Do you think I'm crazy?" Alfred blustered. His face got red and he knew he looked fierce with indignation. But Sam Carr, standing by the door

with his blue eyes shining bright behind his glasses and his lips moving underneath his gray mustache, only nodded his head a few times, and then Alfred grew very frightened and he didn't know what to say. Slowly he raised his hand and dipped it into his pocket, and with his eyes never meeting Sam Carr's eyes, he took out a blue compact and two tubes of toothpaste and a lipstick, and he laid them one by one on the counter.

"Petty thieving, eh, Alfred?" Sam Carr said. "And maybe you'd be good enough to tell me how long this has been going on."

"This is the first time I ever took anything."

"So now you think you'll tell me a lie, eh? What kind of a sap do I look like, huh? I don't know what goes on in my own store, eh? I tell you you've been doing this pretty steady," Sam Carr said as he went over and stood behind the cash register.

Ever since Alfred had left school he had been getting into trouble wherever he worked. He lived at home with his mother and his father, who was a printer. His two older brothers were married and his sister had got married last year, and it would have been all right for his parents now if Alfred had only been able to keep a job.

While Sam Carr smiled and stroked the side of his face very delicately with the tips of his fingers, Alfred began to feel that familiar terror growing in him that had been in him every time he had got into such trouble.

"I liked you," Sam Carr was saying. "I liked you and would have trusted you, and now look what I got to do." While Alfred watched with his alert, frightened blue eyes, Sam Carr drummed with his fingers on the counter. "I don't like to call a cop in point-blank," he was saying as he looked very worried. "You're a fool, and maybe I should call your father and tell him you're a fool. Maybe I should let them know I'm going to have you locked up."

"My father's not at home. He's a printer. He works nights," Alfred said.

"Who's at home?"

"My mother, I guess."

"Then we'll see what she says." Sam Carr went to the phone and dialed the number. Alfred was not so much ashamed, but there was that deep fright growing in him, and he blurted out arrogantly, like a strong, full-grown man, "Just a minute. You don't need to draw anybody else in. You don't need to tell her." He wanted to sound like a swaggering, big guy who could look after himself, yet the old, childish hope was in him, the longing that someone at home would come and help him. "Yeah, that's right, he's in trouble," Mr. Carr was saying. "Yeah, your boy works for me. You'd better come down in a hurry." And when he was finished Mr. Carr went over to the door and looked out at the street and watched the people passing in the late summer night. "I'll keep my eye out for a cop" was all he said.

Alfred knew how his mother would come rushing in; she would rush in with her eyes blazing, or maybe she would be crying, and she would push him away when he tried to talk to her, and make him feel her dreadful contempt; yet he longed that she might come before Mr. Carr saw the cop on the beat passing the door.

While they waited—and it seemed a long time—they did not speak, and when at last they heard someone tapping on the closed door, Mr. Carr, turning the latch, said crisply, "Come in, Mrs. Higgins." He looked hard-faced and stern.

Mrs. Higgins must have been going to bed when he telephoned, for her hair was tucked in loosely under her hat, and her hand at her throat held her light coat tight across her chest so her dress would not show. She came in, large and plump, with a little smile on her friendly face. Most of the store lights had been turned out and at first she did not see Alfred, who was standing in the shadow at the end of the counter. Yet as soon as she saw him she did not look as Alfred thought she would look: she smiled, her blue eyes never wavered, and with a calmness and dignity that made them forget that her clothes seemed to have been thrown on her, she put out her hand to Mr. Carr and said politely, "I'm Mrs. Higgins. I'm Alfred's mother."

Mr. Carr was a bit embarrassed by her lack of terror and her simplicity, and he hardly knew what to say to her, so she asked, "Is Alfred in trouble?"

"He is. He's been taking things from the store. I caught him red-handed. Little things like compacts and toothpaste and lipsticks. Stuff he can sell easily," the proprietor said.

As she listened Mrs. Higgins looked at Alfred sometimes and nodded her head sadly, and when Sam Carr had finished she said gravely, "Is it so, Alfred?"

"Yes."

"Why have you been doing it?"

"I been spending money, I guess."

"On what?"

"Going around with the guys, I guess," Alfred said.

Mrs. Higgins put out her hand and touched Sam Carr's arm with an understanding gentleness, and speaking as though afraid of disturbing him, she said, "If you would only listen to me before doing anything." Her simple earnestness made her shy; her humility made her falter and look away, but in a moment she was smiling gravely again, and she said with a kind of patient dignity, "What did you intend to do, Mr. Carr?"

"I was going to get a cop. That's what I ought to do."

"Yes, I suppose so. It's not for me to say, because he's my son. Yet I sometimes think a little good advice is the best thing for a boy when he's at a certain period in his life," she said.

Alfred couldn't understand his mother's quiet composure, for if they had been at home and someone had suggested that he was going to be arrested, he knew she would be in a rage and would cry out against him. Yet now she was standing there with that gentle, pleading smile on her face, saying, "I wonder if you don't think it would be better just to let him come home with me. He looks a big fellow, doesn't he? It takes some of them a long time to get any sense," and they both stared at Alfred, who shifted away with a bit of light shining for a moment on his thin face and the tiny pimples over his cheekbone.

But even while he was turning away uneasily Alfred was realizing that Mr. Carr had become aware that his mother was really a fine woman; he knew that Sam Carr was puzzled by his mother, as if he had expected her to come in and plead with him tearfully, and instead he was being made feel a bit ashamed by her vast tolerance. While there was only the sound of the mother's soft, assured voice in the store, Mr. Carr began to nod his head encouragingly at her. Without being alarmed, while being just large and still and simple and hopeful, she was becoming dominant there in the dimly lit store. "Of course, I don't want to be harsh," Mr. Carr was saying. "I'll tell you what I'll do. I'll just fire him and let it go at that. How's that?" and he

got up and shook hands with Mrs. Higgins, bowing low to her in deep respect.

There was such warmth and gratitude in the way she said, "I'll never forget your kindness," that Mr. Carr began to feel warm and genial himself.

"Sorry we had to meet this way," he said. "But I'm glad I got in touch with you. Just wanted to do the right thing, that's all," he said.

"It's better to meet like this than never, isn't it?" she said. Suddenly they clasped hands as if they liked each other, as if they had known each other a long time. "Good night, sir," she said.

"Good night, Mrs. Higgins. I'm truly sorry," he said.

The mother and son walked along the street together, and the mother was taking a long, firm stride as she looked ahead with her stern face full of worry. Alfred was afraid to speak to her; he was afraid of the silence that was between them, so he only looked ahead too, for the excitement and relief was still pretty strong in him; but in a little while, going along like that in silence made him terribly aware of the strength and the sternness in her; he began to wonder what she was thinking of as she stared ahead so grimly; she seemed to have forgotten that he walked beside her; so when they were passing under the Sixth Avenue elevated and the rumble of the train seemed to break the silence, he said in his old, blustering way, "Thank God it turned out like that. I certainly won't get in a jam like that again."

"Be quiet. Don't speak to me. You've disgraced me again and again," she said bitterly.

"That's the last time. That's all I'm saying."

"Have the decency to be quiet," she snapped. They kept on their way, looking straight ahead.

When they were at home and his mother

took off her coat, Alfred saw that she was really only half-dressed, and she made him feel afraid again when she said, without even looking at him, "You're a bad lot. God forgive you. It's one thing after another and always has been. Why do you stand there stupidly? Go to bed, why don't you?" When he was going, she said, "I'm going to make myself a cup of tea. Mind, now, not a word about tonight to your father."

While Alfred was undressing in his bedroom, he heard his mother moving around the kitchen. She filled the kettle and put it on the stove. She moved a chair. And as he listened there was no shame in him, just wonder and a kind of admiration of her strength and repose. He could still see Sam Carr nodding his head encouragingly to her; he could hear her talking simply and earnestly, and as he sat on his bed he felt a pride in her strength. "She certainly was smooth," he thought. "Gee, I'd like to tell her she sounded swell."

And at last he got up and went along to the kitchen, and when he was at the door he saw his mother pouring herself a cup of tea. He watched and he didn't move. Her face, as she sat there, was a frightened, broken face utterly unlike the face of the woman who had been so assured a little while ago in the drugstore. When she reached out and lifted the kettle to pour hot water in her cup, her hand trembled and the water splashed on the stove. Leaning back in the chair, she sighed and lifted the cup to her lips, and her lips were groping loosely as if they would never reach the cup. She swallowed the hot tea eagerly, and then she straightened up in relief, though her hand holding the cup still trembled. She looked very old.

It seemed to Alfred that this was the way it had been every time he had been in trouble before, that this trembling had really been in her as she hurried out half-dressed to the drugstore. He understood why she had sat alone in the kitchen the night his young sister had kept repeating doggedly that she was getting married. Now he felt all that his mother had been thinking of as they walked along the street together a little while ago. He watched his mother, and he never spoke, but at that moment his youth seemed to be over; he knew all the years of her life by the way her hand trembled as she raised the cup to her lips. It seemed to him that this was the first time he had ever looked upon his mother.

FOR DISCUSSION

1. Twice in this story Alfred sees unexpected sides of his mother. How is her manner with Mr. Carr different from what he expected? How does she change on the way home with him and later as she sits alone in the kitchen?

2. As Mr. Carr calls his home, Alfred feels "the old, childish hope . . . that someone at home would come and help him." What happens between that moment of childish de-pendence and the end of the story to make him feel that "his youth seemed to be over"? In what way has he become older?

FOR COMPOSITION

• What is going through Mrs. Higgins's head as she sits at the kitchen table? How does she feel about her son? Write what she might be thinking, including memories of the past and thoughts about the future.

THE ADVERSARY

PHYLLIS McGINLEY

A mother's hardest to forgive.
Life is the fruit she longs to hand you,
Ripe on a plate. And while you live,
Relentlessly she understands you.

FOR DISCUSSION

1. The combination of "relentless" with "understanding" is unexpected. In what context is "relentless" usually used? What does it mean here? Can you think of a situation in which a son or daughter might wish that his mother didn't understand him so well?

2. The title "The Adversary" suggests conflict between mother and child, yet the poem speaks only of giving and understanding. How does even the most loving mother become an adversary from her offsprings' point of view?

Mayo found fault with everything. "The only thing that didn't bore him was the idea of hunting, but his father wouldn't buy him a gun. . . ."

THE PHEASANT HUNTER
WILLIAM SAROYAN

MAYO MALONEY at eleven was a little runt of a fellow who was not rude so much as he was rudeness itself, for he couldn't even step inside a church, for instance, without giving everybody who happened to see him an uncomfortable feeling that he, Mayo, despised the place and its purpose.

It was much the same everywhere else that Mayo went: school, library, theater, home. Only his mother felt that Mayo was not a rude boy, but his father frequently asked Mayo to get down off his high horse and act like everybody else. By this, Michael Maloney meant that Mayo ought to take things easy and stop finding so much fault with everything.

Mayo was the most self-confident boy in the world, and he found fault with everything, or so at least it seemed. He found fault with his mother's church activities. He found fault with his father's interest in Shakespeare and Mozart. He found fault with the public-school system, the Government, the United Nations, the entire population of the world. And he did all this fault-finding without so much as going into detail about anything. He did it by being alive, by being on hand at all. He did it by being nervous, irritable, swift, wise, and bored. In short, he was a perfectly normal boy. He had contempt for

everything and everybody, and he couldn't help it. His contempt was unspoken but unmistakable. He was slight of body, dark of face and hair, and he went at everything in a hurry because everything was slow and stupid and weak.

The only thing that didn't bore him was the idea of hunting, but his father wouldn't buy him a gun, not even a .22-caliber single-shot rifle. Michael Maloney told Mayo that as soon as he was sure that Mayo had calmed down a little, he would think about buying him a gun. Mayo tried to calm down a little, so he could have his gun, but he gave it up after a day and a half.

"O.K.," his father said, "if you don't want your gun, you don't have to try to earn it."

"I did try to earn it," Mayo said.

"When?"

"Yesterday and today."

"I had in mind," his father said, "a trial covering a period of at least a month."

"A month?" Mayo said. "How do you expect a fellow to stay calm all through October with pheasant to shoot in the country?"

"I don't know how," Mike Maloney said, "but if you want a gun, you've got to calm down enough so I can believe you won't shoot the neighbors with it. Do you think my father so much as let me sit down to my dinner if I hadn't done something to earn it? He didn't invite me to earn any gun to shoot pheasant with. He told me to earn my food, and he didn't wait until I was eleven, either. I started earning it when I was no more than eight. The whole trouble with you is you're too pent-up from not doing any kind of work at all for your food or shelter or clothing to be decently tired and ordinary like everybody else. You're not human, almost. Nobody's human who doesn't know how hard it is to earn his food and the other basic things. It's the fault of your mother and father that you're such a sarcastic and fault-finding man instead of a calm, handsome one. Everybody in this whole town is talking about how your mother and father have turned you into an arrogant ignoramus of a man by not making you earn your right to judge things."

Mr. Maloney spoke as much to the boy's mother as to the boy himself, and he spoke as well to the boy's younger brother and younger sister, for he had left his office at half past four, as he did once a week, to sit down with the whole family for early supper, and it was his intention to make these mid-week gatherings at the table memorable to everyone, including himself.

"Now, Mike," Mrs. Maloney said. "Mayo's not as bad as all that. He just wants a gun to hunt pheasant with."

Mike Maloney laid down his fork that was loaded with macaroni baked with tomatoes and cheese, and he stared at his wife a long time, rejecting one by one two dozen angry remarks he knew would do no one present any good at all to hear, and only make the gathering *unpleasantly* memorable.

At last he said, "I suppose you think I ought to get him a gun, just like that?"

"Mayo isn't really rude or anything like that," the boy's mother said. "It's just that he's restless, the way every human being's got to be once in his lifetime for a while."

Mayo didn't receive this defense of himself with anything like gratitude. If any-

thing, it appeared as if he were sick and tired of having so much made of a simple little matter like furnishing him with an inexpensive .22-caliber single-shot rifle.

"Now don't you go to work and try to speak up for him," Mike Maloney said to his wife, "because, as you can see for yourself, he doesn't like it. He doesn't enjoy being spoken up for, not even by his mother, poor woman, and you can see how much he thinks of what his father's saying this minute."

"What did I say?" Mayo asked.

"You didn't say anything," his father said. "You didn't need to." He turned to Mrs. Maloney. "Is it a gun I must buy for him now?" he said.

Mrs. Maloney didn't quite know how to say that it was. She remained silent and tried not to look at either her husband or her son.

"O.K.," Mike Maloney said to both his wife and his son. "I have to go back to the office a minute, so if you'll come along with me I'll drop into Archie Cannon's and buy you a gun."

He got up from the table and turned to Mrs. Maloney.

"Provided, of course," he said, "that that meets with your approval."

"Aren't you going to finish your food?" Mrs. Maloney said.

"No, I'm not," Mike Maloney said. "And I'll tell you why, too. I don't want him to be denied anything he wants or anything his mother wants him to have, without earning it, for one unnecessary moment, and as you can see, his cap's on his head, he's at the door, and every moment I stand here explaining is unnecessary."

"Couldn't you both finish your food first?" Mrs. Maloney said.

"Who wants to waste time eating," Mike Maloney said, "when it's time to buy a gun?"

"Well," Mrs. Maloney said, "perhaps

you'll have something after you buy the gun."

"We should have been poor," Mike Maloney said. "Being poor would have helped us in this problem."

Mike Maloney went to the door where his nervous son was standing waiting for him to shut up and get going.

He turned to his wife and said, "I won't be able to account for him after I turn the gun over to him, but I'll be gone no more than an hour. If we'd been poor and couldn't afford it, he'd know the sinfulness of provoking me into this sort of bitter kindness."

When he stepped out of the house onto the front porch, he saw that his son was at the corner, trying his best not to run. He moved quickly and caught up with him, and he moved along as swiftly as his son did.

At last he said, "Now, I'm willing to walk the half mile to Archie Cannon's, but I'm not going to run, so if you've got to run, go ahead, and I'll meet you outside the place as soon as I get there."

He saw the boy break loose and disappear far down the street. When he got to Archie Cannon's, the boy was waiting for him. They went in and Mike Maloney asked Archie to show him the guns.

"What kind of a gun do you want, Mike?" Archie said. "I didn't know you were interested in hunting?"

"It's not for myself," Mike Maloney said. "It's for Mayo here, and it ought to be suitable for pheasant shooting."

"That would be a shotgun," Archie said.

"Would that be what it would be?" Mike Maloney asked his son, and although the boy hadn't expected anything so precisely suitable for pheasant shooting, he said that a shotgun would be what it would be.

"O.K., Archie," Mike Maloney said. "A shotgun."

"Well, Mike," Archie said, "I wouldn't like to think a shotgun would be the proper gun to turn over to a boy."

"Careful," Mike Maloney said. "He's right here with us, you know. Let's not take any unnecessary liberties. I believe he indicated the gun ought to be a shotgun."

"Well, anyway," Archie said, "it's going to have a powerful kick."

"A powerful kick," Mike Maloney repeated, addressing the three words to his son, who received them with disdain.

"That is no matter to him," Mike Maloney said to Archie Cannon.

"Well, then," Archie Cannon said, "this here's a fine double-barrel twelve-gauge shotgun and it's just about the best bargain in the store."

"You shouldn't have said that, Archie," Mike Maloney said. "This man's not interested in bargains. What he wants is the best shotgun you've got that's suitable for pheasant shooting."

"That would be this twelve-gauge repeater," Archie Cannon said, "that sells for ninety-eight fifty, plus tax, of course. It's the best gun of its kind."

"Anybody can see it's a better gun," Mike Maloney said. "No need to waste time with inferior firearms."

He handed the gun to Mayo Maloney, who held it barrel down, resting over his right arm, precisely as a gun, loaded or not, ought to be held.

"I'll show you how it works," Archie Cannon made the mistake of saying to Mayo Maloney. The boy glanced at Archie in a way that encouraged him to say quickly, "Anything else, then? Fishing tackle, hooks, boxing gloves, rowing machines, tennis rackets?"

"Anything else?" Mike Maloney said to his son, who said nothing, but with such irritation that Mike quickly said to Archie Cannon, "Shells, of course. What good is a shotgun without shells?"

Archie Cannon jumped to get three

boxes of his best shotgun shells, and as he turned them over to Mike Maloney, who turned them over to Mayo, Archie said, "A hunting coat in which to carry the shells? A red hunting cap?"

Mayo Maloney was gone, however.

"He didn't want those things," Mike Maloney said.

"Some hunters go to a lot of trouble about costume," Archie Cannon said.

"He doesn't," Mike Maloney said. "What do I owe you?"

"One hundred and five dollars and sixty-nine cents, including tax," Archie said. "Has he got a license?"

"To hunt?" Mike Maloney said. "He hasn't got a license to eat, but damned if I don't halfway admire him sometimes. He must know something to be so sure of himself and so contemptuous of everybody else."

"To tell you the truth," Archie Cannon said, "I thought you were kidding, Mike. I thought you were kidding the way you sometimes do in court when you're helping a small man fight a big company. I didn't expect you to actually buy a gun and turn it over to an eleven-year-old boy. Are you sure it's all right?"

"Of course it's all right," Mike Maloney said. "You saw for yourself the way he held the gun." He began to write a check. "Now, what did you say it came to?"

"A hundred and five sixty-nine," Archie Cannon said. "I hope you know there's no pheasant to speak of anywhere near here. The Sacramento Valley is where the pheasant shooting is."

"Where you going to be around ten o'clock tonight?" Mike Maloney said.

"Home, most likely," Archie Cannon said. "Why?"

"Will you be up?"

"Oh, yes," Archie said. "I never get to bed before midnight. Why?"

"Would you like to drop over to my house for a couple of bottles of beer around ten?" Mike said.

"I'd like that very much," Archie said. "Why?"

"Well," Mike said, "the way I figure is this: It's a quarter after five now. It'll take him about three minutes to hitch a ride with somebody going out to Riverdale, which is about twenty-five miles from here. That would take an average driver forty or forty-five minutes to make, but he'll get the driver, whoever he is, or she is, for that matter, to make it in about half an hour or a little under. He'll do it by being excited, not by saying anything. He'll get the driver to go out of his or her way to let him off where the hunting is, too, so he'll start hunting right away, or a little before six. He'll hunt until after dark, walking a lot in the meantime. He won't get lost or anything like that, but he'll have to walk back to a road with a little traffic. He'll hitch a ride back, and he'll be home a little before or a little after ten."

"How do you know?" Archie said. "How do you even know he's going hunting at all tonight? He just got the gun, and he may not even know how to work it."

"You saw him take off, didn't you?" Mike Maloney said. "He took off to go hunting. And you can be sure he either knows how to work the gun or will find out by himself in a few minutes."

"Well," Archie said, "I certainly would like to drop by for some beer, Mike, if you're serious."

"Of course I'm serious," Mike said.

"I suppose you want to have somebody to share your amusement with when he gets back with nothing shot and his body all sore from the powerful kick of the gun," Archie said.

"Yes," Mike said. "I want to have somebody to share my amusement with but not for those reasons. He may be a little sore from the powerful kick of the gun, but I think he'll come back with something."

"I've never heard of anybody shooting any pheasant around Riverdale," Archie said. "There's a little duck shooting out there in season, and jack rabbits of course."

"He said pheasants," Mike Maloney said. "Here's my check. Better make it a little before ten, just in case."

"I thought you were only kidding about the gun," Archie said. "Are you sure you did the right thing? I mean, considering he's only eleven years old, hasn't got a hunting license and the pheasant-shooting season doesn't open for almost a month?"

"That's one of the reasons I want you to come by for some beer," Mike said.

"I don't get it," Archie said.

"You're game warden of this area, aren't you?"

"I am."

"O.K.," Mike said. "If it turns out that he's broken the law, I want you to know it."

"Well," Archie said, "I wouldn't want to bother about a small boy shooting a few days out of season or without a license."

"I'll pay his fine," Mike Maloney said.

"I don't think he'll get anything," Archie said, "so of course there won't be any fine to be paid."

"I'll see you a little before ten, then," Mike Maloney said.

He spent a half hour at his office, then walked home slowly, to find the house quiet and peaceful, the kids in bed and his wife doing the dishes. He took the dish towel and began to dry and put the clean dishes into the cupboard.

"I bought him the best shotgun Archie Cannon had for pheasant shooting," he said.

"I hope he didn't make you too angry," Mrs. Maloney said.

"He did for a while," Mike said, "but all of a sudden he didn't, if you know what I mean."

"I don't know what you mean," Mrs. Maloney said.

"I mean," Mike said, "it's all right not being poor."

"What's being poor got to do with it?" Mrs. Maloney said.

"I mean it's all right, that's all," Mike said.

"Well, that's fine," Mrs. Maloney said. "But where is he?"

"Hunting, of course," Mike said. "You don't think he wanted a gun to look at."

"I don't know what I think now," Mrs. Maloney said. "You've had so much trouble with him all along, and now all of a sudden you buy him an expensive gun and believe it's perfectly all right for him to go off hunting in the middle of the night on the third day of October. Why?"

"Well," Mike Maloney said, "it's because while I was preaching to him at the table something began to happen. It was as if my own father were preaching to me thirty years ago when I was Mayo's age. Oh, I did earn my food, as I said, and I wanted a gun, too, just as he's been wanting one. Well, my father preached to me, and I didn't get the gun. I mean, I didn't get it until almost five years later, when it didn't mean very much to me any more. Well, while I was preaching to him this afternoon I remembered that when my father preached to me I was sure he was mistaken to belittle me so, and I even believed that somehow—somehow or other, perhaps because we were so poor, if that makes sense—he would suddenly stop preaching and take me along without any fuss of any kind and buy me a gun. But of course he didn't. And I *remembered* that he didn't, and I decided that perhaps I'd do for my son what my father had not done for me, if you know what I mean."

"Do you mean you and Mayo are alike?" Mrs. Maloney said.

"I do," Mike said. "I do indeed."

"Very much alike?"

"Almost precisely," Mike said. "Oh, he'll not be the great man he is now for long, and I don't want to be the one to cheat him out of a single moment of his greatness."

"You must be joking," Mrs. Maloney said.

"I couldn't be more serious," Mike said. "Archie Cannon thought I was joking, too, but why would I be joking? I bought him the gun and shells, and off he went to hunt, didn't he?"

"Well, I hope he doesn't hurt himself," Mrs. Maloney said.

"We'll never know if he does," Mike said. "I've asked Archie to come by around ten for some beer because I figure he'll be back by then."

"Is Mrs. Cannon coming with Archie?"

"I don't think so," Mike said. "Her name wasn't mentioned."

"Then I suppose you don't want me to sit up with you," Mrs. Maloney said.

"I don't know why not, if you want to," Mike said.

But Mrs. Maloney knew it wouldn't do to sit up, so she said, "No, I'll be getting to bed long before ten."

Mike Maloney went out on the front porch with his wife, and they sat and talked about their son Mayo and their other kids until a little after nine, and then Mrs. Maloney went inside to see if the beer was in the ice box and to put some stuff out on the kitchen table, to go with the beer. Then she went to bed.

Around a quarter to ten Archie Cannon came walking up the street and sat down in the rocker on the front porch.

"I've been thinking about what you did," he said, "and I still don't know if you did right."

"I did right all right," Mike Maloney said. "Let's go inside and have some beer. He'll be along pretty soon."

They went inside and sat down at the kitchen table. Mike lifted the caps off two bottles of cold beer, filled two tall glasses, and they began to drink. There was a plate loaded with cold roast beef, ham, bologna and sliced store cheese, and another plate with rye bread on it, already buttered.

When it was almost twelve and Mayo Maloney hadn't come home, Archie Cannon wondered if he shouldn't offer to get up and go home or maybe even offer to get his car and go looking for the boy, but he decided he'd better not. Mike Maloney seemed excited and angry at himself for having done such a foolish thing, and he might not like Archie to rub it in. They had stopped talking about Mayo Maloney around eleven, and Archie knew Mike wanted the situation to remain that way indefinitely.

A little before one in the morning, after they had finished a half dozen bottles of beer apiece and all the food Mrs. Maloney had set out for them, and talked about everything in the world excepting Mayo Maloney, they heard footsteps on the back stairs, and then on the porch, and after a moment he came into the kitchen.

He was a tired man. His face was dirty and flushed, and his clothes were dusty and covered with prickly burs of several kinds. His hands were scratched and almost black with dirt. His gun was slung over his right arm, and nested in his left arm were two beautiful pheasants.

He set the birds on the kitchen table, and then broke his gun up for cleaning. He wrapped a dry dish towel around the pieces and put the bundle in the drawer in which he kept his junk. He then brought six unused shells out of his pockets and placed them in the drawer, too, locked the drawer with his key and put the key back into his pocket. Then he went to the kitchen sink and rolled up his sleeves and washed his hands and arms and face and neck, and after he'd dried himself, he looked into the refrigerator and brought out some bologna wrapped in butcher paper, and began to eat it without bread while he fetched bread and butter and a chair. He sat down and began to put three thick slices of bologna between two slices of buttered bread. Mike Maloney had never before seen him eat so heartily.

He didn't look restless and mean any more, either.

Mike Maloney got up with Archie Cannon, and they left the house by the back door in order not to disturb Mrs. Maloney and the sleeping kids.

When they were in the back yard, Archie Cannon said, "Well, aren't you going to ask him where he got them?"

"He's not ready to talk about it just yet," Mike said. "What's the fine?"

"Well," Archie said, "there won't be any fine because there's not supposed to be any pheasants in the whole area of which I'm game warden. I didn't believe he'd get anything, let alone pheasants, and both of them cocks, too. Damned if I don't admire him a little myself."

"I'll walk you home," Mike said.

In the kitchen, the boy finished his sandwich, drank a glass of milk, and rubbed his shoulder.

The whole evening and night had been unbelievable. Suddenly at the table, when his father had been preaching to him, he'd begun to understand his father a little better, and himself, too, but he'd known he couldn't immediately stop being the way he had been for so long, the way that was making everybody so uncomfortable. He'd known he'd have to go on for a while longer and see the thing through. He'd have to go along with his father. He'd known all this very clearly, because his father had suddenly stopped being a certain way—the way everybody believed a father ought to be—and Mayo had known

it was going to be necessary for him to stop being a certain way, too—the way he had believed he had to be. But he'd known he couldn't stop until he had seen the thing through.

In the kitchen, almost asleep from weariness, he decided he'd tell his father exactly what he'd done, but he'd wait a while first, maybe ten years.

He'd had a devil of a time finding out how the gun worked, and he hadn't been able to hitch a ride at all, so he'd walked and run six miles to the countryside around Clovis, and there he'd loaded the gun and aimed it at a blackbird in a tree leaning over Clovis Creek, and pressed the trigger.

The kick had knocked him down and he had missed the bird by a mile. He'd had to walk a long way through tall dry grass and shrubs for something else to shoot at, but all it was was another blackbird, and again the kick had knocked him down and he'd missed it by a mile.

It was getting dark fast by then and there didn't seem to be anything alive around at all, so he began to shoot the gun just to get used to it. Pretty soon he could shoot it and not get knocked down. He kept shooting and walking, and finally it was dark and it seemed he was lost. He stumbled over a big rock and fell and shot the gun by accident and got a lot of dirt in his eyes. He got up and almost cried, but he managed not to, and then he found a road, but he had no idea where it went to or which direction to take. He was scratched and sore all over, and not very happy about the way he'd shot the gun by accident. That should never have happened. He was scared, too, and he said a prayer a minute and meant every word of what he said. And he understood for the first time in his life why people liked to go to church.

"Please don't let me make a fool of myself," he prayed. "Please let me start walking in the right direction on this road."

He started walking down the road, hoping he was getting nearer home, or at least to a house with a light in it, or a store or something that would be open. He felt a lot of alive things in the dark that he knew must be imaginary, and he said, "Please don't let me get so scared." And pretty soon he felt so tired and small and lost and hopeless and foolish that he could barely keep from crying, and he said, "Please don't let me cry."

He walked a long time, and then far down the road he saw a small light, and he began to walk faster. It was a country store with a gasoline pump out front and a new pickup truck beside the pump. Inside the store was the driver of the truck and the storekeeper, and he saw that it was twenty minutes to twelve. The storekeeper was an old man with a thick white mustache who was sitting on a box talking to the driver of the truck, who was about as old as the boy's father.

He saw the younger man wink at the older one, and he thanked God for both of them, and for the wink, because he didn't think people who could wink could be unfriendly.

He told them exactly what he had done, and why, and the men looked at him and at each other until he was all through talking. They both examined the brand-new gun, too. Then the storekeeper handed the gun back to the boy and said to the younger man, "I'll be much obliged to you, Ed, if you'll get this man home in our truck."

They were a father and a son, too, apparently, and good friends, besides. Mayo Maloney admired them very much, and on account of them, he began to like people in general, too.

"Not at all," the younger man said.

"And I'd like to think we might rustle up a couple of pheasant for him to take home, too."

"That might not be easy to do this hour of the night," the younger man said, "but we could try."

"Isn't there an all-night Chinese restaurant in town that serves pheasant in and out of season?" the old man said. "Commercial pheasant, that is?"

"I don't know," the younger man said, "but we could phone and find out."

"No," the older man said. "No use phoning. They wouldn't be apt to understand what we were talking about. Better just drive up to it and go on in and find out. It's on Kern Street between F and G, but I forget the name. Anyhow, it's open all night, and I've heard you can get pheasant there any time you like."

"It certainly is worth looking into," the younger man said.

The younger man got up, and Mayo Maloney, speechless with amazement, got up, too. He tried to say something courteous to the older man, but nothing seemed to want to come out of his dry mouth. He picked up his gun and went out to the truck and got in beside the younger man, and they went off. He saw the older man standing in the doorway of the store, watching.

The younger man drove all the way to town in silence, and when the boy saw familiar places, he thought in prayer again, saying, *I certainly don't deserve this, and I'm never going to forget it.*

The truck crossed the Southern Pacific tracks to Chinatown, and the driver parked in front of Willie Fong's, which was, in fact, open, although nobody was inside eating. The driver stepped out of the truck and went into the restaurant, and the boy saw him talking to a waiter. The waiter disappeared and soon came back with a man in a business suit. This man and the driver of the truck talked a few minutes, and then they both disappeared into the back of the restaurant, and after a few minutes the driver of the truck came back, and he was holding something that was wrapped in newspaper. He came out of the restaurant and got back into the truck, and they drove off again.

"How's your father?" the man said suddenly.

"He's fine," Mayo managed to say.

"I mean," the man said, "you *are* Mike Maloney's boy, aren't you?"

"Yes, I am," Mayo Maloney said.

"I thought you were," the man said. "You look alike and have a lot in common. You don't have to tell me where you live. I know where it is. And I know you want to know who I am, but don't you think it would be better if I didn't tell you? I've had dealings with your father, and he lent me some money when I needed it badly and we both weren't sure I'd ever be able to pay him back. So it's all right. I mean, nobody's going to know anything about this from me."

"Did they have any pheasants?" the boy said.

"Oh, yes," the man said. "I'm sorry I forgot to tell you. They're in that newspaper. Just throw the paper out the window."

The boy removed the paper from around the birds and looked at them. They were just about the most wonderful-looking things in the whole world.

"Do they have any shot in them?" he asked. "Because they ought to."

"No, I'm afraid they don't," the driver said, "but we'll drive out here a little where it's quiet and we won't disturb too many sleeping farmers, and between the two of us we'll get some shot into them. You can do the shooting, if you like."

"I might spoil them," the boy said.

"I'll be glad to attend to it, then," the driver said.

They drove along in silence a few minutes, and then the truck turned into a lonely road and stopped. The driver got out and placed the two birds on some grass by the side of the road in the light of the truck's lights about twenty yards off. Then he took the gun, examined it, aimed, fired once, unloaded the gun, fetched the birds, got back into the truck, and they drove off again.

"They're just right now," he said.

"Thanks," the boy said.

When the truck got into his neighborhood Mayo said, "Could I get off a couple of blocks from my house, so nobody will see this truck accidentally?"

"Yes, that's a good idea," the driver said.

The truck stopped. The boy carefully nested the two birds in his left arm, then got out, and the driver helped him get the gun slung over his right arm.

"I never expected anything like this to happen," the boy said.

"No, I suppose not," the man said. "I never expected to find a man like your father when I needed him, either, but I guess things like that happen just the same. Well, good night."

"Good night," the boy said.

The man got into the truck and drove off, and the boy hurried home and into the house.

When Mike Maloney got back from walking Archie Cannon home, he was surprised to find the boy asleep on his folded arms on the kitchen table. He shook the boy gently, and Mayo Maloney sat up with a start, his eyes bloodshot and his ears red.

"You better get to bed," Mike said.

"I didn't want to go," the boy said, "until you got back, so I could thank you for the gun."

"That wasn't necessary," the man said. "That wasn't necessary at all."

The boy got up and barely managed to drag himself out of the room without falling.

Alone in the kitchen, the father picked up the birds and examined them, smiling because he knew whatever was behind their presence in the house, it was certainly something as handsome as the birds themselves.

FOR DISCUSSION

1. Everyone agrees that there are no pheasant in the area, yet Mayo comes home carrying two. Does anyone (Mayo, Mike, Archie, the storekeeper and his son) believe that Mayo really shot the pheasant? If not, why do they pretend that he did?

2. At what point in the story does Mayo begin to change from a cocky, fault-finding, rude boy into one who prays, admires other people, and says "thank you"? What happens to cause this transformation?

3. Mike Maloney's first analysis of Mayo's problem is that the boy needs real work to use up his energy and to give him responsibility, that not being poor has spoiled him. What occurs to him in the middle of a lecture on "when I was a boy" that makes Mike change his mind?

FOR COMPOSITION

• What do you think of Mike's decision to let Mayo go off alone with the shotgun? Based on his understanding of Mayo and his memories of his own childhood, what did he expect to happen? Would the plan have been a failure if Mayo hadn't met the storekeeper and his son?

OLD AGE STICKS

E. E. CUMMINGS

old age sticks
up Keep
Off
signs)&

youth yanks them   5
down(old
age
cries No

Tres)&(pas)
youth laughs   10
(sing
old age

scolds Forbid
den Stop
Must   15
n't Don't

&)youth goes
right on
gr
owing old   20

FOR DISCUSSION

1. What contrast does the poem develop? How are the last two words a surprising ending to this development?

2. "Keep off" and "no trespassing" signs are usually only a warning to stay off other people's land. What larger meaning do they have in this poem?

Can you imagine a future in which intelligence and good looks would be considered dangerous? Kurt Vonnegut can.

HARRISON BERGERON

KURT VONNEGUT, JR.

THE YEAR WAS 2081, and everybody was finally equal. They weren't only equal before God and the law. They were equal every which way. Nobody was smarter than anybody else. Nobody was better looking than anybody else. Nobody was stronger or quicker than anybody else. All this equality was due to the 211th, 212th, and 213th Amendments to the Constitution, and to the unceasing vigilance of agents of the United States Handicapper General.

Some things about living still weren't quite right, though. April, for instance, still drove people crazy by not being springtime. And it was in that clammy month that the H-G men took George and Hazel Bergeron's fourteen-year-old son, Harrison, away.

It was tragic, all right, but George and Hazel couldn't think about it very hard. Hazel had a perfectly average intelligence, which meant she couldn't think about anything except in short bursts. And George, while his intelligence was way above normal, had a little mental handicap radio in his ear. He was required by law to wear it at all times. It was tuned to a government transmitter. Every twenty seconds or so, the transmitter would send out some sharp noise to keep people like George from taking unfair advantage of their brains.

George and Hazel were watching television. There were tears on Hazel's cheeks,

From *Welcome to the Monkey House* by Kurt Vonnegut, Jr. Copyright © 1968 by Kurt Vonnegut, Jr. A Seymour Lawrence Book/Delacorte Press. Used by permission.

but she'd forgotten for the moment what they were about.

On the television screen were ballerinas.

A buzzer sounded in George's head. His thoughts fled in panic, like bandits from a burglar alarm.

"That was a real pretty dance, that dance they just did," said Hazel.

"Huh?" said George.

"That dance—it was nice," said Hazel.

"Yup," said George. He tried to think a little about the ballerinas. They weren't really very good—no better than anybody else would have been, anyway. They were burdened with sashweights and bags of birdshot, and their faces were masked, so that no one, seeing a free and graceful gesture or a pretty face, would feel like something the cat drug in. George was toying with the vague notion that maybe dancers shouldn't be handicapped. But he didn't get very far with it before another noise in his ear radio scattered his thoughts.

George winced. So did two out of the eight ballerinas.

Hazel saw him wince. Having no mental handicap herself, she had to ask George what the latest sound had been.

"Sounded like somebody hitting a milk bottle with a ball-peen hammer," said George.

"I'd think it would be real interesting, hearing all the different sounds," said Hazel, a little envious. "All the things they think up."

"Um," said George.

"Only, if I was Handicapper General, you know what I would do?" said Hazel. Hazel, as a matter of fact, bore a strong resemblance to the Handicapper General, a woman named Diana Moon Glampers. "If I was Diana Moon Glampers," said Hazel, "I'd have chimes on Sunday—just chimes. Kind of in honor of religion."

"I could think, if it was just chimes," said George.

"Well—maybe make 'em real loud," said Hazel. "I think I'd make a good Handicapper General."

"Good as anybody else," said George.

"Who knows better'n I do what normal is?" said Hazel.

"Right," said George. He began to think glimmeringly about his abnormal son who was now in jail, about Harrison, but a twenty-one-gun salute in his head stopped that.

"Boy!" said Hazel, "that was a doozy, wasn't it?"

It was such a doozy that George was white and trembling, and tears stood on the rims of his red eyes. Two of the eight ballerinas had collapsed to the studio floor, were holding their temples.

"All of a sudden you look so tired," said Hazel. "Why don't you stretch out on the sofa, so's you can rest your handicap bag on the pillows, honeybunch." She was referring to the forty-seven pounds of bird-shot in a canvas bag, which was padlocked around George's neck. "Go on and rest the bag for a little while," she said. "I don't care if you're not equal to me for a while."

George weighed the bag with his hands. "I don't mind it," he said. "I don't notice it any more. It's just a part of me."

"You been so tired lately—kind of wore out," said Hazel. "If there was just some way we could make a little hole in the bottom of the bag, and just take out a few of them lead balls. Just a few."

"Two years in prison and two thousand dollars fine for every ball I took out," said George. "I don't call that a bargain."

"If you could just take a few out when you came home from work," said Hazel. "I mean—you don't compete with anybody around here. You just set around."

"If I tried to get away with it," said George, "then other people'd get away with it—and pretty soon we'd be right back to the dark ages again, with everybody competing against everybody else. You wouldn't like that, would you?"

"I'd hate it," said Hazel.

"There you are," said George. "The minute people start cheating on laws, what do you think happens to society?"

If Hazel hadn't been able to come up with an answer to this question, George couldn't have supplied one. A siren was going off in his head.

"Reckon it'd fall all apart," said Hazel.

"What would?" said George blankly.

"Society," said Hazel uncertainly. "Wasn't that what you just said?"

"Who knows?" said George.

The television program was suddenly interrupted for a news bulletin. It wasn't clear at first as to what the bulletin was about, since the announcer, like all announcers, had a serious speech impediment. For about half a minute, and in a state of high excitement, the announcer tried to say, "Ladies and gentlemen—"

He finally gave up, handed the bulletin to a ballerina to read.

"That's all right—" Hazel said of the announcer, "he tried. That's the big thing. He tried to do the best he could with what God gave him. He should get a nice raise for trying so hard."

"Ladies and gentlemen—" said the ballerina, reading the bulletin. She must have been extraordinarily beautiful, because the mask she wore was hideous. And it was easy to see that she was the strongest and most graceful of all the dancers, for her handicap bags were as big as those worn by two-hundred-pound men.

And she had to apologize at once for her voice, which was a very unfair voice for a woman to use. Her voice was a warm, luminous, timeless melody. "Excuse me—" she said, and she began again, making her voice absolutely uncompetitive.

"Harrison Bergeron, age fourteen," she said in a grackle squawk, "has just escaped from jail, where he was held on suspicion of plotting to overthrow the government. He is a genius and an athlete, is under-handicapped, and should be regarded as extremely dangerous."

A police photograph of Harrison Bergeron was flashed on the screen upside down, then sideways, upside down again, then right side up. The picture showed the full length of Harrison against a background calibrated in feet and inches. He was exactly seven feet tall.

The rest of Harrison's appearance was Halloween and hardware. Nobody had ever borne heavier handicaps. He had outgrown hindrances faster than the H-G men could think them up. Instead of a little ear radio for a mental handicap, he wore a tremendous pair of earphones, and spectacles with thick wavy lenses. The spectacles were intended to make him not only half blind, but to give him whanging headaches besides.

Scrap metal was hung all over him. Ordinarily, there was a certain symmetry, a military neatness to the handicaps issued to strong people, but Harrison looked like a walking junkyard. In the race of life, Harrison carried three hundred pounds.

And to offset his good looks, the H-G men required that he wear at all times a red rubber ball for a nose, keep his eyebrows shaved off, and cover his even white teeth with black caps at snaggle-tooth random.

"If you see this boy," said the ballerina, "do not—I repeat, do not—try to reason with him."

There was the shriek of a door being torn from its hinges.

Screams and barking cries of consternation came from the television set. The photograph of Harrison Bergeron on the screen jumped again and again, as though dancing to the tune of an earthquake.

George Bergeron correctly identified the earthquake, and well he might have—for many was the time his own home had danced to the same crashing tune. "My God—" said George, "that must be Harrison!"

The realization was blasted from his mind instantly by the sound of an automobile collision in his head.

When George could open his eyes again, the photograph of Harrison was gone. A living, breathing Harrison filled the screen.

Clanking, clownish, and huge, Harrison stood in the center of the studio. The knob of the uprooted studio door was still in his hand. Ballerinas, technicians, musicians, and announcers cowered on their knees before him, expecting to die.

"I am the Emperor!" cried Harrison. "Do you hear? I am the Emperor! Everybody must do what I say at once!" He stamped his foot and the studio shook.

"Even as I stand here—" he bellowed, "crippled, hobbled, sickened—I am a greater ruler than any man who ever lived! Now watch me become what I *can* become!"

Harrison tore the straps of his handicap harness like wet tissue paper, tore straps guaranteed to support five thousand pounds.

Harrison's scrap-iron handicaps crashed to the floor.

Harrison thrust his thumbs under the bar of the padlock that secured his head harness. The bar snapped like celery. Harrison smashed his headphones and spectacles against the wall.

He flung away his rubber-ball nose, revealed a man that would have awed Thor, the god of thunder.

"I shall now select my Empress!" he said, looking down on the cowering people. "Let the first woman who dares rise to her feet claim her mate and her throne!"

A moment passed, and then a ballerina arose, swaying like a willow.

Harrison plucked the mental handicap from her ear, snapped off her physical handicaps with marvelous delicacy. Last of all, he removed her mask.

She was blindingly beautiful.

"Now—" said Harrison, taking her hand, "shall we show the people the meaning of the word dance? Music!" he commanded.

The musicians scrambled back into their chairs, and Harrison stripped them of their handicaps, too. "Play your best," he told

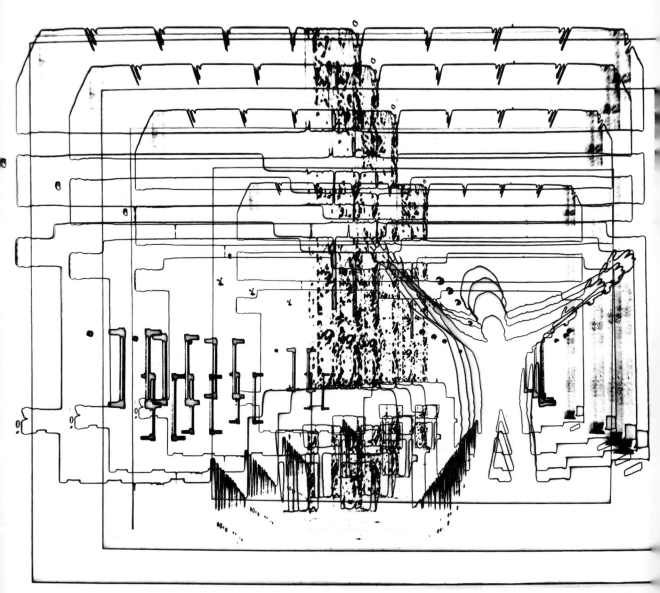

them, "and I'll make you barons and dukes and earls."

The music began. It was normal at first —cheap, silly, false. But Harrison snatched two musicians from their chairs, waved them like batons as he sang the music as he wanted it played. He slammed them back into their chairs.

The music began again and was much improved.

Harrison and his Empress merely listened to the music for a while—listened gravely, as though synchronizing their heartbeats with it.

They shifted their weights to their toes.

Harrison placed his big hands on the girl's tiny waist, letting her sense the weightlessness that would soon be hers.

And then, in an explosion of joy and grace, into the air they sprang!

Not only were the laws of the land abandoned, but the law of gravity and the laws of motion as well.

They reeled, whirled, swiveled, flounced, capered, gamboled, and spun.

They leaped like deer on the moon.

The studio ceiling was thirty feet high, but each leap brought the dancers nearer to it.

It became their obvious intention to kiss the ceiling.

They kissed it.

And then, neutralizing gravity with love and pure will, they remained suspended in air inches below the ceiling, and they kissed each other for a long, long time.

It was then that Diana Moon Glampers, the Handicapper General, came into the studio with a double-barreled ten-gauge shotgun. She fired twice, and the Emperor and the Empress were dead before they hit the floor.

Diana Moon Glampers loaded the gun again. She aimed it at the musicians and told them they had ten seconds to get their handicaps back on.

It was then that the Bergerons' television tube burned out.

Hazel turned to comment about the blackout to George. But George had gone out into the kitchen for a can of beer.

George came back in with the beer, paused while a handicap signal shook him up. And then he sat down again. "You been crying?" he said to Hazel.

"Yup," she said.

"What about?" he said.

"I forget," she said. "Something real sad on television."

"What was it?" he said.

"It's all kind of mixed up in my mind," said Hazel.

"Forget sad things," said George.

"I always do," said Hazel.

"That's my girl," said George. He winced. There was the sound of a rivetting gun in his head.

"Gee—I could tell that one was a doozy," said Hazel.

"You can say that again," said George.

"Gee—" said Hazel, "I could tell that one was a doozy."

FOR DISCUSSION

1. George and Hazel Bergeron forget their son's death a few minutes after it happens. Why? Does the author seem to see this lack of sorrow as a good thing?

2. Many people believe that competition is harmful because it rewards only those with outstanding ability. A better system, from this point of view, is one which encourages people to compete only against themselves, to do their best without being discouraged by the "experts." In some sports the best players are assigned handicaps to give everyone a nearly equal chance of winning. Kurt Vonnegut shows this philosophy carried to its ridiculous extreme. In the world of "Harrison Bergeron," what has been lost by eliminating envy, competition, and failure? How do George Bergeron, the television announcer, the technicians, the dancers, and the musicians illustrate this loss?

3. Why do you think it is fourteen-year-old Harrison and not his father who rebels against the Handicapper General?

FOR COMPOSITION

• What does "equality" mean in Kurt Vonnegut's story? How is it different from "equality before God and the law"? What form of equality would you like to see in an ideal future world?

Through the death of his grandmother a boy learns something of his own identity.

FROM

HOUSE MADE OF DAWN
N. SCOTT MOMADAY

I RETURNED TO Rainy Mountain in July. My grandmother had died in the spring, and I wanted to be at her grave. She had lived to be very old and at last infirm. Her only living daughter was with her when she died, and I was told that in death her face was that of a child.

I like to think of her as a child. When she was born, the Kiowas were living the last great moment of their history. For more than a hundred years they had controlled the open range from the Smoky Hill River to the Red, from the headwaters of the Canadian to the fork of the Arkansas and Cimarron. In alliance with the Comanches, they had ruled the whole of the Southern Plain. War was their sacred business, and they were the finest horsemen the world has ever known. But warfare for the Kiowas was pre-eminently a matter of disposition rather than survival, and they never understood the grim, unrelenting advance of the U.S. Cavalry. When at last, divided and ill-provisioned, they were driven onto the Staked Plain in the cold of autumn, they fell into panic. In Palo Duro Canyon they abandoned their crucial stores to pillage[1] and had nothing then but their lives. In order to save themselves, they surrendered to the soldiers at Fort Sill and were imprisoned in the old stone corral that now stands as a military museum. My grandmother was spared the humiliation of those high gray walls by eight or ten years, but she must have known from birth the affliction of defeat, the dark brooding of old warriors.

Her name was Aho, and she belonged to the last culture to evolve in North America. Her forebears came down from the high north country nearly three centuries ago. The earliest evidence of their existence places them close to the source of the Yellowstone River in western Montana. They were a mountain people, a mysterious tribe of hunters whose language has never been classified in any major group. In the late seventeenth century they began a long migration to the south and east. It was a journey toward the dawn, and it led to a golden age. Along the way the Kiowas were befriended by the Crows, who gave them the culture and religion of the plains. They acquired horses, and their ancient nomadic spirit was suddenly free of the ground. They acquired Tai-me, the sacred sun dance doll, from that moment the chief object and symbol of their worship, and so shared in the divinity of the sun. Not least, they acquired the sense of destiny, therefore courage and pride. When they entered upon the Southern Plains, they had been transformed. No longer were they slaves

---

[1] PILLAGE: to rob of goods by violent seizure.

Pp. 128–136 in *House Made of Dawn* by N. Scott Momaday. Copyright © 1968 by N. Scott Momaday. Reprinted by permission of Harper & Row, Publishers, Inc.

to the simple necessity of survival; they were a lordly and dangerous society of fighters and thieves, hunters and priests of the sun. According to their origin myth, they entered the world through a hollow log. From one point of view, their migration was the fruit of an old prophecy, for indeed they emerged from a sunless world.

I could see that. I followed their ancient way to my grandmother's grave. Though she lived out her long life in the shadow of Rainy Mountain, the immense landscape of the continental interior—all of its seasons and its sounds—lay like memory in her blood. She could tell of the Crows, whom she had never seen, and of the Black Hills, where she had never been. I wanted to see in reality what she had seen more perfectly in the mind's eye.

I began my pilgrimage on the course of the Yellowstone. There, it seemed to me, was the top of the world, a region of deep lakes and dark timber, canyons and waterfalls. But, beautiful as it is, one might have the sense of confinement there. The skyline in all directions is close at hand, the high wall of the woods and deep cleavages of shade. There is a perfect freedom in the mountains, but it belongs to the eagle and the elk, the badger and the bear. The Kiowas reckoned their stature by the distance they could see, and they were bent and blind in the wilderness.

Descending eastward, the highland meadows are a stairway to the plain. In July the inland slope of the Rockies is luxuriant with flax[1] and buckwheat, stonecrop[2] and larkspur. The earth unfolds and the limit of the land recedes. Clusters of trees, and animals grazing far in the distance, cause the vision to reach away and wonder to build upon the mind. The sun follows a longer course in the day, and the sky is

[1] FLAX: blue-flowered plant whose seeds yield linseed oil.
[2] STONECROP: plant with brightly colored flowers.

immense beyond all comparison. The great billowing clouds that sail upon it are shadows that move the grass and grain like water, dividing light. Farther down, in the land of the Crows and the Blackfeet, the plain is yellow. Sweet clover takes hold of the hills and bends upon itself to cover and seal the soil. There the Kiowas paused on their way; they had come to the place where they must change their lives. The sun is at home on the plains. Precisely there does it have the certain character of a god. When the Kiowas came to the land of the Crows, they could see the dark lees of the hills at dawn across the Bighorn River, the profusion of light on the grain shelves, the oldest deity ranging after the solstices. Not yet would they veer south to the caldron of the land that lay below; they must wean their blood from the northern winter and hold the mountains a while longer in their view. They bore Tai-me in procession to the east.

A dark mist lay over the Black Hills, and the land was like iron. At the top of a ridge I caught sight of Devils Tower—the uppermost extremity of it, like a file's end on the gray sky—and then it fell away behind the land. I was a long time then in coming upon it, and I did not see it again until I saw it whole, suddenly there across the valley, as if in the birth of time the core of the earth had broken through its crust and the motion of the world was begun. It stands in motion, like certain timeless trees that aspire too much into the sky, and imposes an illusion on the land. There are things in nature which engender an awful quiet in the heart of man; Devils Tower is one of them. Man must account for it. He must never fail to explain such a thing to himself, or else he is estranged forever from the universe. Two centuries ago, because they could not do otherwise, the Kiowas made a legend at the base of the rock. My grandmother said:

Eight children were there at play, seven sisters and their brother. Suddenly the boy was struck dumb; he trembled and began to run upon his hands and feet. His fingers became claws, and his body was covered with fur. There was a bear where the boy had been. The sisters were terrified; they ran, and the bear after them. They came to the stump of a great tree, and the tree spoke to them. It bade them climb upon it, and as they did so it began to rise into the air. The bear came to kill them, but they were just beyond its reach. It reared against the tree and scored the bark all around with its claws. The seven sisters were borne into the sky, and they became the stars of the Big Dipper.

From that moment, and so long as the legend lives, the Kiowas have kinsmen in the night sky. Whatever they were in the mountains, they could be no more. However tenuous their well-being, however much they had suffered and would suffer again, they had found a way out of the wilderness.

The first man among them to stand on the edge of the Great Plains saw farther over land than he had ever seen before. There is something about the heart of the continent that resides always in the end of vision, some essence of the sun and wind. That man knew the possible quest. There was nothing to prevent his going out; he could enter upon the land and be alive, could bear at once the great hot weight of its silence. In a sense the question of survival had never been more imminent, for no land is more the measure of human strength. But neither had wonder been more accessible to the mind nor destiny to the will.

My grandmother had a reverence for the sun, a certain holy regard which now is all but gone out of mankind. There was a wariness in her, and an ancient awe. She was a Christian in her later years, but she had come a long way about, and she never forgot her birthright. As a child, she had been to the sun dances; she had taken part in that annual rite, and by it she had learned the restoration of her people in the presence of Tai-me. She was about seven years old when the last Kiowa sun dance was held in 1887 on the Washita River above Rainy Mountain Creek. The buffalo were gone. In order to consummate the ancient sacrifice—to impale the head of a buffalo bull upon the Tai-me tree—a delegation of old men journeyed into Texas, there to beg and barter for an animal from the Goodnight herd. She was ten when the Kiowas came together for the last time as a living sun dance culture. They could find no buffalo; they had to hang an old hide from the sacred tree. That summer was known to my grandmother as Ä'poto Etódǎ-de K'ádó, Sun Dance When the Forked Poles Were Left Standing, and it is entered in the Kiowa calendars as the figure of a tree standing outside the unfinished framework of a medicine lodge. Before the dance could begin, a company of armed soldiers rode out from Fort Sill under orders to disperse the tribe. Forbidden without cause the essential act of their faith, having seen the wild herds slaughtered and left to rot upon the ground, the Kiowas backed away forever from the tree. That was July 20, 1890, at the great bend of the Washita. My grandmother was there. Without bitterness, and for as long as she lived, she bore a vision of deicide.

Now that I can have her only in memory, I see my grandmother in the several postures that were peculiar to her: standing at the wood stove on a winter morning and turning meat in a great iron skillet; sitting at the south window, bent above her beadwork, and afterward, when her vision failed, looking down for a long time into the fold of her hands; going out

upon a cane, very slowly as she did when the weight of age came upon her; praying. I remember her most often at prayer. She made long, rambling prayers out of suffering and hope, having seen many things. . . .

Houses are like sentinels in the plain, old keepers of the weather watch. There, in a very little while, wood takes on the appearance of great age. All colors soon wear away in the wind and rain, and then the wood is burned gray and the grain appears and the nails turn red with rust. The windowpanes are black and opaque; you imagine there is nothing within, and indeed there are many ghosts, bones given up to the land. They stand here and there against the sky, and you approach them for a longer time than you expect. They belong in the distance; it is their domain.

My grandmother lived in a house near the place where Rainy Mountain Creek runs into the Washita River. Once there was a lot of sound in the house, a lot of coming and going, feasting and talk. The summers there were full of excitement and reunion. The Kiowas are a summer people; they abide the cold and keep to themselves, but when the season turns and the land becomes warm and vital they cannot hold still; an old love of going returns upon them. The old people have a fine sense of pageantry and a wonderful notion of decorum. The aged visitors who came to my grandmother's house when I was a child were men of immense character, full of wisdom and disdain. They dealt in a kind of infallible quiet and gave but one face away; it was enough. They were made of lean and leather, and they bore themselves upright. They wore great black hats and bright ample shirts that shook in the wind. They rubbed fat upon their hair and wound their braids with strips of colored cloth. Some of them painted their faces and carried the scars of old and cherished enmities. They were an old council of war lords, come to remind and be reminded of who they were. Their wives and daughters served them well. The women might indulge themselves; gossip was at once the mark and compensation of their servitude. They made loud and elaborate talk among themselves, full of jest and gesture, fright and false alarm. They went abroad in fringed and flowered shawls, bright beadwork and German silver. They were at home in the kitchen, and they prepared meals that were banquets.

There were frequent prayer meetings, and great nocturnal feasts. When I was a child, I played with my cousins outside, where the lamplight fell upon the ground and the singing of the old people rose up around us and carried away into the darkness. There were a lot of good things to eat, a lot of laughter and surprise. And afterward, when the quiet returned, I lay down with my grandmother and could hear the frogs away by the river and feel the motion of the air.

Now there is a funereal silence in the rooms, the endless wake of some final word. The walls have closed in upon my grandmother's house. When I returned to it in mourning, I saw for the first time in my life how small it was. It was late at night, and there was a white moon, nearly full. I sat for a long time on the stone steps by the kitchen door. From there I could see out across the land; I could see the long row of trees by the creek, the low light upon the rolling plains, and the stars of the Big Dipper. Once I looked at the moon and caught sight of a strange thing. A cricket had perched upon the handrail, only a few inches away from me. My line of vision was such that the creature filled the moon like a fossil. It had gone there, I thought, to live and die, for there of all places was its small definition made whole and eternal. A warm wind rose up and purled like the longing within me.

The next morning I awoke at dawn and went out of my grandmother's house to the scaffold of the well that stands near the arbor. There was a stillness all around, and night lay still upon the pecan groves away by the river. The sun rose out of the ground, powerless for a long time to burn the air away, dim and nearly cold like the moon. The orange arc grew upon the land, curving out and downward to an impossible diameter. It must not go on, I thought, and I began to be afraid; then the air dissolved and the sun backed away. But for a moment I had seen to the center of the world's being. Every day in the plains proceeds from that strange eclipse.

I went out on the dirt road to Rainy Mountain. It was already hot, and the grasshoppers began to fill the air. Still, it was early in the morning, and birds sang out of the shadows. The long yellow grass on the mountain shone in the bright light, and a scissortail hied above the land. There, where it ought to be, at the end of a long and legendary way, was my grandmother's grave. She had at last succeeded to that holy ground. Here and there on the dark stones were the dear ancestral names. Looking back once, I saw the mountain and came away.

FOR DISCUSSION

1. In the narrator's mind as in his grandmother's, history and myth mingle with recent memories. His grandmother spoke of tribes and places she had never seen and events that happened centuries ago. What does he mean, "I wanted to see in reality what she had seen more perfectly in the mind's eye"? How is this trip a "pilgrimage" for him?

2. "When they entered upon the Southern Plains, they had been transformed." What were the steps in the transformation of the Kiowas from mountain hunters to plains warriors? How was their religion shaped by the change in their experience? What was the act of "deicide" that finally ended their existence as a sun dance culture?

3. The old war lords came together "to remind and be reminded of who they were." In the same way, the narrator makes his trip to remind himself who his grandmother was and who he is. What does he admire most about his grandmother? Although they are two generations apart, what parts of her experience is he able to share?

FOR COMPOSITION

• Think of the times that you have spent with your grandparents or other older members of your family. Without placing too much emphasis on organization, write two or three pages of memories of such times as they come into your head: sights, smells, tastes, conversations, feelings you had. Using your notes, develop one memory into a form to be shared with the class. It could be a character sketch such as that of the grandmother, thoughts about the influence a relative has had on you, or a description of a scene such as the family reunion on page 481.

PATTERNS

PAUL SIMON

The night set softly
With the hush of falling leaves
Casting shivering shadows
On the houses through the trees.
And the light from a street lamp   5
Paints a pattern on my wall
Like the pieces of a puzzle
Or a child's uneven scrawl.

Up a narrow flight of stairs
In a narrow little room   10
As I lie upon my bed
In the early evening gloom
Impaled on my wall
My eyes can dimly see
The pattern of my life   15
And the puzzle that is me.

From the moment of my birth
To the instant of my death
There are patterns I must follow
Just as I must breathe each breath.   20
Like a rat in a maze
The path before me lies
And the pattern never alters
Until the rat dies.

And the pattern still remains   25
On the wall where darkness fell
And it's fitting that it should
For in darkness I must dwell.
Like the color of my skin
Or the day that I grow old   30
My life is made of patterns
That can scarcely be controlled.

FOR DISCUSSION

• In the first stanza the light from a street lamp throws patterns on his wall that remind the poet of parts of a puzzle. How does he see the pattern and the puzzle as metaphors for his own life? What does his mood seem to be as he ponders this metaphor?

In Summary

FOR DISCUSSION

1. In which of the stories in this unit does the relationship between parent or grandparent and child seem to be the closest? In which story does there seem to be the least communication and affection between generations?

2. In three of the stories a boy sees a parent or grandparent in a new light: "All the Years of Her Life," "The Pheasant Hunter," and "House Made of Dawn." What causes this to happen in each story? Are there any similarities among the discoveries that the three boys make?

3. Generations ago, most Americans lived on farms or in small towns and traveled around very little. Children grew up knowing and being known by many adults of all ages. Family and community traditions were often very strong.

Now this "extended family" has been replaced in most cases by a "nuclear family" of parents and children who may rarely see other relatives, and who have few traditions to help them understand who they are. In the stories in this unit, which boys have contact with some kind of "extended family" beyond their own parents? Which ones are aware of a tradition handed down from their ancestors? Do these contacts with other people and other times seem to be helpful to them?

4. The women in "All the Years of Her Life" and "House Made of Dawn" are strong individuals, but the mothers in "Thus I Refute Beelzy," "The Hero," "The Pheasant Hunter," and "Harrison Bergeron" are types. What do they all have in common? Where have you encountered this stereotype before?

OTHER THINGS TO DO

1. Make a collage of photographs, symbols, and other materials representing the forces that divide the generations and those that draw them together.

2. Write two or more pages of dialogue between a parent and child who are in conflict. The writing will be easier if it is preceded by role playing: one student plays the parent, another the child; someone suggests a situation, and they begin improvising. Several small groups may do this with a tape recorder or secretary to record their best efforts, or role playing in class may be used to inspire each student to write his own dialogue. If you are pleased with your results, try the same assignment with three or more characters, possibly adding a grandparent.

3. Describe the same event as it would be seen by members of different generations. For example, how would a school strike be described by a student talking to his friend on the phone, a parent speaking at a School Board meeting, and a grandparent writing to an old friend?

4. Poll students in your school and their parents about issues which often cause disagreement. Summarizing your results will be easiest if you ask yes/no or multiple choice questions, for example:

Students should be free to wear whatever style of clothing they prefer.

    Agree———   Disagree———

A reasonable week-night curfew for fifteen-year-olds would be:———

    a. Before 9:00
    b. 9:00
    c. 10:00
    d. 11:00
    e. Midnight
    f. After midnight

On the other hand, you will often get interesting answers to open-ended questions such as:

What one thing about your son or daughter (or parent) would you most like to change?

Present your results in an oral report. If several students choose this project, you might follow the reports with a panel discussion.

The World of Words

THUS I REFUTE BEELZY

The word *fantasy* occurs several times in this story. Its meaning is related to the meanings of *fancy* and *imagination,* in that all three words refer to the power of the mind to create images. What differences do you find in the meanings of these three words? Is *fantasy* the proper word to use in this story?

THE HERO

If the word *hero* in the title refers to Mr. Whalen, the use of the word appears ironic. How do we usually use the word? To whom in the story would we likely apply it? Yet the origin of the word *hero* might leave room for Mr. Whalen. It comes from an early root meaning "to protect." It came into Latin as *servare,* meaning "to keep or preserve," from which we get our words *conserve* and *preserve.* It came into Greek as *heros,* meaning "protector." Considering these origins of the word, is there any clear sense in which Mr. Whalen might be called a "hero"?

ALL THE YEARS OF HER LIFE

When Sam Carr decides to call Alfred's mother, Alfred, we are told, speaks "arrogantly." *Arrogantly* is the adverb form of the adjective *arrogant,* which can be defined as "overbearingly proud or haughty." The words *proud* and *haughty* are regarded as synonyms of *arrogant,* yet there are differences in the meanings of these words. What are those differences? Would it be just as accurate to call Alfred proud or haughty instead of arrogant? The words *bluster* and *swagger* are also applied to Alfred. How do these words relate to *arrogant?*

THE PHEASANT HUNTER

Mike Maloney tells his son: "The whole trouble with you is you're too pent up from not doing any kind of work. . . ." The phrase *pent up* is a common one, and its meaning comes from its origin. What is the origin of *pent up,* and what does it mean? Mike also calls his son "sarcastic." *Sarcastic* comes from *sarcasm,* and *sarcasm* refers to remarks that cut or wound. Look up the origin of *sarcasm* and explain how that origin relates to the present meaning of the word.

HARRISON BERGERON

Harrison Bergeron's mother, Hazel, does not need any handicaps, we are told, because she "had a perfectly average intelligence." All words have histories and the word *average* has an especially interesting history. It began as the word *awar,* an Arabic word meaning "fault or blemish," which became *awariyah,* meaning "damaged goods." This word came into Italian as *avaria,* from there into French as *avarie,* meaning "damage to shipping," and from there into English as *average.* In its French form, *avarie,* it referred to the loss of money that was incurred when goods were damaged or lost at sea. Such losses were shared in equal portions by all those who had invested their money in the business. From this idea of equalizing the loss, we get the idea of a numerical average and the other meanings the word has taken on. The study of the origins and histories of words is called "etymology." What is the etymology of *etymology?*

HOUSE MADE OF DAWN

Speaking of his grandmother, Momaday says that "she belonged to the last culture to evolve in North America." Like most all words, *culture* has a number of different meanings. What are its most common meanings? Which meaning is more appropriate in this selection? Why do you say so? Earlier Momaday has said that when his grandmother died, "her face was that of a child." We sometimes speak of adults as "childlike" or as "childish." Do the two words mean the same thing? If not, what is the difference?

Reader's Choice

The Ark, *by Margot Benary-Isbert.*

Their father in prison camp, their brother shot, the Lechow family struggles to find food and shelter in postwar Germany. Shy Margret's love of animals finally leads them to a farm where they find work and an old railroad car, the Ark, which becomes a new home for the reunited family.

Big Doc's Girl, *by Mary Medearis.*

Sixteen-year-old Mary Clayborne, the oldest child of an Arkansas back-country doctor, hopes to study music in the city someday. When her mother is hospitalized with TB she finds herself instead caring for her sisters and brothers and helping her father with his heavy responsibilities.

The Chosen, *by Chaim Potok.*

Because the leadership of a Hasidic Jewish congregation is handed down from father to son, everyone assumes that Danny Saunders will follow in his father's footsteps. But Danny is interested in Freudian psychology and other heretical ideas. What is more, his best friend is Reuven Malter, whose father leads a Zionist movement of which Rabbi Saunders strongly disapproves. In the resulting conflict Danny finds himself torn between opposing loyalties.

Good-bye, Mr. Chips, *by James Hilton.*

When Mr. Chipping came to the Brookfield School as a young teacher of twenty-two, he didn't guess that he would still be there sixty-three years later. Three generations of English students became "his boys," laughing at his legendary jokes even while German bombs were falling outside. So many people have laughed and cried over this book that it has become a modern classic.

I'm Really Dragged But Nothing Gets Me Down, *by Nat Hentoff.*

Jeremy Wolf, high school senior, struggles with demands from all sides. Can his country make him kill? Can his father make him "respectable"? Told from first Jeremy's and then his father's point of view, this novel explores both sides of the generation gap with humor and understanding.

The Light in the Forest, *by Conrad Richter.*

" 'Who is my father?' the boy cried in despair." Captured by the Lenni Lenape as a baby, True Son grows up believing himself an Indian and is heartbroken to be returned to the whites. Can he become an Indian again if it means making war on his own flesh and blood?

The Pigman, *by Paul Zindel.*

John and Lorraine are high school sophomores who hate school and don't get along with their parents. When they meet Mr. Pignati, an old man who lives for his memories and his visits to the baboon at the zoo, they feel sorry for him at first. Then a strange friendship grows up between them as his house becomes a refuge where they are accepted for themselves in their craziest or most serious moods.

To Kill a Mockingbird, *by Harper Lee.*

"Atticus was feeble: he was nearly fifty . . . our father didn't do anything that could possibly arouse the admiration of anyone." But when their father defends Tom Robinson, a black man, against the accusations of a white woman, Jed and Scout discover that they—and the small Southern town in which they live—have a great deal to learn from Atticus.

When the Legends Die, *by Hal Borland.*

"When the legends die, the dreams end." Thomas Black Bull's dreams seem to end when his parents die and he is forced to live in the white man's school. Everything there is alien to him but the horses. Taking out his hatred on the meanest of broncos, he becomes a famous rodeo rider—but always he hears the call of the old legends, his ancestors' songs, and his wilderness home.

EPIC POETRY

AN *epic* is a long poem that celebrates the feats of a hero representative of a nation or a race. In other words, epics unfold worlds larger than life, peopled by supermen in whom we see our own imperfect selves reflected whole and on a grand scale. No race or nation·is fortunate enough to boast of many epics. In American literature, no true epic exists, and English literature contains only one, Milton's *Paradise Lost*. The ancestor of English, Anglo-Saxon, produced the epic *Beowulf;* Latin produced the *Aeneid,* but ancient Greek literature produced two epics, and the two greatest of all, written by Homer probably in the ninth century B.C. One is the *Iliad,* about the fall of Troy, or Ilium. The other epic is the *Odyssey.* It is from that second great work that the following selections come.

By the stratagem of a hollow wooden horse, filled with soldiers and admitted within the enemy's walls, the Greeks finally had won their ten-year war against Troy in Asia Minor. Subsequently the Greek armies disbanded. The *Odyssey* tells what happened to Odysseus (ō·dĭs'yüs), one of the Greek princes and leaders in that war, between the time he left Troy and the time, ten years later, when he finally reached his home in Ithaka and was reunited with his faithful wife Penélopê (pə·nĕl'ə·pē). All his life Odysseus had been known for his cleverness, and in the decade of wandering that followed the Greek victory, he was to need every bit of skill and craft that he could muster. For he and his fleet of twelve ships traveling the Mediterranean met with a series of fantastic adventures, including shipwreck, storms, and monstrous combats, that would have taxed any man's courage and wisdom.

Philip McFarland

While Odysseus wanders in search of home, his wife Penélopê finds herself beseiged with suitors who help themselves to Odysseus' wealth while waiting for her to decide which of them she will marry. For years she put them off by telling them she must first weave a shroud for her father-in-law, Laërtês (lä·ėr′tās). Every night she secretly undid the weaving from the day before until one of her handmaidens finally revealed the secret. Now Penélopê and her son Telémakhos (tə·lĕm′ə·kas) are helpless to send the suitors away.

Book One opens with a meeting of the gods on Mount Olympos at which Athena pleads for mercy for Odysseus.

FROM

THE ODYSSEY
HOMER

BOOK ONE

SING IN ME, MUSE, and through me tell the story
of that man skilled in all ways of contending,
the wanderer, harried for years on end,
after he plundered the stronghold
on the proud height of Troy.   5
                        He saw the townlands
and learned the minds of many distant men,
and weathered many bitter nights and days
in his deep heart at sea, while he fought only
to save his life, to bring his shipmates home.   10
But not by will nor valor could he save them,
for their own recklessness destroyed them all—
children and fools, they killed and feasted on
the cattle of Lord Hêlios, the Sun,
and he who moves all day through heaven   15
took from their eyes the dawn of their return.

Of these adventures, Muse, daughter of Zeus,
tell us in our time, lift the great song again.
Begin when all the rest who left behind them
headlong death in battle or at sea   20
had long ago returned, while he alone still hungered
for home and wife. Her ladyship Kalypso

clung to him in her sea-hollowed caves—
a nymph, immortal and most beautiful,
who craved him for her own.   25
                    And when long years and seasons
wheeling brought around that point of time
ordained for him to make his passage homeward,
trials and dangers, even so, attended him
even in Ithaka, near those he loved.   30
Yet all the gods had pitied Lord Odysseus,
all but Poseidon,* raging cold and rough
against the brave king till he came ashore
at last on his own land.
                  But now that god   35
had gone far off among the sunburnt races,
most remote of men, at earth's two verges,
in sunset lands and lands of the rising sun,
to be regaled by smoke of thighbones burning,
haunches of rams and bulls, a hundred fold.   40
He lingered delighted at the banquet side.

In the bright hall of Zeus upon Olympos
the other gods were all at home, and Zeus,
the father of gods and men, made conversation.
For he had meditated on Aigísthos,* dead   45
by the hand of Agamémnon's son, Orestês,
and spoke his thought aloud before them all:

"My word, how mortals take the gods to task!
All their afflictions come from us, we hear.
And what of their own failings? Greed and folly   50
double the suffering in the lot of man.
See how Aigísthos, for his double portion,
stole Agamémnon's wife and killed the soldier
on his homecoming day. And yet Aigísthos
knew that his own doom lay in this. We gods   55
had warned him, sent down Hermês Argeiphontês,*
our most observant courier, to say:
'Don't kill the man, don't touch his wife,
or face a reckoning with Orestês
the day he comes of age and wants his patrimony.'*   60
Friendly advice—but would Aigísthos take it?
Now he has paid the reckoning in full."

---

32 POSEIDON (pō·sā′don): god of the sea; producer of earthquakes. 45 AIGIS-
THOS: ī·jĭs′thos. 56 ARGEIPHONTES: ar·jā·fon′tās. 60 PATRIMONY (pat′rə·mō-
nē): inheritance from a father or other ancestor.

The gray-eyed goddess Athena replied to Zeus:

"O Majesty, O Father of us all,
that man is in the dust indeed, and justly. 65
So perish all who do what he had done.
But my own heart is broken for Odysseus,
the master mind of war, so long a castaway
upon an island in the running sea;
a wooded island, in the sea's middle, 70
and there's a goddess in the place, the daughter
of one whose baleful mind knows all the deeps
of the blue sea—Atlas, who holds the columns
that bear from land the great thrust of the sky.
His daughter will not let Odysseus go, 75
poor mournful man; she keeps on coaxing him
with her beguiling talk, to turn his mind
from Ithaka. But such desire is in him
merely to see the hearthsmoke leaping upward
from his own island, that he longs to die. 80
Are you not moved by this, Lord of Olympos?
Had you no pleasure from Odysseus' offerings
beside the Argive ships, on Troy's wide seaboard?
O Zeus, what do you hold against him now?"

To this the summoner of cloud replied: 85

"My child, what strange remarks you let escape you.
Could I forget that kingly man, Odysseus?
There is no mortal half so wise; no mortal
gave so much to the lords of open sky.
Only the god who laps the land in water, 90
Poseidon, bears the fighter an old grudge
since he poked out the eye of Polyphêmos,*
brawniest of the Kyklopês.* Who bore
that giant lout? Thoösa, daughter of Phorkys,
an offshore sea lord: for this nymph had lain 95
with Lord Poseidon in her hollow caves.
Naturally, the god, after the blinding—
mind you, he does not kill the man;
he only buffets him away from home.
But come now, we are all at leisure here, 100
let us take up this matter of his return.
How should he sail? Poseidon must relent,

---

⁹² Polyphemos: pol·ē·fām′os.   ⁹³ Kyklopes: kē·klō′pās.

for being quarrelsome will get him nowhere,
one god, flouting the will of all the gods."

The gray-eyed goddess Athena answered him: 105

"O Majesty, O Father of us all,
if it now please the blissful gods
that wise Odysseus reach his home again,
let the Wayfinder, Hermês, cross the sea
to the island of Ogýgia; let him tell   110
our fixed intent to the nymph with pretty braids,
and let the steadfast man depart for home.
For my part, I shall visit Ithaka
to put more courage in the son, and rouse him
to call an assembly of the islanders,   115
Akhaian* gentlemen with flowing hair.
He must warn off that wolf pack of the suitors
who prey upon his flocks and dusky cattle.
I'll send him to the mainland then, to Sparta
by the sand beach of Pylos; let him find   120
news of his dear father where he may
and win his own renown about the world."

She bent to tie her beautiful sandals on,
ambrosial, golden, that carry her over water
or over endless land on the wings of the wind,   125
and took the great haft of her spear in hand—
that bronzeshod spear this child of Power can use
to break in wrath long battle lines of fighters.

Flashing down from Olympos' height she went
to stand in Ithaka, before the Manor,   130
just at the doorsill of the court. She seemed
a family friend, the Taphian captain, Mentês,
waiting, with a light hand on her spear.
Before her eyes she found the lusty suitors
casting dice inside the gate, at ease   135
on hides of oxen—oxen they had killed.
Their own retainers made a busy sight
with houseboys, mixing bowls of water and wine,
or sopping water up in sponges, wiping
tables to be placed about in hall,   140
or butchering whole carcasses for roasting.

---

116 AKHAIAN (a·kī′ən): one of Odysseus' men.

Long before anyone else, the prince Telémakhos
now caught sight of Athena—for he, too,
was sitting there, unhappy among the suitors,
a boy, daydreaming. What if his great father   145
came from the unknown world and drove these men
like dead leaves through the place, recovering
honor and lordship in his own domains?
Then he who dreamed in the crowd gazed out at Athena.

Straight to the door he came, irked with himself   150
to think a visitor had been kept there waiting,
and took her right hand, grasping with his left
her tall bronze-bladed spear. Then he said warmly:

"Greetings, stranger! Welcome to our feast.
There will be time to tell your errand later."   155

He led the way, and Pallas Athena followed
into the lofty hall. The boy reached up
and thrust her spear high in a polished rack
against a pillar, where tough spear on spear
of the old soldier, his father, stood in order.   160
Then, shaking out a splendid coverlet,
he seated her on a throne with footrest—all
finely carved—and drew his painted armchair
near her, at a distance from the rest.
To be amid the din, the suitors' riot   165
would ruin his guest's appetite, he thought,
and he wished privacy to ask for news
about his father, gone for years.
                                A maid
brought them a silver finger bowl and filled it   170
out of a beautiful spouting golden jug,
then drew a polished table to their side.
The larder* mistress with her tray came by
and served them generously. A carver lifted
cuts of each roast meat to put on trenchers*   175
before the two. He gave them cups of gold,
and these the steward as he went his rounds
filled and filled again.
                        Now came the suitors,
young bloods trooping in to their own seats   180
on thrones or easy chairs. Attendants poured

---

[173] LARDER: room for keeping meat and other foods.   [175] TRENCHERS:
wooden boards or plates on which meat is carved.

water over their fingers, while the maids
piled baskets full of brown loaves near at hand,
and houseboys brimmed the bowls with wine.
Now they laid hands upon the ready feast   185
and thought of nothing more. Not till desire
for food and drink had left them were they mindful
of dance and song, that are the grace of feasting.
A herald gave a shapely eithern harp
to Phêmios, whom they compelled to sing—   190
and what a storm he plucked upon the strings
for prelude! High and clear the song arose.

Telémakhos now spoke to gray-eyed Athena,
his head bent close, so no one else might hear:

"Dear guest, will this offend you, if I speak?   195
It is easy for these men to like these things,
harping and song; they have an easy life,
scot free, eating the livestock of another—
a man whose bones are rotting somewhere now,
white in the rain on dark earth where they lie,   200
or tumbling in the groundswell of the sea.
If he returned, if these men ever saw him,
faster legs they'd pray for, to a man,
and not more wealth in handsome robes or gold.
But he is lost; he came to grief and perished,   205
and there's no help for us in someone's hoping
he still may come; that sun has long gone down.
But tell me now, and put it for me clearly—
who are you? Where do you come from? Where's your home
and family? What kind of ship is yours,   210
and what course brought you here? Who are your sailors?
I don't suppose you walked here on the sea.
Another thing—this too I ought to know—
is Ithaka new to you, or were you ever
a guest here in the old days? Far and near   215
friends knew this house; for he whose home it was
had much acquaintance in the world."

                      To this
the gray-eyed goddess answered:
                         "As you ask,   220
I can account most clearly for myself.
Mentês I'm called, son of the veteran
Ankhíalos; I rule seafaring Taphos.

I came by ship, with a ship's company,
sailing the winedark sea for ports of call   225
on alien shores—to Témesê, for copper,
bringing bright bars of iron in exchange.
My ship is moored on a wild strip of coast
in Reithron Bight, under the wooded mountain.
Years back, my family and yours were friends,   230
as Lord Laërtês knows; ask when you see him.
I hear the old man comes to town no longer,
stays up country, ailing, with only one
old woman to prepare his meat and drink
when pain and stiffness take him in the legs   235
from working on his terraced plot, his vineyard.
As for my sailing here—
The tale was that your father had come home,
therefore I came. I see the gods delay him.
But never in this world is Odysseus dead—   240
only detained somewhere on the wide sea,
upon some island, with wild islanders;
savages, they must be, to hold him captive.
Well, I will forecast for you, as the gods
put the strong feeling in me—I see it all,   245
and I'm no prophet, no adept in bird-signs.
He will not, now, be long away from Ithaka,
his father's dear land; though he be in chains
he'll scheme a way to come; he can do anything.

But tell me this now, make it clear to me: 250
You must be, by your looks, Odysseus' boy?
The way your head is shaped, the fine eyes—yes,
how like him! We took meals like this together
many a time, before he sailed for Troy
with all the lords of Argos in the ships.   255
I have not seen him since, nor has he seen me."

And thoughtfully Telémakhos replied:
"Friend, let me put it in the plainest way.
My mother says I am his son; I know not
surely. Who has known his own engendering?   260
I wish at least I had some happy man
as father, growing old in his own house—
but unknown death and silence are the fate
of him that, since you ask, they call my father."

Then gray-eyed Athena said: 265
                              "The gods decreed
no lack of honor in this generation:

such is the son Penélopê bore in you.
But tell me now, and make this clear to me:
what gathering, what feast is this? Why here?   270
A wedding? Revel? At the expense of all?
Not that, I think. How arrogant they seem,
these gluttons, making free here in your house!
A sensible man would blush to be among them."

To this Telémakhos answered: 275

"Friend, now that you ask about these matters,
our house was always princely, a great house,
as long as he of whom we speak remained here.
But evil days the gods have brought upon it,
making him vanish, as they have, so strangely.   280
Were his death known, I could not feel such pain—
if he had died of wounds in Trojan country
or in the arms of friends, after the war.
They would have made a tomb for him, the Akhaians,
and I should have all honor as his son.   285
Instead, the whirlwinds got him, and no glory.
He's gone, no sign, no word of him; and I inherit
trouble and tears—and not for him alone,
the gods have laid such other burdens on me.
For now the lords of the islands,   290
Doulíkhion* and Samê,* wooded Zakynthos,*
and rocky Ithaka's young lords as well,
are here courting my mother; and they use
our house as if it were a house to plunder.
Spurn them she dare not, though she hates that marriage,   295
nor can she bring herself to choose among them.
Meanwhile they eat their way through all we have,
and when they will, they can demolish me."

Pallas Athena was disturbed, and said:

"Ah, bitterly you need Odysseus, then!   300
High time he came back to engage these upstarts.
I wish we saw him standing helmeted
there in the doorway, holding shield and spear,
looking the way he did when I first knew him.
That was at our house, where he drank and feasted   305
after he left Ephyra, homeward bound
from a visit to the son of Mérmeris, Ilos.
He took his fast ship down the gulf that time

---

²⁹¹ Doulíkhion, Samê, Zakynthos: du·lĭk′ĭ·on; sä′mā; zä·kĭn′thos.

for a fatal drug to dip his arrows in
and poison the bronze points; but young Ilos   310
turned him away, fearing the god's wrath.
My father gave it, for he loved him well.
I wish these men could meet the man of those days!
They'd know their fortune quickly: a cold bed.
Aye! but it lies upon the god's great knees   315
whether he can return and force a reckoning
in his own house, or not.
                               If I were you,
I should take steps to make these men disperse.
Listen, now, and attend to what I say: 320
at daybreak call the islanders to assembly,
and speak your will, and call the gods to witness:
the suitors must go scattering to their homes.
Then here's a course for you, if you agree:
get a sound craft afloat with twenty oars   325
and go abroad for news of your lost father—
perhaps a traveler's tale, or rumored fame
issued from Zeus abroad in the world of men.
Talk to that noble sage at Pylos, Nestor,
then go to Meneláos, the red-haired king   330
at Sparta, last man home of all the Akhaians.
Stay a full year. You may learn he's alive
and coming home; or else you may hear nothing,
or learn that he is dead and gone. If so,
then you can come back to your own dear country   335
and raise a mound* for him, and burn his gear,
with all the funeral honors due the man,
and give your mother to another husband.

When you have done all this, or seen it done,
it will be time to ponder   340
concerning these contenders in your house—
how you should kill them, outright or by guile.*
You need not bear this insolence of theirs,
you are a child no longer. Have you heard
what glory young Orestês won   345
when he cut down that two-faced man, Aigísthos,
for killing his illustrious father?
Dear friend, you are tall and well set up, I see;
be brave—you, too—and men in times to come
will speak of you respectfully.   350

---

[336] RAISE A MOUND: prepare a memorial.   [342] GUILE (gīl): craftiness.

Now I must join my ship;
my crew will grumble if I keep them waiting.
Look to yourself; remember what I told you."
Telémakhos replied:
                "Friend, you have done me   355
kindness, like a father to his son,
and I shall not forget your counsel ever.
You must get back to sea, I know, but come
take a hot bath, and rest; accept a gift
to make your heart lift up when you embark—   360
some precious thing, and beautiful, from me,
a keepsake, such as dear friends give their friends."

But the gray-eyed goddess Athena answered him:

"Do not delay me, for I love the sea ways.
As for the gift your heart is set on giving,   365
let me accept it on my passage home,
and you shall have a choice gift in exchange."

With this Athena left him
as a bird rustles upward, off and gone.
But as she went she put new spirit in him,   370
a new dream of his father, clearer now,
so that he marveled to himself
divining that a god had been his guest.
Then godlike in his turn he joined the suitors.

The famous minstrel still sang on before them,   375
and they sat still and listened, while he sang
that bitter song, the Homecoming of Akhaians—
how by Athena's will they fared from Troy;
and in her high room careful Penélopê,
Ikários' daughter, heeded the holy song.   380
She came, then, down the long stairs of her house,
this beautiful lady, with two maids in train
attending her as she approached the suitors;
and near a pillar of the roof she paused,
her shining veil drawn over across her cheeks,   385
the two girls close to her and still,
and through her tears spoke to the noble minstrel:

"Phêmios, other spells you know, high deeds
of gods and heroes, as the poets tell them;
let these men hear some other, while they sit   390

silent and drink their wine. But sing no more
this bitter tale that wears my heart away.
It opens in me again the wound of longing
for one incomparable, ever in my mind—
his fame all Hellas knows, and midland Argos."   395

But Telémakhos intervened and said to her:

"Mother, why do you grudge our own dear minstrel
joy of son, wherever his thought may lead?
Poets are not to blame, but Zeus who gives
what fate he pleases to adventurous men.   400
Here is no reason for reproof: to sing
the news of the Danaans!* Men like best
a song that rings like morning on the ear.
But you must nerve yourself and try to listen.
Odysseus was not the only one at Troy   405
never to know the day of his homecoming.
Others, how many others, lost their lives!"

The lady gazed in wonder and withdrew,
her son's clear wisdom echoing in her mind.
But when she had mounted to her rooms again   410
with her two handmaids, then she fell to weeping
for Odysseus, her husband. Gray-eyed Athena
presently cast a sweet sleep on her eyes.

Meanwhile the din grew loud in the shadowy hall
as every suitor swore to lie beside her,   415
but Telémakhos turned now and spoke to them:

"You suitors of my mother! Insolent men,
now we have dined, let us have entertainment
and no more shouting. There can be no pleasure
so fair as giving heed to a great minstrel   420
like ours, whose voice itself is pure delight.
At daybreak we shall sit down in assembly
and I shall tell you—take it as you will—
you are to leave this hall. Go feasting elsewhere,
consume your own stores. Turn and turn about,   425
use one another's houses. If you choose
to slaughter one man's livestock and pay nothing,
this is rapine;* and by the eternal gods

---

402 DANAANS (dǎ′nē·ənz): Greeks.   428 RAPINE: plundering.

I beg Zeus you shall get what you deserve:
a slaughter here, and nothing paid for it!"   430

By now their teeth seemed fixed in their under-lips,
Telémakhos' bold speaking stunned them so.
Antínoös, Eupeithês' son, made answer:

"Telémakhos, no doubt the gods themselves
are teaching you this high and mighty manner.   435
Zeus forbid you should be king in Ithaka,
though you are eligible as your father's son."

Telémakhos kept his head and answered him:

"Antínoös, you may not like my answer,
but I would happily be king, if Zeus   440
conferred the prize. Or do you think it wretched?
I shouldn't call it bad at all. A king
will be respected, and his house will flourish.
But there are eligible men enough,
heaven knows, on the island, young and old,   445
and one of them perhaps may come to power
after the death of King Odysseus.
All I insist on is that I rule our house
and rule the slaves my father won for me."

Eurýmakhos, Pólybos' son, replied: 450
"Telémakhos, it is on the gods' great knees
who will be king in sea-girt Ithaka.
But keep your property, and rule your house,
and let no man, against your will, make havoc
of your possessions, while there's life on Ithaka.   455
But now, my brave young friend,
a question or two about the stranger.
Where did your guest come from? Of what country?
Where does he say his home is, and his family?
Has he some message of your father's coming,   460
or business of his own, asking a favor?
He left so quickly that one hadn't time
to meet him, but he seemed a gentleman."

Telémakhos made answer, cool enough:

"Eurýmakhos, there's no hope for my father.   465
I would not trust a message, if one came,

nor any forecaster my mother invites
to tell by divination of time to come.
My guest, however, was a family friend,
Mentês, son of Ankhíalos.   470
He rules the Taphian people of the sea."

So said Telémakhos, though in his heart
he knew his visitor had been immortal.
But now the suitors turned to play again
with dance and haunting song. They stayed till nightfall,   475
indeed black night came on them at their pleasure,
and half asleep they left, each for his home.

Telémakhos' bedroom was above the court,
a kind of tower, with a view all round;
here he retired to ponder in the silence,   480
while carrying brands of pine alight beside him
Eurýkleia* went padding, sage and old.
Her father had been Ops, Peisênor's son,
and she had been a purchase of Laërtês
when she was still a blossoming girl. He gave   485
the price of twenty oxen for her, kept her
as kindly in his house as his own wife,
though, for the sake of peace, he never touched her.
No servant loved Telémakhos as she did,
she who had nursed him in his infancy.   490
So now she held the light, as he swung open
the door of his neat freshly painted chamber.
There he sat down, pulling his tunic off,
and tossed it into the wise old woman's hands.
She folded it and smoothed it, and then hung it   495
beside the inlaid bed upon a bar;
then, drawing the door shut by its silver handle
she slid the catch in place and went away.
And all night long, wrapped in the finest fleece,
he took in thought the course Athena gave him.   500

⁴⁸² Eurýkleia: ū·rē′klē·a.

FOR DISCUSSION

1. How is Pallas Athena received when she visits Telémakhos in disguise? What does she say to stir the young man to action? How is he changed because of her visit?

2. At the council of the gods, what arguments are presented for and against releasing Odysseus? Why does Poseidon alone of all the gods oppose Odysseus' return home? How is a decision finally reached?

3. Zeus complains that men blame all evil on the gods, and gives Aigísthos as an example of a man who caused his own suffering through wrongdoing. What evidence is there in Book One that the gods do, in fact, play an important part in human affairs?

4. Odysseus does not appear at all in the first four books. How is he kept in the audience's mind? What opinion do the gods, his family, and men in general have of him? What effect does it have on our opinion of him that Homer begins his story on Mt. Olympos?

Having obtained release from Kalypso's island through the intervention of Hermes, Odysseus sails again toward home. On the way he is helped by Alkínoös, king of the Phaiakians. Book Nine is part of a flashback in which Odysseus tells the Phaiakians of his adventures in the years between the fall of Troy and his capture by Kalypso.

BOOK NINE

Now this was the reply Odysseus made:
"Alkínoös, king and admiration of men,
how beautiful this is, to hear a minstrel
gifted as yours: a god he might be, singing!
There is no boon in life more sweet, I say,   5
than when a summer joy holds all the realm,
and banqueters sit listening to a harper
in a great hall, by rows of tables heaped
with bread and roast meat, while a steward goes
to dip up wine and brim your cups again.   10
Here is the flower of life, it seems to me!
But now you wish to know my cause for sorrow—
and thereby give me cause for more.
                         What shall I
say first? What shall I keep until the end?   15
The gods have tried me in a thousand ways.
But first my name: let that be known to you,
and if I pull away from pitiless death,
friendship will bind us, though my land lies far.

I am Laërtês' son, Odysseus.   20
                 Men hold me
formidable for guile* in peace and war:
this fame has gone abroad to the sky's rim.

---

²² FORMIDABLE (for′məd·ə·bəl) FOR GUILE: well-known for craftiness.

My home is on the peaked sea-mark of Ithaka
under Mount Neion's* wind-blown robe of leaves,   25
in sight of other islands—Doulíkhion,
Samê, wooded Zakynthos—Ithaka
being most lofty in that coastal sea,
and northwest, while the rest lie east and south.
A rocky isle, but good for a boy's training;   30
I shall not see on earth a place more dear,
though I have been detained long by Kalypso,
loveliest among goddesses, who held me
in her smooth caves, to be her heart's delight,
as Kirkê of Aiaia,* the enchantress,   35
desired me, and detained me in her hall.
But in my heart I never gave consent.
Where shall a man find sweetness to surpass
his own home and his parents? In far lands
he shall not, though he find a house of gold.   40

What of my sailing, then, from Troy?
                                        What of those years
of rough adventure, weathered under Zeus?
The wind that carried west from Ilion
brought me to Îsmaros, on the far shore,   45
a strongpoint on the coast of Kikonês.*
I stormed that place and killed the men who fought.
Plunder we took, and we enslaved the women,
to make division, equal shares to all—
but on the spot I told them: 'Back, and quickly!   50
Out to sea again!' My men were mutinous,
fools, on stores of wine. Sheep after sheep
they butchered by the surf, and shambling cattle,
feasting—while fugitives went inland, running
to call to arms the main force of Kikonês.   55
This was an army, trained to fight on horseback
or, where the ground required, on foot. They came
with dawn over that terrain like the leaves
and blades of spring. So doom appeared to us,
dark word of Zeus for us, our evil days.   60
My men stood up and made a fight of it—
backed on the ships, with lances kept in play,
from bright morning through the blaze of noon
holding our beach, although so far outnumbered;

---

²⁵ Neion's: nā′ŏnz.   ³⁵ Kirkê of Aiaia: ker′kā, ī·ī′ə.   ⁴⁶ Kikonês: kē·kŏn′ās.

but when the sun passed toward unyoking time,*   65
then the Akhaians, one by one, gave way.
Six benches were left empty in every ship
that evening when we pulled away from death.
And this new grief we bore with us to sea:
our precious lives we had, but not our friends.   70
No ship made sail next day until some shipmate
had raised a cry, three times, for each poor ghost
unfleshed by the Kikonês on that field.

Now Zeus the lord of cloud roused in the north
a storm against the ships, and driving veils   75
of squall moved down like night on land and sea.
The bows went plunging at the gust; sails
cracked and lashed out strips in the big wind.
We saw death in that fury, dropped the yards,
unshipped the oars, and pulled for the nearest lee:*   80
then two long days and nights we lay offshore
worn out and sick at heart, tasting our grief,
until a third Dawn came with ringlets shining.
Then we put up our masts, hauled sail, and rested,
letting the steersmen and the breeze take over.   85

I might have made it safely home, that time,
but as I came round Malea* the current
took me out to sea, and from the north
a fresh gale drove me on, past Kythera.*
Nine days I drifted on the teeming sea   90
before dangerous high winds. Upon the tenth
we came to the coastline of the Lotus Eaters,
who lived upon that flower. We landed there
to take on water. All ships' companies
mustered alongside for the mid-day meal.   95
Then I sent out two picked men and a runner
to learn what race of men that land sustained.
They fell in, soon enough, with Lotus Eaters,
who showed no will to do us harm, only
offering the sweet Lotus to our friends—   100
but those who ate this honeyed plant, the Lotus,
never cared to report, nor to return:
they longed to stay forever, browsing on
that native bloom, forgetful of their homeland.

---

[65] UNYOKING TIME: sunset. According to Greek mythology the sun was
drawn by horses across the sky each day.   [80] LEE: shelter.   [87] MALEA:
mä·lā′ə.   [89] KYTHERA: kith′er·ə.

I drove them, all three wailing, to the ships,   105
tied them down under their rowing benches,
and called the rest: 'All hands aboard;
come, clear the beach and no one taste
the Lotus, or you lose your hope of home.'
Filing in to their places by the rowlocks   110
my oarsmen dipped their long oars in the surf,
and we moved out again on our sea faring.

In the next land we found were Kyklopês,
giants, louts, without a law to bless them.
In ignorance leaving the fruitage of the earth in mystery   115
to the immortal gods, they neither plow
nor sow by hand, nor till the ground, though grain—
wild wheat and barley—grows untended, and
wine-grapes, in clusters, ripen in heaven's rain.
Kyklopês have no muster* and no meeting,   120
no consultation or old tribal ways,
but each one dwells in his own mountain cave
dealing out rough justice to wife and child,
indifferent to what the others do.
              Well, then: 125
across the wide bay from the mainland
there lies a desert island, not far out,
but still not close inshore. Wild goats in hundreds
breed there; and no human being comes
upon the isle to startle them—no hunter   130
of all who ever tracked with hounds through forests
or had rough going over mountain trails.
The isle, unplanted and untilled, a wilderness,
pastures goats alone. And this is why:
good ships like ours with cheekpaint at the bows   135
are far beyond the Kyklopês. No shipwright
toils among them, shaping and building up
symmetrical trim hulls to cross the sea
and visit all the seaboard towns, as men do
who go and come in commerce over water.   140
This isle—seagoing folk would have annexed it
and built their homesteads on it: all good land,
fertile for every crop in season: lush
well-watered meads* along the shore, vines in profusion,
prairie, clear for the plow, where grain would grow   145
chin high by harvest time, and rich sub-soil.
The island cove is landlocked, so you need

---

[120] MUSTER: assembly.   [144] MEADS: meadows.

no hawsers* out astern, bow-stones or mooring:
run in and ride there till the day your crews
chafe to be under sail, and a fair wind blows.   150
You'll find good water flowing from a cavern
through dusky poplars into the upper bay.
Here we made harbor. Some god guided us
that night, for we could barely see our bows
in the dense fog around us, and no moonlight   155
filtered through the overcast. No look-out,
nobody saw the island dead ahead,
nor even the great landward rolling billow
that took us in: we found ourselves in shallows,
keels grazing shore: so furled our sails   160
and disembarked where the low ripples broke.
There on the beach we lay, and slept till morning.

When Dawn spread out her finger tips of rose
we turned out marveling, to tour the isle,
while Zeus's shy nymph daughters flushed wild goats   165
down from the heights—a breakfast for my men.
We ran to fetch our hunting bows and long-shanked
lances from the ships, and in three companies
we took our shots. Heaven gave us game a-plenty:
for every one of twelve ships in my squadron   170
nine goats fell to be shared; my lot was ten.
So there all day, until the sun went down,
we made our feast on meat galore, and wine—
wine from the ship, for our supply held out,
so many jars were filled at Ísmaros   175
from stores of the Kikonês that we plundered.
We gazed, too, at Kyklopês Land, so near,
we saw their smoke, heard bleating from their flocks.
But after sundown, in the gathering dusk,
we slept again above the wash of ripples.   180

¹⁴⁸ HAWSERS: ropes for securing a ship to an anchorage.

FOR DISCUSSION

1. How do the episodes with the Kikonês and the Lotus-Eaters show Odysseus' abilities as a leader? Because Homer makes no judgments about his characters, we have to learn about them through their words and actions. What else have we learned about Odysseus so far? (Note especially what he says about himself in his introduction to the Phaiakians.)

2. From the Greeks' point of view, the Kyklopês are uncivilized "ignorant louts." How do the Greeks and the Kyklopês differ in social organization, law, religion, farming, and transportation? Is there anything about the Greeks that would be considered "uncivilized" by our standards?

When the young Dawn with finger tips of rose
came in the east, I called my men together
and made a speech to them:

                   'Old shipmates, friends,
the rest of you stand by; I'll make the crossing   185
in my own ship, with my own company,
and find out what the mainland natives are—
for they may be wild savages, and lawless,
or hospitable and god fearing men.'

At this I went aboard, and gave the word   190
to cast off by the stern. My oarsmen followed,
filing in to their benches by the rowlocks,
and all in line dipped oars in the gray sea.

As we rowed on, and nearer to the mainland,
at one end of the bay, we saw a cavern   195
yawning above the water, screened with laurel,
and many rams and goats about the place
inside a sheepfold—made from slabs of stone
earthfast between tall trunks of pine and rugged
towering oak trees.   200

                  A prodigious* man
slept in this cave alone and took his flocks
to graze afield—remote from all companions,
knowing none but savage ways, a brute
so huge, he seemed no man at all of those   205
who eat good wheaten bread,* but he seemed rather
a shaggy mountain reared in solitude.
We beached there, and I told the crew
to stand by and keep watch over the ship;
as for myself I took my twelve best fighters   210
and went ahead. I had a goatskin full
of that sweet liquor that Euanthês'* son,
Maron, had given me. He kept Apollo's
holy grove at Ismaros; for kindness
we showed him there, and showed his wife and child,   215
he gave me seven shining golden talents*
perfectly formed, a solid silver winebowl,
and then this liquor—twelve two-handled jars
of brandy, pure and fiery. Not a slave
in Maron's household knew this drink; only   220

---

[201] PRODIGIOUS (prə·dij′əs): monstrous. [205–206] SO HUGE . . . BREAD: so large
that he was not like ordinary human beings. [212] EUANTHÊS': yü·än′thäs.
[216] TALENTS: coins of great value.

he, his wife and the storeroom mistress knew;
and they would put one cupful—ruby-colored,
honey-smooth—in twenty more of water,
but still the sweet scent hovered like a fume
over the winebowl. No man turned away   225
when cups of this came round.
                    A wineskin full
I brought along, and victuals in a bag,
for in my bones I knew some towering brute
would be upon us soon—all outward power,   230
a wild man, ignorant of civility.

We climbed, then, briskly to the cave. But Kyklops
had gone afield, to pasture his fat sheep,
so we looked round at everything inside:
a drying rack that sagged with cheeses, pens   235
crowded with lambs and kids, each in its class:
firstlings apart from middlings, and the "dewdrops,"
or newborn lambkins, penned apart from both.
And vessels full of whey were brimming there—
bowls of earthenware and pails for milking.   240
My men came pressing round me, pleading:
                       'Why not
take these cheeses, get them stowed, come back,
throw open all the pens, and make a run for it?
We'll drive the kids and lambs aboard. We say   245
put out again on good salt water!'
                      Ah,
how sound that was! Yet I refused. I wished
to see the caveman, what he had to offer—
no pretty sight, it turned out, for my friends.   250
We lit a fire, burnt an offering,
and took some cheese to eat; then sat in silence
around the embers, waiting. When he came
he had a load of dry boughs on his shoulder
to stoke his fire at suppertime. He dumped it   255
with a great crash into that hollow cave,
and we all scattered fast to the far wall.

Then over the broad cavern floor he ushered
the ewes he meant to milk. He left his rams
and he-goats in the yard outside, and swung   260
high overhead a slab of solid rock
to close the cave. Two dozen four-wheeled wagons,
with heaving wagon teams, could not have stirred

Continued on page 522

IDEAS AND THE ARTS

For twenty-five hundred years generation after generation has been fascinated by the two great narratives by the man we know as Homer. We do not know who Homer was. We do not really know if there was a Homer. We do not know if the *Iliad* and the *Odyssey* were written by one man, by two, or by more. It may be that they were written by a number of men and were put together by one or more of them.

For the ordinary reader, however, each poem hangs together so well that there seems little point in worrying about how they were written. Moreover, the two poems complement each other so neatly that they ought to have been written by one man. They seem to go together like salt and pepper or bread and butter. The reason for this feeling is that the two poems taken together seem to cover the major parts of human life.

The sense of completeness requires that the themes of both poems be taken together. The *Iliad* is a poem of concentration; the *Odyssey* is a poem of expansion. The *Iliad* is a poem of struggle and of conflict between men and groups of men. Although there is struggle in the *Odyssey*, it is essentially the story of a man who is trying to get home again. The *Iliad* is like a great wave that crests in foam and crashes. The *Odyssey* is like a river that finds its way to the sea.

The *Iliad* reflects a major aspect of our lives. Although we do not live on the battlefield as Homer's warriors did, conflict and struggle between men and groups of men is the daily substance of our lives. Even to drive an automobile on our busy streets is a kind of Homeric heroism. But in the *Iliad* the reason for the war is almost forgotten. Nobody seems to care about it one way or the other. It seems that struggle and conflict are important for their own sakes. The *Iliad* reminded a great German poet of hell, because he found no purpose in the struggle. Whatever purpose there seemed to be appeared trivial, even silly.

In everyday life the struggle and conflict are so endless that we often wonder whether or not there is any purpose in our efforts. We go to work or to school, struggle with problems and strive to overcome obstacles and resolve conflicts. We come home and then the next day we do the same thing all over again. Unless we have a goal clearly in mind, it is not surprising that we sometimes wonder what we are doing and why we are doing it. Everyone, from time to time, feels that he is living the life of the *Iliad.*

After the nightmare of the *Iliad,* the *Odyssey* comes as a relief, because it is a poem about a purpose. In all kinds of games, children's games and baseball, the purpose of the players is to get home safe. These games never lose their appeal because instead of pointless struggle they give the players the opportunity to experience purposeful activity. The *Odyssey* reflects that kind of experience.

The *Iliad* reflects the experience of purposelessness. But that is only half the story. The other half is the conviction that one's life has purpose. It is the feeling that one is going "home." In the *Odyssey* the purposeful effort to get home is half the story. The other half is to have other people recognize that Odysseus has gotten home. The poem is saying that to be satisfying our life must have a purpose and that purpose and its achievement must be acknowledged by other people. "Home" is a place where you feel you belong. To have a purpose gives the conviction that we belong in this life and in this world.

Morse Peckham

ART

The following paintings are some examples of the ways in which Homer's poems, the *Iliad* and the *Odyssey,* have captured the imaginations of artists.

Aristotle Contemplating the Bust of Homer was painted by the great Dutch painter Rembrandt. It shows Aristotle not in ancient Greek costume but in clothing of the seventeenth century. In this way Rembrandt wishes to indicate the timelessness of both Aristotle and Homer. Aristotle was a great Greek philosopher, one of the greatest philosophers who has ever lived. He wished to create a clear picture of human life by explaining it in rational and understandable principles. The poet Homer had shown life in all its conflicts, confusions, and suffering. By presenting his figures as he does, Rembrandt suggests that Aristotle feels his vision of human life is less significant.

The Apotheosis of Homer, by the nineteenth-century French painter Jean Ingres presents a different kind of tribute. It celebrates the public recognition of a man of genius by other men of genius, or the greatest artistic genius by men who acknowledge that he is greater than they are. *Apotheosis* means "ascent to God." Here it means ascent to the highest level of artistic greatness. The figure crowning Homer is not a heavenly angel. It is the Greek goddess of Victory, always shown with wings to show that she is a divine messenger. At Homer's feet at the left a figure with a sword stands for the *Iliad.* At the right a figure with an oar stands for the *Odyssey.* The figures standing in the middle are from the ancient world of Greece and Rome, except for Raphael who stands fourth from the left. In the foreground at the foot of the steps are figures from the modern world. Shakespeare is at the extreme left.

Long before Ingres painted this picture a Greek sculptor of the second century B.C. had used the same subject. He was Archelaos of Priene. His bas relief was found during the seventeenth century in a little town south of Rome. It is quite probable that Ingres saw it when he studied in Rome early in the nineteenth century. Homer is seated at the bottom on the left with figures from the *Iliad* and the *Odyssey* beside him, as in Ingres' painting. Before him various figures are worshiping his memory. From left to right these are Myth, History, Poetry, and Tragedy and Comedy. Above is Mount Helicon, the home of the Muses. These Muses are the goddesses who inspire the artistic and intellectual activities of man. Their leader is Apollo, who is shown with a lyre. At the top is Zeus gazing at Memory (or Mnemosyne), the mother of the Muses. The idea of this work is that Homer, the greatest of poets, is under the protection of Zeus, the chief of the Gods, and of Apollo and the Muses.

The next painting shows one of the most powerful and moving passages in the *Iliad.* It is *Priam Pleading with Achilles for the Body of Hector,* by the eighteenth-century English painter Gavin Hamilton. This is one of the great moments of the *Iliad.* It reveals both the passion and the suffering of war and the way man can rise above his passions and suffering to a higher level of compassion. Hector, the Trojan hero, had killed Patroclus, Achilleus' closest friend. In great anger Achilleus then killed Hector and dragged his body behind his chariot back to the Greek camp. Hector's father, King Priam of Troy, comes secretly at night to the enemy camp to beg for the body of his son. Achilleus is moved by Priam's plea and consents to the return of the body. But he insists that the body be kept covered, for if he looks upon it his anger might once again be aroused.

The next two paintings refer to episodes in the *Odyssey*. The first is *Ulysses Deriding Polyphemus* by J. M. W. Turner, the great English painter of the nineteenth century. (*Ulysses* is the Latin name for Odysseus.) Polyphemus was a one-eyed giant, a son of the sea god Poseidon. He lived in a cave and kept a flock of sheep. While wandering in search of food Ulysses entered the cave with some of his companions. Polyphemus discovered them eating his cheeses. He blocked the entrance with a great rock and proceeded to eat several of Ulysses' men. Ulysses and those remaining got him drunk and put out his single eye. Then they escaped back to their ship. As they set sail Ulysses derided Polyphemus, shouting scornful remarks at him, and Polyphemus threw huge rocks at them. Turner has painted their escape in this glowing picture.

The next painting is by Dosso Dossi, a sixteenth-century Italian. Entitled *Circe,* the painting depicts Kirke (Circe is the Latin form), the sorceress who drugged Odysseus' men. Odysseus himself was protected by the god Hermes. The painting shows Circe in an oriental costume, brandishing a wand in fire. On the right we see a dog and some birds (probably representing men she has formerly transformed) and empty armor. The quality is poetic and magical, even enchanted. Dossi has definitely shown her as Circe the sorceress. She even holds a tablet with formulas on it (undoubtedly magical formulas). Miniature men appear in a tree to the left, and they may represent the souls of transformed men.

Morse Peckham

REMBRANDT VAN RIJN (1606-1669) *ARISTOTLE CONTEMPLATING THE BUST OF HOMER.* Metropolitan Museum of Art, New York.

JEAN AUGUSTE DOMINIQUE INGRES (1780-1867) *THE APOTHEOSIS OF HOMER.* Musée du Louvre.

Photo: Telarci-Giraudon

ARCHELAOS OF PRIENE (2nd century B.C.) *THE APOTHEOSIS OF HOMER*. British Museum, London.

517

518

JOSEPH MALLORD WILLIAM TURNER (1775-1851) *ULYSSES DERIDING POLYPHEMUS*. National Gallery, London.

DOSSO DOSSI (c.1490-1542) *CIRCE.* Borghese Gallery, Rome.

MUSIC

FRANZ LISZT:
LES PRÉLUDES
[A number of recordings available]

The *Iliad* and the *Odyssey* present two quite different ways of understanding human experience. In the *Iliad,* the warriors of Greece and Troy seem to be driven by forces they do not understand. Everyone seems to be trapped into actions they do not want to be involved in. The main story has to do with the anger of Achilleus, and he himself is helpless before the violence of his emotions. The poem ends only when his angry emotions have died away. Achilleus and the other warriors act without a clear purpose in a war over an unworthy cause.

The idea that human life has no clear purpose explains a great deal about human behavior. But it does not explain everything. It is at best only a half truth. The *Odyssey* gives the other half. Odysseus is always referred to as the "wise Odysseus." He has a purpose and he has a goal. His goal is his home, and his purpose is to get there. The story of the *Odyssey* suggests that human life has meaning because it has a purpose.

Like a great many other stories, the *Odyssey* illustrates the theme of the quest. Such stories about seeking for something are found all over the world. Sometimes the search is for treasure, as in *Treasure Island,* by Robert Louis Stevenson. In the Middle Ages a very popular story was the search, or quest, for the Holy Grail, the cup from which Jesus was supposed to have drunk at his crucifixion. The important thing about the *Odyssey* is not that Odysseus' goal is to get home; the important thing is that he had a purpose.

The sense of having or not having a purpose in our lives creates certain feelings within us. It is probably true that we cannot be happy unless we feel that our lives have purpose. But it is also true that we need relief from that feeling. We need vacations from always directing our actions toward some specific goal. At the same time, if we are too long without a purpose, we often become depressed and miserable. We must then find a purpose to restore our feelings.

Long ago a great philosopher said that the upward motion of musical melody means an expression of the will, which is another way of talking about purpose. He was probably right. Thus when the melody moves downward, the music says that the will or purpose is being defeated or is being given up. When music hovers and wanders around a single note, aimlessness or purposelessness is being expressed. This expression can be happy or not, satisfactory or not.

Liszt's *Les Préludes* is a piece of music that expresses our feelings about human experiences. It consists of five easily distinguishable sections. It begins with the birth or creation of purpose. There is a struggle to achieve that purpose, and then the purpose is given up. The second section is without effort and tension. It is a vacation, a rest. In the next section the struggle is renewed, this time with greater violence and energy. Then once again the music turns to rest and recovery, to simple aimless happiness. Finally, the struggle is begun once more, and this time it is successful. The music ends in triumph; the goal is achieved; the purpose is fulfilled. Throughout the course of the music the opening theme is heard again and again. That theme is a great musical statement of the sense of purpose.

Morse Peckham

the tonnage of that rock from where he wedged it
over the doorsill. Next he took his seat   265
and milked his bleating ewes. A practiced job
he made of it, giving each ewe her suckling;
thickened his milk, then, into curds and whey,
sieved out the curds to drip in withy* baskets,
and poured the whey to stand in bowls   270
cooling until he drank it for his supper.
When all these chores were done, he poked the fire,
heaping on brushwood. In the glare he saw us.

'Strangers,' he said, 'who are you? And where from?
What brings you here by sea ways—a fair traffic?   275
Or are you wandering rogues, who cast your lives
like dice, and ravage other folk by sea?'

We felt a pressure on our hearts, in dread
of that deep rumble and that mighty man.
But all the same I spoke up in reply: 280

'We are from Troy, Akhaians, blown off course
by shifting gales on the Great South Sea;
homeward bound, but taking routes and ways
uncommon; so the will of Zeus would have it.
We served under Agamémnon,* son of Atreus—   285
the whole world knows what city
he laid waste, what armies he destroyed.
It was our luck to come here; here we stand,
beholden for* your help, or any gifts
you give—as custom is to honor strangers.   290
We would entreat you, great Sir, have a care
for the gods' courtesy; Zeus will avenge
the unoffending guest.'
                                He answered this
from his brute chest, unmoved: 295
                                'You are a ninny,
or else you come from the other end of nowhere,
telling me, mind the gods! We Kyklopês
care not a whistle for your thundering Zeus
or all the gods in bliss; we have more force by far.   300
I would not let you go for fear of Zeus—
you or your friends—unless I had a whim to.
Tell me, where was it, now, you left your ship—

---

269 WITHY: willow.   285 AGAMÉMNON (ä′gä·mem′nōn): leader of the Greeks
against Troy.   289 BEHOLDEN FOR: dependent on.

around the point, or down the shore, I wonder?'

He thought he'd find out, but I saw through this,   305
and answered with a ready lie:
                                    'My ship?
Poseidon Lord, who sets the earth a-tremble,
broke it up on the rocks at your land's end.
A wind from seaward served him, drove us there.   310
We are survivors, these good men and I.'

Neither reply nor pity came from him,
but in one stride he clutched at my companions
and caught two in his hands like squirming puppies
to beat their brains out, spattering the floor.   315
Then he dismembered them and made his meal,
gaping and crunching like a mountain lion—
everything: innards, flesh, and marrow bones.
We cried aloud, lifting our hands to Zeus,
powerless, looking on at this, appalled;   320
but Kyklops went on filling up his belly
with manflesh and great gulps of whey,
then lay down like a mast among his sheep.
My heart beat high now at the chance of action,
and drawing the sharp sword from my hip I went   325
along his flank to stab him where the midriff
holds the liver. I had touched the spot
when sudden fear stayed me: if I killed him
we perished there as well, for we could never
move his ponderous doorway slab aside.   330
So we were left to groan and wait for morning.

When the young Dawn with finger tips of rose
lit up the world, the Kyklops built a fire
and milked his handsome ewes, all in due order,
putting the sucklings to the mothers. Then,   335
his chores being all dispatched, he caught
another brace of men to make his breakfast,
and whisked away his great door slab
to let his sheep go through—but he, behind,
reset the stone as one would cap a quiver.   340
There was a din of whistling as the Kyklops
rounded his flock to higher ground, then stillness.
And now I pondered how to hurt him worst,
if but Athena granted what I prayed for.
Here are the means I thought would serve my turn: 345

a club, or staff, lay there along the fold—
an olive tree, felled green and left to season
for Kyklops' hand. And it was like a mast
a lugger of twenty oars, broad in the beam—
a deep-sea-going craft—might carry: 350
so long, so big around, it seemed. Now I
chopped out a six foot section of this pole
and set it down before my men, who scraped it;
and when they had it smooth, I hewed again
to make a stake with pointed end. I held this   355
in the fire's heart and turned it, toughening it,
then hid it, well back in the cavern, under
one of the dung piles in profusion there.
Now came the time to toss for it: who ventured
along with me? whose hand could bear to thrust   360
and grind that spike in Kyklops' eye, when mild
sleep had mastered him? As luck would have it,
the men I would have chosen won the toss—
four strong men, and I made five as captain.

At evening came the shepherd with his flock,   365
his woolly flock. The rams as well, this time,
entered the cave: by some sheep-herding whim—
or a god's bidding—none were left outside.
He hefted his great boulder into place
and sat him down to milk the bleating ewes   370
in proper order, put the lambs to suck,
and swiftly ran through all his evening chores.
Then he caught two more men and feasted on them.
My moment was at hand, and I went forward
holding an ivy bowl of my dark drink,   375
looking up, saying:
                    'Kyklops, try some wine.
Here's liquor to wash down your scraps of men.
Taste it, and see the kind of drink we carried
under our planks. I meant it for an offering   380
if you would help us home. But you are mad,
unbearable, a bloody monster! After this,
will any other traveler come to see you?'

He seized and drained the bowl, and it went down
so fiery and smooth he called for more: 385

'Give me another, thank you kindly. Tell me,
how are you called? I'll make a gift will please you.
Even Kyklopês know the wine-grapes grow

out of grassland and loam in heaven's rain,
but here's a bit of nectar and ambrosia!'*   390

Three bowls I brought him, and he poured them down.
I saw the fuddle and flush come over him,
then I sang out in cordial tones:
                              'Kyklops,
you ask my honorable name? Remember   395
the gift you promised me, and I shall tell you.
My name is Nohbdy: mother, father, and friends,
everyone calls me Nohbdy.'
                              And he said:
'Nohbdy's my meat, then, after I eat his friends.   400
Others come first. There's a noble gift, now.'

Even as he spoke, he reeled and tumbled backward,
his great head lolling to one side; and sleep
took him like any creature. Drunk, hiccuping,
he dribbled streams of liquor and bits of men.   405

Now, by the gods, I drove my big hand spike
deep in the embers, charring it again,
and cheered my men along with battle talk
to keep their courage up: no quitting now.
The pike of olive, green though it had been,   410
reddened and glowed as if about to catch.
I drew it from the coals and my four fellows
gave me a hand, lugging it near the Kyklops
as more than natural force nerved them; straight
forward they sprinted, lifted it, and rammed it   415
deep in his crater eye, and I leaned on it
turning it as a shipwright turns a drill
in planking, having men below to swing
the two-handled strap that spins it in the groove.
So with our brand we bored that great eye socket   420
while blood ran out around the red hot bar.
Eyelid and lash were seared; the pierced ball
hissed broiling, and the roots popped.
                              In a smithy
one sees a white-hot axehead or an adze   425
plunged and wrung in a cold tub, screeching steam—
the way they make soft iron hale and hard—:
just so that eyeball hissed around the spike.

390 NECTAR AND AMBROSIA: the drink and food of the gods.

The Kyklops bellowed and the rock roared round him,
and we fell back in fear. Clawing his face   430
he tugged the bloody spike out of his eye,
threw it away, and his wild hands went groping;
then he set up a howl for Kyklopês
who lived in caves on windy peaks nearby.
Some heard him; and they came by divers ways   435
to clump around outside and call:
                                    'What ails you,
Polyphêmos? Why do you cry so sore
in the starry night? You will not let us sleep.
Sure no man's driving off your flock? No man   440
has tricked you, ruined you?'
                                    Out of the cave
the mammoth Polyphêmos roared in answer:
'Nohbdy, Nohbdy's tricked me, Nohbdy's ruined me!'

To this rough shout they made a sage reply: 445
'Ah well, if nobody has played you foul
there in your lonely bed, we are no use in pain
given by great Zeus. Let it be your father,
Poseidon Lord, to whom you pray.'
                                    So saying   450
they trailed away. And I was filled with laughter
to see how like a charm the name deceived them.
Now Kyklops, wheezing as the pain came on him,
fumbled to wrench away the great doorstone
and squatted in the breach with arms thrown wide   455
for any silly beast or man who bolted—
hoping somehow I might be such a fool.
But I kept thinking how to win the game:
death sat there huge; how could we slip away?
I drew on all my wits, and ran through tactics,   460
reasoning as a man will for dear life,
until a trick came—and it pleased me well.
The Kyklops' rams were handsome, fat, with heavy
fleeces, a dark violet.
                                    Three abreast   465
I tied them silently together, twining
cords of willow from the ogre's bed;
then slung a man under each middle one
to ride there safely, shielded left and right.
So three sheep could convey each man. I took   470
the woolliest ram, the choicest of the flock,
and hung myself under his kinky belly,
pulled up tight, with fingers twisted deep

in sheepskin ringlets for an iron grip.
So, breathing hard, we waited until morning.   475

When Dawn spread out her finger tips of rose
the rams began to stir, moving for pasture,
and peals of bleating echoed round the pens
where dams with udders full called for a milking.
Blinded, and sick with pain from his head wound,   480
the master stroked each ram, then let it pass,
but my men riding on the pectoral* fleece
the giant's blind hands blundering never found.
Last of them all my ram, the leader, came,
weighted by wool and me with my meditations.   485
The Kyklops patted him, and then he said:

'Sweet cousin ram, why lag behind the rest
in the night cave? You never linger so,
but graze before them all, and go afar
to crop sweet grass, and take your stately way   490
leading along the streams, until at evening
you run to be the first one in the fold.
Why, now, so far behind? Can you be grieving
over your Master's eye? That carrion* rogue
and his accurst companions burnt it out   495
when he had conquered all my wits with wine.
Nohbdy will not get out alive, I swear.
Oh, had you brain and voice to tell
where he may be now, dodging all my fury!
Bashed by this hand and bashed on this rock wall   500
his brains would strew the floor, and I should have
rest from the outrage Nohbdy worked upon me.'
He sent us into the open, then. Close by,
I dropped and rolled clear of the ram's belly,
going this way and that to untie the men.   505
With many glances back, we rounded up
his fat, stiff-legged sheep to take aboard,
and drove them down to where the good ship lay.
We saw, as we came near, our fellows' faces
shining; then we saw them turn to grief   510
tallying those who had not fled from death.
I hushed them, jerking head and eyebrows up,
and in a low voice told them: 'Load this herd;
move fast, and put the ships' head toward the breakers.'
They all pitched in at loading, then embarked   515

482 PECTORAL: of the chest.   494 CARRION: rotten.

and struck their oars into the sea. Far out,
as far off shore as shouted words would carry,
I sent a few back to the adversary:

'O Kyklops! Would you feast on my companions?
Puny, am I, in a Caveman's hands?   520
How do you like the beating that we gave you,
you damned cannibal? Eater of guests
under your roof! Zeus and the gods have paid you!'

The blind thing in his doubled fury broke
a hilltop in his hands and heaved it after us.   525
Ahead of our black prow it struck and sank
whelmed in a spuming geyser, a giant wave
that washed the ship stern foremost back to shore.
I got the longest boathook out and stood
fending us off, with furious nods to all   530
to put their backs into a racing stroke—
row, row, or perish. So the long oars bent
kicking the foam sternward, making head
until we drew away, and twice as far.
Now when I cupped my hands I heard the crew   535
in low voices protesting:
                          'Godsake, Captain!
Why bait the beast again? Let him alone!'
'That tidal wave he made on the first throw
all but beached us.'   540
                'All but stove us in!'
'Give him our bearing with your trumpeting,
he'll get the range and lob a boulder.'
                              'Aye
He'll smash our timbers and our heads together!'   545

I would not heed them in my glorying spirit,
but let my anger flare and yelled:
                          'Kyklops,
if ever mortal man inquire
how you were put to shame and blinded, tell him   550
Odysseus, raider of cities, took your eye:
Laërtês' son, whose home's on Ithaka!'

At this he gave a mighty sob and rumbled:
'Now comes the weird* upon me, spoken of old.
A wizard, grand and wondrous, lived here—Télemos,*   555

---

⁵⁵⁴ WEIRD: disastrous fate.   ⁵⁵⁵ TELEMOS: tel'ə·mos.

a son of Eurymos; great length of days
he had in wizardry among the Kyklopês,
and these things he foretold for time to come:
my great eye lost, and at Odysseus' hands.
Always I had in mind some giant, armed   560
in giant force, would come against me here.
But this, but you—small, pitiful and twiggy—
you put me down with wine, you blinded me.
Come back, Odysseus, and I'll treat you well,
praying the god of earthquake to befriend you—   565
his son I am, for he by his avowal
fathered me, and, if he will, he may
heal me of this black wound—he and no other
of all the happy gods or mortal men.'

Few words I shouted in reply to him: 570
'If I could take your life I would and take
your time away, and hurl you down to hell!
The god of earthquake could not heal you there!'

At this he stretched his hands out in his darkness
toward the sky of stars, and prayed Poseidon: 575

'O hear me, lord, blue girdler of the islands,
if I am thine indeed, and thou art father:
grant that Odysseus, raider of cities, never
see his home: Laërtês' son, I mean,
who kept his hall on Ithaka. Should destiny   580
intend that he shall see his roof again
among his family in his father land,
far be that day, and dark the years between.
Let him lose all companions, and return
under strange sail to bitter days at home.'   585

In these words he prayed, and the god heard him.
Now he laid hands upon a bigger stone
and wheeled around, titanic for the cast,*
to let it fly in the back-prowed vessel's track.
But it fell short, just aft the steering oar,   590
and whelming seas rose giant above the stone
to bear us onward toward the island.
                                    There
as we ran in we saw the squadron waiting,
the trim ships drawn up side by side, and all   595
our troubled friends who waited, looking seaward.

588 TITANIC . . . CAST: gigantic . . . throw.

We beached her, grinding keel in the soft sand,
and waded in, ourselves, on the sandy beach.
Then we unloaded all the Kyklops' flock
to make division, share and share alike,   600
only my fighters voted that my ram,
the prize of all, should go to me. I slew him
by the sea side and burnt his long thighbones
to Zeus beyond the stormcloud, Kronos' son,
who rules the world. But Zeus disdained my offering;   605
destruction for my ships he had in store
and death for those who sailed them, my companions.
Now all day long until the sun went down
we made our feast on mutton and sweet wine,
till after sunset in the gathering dark   610
we went to sleep above the wash of ripples.

When the young Dawn with finger tips of rose
touched the world, I roused the men, gave orders
to ma.. the ships, cast off the mooring lines;
and filing in to sit beside the rowlocks   615
oarsmen in line dipped oars in the gray sea.
So we moved out, sad in the vast offing,
having our precious lives, but not our friends.

FOR DISCUSSION

1. Kyklops declares that his people "care not a whistle" for the gods, yet he himself prays to Poseidon, god of the sea and of earthquakes, to curse Odysseus. From what you learned in Book One, is the curse effective? How else do the characters attempt to persuade the gods to help them?

2. Which details of the Greeks' stay in Kyklops' cave were most horrible to you? What comparisons does Homer use to describe the enormous size and strength of the giant?

3. Review the tricks Odysseus uses to outwit Kyklops. What does he gain by calling himself "nohbdy"?

4. Homer's characters, legendary though they may be, are individuals with human weaknesses and contradictions. In the first part of Book Nine Odysseus shows prudence and self-control; then in the episode with Kyklops he ignores his men's good advice several times. What other traits in him overrule his judgment? To what extent is he responsible for the loss of his men?

5. Memorizing a poem as long as the *Odyssey* was an enormous task. To simplify it, poets often repeated phrases such as "the wine-dark sea" and "Zeus, lord of clouds." There was pleasure for the audience, too, in recognizing familiar lines, especially since the poems were recited in installments rather than all at one sitting. What other repetitions have you noticed?

In Summary

FOR DISCUSSION

1. Odysseus was one of the greatest heroes of Greek literature. Judging from what others say about him in the story, what qualities in him were most admired? What were the abilities that set him above ordinary men? What, on the other hand, made him only a "godlike" hero and not a god?

2. Is there any equivalent of the epic hero in our time? How have our heroic ideals changed since Homer's time?

3. A great deal can be learned about ancient Greek religion from reading even a small part of the *Odyssey*. What was the relation of the Greek gods to each other? What was their relation to man and nature? Were there any limits on their powers? Was their function ethical (to encourage rightdoing and punish evil), or were they interested mostly in their own power and prestige?

4. Penélopê was considered an ideal wife. Judging from her actions, and from what we see of other women in the story, what were the standards by which women were judged in ancient Greek times? How have these standards changed in the nearly three thousand years since then?

OTHER THINGS TO DO

1. Read the rest of the *Odyssey*. Choose a scene that you enjoy to read or summarize for the class.

2. Draw a map showing Odysseus' stops between Troy and Ithaka. What are the modern equivalents of these places? This could effectively be presented to the class on an overhead projector transparency.

3. Make a model of Odysseus' ship, explaining how it was propelled. What types of ships preceded and followed it in history?

4. Illustrate any two scenes from the *Odyssey*. You will have to do some research into costumes, architecture, weapons, etc., first.

5. Myths and legends are often told briefly, giving only the main action and leaving characterization, dialogue and other details to the reader's imagination. Homer put much of this "flesh" on the bones of the Odysseus legend in his retelling. Try doing the same thing for one of the Greek myths or a part of the Odysseus legend that could be told in more detail. Some possibilities are:

a. Present the story in dramatic form. Start with the basic characters and situation, then improvise.
b. Tell it in comic book form.
c. Write it as a short story.
d. Present it as a puppet show for a younger audience.

The World of Words

THE ODYSSEY

1. The word *odyssey* comes from the name of Homer's hero Odysseus. Used in the title of Homer's epic, it means "the story of Odysseus." (The name sometimes appears in its Latin form Ulysses.) The word *odyssey*, however, is not limited to its use as the title of Homer's epic. It is used in various ways today. What does the word mean today? Give examples in which it is used.

2. In the opening lines of his poem, Homer asks the Muse to help him tell the story of Odysseus. The word *Muse* comes from Greek mythology. It refers to any of the nine daughters of Zeus and Mnemosyne, the goddess of memory. Each daughter, or Muse, represents some aspect of art or science. The nine daughters are Calliope, Clio, Erata, Euterpe, Melpomene, Polyhymnia, Terpsichore, Thalia, and Urania. What aspect of art or science does each of these Muses represent? Which of the Muses would be especially helpful to Homer? The word *museum* comes from a Greek word meaning "place of the Muses." Is this meaning appropriate today? Why or why not?

3. *Calliope* is the name of one of the Muses in Greek mythology, but the word *calliope* is also used in a different way today. What does the word *calliope* refer to? In Homer's poem we find the name *Kalypso*, referring to the sea nymph who delayed Odysseus on her island. It is spelled in this way to bring it as close as possible to its Greek form, but it also appears as *Calypso*, which follows its form in Latin. It also appears in English as the word *calypso*. What does *calypso* refer to? *Kyklops* is the name of a one-eyed giant who tries to destroy Odysseus and his men in Book Nine. The more familiar form of the name is *Cyclops*, and from *Cyclops* we get the word *cyclopean*. What does it mean? How does it relate to *Cyclops*?

Reader's Choice

Gods, Graves and Scholars, *by C. W. Ceram.*

Archeologists who have excavated ancient cities, Troy among them, provide fascinating insights into daily life in the times of Odysseus.

The Hobbit and The Lord of the Rings, *by J. R. R. Tolkien.*

Tolkien creates a world called Middle-earth inhabited by dwarfs, goblins, elves, and other mythical creatures. One of them, a hobbit, is caught up in the quest to save the Ring of Power from the forces of evil that would use it to control the world. The adventure and suspense of these books made them classics.

The Incredible Journey, *by Sheila Burnford.*

The heroes in this odyssey are a Labrador retriever, a bull terrier, and a Siamese cat. Separated from their human owners, they set out on a journey through the Canadian wilderness to find their family hundreds of miles away.

Mythology, *by Edith Hamilton.*

Here, retold in an easily readable style, are the stories of all the Greek gods and heroes, including the Trojan war and the wanderings of Odysseus. Selections from Norse mythology offer interesting comparisons with Greek and Roman beliefs.

2001: A Space Odyssey, *by Arthur C. Clarke.*

A mysterious voyage to the planet Jupiter raises provocative questions about the history and future of man and his relation to other forms of intelligence in the universe. "It occurred to us," said Stanley Kubrick who filmed the book, "that for the Greeks the vast stretches of the sea must have had the same sort of mystery and remoteness that space has for our generation, and that the far-flung islands of Homer's wonderful characters visited were no less remote to them than the planets our spacemen will soon be landing on are to us."

"Ulysses" and "The Lotus-Eaters", *by Alfred, Lord Tennyson.*

These two poems give another poet's interpretation of part of the legend of Odysseus. One describes the sweet seductions of the lotus flowers that held Odysseus' men; the other imagines Odysseus as an old man, restless to be at sea again.

Words from the Myths, *by Isaac Asimov.*

Mr. Asimov explores the Greek myths and legends, emphasizing our many everyday words that come from them.

THE NOVEL

A NOVEL TELLS a fictional story in prose and at some length. Because of the length—longer than what can usually be read at a single sitting—the novel lets us get to know well whatever world and people it describes. Mark Twain's *A Connecticut Yankee at King Arthur's Court* is a novel that included two worlds thirteen hundred years apart, so that before it is finished, we have come to understand, better than we did before, both worlds—of the distant past and of Mark Twain's present—and our own world better as well.

The novel turns on one of man's recurring dreams. All of us have longed on occasion to transcend time: to be put forward or backward in time by means of some machine or magician's wand (always provided we could return to the present at will). Suppose we could walk for one day in Rome's forum at the height of its splendor, see Caesar alive at the capitol. Suppose we could witness an opening performance of one of Shakespeare's great plays at the Globe Theater some spring afternoon in seventeenth-century London, with the playwright himself taking one of the roles. Or suppose we could be in the crowd at the dedicatory ceremony at Gettysburg and see the President rise and give his little talk, hearing his high-pitched voice through those few, irrecoverable moments of time.

In answering that dream through his novel, Mark Twain has transported backward, to King Arthur's court in sixth-century Britain, a nineteenth-century mechanic from Hartford, Connecticut. But knowledge is power: bearing the knowledge of the present into the past could make anyone the most powerful man alive on earth. The question then would be: how should he use that power?

Philip McFarland

*What effect will a nineteenth-century Yankee with a head full of "new-fangled
inventions" have on the sixth-century court of King Arthur? Mark Twain saw
all of the comic possibilities in this situation and developed them to their fullest.
He also saw his chance to attack the foolishness and inhumanity of medieval
and modern man. This combination of a serious message in an imaginative and
humorous story makes his novel a* satire, *bitter medicine with a sugar coating.*

A CONNECTICUT YANKEE AT KING ARTHUR'S COURT

MARK TWAIN

A WORD OF EXPLANATION

IT WAS in Warwick Castle that I came across the curious stranger whom I am going to talk about. He attracted me by three things: his candid simplicity, his marvelous familiarity with ancient armor, and the restfulness of his company—for he did all the talking. We fell together, as modest people will, in the tail of the herd that was being shown through, and he at once began to say things which interested me. As he talked along, softly, pleasantly, flowingly, he seemed to drift away imperceptibly out of this world and time, and into some remote era and old forgotten country; and so he gradually wove such a spell about me that I seemed to move among the specters and shadows and dust and mold of a gray antiquity, holding speech with a relic of it! Exactly as I would speak of my nearest personal friends or enemies, or my most familiar neighbors, he spoke of Sir Bedivere, Sir Bors de Ganis, Sir Launcelot of the Lake, Sir Galahad, and all the other great names

of the Table Round—and how old, old, unspeakably old and faded and dry and musty and ancient he came to look as he went on! Presently he turned to me and said, just as one might speak of the weather or any other common matter—

"You know about transmigration of souls; do you know about transposition of epochs—and bodies?"

I said I had not heard of it. He was so little interested—just as when people speak of the weather—that he did not notice whether I made him any answer or not. There was half a moment of silence, immediately interrupted by the droning voice of the salaried cicerone.

"Ancient hauberk, date of the sixth century, time of King Arthur and the Round Table; said to have belonged to the knight Sir Sagramore le Desirous; observe the round hole through the chain-mail in the left breast; can't be accounted for; supposed to have been done with a bullet since invention of firearms—perhaps maliciously by Cromwell's soldiers."

My acquaintance smiled—not a modern smile, but one that must have gone out of

Chapters 1–18, 27–30, 34–44 *A Connecticut Yankee at King Arthur's Court* by Mark Twain. Reprinted by permission of Harper & Row, Publishers, Incorporated.

538

general use many, many centuries ago—and muttered apparently to himself:

"Wit ye well, *I saw it done.*" Then, after a pause, added: "I did it myself."

By the time I had recovered from the electric surprise of this remark, he was gone.

All that evening I sat by my fire at the Warwick Arms, steeped in a dream of the olden time, while the rain beat upon the windows, and the wind roared about the eaves and corners. From time to time I dipped into old Sir Thomas Malory's enchanting book and fed at its rich feast of prodigies and adventures, breathed in the fragrance of its obsolete names, and dreamed again. Midnight being come at length, I read another tale, for a nightcap —this which here follows, to wit:

HOW SIR LAUNCELOT SLEW TWO GIANTS, AND MADE A CASTLE FREE

Anon withal came there upon him two great giants, well armed, all save the heads, with two horrible clubs in their hands. Sir Launcelot put his shield afore him, and put the stroke away of the one giant, and with his sword he clave his head asunder. When his fellow saw that, he ran away as he were wood, for fear of the horrible strokes, and Sir Launcelot after him with all his might, and smote him on the shoulder, and clave him to the middle. Then Sir Launcelot went into the hall, and there came afore him three score ladies and damsels, and all kneeled unto him, and thanked God and him of their deliverance. For, sir, said they, the most part of us have been here this seven year their prisoners, and we have worked all manner of silk works for our meat, and we are all great gentlewomen born, and blessed be the time, knight, that ever thou wert born; for thou hast done the most worship that ever did knight in the world, that will we bear record, and we all pray you to tell us your name, that we may tell our friends who delivered us out of prison. Fair damsels, he said, my name is Sir Launcelot du Lake. And so he departed from them and betaught them unto

God. And then he mounted upon his horse, and rode into many strange and wild countries, and through many waters and valleys, and evil was he lodged. And at the last by fortune him happened against a night to come to a fair courtelage, and therein he found an old gentlewoman that lodged him with a good will, and there he had good cheer for him and his horse. And when time was, his host brought him into a fair garret over the gate to his bed. There Sir Launcelot unarmed him, and set his harness by him, and went to bed, and anon he fell on sleep. So, soon after there came one on horseback, and knocked at the gate in great haste. And when Sir Launcelot heard this he arose up, and looked out at the window, and saw by the moonlight three knights come riding after that one man, and all three lashed on him at once with swords, and that one knight turned on them knightly again and defended him. Truly, said Sir Launcelot, yonder one knight shall I help, for it were shame for me to see three knights on one, and if he be slain I am partner of his death. And therewith he took his harness and went out at a window by a sheet down to the four knights, and then Sir Launcelot said on high, Turn you knights unto me, and leave your fighting with that knight. And then they all three left Sir Kay, and turned unto Sir Launcelot, and there began great battle, for they alight all three, and strake many strokes at Sir Launcelot, and assailed him on every side. Then Sir Kay dressed him for to have holpen Sir Launcelot. Nay, sir, said he, I will none of your help, therefore as ye will have my help let me alone with them. Sir Kay for the pleasure of the knight suffered him for to do his will, and so stood aside. And then anon within six strokes Sir Launcelot had stricken them to the earth.

And then they all three cried, Sir knight, we yield us unto you as man of might matchless. As to that, said Sir Launcelot, I will not take your yielding unto me, but so that ye yield you unto Sir Kay the seneschal, on that covenant I will save your lives and else not. Fair knight, said they, that were we loth to do; for as for Sir Kay we chased him hither, and had overcome him had ye not been; therefore, to yield us unto him it were no reason. Well, as to that, said Sir Launcelot, advise you well, for ye may choose whether ye will die or live, for an ye be yielden, it shall be unto Sir Kay. Fair knight, then they said, in saving our lives we will do as thou commandest us. Then shall ye, said Sir Launcelot, on Whitsunday next coming go unto the court of King Arthur, and there shall ye yield you unto Queen Guenever, and put you all three in her grace and mercy, and say that Sir Kay sent you thither to be her prisoners. On the morn Sir Launcelot arose early, and left Sir Kay sleeping: and Sir Launcelot took Sir Kay's armour and his shield and armed him, and so he went to the stable and took his horse, and took his leave of his host, and so he departed. Then soon after arose Sir Kay and missed Sir Launcelot: and then he espied that he had his armour and his horse. Now by my faith I know well that he will grieve some of the court of King Arthur: for on him knights will be bold, and deem that it is I, and that will beguile them; and because of his armour and shield I am sure I shall ride in peace. And then soon after departed Sir Kay, and thanked his host.

As I laid the book down there was a knock at the door, and my stranger came in. I gave him a pipe and a chair and made him welcome. I also comforted him with a hot Scotch whiskey; gave him another one; then still another—hoping always for his story. After a fourth persuader, he drifted into it himself, in a quite simple and natural way:

THE STRANGER'S HISTORY

I am an American. I was born and reared in Hartford, in the State of Connecticut—anyway, just over the river, in the country. So I am a Yankee of the Yankees—and practical; yes, and nearly barren of sentiment, I suppose—or poetry, in other words. My father was a blacksmith, my uncle was a horse doctor, and I was both, along at first. Then I went over to the great arms factory and learned my real trade; learned all there was to it; learned to make everything; guns, revolvers, cannon, boilers, engines, all sorts of labor-saving machinery. Why, I could make anything a body wanted—anything in the world, it didn't make any difference what; and if there wasn't any quick new-fangled way to make a thing, I could invent one—and do it as easy as rolling off a log. I became head superintendent; had a couple of thousand men under me.

Well, a man like that is a man that is full of fight—that goes without saying. With a couple of thousand rough men under one, one has plenty of that sort of amusement. I had, anyway. At last I met my match, and I got my dose. It was during a misunderstanding conducted with crowbars with a fellow we used to call Hercules. He laid me out with a crusher alongside the head that made everything crack, and seemed to spring every joint in my skull and make it overlap its neighbor. Then the world went out in darkness, and I didn't feel anything more, and didn't know anything at all—at least for a while.

When I came to again, I was sitting under an oak tree, on the grass, with a whole beautiful and broad country landscape all to myself—nearly. Not entirely; for there was a fellow on a horse, looking down at me—a fellow fresh out of a picture book. He was in old-time iron armor from head to heel, with a helmet on his head the shape of a nail keg with slits in it; and he had a shield, and a sword, and a prodigious spear; and his horse had armor on, too, and a steel horn projecting from his forehead, and gorgeous red and green silk trappings that hung down all around him like a bed quilt, nearly to the ground.

"Fair sir, will ye just?" said this fellow.

"Will I which?"

"Will ye try a passage of arms for land or lady or for—"

"What are you giving me?" I said. "Get along back to your circus, or I'll report you."

Now what does this man do but fall back a couple of hundred yards and then come rushing at me as hard as he could tear, with his nail keg bent down nearly to his horse's neck and his long spear pointed straight ahead. I saw he meant business, so I was up the tree when he arrived.

He allowed that I was his property, the captive of his spear. There was argument on his side—and the bulk of the advantage—so I judged it best to humor him. We fixed up an agreement whereby I was to go with him and he was not to hurt me. I came down, and we started away, I walking by the side of his horse. We marched comfortably along, through glades and over brooks which I could not remember to have seen before—which puzzled me and made me wonder—and yet we did not come to any circus or sign of a circus. So I gave up the idea of a circus, and concluded he was from an asylum. But we never came to any asylum—so I was up a stump, as you may say. I asked him how far we were from Hartford. He said he had never heard of the place; which I took to be a lie, but allowed it to go at that. At the end of an hour we saw a faraway town sleeping in a valley by a winding river; and beyond it on a hill, a vast gray fortress, with towers and turrets, the first I had ever seen out of a picture.

"Bridgeport?" said I, pointing.

"Camelot," said he.

My stranger had been showing signs of sleepiness. He caught himself nodding, now, and smiled one of those pathetic, obsolete smiles of his, and said:

"I find I can't go on; but come with me, I've got it all written out, and you can read it if you like."

In his chamber, he said: "First, I kept a journal; then by and by, after years, I took the journal and turned it into a book. How long ago that was!"

He handed me his manuscript, and pointed out the place where I should begin:

"Begin here—I've already told you what goes before." He was steeped in drowsiness by this time. As I went out at his door I heard him murmur sleepily: "Give you good den, fair sir."

I sat down by my fire and examined my treasure. The first part of it—the great bulk of it—was parchment, and yellow with age. I scanned a leaf particularly and saw that it was a palimpsest. Under the old dim writing of the Yankee historian appeared traces of a penmanship which was older and dimmer still—Latin words and sentences: fragments from old monkish legends, evidently. I turned to the place indicated by my stranger and began to read—as follows.

CHAPTER 1

"Camelot—Camelot," said I to myself. "I don't seem to remember hearing of it before. Name of the asylum, likely."

It was a soft, reposeful summer landscape, as lovely as a dream, and as lonesome as Sunday. The air was full of the smell of flowers, and the buzzing of insects, and the twittering of birds, and there were no people, no wagons, there was no stir of life, nothing going on. The road was mainly a winding path with hoofprints in it, and now and then a faint trace of wheels on either side in the grass—wheels that apparently had a tire as broad as one's hand.

Presently a fair slip of a girl, about ten years old, with a cataract of golden hair streaming down over her shoulders, came along. Around her head she wore a hoop of flame-red poppies. It was as sweet an outfit as ever I saw, what there was of it. She walked indolently along, with a mind at rest, its peace reflected in her innocent face. The circus man paid no attention to her; didn't even seem to see her. And she —she was no more startled at his fantastic makeup than if she was used to his like every day of her life. She was going by as indifferently as she might have gone by a couple of cows; but when she happened to notice me, *then* there was a change! Up went her hands, and she was turned to stone; her mouth dropped open, her eyes stared wide and timorously, she was the picture of astonished curiosity touched with fear. And there she stood gazing, in a sort of stupefied fascination, till we turned a corner of the wood and were lost to her view. That she should be startled at me instead of at the other man, was too many for me; I couldn't make head or tail of it. And that she should seem to consider me a spectacle, and totally overlook her own merits in that respect, was another puzzling thing, and a display of magnanimity, too, that was surprising in one so young. There was food for thought here. I moved along as one in a dream.

As we approached the town, signs of life began to appear. At intervals we passed a wretched cabin, with a thatched roof, and about it small fields and garden patches in an indifferent state of cultivation. There were people, too; brawny men, with long, coarse, uncombed hair that hung down over their faces and made them look like animals. They and the women, as a rule, wore a coarse tow-linen robe that came well below the knee, and a rude sort of sandals, and many wore an iron collar. The small boys and girls were always naked; but nobody seemed to know it. All of these people stared at me, talked about me, ran into the huts and fetched out their families to gape at me; but nobody ever noticed that other fellow, except to make him humble salutation and get no response for their pains.

In the town were some substantial windowless houses of stone scattered among a wilderness of thatched cabins; the streets were mere crooked alleys, and unpaved; troops of dogs and nude children played in the sun and made life and noise; hogs roamed and rooted contentedly about, and one of them lay in a reeking wallow in the middle of the main thoroughfare and suckled her family. Presently there was a distant blare of military music; it came nearer, still nearer, and soon a noble cavalcade wound into view, glorious with plumed helmets and flashing mail and flaunting banners and rich doublets and horsecloths and gilded spearheads; and through the muck and swine, and naked brats, and joyous dogs, and shabby huts it took its gallant way, and in its wake we followed. Followed through one winding alley and then another—and climbing, always climbing—till at last we gained the breezy height where the huge castle stood. There was an exchange of bugle blasts; then a parley from the walls, where men-at-arms, in hauberk and morion marched back and forth with halberd at shoulder under flapping banners with the rude figure of a dragon displayed upon them; and then the great gates were flung open, the drawbridge was lowered, and the head of the cavalcade swept forward under the frowning arches; and we, following, soon found ourselves in a great paved court, with towers and turrets stretching up into the blue air on all the four sides; and all about us the dismount was going on, and much greeting and ceremony, and running to-and-fro, and a gay display of moving and intermingling colors, and an altogether pleasant stir and noise and confusion.

FOR DISCUSSION

1. When the Yankee first "wakes up" after being hit on the head, he assumes that he is still in Hartford, Connecticut. What is the dramatic irony of the scene that follows?

2. What is it about the "curious stranger" that attracts the attention of the visitor to Warwick Castle? How does he obtain the Yankee's journal?

CHAPTER 2

The moment I got a chance I slipped aside privately and touched an ancient common looking man on the shoulder and said, in an insinuating, confidential way—

"Friend, do me a kindness. Do you belong to the asylum, or are you just here on a visit or something like that?"

He looked me over stupidly, and said—

"Marry, fair, sir, me seemeth—"

"That will do," I said; "I reckon you are a patient."

I moved away, cogitating, and at the same time keeping an eye out for any chance passenger in his right mind that might come along and give me some light. I judged I had found one, presently; so I drew him aside and said in his ear—

"If I could see the head keeper a minute—only just a minute—"

"Prithee do not let me."

"Let you *what*?"

"*Hinder* me, then, if the word please thee better." Then he went on to say he was an undercook and could not stop to gossip, though he would like it another time; for it would comfort his very liver to know where I got my clothes. As he started away he pointed and said yonder was one who was idle enough for my purpose, and was seeking me besides, no doubt. This was an airy slim boy in shrimp-colored tights that made him look like a forked carrot; the rest of his gear was blue silk and dainty laces and ruffles; and he had long yellow curls, and wore a plumed pink satin cap tilted complacently over his ear. By his look, he was good-natured; by his gait, he was satisfied with himself. He was pretty enough to frame. He arrived, looked me over with a smiling and impudent curiosity; said he had come for me, and informed me that he was a page.

"Go 'long," I said; "you ain't more than a paragraph."

It was pretty severe, but I was nettled. However, it never phazed him; he didn't appear to know he was hurt. He began to talk and laugh, in happy, thoughtless, boyish fashion, as we walked along, and made himself old friends with me at once; asked me all sorts of questions about myself and about my clothes, but never waited for an answer—always chattered straight ahead, as if he didn't know he had asked a question and wasn't expecting any reply, until at last he happened to mention that he was born in the beginning of the year 513.

It made the cold chills creep over me! I stopped, and said, a little faintly:

"Maybe I didn't hear you just right. Say it again—and say it slow. What year was it?"

"Five thirteen."

"Five thirteen! You don't look it! Come, my boy, I am a stranger and friendless: be honest and honorable with me. Are you in your right mind?"

He said he was.

"Are these other people in their right minds?"

He said they were.

"And this isn't an asylum? I mean, it isn't a place where they cure crazy people?"

He said it wasn't.

"Well, then," I said, "either I am a lunatic, or something just as awful has happened. Now tell me, honest and true, where am I?"

"In King Arthur's Court."

I waited a minute, to let that idea shudder its way home, and then said:

"And according to your notions, what year is it now?"

"Five twenty-eight—nineteenth of June."

I felt a mournful sinking at the heart, and muttered: "I shall never see my friends again—never, never again. They will not be born for more than thirteen hundred years yet."

I seemed to believe the boy, I didn't know why. *Something* in me seemed to believe him—my consciousness, as you may say; but my reason didn't. My reason straightway began to clamor; that was natural. I didn't know how to go about satisfying it, because I knew that the testimony of men wouldn't serve—my reason would say they were lunatics, and throw out their evidence. But all of a sudden I stumbled on the very thing, just by luck. I knew that the only total eclipse of the sun in the first half of the sixth century occurred on the twenty-first of June, A.D. 528 O. S., and

began at three minutes after twelve noon. I also knew that no total eclipse of the sun was due in what to *me* was the present year—*i.e.*, 1879. So, if I could keep my anxiety and curiosity from eating the heart out of me for forty-eight hours, I should then find out for certain whether this boy was telling me the truth or not.

Wherefore, being a practical Connecticut man, I now shoved this whole problem clear out of my mind till its appointed day and hour should come, in order that I might turn all my attention to the circumstances of the present moment, and be alert and ready to make the most out of them that could be made. One thing at a time, is my motto—and just play that thing for all it is worth, even if it's only two pair and a jack. I made up my mind to two things; if it was still the nineteenth century and I was among lunatics and couldn't get away, I would presently boss that asylum or know the reason why; and if on the other hand it was really the sixth century, all right, I didn't want any softer thing: I would boss the whole country inside of three months; for I judged I would have the start of the best-educated man in the kingdom by a matter of thirteen hundred years and upwards. I'm not a man to waste time after my mind's made up and there's work on hand; so I said to the page—

"Now, Clarence, my boy—if that might happen to be your name—I'll get you to post me up a little if you don't mind. What is the name of that apparition that brought me here?"

"My master and thine? That is the good knight and great lord Sir Kay the Seneschal, foster brother to our liege the king."

"Very good; go on, tell me everything."

He made a long story of it; but the part that had immediate interest for me was this. He said I was Sir Kay's prisoner, and that in the due course of custom I would be flung into a dungeon and left there on scant commons until my friends ransomed me—unless I chanced to rot, first. I saw that the last chance had the best show, but I didn't waste any bother about that; time was too precious. The page said, further, that dinner was about ended in the great hall by this time, and that as soon as the sociability and the heavy drinking should begin, Sir Kay would have me in and exhibit me before King Arthur and his illustrious knights seated at the Table Round, and would brag about his exploit in capturing me, and would probably exaggerate the facts a little, but it wouldn't be good form for me to correct him, and not over safe, either; and when I was done being exhibited, then ho for the dungeon; but he, Clarence, would find a way to come and see me every now and then, and cheer me up, and help me get word to my friends.

Get word to my friends! I thanked him; I couldn't do less; and about this time a lackey came to say I was wanted; so Clarence led me in and took me off to one side and sat down by me.

Well, it was a curious kind of spectacle, and interesting. It was an immense place, and rather naked—yes, and full of loud contrasts. It was very, very lofty; so lofty that the banners depending from the arched beams and girders away up there floated in a sort of twilight; there was a stone-railed gallery at each end, high up, with musicians in the one, and women, clothed in stunning colors, in the other. The floor was of big stone flags laid in black and white squares, rather battered by age and use, and needing repair. As to ornament, there wasn't any, strictly speaking; though on the walls hung some huge tapestries which were probably taxed as works of art; battle pieces, they were, with horses shaped like those which children cut out of paper or create in gingerbread; with

men on them in scale armor whose scales are represented by round holes—so that the man's coat looks as if it had been done with a biscuit punch. There was a fireplace big enough to camp in; and its projecting sides and hood, of carved and pillared stonework, had the look of a cathedral door. Along the walls stood men-at-arms, in breastplate and morion, with halberds for their only weapon—rigid as statues; and that is what they looked like.

In the middle of this groined and vaulted public square was an oaken table which they called the Table Round. It was as large as a circus ring; and around it sat a great company of men dressed in such various and splendid colors that it hurt one's eyes to look at them. They wore their plumed hats, right along, except that whenever one addressed himself directly to the king, he lifted his hat a trifle just as he was beginning his remark.

Mainly they were drinking—from entire ox horns; but a few were still munching bread or gnawing beef bones. There was about an average of two dogs to one man; and these sat in expectant attitudes till a spent bone was flung to them, and then they went for it by brigades and divisions, with a rush, and there ensued a fight which filled the prospect with a tumultuous chaos of plunging heads and bodies and flashing tails, and the storm of howlings and barkings deafened all speech for the time; but that was no matter, for the dogfight was always a bigger interest anyway; the men rose, sometimes, to observe it the better and bet on it, and the ladies and the musicians stretched themselves out over their balusters with the same object; and all broke into delighted ejaculations from time to time. In the end, the winning dog stretched himself out comfortably with his bone between his paws, and proceeded to growl over it, and gnaw it, and grease the floor with it, just as fifty others were already doing; and the rest of the court resumed their previous industries and entertainments.

As a rule the speech and behavior of these people were gracious and courtly; and I noticed that they were good and serious listeners when anybody was telling anything—I mean in a dogfightless interval. And plainly, too, they were a childlike and innocent lot; telling lies of the stateliest pattern with a most gentle and winning naïvete and ready and willing to listen to anybody else's lie, and believe it, too. It was hard to associate them with anything cruel or dreadful; and yet they dealt in tales of blood and suffering with a guileless relish that made me almost forget to shudder.

I was not the only prisoner present. There were twenty or more. Poor devils, many of them were maimed, hacked, carved, in a frightful way; and their hair, their faces, their clothing, were caked with black and stiffened drenchings of blood. They were suffering sharp physical pain, of course; and weariness, and hunger and thirst, no doubt; and at least none had given them the comfort of a wash, or even the poor charity of a lotion for their wounds; yet you never heard them utter a moan or a groan, or saw them show any sign of restlessness, or any disposition to complain. The thought was forced upon me: "The rascals—*they* have served other people so in their day; it being their own turn, now, they were not expecting any better treatment than this; so their philosophical bearing is not an outcome of mental training, intellectual fortitude, reasoning; it is mere animal training; they are white Indians."

FOR DISCUSSION

1. When the Yankee learns that he is trapped in the year 528, he makes an immediate resolve. What is it, and what does it show about his character?

2. King Arthur's hall is "full of loud contrasts." What are some of the contrasts that the Yankee notices on first entering?

CHAPTER 3

Mainly the Round Table talk was monologues—narrative accounts of the adventures in which these prisoners were captured and their friends and backers killed and stripped of their steeds and armor. As a general thing—as far as I could make out —these murderous adventures were not forays undertaken to avenge injuries, nor to settle old disputes or sudden fallings out; no, as a rule they were simple duels between strangers—duels between people who had never even been introduced to each other, and between whom existed no cause of offense whatever. Many a time I had seen a couple of boys, strangers, meet by chance, and say simultaneously, "I can lick you," and go at it on the spot; but I had always imagined until now, that that sort of thing belonged to children only, and was a sign and mark of childhood; but here were these big boobies sticking to it and taking pride in it clear up into full age and beyond. Yet there was something very engaging about these great simplehearted creatures, something attractive and lovable. There did not seem to be brains enough in the entire nursery, so to speak, to bait a fishhook with; but you didn't seem to mind that, after a little, because you soon saw that brains were not needed in a society like that, and, indeed would have marred it, hindered it, spoiled its symmetry—perhaps rendered its existence impossible.

There was a fine manliness observable in almost every face; and in some a certain loftiness and sweetness that rebuked your belittling criticisms and stilled them. A most noble benignity and purity reposed in the countenance of him they called Sir Galahad, and likewise in the king's also; and there was majesty and greatness in the giant frame and high bearing of Sir Launcelot of the Lake.

There was presently an incident which centered the general interest upon this Sir Launcelot. At a sign from a sort of master of ceremonies, six or eight of the prisoners rose and came forward in a body and knelt on the floor and lifted up their hands toward the ladies' gallery and begged the grace of a word with the queen. The most conspicuously situated lady in that massed flower bed of feminine show and finery inclined her head by way of assent, and then the spokesman of the prisoners delivered himself and his fellows into her hands for free pardon, ransom, captivity or death, as she in her good pleasure might elect; and this, as he said, he was doing by command of Sir Kay the Seneschal, whose prisoners they were, he having vanquished them by his single might and prowess in sturdy conflict in the field.

Surprise and astonishment flashed from face to face all over the house; the queen's gratified smile faded out at the name of Sir Kay, and she looked disappointed; and the page whispered in my ear with an accent and manner expressive of extravagant derision—

"Sir *Kay*, forsooth! Oh, call me pet names, dearest, call me a marine! In twice a thousand years shall the unholy invention of man labor at odds to beget the fellow to this majestic lie!"

Every eye was fastened with severe inquiry upon Sir Kay. But he was equal to the occasion. He got up and played his hand like a major—and took every trick. He said he would state the case, exactly according to the facts; he would tell the simple straightforward tale, without comment of his own; "and then," said he, "if ye find glory and honor due, ye will give it unto him who is the mightiest man of his hands that ever bare shield or strake with sword in the ranks of Christian battle—even him that sitteth there!" and he pointed to Sir Launcelot. Ah, he fetched them; it was a rattling good stroke. Then he went on and told how Sir Launcelot, seeking adventures, some brief time gone by, killed seven giants at one sweep of his sword, and set a hundred and forty-two captive maidens free; and then went further, still seeking adventures, and found him (Sir Kay) fighting a desperate fight against nine foreign knights, and straightway took the battle solely into his own hands, and conquered the nine; and that night Sir Launcelot rose quietly, and dressed him in Sir Kay's armor and took Sir Kay's horse and gat him away into distant lands, and vanquished sixteen knights in one pitched battle and thirty-four in another; and all these and the former nine he made to swear that about Whitsuntide they would ride to Arthur's court and yield them to Queen Guenever's hands as captives of Sir Kay the Seneschal, spoil of his knightly prowess; and now here were these half dozen, and the rest would be along as soon as they might be healed of their desperate wounds.

Well, it was touching to see the queen blush and smile, and look embarrassed and happy, and fling furtive glances at Sir

Launcelot that would have got him shot in Arkansas, to a dead certainty.

Everybody praised the valor and magnanimity of Sir Launcelot; and as for me, I was perfectly amazed, that one man, all by himself, should have been able to beat down and capture such battalions of practiced fighters. I said as much to Clarence; but this mocking featherhead only said—

"An Sir Kay had had time to get another skin of sour wine into him, ye had seen the accompt doubled."

I looked at the boy in sorrow; and as I looked I saw the cloud of a deep despondency settle upon his countenance. I followed the direction of his eye, and saw that a very old and white-bearded man, clothed in a flowing black gown, had risen and was standing at the table upon unsteady legs, and feebly swaying his ancient head and surveying the company with his watery and wandering eye. The same suffering look that was in the page's face was observable in all the faces around—the look of dumb creatures who know that they must endure and make no moan.

"Marry, we shall have it again," sighed the boy; "that same old weary tale that he hath told a thousand times in the same words, and that he *will* tell till he dieth, every time he hath gotten his barrel full and feeleth his exaggeration-mill a-working. Would God I had died or I saw this day!"

"Who is it?"

"Merlin, the mighty liar and magician, perdition singe him for the weariness he worketh with his one tale! But that men fear him for that he hath the storms and the lightnings and all the devils that be in hell at his beck and call, they would have dug his entrails out these many years ago to get at that tale and squelch it. He telleth it always in the third person, making believe he is too modest to glorify himself—

maledictions light upon him, misfortune be his dole! Good friend, prithee call me for evensong."

The boy nestled himself upon my shoulder and pretended to go to sleep. The old man began his tale; and presently the lad was asleep in reality; so also were the dogs, and the court, the lackeys, and the files of men-at-arms. The droning voice droned on; a soft snoring arose on all sides and supported it like a deep and subdued accompaniment of wind instruments. Some heads were bowed upon folded arms, some lay back with open mouths that issued unconscious music; the flies buzzed and bit, unmolested, the rats swarmed softly out from a hundred holes, and pattered about, and made themselves at home everywhere; and one of them sat up like a squirrel on the king's head and held a bit of cheese in its hands and nibbled it, and dribbled the crumbs in the king's face with naïve and impudent irreverence. It was a tranquil scene, and restful to the weary eye and the jaded spirit.

This was the old man's tale. He said:

"Right so the king and Merlin departed, and went until an hermit that was a good man and a great leech. So the hermit searched all his wounds and gave him good salves; so the king was there three days, and then were his wounds well amended that he might ride and go, and so departed. And as they rode, Arthur said, I have no sword. No force, said Merlin, hereby is a sword that shall be yours and I may. So they rode till they came to a lake, the which was a fair water and broad, and in the midst of the lake Arthur was ware of an arm clothed in white samite, that held a fair sword in that hand. Lo, said Merlin, yonder is that sword that I spake of. With that they saw a damsel going upon the lake. What damsel is that? said Arthur. That is the Lady of the lake, said Merlin;

and within that lake is a rock, and therein is as fair a place as any on earth, and richly beseen, and this damsel will come to you anon, and then speak ye fair to her that she will give you that sword. Anon withal came the damsel unto Arthur and saluted him, and he her again. Damsel, said Arthur, what sword is that, that yonder the arm holdeth above the water? I would it were mine, for I have no sword. Sir Arthur King, said the damsel, that sword is mine, and if ye will give me a gift when I ask it you, ye shall have it. By my faith, said Arthur, I will give you what gift ye will ask. Well, said the damsel, go ye into yonder barge and row yourself to the sword, and take it and the scabbard with you, and I will ask my gift when I see my time. So Sir Arthur and Merlin alight, and tied their horses to two trees, and so they went into the ship, and when they came to the sword that the hand held, Sir Arthur took it up by the handles, and took it with him. And the arm and the hand went under the water; and so they came into the land and rode forth. And then Sir Arthur saw a rich pavilion. What signifieth yonder pavilion? It is the knight's pavilion, said Merlin, that ye fought with last, Sir Pellinore, but he is out, he is not there; he hath ado with a knight of yours, that hight Egglame, and they have fought together, but at the last Egglame fled, and else he had been dead, and he hath chased him even to Carlion, and we shall meet with him anon in the highway. That is well said, said Arthur, now have I a sword, now will I wage battle with him, and be avenged on him. Sir, ye shall not so, said Merlin, for the knight is weary of fighting and chasing, so that ye shall have no worship to have ado with him; also, he will not lightly be matched of one knight living; and therefore it is my counsel, let him pass, for he shall do you good service in short time, and his sons, after his days. Also ye shall see that day in short space ye shall be right glad to give him your sister to wed. When I see him, I will do as ye advise me, said Arthur. Then Sir Arthur looked on the sword, and liked it passing well. Whether liketh you better, said Merlin, the sword or the scabbard? Me liketh better the sword, said Arthur. Ye are more unwise, said Merlin, for the scabbard is worth ten of the sword, for while ye have the scabbard upon you ye shall never lose no blood, be ye never so sore wounded; therefore, keep well the scabbard always with you. So they rode unto Carlion, and by the way they met with Sir Pellinore; but Merlin had done such a craft that Pellinore saw not Arthur, and he passed by without any words. I marvel, said Arthur, that the knight would not speak. Sir, said Merlin, he saw you not; for and he had seen you ye had not lightly departed. So they came unto Carlion, whereof his knights were passing glad. And when they heard of his adventures they marveled that he would jeopard his person so alone. But all men of worship said it was merry to be under such a chieftain that would put his person in adventure as other poor knights did."

CHAPTER 4

It seemed to me that this quaint lie was most simply and beautifully told; but then I had heard it only once, and that makes a difference; it was pleasant to the others when it was fresh, no doubt.

Sir Dinadan the Humorist was the first to awake, and he soon roused the rest with a practical joke of a sufficiently poor quality. He tied some metal mugs to a dog's tail and turned him loose, and he tore around and around the place in a frenzy of fright, with all the other dogs bellowing after him and battering and crashing against everything that came in their way and making altogether a chaos of confusion and a most deafening din and turmoil; at which every man and woman of the multitude laughed till the tears flowed, and some fell out of their chairs and wallowed on the floor in ecstasy. It was just like so many children. Sir Dinadan was so proud of his exploit that he could not keep from telling over and over again, to weariness, how the immortal idea happened to occur to him; and as is the way with humorists of his breed, he was still laughing at it after everybody else had got through. He was so set up that he concluded to make a speech—of course a humorous speech. I think I never heard so many old played out jokes strung together in my life. He was worse than the minstrels, worse than the clown in the circus. It seemed peculiarly sad to sit here, thirteen hundred years before I was born and listen again to poor, flat, worm-eaten jokes that had given me the dry gripes when I was a boy thirteen hundred years afterwards. It about convinced me that there isn't any such thing as a new joke possible. Everybody laughed at these antiquities—but then they always do; I had noticed that, centuries later. However, of course the scoffer didn't laugh—I mean the boy. No, he scoffed; there wasn't anything he wouldn't scoff at. He said the most of Sir Dinadan's jokes were rotten and the rest were petrified. I said "petrified" was good; as I believed, myself, that the only right way to classify the majestic ages of some of those jokes was by geologic periods. But that neat idea hit the boy in a blank place, for geology hadn't been invented yet. However, I made a note of the remark, and calculated to educate the commonwealth up to it if I pulled through. It is no use to throw

a good thing away merely because the market isn't ripe yet.

Now Sir Kay arose and began to fire up on his history-mill, with me for fuel. It was time for me to feel serious, and I did. Sir Kay told how he had encountered me in a far land of barbarians, who all wore the same ridiculous garb that I did—a garb that was a work of enchantment, and intended to make the wearer secure from hurt by human hands. However, he had nullified the force of the enchantment by prayer, and had killed my thirteen knights in a three-hours' battle, and taken me prisoner, sparing my life in order that so strange a curiosity as I was might be exhibited to the wonder and admiration of the king and the court. He spoke of me all the time, in the blandest way, as "this prodigious giant," and "this horrible sky-towering monster," and "this tusked and taloned man-devouring ogre"; and everybody took in all this bosh in the naïvest way, and never smiled or seemed to notice that there was any discrepancy between these watered statistics and me. He said that in trying to escape from him I sprang into the top of a tree two hundred cubits high at a single bound, but he dislodged me with a stone the size of a cow, which "all-to brast" the most of my bones, and then swore me to appear at Arthur's court for sentence. He ended by condemning me to die at noon on the twenty-first; and was so little concerned about it that he stopped to yawn before he named the date.

I was in a dismal state by this time; indeed, I was hardly enough in my right mind to keep the run of a dispute that sprung up as to how I had better be killed, the possibility of the killing being doubted by some, because of the enchantment in my clothes. And yet it was nothing but an ordinary suit of fifteen-dollar slopshops. Still, I was sane enough to notice this detail, to wit: many of the terms used in the most matter-of-fact way by this great assemblage of the first ladies and gentlemen in the land would have made a Comanche blush. Indelicacy is too mild a term to convey the idea. However, I had read *Tom Jones* and *Roderick Random,* and other books of that kind, and knew that the highest and first ladies and gentlemen in England had remained little or no cleaner in their talk, and in the morals and conduct which such talk implies, clear up to a hundred years ago; in fact clear into our own nineteenth century—in which century, broadly speaking, the earliest samples of the real lady and real gentleman discoverable in English history—or in European history, for that matter—may be said to have made their appearance. Suppose Sir Walter, instead of putting the conversation into the mouths of his characters, had allowed the characters to speak for themselves? We should have had talk from Rachel and Ivanhoe and the soft lady Rowena which would embarrass a tramp in our day. However, to the unconsciously indelicate all things are delicate. King Arthur's people were not aware that they were indecent, and I had presence of mind enough not to mention it.

They were so troubled about my enchanted clothes that they were mightily relieved, at last, when old Merlin swept the difficulty away for them with a commonsense hint. He asked them why they were so dull—why didn't it occur to them to strip me. In half a minute I was as naked as a pair of tongs! And dear, dear, to think of it: I was the only embarrassed person there. Everybody discussed me; and did it as unconcernedly as if I had been a cabbage. Queen Guenever was as naïvely interested as the rest, and said she had never seen anybody with legs just like mine before. It was the only compliment I got— if it was a compliment.

Finally I was carried off in one direction, and my perilous clothes in another. I was shoved into a dark and narrow cell in a dungeon, with some scant remnants for dinner, some moldy straw for a bed, and no end of rats for company.

FOR DISCUSSION

• How does Mark Twain use exaggeration and dramatic irony to show what monstrous liars the knights were? In what other ways does he discredit the idealized picture of King Arthur and his knights? Is there anything about them that the Yankee finds worthy of admiration?

CHAPTER 5

I was so tired that even my fears were not able to keep me awake long.

When I next came to myself, I seemed to have been asleep a very long time. My first thought was, "Well, what an astonishing dream I've had! I reckon I've waked only just in time to keep from being hanged or drowned or burned, or something. . . . I'll nap again till the whistle blows, and then I'll go down to the arms factory and have it out with Hercules."

But just then I heard the harsh music of rusty chains and bolts, a light flashed in my eyes, and that butterfly, Clarence, stood before me! I gasped with surprise; my breath almost got away from me.

"What!" I said, "you here yet? Go along with the rest of the dream! scatter!"

But he only laughed, in his lighthearted way, and fell to making fun of my sorry plight.

"All right," I said resignedly, "let the dream go on; I'm in no hurry."

"Prithee what dream?"

"What dream? Why, the dream that I am in Arthur's court—a person who never existed; and that I am talking to you, who are nothing but a work of the imagination."

"Oh, la, indeed! And is it a dream that you're to be burned tomorrow? Ho-ho—answer me that!"

The shock that went through me was distressing. I now began to reason that my situation was in the last degree serious, dream or no dream; for I knew by past experience of the lifelike intensity of dreams, that to be burned to death, even in a dream, would be very far from being a jest, and was a thing to be avoided, by any means, fair or foul, that I could contrive. So I said beseechingly:

"Ah, Clarence, good boy, only friend I've got—for you *are* my friend, aren't you—don't fail me; help me to devise some way of escaping from this place!"

"Now do but hear thyself! Escape? Why, man, the corridors are in guard and keep of men-at-arms."

"No doubt, no doubt. But how many, Clarence? Not many, I hope?"

"Full a score. One may not hope to escape." After a pause—hesitatingly: "and there be other reasons—and weightier."

"Other ones? What are they?"

"Well, they say—oh, but I daren't, indeed I daren't!"

"Why, poor lad, what is the matter? Why do you blench? Why do you tremble so?"

"Oh, in sooth, there is need! I do want to tell you, but—"

"Come, come, be brave, be a man—speak out, there's a good lad!"

He hesitated, pulled one way by desire, the other way by fear; then he stole to the door and peeped out, listening; and finally crept close to me and put his mouth to my ear and told me his fearful news in a whisper, and with all the cowering apprehension of one who was venturing upon awful ground and speaking of things whose very mention might be freighted with death.

"Merlin, in his malice, has woven a spell about this dungeon, and there bides not the man in these kingdoms that would be desperate enough to essay to cross its lines with you! Now God pity me, I have told it! Ah, be kind to me, be merciful to a poor boy who means thee well; for an thou betray me I am lost!"

I laughed the only really refreshing laugh I had had for some time; and shouted—

"Merlin has wrought a spell! *Merlin,* forsooth! That cheap old humbug, that maundering old ape? Bosh, pure bosh, the silliest bosh in the world! Why, it does seem to me that of all the childish, idiotic, chuckleheaded, chicken-livered superstitions that ev—oh, damn Merlin!"

But Clarence had slumped to his knees before I had half finished, and he was like to go out of his mind with fright.

"Oh, beware! These are awful words! Any moment these walls may crumble upon us if you say such things. Oh call them back before it is too late!"

Now this strange exhibition gave me a good idea and set me to thinking. If everybody about here was so honestly and sincerely afraid of Merlin's pretended magic as Clarence was, certainly a superior man like me ought to be shrewd enough to contrive some way to take advantage of such a state of things. I went on thinking, and worked out a plan. Then I said:

"Get up. Pull yourself together; look me in the eye. Do you know why I laughed?"

"No—but for our blessed Lady's sake, do it no more."

"Well, I'll tell you why I laughed. Because I'm a magician myself."

"Thou!" The boy recoiled a step, and caught his breath, for the thing hit him rather sudden; but the aspect which he took on was very, very respectful. I took quick note of that; it indicated that a humbug didn't need to have a reputation in this asylum; people stood ready to take him at his word, without that. I resumed:

"I've known Merlin seven hundred years, and he—"

"Seven hun—"

"Don't interrupt me. He has died and come alive again thirteen times, and traveled under a new name every time: Smith, Jones, Robinson, Jackson, Peters, Haskins, Merlin—a new alias every time he turns up. I knew him in Egypt three hundred years ago; I knew him in India five hundred years ago—he is always blethering around in my way, everywhere I go; he makes me tired. He don't amount to shucks, as a magician; knows some of the old common tricks, but has never got beyond the rudiments, and never will. He is well enough for the provinces—one-night stands and that sort of thing, you know—but dear me, *he* oughtn't to set up for an expert—anyway not where there's a real artist. Now look here, Clarence, I am going to stand your friend, right along, and in return you must be mine. I want you to do me a favor. I want you to get word to the king that I am a magician myself—and the Supreme Grand High-yu-Mucka-muck and head of the tribe, at that; and I want him to be made to understand that I am just quietly arranging a little calamity here that will make the fur fly in these realms if Sir Kay's project is carried out and any harm comes to me. Will you get that to the king for me?"

The poor boy was in such a state that he could hardly answer me. It was pitiful to see a creature so terrified, so unnerved, so demoralized. But he promised everything; and on my side he made me promise over and over again that I would remain his friend, and never turn against him or cast any enchantments upon him. Then he worked his way out, staying himself with his hand along the wall, like a sick person.

Presently this thought occurred to me: how heedless I have been! When the boy gets calm, he will wonder why a great magician like me should have begged a boy like him to help me get out of this place; he will put this and that together, and will see that I am a humbug.

I worried over that heedless blunder for an hour, and called myself a great many hard names, meantime. But finally it occurred to me all of a sudden that these animals didn't reason; that *they* never put this and that together; that all their talk showed that they didn't know a discrepancy when they saw it. I was at rest, then.

But as soon as one is at rest, in this world, off he goes on something else to worry about. It occurred to me that I had made another blunder: I had sent the boy off to alarm his betters with a threat—I intending to invent a calamity at my leisure; now the people who are the readiest and eagerest and willingest to swallow miracles are the very ones who are the hungriest to see you perform them; suppose I should be called on for a sample? Suppose I should be asked to name my calamity? Yes, I had made a blunder; I ought to have invented my calamity first. "What shall I do? what can I say, to gain a little time?" I was in trouble again; in the deepest kind of trouble: . . . "There's a footstep—they're coming! If I had only just a moment to think. . . . Good, I've got it. I'm all right."

You see, it was the eclipse. It came into my mind, in the nick of time, how Columbus, or Cortez, or one of those people, played an eclipse as a saving trump once, on some savages, and I saw my chance. I could play it myself, now; and it wouldn't be any plagiarism, either, because I should get it in nearly a thousand years ahead of those parties.

Clarence came in, subdued, distressed, and said:

"I hasted the message to our liege the king, and straightway he had me to his presence. He was frighted even to the marrow, and was minded to give order for your instant enlargement, and that you be clothed in fine raiment and lodged as befitted one so great; but then came Merlin and spoiled all; for he persuaded the king that you are mad, and know not whereof you speak; and said your threat is but foolishness and idle vaporing. They disputed long, but in the end, Merlin, scoffing, said, 'Wherefore hath he not *named* his brave calamity? Verily it is because he cannot.' This thrust did in a most sudden sort close the king's mouth, and he could offer naught to turn the argument; and so, reluctant, and full loth to do you the discourtesy, he yet prayeth you to consider his perplexed case, as noting how the matter stands, and name the calamity—if so be you have determined the nature of it and the time of its coming. Oh, prithee delay not; to delay at such a time were to double and treble the perils that already compass thee about. Oh, be thou wise—name the calamity!"

I allowed silence to accumulate while I got my impressiveness together, and then said:

"How long have I been shut up in this hole?"

"Ye were shut up when yesterday was well spent. It is nine of the morning now."

"No! Then I have slept well, sure enough. Nine in the morning now! And yet it is the very complexion of midnight, to a shade. This is the 20th, then?"

"The 20th—yes."

"And I am to be burned alive tomorrow." The boy shuddered.

"At what hour?"

"At high noon."

"Now then, I will tell you what to say." I paused, and stood over that cowering lad a whole minute in awful silence; then in a voice deep, measured, charged with doom, I began, and rose by dramatically graded stages to my colossal climax, which I delivered in as sublime and noble a way as ever I did such a thing in my life: "Go back and tell the king that at that hour I will smother the whole world in dead blackness of midnight; I will blot out the sun, and he shall never shine again; the fruits of the earth shall rot for lack of light and warmth, and the peoples of the earth shall famish and die, to the last man!"

I had to carry the boy out myself, he sunk into such a collapse. I handed him over to the soldiers, and went back.

CHAPTER 6

In the stillness and the darkness, realization soon began to supplement knowledge. The mere knowledge of a fact is pale; but when you come to *realize* your fact, it takes on color. It is all the difference between hearing of a man being stabbed to the heart, and seeing it done. In the stillness and the darkness, the knowledge that I was in deadly danger took to itself deeper and deeper meaning all the time;

a something which was realization crept inch by inch through my veins and turned me cold.

But it is a blessed provision of nature that at times like these, as soon as a man's mercury has got down to a certain point there comes a revulsion, and he rallies. Hope springs up, and cheerfulness along with it, and then he is in good shape to do something for himself, if anything can be done. When my rally came, it came with a bound. I said to myself that my eclipse would be sure to save me, and make me the greatest man in the kingdom besides; and straightway my mercury went up to the top of the tube, and my solicitudes all vanished. I was as happy a man as there was in the world. I was even impatient for tomorrow to come, I so wanted to gather in that great triumph and be the center of all the nation's wonder and reverence. Besides, in a business way it would be the making of me; I knew that.

Meantime there was one thing which had got pushed into the background of my mind. That was the half conviction that when the nature of my proposed calamity should be reported to those superstitious people, it would have such an effect that they would want to compromise. So, by and by when I heard footsteps coming, that thought was recalled to me, and I said to myself, "As sure as anything, it's the compromise. Well, if it is good, all right, I will accept; but if it isn't, I mean to stand my ground and play my hand for all it is worth."

The door opened, and some men-at-arms appeared. The leader said—

"The stake is ready. Come!"

The stake! The strength went out of me, and I almost fell down. It is hard to get one's breath at such a time, such lumps come into one's throat, and such gaspings, but as soon as I could speak, I said:

"But this is a mistake—the execution is tomorrow."

"Order changed; been set forward a day. Haste thee!"

I was lost. There was no help for me. I was dazed, stupefied; I had no command over myself; I only wandered purposelessly about, like one out of his mind; so the soldiers took hold of me, and pulled me along with them, out of the cell and along the maze of underground corridors, and finally into the fierce glare of daylight and the upper world. As we stepped into the vast inclosed court of the castle I got a shock; for the first thing I saw was the stake, standing in the center, and near it the piled fagots and a monk. On all four sides of the court the seated multitudes rose rank above rank, forming sloping terraces that were rich with color. The king and the queen sat in their thrones, the most conspicuous figures there, of course.

To note all this occupied but a second. The next second Clarence had slipped from some place of concealment and was pouring news into my ear, his eyes beaming with triumph and gladness. He said:

"'Tis through *me* the change was wrought! And main hard have I worked to do it, too. But when I revealed to them the calamity in store, and saw how mighty was the terror it did engender, then saw I also that this was the time to strike! Wherefore I diligently pretended, unto this and that and the other one, that your power against the sun could not reach its full until the morrow; and so if any would save the sun and the world, you must be slain today, whilst your enchantments are but in the weaving and lack potency. Odsbodikins, it was but a dull lie, a most indifferent invention, but you should have seen them seize it and swallow it, in the frenzy of their fright, as it were salvation sent from heaven; and all the while was I laughing in my sleeve the one moment, to see them so cheaply deceived, and glorifying God the next, that He was content to let the meanest of His creatures be His instrument to the saving of thy life. Ah, how happy has the matter sped! You will not need to do the sun a *real* hurt—ah, forget not that, on your soul forget it not! Only make a little darkness—only the littlest little darkness, mind, and cease with that. It will be sufficient. They will see that I spoke falsely, —being ignorant as they will fancy—and with the falling of the first shadow of that darkness you shall see them go mad with fear; and they will set you free and make you great! Go to thy triumph, now! But remember—ah, good friend, I implore thee remember my supplication, and do the blessed sun no hurt. For *my* sake, thy true friend."

I choked out some words through my grief and misery; as much as to say I would spare the sun; for which the lad's eyes paid me back with such deep and loving gratitude that I had not the heart to tell him his good-hearted foolishness had ruined me and sent me to my death.

As the soldiers assisted me across the court the stillness was so profound that if I had been blindfolded I should have supposed I was in a solitude instead of walled in by four thousand people. There was not a movement perceptible in those masses of humanity; they were as rigid as stone images, and as pale; and dread sat upon every countenance. This hush continued while I was being chained to the stake; it still continued while the fagots were carefully and tediously piled about my ankles, my knees, my thighs, my body. Then there was a pause, and a deeper hush, if possible, and a man knelt down at my feet with a blazing torch; the multitude strained forward, gazing, and parting slightly from their seats without knowing it; the monk raised his hands above my head, and his eyes toward the blue sky, and began some words in Latin; in this attitude he droned on and on, a little while, and then stopped. I waited two or three moments: then looked up; he was standing there petrified. With a common impulse the multitude rose slowly up and stared into the sky. I followed their eyes; as sure as guns, there was my eclipse beginning! The life went boiling through my veins; I was a new man! The rim of black spread slowly into the sun's disk, my heart beat higher and higher, and still the assemblage and the priest stared into the sky, motionless. I knew that this gaze would be turned upon me, next. When it was, I was ready. I was in one of the most grand attitudes I ever struck, with my arm stretched up pointing to the sun. It was a noble effect. You could *see* the shudder sweep the mass like a wave. Two shouts rang out, one close upon the heels of the other:

"Apply the torch!"

"I forbid it!"

The one was from Merlin, the other from the king. Merlin started from his place—to apply the torch himself, I judged. I said:

"Stay where you are. If any man moves —even the king—before I give him leave, I will blast him with thunder, I will consume him with lightnings!"

The multitude sank meekly into their seats, and I was just expecting they would. Merlin hesitated a moment or two, and I was on pins and needles during that little while. Then he sat down, and I took a good breath; for I knew I was master of the situation now. The king said:

"Be merciful, fair sir, and essay no further in this perilous matter, lest disaster follow. It was reported to us that your powers could not attain unto their full strength until the morrow; but—"

"Your Majesty thinks the report may

have been a lie? It *was* a lie."

That made an immense effect; up went appealing hands everywhere, and the king was assailed with a storm of supplications that I might be bought off at any price, and the calamity stayed. The king was eager to comply. He said:

"Name any terms, reverend sir, even to the halving of my kingdom; but banish this calamity, spare the sun!"

My fortune was made. I would have taken him up in a minute, but *I* couldn't stop an eclipse; the thing was out of the question. So I asked time to consider. The king said—

"How long—ah, how long, good sir? Be merciful; look it groweth darker, moment by moment. Prithee how long?"

"Not long. Half an hour—maybe an hour."

There were a thousand pathetic protests, but I couldn't shorten up any, for I couldn't remember how long a total eclipse lasts. I was in a puzzled condition, anyway, and wanted to think. Something was wrong about that eclipse, and the fact was very unsettling. If this wasn't the one I was after, how was I to tell whether this was the sixth century, or nothing but a dream? Dear me, if I could only prove it was the latter! Here was a glad new hope. If the boy was right about the date, and this was the twentieth, it *wasn't* the sixth century. I reached for the monk's sleeve, in considerable excitement, and asked him what day of the month it was.

Hang him, he said it was the *twenty-first!* It made me turn cold to hear him. I begged him not to make any mistake about it; but he was sure; he knew it was the twenty-first. So, that featherheaded boy had botched things again! The time of the day was right for the eclipse; I had seen that for myself, in the beginning, by the dial that was nearby. Yes, I *was* in King Arthur's court, and I might as well make the most out of it I could.

The darkness was steadily growing, the people becoming more and more distressed. I now said:

"I have reflected, Sir King. For a lesson, I will let this darkness proceed, and spread night in the world; but whether I blot out the sun for good, or restore it, shall rest with you. These are the terms, to wit: You shall remain king over all your dominions, and receive all the glories and honors that belong to the kingship; but you shall appoint me your perpetual minister and executive, and give me for my services one per cent of such actual increase of revenue over and above its present amount as I may succeed in creating for the state. If I can't live on that, I shan't ask anybody to give me a lift. Is it satisfactory?"

There was a prodigious roar of applause, and out of the midst of it the king's voice rose, saying:

"Away with his bonds and set him free! and do him homage, high and low, rich and poor, for he is become the king's right hand, is clothed with power and authority, and his seat is upon the highest step of the throne! Now sweep away this creeping night, and bring the light and cheer again, that all the world may bless thee."

But I said:

"That a common man should be shamed before the world, is nothing; but it were dishonor to the *king* if any that saw his minister naked should not also see him delivered from his shame. If I might ask that my clothes be brought again—"

"They are not meet," the king broke in. "Fetch raiment of another sort; clothe him like a prince!"

My idea worked. I wanted to keep things as they were till the eclipse was total, otherwise they would be trying again to get me to dismiss the darkness, and of course I couldn't do it. Sending for the clothes gained some delay, but not enough. So I had to make another excuse. I said it would be but natural if the king should change his mind and repent to some extent of what he had done under excitement; therefore I would let the darkness grow a while, and if at the end of a reasonable time the king had kept his mind the same, the darkness should be dismissed. Neither the king nor anybody else was satisfied with that arrangement, but I had to stick to my point.

It grew darker and darker and blacker and blacker, while I struggled with those awkward sixth-century clothes. It got to be pitch dark, at last, and the multitude groaned with horror to feel the cold uncanny night breezes fan through the place and see the stars come out and twinkle in the sky. At last the eclipse was total, and I was very glad of it, but everybody else was in misery; which was quite natural. I said:

"The king, by his silence, still stands to the terms." Then I lifted up my hands—stood just so a moment—then I said, with the most awful solemnity: "Let the enchantment dissolve and pass harmless away!"

There was no response, for a moment, in that deep darkness and that graveyard hush. But when the silver rim of the sun pushed itself out a moment or two later, the assemblage broke loose with a vast shout and came pouring down like a deluge to smother me with blessings and gratitude; and Clarence was not the last of the wash, be sure.

FOR DISCUSSION

1. How does the Yankee use his knowledge of the eclipse to escape being burned at the stake? What abilities enable him to make the hoax succeed?

2. Clarence, the king, and Merlin are made to look very foolish in these last two chapters. What is Mark Twain satirizing through their actions?

3. What terms does the Yankee demand for restoring the sun? How do they show him to be a "typical Yankee" businessman?

CHAPTER 7

Inasmuch as I was now the second personage in the Kingdom, as far as political power and authority were concerned, much was made of me. My raiment was of silks and velvets and cloth of gold, and by consequence was very showy, also uncomfortable. But habit would soon reconcile me to my clothes; I was aware of that. I was given the choicest suite of apartments in the castle, after the king's. They were aglow with loud-colored silken hangings, but the stone floors had nothing but rushes on them for a carpet, and they were misfit rushes at that, being not all of one breed. As for conveniences, properly speaking, there weren't any. I mean *little* conveniences; it is the little conveniences that make the real comfort of life. The big oaken chairs, graced with rude carvings, were well enough, but that was the stopping place. There was no soap, no matches, no looking glass—except a metal one, about as powerful as a pail of water. And not a chromo. I had been used to chromos for years, and I saw now that without my suspecting it a passion for art had got worked into the fabric of my being, and was become a part of me. It made me homesick to look around over this proud and gaudy but heartless barrenness and remember that in our house in East Hartford, all unpretending as it was, you couldn't go into a room but you find an insurance chromo, or at least a three-color God-Bless-Our-Home over the door; and in the parlor we had nine. But here, even in my grand room of state, there wasn't anything in the nature of a picture except a thing the size of a bed quilt, which was either woven or knitted (it had darned places in it), and nothing in it was the right color or the right shape; and as for proportions, even Raphael himself couldn't have botched them more formidably, after all his practice on those nightmares they call his "celebrated Hampton Court cartoons." Raphael was a bird. We had several of his chromos; one was his "Miraculous Draught of Fishes," where he puts in a miracle of his own—puts three men into a canoe which wouldn't have held a dog without upsetting. I always admired to study R.'s art, it was so fresh and unconventional.

There wasn't even a bell or a speaking tube in the castle. I had a great many servants, and those that were on duty lolled in the anteroom; and when I wanted one of them I had to go and call for him. There was no gas, there were no candles; a bronze dish half full of boardinghouse butter with a blazing rag floating in it was the thing that produced what was regarded as light. A lot of these hung along the walls and modified the dark, just toned it down enough to make it dismal. If you went out at night, your servants carried torches. There were no books, pens, paper, or ink, and no glass in the openings they believed to be windows. It is a little thing—glass is —until it is absent, then it becomes a big thing. But perhaps the worst of all was, that there wasn't any sugar, coffee, tea, or

tobacco. I saw that I was just another Robinson Crusoe cast away on an uninhabited island, with no society but some more or less tame animals, and if I wanted to make life bearable I must do as he did—invent, contrive, create, reorganize things; set brain and hand to work, and keep them busy. Well, that was in my line.

One thing troubled me along at first—the immense interest which people took in me. Apparently the whole nation wanted a look at me. It soon transpired that the eclipse had scared the British world almost to death: that while it lasted the whole country, from one end to the other, was in a pitiable state of panic, and the churches, hermitages, and monkeries overflowed with praying and weeping poor creatures who thought the end of the world was come. Then had followed the news that the producer of this awful event was a stranger, a mighty magician at Arthur's court; that he could have blown out the sun like a candle, and was just going to do it when his mercy was purchased, and he then dissolved his enchantments, and was now recognized and honored as the man who had by his unaided might saved the globe from destruction and its peoples from extinction. Now if you consider that everybody believed that, and not only believed it but never even dreamed of doubting it, you will easily understand that there was not a person in all Britain that would not have walked fifty miles to get a sight of me. Of course I was all the talk—all other subjects were dropped; even the king became suddenly a person of minor interest and notoriety. Within twenty-four hours the delegations began to arrive, and from that time onward for a fortnight they kept coming. The village was crowded, and all the countryside. I had to go out a dozen times a day and show myself to these reverent and awe-stricken multitudes. It came to be a great burden, as to time and trouble, but of course it was at the same time compensatingly agreeable to be so celebrated and such a center of homage. It turned Brer Merlin green with envy and spite, which was a great satisfaction to me. But there was one thing I couldn't understand; nobody had asked for an autograph. I spoke to Clarence about it. By George, I had to explain to him what it was. Then he said nobody in the country could read or write but a few dozen priests. Land! think of that.

There was another thing that troubled me a little. Those multitudes presently began to agitate for another miracle. That was natural. To be able to carry back to their far homes the boast that they had seen the man who could command the sun, riding in the heavens, and be obeyed, would make them great in the eyes of their neighbors, and envied by them all; but to be able to also say they had seen him work a miracle themselves—why, people would come a distance to see *them*. The pressure got to be pretty strong. There was going to be an eclipse of the moon, and I knew the date and hour, but it was too far away. Two years. I would have given a good deal for license to hurry it up and use it now when there was a big market for it. It seemed a great pity to have it wasted so, and come lagging along at a time when a body wouldn't have any use for it as like as not. If it had been booked for only a month away, I could have sold it short; but as matters stood, I couldn't seem to cipher out any way to make it do me any good, so I gave up trying. Next, Clarence found that old Merlin was making himself busy on the sly among those people. He was spreading a report that I was a humbug, and that the reason I didn't accommodate the people with a miracle was because I couldn't. I saw that I must do something. I presently thought out a plan.

By my authority as executive I threw Merlin into prison—the same cell I had occupied myself. Then I gave public notice by herald and trumpet that I should be busy with affairs of state for a fortnight, but about the end of that time I would take a moment's leisure and blow up Merlin's stone tower by fires from heaven; in the meantime, whoso listened to evil reports about me, let him beware. Furthermore, I would perform but this one miracle at this time, and no more; if it failed to satisfy and any murmured, I would turn the murmurers into horses, and make them useful. Quiet ensued.

I took Clarence into my confidence, to a certain degree, and we went to work privately. I told him that this was a sort of miracle that required a trifle of preparation; and that it would be sudden death to ever talk about these preparations to anybody. That made his mouth safe enough. Clandestinely we made a few bushels of first-rate blasting powder, and I superintended my armorers while they constructed a lightning rod and some wires. This old stone tower was very massive—and rather ruinous, too, for it was Roman, and four hundred years old. Yes, and handsome, after a rude fashion, and clothed with ivy from base to summit, as with a shirt of scale mail. It stood on a lonely eminence, in good view from the castle, and about half a mile away.

Working by night, we stowed the powder in the tower—dug stones out, on the inside, and buried the powder in the walls themselves, which were fifteen feet thick at the base. We put in a peck at a time, in a dozen places. We could have blown up the Tower of London with these charges. When the thirteenth night was come we put up our lightning rod, bedded it in one of the batches of powder, and ran wires from it to the other batches. Everybody had shunned that locality from the day of my proclamation, but on the morning of the fourteenth I thought best to warn the people, through the heralds, to keep clear away —a quarter of a mile away. Then added, by command, that at some time during the twenty-four hours I would consummate the miracle, but would first give a brief notice; by flags on the castle towers, if in the daytime, by torch baskets in the same places if at night.

Thundershowers had been tolerantly frequent, of late, and I was not much afraid of a failure; still, I shouldn't have cared for a delay of a day or two; I should have explained that I was busy with affairs of state, yet, and the people must wait.

Of course we had a blazing sunny day —almost the first one without a cloud for three weeks; things always happen so. I kept secluded, and watched the weather. Clarence dropped in from time to time and said the public excitement was growing and growing all the time, and the whole country filling with human masses as far as one could see from the battlements. At last the wind sprang up and a cloud appeared—in the right quarter, too, and just at nightfall. For a little while I watched that distant cloud spread and blacken, then I judged it was time for me to appear. I ordered the torch baskets to be lit, and Merlin liberated and sent to me. A quarter of an hour later I ascended the parapet and there found the king and the court assembled and gazing off in the darkness toward Merlin's tower. Already the darkness was so heavy that one could not see far; these people, and the old turrets, being partly in deep shadow and partly in the red glow from the great torch baskets overhead, made a good deal of a picture.

Merlin arrived in a gloomy mood. I said:

"You wanted to burn me alive when I had not done you any harm, and latterly you have been trying to injure my professional reputation. Therefore I am going to call down fire and blow up your tower, but it is only fair to give you a chance; now if you think you can break my enchantments and ward off the fires, step to the bat, it's your innings."

"I can, fair sir, and I will. Doubt it not."

He drew an imaginary circle on the stones of the roof, and burnt a pinch of powder in it which sent up a small cloud of aromatic smoke, whereat everybody fell back, and began to cross themselves and get uncomfortable. Then he began to mutter and make passes in the air with his hands. He worked himself up slowly and gradually into a sort of frenzy, and got to thrashing around with his arms like the sails of a windmill. By this time the storm had about reached us; the gusts of wind were flaring the torches and making the shadows swash about, the first heavy drops of rain were falling, the world abroad was black as pitch, the lightning began to wink fitfully. Of course my rod would be loading itself now. In fact, things were imminent. So I said:

"You have had time enough. I have given you every advantage, and not interfered. It is plain your magic is weak. It is only fair that I begin now."

I made about three passes in the air, and then there was an awful crash and that old tower leaped into the sky in chunks, along with a vast volcanic fountain of fire that turned night to noonday, and showed a thousand acres of human beings groveling on the ground in a general collapse of consternation. Well, it rained mortar and masonry the rest of the week. This was the report; but probably the facts would have modified it.

It was an effective miracle. The great bothersome temporary population vanished. There were a good many thousand tracks in the mud the next morning, but they were all outward bound. If I had advertised another miracle I couldn't have raised an audience with a sheriff.

Merlin's stock was flat. The king wanted to stop his wages; he even wanted to banish him, but I interfered. I said he would be useful to work the weather, and attend to small matters like that, and I would give him a lift now and then when his poor little parlor magic soured on him. There wasn't a rag of his tower left, but I had the government rebuild it for him, and advised him to take boarders; but he was too high-toned for that. And as for being grateful, he never even said thank-you. He was a rather hard lot, take him how you might; but then you couldn't fairly expect a man to be sweet that had been set back so.

FOR DISCUSSION

1. What "new miracle" does the Yankee perform? What is its effect?

2. Why does no one ask for his autograph?

3. What does his "Robinson Crusoe" remark (page 560) reveal about his attitudes?

4. What "modern convenience" does the Yankee miss most?

CHAPTER 8

To be vested with enormous authority is a fine thing; but to have the onlooking world consent to it is a finer. The tower episode solidified my power, and made it impregnable. If any were perchance disposed to be jealous and critical before that, they experienced a change of heart, now. There was not anyone in the kingdom who would have considered it good judgment to meddle with my matters.

I was fast getting adjusted to my situation and circumstances. For a time, I used to wake up mornings, and smile at my "dream," and listen for the Colt's factory whistle; but that sort of thing played itself out, gradually, and at last I was fully able to realize that I was actually living in the sixth century, and in Arthur's court, not a lunatic asylum. After that, I was just as much at home in that century as I could have been in any other; and as for preference, I wouldn't have traded it for the twentieth. Look at the opportunities here for a man of knowledge, brains, pluck, and enterprise to sail in and grow up with the country. The grandest field that ever was; and all my own; not a competitor; not a man who wasn't a baby to me in acquirements and capacities; whereas, what would I amount to in the twentieth century? I should be foreman of a factory, that is about all; and could drag a seine downstreet any day and catch a hundred better men than myself.

What a jump I had made! I couldn't keep from thinking about it, and contemplating it, just as one does who has struck oil. There was nothing back of me that could approach it, unless it might be Joseph's case; and Joseph's only approached it, it didn't equal it, quite. For it stands to reason that as Joseph's splendid financial ingenuities advantaged nobody but the king, the general public must have regarded him with a good deal of disfavor, whereas I had done my entire public a kindness in sparing the sun, and was popular by reason of it.

I was no shadow of a king; I was the substance; the king himself was the shadow. My power was colossal; and it was not a mere name, as such things have generally been, it was the genuine article. I stood here, at the very spring and source of the second great period of the world's history; and could see the trickling stream of that history gather, and deepen and broaden, and roll its mighty tides down the far centuries; and I could note the upspringing of adventurers like myself in the shelter of its long array of thrones: De Montforts, Gavestons, Mortimers, Villierses; the warmaking, campaign-directing wantons of France, and Charles the Second's scepter-wielding drabs; but nowhere in the procession was my full-sized fellow visible. I was a Unique; and glad to know that that fact could not be dislodged or challenged for thirteen centuries and a half, for sure.

Yes, in power I was equal to the king. At the same time there was another power that was a trifle stronger than both of us put together. That was the Church. I do not wish to disguise that fact. I couldn't, if I wanted to. But never mind about that, now; it will show up, in its proper place, later on. It didn't cause me any trouble in the beginning—at least any of consequence.

Well, it was a curious country, and full of interest. And the people! They were the quaintest and simplest and trustingest race; why, they were nothing but rabbits. It was pitiful for a person born in a wholesome free atmosphere to listen to their humble and hearty outpourings of loyalty toward their king and Church and nobility; as if they had any more occasion to love and honor king and Church and noble than a slave has to love and honor the lash, or a dog has to love and honor the stranger that kicks him! Why, dear me, *any* kind of royalty, howsoever modified, *any* kind of aristocracy, howsoever pruned, is rightly an insult; but if you are born and brought up under that sort of arrangement you probably never find it out for yourself, and

don't believe it when somebody else tells you. It is enough to make a body ashamed of his race to think of the sort of froth that has always occupied its thrones without shadow of right or reason, and the seventh-rate people that have always figured as its aristocracies—a company of monarchs and nobles who, as a rule, would have achieved only poverty and obscurity if left, like their betters, to their own exertions.

The most of King Arthur's British nation were slaves, pure and simple, and bore that name, and wore the iron collar on their necks; and the rest were slaves in fact, but without the name; they imagined themselves men and freemen, and called themselves so. The truth was, the nation as a body was in the world for one object, and one only: to grovel before king and Church and noble; to slave for them, sweat blood for them, starve that they might be fed, work that they might play, drink misery to the dregs that they might be happy, go naked that they might wear silks and jewels, pay taxes that they might be spared from paying them, be familiar all their lives with the degrading language and postures of adulation that they might walk in pride and think themselves the gods of this world. And for all this, the thanks they got were cuffs and contempt; and so poor-spirited were they that they took even this sort of attention as an honor.

Inherited ideas are a curious thing, and interesting to observe and examine. I had mine, the king and his people had theirs. In both cases they flowed in ruts worn deep by time and habit, and the man who should have proposed to divert them by reason and argument would have had a long contract on his hands. For instance, those people had inherited the idea that all men without title and a long pedigree, whether they had great natural gifts and acquirements or hadn't, were creatures of no more consideration than so many animals, bugs, insects; whereas I had inherited the idea that human daws who can consent to masquerade in the peacock-shams of inherited dignities and unearned titles are of no good but to be laughed at. The way I was looked upon was odd, but it was natural. You know how the keeper and the public regard the elephant in the menagerie: well, that is the idea. They are full of admiration of his vast bulk and his prodigious strength; they speak with pride of the fact that he can do a hundred marvels which are far and away beyond their own powers; and they speak with the same pride of the fact that in his wrath he is able to drive a thousand men before him. But does that make him one of *them?* No; the raggedest tramp in the pit would smile at the idea. He couldn't comprehend it; couldn't take it in; couldn't in any remote way conceive of it. Well, to the king, the nobles, and all the nation, down to the very slaves and tramps, I was just that kind of an elephant, and nothing more. I was admired, also feared; but it was as an animal is admired and feared. The animal is not reverenced, neither was I; I was not even respected. I had no pedigree, no inherited title; so in the king's and nobles' eyes I was mere dirt; the people regarded me with wonder and awe, but there was no reverence mixed with it; through the force of inherited ideas they were not able to conceive of anything being entitled to that except pedigree and lordship. There you see the hand of that power, the Church. In two or three little centuries it had converted a nation of men to a nation of worms. Before the day of the Church's supremacy in the world, men were men, and held their heads up, and had a man's pride and spirit and independence; and what of greatness and position a person got, he got mainly by achievement, not by birth. But then the Church came to the front, with an ax to grind; and she was wise, subtle, and knew more than one way to skin a cat—or a nation; she invented "divine right of kings," and propped it all around, brick by brick, with the Beatitudes—wrenching them from their good purpose to make them fortify an evil one; she preached (to the commoner) humility, obedience to superiors, the beauty of self-sacrifice; she preached (to the commoner) meekness under insult; preached (still to the commoner, always to the commoner) patience, meanness of spirit, nonresistance under oppression; and she introduced heritable ranks and aristocracies, and taught all the Christian populations of the earth to bow down to them and worship them. Even down to my birth century that poison was still in the blood of Christendom, and the best of English commoners was still content to see his inferiors impudently continuing to hold a number of positions, such as lordships and the throne, to which the grotesque laws of his country did not allow him to aspire; in fact he was not merely contented with this strange condition of things, he was even able to persuade himself that he was proud of it. It seems to show that there isn't anything you can't stand, if you are only born and bred to it. Of course that taint, that reverence for rank and title, had been in our American blood, too—I know that; but when I left America it had disappeared—at least to all intents and purposes. The remnant of it was restricted to the dudes and dudesses. When a disease has worked its way down to that level, it may fairly be said to be out of the system.

But to return to my anomalous position in King Arthur's kingdom. Here I was, a giant among pigmies, a man among children, a master intelligence among intellectual moles: by all rational measurement the one and only actually great man in that whole British world; and yet there and then, just as in the remote England of my birth time, the sheep-witted earl who could claim long descent from a king's leman, acquired at secondhand from the slums of London, was a better man than I was. Such a personage was fawned upon in Arthur's realm and reverently looked up to by everybody, even though his dispositions were as mean as his intelligence, and his morals as base as his lineage. There were times when *he* could sit down in the king's presence, but I couldn't. I could have got a title easily enough, and that would have raised me a large step in everybody's eyes; even in the king's, the giver of it. But I didn't ask for it; and I declined it when it was offered. I couldn't have enjoyed such a thing with my notions; and it wouldn't have been fair, anyway, because as far back as I could go, our tribe had always been short of the bar sinister. I couldn't have felt really and satisfactorily fine and proud and set up over any title except one that should come from the nation itself, the only legitimate source; and such an one I hoped to win; and in the course of years of honest and honorable endeavor, I did win it and did wear it with a high and clean pride. This title fell casually from the lips of a blacksmith, one day, in a village, was caught up as a happy thought and tossed from mouth to mouth with a laugh and an affirmative vote; in ten days it had swept the kingdom, and was become as familiar as the king's name. I was never known by any other designation afterward, whether in the nation's talk or in grave debate upon the matters of state at the council board of the sovereign. This title, translated into modern speech, would be THE BOSS. Elected by the nation. That suited me. And it was a pretty high title. There were very few THE's, and I was one of them. If you spoke of the duke, or the earl, or the bishop, how could anybody tell which one you meant? But if you spoke of The King or The Queen or The Boss, it was different.

Well, I liked the king, and *as* king I respected him—respected the office; at least respected it as much as I was capable of respecting any unearned supremacy; but as *men* I looked down upon him and his nobles—privately. And he and they liked me, and respected my office; but as an animal, without birth or sham title, they looked down upon me—and were not particularly private about it, either. I didn't charge for my opinion about them, and they didn't charge for their opinion about me: the account was square, the books balanced, everybody was satisfied.

FOR DISCUSSION

1. How does the Yankee view himself in relation to a) other men of the sixth century, b) other great men of history, and c) other "modern" men? What is the irony of his view?

2. The Yankee makes a long-winded speech attacking various medieval ideas and institutions. Which ones are most offensive to his democratic spirit?

3. Why does he see himself as a kind of sixth-century elephant?

4. In spite of his contempt for titles, what title does the Yankee finally accept? What makes it preferable, from his point of view, to "duke" or "earl"?

CHAPTER 9

They were always having grand tournaments there at Camelot; and very stirring and picturesque and ridiculous human bullfights they were, too, but just a little wearisome to the practical mind. However, I was generally on hand—for two reasons: a man must not hold himself aloof from the things which his friends and his community have at heart if he would be liked—especially as a statesman; and both as businessman and statesman I wanted to study the tournament and see if I couldn't invent an improvement on it. That reminds me to remark, in passing, that the very first official thing I did, in my administration—and it was on the very first day of it, too—was to start a patent office; for I knew that a country without a patent office and good patent laws was just a crab, and couldn't travel any way but sideways or backwards.

Things ran along, a tournament nearly every week; and now and then the boys used to want me to take a hand—I mean Sir Launcelot and the rest—but I said I would by and by; no hurry yet, and too much government machinery to oil up and set to rights and start a-going.

We had one tournament which was continued from day to day during more than a week, and as many as five hundred knights took part in it, from first to last. They were weeks gathering. They came on horseback from everywhere; from the very ends of the country, and even from beyond the sea; and many brought ladies and all brought squires, and troops of servants. It was a most gaudy and gorgeous crowd, as to costumery, and very characteristic of the country and the time, in the way of high animal spirits, innocent indecencies of language, and happy-hearted indifference to morals. It was fight or look on, all day and every day; and sing, gamble, dance, carouse, half the night every night. They had

a most noble good time. You never saw such people. Those banks of beautiful ladies, shining in their barbaric splendors, would see a knight sprawl from his horse in the lists with a lance shaft the thickness of your ankle clean through him and the blood spouting, and instead of fainting they would clap their hands and crowd each other for a better view; only sometimes one would dive into her handkerchief, and look ostentatiously brokenhearted, and then you could lay two to one that there was a scandal there somewhere and she was afraid the public hadn't found it out.

The noise at night would have been annoying to me ordinarily, but I didn't mind it in the present circumstances, because it kept me from hearing the quacks detaching legs and arms from the day's cripples. They ruined an uncommon good old crosscut saw for me, and broke the sawbuck, too, but I let it pass. And as for my ax—well, I made up my mind that the next time I lent an ax to a surgeon I would pick my century.

I not only watched this tournament from day to day, but detailed an intelligent priest from my Department of Public Morals and Agriculture, and ordered him to report it; for it was my purpose by and by, when I should have gotten the people along far enough, to start a newspaper. The first thing you want in a new country is a patent office; then work up your school system; and after that, out with your paper. A newspaper has its faults, and plenty of them, but no matter, it's hark from the tomb for a dead nation, and don't you forget it. You can't resurrect a dead nation without it; there isn't any way. So I wanted to sample things, and be finding out what sort of reporter material I might be able to rake together out of the sixth century when I should come to need it.

Well, the priest did very well, considering. He got in all the details, and that is a good thing in a local item: you see he had kept books for the undertaker department of his church when he was younger, and there, you know, the money's in the details; the more details, the more swag: bearers, mutes, candles, prayers—everything counts; and if the bereaved don't buy prayers enough you mark up your candles with a forked pencil, and your bill shows up all right. And he had a good knack at getting in the complimentary thing here and there about a knight that was likely to advertise —no, I mean a knight that had influence; and he also had a neat gift of exaggeration, for in his time he had kept door for a pious hermit who lived in a sty and worked miracles.

Of course this novice's report lacked whoop and crash and lurid description, and therefore wanted the true ring; but its antique wording was quaint and sweet and simple, and full of the fragrances and flavors of the time, and these little merits made up in a measure for its more important lacks. Here is an extract from it:

Then Sir Brian de les Isles and Grummore Grummorsum, knights of the castle, encountered with Sir Aglovale and Sir Tor, and Sir Tor smote down Sir Grummore Grummorsum to the earth. Then came in Sir Carados of the dolorous tower, and Sir Turquine, knights of the castle, and there encountered with them Sir Percivale de Galis and Sir Lamorak de Galis, that were two brethren, and there encountered Sir Percivale with Sir Carados, and either brake their spears unto their hands, and then Sir Turquine with Sir Lamorak, and either of them smote down other, horse and all, to the earth, and either parties rescued other and horsed them again.

Well, to proceed: I sat in the private box set apart for me as the king's minister. While Sir Dinadan was waiting for his turn to enter the lists, he came in there and sat down and began to talk; for he was always making up to me, because I was a stranger and he liked to have a fresh market for his jokes, the most of them having reached that stage of wear where the teller has to do the laughing himself while the other person looks sick. I had always responded to his efforts as well as I could, and felt a very deep and real kindness for him, too, for the reason that if by malice of fate he knew the one particular anecdote which I had heard oftenest and had most hated and most loathed all my life, he had at least spared it me. It was one which I had heard attributed to every humorous person who had ever stood on American soil, from Columbus down to Artemus Ward. It was about a humorous lecturer who flooded an ignorant audience with the killingest jokes for an hour and never got a laugh; and then when he was leaving, some gray simpletons wrung him gratefully by the hand and said it had been the funniest thing they had ever heard, and "it was all they could do to keep from laughin' right out in meetin'." That anecdote never saw the day that it was worth the telling; and yet I had sat under the telling of it hundreds and thousands and millions and billions of times, and cried and cursed all the way through. Then who can hope to know what my feelings were, to hear this armor-plated ape start on it again, in the murky twilight of tradition, before the dawn of history, while even Lactantius might be referred to as "the late Lactantius," and the Crusades wouldn't be born for five hundred years yet? Just as he finished, the call boy came; so, hawhawing like a demon, he went rattling and clanking out like a crate of loose castings, and I knew nothing more. It was some minutes before I came to, and then I opened my eyes just in time to see Sir Gareth fetch him an awful welt, and I unconsciously out with the prayer, "I hope to gracious he's killed!" But by ill luck, before I had got half through with the words, Sir Gareth crashed into Sir Sagramor le Desirous and sent him thundering over his horse's crupper, and Sir Sagramor caught my remark and thought I meant it for *him*.

Well, whenever one of those people got a thing into his head, there was no getting it out again. I knew that, so I saved my breath, and offered no explanations. As soon as Sir Sagramor got well, he notified me that there was a little account to settle between us, and he named a day three or four years in the future; place of settlement, the lists where the offense had been given. I said I would be ready when he got back. You see, he was going for the Holy Grail. The boys all took a flier at the Holy Grail now and then. It was several years' cruise. They always put in the long absence snooping around, in the most conscientious way, though none of them had any idea where the Holy Grail really was, and I don't think any of them actually expected to find it, or would have known what to do with it if he *had* run across it. You see, it was just the Northwest Passage of that day, as you may say; that was all. Every year expeditions went out holy grailing, and next year relief expeditions went out to hunt for *them*. There was worlds of reputation in it, but no money. Why, they actually wanted *me* to put in! Well, I should smile.

FOR DISCUSSION

1. Placing incompatible things together is known as *incongruity*. This technique is the basis of much of Mark Twain's humor. For example, referring to Sir Launcelot and the other knights as "the boys" is incongruous, as is a "Department of Public Morals and Agriculture." What other examples can you find?

2. What aspects of medieval life does Mark Twain satirize in this chapter? How does he make his attack humorous?

3. Of all the changes that he hopes to make, which ones does the Yankee begin first? Why?

4. Why does Sir Sagramor challenge the Yankee to joust?

CHAPTER 10

The Round Table soon heard of the challenge, and of course it was a good deal discussed, for such things interested the boys. The king thought I ought now to set forth in quest of adventures, so that I might gain renown and be the more worthy to meet Sir Sagramor when the several years should have rolled away. I excused myself for the present; I said it would take me three or four years yet to get things well fixed up and going smoothly; then I should be ready; all the chances were that at the end of that time Sir Sagramor would still be out grailing, so no valuable time would be lost by the postponement; I should then have been in office six or seven years, and I believed my system and machinery would be so well developed that I could take a holiday without its working any harm.

I was pretty well satisfied with what I had already accomplished. In various quiet nooks and corners I had the beginnings of all sorts of industries under way—nuclei of future vast factories, the iron and steel missionaries of my future civilization. In these were gathered together the brightest young minds I could find, and I kept agents out raking the country for more, all the time. I was training a crowd of ignorant folk into experts—experts in every sort of handi-work and scientific calling. These nurseries of mine went smoothly and privately along undisturbed in their obscure country re-treats, for nobody was allowed to come into their precincts without a special permit—for I was afraid of the Church.

I had started a teacher factory and a lot of Sunday schools the first thing; as a re-sult, I now had an admirable system of graded schools in full blast in those places, and also a complete variety of Protestant congregations all in a prosperous and growing condition. Everybody could be any kind of a Christian he wanted to; there was perfect freedom in that matter. But I confined public religious teaching to the churches and the Sunday schools, permit-ting nothing of it in my other educational buildings. I could have given my own sect the preference and made everybody a Pres-byterian without any trouble, but that would have been to affront a law of hu-man nature: spiritual wants and instincts are as various in the human family as are physical appetites, complexions, and fea-tures, and a man is only at his best, mor-ally, when he is equipped with the reli-gious garment whose color and shape and size most nicely accommodate themselves to the spiritual complexion, angularities, and stature of the individual who wears it; and besides I was afraid of a united Church; it makes a mighty power, the mightiest conceivable, and then when it by and by gets into selfish hands, as it is always bound to do, it means death to hu-man liberty, and paralysis to human thought.

All mines were royal property, and there were a good many of them. They had formerly been worked as savages always work mines—holes grubbed in the earth and the mineral brought up in sacks of hide by hand, at the rate of a ton a day; but I had begun to put the mining on a scien-tific basis as early as I could.

Yes, I had made pretty handsome prog-ress when Sir Sagramor's challenge struck me.

Four years rolled by—and then! Well, you would never imagine it in the world. Unlimited power *is* the ideal thing when it is in safe hands. The despotism of heaven is the one absolutely perfect government. An earthly despotism would be the abso-lutely perfect earthly government, if the conditions were the same, namely, the despot the perfectest individual of the hu-man race, and his lease of life perpetual. But as a perishable perfect man must die, and leave his despotism in the hands of an imperfect successor, an earthly despo-tism is not merely a bad form of govern-ment, it is the worst form that is possible.

My works showed what a despot could do with the resources of a kingdom at his command. Unsuspected by this dark land, I had the civilization of the nineteenth cen-tury booming under its very nose! It was fenced away from the public view, but there it was, a gigantic and unassailable fact—and to be heard from, yet, if I lived and had luck. There it was, as sure a fact, and as substantial a fact as any serene vol-cano, standing innocent with its smokeless summit in the blue sky and giving no sign of the rising hell in its bowels. My schools and churches were children four years be-fore; they were grown up, now; my shops of that day were vast factories, now; where I had a dozen trained men then, I had a thousand, now; where I had one brilliant expert then, I had fifty now. . . . But I was not going to do the thing in that sudden way. It was not my policy. The people could not have stood it; and moreover I should have had the Established Church on my back in a minute.

No, I had been going cautiously all the while. I had had confidential agents trickling through the country some time, whose office was to undermine knighthood by imperceptible degrees, and to gnaw a little at this and that and the other superstition, and so prepare the way gradually for a better order of things. I was turning on my light one candlepower at a time, and meant to continue to do so.

I had scattered some branch schools secretly about the kingdom, and they were doing very well. I meant to work this racket more and more, as time wore on, if nothing occurred to frighten me. One of my deepest secrets was my West Point—my military academy. I kept that most jealously out of sight; and I did the same with my naval academy which I had established at a remote seaport. Both were prospering to my satisfaction.

Clarence was twenty-two now, and was my head executive, my right hand. He was a darling; he was equal to anything; there wasn't anything he couldn't turn his hand to. Of late I had been training him for journalism, for the time seemed about right for a start in the newspaper line; nothing big, but just a small weekly for experimental circulation in my civilization-nurseries. He took to it like a duck; there was an editor concealed in him, sure. Already he had doubled himself in one way; he talked sixth century and wrote nineteenth. His journalistic style was climbing, steadily; it was already up to the back settlement Alabama mark, and couldn't be told from the editorial output of that region either by matter or flavor.

We had another large departure on hand, too. This was a telegraph and a telephone; our first venture in this line. These wires were for private service only, as yet, and must be kept private until a riper day should come. We had a gang of men on the road, working mainly by night. They were stringing ground wires; we were afraid to put up poles, for they would attract too much inquiry. Ground wires were good enough, in both instances, for my wires were protected by an insulation of my own invention which was perfect. My men had orders to strike across country, avoiding roads, and establishing connection with any considerable towns whose lights betrayed their presence, and leaving experts in charge. Nobody could tell you how to find any place in the kingdom, for nobody ever went intentionally to any place, but only struck it by accident in his wanderings, and then generally left it without thinking to inquire what its name was. At one time and another we had sent out topographical expeditions to survey and map the kingdom, but the priests had always interfered and raised trouble. So we had given the thing up, for the present; it would be poor wisdom to antagonize the Church.

As for the general condition of the country, it was as it had been when I arrived in it, to all intents and purposes. I had made changes, but they were necessarily slight, and they were not noticeable. Thus far, I had not even meddled with taxation, outside of the taxes which provided the royal revenues. I had systematized those, and put the service on an effective and righteous basis. As a result, these revenues were already quadrupled, and yet the burden was so much more equably distributed than before, that all the kingdom felt a sense of relief, and the praises of my administration were hearty and general.

Personally, I struck an interruption, now, but I did not mind it, it could not have happened at a better time. Earlier it could have annoyed me, but now everything was in good hands and swimming right along. The king had reminded me several times, of late, that the postponement I had asked for, four years before, had about run out, now. It was a hint that I ought to be starting out to seek adventures and get up a reputation of a size to make me worthy of the honor of breaking a lance with Sir Sagramor, who was still out grailing, but was being hunted for by various relief expeditions, and might be found any year, now. So you see I was expecting this interruption; it did not take me by surprise.

FOR DISCUSSION

1. What are eight elements of civilization introduced by "the Boss"? Is there anything humorous in his telling of this?

2. Who does he consider his main antagonist? Why?

3. Why does the Yankee compare his improvements to a volcano?

CHAPTER 11

There never was such a country for wandering liars; and they were of both sexes. Hardly a month went by without one of these tramps arriving; and generally loaded with a tale about some princess or other wanting help to get her out of some faraway castle where she was held in captivity by a lawless scoundrel, usually a giant. Now you would think that the first thing the king would do after listening to such a novelette from an entire stranger, would be to ask for credentials—yes, and a pointer or two as to locality of castle, best route to it, and so on. But nobody ever thought of so simple and commonsense a thing as that. No, everybody swallowed these people's lies whole, and never asked a question of any sort or about anything. Well, one day when I was not around, one of these people came along—it was a she one, this time—and told a tale of the usual pattern. Her mistress was a captive in a vast and gloomy castle, along with forty-four other young and beautiful girls, pretty much all of them princesses; they had been languishing in that cruel captivity for twenty-six years; the masters of the castle were three stupendous brothers, each with four arms and one eye—the eye in the center of the forehead, and as big as a fruit. Sort of fruit not mentioned; their usual slovenliness in statistics.

Would you believe it? The king and the whole Round Table were in raptures over this preposterous opportunity for adventure. Every knight of the Table jumped for the chance, and begged for it; but to their vexation and chagrin the king conferred it upon me, who had not asked for it at all.

By an effort, I contained my joy when Clarence brought me the news. But he—he could not contain his. His mouth gushed delight and gratitude in a steady discharge—delight in my good fortune, gratitude to the king for this splendid mark of his favor for me. He could keep neither his legs nor his body still, but pirouetted about the place in an airy ecstasy of happiness.

On my side, I could have cursed the kindness that conferred upon me this benefaction, but I kept my vexation under the surface for policy's sake, and did what I could to let on to be glad. Indeed, I *said* I was glad. And in a way it was true; I was as glad as a person is when he is scalped.

Well, one must make the best of things, and not waste time with useless fretting, but get down to business and see what can be done. In all lies there is wheat among the chaff; I must get at the wheat in this case: so I sent for the girl and she came. She was a comely enough creature, and soft and modest, but if signs went for anything, she didn't know as much as a lady's watch. I said—

"My dear, have you been questioned as to particulars?"

She said she hadn't.

"Well, I didn't expect you had, but I thought I would ask to make sure; it's the way I've been raised. Now you mustn't take it unkindly if I remind you that as we don't know you, we must go a little slow. You may be all right, of course, and we'll hope that you are; but to take it for granted isn't business. *You* understand that. I'm obliged to ask you a few questions; just answer up fair and square, and don't be afraid. Where do you live, when you are at home?"

"In the land of Moder, fair sir."

"Land of Moder. I don't remember hearing of it before. Parents living?"

"As to that, I know not if they be yet on live, sith it is many years that I have lain shut up in the castle."

"Your name, please?"

"I hight the Demoiselle Alisande la Carteloise, an it please you."

"Do you know anybody here who can identify you?"

"That were not likely, fair lord, I being come hither now for the first time."

"Have you brought any letters—any documents—any proofs that you are trustworthy and truthful?"

"Of a surety, no; and wherefore should I? Have I not a tongue, and cannot I say all that myself?"

"But *your* saying it, you know, and somebody else's saying it, is different."

"Different? How might that be? I fear me I do not understand."

"Don't *understand?* Land of—why, you see—you see—why, great Scott, can't you understand a little thing like that? Can't you understand the difference between your—*why* do you look so innocent and idiotic!"

"I? In truth I know not, but an it were the will of God."

"Yes, yes, I reckon that's about the size of it. Don't mind my seeming excited; I'm not. Let us change the subject. Now as to this castle, with forty-five princesses in it, and three ogres at the head of it, tell me—where is this harem?"

"Harem?"

"The *castle,* you understand; where is the castle?"

"Oh, as to that, it is great, and strong, and well beseen, and lieth in a far country. Yes, it is many leagues."

"*How* many?"

"Ah, fair sir, it were woundily hard to tell, they are so many, and do so lap the one upon the other, and being made all in the same image and tincted with the same color, one may not know the one league from its fellow, nor how to count them except they be taken apart, and ye wit well it were God's work to do that, being not within man's capacity; for ye will note—"

"Hold on, hold on, never mind about the distance; *whereabouts* does the castle lie? What's the direction from here?"

"Ah, please you sir, it hath no direction from here; by reason that the road lieth not straight, but turneth evermore; wherefore the direction of its place abideth not, but is sometime under the one sky and anon under another, whereso if ye be minded that it is in the east, and wend thitherward, ye shall observe that the way of the road doth yet again turn upon itself by the space of half a circle, and this marvel happing again and yet again and still again, it will grieve you that you had thought by vanities of the mind to thwart and bring to naught the will of Him that giveth not a castle a direction from a place except it pleaseth Him, and if it please Him not, will the rather that even all castles and all directions thereunto vanish out of the earth, leaving the places wherein they tarried desolate and vacant, so warning His creatures that where He will He will, and where He will not He—"

"Oh, that's all right, that's all right, give us a rest; never mind about the direction, *hang* the direction—I beg pardon, I beg a thousand pardons, I am not well today; pay no attention when I soliloquize, it is an old habit, an old, bad habit, and hard to get rid of when one's digestion is all disordered with eating food that was raised forever and ever before he was born; good land! a man can't keep his functions regular on spring chickens thirteen hundred years old. But come—never mind about that; let's—have you got such a thing as a map of that region about you? Now a good map—"

"Is it peradventure that manner of thing which of late the unbelievers have brought from over the great seas, which, being boiled in oil, and an onion and salt added thereto, doth—"

"What, a map? What are you talking about? Don't you know what a map is? There, there, never mind, don't explain, I hate explanations; they fog a thing up so that you can't tell anything about it. Run along, dear; good-day; show her the way, Clarence."

Oh, well, it was reasonably plain, now, why these donkeys didn't prospect these liars for details. It may be that this girl had a fact in her somewhere, but I don't believe you could have sluiced it out with a hydraulic; nor got it with the earlier forms of blasting, even; it was a case for dynamite. Why, she was a perfect sap; and yet the king and his knights had listened to her as if she had been a leaf out of the gospel. It kind of sizes up the whole party. And think of the simple ways of this court: this wandering wench hadn't any more trouble to get access to the king in his palace than she would have had to get into the poorhouse in my day and country. In fact he was glad to see her, glad to hear her tale; with that adventure of hers to offer, she was as welcome as a corpse is to a coroner.

Just as I was ending up these reflections, Clarence came back. I remarked upon the barren result of my efforts with the girl; hadn't got hold of a single point that could help me to find the castle. The youth looked a little surprised, or puzzled, or something, and intimated that he had been wondering to himself what I had wanted to ask the girl all those questions for.

"Why, great guns," I said, "don't I want to find the castle? And how else would I go about it?"

"La, sweet your worship, one may lightly answer that, I ween. She will go with thee. They always do. She will ride with thee."

"Ride with me? Nonsense!"

"But of a truth she will. She will ride with thee. Thou shalt see."

"What? She browse around the hills and scour the woods with me—alone—and I as good as engaged to be married? Why, it's scandalous. Think how it would look."

My, the dear face that rose before me! The boy was eager to know all about this tender matter. I swore him to secrecy and then whispered her name. He looked disappointed, and said he didn't remember the countess. How natural it was for the little courtier to give her a rank. He asked me where she lived.

"In East Har—" I came to myself and stopped, a little confused; then I said, "Never mind, now; I'll tell you sometime."

And might he see her? Would I let him see her some day?

It was but a little thing to promise—thirteen hundred years or so—and he so eager; so I said Yes. But I sighed; I couldn't help it. And yet there was no sense in sighing, for she wasn't born yet. But that is the way we are made: we don't reason, where we feel; we just feel.

My expedition was all the talk that day and that night, and the boys were very good to me, and made much of me, and seemed to have forgotten their vexation and disappointment, and come to be as anxious for me to hive those ogres and set those ripe old virgins loose as if it were themselves that had the contract. Well, they *were* good children—but just children, that is all. And they gave me no end of points about how to scout for giants, and how to scoop them in; and they told me all sorts of charms against enchantments, and gave me salves and other rubbish to put on my wounds. But it never occurred to one of them to reflect that if I was such a wonderful necromancer as I was pretending to be, I ought not to need salves or instructions, or charms against enchantments, and least of all, arms and armor, on a foray of any kind—even against fire-spouting dragons, and devils hot from perdition, let alone such poor adversaries as these I was after, these commonplace ogres of the back settlements.

I was to have an early breakfast, and start at dawn, for that was the usual way; but I had the demon's own time with my armor, and this delayed me a little. It is troublesome to get into, and there is so much detail. First you wrap a layer or two of blanket around your body, for a sort of cushion and to keep off the cold iron; then you put on your sleeves and shirt of chain mail—these are made of small steel links woven together, and they form a fabric so flexible that if you toss your shirt onto the floor, it slumps into a pile like a peck of wet fishnet; it is very heavy and is nearly the uncomfortablest material in the world for a nightshirt, yet plenty used it for that—tax collectors, and reformers, and one-horse kings with a defective title, and those sorts of people; then you put on your shoes—flatboats roofed over with interleaving bands of steel—and screw your clumsy spurs into the heels. Next you buckle your greaves on your legs, and your cuisses on your thighs; then come your backplate and your breastplate, and you begin to feel crowded; then you hitch onto the breastplate and the half-petticoat of broad overlapping bands of steel which hangs down in front but is scalloped out behind so you can sit down, and isn't any real improvement on an inverted coal scuttle, either for looks or for wear, or to wipe your hands on; next you belt on your sword; then you put your stovepipe joints onto your arms, your iron gauntlets onto your hands, your iron rattrap onto your head, with a rag of steel web hitched onto it to hang over the back of your neck—and there you are, snug as a candle in a candle mold. This is no time to dance. Well, a man that is packed away like that, is a nut that isn't worth the cracking, there is so little of the meat, when you get down to it, by comparison with the shell.

The boys helped me, or I never could have got in. Just as we finished, Sir Bedivere happened in, and I saw that as like as not I hadn't chosen the most convenient outfit for a long trip. How stately he looked; and tall and broad and grand. He had on his head a conical steel casque that only came down to his ears, and for visor had only a narrow steel bar that extended down to his upper lip and protected his nose; and all the rest of him, from neck to heel, was flexible chain mail, trousers and all. But pretty much all of him was hidden under his outside garment, which of course was of chain mail, as I said, and hung straight from his shoulders to his ankles; and from his middle to the bottom, both before and behind, was divided, so that he could ride and let the skirts hang down on each side. He was going grailing, and it was just the outfit for it, too. I would have given a good deal for that ulster, but it was too late now to be fooling around. The sun was just up, the king and the court were all on hand to see me off and wish me luck; so it wouldn't be etiquette for me to tarry. You don't get on your horse yourself; no, if you tried it you would get disappointed. They carry you out, just as they carry a sunstruck man to the drug store, and put you on, and help get you to rights, and fix your feet in the stirrups; and all the while you do feel so strange and stuffy and like somebody else—like somebody that has been married on a sudden, or struck by lightning, or something like that, and hasn't quite fetched around, yet, and is sort of numb, and can't just get his bearings. Then they stood up the mast they called a spear, in its socket by my left foot, and I gripped it with my hand; lastly they hung my shield around my neck, and I was all complete and ready to up anchor and get to sea. Everybody was as good to me as they could be, and a maid of honor gave me the stirrup cup her own self. There was nothing more to do, now, but for that damsel to get up behind me on a pillion, which she did, and put an arm or so around me to hold on.

And so we started; and everybody gave us a good-bye and waved their handkerchiefs or helmets. And everybody we met, going down the hill and through the village was respectful to us, except some shabby little boys on the outskirts. They said—

"Oh, what a guy!" And hove clods at us.

In my experience boys are the same in all ages. They don't respect anything, they don't care for anything or anybody. They say "Go up, baldhead" to the prophet going his unoffending way in the gray of antiquity; they sass me in the holy gloom of the Middle Ages; and I had seen them act the same way in Buchanan's administration; I remember, because I was there and helped. The prophet had his bears and settled with his boys; and I wanted to get down and settle with mine, but it wouldn't answer, because I couldn't have got up again. I hate a country without a derrick.

CHAPTER 12

Straight off, we were in the country. It was most lovely and pleasant in those sylvan solitudes in the early cool morning in the first freshness of autumn. From hilltops we saw fair green valleys lying spread out below, with streams winding through them, and island groves of trees here and there, and huge lonely oaks scattered about and casting black blots of shade; and beyond the valleys we saw the ranges of hills, blue with haze, stretching away in billowy perspective to the horizon, with at wide intervals a dim fleck of white or gray on a wave summit, which we knew was a castle. We crossed broad natural lawns sparkling with dew, and we moved like spirits, the cushioned turf giving out no sound of footfall; we dreamed along through glades in a mist of green light that got its tint from the sundrenched roof of leaves overhead, and by our feet the clearest and coldest of runlets went frisking and gossiping over its reefs and making a sort of whispering music comfortable to hear; and at times we left the world behind and entered into the solemn great deeps and rich gloom of the forest, where furtive wild things whisked and scurried by and were gone before you could even get your eye on the place where the noise was; and where only the earliest birds were turning out and getting to business with a song here and a quarrel yonder and a mysterious far-off hammering and drumming for worms on a tree trunk away somewhere in the impenetrable remotenesses of the woods. And by and by out we would swing again into the glare.

About the third or fourth or fifth time that we swung out into the glare—it was along there somewhere, a couple of hours or so after sunup—it wasn't as pleasant as it had been. It was beginning to get hot. This was quite noticeable. We had a very long pull, after that, without any shade. Now it is curious how progressively little frets grow and multiply after they once get a start. Things which I didn't mind at all, at first, I began to mind now—and more and more, too, all the time. The first ten or fifteen times I wanted my handkerchief I didn't seem to care; I got along, and said never mind, it isn't any matter, and dropped it out of my mind. But now it was different; I wanted it all the time; it was nag, nag, nag, right along, and no rest; I couldn't get it out of my mind; and so at last I lost my temper and said hang a man that would make a suit of armor without any pockets in it. You see I had my handkerchief in my helmet; and some other things; but it was that kind of a helmet that you can't take off by yourself. That hadn't occurred to me when I put it there; and in fact I didn't know it. I supposed it would be particularly convenient there. And so now, the thought of its being there, so handy and close by, and yet not get-at-able, made it all the worse and the harder to bear. Yes, the thing that you can't get is the thing that you want, mainly; everyone has noticed that. Well, it took my mind

off from everything else; took it clear off, and centered it in my helmet; and mile after mile, there it stayed, imagining the handkerchief, picturing the handkerchief; and it was bitter and aggravating to have the salt sweat keep trickling down into my eyes, and I couldn't get at it. It seems like a little thing, on paper, but it was not a little thing at all; it was the most real kind of misery. I would not say it if it was not so. I made up my mind that I would carry along a reticule next time, let it look how it might, and people say what they would. Of course these iron dudes of the Round Table would think it was scandalous, and maybe raise Sheol about it, but as for me, give me comfort first, and style afterwards. So we jogged along, and now and then we struck a stretch of dust, and it would tumble up in clouds and get into my nose and make me sneeze and cry; and of course I said things I oughtn't to have said, I don't deny that. I am not better than others. We couldn't seem to meet anybody in this lonesome Britain, not even an ogre; and in the mood I was in then, it was well for the ogre; that is, an ogre with a handkerchief. Most knights would have thought of nothing but getting his armor; but so I got his bandanna, he could keep his hardware, for all me.

Meantime it was getting hotter and hotter in there. You see, the sun was beating down and warming up the iron more and more all the time. Well, when you are hot, that way, every little thing irritates you. When I trotted, I rattled like a crate of dishes, and that annoyed me; and moreover I couldn't seem to stand that shield slatting and banging, now about my breast, now around my back; and if I dropped into a walk my joints creaked and screeched in that wearisome way that a wheelbarrow does, and as we didn't create any breeze at that gait, I was like to get fried in that stove; and besides, the quieter you went the heavier the iron settled down on you and the more and more tons you seemed to weigh every minute. And you had to be always changing hands, and passing your spear over to the other foot, it got so irksome for one hand to hold it long at a time.

Well, you know, when you perspire that way, in rivers, there comes a time when you—when you—well, when you itch. You are inside, your hands are outside; so there you are; nothing but iron between. It is not a light thing, let it sound as it may. First it is one place; then another; then some more; and it goes on spreading and spreading, and at last the territory is all occupied, and nobody can imagine what you feel like, nor how unpleasant it is. And when it had got to the worst, and it seemed to me that I could not stand anything more, a fly got in through the bars and settled on my nose, and the bars were stuck and wouldn't work, and I couldn't get the visor up; and I could only shake my head, which was baking hot by this time, and the fly—well, you know how a fly acts when he has got a certainty—he only minded the shaking long enough to change from nose to lip, and lip to ear, and buzz and buzz all around in there, and keep on lighting and biting, in a way that a person already so distressed as I was, simply could not stand. So I gave in, and got Alisande to unship the helmet and relieve me of it. Then she emptied the conveniences out of it and fetched it full of water, and I drank and then stood up and she poured the rest down inside the armor. One cannot think how refreshing it was. She continued to fetch and pour until I was well soaked and thoroughly comfortable.

It was good to have a rest—and peace. But nothing is quite perfect in this life, at any time. I had made a pipe a while back, and also some pretty fair tobacco; not the real thing, but what some of the Indians use: the inside bark of the willow, dried. These comforts had been in the helmet, and now I had them again, but no matches.

Gradually, as the time wore along, one annoying fact was borne in upon my understanding—that we were weather-bound. An armed novice cannot mount his horse without help and plenty of it. Sandy was not enough; not enough for me, anyway. We had to wait until somebody should come along. Waiting, in silence, would have been agreeable enough, for I was full of matter for reflection, and wanted to give it a chance to work. I wanted to try and think out how it was that rational or even half-rational men could ever have learned to wear armor, considering its inconveniences; and how they had managed to keep up such a fashion for generations when it was plain that what I had suffered today they had had to suffer all the days of their lives. I wanted to think that out; and moreover I wanted to think out some way to reform this evil and persuade the people to let the foolish fashion die out; but thinking was out of the question in the circumstances. You couldn't think, where Sandy was. She was a quite biddable creature and good-hearted, but she had a flow of talk that was as steady as a mill, and made your head sore like the drays and wagons in a city. If she had had a cork she would have been a comfort. But you can't cork that kind; they would die. Her clack was going all day, and you would think something would surely happen to her works, by and by; but no, they never got out of order; and she never had to slack up for words. She could grind, and pump, and churn and buzz by the week, and never stop to oil up or blow out. And yet the result was just nothing but wind. She never had any ideas, any more than a fog has. She was a perfect blatherskite; I mean for jaw, jaw, jaw, talk, talk, talk, jabber, jabber, jabber; but just as good as she could be. I hadn't minded her mill that morning, on account of having that hornet's nest of other troubles; but more than once in the afternoon I had to say—

"Take a rest, child; the way you are using up all the domestic air, the kingdom will have to go to importing it by tomorrow, and it's a low enough treasury without that."

FOR DISCUSSION

1. Chapter 11 illustrates a gigantic generation gap. What sixth-century and nineteenth-century attitudes and values come into conflict?

2. The humor in Chapter 12 becomes purely ridiculous. What are some elements of incongruity and exaggeration that make it so?

CHAPTER 13

Yes, it is strange how little a while at a time a person can be contented. Only a little while back, when I was riding and suffering, what a heaven this peace, this rest, this sweet serenity in this secluded shady nook by this purling stream would have seemed, where I could keep perfectly comfortable all the time by pouring a dipper of water into my armor now and then; yet already I was getting dissatisfied; partly because I could not light my pipe—for although I had long ago started a match factory, I had forgotten to bring matches with me—and partly because we had nothing to eat. Here was another illustration of the childlike improvidence of this age and people. A man in armor always trusted to chance for his food on a journey, and would have been scandalized at the idea of hanging a basket of sandwiches on his spear. There was probably not a knight of all the Round Table combination who would not rather have died than been caught carrying such a thing as that on his flagstaff. And yet there could not be anything more sensible. It had been my intention to smuggle a couple of sandwiches into my helmet, but I was interrupted in the act, and had to make an excuse and lay them aside, and a dog got them.

Night approached, and with it a storm. The darkness came on fast. We must camp, of course. I found a good shelter for the demoiselle under a rock, and went off and found another for myself. But I was obliged to remain in my armor, because I could not get it off by myself and yet could not allow Alisande to help, because it would have seemed so like undressing before folk. It would not have amounted to that in reality, because I had clothes on underneath; but the prejudices of one's breeding are not gotten rid of just at a jump, and I knew that when it came to stripping off that bobtailed iron petticoat I should be embarrassed.

With the storm came a change of weather; and the stronger the wind blew, and the wilder the rain lashed around, the colder and colder it got. Pretty soon, various kinds of bugs and ants and worms and things began to flock in out of the wet and crawl down inside my armor to get warm; and while some of them behaved well enough, and snuggled up among my clothes and got quiet, the majority were of a restless, uncomfortable sort, and never

stayed still, but went on prowling and hunting for they did not know what; especially the ants, which went tickling along in wearisome procession from one end of me to the other by the hour, and are a kind of creatures which I never wish to sleep with again. It would be my advice to persons situated in this way, to not roll or thrash around, because this excites the interest of all the different sorts of animals and makes every last one of them want to turn out and see what is going on, and this makes things worse than they were before, and of course makes you objurgate harder, too, if you can. Still, if one did not roll and thrash around he would die; so perhaps it is as well to do one way as the other, there is no real choice. Even after I was frozen solid I could still distinguish that tickling, just as a corpse does when he is taking electric treatment. I said I would never wear armor after this trip.

All those trying hours whilst I was frozen and yet was in a living fire, as you may say, on account of that swarm of crawlers, that same unanswerable question kept circling and circling through my tired head: How do people stand this miserable armor? How have they managed to stand it all these generations? How can they sleep at night for dreading the tortures of next day?

When the morning came at last, I was in a bad enough plight: seedy, drowsy, fagged, from want of sleep; weary from thrashing around, famished from long fasting; pining for a bath, and to get rid of the animals; and crippled with rheumatism. And how had it fared with the nobly born, the titled aristocrat, the Demoiselle Alisande la Carteloise? Why, she was as fresh as a squirrel; she had slept like the dead; and as for a bath, probably neither she nor any other noble in the land had ever had one, and so she was not missing it. Measured by modern standards, they were

merely modified savages, those people. This noble lady showed no impatience to get to breakfast—and that smacks of the savage, too. On their journeys those Britons were used to long fasts, and knew how to bear them; and also how to freight up against probable fasts before starting, after the style of the Indian and the anaconda. As like as not, Sandy was loaded for a three-day stretch.

We were off before sunrise, Sandy riding and I limping along behind. In half an hour we came upon a group of ragged poor creatures who had assembled to mend the thing which was regarded as a road. They were as humble as animals to me; and when I proposed to breakfast with them, they were so flattered, so overwhelmed by this extraordinary condescension of mine that at first they were not able to believe that I was in earnest. My lady put up her scornful lip and withdrew to one side; she said in their hearing that she would as soon think of eating with the other cattle—a remark which embarrassed these poor devils merely because it referred to them, and not because it insulted or offended them, for it didn't. And yet they were not slaves, not chattels. By a sarcasm of law and phrase they were freemen. Seventenths of the free population of the country were of just their class and degree: small "independent" farmers, artisans, etc.; which is to say, they were the nation, the actual Nation; they were about all of it that was useful, or worth saving, or really respectworthy; and to subtract them would have been to subtract the Nation and leave behind some dregs, some refuse, in the shape of a king, nobility and gentry, idle, unproductive, acquainted mainly with the arts of wasting and destroying, and no sort of use or value in any rationally constructed world. And yet, by ingenious contrivance, this gilded minority, instead of being in the tail of the procession where it belonged, was marching head up and banners flying, at the other end of it; had elected itself to be the Nation, and these innumerable clams had permitted it so long that they had come at last to accept it as a truth; and not only that, but to believe it right and as it should be. The priests had told their fathers and themselves that this ironical state of things was ordained of God; and so, not reflecting upon how unlike God it would be to amuse himself with sarcasms, and especially such poor transparent ones as this, they had dropped the matter there and become respectfully quiet.

The talk of these meek people had a strange enough sound in a formerly American ear. They were freemen, but they could not leave the estates of their lord or their bishop without his permission; they could not prepare their own bread, but must have their corn ground and their bread baked at his mill and his bakery, and pay roundly for the same; they could not sell a piece of their own property without paying him a handsome percentage of the proceeds, nor buy a piece of somebody else's without remembering him in cash for the privilege; they had to harvest his grain for him gratis, and be ready to come at a moment's notice, leaving their own crop to destruction by the threatened storm; they had to let him plant fruit trees in their fields, and then keep their indignation to themselves when his heedless fruit gatherers trampled the grain around the trees; they had to smother their anger when his hunting parties galloped through their fields laying waste the result of their patient toil; they were not allowed to keep doves themselves, and when the swarms from my lord's dovecot settled on their crops they must not lose their temper and kill a bird, for awful would the penalty be; when the harvest was at last gathered, then came the procession of robbers to levy their

blackmail upon it: first the Church carted off its fat tenth, then the king's commissioner took his twentieth, then my lord's people made a mighty inroad upon the remainder; after which, the skinned freeman had liberty to bestow the remnant in his barn, in case it was worth the trouble; there were taxes, and taxes, and taxes, and more taxes, and taxes again, and yet other taxes—upon this free and independent pauper, but none upon his lord the baron or the bishop, none upon the wasteful nobility or the all-devouring Church; if the baron would sleep unvexed, the freeman must sit up all night after his day's work and whip the ponds to keep the frogs quiet; if the freeman's daughter—but no, that last infamy of monarchical government is unprintable; and finally, if the freeman, grown desperate with his tortures, found his life unendurable under such conditions, and sacrificed it and fled to death for mercy and refuge, the gentle Church condemned him to eternal fire, the gentle law buried him at midnight at the crossroads with a stake through his back, and his master the baron or the bishop confiscated all his property and turned his widow and his orphans out of doors.

And here were these freemen assembled in the early morning to work on their lord the bishop's road three days each— gratis; every head of a family, and every son of a family, three days each, gratis, and a day or so added for their servants. Why, it was like reading about France and the French, before the ever-memorable and blessed Revolution, which swept a thousand years of such villainy away in one swift tidal wave of blood—one: a settlement of that hoary debt in the proportion of half a drop of blood for each hogshead of it that had been pressed by slow tortures out of that people in the weary stretch of ten centuries of wrong and shame and misery the like of which was not to be mated but in hell. There were two "Reigns of Terror," if we would but remember it and consider it; the one wrought murder in hot passion, the other in heartless cold blood; the one lasted mere months, the other had lasted a thousand years; the one inflicted death upon ten thousand persons, the other upon a hundred millions; but our shudders are all for the "horrors" of the minor Terror, the momentary Terror, so to speak; whereas, what is the horror of swift death by the ax, compared with lifelong death from hunger, cold, insult, cruelty, and heartbreak? What is swift death by lightning compared with death by slow fire at the stake? A city cemetery could contain the coffins filled by that brief Terror which we have all been so diligently taught to shiver at and mourn over; but all France could hardly contain the coffins filled by that older and real Terror—that unspeakably bitter and awful Terror which none of us has been taught to see in its vastness or pity as it deserves.

These poor ostensible freemen who were sharing their breakfast and their talk with me, were as full of humble reverence for their king and Church and nobility as their worst enemy could desire. There was something pitifully ludicrous about it. I asked them if they supposed a nation of people ever existed, who, with a free vote in every man's hand, would elect that a single family and its descendants should reign over it forever, whether gifted or boobies, to the exclusion of all other families—including the voter's; and would also elect that a certain hundred families should be raised to dizzy summits of rank, and clothed on with offensive transmissible glories and privileges to the exclusion of the rest of the nation's families—*including his own.*

They all looked unhit, and said they didn't know; that they had never thought about it before, and it hadn't ever occurred to them that a nation could be so situated that every man *could* have a say in the government. I said I had seen one—and that it would last until it had an Established Church. Again they were all unhit—at first. But presently one man looked up and asked me to state that proposition again; and state it slowly, so it could soak into his understanding. I did it; and after a little he had the idea, and he brought his fist down and said *he* didn't believe a nation where every man had a vote would voluntarily get down in the mud and dirt in any such way; and that to steal from a nation its will and preference must be a crime and the first of all crimes.

I said to myself:

"This one's a man. If I were backed by enough of his sort, I would make a strike for the welfare of this country, and try to prove myself its loyalest citizen by making a wholesome change in its system of government."

You see my kind of loyalty was loyalty to one's country, not to its institutions or its officeholders. The country is the real thing, the substantial thing, the eternal thing; it is the thing to watch over, and care for, and be loyal to; institutions are extraneous, they are its mere clothing, and clothing can wear out, become ragged, cease to be comfortable, cease to protect the body from winter, disease, and death. To be loyal to rags, to shout for rags, to worship rags, to die for rags—that is a loyalty of unreason, it is pure animal; it belongs to monarchy, was invented by monarchy; let monarchy keep it. I was from Connecticut, whose Constitution declares "that all political power is inherent in the people, and all free governments are founded on their authority and instituted for their benefit; and that they have *at all times* an undeniable and indefeasible right to *alter their form of government* in such a manner as they may think expedient."

Under that gospel, the citizen who thinks he sees that the commonwealth's political clothes are worn out, and yet holds his peace and does not agitate for a new suit, is disloyal; he is a traitor. That he may be the only one who thinks he sees this decay, does not excuse him; it is his duty to agitate any way, and it is the duty of the others to vote him down if they do not see the matter as he does.

And now here I was, in a country where a right to say how the country should be governed was restricted to six persons in each thousand of its population. For the nine hundred and ninety-four to express dissatisfaction with the regnant system and propose to change it, would have made the whole six shudder as one man, it would have been so disloyal, so dishonorable, such putrid black treason. So to speak, I was become a stockholder in a corporation where nine hundred and ninety-four of the members furnished all the money and did all the work, and the other six elected themselves a permanent board of direction and took all the dividends. It seemed to me that what the nine hundred and ninety-four dupes needed was a new deal. The thing that would have best suited the circus side of my nature would have been to resign the Boss-ship and get up an insurrection and turn it into a revolution; but I knew that the Jack Cade or the Wat Tyler who tries such a thing without first educating his materials up to revolution grade is almost absolutely certain to get left. I had never been accustomed to getting left, even if I do say it myself. Wherefore, the "deal" which had been for some time working into shape in my mind was of a quite different pattern from the Cade-Tyler sort.

So I did not talk blood and insurrection to that man there who sat munching black bread with that abused and mistaught herd of human sheep, but took him aside and talked matter of another sort to him. After I had finished, I got him to lend me a little ink from his veins; and with this and a sliver I wrote on a piece of bark—

Put him in the Man Factory—

and gave it to him, and said—

"Take it to the palace at Camelot and give it into the hands of Amyas le Poulet, whom I call Clarence, and he will understand."

"He is a priest, then," said the man, and some of the enthusiasm went out of his face.

"How—a priest? Didn't I tell you that no chattel of the Church can enter my Man Factory? Didn't I tell you that *you* couldn't enter unless your religion, whatever it might be, was your own free property?"

"Marry, it is so, and for that I was glad; wherefore it liked me not, and bred in me a cold doubt, to hear of this priest being there."

"But he isn't a priest, I tell you."

The man looked far from satisfied. He said:

"He is not a priest, and yet can read?"

"He is not a priest and yet can read—yes, and write, too, for that matter. I taught him myself." The man's face cleared. "And it is the first thing that you yourself will be taught in that Factory—"

"I? I would give blood out of my heart to know that art. Why, I will be your slave, your—"

"No you won't, you won't be anybody's slave. Take your family and go along. Your lord the bishop will confiscate your small property, but no matter, Clarence will fix you all right."

1. What is ironic about the Yankee's calling Sandy a "savage"?

2. Mark Twain launches into another long attack in this chapter. What about the freemen's life makes him so angry? What are some of the comparisons (metaphors and analogies) that he uses to show how wrong the system of government is?

3. The Yankee admits that "it would have suited the circus side of my nature" to start a revolution. Why doesn't he? What does he plan instead?

CHAPTER 14

I paid three pennies for my breakfast, and a most extravagant price it was, too, seeing that one could have breakfasted a dozen persons for that money; but I was feeling good by this time, and I had always been a kind of spendthrift any way; and then these people had wanted to give me the food for nothing, scant as their provision was, and so it was a grateful pleasure to emphasize my appreciation and sincere thankfulness with a good big financial lift where the money would do so much more good than it would in my helmet, where, these pennies being made of iron and not stinted in weight, my half dollar's worth was a good deal of a burden to me. I spent money rather too freely in those days, it is true; but one reason for it was that I hadn't got the proportions of things entirely adjusted, even yet, after so long a sojourn in Britain—hadn't got along to where I was able to absolutely realize that a penny in Arthur's land and a couple of dollars in Connecticut were about one and the same thing: just twins, as you may say, in purchasing power. If my start from Camelot could have been delayed a very few days I could have paid these people in beautiful new coins from our own mint, and that would have pleased me; and them, too, not less. I had adopted the American values exclusively. In a week or two now, cents, nickels, dimes, quarters and half dollars, and also a trifle of gold, would be trickling in thin but steady streams all through the commercial veins of the kingdom, and I looked to see this new blood freshen up its life.

The farmers were bound to throw in something, to sort of offset my liberality, whether I would or no; so I let them give me a flint and steel; and as soon as they had comfortably bestowed Sandy and me on our horse, I lit my pipe. When the first blast of smoke shot out through the bars of my helmet, all those people broke for the woods, and Sandy went over backwards and struck the ground with a dull thud. They thought I was one of those fire-belching dragons they had heard so much about from knights and other professional liars. I had infinite trouble to persuade those people to venture back within explaining distance. Then I told them that this was only a bit of enchantment which would work harm to none but my enemies. And I promised, with my hand on my heart, that if all who felt no enmity toward me would come forward and pass before me they should see that only those who remained behind would be struck dead. The procession moved with a good deal of promptness. There were no casualties to report, for nobody had curiosity enough to remain behind to see what would happen.

I lost some time, now, for these big children, their fears gone, became so ravished with wonder over my awe-compelling fire-works that I had to stay there and smoke a couple of pipes out before they would let me go. Still the delay was not wholly un-productive, for it took all that time to get Sandy thoroughly wonted to the new thing, she being so close to it, you know. It plugged up her conversation-mill, too, for a considerable while, and that was a gain. But above all other benefits accruing, I had learned something. I was ready for any giant or any ogre that might come along, now.

We tarried with a holy hermit, that night, and my opportunity came about the middle of the next afternoon. We were crossing a vast meadow by way of short-cut, and I was musing absently, hearing nothing, seeing nothing, when Sandy sud-denly interrupted a remark which she had begun that morning, with the cry—

"Defend thee, lord—peril of life is to-ward!"

And she slipped down from the horse and ran a little way and stood. I looked up and saw, far off in the shade of a tree, half a dozen armed knights and their squires; and straightway there was bustle among them and tightening of saddle girths for the mount. My pipe was ready and would have been lit, if I had not been lost in thinking about how to banish oppression from this land and restore to all its people their stolen rights and manhood without disobliging anybody. I lit up at once, and by the time I had got a good head of re-served steam on, here they came. All to-gether, too; none of those chivalrous mag-nanimities which one reads so much about —one courtly rascal at a time, and the rest standing by to see fair play. No, they came in a body, they came with a whirr and a rush, they came like a volley from a bat-tery; came with heads low down, plumes

streaming out behind, lances advanced at a level. It was a handsome sight, a beautiful sight—for a man up a tree. I laid my lance in rest and waited, with my heart beating, till the iron wave was just ready to break over me, then spouted a column of white smoke through the bars of my helmet. You should have seen the wave go to pieces and scatter! This was a finer sight than the other one.

But these people stopped, two or three hundred yards away, and this troubled me. My satisfaction collapsed, and fear came; I judged I was a lost man. But Sandy was radiant; and was going to be eloquent, but I stopped her, and told her my magic had miscarried, somehow or other, and she must mount, with all dispatch, and we must ride for life. No, she wouldn't. She said that my enchantment had disabled those knights; they were not riding on, because they couldn't; wait, they would drop out of their saddles presently, and we would get their horses and harness. I could not de-ceive such trusting simplicity, so I said it was a mistake; that when my fireworks killed at all, they killed instantly; no, the men would not die, there was something wrong about my apparatus, I couldn't tell what; but we must hurry and get away, for those people would attack us again, in a minute. Sandy laughed, and said—

"Lackaday, sir, they be not of that breed! Sir Launcelot will give battle to dragons, and will abide by them, and will assail them again, and yet again, and still again, until he do conquer and destroy them; and so likewise will Sir Pellinore and Sir Aglovale and Sir Carados, and mayhap others, but there be none else that will venture it, let the idle say what the idle will. And, la, as to yonder base rufflers, think ye they have not their fill, but yet desire more?"

"Well, then, what are they waiting for? Why don't they leave? Nobody's hindering.

Good land, I'm willing to let bygones be bygones, I'm sure."

"Leave, is it? Oh, give thyself easement as to that. They dream not of it, no, not they. They wait to yield them."

"Come—really, is that 'sooth'—as you people say? If they want to, why don't they?"

"It would like them much; but an ye wot how dragons are esteemed, ye would not hold them blamable. They fear to come."

"Well, then, suppose I go to them instead, and—"

"Ah, wit ye well they would not abide your coming. I will go."

And she did. She was a handy person to have along on a raid. I would have considered this a doubtful errand, myself. I presently saw the knights riding away, and

Sandy coming back. That was a relief. I judged she had somehow failed to get the first innings—I mean in the conversation; otherwise the interview wouldn't have been so short. But it turned out that she had managed the business well; in fact admirably. She said that when she told those people I was The Boss, it hit them where they lived: "smote them sore with fear and dread" was her word; and then they were ready to put up with anything she might require. So she swore them to appear at Arthur's court within two days and yield them, with horse and harness, and be my knights henceforth, and subject to my command. How much better she managed that thing than I should have done it myself! She was a daisy.

CHAPTER 15

"And so I'm proprietor of some knights," said I, as we rode off. "Who would ever have supposed that I should live to list up assets of that sort. I shan't know what to do with them; unless I raffle them off. How many of them are there, Sandy?"

"Seven, please you, sir, and their squires."

"It is a good haul. Who are they? Where do they hang out?"

"Where do they hang out?"

"Yes, where do they live?"

"Ah, I understood thee not. That will I tell thee eftsoons." Then she said musingly, and softly, turning the words daintily over her tongue: "Hang they out—hang they out—where hang—where do they hang out; eh, right so; where do they hang out. Of a truth the phrase hath a fair and winsome grace, and is prettily worded withal. I will repeat it anon and anon in mine idlesse, whereby I may peradventure learn

it. Where do they hang out. Even so! Already it falleth trippingly from my tongue, and forasmuch as—"

"Don't forget the cowboys, Sandy."

"Cowboys?"

"Yes; the knights, you know: You were going to tell me about them. A while back, you remember. Figuratively speaking, game's called."

"Game—"

"Yes, yes, yes! Go to the bat. I mean, get to work on your statistics, and don't burn so much kindling getting your fire started. Tell me about the knights."

"I will well, and lightly will begin. So they two departed and rode into a great forest. And—"

"Great Scott!"

You see, I recognized my mistake at once. I had set her works agoing; it was my own fault; she would be thirty days getting down to those facts. And she generally began without a preface and finished without a result. If you interrupted her she would either go right along without noticing, or answer with a couple of words, and go back and say the sentence over again. So, interruptions only did harm; and yet I had to interrupt, and interrupt pretty frequently, too, in order to save my life; a person would die if he let her monotony drip on him right along all day.

"Great Scott!" I said in my distress. She went right back and began over again:

"So they two departed and rode into a great forest. And—"

"Which two?"

"Sir Gawaine and Sir Uwaine. And so they came to an abbey of monks, and there were well lodged. So on the morn they heard their masses in the abbey, and so they rode forth till they came to a great forest; then was Sir Gawaine ware in a valley by a turret, of twelve fair damsels, and two knights armed on great horses, and the damsels went to and fro by a tree. And then was Sir Gawaine ware how there hung a white shield on that tree, and ever as the damsels came by it they spit upon it, and some threw mire upon the shield—"

"Now, if I hadn't seen the like myself in this country, Sandy, I wouldn't believe it. But I've seen it, and I can just see those creatures now, parading before that shield and acting like that. The women here do certainly act like all possessed. Yes, and I mean your best, too, society's very choicest brands. The humblest hello-girl along ten thousand miles of wire could teach gentleness, patience, modesty, manners, to the highest duchess in Arthur's land."

"Hello-girl?"

"Yes, but don't you ask me to explain; it's a new kind of girl; they don't have them here; one often speaks sharply to them when they are not the least in fault, and he can't get over feeling sorry for it

and ashamed of himself in thirteen hundred years, it's such shabby mean conduct and so unprovoked; the fact is, no gentleman ever does it—though I—well, I myself, if I've got to confess—"

"Peradventure she—"

"Never mind her; never mind her; I tell you I couldn't ever explain her so you would understand."

"Even so be it, sith ye are so minded. Then Sir Gawaine and Sir Uwaine went and saluted them, and asked them why they did that despite to the shield. Sirs, said the damsels, we shall tell you. There is a knight in this country that owneth this white shield, and he is a passing good man of his hands, but he hateth all ladies and gentlewomen, and therefore we do all this despite to the shield. I will say you, said Sir Gawaine, it beseemeth evil a good knight to despise all ladies and gentlewomen, and peradventure though he hate you he hath some cause, and peradventure he loveth in some other places ladies and gentlewomen, and to be loved again, and he such a man of prowess as ye speak of—"

"Man of prowess—yes, that is the man to please them, Sandy. Man of brains—that is a thing they never think of. Tom Sayers —John Heenan—John L. Sullivan—pity but you could be here. You would have your legs under the Round Table and a Sir in front of your names within the twenty-four hours; and you could bring about a new distribution of the married princesses and duchesses of the Court in another twenty-four. The fact is, it is just a sort of polished up court of Comanches, and there isn't a squaw in it who doesn't stand ready at the dropping of a hat to desert to the buck with the biggest string of scalps at his belt."

"—and he be such a man of prowess as ye speak of, said Sir Gawaine. Now what is his name? Sir, said they, his name is

Marhaus the king's son of Ireland."

"Son of the king of Ireland, you mean; the other form doesn't mean anything. And look out and hold on tight, now, we must jump this gully. . . . There, we are all right now. This horse belongs in the circus; he is born before his time."

"I know him well, said Sir Uwaine, he is a passing good knight as any is on live."

"*On live.* If you've got a fault in the world, Sandy, it is that you are a shade too archaic. But it isn't any matter."

"—for I saw him once proved at a jousts where many knights were gathered, and that time there might no man withstand him. Ah, said Sir Gawaine, damsels, methinketh ye are to blame, for it is to suppose he that hung that shield there will not be long therefrom, and then may those knights match him on horseback, and that is more your worship than thus; for I will abide no longer to see a knight's shield dishonored. And therewith Sir Uwaine and Sir Gawaine departed a little from them, and then were they ware where Sir Marhaus came riding on a great horse straight toward them. And when the twelve damsels saw Sir Marhaus they fled into the turret as they were wild, so that some of them fell by the way. Then the one of the knights of the tower dressed his shield, and said on high, Sir Marhaus defend thee. And so they ran together that the knight brake his spear on Marhaus, and Sir Marhaus smote him so ward that he brake his neck and the horse's back—"

"Well, that is just the trouble about this state of things, it ruins so many horses."

"That saw the other knight of the turret, and dressed him toward Marhaus, and they went so eagerly together, that the knight of the turret was soon smitten down, horse and man, stark dead—"

"*Another* horse gone; I tell you it is a custom that ought to be broken up. I don't see how people with any feeling can applaud and support it."

"So these two knights came together with great random—"

I saw that I had been asleep and missed a chapter, but I didn't say anything. I judged that the Irish knight was in trouble with the visitors by this time, and this turned out to be the case.

"—that Sir Uwaine smote Sir Marhaus that his spear brast in pieces on the shield, and Sir Marhaus smote him so sore that horse and man he bare to the earth, and hurt Sir Uwaine on the left side—"

"The truth is, Alisande, these archaics are a little *too* simple; the vocabulary is too limited, and so, by consequence, descriptions suffer in the matter of variety; they run too much to level Saharas of fact, and not enough to picturesque detail; this throws about them a certain air of the monotonous; in fact the fights are all alike: a couple of people come together with great random—random is a good word, and so is exegesis, for that matter, and so is holocaust, and defalcation, and usufruct and a hundred others, but land! a body ought to discriminate—they come together with great random, and a spear is brast, and one party brake his shield and the other one goes down, horse and man, over his horsetail and brake his neck, and then the next candidate comes randoming in, and brast *his* spear, and the other man brast his shield, and down *he* goes, horse and man, over his horsetail, and brake *his* neck, and then there's another elected, and another and another and still another, till the material is all used up; and when you come to figure up results, you can't tell one fight from another, nor who whipped; and as a *picture*, of living, raging, roaring battle, sho! why, it's pale and noiseless—just ghosts scuffling in a fog. Dear me, what would this barren vocabulary get out of the mightiest spectacle—the burning of Rome in Nero's time, for instance? Why, it would merely say, 'Town burned down; no insurance; boy brast a window, fireman brake his neck!' Why, *that* ain't a picture!"

It was a good deal of a lecture, I thought, but it didn't disturb Sandy, didn't turn a feather; her steam soared steadily up again, the minute I took off the lid:

"Then Sir Marhaus turned his horse and rode toward Gawaine with his spear. And when Sir Gawaine saw that, he dressed his shield, and they aventred their spears, and they came together with all the might of their horses, that either knight smote other so hard in the midst of their shields, but Sir Gawaine's spear brake—"

"I knew it would."

"—but Sir Marhaus's spear held; and therewith Sir Gawaine and his horse rushed down to the earth—"

"Just so—and brake his back."

"—and lightly Sir Gawaine rose upon his feet and pulled out his sword, and dressed him toward Sir Marhaus on foot, and therewith either came unto other eagerly, and smote together with their swords, that their shields flew in cantles, and they bruised their helms and their hauberks, and wounded either other. But Sir Gawaine, fro it passed nine of the clock, waxed by the space of three hours ever stronger and stronger, and thrice his might was increased. All this espied Sir Marhaus, and had great wonder how his might increased, and so they wounded other passing sore; and then when it was come noon—"

The pelting singsong of it carried me forward to scenes and sounds of my boyhood days:

"Ne-e-ew Haven! ten minutes for refreshments—knductr 'll strike the gong-bell two minutes before train leaves—pas-

sengers for the Shore-line please take seats in the rear k'yar, this k'yar don't go no furder—*ahh*-pls, *aw*-rnjz, b'*nan*ners, *s-a-n-d*'ches, p—*op*-corn!"

"—and waxed past noon and drew towards evensong. Sir Gawaine's strength feebled and waxed passing faint, that unnethes he might dure any longer, and Sir Marhaus was then bigger and bigger—"

"Which strained his armor, of course; and yet little would one of these people mind a small thing like that."

"—and so, Sir Knight, said Sir Marhaus, I have well felt that ye are a passing good knight, and a marvelous man of might as ever I felt any, while it lasteth, and our quarrels are not great, and therefore it were a pity to do you hurt, for I feel you are passing feeble. Ah, said Sir Gawaine, gentle knight, ye say the word that I should say. And therewith they took off their helms and either kissed other, and there they swore together either to love other as brethren—"

But I lost the thread there, and dozed off to slumber, thinking about what a pity it was that men with such superb strength—strength enabling them to stand up cased in cruelly burdensome iron and drenched with perspiration, and hack and batter and bang each other for six hours on a stretch—should not have been born at a time when they could put it to some useful purpose. Take a jackass, for instance: a jackass has that kind of strength, and puts it to a useful purpose, and is valuable to this world because he *is* a jackass; but a nobleman is not valuable because he is a jackass. It is a mixture that is always ineffectual, and should never have been attempted in the first place. And yet, once you start a mistake, the trouble is done and you never know what is going to come of it.

When I came to myself again and began to listen, I perceived that I had lost another chapter, and that Alisande had wandered a long way off with her people.

"And so they rode and came into a deep valley full of stones, and thereby they saw a fair stream of water; above thereby was the head of the stream, a fair fountain, and three damsels sitting thereby. In this country, said Sir Marhaus, came never knight since it was christened, but he found strange adventures—"

"This is not good form, Alisande. Sir Marhaus the king's son of Ireland talks like all the rest; you ought to give him a brogue, or at least a characteristic expletive; by this means one would recognize him as soon as he spoke, without his ever being named. It is a common literary device with the great authors. You should make him say, 'In this country, be jabers, came never knight since it was christened, but he found strange adventures, be jabers.' You see how much better that sounds."

"—came never knight but he found strange adventures, be jabers. Of a truth it doth indeed, fair lord, albeit 'tis passing hard to say, though peradventure that will not tarry but better speed with usage. And then they rode to the damsels, and either saluted other, and the eldest had a garland of gold about her head, and she was three-score winter of age or more—"

"The *damsel* was?"

"Even so, dear lord—and her hair was white under the garland—"

"Celluloid teeth, nine dollars a set, as like as not—the loose-fit kind, that go up and down like a portcullis when you eat, and fall out when you laugh."

"The second damsel was of thirty winter of age, with a circlet of gold about her head. The third damsel was but fifteen year of age—"

Billows of thought came rolling over my soul, and the voice faded out of my hearing!

Fifteen! Break—my heart! Oh, my lost darling! Just her age who was so gentle, and lovely, and all the world to me, and whom I shall never see again! How the thought of her carries me back over wide seas of memory to a vague dim time, a happy time, so many, many centuries hence, when I used to wake in the soft summer mornings, out of sweet dreams of her, and say "Hello, Central!" just to hear her dear voice come melting back to me with a "Hello, Hank!" that was music of the spheres to my enchanted ear. She got three dollars a week, but she was worth it.

I could not follow Alisande's further explanation of who our captured knights were, now—I mean in case she should ever get to explaining who they were. My interest was gone, my thoughts were far away, and sad. By fitful glimpses of the drifting tale, caught here and there and now and then, I merely noted in a vague way that each of these three knights took one of these three damsels up behind him on his horse, and one rode north, another east, the other south, to seek adventures, and meet again and lie, after year and day. Year and day—and without baggage. It was of a piece with the general simplicity of the country.

The sun was now setting. It was about three in the afternoon when Alisande had begun to tell me who the cowboys were; so she had made pretty good progress with it—for her. She would arrive some time or other, no doubt, but she was not a person who could be hurried.

We were approaching a castle which stood on high ground: a huge, strong, venerable structure, whose gray towers and battlements were charmingly draped with ivy, and whose whole majestic mass was drenched wih splendors flung from the sinking sun. It was the largest castle we had seen, and so I thought it might be the one we were after, but Sandy said no. She did not know who owned it; she said she had passed it without calling, when she went down to Camelot.

FOR DISCUSSION

1. What change of attitude does the Yankee undergo in Chapter 14?

2. Almost all the humor in Chapter 15 comes from the language. How do parody, sarcasm, exaggeration, and incongruity contribute to this?

CHAPTER 16

If knights-errant were to be believed, not all castles were desirable places to seek hospitality in. As a matter of fact, knights-errant were *not* persons to be believed—that is, measured by modern standards of veracity; yet, measured by the standards of their own time, and scaled accordingly, you got the truth. It was very simple: you discounted a statement ninety-seven percent; the rest was fact. Now after making this allowance, the truth remained that if I could find out something about a castle before ringing the doorbell—I mean hailing the warders—it was the sensible thing to do. So I was pleased when I saw in the distance a horseman making the bottom turn of the road that wound down from this castle.

As we approached each other, I saw that he wore a plumed helmet, and seemed to be otherwise clothed in steel, but bore a curious addition also—a stiff square garment like a herald's tabard. However, I had to smile at my own forgetfulness when I got nearer and read this sign on his tabard:

*"Persimmon's Soap—
All the Prime-Donne Use It."*

That was a little idea of my own, and had several wholesome purposes in view toward the civilizing and uplifting of this nation. In the first place, it was a furtive, underhand blow at this nonsense of knight errantry, though nobody suspected that but me. I had started a number of these people out—the bravest knights I could get—each sandwiched between bulletin boards bearing one device or another, and I judged that by and by when they got to be numerous enough they would begin to look ridiculous; and then, even the steel-clad ape that *hadn't* any board would himself begin to look ridiculous because he was out of the fashion.

Secondly, these missionaries would gradually, and without creating suspicion or exciting alarm, introduce a rudimentary cleanliness among the nobility, and from them it would work down to the people, if the priests could be kept quiet. This would undermine the Church. I mean it would be a step toward that. Next, education—next, freedom—and then she would begin to crumble. It being my conviction that any Established Church is an established crime, an established slave pen, I had no scruples, but was willing to assail it in any way or with any weapon that promised to hurt it. Why, in my own former day—in remote centuries not yet stirring in the womb of time—there were old Englishmen who imagined that they had been born in a free country: a "free" country with the Corporation Act and the Test still in force in it—

timbers propped against men's liberties and dishonored consciences to shore up an Established Anachronism with.

My missionaries were taught to spell out the gilt signs on their tabards—the showy gilding was a neat idea, I could have got the king to wear a bulletin board for the sake of that barbaric splendor—they were to spell out these signs and then explain to the lords and ladies what soap was; and if the lords and ladies were afraid of it, get them to try it on a dog. The missionary's next move was to get the family together and try it on himself; he was to stop at no experiment, however desperate, that could convince the nobility that soap was harmless; if any final doubt remained, he must catch a hermit—the woods were full of them; saints they called themselves, and saints they were believed to be. They were unspeakably holy, and worked miracles, and everybody stood in awe of them. If a hermit could survive a wash, and that failed to convince a duke, give him up, let him alone.

Whenever my missionaries overcame a knight errant on the road they washed him, and when he got well they swore him to go and get a bulletin board and disseminate soap and civilization the rest of his days. As a consequence the workers in the field were increasing by degrees, and the reform was steadily spreading. My soap factory felt the strain early. At first I had only two hands; but before I had left home I was already employing fifteen, and running night and day; and the atmospheric result was getting so pronounced that the king went sort of fainting and gasping around and said he did not believe he could stand it much longer, and Sir Launcelot got so that he did hardly anything but walk up and down the roof and swear, although I told him it was worse up there than anywhere else, but he said he wanted plenty of air; and he was always complaining that a pal-

ace was no place for a soap factory, anyway, and said if a man was to start one in his house he would be damned if he wouldn't strangle him. There were ladies present, too, but much these people ever cared for that; they would swear before children, if the wind was their way when the factory was going.

This missionary knight's name was La Cote Male Taile, and he said that this castle was the abode of Morgan le Fay, sister of King Arthur, and wife of King Uriens, monarch of a realm about as big as the District of Columbia—you could stand in the middle of it and throw bricks into the next kingdom. "Kings" and "Kingdoms" were as thick in Britain as they had been in little Palestine in Joshua's time, when people had to sleep with their knees pulled up because they couldn't stretch out without a passport.

La Cote was much depressed, for he had scored here the worst failure of his campaign. He had not worked off a cake; yet he had tried all the tricks of the trade, even to the washing of a hermit; but the hermit died. This was indeed a bad failure, for this animal would now be dubbed a martyr, and would take his place among the saints of the Roman calendar. Thus made he his moan, his poor Sir La Cote Male Taile, and sorrowed passing sore. And so my heart bled for him, and I was moved to comfort and stay him. Wherefore I said—

"Forbear to grieve fair knight, for this is not a defeat. We have brains, you and I; and for such as have brains there are no defeats, but only victories. Observe how we will turn this seeming disaster into an advertisement; an advertisement for our soap; and the biggest one, to draw, that was ever thought of; an advertisement that will transform that Mount Washington defeat into a Matterhorn victory. We will put on your bulletin board, '*Patronized by the Elect.*' How does that strike you?"

"Verily, it is wonderly bethought!"

"Well, a body is bound to admit that for just a modest little one-line ad, it's a corker."

So the poor colporteur's griefs vanished away. He was a brave fellow, and had done mighty feats of arms in his time. His chief celebrity rested upon the events of an excursion like this one of mine, which he had once made with a damsel named Maledisant, who was as handy with her tongue as was Sandy, though in a different way, for her tongue churned forth only railings and insult, whereas Sandy's music was of a kindlier sort. I knew his story well, and so I knew how to interpret the compassion that was in his face when he bade me farewell. He supposed I was having a bitter hard time of it.

Sandy and I discussed his story, as we rode along, and she said that La Cote's bad luck had begun with the very beginning of that trip; for the king's fool had overthrown him on the first day, and in such cases it was customary for the girl to desert to the conqueror, but Maledisant didn't do it; and also persisted afterward in sticking to him, after all his defeats. But, said I, suppose the victor should decline to accept his spoil? She said that that wouldn't answer —he must. He couldn't decline; it wouldn't be regular. I made a note of that. If Sandy's music got to be too burdensome, sometime I would let a knight defeat me, on the chance that she would desert to him.

In due time we were challenged by the warders, from the castle walls, and after a parley admitted. I have nothing pleasant to tell about that visit. But it was not a disappointment, for I knew Mrs. le Fay by reputation, and was not expecting anything pleasant. She was held in awe by the whole realm, for she had made everybody believe she was a great sorceress. All her ways were wicked, all her instincts devilish. She was loaded to the eyelids with cold malice.

All her history was black with crime; and among her crimes murder was common. I was most curious to see her; as curious as I could have been to see Satan. To my surprise she was beautiful; black thoughts had failed to make her expression repulsive, age had failed to wrinkle her satin skin or mar its bloomy freshness. She could have passed for old Uriens's granddaughter, she could have been mistaken for sister to her own son.

As soon as we were fairly within the castle gates we were ordered into her presence. King Uriens was there, a kind-faced old man with a subdued look; and also the son, Sir Uwaine le Blanchemains, in whom I was of course interested on account of the tradition that he had once done battle with thirty knights, and also on account of his trip with Sir Gawaine and Sir Marhaus, which Sandy had been aging me with. But Morgan was the main attraction, the conspicuous personality here; she was head chief of this household, that was plain. She caused us to be seated, and then she began, with all manner of pretty graces and graciousnesses, to ask me questions. Dear me, it was like a bird or a flute, or something, talking. I felt persuaded that this woman must have been misrepresented, lied about. She trilled along, and trilled along, and presently a handsome young page, clothed like the rainbow, and as easy and undulatory of movement as a wave, came with something on a golden salver, and kneeling to present it to her, overdid his graces and lost his balance, and so fell lightly against her knee. She slipped a dirk into him in as matter-of-course a way as another person would have harpooned a rat!

Poor child, he slumped to the floor, twisted his silken limbs in one great straining contortion of pain, and was dead. Out of the old king was wrung an involuntary "O-h!" of compassion. The look he got, made him cut it suddenly short and not put any more hyphens in it. Sir Uwaine, at a sign from his mother, went to the anteroom and called some servants, and meanwhile madame went rippling sweetly along with her talk.

I saw that she was a good housekeeper, for while she talked she kept a corner of her eye on the servants to see that they made no balks in handling the body and getting it out; when they came with fresh clean towels, she sent back for the other kind; and when they had finished wiping the floor and were going, she indicated a crimson fleck the size of a tear which their duller eyes had overlooked. It was plain to me that La Cote Male Taile had failed to see the mistress of the house. Often, how louder and clearer than any tongue, does dumb circumstantial evidence speak.

Morgan le Fay rippled along as musically as ever. Marvelous woman. And what a glance she had: when it fell in reproof upon those servants, they shrunk and quailed as timid people do when the lightning flashes out of a cloud. I could have got the habit myself. It was the same with that poor old Brer Uriens; he was always on the ragged edge of apprehension; she could not even turn towards him but he winced.

In the midst of the talk I let drop a complimentary word about King Arthur, forgetting for the moment how this woman hated her brother. That one little compliment was enough. She clouded up like a storm; she called for her guards, and said—

"Hale me those varlets to the dungeons!"

That struck cold on my ears, for her dungeons had a reputation. Nothing occurred to me to say—or do. But not so with Sandy. As the guard laid a hand upon me, she piped up with the tranquilest confidence, and said—

"Dost thou covet destruction, thou maniac? It is The Boss!"

Now what a happy idea that was—and so simple; yet it would never have occurred to me. I was born modest; not all over, but in spots; and this was one of the spots.

The effect upon madame was electrical. It cleared her countenance and brought back her smiles and all her persuasive graces and blandishments; but nevertheless she was not able to entirely cover up with them the fact that she was in a ghastly fright. She said:

"La, but do list to thine handmaid! As if one gifted with powers like to mine might say the thing which I have said unto one who has vanquished Merlin, and not be jesting. By mine enchantments I foresaw your coming, and by them I knew you when you entered here. I did but play this little jest with hope to surprise you into some display of your art, as not doubting you would blast the guards with occult fires, consuming them to ashes on the spot, a marvel much beyond mine own ability, yet one which I have long been childishly curious to see."

The guards were less curious, and got out as soon as they got permission.

FOR DISCUSSION

1. What were the Yankee's purposes in starting knight-billboards?

2. What is the irony of his soap factory?

3. Why does Morgan le Fay invite the Yankee's sarcasm? Give examples.

CHAPTER 17

Madame, seeing me pacific and unresentful, no doubt judged that I was deceived by her excuse; for her fright dissolved away, and she was soon so importunate to have me give an exhibition and kill somebody, that the thing grew to be embarrassing. However, to my relief she was presently interrupted by the call to prayers. I will say this much for the nobility: that, tyrannical, murderous, rapacious and morally rotten as they were, they were deeply and enthusiastically religious. Nothing could divert them from the regular and faithful performance of the pieties enjoined by the Church. More than once I had seen a noble who had gotten his enemy at a disadvantage, stop to pray before cutting his throat; more than once I had seen a noble, after ambushing and dispatching his enemy, retire to the nearest wayside shrine and humbly give thanks, without even waiting to rob the body. There was to be nothing finer or sweeter in the life of even Benvenuto Cellini, that roughhewn saint, ten centuries later. All the nobles of Britain, with their families, attended divine service morning and night daily, in their private chapels, and even the worst of them had family worship five or six times a day besides. The credit of this belonged entirely to the Church. Although I was no friend to that Church, I was obliged to admit this. And often, in spite of me, I found myself saying, "What would this country be without the Church?"

After prayers we had dinner in a great banqueting hall which was lighted by hundreds of grease jets, and everything was as fine and lavish and rudely splendid as might become the royal degree of the hosts. At the head of the hall, on a dais, was the table of the king, queen, and their son, Prince Uwaine. Stretching down the hall from this, was the general table, on the floor. At this, above the salt, sat the visiting nobles and the grown members of their families, of both sexes—the resident Court, in effect—sixty-one persons; below the salt sat minor officers of the household, with their principal subordinates: altogether a hundred and eighteen persons sitting, and about as many liveried servants standing behind their chairs, or serving in one capacity or another. It was a very fine show. In a gallery a band with cymbals, horns, harps, and other horrors opened the proceedings with what seemed to be the crude first draft or original agony of the wail known to later centuries as "In the Sweet Bye and Bye." It was new, and ought to have been rehearsed a little more. For some reason or other the queen had the composer hanged, after dinner.

After this music, the priest who stood behind the royal table said a noble long grace in ostensible Latin. Then the battalion of waiters broke away from their posts, and darted, rushed, flew, fetched, and carried, and the mighty feeding began; no words anywhere, but absorbing attention to business. The rows of chops opened and shut in vast unison, and the sound of it was like to the muffled burr of subterranean machinery.

The havoc continued an hour and a half, and unimaginable was the destruction of substantials. Of the chief feature of the feast—the huge wild boar that lay stretched out so portly and imposing at the start—nothing was left but the semblance of a hoopskirt; and he was but the type and symbol of what had happened to all the other dishes.

With the pastries and so on, the heavy drinking began—and the talk. Gallon after gallon of wine and mead disappeared, and everybody got comfortable, then happy, then sparklingly joyous—both sexes—and by and by pretty noisy. Men told anecdotes that were terrific to hear, but nobody blushed; and when the nub was sprung, the assemblage let go with a horselaugh that shook the fortress. Ladies answered back with historiettes that would almost have made Queen Margaret of Navarre or even the great Elizabeth of England hide behind a handkerchief, but nobody hid here, but only laughed—howled, you may say. In pretty much all of these dreadful stories, ecclesiastics were the hardy heroes, but that didn't worry the chaplain any, he had his laugh with the rest; more than that, upon invitation he roared out a song which was of as daring a sort as any that was sung that night.

By midnight everybody was fagged out, and sore with laughing; and as a rule, drunk: some weepingly, some affectionately, some hilariously, some quarrelsomely, some dead and under the table. Of the ladies, the worst spectacle was a lovely young duchess, whose wedding eve this was; and indeed she was a spectacle, sure enough. Just as she was she could have sat in advance for the portrait of the young daughter of the Regent d'Orleans, at the famous dinner whence she was carried, foulmouthed, intoxicated, and helpless, to her bed, in the lost and lamented days of the Ancient Regime.

Suddenly, even while the priest was lifting his hands, and all conscious heads were bowed in reverent expectation of the coming blessing, there appeared under the arch of the far-off door at the bottom of the hall, an old and bent and white-haired lady, leaning upon a crutchstick; and she lifted the stick and pointed it toward the queen and cried out—

"The wrath and curse of God fall upon you, woman without pity, who have slain mine innocent grandchild and made desolate this old heart that had nor chick nor friend nor stay nor comfort in all this world but him!"

Everybody crossed himself in a grisly fright, for a curse was an awful thing to those people; but the queen rose up majestic, with the death light in her eye, and flung back this ruthless command:

"Lay hands on her! To the stake with her!"

The guards left their posts to obey. It was a shame; it was a cruel thing to see. What could be done? Sandy gave me a look; I knew she had another inspiration. I said—

"Do what you choose."

She was up and facing toward the queen in a moment. She indicated me, and said:

"Madame, *he* saith this may not be. Recall the commandment, or he will dissolve the castle and it shall vanish away like the instable fabric of a dream!"

Confound it, what a crazy contract to pledge a person to! What if the queen—

But my consternation subsided there, and my panic passed off; for the queen, all in a collapse, made no show of resistance but gave a countermanding sign and sunk into her seat. When she reached it she was sober. So were many of the others. The assemblage rose, whiffed ceremony to the winds, and rushed for the door like a mob, overturning chairs, smashing crockery, tugging, struggling, shouldering, crowding—anything to get out before I should change my mind and puff the castle into the measureless dim vacancies of space. Well, well, well, they *were* a superstitious lot. It is all a body can do to conceive of it.

The poor queen was so scared and humbled that she was even afraid to hang the composer without first consulting me. I was very sorry for her—indeed anyone would

have been, for she was really suffering; so I was willing to do anything that was reasonable, and had no desire to carry things to wanton extremities. I therefore considered the matter thoughtfully, and ended by having the musicians ordered into our presence to play that Sweet Bye and Bye again, which they did. Then I saw that she was right, and gave her permission to hang the whole band. This little relaxation of sternness had a good effect upon the queen. A statesman gains little by the arbitrary exercise of ironclad authority upon all occasions that offer, for this wounds the just pride of his subordinates, and thus tends to undermine his strength. A little concession, now and then, where it can do no harm, is the wiser policy.

Now that the queen was at ease in her mind once more, and measurably happy, her wine naturally began to assert itself again, and it got a little the start of her. I mean it set her music going—her silver bell of a tongue. Dear me, she was a master talker. It would not become me to suggest that it was pretty late and that I was a tired man and very sleepy. I wished I had gone off to bed when I had the chance. Now I must stick it out; there was no other way. So she tinkled along and along, in the otherwise profound and ghostly hush of the sleeping castle, until by and by there came, as if from deep down under us, a faraway sound, as of a muffled shriek—with an expression of agony about it that made my flesh crawl. The queen stopped, and her eyes lighted with pleasure; she tilted her graceful head as a bird does when it listens. The sound bored its way up through the stillness again.

"What is it?" I said.

"It is truly a stubborn soul, and endureth long. It is many hours now."

"Endureth what?"

"The rack. Come—ye shall see a blithe sight. An he yield not his secret now, ye shall see him torn asunder."

What a silky smooth hellion she was; and so composed and serene, when the cords all down my legs were hurting in sympathy with that man's pain. Conducted by mailed guards bearing flaring torches, we tramped along echoing corridors, and down stone stairways dank and dripping, and smelling of mold and ages of imprisoned night—a chill, uncanny journey and a long one, and not made the shorter or the cheerier by the sorceress' talk, which was about this sufferer and his crime. He had been accused by an anonymous informer, of having killed a stag in the royal preserves. I said—

"Anonymous testimony isn't just the right thing, your Highness. It were fairer to confront the accused with the accuser."

"I had not thought of that, it being but of small consequence. But an I would, I could not, for that the accuser came masked by night, and told the forester, and straightway got him hence again, and so the forester knoweth him not."

"Then is this Unknown the only person who saw the stag killed?"

"Marry, *no man saw* the killing, but this Unknown saw this hardy wretch near to the spot where the stag lay, and came with right loyal zeal and betrayed him to the forester."

"So the Unknown was near the dead stag, too? Isn't it just possible that he did the killing himself? His loyal zeal—in a mask—looks just a shade suspicious. But what is your Highness' idea for racking the prisoner? Where is the profit?"

"He will not confess, else; and then were his soul lost. For his crime his life is forfeited by the law—and of a surety will I see that he payeth it—but it were peril to my own soul to let him die unconfessed and unabsolved. Nay, I were a fool to fling me into hell for *his* accommodation."

"But, your Highness, suppose he has

nothing to confess?"

"As to that, we shall see, anon. An I rack him to death and he confess not, it will peradventure show that he had indeed naught to confess—ye will grant that that is sooth? Then shall I not be damned for an unconfessed man that had naught to confess—wherefore, I shall be safe."

It was the stubborn unreasoning of the time. It was useless to argue with her. Arguments have no chance against petrified training; they wear it as little as the waves wear a cliff. And her training was everybody's. The brightest intellect in the land would not have been able to see that her position was defective.

As we entered the rack cell I caught a picture that will not go from me; I wish it would. A native young giant of thirty or thereabouts, lay stretched upon the frame on his back, with his wrists and ankles tied to ropes which led over windlasses at either end. There was no color in him; his features were contorted and set, and sweat drops stood upon his forehead. A priest bent over him on each side; the executioner stood by; guards were on duty; smoking torches stood in sockets along the walls; in a corner crouched a poor young creature, her face drawn with anguish, a half-wild and hunted look in her eyes, and in her lap lay a little child asleep. Just as we stepped across the threshold the executioner gave his machine a slight turn, which wrung a cry from both the prisoner and the woman; but I shouted and the executioner released the strain without waiting to see who spoke. I could not let this horror go on; it would have killed me to see it. I asked the queen to let me clear the place and speak to the prisoner privately; and when she was going to object I spoke in a low voice and said I did not want to make a scene before her servants, but I must have my way; for I was King Arthur's representative, and was speaking in his name. She

saw she had to yield. I asked her to endorse me to these people, and then leave me. It was not pleasant for her, but she took the pill; and even went further than I was meaning to require. I only wanted the backing of her own authority; but she said—

"Ye will do in all things as this lord shall command. It is The Boss."

It was certainly a good word to conjure with: you could see it by the squirming of these rats. The queen's guards fell into line, and she and they marched away, with their torchbearers, and woke the echoes of the cavernous tunnels with the measured beat of their retreating footfalls. I had the prisoner taken from the rack and placed upon his bed, and medicaments applied to his hurts, and wine given him to drink. The woman crept near and looked on, eagerly, lovingly, but timorously—like one who fears a repulse; indeed, she tried furtively to touch the man's forehead, and jumped back, the picture of fright, when I turned unconsciously toward her. It was pitiful to see.

"Lord," I said, "stroke him, lass, if you want to. Do anything you're a mind to; don't mind me."

Why, her eyes were as grateful as an animal's, when you do it a kindness that it understands. The baby was out of her way and she had her cheek against the man's in a minute, and her hands fondling his hair, and her happy tears running down. The man revived, and caressed his wife with his eyes, which was all he could do. I judged I might clear the den, now, and I did; cleared it of all but the family and myself. Then I said—

"Now my friend, tell me your side of this matter; I know the other side."

The man moved his head in sign of refusal. But the woman looked pleased—as it seemed to me—pleased with my suggestion. I went on:

"You know of me?"

"Yes. All do, in Arthur's realms."

"If my reputation has come to you right and straight, you should not be afraid to speak."

The woman broke in, eagerly:

"Ah, fair my lord, do thou persuade him! Thou canst an thou wilt. Ah, he suffereth so; and it is for me—for *me!* And how can I bear it? I would I might see him die—a sweet, swift death; oh, my Hugo, I cannot bear this one!"

And she fell to sobbing and groveling about my feet, and still imploring. Imploring what? The man's death? I could not quite get the bearings of the thing. But Hugo interrupted her and said—

"Peace! Ye wit not what ye ask. Shall I starve whom I love, to win a gentle death? I wend thou knewest me better."

"Well," I said, "I can't quite make this out. It is a puzzle. Now—"

"Ah, dear my lord, an ye will but persuade him! Consider how these his tortures wound me! Oh, and he will not speak—whereas, the healing, the solace that lie in a blessed swift death—"

"What *are* you maundering about? He's going out from here a free man and whole—he's not going to die."

The man's white face lit up, and the woman flung herself at me in a most surprising explosion of joy, and cried out—

"He is saved—for it is the king's word by the mouth of the king's servant—Arthur, the king whose word is gold!"

"Well, then you do believe I can be trusted, after all. Why didn't you before?"

"Who doubted? Not I, indeed; and not she."

"Well, why wouldn't you tell me your story, then?"

"Ye had made no promise; else had it been otherwise."

"I see, I see. . . . And yet I believe I don't quite see, after all. You stood the torture and refused to confess; which shows plain enough to even the dullest understanding that you had nothing to confess—"

"*I*, my lord? How so? It was I that killed the deer!"

"You *did?* Oh, dear, this is the most mixed-up business that ever—"

"Dear Lord, I begged him on my knees to confess, but—"

"You *did!* It gets thicker and thicker. What did you want him to do that for?"

"Sith it would bring him a quick death and save him all this cruel pain."

"Well—yes, there is reason in that. But *he* didn't want the quick death."

"He? Why, of a surety he *did.*"

"Well, then, why in the world *didn't* he confess?"

"Ah, sweet sir, and leave my wife and chick without bread and shelter?"

"Oh, heart of gold, now I see it! The bitter law takes the convicted man's estate and beggars his widow and his orphans. They could torture you to death, but without conviction or confession they could not rob your wife and baby. You stood by them like a man; and *you*—true wife and true woman that you are—you would have bought him release from torture at cost to yourself of slow starvation and death—well, it humbles a body to think what your sex can do when it comes to self-sacrifice. I'll book you both for my colony; you'll like it there; it's a Factory where I'm going to turn groping and grubbing automata into *men.*"

CHAPTER 18

Well, I arranged all that; and I had the man sent to his home. I had a great desire to rack the executioner; not because he was a good, painstaking and paingiving official— for surely it was not to his discredit that he performed his functions well—but to pay him back for wantonly cuffing and otherwise distressing that young woman. The priests told me about this, and were generously hot to have him punished. Something of this disagreeable sort was turning up every now and then. I mean, episodes that showed that not all priests were frauds and self-seekers, but that many, even the great majority, of these that were down on the ground among the common people, were sincere and right-hearted, and devoted to the alleviation of human troubles and sufferings. Well, it was a thing which could not be helped, so I seldom fretted about it, and never many minutes at a time; it has never been my way to bother much about things which you can't cure. But I did not like it, for it was just the sort of thing to keep people reconciled to an Established Church. We *must* have a religion—it goes without saying—but my idea is, to have it cut up into forty free sects, so that they will police each other, as had been the case in the United States in my time. Concentration of power in a political machine is bad; and an Established Church is only a political machine; it was invented for that; it is nursed, cradled, preserved for that; it is an enemy to human liberty, and does no good which it could not better do in a split-up and scattered condition. That wasn't law; it wasn't gospel: it was only an opinion—my opinion, and I was only a man, one man: so it wasn't worth any more than the Pope's—or any less, for that matter.

Well, I couldn't rack the executioner, neither would I overlook the just complaint of the priests. The man must be punished somehow or other, so I degraded him from his office and made him leader of the band —the new one that was to be started. He begged hard, and said he couldn't play— a plausible excuse, but too thin; there wasn't a musician in the country that could.

The queen was a good deal outraged, next morning, when she found she was going to have neither Hugo's life nor his property. But I told her she must bear this cross; that while by law and custom she certainly was entitled to both the man's life and his property, there were extenuating circumstances, and so in Arthur the king's name I had pardoned him. The deer was ravaging the man's fields, and he had killed it in sudden passion, and not for gain; and he had carried it into the royal forest in the hope that that might make detection of the misdoer impossible. Confound her, I couldn't make her see that sudden passion is an extenuating circumstance in the killing of venison—or of a person—so I gave it up and let her sulk it out. I *did* think I was going to make her see it by remarking that her own sudden passion in the case of the page modified that crime.

"Crime!" she exclaimed. "How thou talkest! Crime, forsooth! Man, I am going to *pay* for him!"

Oh, it was no use to waste sense on her. Training—training is everything; training is all there is *to* a person. We speak of nature; it is folly; there is no such thing as nature; what we call by that misleading name is merely heredity and training. We have no thoughts of our own, no opinions of our own; they are transmitted to us, trained into us. All that is original in us, and therefore fairly creditable or discreditable to us, can be covered up and hidden by the point of a cambric needle, all the rest being atoms contributed by, and inherited from, a procession of ancestors that stretches back a billion years to the Adam-clam or grasshopper or monkey from whom our race has been so tediously and ostentatiously and unprofitably developed. And as for me, all that I think about in this plodding sad pilgrimage, this pathetic drift between the eternities, is to look out and humbly live a pure and high and blameless life, and save that one microscopic atom in me that is truly *me:* the rest may land in Sheol and welcome for all I care.

No, confound her, her intellect was good, she had brains enough, but her training made her a sap—that is, from a many-centuries-later point of view. To kill the page was no crime—it was her right; and upon her right she stood, serenely and unconscious of offense. She was a result of generations of training in the unexamined and unassailed belief that the law which permitted her to kill a subject when she chose was a perfectly right and righteous one.

Well, we must give even Satan his due. She deserved a compliment for one thing; and I tried to pay it, but the words stuck in my throat. She had a right to kill the boy, but she was in no wise obliged to pay for him. That was law for some other people, but not for her. She knew quite well that she was doing a large and generous thing to pay for that lad, and that I ought in common fairness to come out with something handsome about it, but I couldn't—my mouth refused. I couldn't help seeing, in my fancy, that poor old grandam with the broken heart, and that fair young creature lying butchered, his little silken pomps and vanities laced with his golden blood. How could she *pay* for him? *Whom* could she pay? And so, well knowing that this woman, trained as she had been, deserved praise, even adulation, I was yet not able to utter it, trained as *I*

had been. The best I could do was to fish up a compliment from outside, so to speak—and the pity of it was, that it was true:

"Madame, your people will adore you for this."

Quite true, but I meant to hang her for it some day, if I lived. Some of those laws were too bad, altogether too bad. A master might kill his slave for nothing: for mere spite, malice, or to pass the time—just as we have seen that the crowned head could do it with *his* slave, that is to say, anybody. A gentleman could kill a free commoner, and pay for him—cash or garden truck. A noble could kill a noble without expense, as far as the law was concerned, but reprisals in kind were to be expected. *Any*body could kill *some*body, except the commoner and the slave; these had no privileges. If they killed, it was murder, and the law wouldn't stand murder. It made short work of the experimenter—and of his family too, if he murdered somebody who belonged up among the ornamental ranks. If a commoner gave a noble even so much as a Damiens-scratch which didn't kill or even hurt, he got Damiens's dose for it just the same; they pulled him to rags and tatters with horses, and all the world came to see the show, and crack jokes, and have a good time; and some of the performances of the best people present were as tough, and as properly unprintable, as any that have been printed by the pleasant Casanova in his chapter about the dismemberment of Louis XV's poor awkward enemy.

I had had enough of this grisly place by this time, and wanted to leave, but I couldn't, because I had something on my mind that my conscience kept prodding me about, and wouldn't let me forget. If I had the remaking of man, he wouldn't have any conscience. It is one of the most disagreeable things connected with a person; and although it certainly does a great deal of good, it cannot be said to pay, in the long run; it would be much better to have less good and more comfort. Still, this is only my opinion, and I am only one man; others, with less experience, may think differently. They have a right to their view. I only stand to this: I have noticed my conscience for many years, and I know it is more trouble and bother to me than anything else I started with. I suppose that in the beginning I prized it, because we prize anything that is ours; and yet how foolish it was to think so. If we look at it in another way, we see how absurd it is: if I had an anvil in me would I prize it? Of course not. And yet when you come to think, there is no real difference between a conscience and an anvil—I mean for comfort. I have noticed it a thousand times. And you could dissolve an anvil with acids, when you couldn't stand it any longer; but there isn't any way that you can work off a conscience —at least so it will stay worked off; not that I know of, anyway.

There was something I wanted to do before leaving, but it was a disagreeable matter, and I hated to go at it. Well, it bothered me all the morning. I could have mentioned it to the old king, but what would be the use—he was but an extinct volcano; he had been active in his time, but his fire was out, this good while, he was only a stately ash pile, now; gentle enough, and kindly enough for my purpose, without doubt, but not usable. He was nothing, this so-called king: the queen was the only power there. And she was a Vesuvius. As a favor, she might consent to warm a flock of sparrows for you, but then she might take that very opportunity to turn herself loose and bury a city. However, I reflected that as often as any other way, when you are expecting the worst, you get something that is not so bad, after all.

So I braced up and placed my matter before her royal Highness. I said I had

been having a general jail delivery at Camelot and among neighboring castles, and with her permission I would like to examine her collection, her bric-a-brac—that is to say, her prisoners. She resisted; but I was expecting that. But she finally consented. I was expecting that, too, but not so soon. That about ended my discomfort. She called her guards and torches, and we went down into the dungeons. These were down under the castle's foundations, and mainly were small cells hollowed out of the living rock. Some of these cells had no light at all. In one of them was a woman, in foul rags, who sat on the ground, and would not answer a question, or speak a word, but only looked up at us once or twice, through a cobweb of tangled hair, as if to see what casual thing it might be that was disturbing with sound and light the meaningless dull dream that was become her life; after that, she sat bowed, with her dirt-caked fingers idly interlocked in her lap, and gave no further sign. This poor rack of bones was a woman of middle age, apparently; but only apparently; she had been there nine years, and was eighteen when she entered. She was a commoner, and had been sent here on her bridal night by Sir Breuse Sance Pité, a neighboring lord whose vassal her father was, and to which said lord she had refused what has since been called *le droit du Seigneur;* and moreover, had opposed violence to violence and spilt half a gill of his almost sacred blood. The young husband had interfered at that point, believing the bride's life in danger, and had flung the noble out into the midst of the humble and trembling wedding guests, in the parlor, and left him there astonished at this strange treatment, and implacably embittered against both bride and groom. The said lord being cramped for dungeon room had asked the queen to accommodate his two criminals, and here in her bastille they had been ever since; hither indeed, they had come before their crime was an hour old, and had never seen each other since. Here they were, kerneled like toads in the same rock; they had passed nine pitch dark years within fifty feet of each other, yet neither knew whether the other was alive or not. All the first years, their only question had been— asked with beseechings and tears that might have moved stones, in time, perhaps, but hearts are not stones: "Is he alive?" "Is she alive?" But they had never got an answer; and at last that question was not asked any more—or any other.

I wanted to see the man, after hearing all this. He was thirty-four years old, and looked sixty. He sat upon a squared block of stone, with his head bent down, his forearms resting on his knees, his long hair hanging like a fringe before his face, and he was muttering to himself. He raised his chin and looked us slowly over, in a list-less dull way, blinking with the distress of the torchlight, then dropped his head and fell to muttering again and took no further notice of us. There were some pathetically suggestive dumb witnesses present. On his wrists and ankles were cicatrices, old smooth scars, and fastened to the stone on which he sat was a chain with manacles and fetters attached; but this apparatus lay idle on the ground, and was thick with rust. Chains cease to be needed after the spirit has gone out of a prisoner.

I could not rouse the man; so I said we would take him to her, and see—to the bride who was the fairest thing in the earth to him, once—roses, pearls, and dew made flesh, for him; a wonderwork, the master-work of nature: with eyes like no other eyes, and voice like no other voice, and a freshness, and lithe young grace, and beauty that belonged properly to the crea-tures of dreams—as he thought—and to no other. The sight of her would set his

stagnant blood leaping; the sight of her—

But it was a disappointment. They sat together on the ground and looked dimly wondering into each other's faces awhile, with a sort of weak animal curiosity; then forgot each other's presence, and dropped their eyes, and you saw that they were away again and wandering in some far land of dreams and shadows that we know nothing about.

I had them taken out and sent to their friends. The queen did not like it much. Not that she felt any personal interest in the matter, but she thought it disrespectful to Sir Breuse Sance Pité. However, I as-sured her that if he found he couldn't stand it I would fix him so that he could.

I set forty-seven prisoners loose out of those awful ratholes, and left only one in captivity. He was a lord, and had killed another lord, a sort of kinsman of the queen. That other lord had ambushed him to assassinate him, but this fellow had got the best of him and cut his throat. How-ever, it was not for that that I left him jailed, but for maliciously destroying the only public well in one of his wretched vil-lages. The queen was bound to hang him for killing her kinsman, but I would not allow it: it was no crime to kill an assassin. But I said I was willing to let her hang him for destroying the well; so she concluded to put up with that, as it was better than nothing.

Dear me, for what trifling offenses the most of those forty-seven men and women were shut up there! Indeed some were there for no distinct offense at all, but only to gratify somebody's spite; and not al-ways the queen's by any means, but a friend's. The newest prisoner's crime was a mere remark which he had made. He said he believed that men were about all alike, and one man as good as another, barring clothes. He said he believed that if you were to strip the nation naked and send a stranger through the crowd, he couldn't tell the king from a quack doctor, nor a duke from a hotel clerk. Apparently here was a man whose brains had not been reduced to an ineffectual mush by idiotic training. I set him loose and sent him to the Factory.

Some of the cells carved in the living rock were just behind the face of the precipice, and in each of these an arrow-slit had been pierced outward to the daylight, and so the captive had a thin ray from the blessed sun for his comfort. The case of one of these poor fellows was particularly hard. From his dusky swallow's hole high up in that vast wall of native rock he could peer out through the arrow-slit and see his own home off yonder in the valley; and for twenty-two years he had watched it, with heartache and longing, through that crack. He could see the lights shine there at night, and in the daytime he could see figures go in and come out— his wife and children, some of them, no doubt, though he could not make out, at that distance. In the course of years he noted festivities there, and tried to rejoice, and wondered if they were weddings or what they might be. And he noted funerals; and they wrung his heart. He could make out the coffin, but he could not determine its size, and so could not tell whether it was wife or child. He could see the procession form, with priests and mourners, and move solemnly away, bearing the secret with them. He had left behind him five children and a wife; and in nineteen years he had seen five funerals issue, and none of them humble enough in pomp to denote a servant. So he had lost five of his treasures; there must still be one remaining—one now infinitely, unspeakably precious—but *which* one? Wife, or child? That was the question that tortured him, by night and by day, asleep and awake. Well, to have an interest of some

sort, and half a ray of light, when you are in a dungeon, is a great support to the body and preserver of the intellect. This man was in pretty good condition yet. By the time he had finished telling me his distressful tale, I was in the same state of mind that you would have been in yourself, if you have got average human curiosity: that is to say, I was as burning up as he was, to find out which member of the family it was that was left. So I took him over home myself; and an amazing kind of a surprise party it was, too—typhoons and cyclones of frantic joy, and whole Niagaras of happy tears; and by George we found the aforetime young matron graying toward the imminent verge of her half century, and the babies all men and women, and some of them married and experimenting familywise themselves—for not a soul of the tribe was dead! Conceive of the ingenious devilishness of that queen: she had a special hatred for this prisoner, and she had *invented* all those funerals herself, to scorch his heart with; and the sublimest stroke of genius of the whole thing was leaving the family invoice a funeral *short,* so as to let him wear his poor old soul out guessing.

But for me, he never would have got out. Morgan le Fay hated him with her whole heart, and she never would have softened toward him. And yet his crime was committed more in thoughtlessness than deliberate depravity. He had said she had red hair. Well, she had; but that was no way to speak of it. When red-headed people are above a certain social grade, their hair is auburn.

Consider it: among these forty-seven captives, there were five whose names, offenses and dates of incarceration were no longer known! One woman and four men—all bent, and wrinkled, and mind-extinguished patriarchs. They themselves had long ago forgotten these details; at any rate they had mere vague theories about them, nothing definite and nothing that they repeated twice in the same way. The succession of priests whose office it had been to pray daily with the captives and remind them that God had put them there, for some wise purpose or other, and teach them that patience, humbleness, and submission to oppression was what He loved to see in parties of a subordinate rank, had traditions about these poor old human ruins, but nothing more. These traditions went but little way, for they concerned the length of the incarceration only, and not the names or the offenses. And even by the help of tradition the only thing that could be proven was that none of the five had seen daylight for thirty-five years: how much longer this privation had lasted was not guessable. The king and the queen knew nothing about these poor creatures, except that they were heirlooms, assets inherited, along with the throne, from the former firm. Nothing of their history had been transmitted with their persons, and so the inheriting owners had considered them of no value, and had felt no interest in them. I said to the queen—

"Then why in the world didn't you set them free?"

The question was a puzzler. She didn't know *why* she hadn't; the thing had never come up in her mind. So here she was, forecasting the veritable history of future prisoners of the castle d'If, without knowing it. It seemed plain to me now, that with her training, those inherited prisoners were merely property—nothing more, nothing less. Well, when we inherit property, it does not occur to us to throw it away, even when we do not value it.

When I brought my procession of human bats up into the open world and the glare of the afternoon sun—previously blindfolding them, in charity for eyes so long untortured by light—they were a spectacle to look at. Skeletons, scarecrows, goblins, pathetic frights, every one: legitimatest possible children of Monarchy by the Grace of God and the Established Church. I muttered absently—

"I *wish* I could photograph them!"

You have seen that kind of people who will never let on that they don't know the meaning of a new big word. The more ignorant they are, the more pitifully certain they are to pretend you haven't shot over their heads. The queen was just one of that sort, and was always making the stupidest blunders by reason of it. She hesitated a moment; then her face brightened up with sudden comprehension, and she said she would do it for me.

I thought to myself: She? why what can she know about photography? But it was a poor time to be thinking. When I looked around, she was moving on the procession with an ax!

Well, she certainly was a curious one, was Morgan le Fay. I have seen a good many kinds of women in my time, but she laid over them all, for variety. And how sharply characteristic of her this episode was. She had no more idea than a horse of how to photograph a procession; but being in doubt, it was just like her to try to do it with an ax.

FOR DISCUSSION

1. What pathetic sights does the Yankee find in the queen's rack-cell and dungeons?

2. Explain how the incidents with the musicians and the "photography" provide a kind of comic relief from the horrors of Morgan le Fay's castle.

3. What is the Yankee's theory about the importance of training (pages 603–604)? What evidence does he present for it? Do you agree with him?

The Yankee and Sandy continue on their travels, finding Sandy's ogre's castle "transformed" into a pigsty full of hogs whom Sandy insists are nobility. They pass a band of slaves and must watch a husband and wife parted. Joining a band of pilgrims headed for a miraculous fountain in the Valley of Holiness, they find the fountain dried up, and the Boss "miraculously" restores it.

Later, the king decides to join the Yankee in his plan to tour the country in humble disguise in order to find out how the people live.

CHAPTER 27

About bedtime I took the king to my private quarters to cut his hair and help him get the hang of the lowly raiment he was to wear. The high classes wore their hair banged across the forehead but hanging to the shoulders the rest of the way around, whereas the lowest ranks of commoners were banged fore and aft both; the slaves were bangless, and allowed their hair free growth. So I inverted a bowl over his head and cut away all the locks that hung below it. I also trimmed his whiskers and mustache until they were only about a half inch long; and tried to do it inartistically, and succeeded. It was a villainous disfigurement. When he got his lubberly sandals on, and his long robe of coarse brown linen cloth, which hung straight from his neck to his anklebones, he was no longer the comeliest man in his kingdom, but one of the unhandsomest and most commonplace and unattractive. We were dressed and barbered alike, and could pass for small farmers, or farm bailiffs, or shepherds, or carters; yes, or for village artisans, if we chose, our costumes being in effect universal among the poor, because of its strength and cheapness. I don't mean that it was really cheap to a very poor person, but I do mean that it was the cheapest material there was for male attire—manufactured material, you understand.

We slipped away an hour before dawn, and by broad sunup had made eight or ten miles, and were in the midst of a sparsely settled country. I had a pretty heavy knapsack; it was laden with provisions—provisions for the king to taper down on, till he could take to the coarse fare of the country without damage.

I found a comfortable seat for the king by the roadside, and then gave him a morsel or two to stay his stomach with. Then I said I would find some water for him, and strolled away. Part of my project was to get out of sight and sit down and rest a little myself. It had always been my custom to stand, when in his presence; even at the council board, except upon those rare occasions when the sitting was a very long one, extending over hours; then I had a trifling little backless thing which was like a reversed culvert and was as comfortable as the toothache. I didn't want to break him in suddenly, but do it by degrees. We should have to sit together now when in company, or people would notice; but it would not be good politics for me to be playing equality with him when there was no necessity for it.

I found the water, some three hundred yards away, and had been resting about twenty minutes, when I heard voices. That is all right, I thought—peasants going to work; nobody else likely to be stirring this early. But the next moment these comers jingled into sight around a turn of the road—smartly clad people of quality, with luggage-mules and servants in their train! I was off like a shot through the bushes, by the shortest cut. For a while it did seem that these people would pass the king before I could get to him; but desperation gives you wings, you know, and I canted my body forward, inflated my breast, and held my breath and flew. I arrived. And in plenty good enough time, too.

"Pardon, my king, but it's no time for ceremony—jump! Jump to your feet—some quality are coming!"

"Is that a marvel? Let them come."

"But my liege! You must not be seen sitting. Rise—and stand in humble posture while they pass! You are a peasant, you know."

"True—I had forgot it, so lost was I in planning of a huge war with Gaul"—he was up by this time, but a farm could have got up quicker, if there was any kind of a boom in real estate—"and right-so a thought came randoming overthwart this majestic dream the which—"

"A humbler attitude, my lord the king—and quick! Duck your head—more—still more—droop it!"

He did his honest best, but lord it was not great things. He looked as humble as the leaning tower at Pisa. It is the most you could say of it. Indeed it was such a thundering poor success that it raised wondering scowls all along the line, and a gorgeous flunkey at the tail end of it raised his whip; but I jumped in time and was under it when it fell; and under cover of the volley of coarse laughter which followed, I spoke up sharply and warned the king to take no notice. He mastered himself for the moment, but it was a sore tax; he wanted to eat up the procession. I said:

"It would end our adventures at the very start; and we, being without weapons, could do nothing with that armed gang. If we are going to succeed in our emprise, we must not only look the peasant but act the peasant."

"It is wisdom; none can gainsay it. Let us go on, Sir Boss. I will take note and learn, and do the best I may."

He kept his word. He did the best he could, but I've seen better. If you have ever seen an active, heedless, enterprising child going diligently out of one mischief and into another all day long, and an anxious mother at its heels all the while, and just saving it by a hair from drowning itself or breaking its neck with each new experiment, you've seen the king and me.

If I could have foreseen what the thing was going to be like, I should have said, No, if anybody wants to make his living exhibiting a king as a peasant, let him take the layout; I can do better with a menagerie, and last longer. And yet, during the first three days I never allowed him to enter a hut or other dwelling. If he could pass muster anywhere, during his early noviciate, it would be in small inns and on the road; so to these places we confined ourselves. Yes, he certainly did the best he could, but what of that? He didn't improve a bit that I could see.

He was always frightening me, always breaking out with fresh astonishers, in new and unexpected places. Toward evening on the second day, what does he do but blandly fetch out a dirk from inside his robe!

"Great guns, my liege, where did you get that?"

"From a smuggler at the inn, yester eve."

"What in the world possessed you to buy it?"

"We have escaped divers dangers by wit —thy wit—but I have bethought me that it were but prudence if I bore a weapon, too. Thine might fail thee in some pinch."

"But people of our condition are not allowed to carry arms. What would a lord say—yes, or any other person of whatever condition—if he caught an upstart peasant with a dagger on his person?"

It was a lucky thing for us that nobody

came along just then. I persuaded him to throw the dirk away; and it was as easy as persuading a child to give up some bright fresh new way of killing itself. We walked along, silent and thinking. Finally the king said:

"When ye know that I meditate a thing inconvenient, or that hath a peril in it, why do you not warn me to cease from that project?"

It was a startling question, and a puzzler. I didn't quite know how to take hold of it, or what to say, and so of course I ended by saying the natural thing:

"But sire, how can *I* know what your thoughts are?"

The king stopped dead in his tracks, and stared at me.

"I believed thou wert greater than Merlin; and truly in magic thou art. But prophecy is greater than magic. Merlin is a prophet."

I saw I had made a blunder. I must get back my lost ground. After deep reflection and careful planning, I said:

"Sire, I have been misunderstood. I will explain. There are two kinds of prophecy. One is the gift to foretell things that are but a little way off, the other is the gift to foretell things that are whole ages and centuries away. Which is the mightier gift, do you think?"

"Oh, the last, most surely!"

"True. Does Merlin possess it?"

"Partly, yes. He foretold mysteries about my birth and future kingships that were twenty years away."

"Has he ever gone beyond that?"

"He would not claim more, I think."

"It is probably his limit. All prophets have their limit. The limit of some of the great prophets has been a hundred years."

"These are few, I ween."

"There have been two still greater ones, whose limit was four hundred and six hundred years, and one whose limit compassed even seven hundred and twenty."

"Gramercy, it is marvelous!"

"But what are these in comparison with me? They are nothing."

"What? Canst thou truly look beyond even so vast a stretch of time as—"

"Seven hundred years? My liege, as clear as the vision of an eagle does my prophetic eye penetrate and lay bare the future of this world for nearly thirteen centuries and a half!"

My land, you should have seen the king's eyes spread slowly open, and lift the earth's entire atmosphere as much as an inch! That settled Brer Merlin. One never had any occasion to prove his facts, with these people; all he had to do was state them. It never occurred to anybody to doubt the statement.

"Now, then," I continued, "I *could* work both kinds of prophecy—the long and the short—if I chose to take the trouble to keep in practice; but I seldom exercise any but the long kind, because the other is beneath my dignity. It is properer to Merlin's sort—stump-tail prophets, as we call them in the profession. Of course I whet up now and then and flirt out a minor prophecy, but not often—hardly ever, in fact. You will remember that there was great talk, when you reached the Valley of Holiness, about my having prophesied your coming and the very hour of your arrival, two or three days beforehand."

"Indeed, yes, I mind it now."

"Well, I could have done it as much as forty times easier, and piled on a thousand times more detail into the bargain, if it had been five hundred years away instead of two or three days."

"How amazing that it should be so!"

"Yes, a genuine expert can always foretell a thing that is five hundred years away easier than he can a thing that's only five hundred seconds off."

"And yet in reason it should clearly be the other way: it should be five hundred times as easy to foretell the last as the first, for indeed it is so close by that one uninspired might almost see it. In truth the law of prophecy doth contradict the likelihoods, most strangely making the difficult easy, and the easy difficult."

It was a wise head. A peasant's cap was no safe disguise for it; you could know it for a king's, under a diving bell, if you could hear it work its intellect.

I had a new trade, now, and plenty of business in it. The king was as hungry to find out everything that was going to happen during the next thirteen centuries as if he were expecting to live in them. From that time out, I prophesied myself baldheaded trying to supply the demand. I have done some indiscreet things in my day, but this thing of playing myself for a prophet was the worst. Still, it had its ameliorations. A prophet doesn't have to have any brains. They are good to have, of course, for the ordinary exigencies of life, but they are no use in professional work. It is the restfulest vocation there is. When the spirit of prophecy comes upon you, you merely take your intellect and lay it off in a cool place for a rest, and unship your jaw and leave it alone; it will work itself: the result is prophecy.

Everyday a knight-errant or so came along, and the sight of them fired the king's martial spirit every time. He would have forgotten himself, sure, and said something to them in a style a suspicious shade or so above his ostensible degree, and so I always got him well out of the road in time. Then he would stand, and look with all his eyes; and a proud light would flash from them, and his nostrils would inflate like a warhorse's, and I knew he was longing for a brush with them. But about noon of the third day I had stopped in the road to take a precaution which had been suggested by the whip stroke that had fallen to my share two days before; a precaution which I had afterward decided to leave untaken, I was

so loath to institute it; but now I had just had a fresh reminder: while striding heedlessly along, with jaw spread and intellect at rest, for I was prophesying, I stubbed my toe and fell sprawling. I was so pale I couldn't think, for a moment; then I got softly and carefully up and unstrapped my knapsack. I had that dynamite bomb in it, done up in wool, in a box. It was a good thing to have along; the time would come when I could do a valuable miracle with it, maybe, but it was a nervous thing to have about me, and I didn't like to ask the king to carry it. Yet I must either throw it away or think up some safe way to get along with its society. I got it out and slipped it into my scrip, and just then, here came a couple of knights. The king stood, stately as a statue, gazing toward them—had forgotten himself again, of course—and before I could get a word of warning out, it was time for him to skip, and well that he did it, too. He supposed they would turn aside. Turn aside to avoid trampling peasant dirt under foot? When had he ever turned aside himself—or ever had the chance to do it, if a peasant saw him or any other noble knight in time to judiciously save him the trouble? The knights paid no attention to the king at all; it was his place to look out himself, and if he hadn't skipped he would have been placidly ridden down, and laughed at besides.

The king was in a flaming fury, and launched out his challenge and epithets with a most royal vigor. The knights were some little distance by, now. They halted, greatly surprised, and turned in their saddles and looked back, as if wondering if it might be worth while to bother with such scum as we. Then they wheeled and started for us. Not a moment must be lost. I started for *them*. I passed them at a rattling gait, and as I went by I flung out a hair-lifting soul-scorching thirteen-jointed insult which made the king's effort poor

and cheap by comparison. I got it out of the nineteenth century where they know how. They had such headway that they were nearly to the king before they could check up; then, frantic with rage, they stood up their horses on their hind hoofs and whirled them around, and the next moment here they came, breast to breast. I was seventy yards off, then, and scrambling up a great boulder at the roadside. When they were within thirty yards of me they let their long lances droop to a level, depressed their mailed heads, and so, with their horsehair plumes streaming straight out behind, most gallant to see, this lightning express came tearing for me! When they were within fifteen yards, I sent that bomb with a sure aim, and it struck the ground just under the horses' noses.

Yes, it was a neat thing, very neat and pretty to see. It resembled a steamboat explosion on the Mississippi; and during the next fifteen minutes we stood under a steady drizzle of microscopic fragments of knights and hardware and horseflesh. I say

we, for the king joined the audience, of course, as soon as he had got his breath again. There was a hole there which would afford steady work for all the people in that region for some years to come—in trying to explain it, I mean; as for filling it up, that service would be comparatively prompt, and would fall to the lot of a select few—peasants of that siegnory, and they wouldn't get anything for it, either.

But I explained it to the king myself. I said it was done with a dynamite bomb. This information did him no damage, because it left him as intelligent as he was before. However, it was a noble miracle, in his eyes, and was another settler for Merlin. I thought it well enough to explain that this was a miracle of so rare a sort that it couldn't be done except when the atmospheric conditions were just right. Otherwise he would be encoring it every time we had a good subject, and that would be inconvenient, because I hadn't any more bombs along.

CHAPTER 28

On the morning of the fourth day, when it was just sunrise, and we had been tramping an hour in the chill dawn, I came to a resolution: the king *must* be drilled; things could not go on so, he must be taken in hand and deliberately and conscientiously drilled, or we couldn't even venture to enter a dwelling; the very cats would know this masquerader for a humbug and no peasant. So I called a halt and said:

"Sire, as between clothes and countenance, you are all right, there is no discrepancy; but as between your clothes and your bearing, you are all wrong, there is a most noticeable discrepancy. Your soldierly stride, your lordly port—these will not do. You stand too straight, your looks are too high, too confident. The cares of a kingdom

do not stoop the shoulders, they do not droop the chin, they do not depress the high level of the eye glance, they do not put doubt and fear in the heart and hang out the signs of them in slouching body and unsure step. It is the sordid cares of the lowly born that do these things. You must learn the trick; you must imitate the trademarks of poverty, misery, oppression, insult, and the other several and common inhumanities that sap the manliness out of a man and make him a loyal and proper and approved subject and a satisfaction to his masters, or the very infants will know you for better than your disguise, and we shall go to pieces at the first hut we stop at. Pray try to walk like this."

The king took careful note, and then

tried an imitation.

"Pretty fair—pretty fair. Chin a little lower, please—there, very good. Eyes too high; pray don't look at the horizon, look at the ground, ten steps in front of you. Ah—that is better, that is very good. Wait, please; you betray too much vigor, too much decision; you want more of a shamble. Look at me, please—this is what I mean. . . . Now you are getting it; that is the idea—at least, it sort of approaches it. . . . Yes, that is pretty fair. *But!* There is a great big something wanting, I don't quite know what it is. Please walk thirty yards, so that I can get a perspective on the thing. . . . Now, then—your head's right, speed's right, shoulders right, eyes right, chin right, gait, carriage, general style right—everything's right! And yet the fact remains, the aggregate's wrong. The account don't balance. Do it again, please . . . *now* I think I begin to see what it is. Yes, I've struck it. You see, the genuine, spiritlessness is wanting; that's what's the trouble. It's all *amateur*—mechanical details all right, almost to a hair; everything about the delusion perfect, except that it don't delude."

"What, then, must one do to prevail?"

"Let me think . . . I can't seem to quite get at it. In fact there isn't anything that can right the matter but practice. This is a good place for it: roots and stony ground to break up your stately gait, a region not liable to interruption, only one field and one hut in sight, and they so far away that nobody could see us from there. It will be well to move a little off the road and put in the whole day drilling you, sire."

After the drill had gone on a little while, I said:

"Now, sire, imagine that we are at the door of the hut yonder, and the family are before us. Proceed, please—accost the head of the house."

The king unconsciously straightened up like a monument and said, with frozen austerity:

"Varlet, bring a seat; and serve to me what cheer ye have."

"Ah, your grace, that is not well done."

"In what lacketh it?"

"These people do not call *each other* varlets."

"Nay, is that true?"

"Yes; only those above them call them so."

"Then must I try again. I will call him villein."

"No-no; for he may be a freeman."

"Ah—so. Then peradventure I should call him goodman."

"That would answer, your grace, but it would be still better if you said friend, or brother."

"Brother! To dirt like that?"

"Ah, but *we* are pretending to be dirt like that, too."

"It is even true. I will say it. Brother, bring a seat, and thereto what cheer ye have, withal. *Now* 'tis right."

"Not quite, not wholly right. You have asked for one, not *us*—for one, not both; food for one, a seat for one."

The king looked puzzled—he wasn't a very heavy weight, intellectually. His head was an hourglass; it could stow an idea, but it had to do it a grain at a time, not the whole idea at once.

"Would *you* have a seat also—and sit?"

"If I did not sit, the man would perceive that we were only pretending to be equals—and playing the deception pretty poorly, too."

"It is well and truly said! How wonderful is truth, come it in whatsoever unexpected form it may! Yes, he must bring out seats and food for both, and in serving us present not ewer and napkin with more show of respect to the one than to the other."

"And there is even yet a detail that needs correcting. He must bring nothing outside—we will go in—in among the dirt, and possibly other repulsive things—and take the food with the household, and after the fashion of the house, and all on equal terms, except the man be of the serf class; and finally, there will be no ewer and no napkin, whether he be serf or free. Please walk again, my liege. There—it is better—it is the best yet; but not perfect. The shoulders have known no ignobler burden than iron mail, and they will not stoop."

"Give me, then, the bag. I will learn the spirit that goeth with burdens that have not honor. It is the spirit that stoopeth the shoulders, I ween, and not the weight; for armor is heavy, yet it is a proud burden, and a man standeth straight in it. . . . Nay, but me no buts, offer me no objections. I will have the thing. Strap it upon my back."

He was complete, now, with that knapsack on, and looked as little like a king as any man I had ever seen. But it was an obstinate pair of shoulders; they could not seem to learn the trick of stooping with any sort of deceptive naturalness. The drill went on, I prompting and correcting:

"Now, make believe you are in debt, and eaten up by relentless creditors: you are out of work—which is horseshoeing, let us say—and can get none; and your wife is sick, your children are crying because they are hungry—"

And so on, and so on. I drilled him as representing in turn, all sorts of people out of luck and suffering dire privations and misfortunes. But lord it was only just words, words—they meant nothing in the world to him, I might just as well have whistled. Words realize nothing, vivify nothing to you, unless you have suffered in your own person the thing which the words try to describe. There are wise people who talk ever so knowingly and complacently about "the working classes," and satisfy themselves that a day's hard intellectual work is very much harder than a day's hard manual toil, and is righteously entitled to much bigger pay. Why, they really think that, you know, because they know all about the one, but haven't tried the other. But I know all about both; and so far as I am concerned, there isn't money enough in the universe to hire me to swing a pickax thirty days, but I will do the hardest kind of intellectual work for just as near nothing as you can cipher it down—and I will be satisfied, too.

Intellectual "work" is misnamed; it is a pleasure, a dissipation, and is its own highest reward. The poorest paid architect, engineer, general, author, sculptor, painter, lecturer, advocate, legislator, actor, preacher, singer is constructively in heaven when he is at work; and as for the magician with the fiddle bow in his hand who sits in the midst of a great orchestra with the ebbing and flowing tides of divine sounds washing over him—why, certainly, he is at work, if you wish to call it that, but lord, it's a sarcasm just the same. The law of work does seem utterly unfair—but there it is: and nothing can change it: the higher the pay in enjoyment the worker gets out of it, the higher shall be his pay in cash, also. And it's also the very law of those transparent swindles, transmissible nobility and kingship.

FOR DISCUSSION

1. What steps does the Yankee take to disguise the king? Why does the king not seem to be a peasant in spite of the change in his appearance?

2. What parts of sixth-century life is Mark Twain satirizing in these two chapters?

CHAPTER 29

When we arrived at that hut at midafternoon, we saw no signs of life about it. The field near by had been denuded of its crop some time before, and had a skinned look, so exhaustively had it been harvested and gleaned. Fences, sheds, everything had a ruined look, and were eloquent of poverty. No animal was around anywhere, no living thing in sight. The stillness was awful, it was like the stillness of death. The cabin was a one-story one, whose thatch was black with age, and ragged from lack of repair.

The door stood a trifle ajar. We approached it stealthily—on tiptoe and at half breath—for that is the way one's feeling makes him do, at such a time. The king knocked. We waited. No answer. Knocked again. No answer. I pushed the door softly open and looked in. I made out some dim forms, and a woman started up from the ground and stared at me, as one does who is wakened from sleep. Presently she found her voice—

"Have mercy!" she pleaded. "All is taken, nothing is left."

"I have not come to take anything, poor woman."

"You are not a priest?"

"No."

"Nor come not from the lord of the manor?"

"No, I am a stranger."

"Oh, then, for the fear of God, who visits with misery and death such as be harmless, tarry not here, but fly! This place is under his curse—and his Church's."

"Let me come in and help you—you are sick and in trouble."

I was better used to the dim light, now. I could see her hollow eyes fixed upon me. I could see how emaciated she was.

"I tell you the place is under the Church's ban. Save yourself—and go, before some straggler see thee here, and report it."

"Give yourself no trouble about me; I don't care anything for the Church's curse. Let me help you."

"Now all good spirits—if there be any such—bless thee for that word. Would God I had a sup of water—but hold, hold, forget I said it, and fly; for there is that here that even he that feareth not the Church must fear: this disease whereof we die. Leave us, thou brave, good stranger, and take with thee such whole and sincere blessings as them that be accursed can give."

But before this I had picked up a wooden bowl and was rushing past the king on my way to the brook. It was ten yards away. When I got back and entered, the king was within, and was opening the shutter that closed the window hole, to let in air and light. The place was full of a foul stench. I put the bowl to the woman's lips, and as she gripped it with her eager talons the shutter came open and a strong light flooded her face. Smallpox!

I sprang to the king, and said in his ear:

"Out of the door on the instant, sire! the woman is dying of that disease that wasted the skirts of Camelot two years ago."

He did not budge.

"Of a truth I shall remain—and likewise help."

I whispered again:

"King, it must not be. You must go."

"Ye mean well, and ye speak not unwisely. But it were shame that a king should know fear, and shame that belted knight should withhold his hand where be such as need succor. Peace, I will not go. It is you who must go. The Church's ban is not upon me, but it forbiddeth you to be here, and she will deal with you with a heavy hand an word come to her of your trespass."

It was a desperate place for him to be in, and might cost him his life, but it was no use to argue with him. If he considered his knightly honor at stake here, that was the end of argument; he would stay, and nothing could prevent it; I was aware of that. And so I dropped the subject. The woman spoke:

"Fair sir, of your kindness will ye climb the ladder there, and bring me news of what ye find? Be not afraid to report, for times can come when even a mother's heart is past breaking—being already broke."

"Abide," said the king, "and give the woman to eat. I will go." And he put down the knapsack.

I turned to start but the king had already started. He halted, and looked down upon a man who lay in a dim light, and had not noticed us, thus far, or spoken.

"Is it your husband?" the king asked.

"Yes."

"Is he asleep?"

"God be thanked for that one charity, yes—these three hours. Where shall I pay to the full, my gratitude! For my heart is bursting with it for that sleep he sleepeth now."

I said:

"We will be careful. We will not wake him."

"Ah, no, that ye will not, for he is dead."

"Dead?"

"Yes, what triumph it is to know it! None can harm him, none insult him more. He is in heaven, now, and happy; or if not there, he bides in hell and is content; for in that place he will find neither abbot nor yet bishop. We were boy and girl together; we were man and wife these five and twenty years, and never separated till this day. Think how long that is, to love and suffer together. This morning he was out of his mind, and in his fancy we were boy and girl again and wandering in the happy fields; and so in that innocent glad converse wandered he far and farther, still lightly gossiping, and entered into those other fields we know not of, and was shut away from mortal sight. And so there was no parting, for in his fancy I went with him; he knew not but I went with him, my hand in his—my young soft hand, not this withered claw. Ah, yes, to go, and know it not; to separate and know it not; how could one go peacefuler than that? It was his reward for a cruel life patiently borne."

There was a slight noise from the direction of the dim corner where the ladder was. It was the king, descending. I could see that he was bearing something in one arm, and assisting himself with the other. He came forward into the light; upon his breast lay a slender girl of fifteen. She was but half conscious; she was dying of smallpox. Here was heroism at its last and loftiest possibility, its utmost summit; this was challenging death in the open field unarmed, with all the odds against the challenger, no reward set upon the contest, and no admiring world in silks and cloth of gold to gaze and applaud; and yet the king's bearing was as serenely brave as it had always been in those cheaper contests where knight meets knight in equal fight and clothed in protecting steel. He was great, now; sublimely great. The rude statues of his ancestors in his palace should have an addition—I would see to that; and it would not be a mailed king killing a giant or a dragon, like the rest, it would be a king in commoner's garb bearing death in his arms that a peasant mother might look her last upon her child and be comforted.

He laid the girl down by her mother, who poured out endearments and caresses from an overflowing heart, and one could detect a flickering faint light of response in the child's eyes, but that was all. The mother hung over her, kissing her, petting her, and imploring her to speak, but the lips only moved and no sound came. I snatched my liquor flask from my knapsack, but the woman forbade me, and said:

"No—she does not suffer; it is better so. It might bring her back to life. None that be so good and kind as ye are, would do her that cruel hurt. For look you—what is left to live for? Her brothers are gone, her father is gone, her mother goeth, the Church's curse is upon her, and none may shelter or befriend her even though she lay perishing in the road. She is desolate. I have not asked you, good heart, if her sister be still on live, here overhead; I had no need; ye had gone back, else, and not left the poor thing forsaken—"

"She lieth at peace," interrupted the king, in a subdued voice.

"I would not change it. How rich is this day in happiness! Ah, my Annis, thou shalt join thy sister soon—thou'rt on thy way, and these be merciful friends, that will not hinder."

And so she fell to murmuring and cooing over the girl again, and softly stroking her face and hair, and kissing her and calling her by endearing names; but there was scarcely sign of response, now, in the glazing eyes. I saw tears well from the king's eyes, and trickle down his face. The woman noticed them, too, and said:

"Ah, I know that sign: thou'st a wife at home, poor soul, and you and she have gone hungry to bed, many's the time, that the little ones might have your crust; you know what poverty is, and the daily insults of your betters, and the heavy hand of the Church and the king."

The king winced under this accidental home shot, but kept still; he was learning his part; and he was playing it well, too, for a pretty dull beginner. I struck up a diversion. I offered the woman food and liquor, but she refused both. She would allow nothing to come between her and the release of death. Then I slipped away and brought the dead child from aloft, and laid

it by her. This broke her down again, and there was another scene that was full of heartbreak. By and by I made another diversion, and beguiled her to sketch her story.

"Ye know it well, yourselves, having suffered it—for truly none of our condition in Britain escape it. It is the old, weary tale. We fought and struggled and succeeded; meaning by success, that we lived and did not die; more than that is not to be claimed. No troubles came that we could not outlive, till this year brought them; then came they all at once, as one might say, and overwhelmed us. Years ago the lord of the manor planted certain fruit trees on our farm; in the best part of it, too—a grievous wrong and shame—"

"But it was his right," interrupted the king.

"None denieth that, indeed; an the law mean anything, what is the lord's is his, and what is mine is his also. Our farm was ours by lease, therefore 'twas likewise his, to do with it as he would. Some little time ago, three of those trees were found hewn down. Our three grown sons ran frightened to report the crime. Well, in his lordship's dungeon there they lie, who saith there shall they lie and rot till they confess. They have naught to confess, being innocent, wherefore there will they remain until they die. Ye know that right well, I ween. Think how this left us: a man, a woman, and two children, to gather a crop that was planted by so much greater force, yes, and protect it night and day from pigeons and prowling animals that be sacred and must not be hurt by any of our sort. When my lord's crop was nearly ready for the harvest, so also was ours; when his bell rang to call us to his fields to harvest his crops for nothing, he would not allow that I and my two girls should count for our three captive sons, but for only two of them; so, for the lacking one were we daily fined. All this time

our own crop was perishing through neglect; and so both the priest and his lordship fined us because their shares of it were
suffering through damage. In the end the
fines ate up our crop—and they took it all;
they took it all and made us harvest it for
them, without pay or food, and we starving.
Then the worst came when I, being out of
my mind with hunger and loss of my boys,
and grief to see my husband and my little
maids in rags and misery and despair, uttered a deep blasphemy—oh, a thousand of
them—against the Church and the
Church's ways. It was ten days ago. I had
fallen sick with this disease, and it was to
the priest I said the words, for he was come
to chide me for lack of due humility under
the chastening hand of God. He carried my
trespass to his betters; I was stubborn;
wherefore, presently upon my head and
upon all heads that were dear to me, fell

the curse of Rome.

"Since that day, we are avoided, shunned
with horror. None has come near this hut
to know whether we live or not. The rest
of us were taken down. Then I roused me
and got up, as wife and mother will. It was
little they could have eaten in any case; it
was less than little they had to eat. But
there was water, and I gave them that. How
they craved it! And how they blessed it!
But the end came yesterday; my strength
broke down. Yesterday was the last time I
ever saw my husband and this youngest
child alive. I have lain here all these hours
—these ages, ye may say—listening, listening, for any sound up there that—"

She gave a sharp quick glance at her eldest daughter, then cried out, "Oh, my darling!" and feebly gathered the stiffening
form to her sheltering arms. She had recognized the death rattle.

CHAPTER 30

At midnight all was over, and we sat in the
presence of four corpses. We covered them
with such rags as we could find, and started
away, fastening the door behind us. Their
home must be these people's grave, for
they could not have Christian burial, or be
admitted to consecrated ground. They were
as dogs, wild beasts, lepers, and no soul
that valued its hope of eternal life would
throw it away by meddling in any sort with
these rebuked and smitten outcasts.

We had not moved four steps when I
caught a sound as of footsteps upon gravel.
My heart flew to my throat. We must not
be seen coming from that house. I plucked
at the king's robe and we drew back and
took shelter behind the corner of the cabin.

"Now we are safe," I said, "but it was a
close call—so to speak. If the night had
been lighter he might have seen us, no
doubt, he seemed to be so near."

"Mayhap it is but a beast and not a man
at all."

"True. But man or beast, it will be wise
to stay here a minute and let it get by and
out of the way."

"Hark! It cometh hither."

True again. The step was coming toward
us—straight toward the hut. It must be a
beast, then, and we might as well have
saved our trepidation. I was going to step
out, but the king laid his hand upon my
arm. There was a moment of silence, then
we heard a soft knock on the cabin door.
It made me shiver. Presently the knock was
repeated, and then we heard these words
in a guarded voice:

"Mother! Father! Open—we have got
free, and we bring news to pale your cheeks
but glad your hearts; and we may not tarry,
but must fly! And—but they answer not.
Mother! Father!—"

I drew the king toward the other end of the hut and whispered:

"Come—now we can get to the road."

The king hesitated, was going to demur; but just then we heard the door give way, and knew that those desolate men were in the presence of their dead.

"Come, my liege! In a moment they will strike a light, and then will follow that which it would break your heart to hear."

He did not hesitate this time. The moment we were in the road, I ran; and after a moment he threw dignity aside and followed. I did not want to think of what was happening in the hut—I couldn't bear it; I wanted to drive it out of my mind; so I struck into the first subject that lay under that one in my mind:

"I have had the disease those people died of, and so have nothing to fear; but if you have not had it also—"

He broke in upon me to say he was in trouble, and it was his conscience that was troubling him:

"These young men have got free, they say—but *how?* It is not likely that their lord hath set them free."

"Oh, no, I make no doubt they escaped."

"That is my trouble; I have a fear that this is so, and your suspicion doth confirm it, you having the same fear."

"I should not call it by that name though. I do suspect that they escaped, but if they did, I am not sorry, certainly."

"I am not sorry, I *think*—but—"

"What is it? What is there for one to be troubled about?"

"*If* they did escape, then are we bound in duty to lay hands upon them and deliver them again to their lord; for it is not seemly that one of his quality should suffer a so insolent and high-handed outrage from persons of their base degree."

There it was, again. He could see only one side of it. He was born so, educated so, his veins were full of ancestral blood that was rotten with this sort of unconscious brutality, brought down by inheritance from a long procession of hearts that had each done its share toward poisoning the stream. To imprison these men without proof, and starve their kindred, was no harm, for they were merely peasants and subject to the will and pleasure of their lord, no matter what fearful form it might take; but for these men to break out of unjust captivity was insult and outrage, and a thing not to be countenanced by any conscientious person who knew his duty to his sacred caste.

I worked more than half an hour before I got him to change the subject—and even then an outside matter did it for me. This was a something which caught our eyes as we struck the summit of a small hill—a red glow, a good way off.

"That's a fire," said I.

Fires interested me considerably, because I was getting a good deal of an insurance business started, and was also training some horses and building some steam fire engines, with an eye to a paid fire department by and by. The priests opposed both my fire and life insurance, on the ground that it was an insolent attempt to hinder the decrees of God; and if you pointed out that they did not hinder the decrees in the least, but only modified the hard consequences of them if you took out policies and had luck, they retorted that that was gambling against the decrees of God, and was just as bad. So they managed to damage those industries more or less, but I got even on my Accident business. As a rule, a knight is a lummux, and sometimes even a labrick, and hence open to pretty poor arguments when they come glibly from a superstition monger, but even *he* could see the practical side of a thing once in a while; and so of late you couldn't clean up a tournament and pile the result without finding one of my accident-tickets in every helmet.

We stood there awhile, in the thick darkness and stillness, looking toward the red blur in the distance and trying to make out the meaning of a far away murmur that rose and fell fitfully on the night. Sometimes it swelled up and for a moment seemed less remote; but when we were hopefully expecting it to betray its cause and nature, it dulled and sank again, carrying its mystery with it. We started down the hill in its direction, and the winding road plunged us at once into almost solid darkness—darkness that was packed and crammed in between two tall forest walls. We groped along down for half a mile, perhaps, that murmur growing more and more distinct all the time, the coming storm threatening more and more, with now and then a little shiver of wind, a faint show of lightning, and dull grumblings of distant thunder. I was in the lead. I ran against something—a soft heavy something which gave, slightly, to the impulse of my weight; at the same moment the lightning glared out, and within a foot of my face was the writhing face of a man who was hanging from the limb of a tree! That is, it seemed to be writhing, but it was not. It was a gruesome sight. Straightway there was an earsplitting explosion of thunder, and the bottom of heaven fell out; the rain poured down in a deluge. No matter, we must try to cut this man down, on the chance that there might be life in him yet, mustn't we? The lightning came quick and sharp, now, and the place was alternately noonday and midnight. One moment the man would be hanging before me in an intense light, and the next he was blotted out again in the darkness. I told the king we must cut him down. The king at once objected.

"If he hanged himself, he was willing to lose his property to his lord; so let him be. If others hanged him, belike they had the right—let him hang."

"But"—

"But me no buts, but even leave him as

he is. And for yet another reason. When the lightning cometh again—there, look abroad."

Two others hanging, within fifty yards of us!

"It is not weather meet for doing useless courtesies unto dead folk. They are past thanking you. Come—it is unprofitable to tarry here."

There was reason in what he said, so we moved on. Within the next mile we counted six more hanging forms by the blaze of the lightning, and altogether it was a grisly excursion. That murmur was a murmur no longer, it was a roar; a roar of men's voices. A man came flying by, now, dimly through the darkness, and other men chasing him. They disappeared. Presently another case of the kind occurred, and then another and another. Then a sudden turn of the road brought us in sight of that fire—it was a large manor house, and little or nothing was left of it—and everywhere men were flying and other men raging after them in pursuit.

I warned the king that this was not a safe place for strangers. We would better get away from the light, until matters should improve. We stepped back a little, and hid in the edge of the wood. From this hiding place we saw both men and women hunted by the mob. The fearful work went on until nearly dawn. Then, the fire being out and the storm spent, the voices and flying footsteps presently ceased, and darkness and stillness reigned again.

We ventured out, and hurried cautiously away; and although we were worn out and sleepy, we kept on until we had put this place some miles behind us. Then we asked hospitality at the hut of a charcoal burner, and got what was to be had. A woman was up and about, but the man was still asleep, on a straw shakedown, on the clay floor. The woman seemed uneasy until I explained that we were travelers and had lost our way and been wandering in the woods all night. She became talkative, then, and asked if we had heard of the terrible goings-on at the manor house of Abbla-soure. Yes, we had heard of them, but what we wanted now, was rest and sleep. The king broke in:

"Sell us the house and take yourselves away, for we be perilous company, being but late come from people that died of the Spotted Death."

It was good of him, but unnecessary. One of the commonest decorations of the nation was the waffle-iron face. I had early noticed that the woman and her husband were both so decorated. She made us entirely welcome, and had no fears; and plainly she was immensely impressed by the king's proposition; for of course it was a good deal of an event in her life to run across a person of the king's humble appearance who was ready to buy a man's house for the sake of a night's lodging. It gave her a large respect for us, and she strained the lean possibilities of her hovel to their utmost to make us comfortable.

We slept till far into the afternoon, and then got up hungry enough to make cotter fare quite palatable to the king, the more particularly as it was scant in quantity. And also in variety; it consisted solely of onions, salt, and the national black bread —made out of horse feed. The woman told us about the affair of the evening before. At ten or eleven at night, when everybody was in bed, the manor house burst into flames. The countryside swarmed to the rescue, and the family were saved, with one exception, the master. He did not appear. Everybody was frantic over this loss, and two brave yeomen sacrificed their lives in ransacking the burning house seeking that valuable personage. But after a while he was found—what was left of him— which was his corpse. It was in a copse three hundred yards away, bound, gagged, stabbed in a dozen places.

Who had done this? Suspicion fell upon a humble family in the neighborhood who had been lately treated with peculiar harsh-ness by the baron; and from these people the suspicion easily extended itself to their relatives and familiars. A suspicion was enough; my lord's liveried retainers proclaimed an instant crusade against these people, and were promptly joined by the community in general. The woman's husband had been active with the mob, and had not returned home until nearly dawn. He was gone, now, to find out what the general result had been. While we were still talking, he came back from his quest. His report was revolting enough. Eighteen persons hanged or butchered, and two yeomen and thirteen prisoners lost in the fire.

"And how many prisoners were there altogether, in the vaults?"

"Thirteen."

"Then every one of them was lost."

"Yes, all."

"But the people arrived in time to save the family; how is it they could save none of the prisoners?"

The man looked puzzled, and said:

"Would one unlock the vaults at such a time? Marry, some would have escaped."

"Then you mean that nobody *did* unlock them?"

"None went near them, either to lock or unlock. It standeth to reason that the bolts were fast; wherefore it was only needful to establish a watch, so that if any broke the bonds he might not escape, but be taken. None were taken."

"Natheless, three did escape," said the king, "and ye will do well to publish it and set justice upon their track, for these mur-thered the baron and fired the house."

I was just expecting he would come out with that. For a moment the man and his wife showed an eager interest in this news and an impatience to go out and spread it; then a sudden something else betrayed it-self in their faces, and they began to ask questions. I answered the questions myself, and narrowly watched the effects produced. I was soon satisfied that the knowledge of who these three prisoners were, had somehow changed the atmosphere; that our hosts' continued eagerness to go and spread the news was now only pretended and not real. The king did not notice the change, and I was glad of that. I worked the conversation around toward other details of the night's proceedings, and noted that these people were relieved to have it take that direction.

The painful thing observable about all this business was, the alacrity with which this oppressed community had turned their cruel hands against their own class in the interest of the common oppressor. This man and woman seemed to feel that in a quarrel between a person of their own class and his lord, it was the natural and proper and rightful thing for that poor devil's whole caste to side with the master and fight his battle for him, without ever stopping to inquire into the rights or wrongs of the matter. This man had been out helping to hang his neighbors, and had done his work with zeal, and yet was aware that there was nothing against them but a mere suspicion, with nothing back of it describable as evidence, still neither he nor his wife seemed to see anything horrible about it.

This was depressing—to a man with the dream of a republic in his head. It reminded me of a time thirteen centuries away, when the "poor whites" of our South who were always despised and frequently insulted, by the slave-lords around them, and who owned their base condition simply to the presence of slavery in their midst, were yet pusillanimously ready to side with slave-lords in all political moves for the upholding and perpetuating of slavery, and did also finally shoulder their muskets and pour out their lives in an effort to prevent the destruction of that very institution

which degraded them. And there was only one redeeming feature connected with that pitiful piece of history; and that was, that secretly the "poor white" did detest the slave-lord, and did feel his own shame. That feeling was not brought to the surface, but the fact that it was there and could have been brought out, under favoring circumstances, was something—in fact it was enough; for it showed that a man is at bottom a man, after all, even if it doesn't show on the outside.

Well, as it turned out, this charcoal burner was just the twin of the Southern "poor white" of the far future. The king presently showed impatience, and said:

"An ye prattle here all the day, justice will miscarry. Think ye the criminals will abide in their father's house? They are fleeing, they are not waiting. You should look to it that a party of horse be set upon their track."

The woman paled slightly, but quite perceptibly, and the man looked flustered and irresolute. I said:

"Come, friend, I will walk a little way with you, and explain which direction I think they would try to take. If they were merely resisters of the gabelle or some kindred absurdity I would try to protect them from capture; but when men murder a person of high degree and likewise burn his house, that is another matter."

The last remark was for the king—to quiet him. On the road the man pulled his resolution together, and began the march with a steady gait, but there was no eagerness in it. By and by I said:

"What relation were these men to you—cousins?"

He turned as white as his layer of charcoal would let him, and stopped trembling.

"Ah, how knew you that?"

"I didn't know it; it was a chance guess."

"Poor lads, they are lost. And good lads they were, too."

"Were you actually going yonder to tell

on them?"

He didn't quite know how to take that; but he said, hesitatingly:

"Ye-s."

"Then I think you are a scoundrel!"

It made him as glad as if I had called him an angel.

"Say the good words again, brother! For surely ye mean that ye would not betray me an I failed of my duty."

"Duty? There is no duty in the matter, except the duty to keep still and let those men get away. They've done a righteous deed."

He looked pleased; pleased, and touched with apprehension at the same time. He looked up and down the road to see that no one was coming, and then said in a cautious voice:

"From what land come you, brother, that you speak such perilous words, and seem not to be afraid?"

"They are not perilous words when spoken to one of my own caste, I take it. You would not tell anybody I said them?"

"I? I would be drawn asunder by wild horses first."

"Well, then, let me say my say. I have no fears of your repeating it. I think devil's work has been done last night upon those innocent poor people. That old baron got only what he deserved. If I had my way, all his kind should have the same luck."

Fear and depression vanished from the man's manner, and gratefulness and a brave animation took their place:

"Even though you be a spy, and your words a trap for my undoing, yet are they such refreshment that to hear them again and others like to them, I would go to the gallows happy, as having had one good feast at least in a starved life. And I will say my say, now, and ye may report it if ye be so minded. I helped to hang my neighbors for that it were peril to my own life to show lack of zeal in the master's cause; the others helped for none other reason. All rejoice today that he is dead, but all do go about seemingly sorrowing, and shedding the hypocrite's tear, for in that lies safety. I have said the words. I have said the words! the only ones that have ever tasted good in my mouth, and the reward of that taste is sufficient. Lead on, an ye will, be it even to the scaffold, for I am ready."

There it was, you see. A man *is* a man, at bottom. Whole ages of abuse and oppression cannot crush the manhood clear out of him. Whoever thinks it a mistake, is himself mistaken. Yes, there is plenty good enough material for a republic in the most degraded people that ever existed—even the Russians; plenty of manhood in them —even in the Germans—if one could but force it out of its timid and suspicious privacy, to overthrow and trample in the mud any throne that ever was set up and any nobility that ever supported it. We should see certain things yet, let us hope and believe. First, a modified monarchy, till Arthur's days were done, then the destruction of the throne, nobility abolished, every member of it bound out to some useful trade, universal suffrage instituted, and the whole government placed in the hands of the men and women of the nation there to remain. Yes, there was no occasion to give up my dream yet awhile.

FOR DISCUSSION

1. "How rich is this day in happiness!" exclaims the old mother as she watches her family die. What hardships have driven her to this extreme?

2. "Here was heroism at its last and loftiest possibility. . . ." What does the king do to merit such admiration from the Yankee? What evidence is there that he is beginning to sympathize with the hard life of his people?

The Yankee and the king (introduced as Jones, a farmer) stay awhile with Marco and his family. Naturally the Yankee tries to teach the villagers something, this time about economics. In the middle of an argument about wages he play-fully accuses the blacksmith of overpaying his help, a crime punishable by imprisonment in the stocks. Immediately the terrified villagers become suspicious of him.

CHAPTER 34

The king joined us, about this time, mightily refreshed by his nap, and feeling good. Anything could make me nervous now, I was so uneasy—for our lives were in danger; and so it worried me to detect a complacent something in the king's eye which seemed to indicate that he had been loading himself up for a performance of some kind or other; confound it, why must he go and choose such a time as this?

I was right. He began, straight off, in the most innocently artful, and transparent, and lubberly way, to lead up to the subject of agriculture. The cold sweat broke out all over me. I wanted to whisper in his ear, "Man, we are in awful danger! Every moment is worth a principality till we get back these men's confidence; *don't* waste any of this golden time." But of course I couldn't do it. Whisper to him? It would look as if we were conspiring. So I had to sit there and look calm and pleasant while the king stood over that dynamite mine and mooned along about his onions and things. At first the tumult of my own thoughts, summoned by the danger signal and swarming to the rescue from every quarter of my skull, kept up such a hurrah and confusion and fifing and drumming that I couldn't take in a word; but presently when my mob of gathering plans began to crystallize and fall into position and form line of battle, a sort of order and quiet ensued and I caught the boom of the king's batteries, as if out of remote distance:

"—were not the best way, methinks, albeit it is not to be denied that authorities differ as concerning this point, some contending that the onion is but an unwholesome berry when stricken early from the tree—"

The audience showed signs of life, and sought each other's eyes in a surprised and troubled way.

"whileas others do yet maintain, with much show of reason, that this is not of necessity the case, instancing that plums and other like cereals do be always dug in the unripe state—"

The audience exhibited distinct distress; yes, and also fear.

"—yet are they clearly wholesome, the more especially when one doth assuage the asperities of their nature by admixture of the tranquilizing juice of the wayward cabbage—"

The wild light of terror began to glow in these men's eyes, and one of them muttered, "These be errors, every one—God hath surely smitten the mind of this farmer." I was in miserable apprehension; I sat upon thorns.

"—and further instancing the known truth that in the case of animals, the young, which may be called the green fruit of the creature, is the better, all confessing that when a goat is ripe, his fur doth heat and sore engame his flesh, the which defect, taken in connection with his several rancid habits, and fulsome appetites, and godless attitudes of mind, and bilious quality of morals—"

They rose and went for him! With a fierce shout, "The one would betray us, the other is mad. Kill them! Kill them!" they flung themselves upon us. What joy flamed up in the king's eye! He might be lame in agriculture, but this kind of thing was just in his line. He had been fasting long, he was hungry for a fight. He hit the blacksmith a crack under the jaw that lifted him clear off his feet and stretched him flat of his back. "St. George for Britain!" And he downed the wheelwright. The mason was big, but I laid him out like nothing. The three gathered themselves up and came again; went down again; came again; and kept on repeating this, with native British pluck, until they were battered to jelly, reeling with exhaustion, and so blind that they couldn't tell us from each other; and yet they kept right on, hammering away with what might was left in them. Hammering each other—for we stepped aside and looked on while they rolled, and struggled, and gouged, and pounded, and bit, with the strict and wordless attention to business of so many bulldogs. We looked on without apprehension, for they were fast getting past ability to go for help against us, and the arena was far enough from the public road to be safe from intrusion.

Well, while they were gradually playing out, it suddenly occurred to me to wonder what had become of Marco. I looked around; he was nowhere to be seen. Oh, but this was ominous! I pulled the king's sleeve, and we glided away and rushed for the hut. No Marco there, no Phyllis there! They had gone to the road for help, sure. I told the king to give his heels wings, and I would explain later. We made good time across the open ground, and as we darted into the shelter of the wood I glanced back and saw a mob of excited peasants swarm

into view, with Marco and his wife at their head. They were making a world of noise, but that couldn't hurt anybody; the wood was dense, and as soon as we were well into its depths we would take to a tree and let them whistle. Ah, but then came another sound—dogs! Yes, that was quite another matter. It magnified our contract—we must find running water.

We tore along at a good gait, and soon left the sounds far behind and modified to a murmur. We struck a stream and darted into it. We waded swiftly down it, in the dim forest light, for as much as three hundred yards, and then came across an oak with a great bough sticking out over the water. We climbed up on this bough, and began to work our way along it to the body of the tree; now we began to hear those sounds more plainly; so the mob had struck our trail. For a while the sounds approached pretty fast. And then for another while they didn't. No doubt the dogs had found the place where we had entered the stream, and were now waltzing up and down the shores trying to pick up the trail again.

When we were snugly lodged in the tree and curtained with foliage, the king was satisfied, but I was doubtful. I believed we could crawl along a branch and get into the next tree, and I judged it worth while to try. We tried it, and made a success of it, though the king slipped, at the junction, and came near failing to connect. We got comfortable lodgement and satisfactory concealment among the foliage, and then we had nothing to do but listen to the hunt.

Presently we heard it coming—and coming on the jump, too; yes, and down both sides of the stream. Louder—louder—next minute it swelled swiftly up into a roar of shoutings, barkings, tramplings, and swept by like a cyclone.

"I was afraid that the overhanging

branch would suggest something to them," said I, "but I don't mind the disappointment. Come, my liege, it were well that we make good use of our time. We've flanked them. Dark is coming on, presently. If we can cross the stream and get a good start, and borrow a couple of horses from somebody's pasture to use for a few hours, we shall be safe enough."

We started down, and got nearly to the lowest limb, when we seemed to hear the hunt returning. We stopped to listen.

"Yes," said I, "they're baffled, they've given it up, they're on their way home. We will climb back to our roost again, and let them go by."

So we climbed back. The king listened a moment and said:

"They still search—I wit the sign. We did best to abide."

He was right. He knew more about hunting than I did. The noise approached steadily, but not with a rush. The king said:

"They reason that we were advantaged by no parlous start of them, and being on foot are as yet no mighty way from where we took the water."

"Yes, sire, that is about it, I am afraid, though I was hoping better things."

The noise drew nearer and nearer, and soon the van was drifting under us, on both sides of the water. A voice called a halt from the other bank, and said:

"An they were so minded, they could get to yon tree by this branch that overhangs, and yet not touch ground. Ye will do well to send a man up it."

"Marry, that will we do!"

I was obliged to admire my cuteness in foreseeing this very thing and swapping trees to beat it. But don't you know, there are some things that can beat smartness and foresight? Awkwardness and stupidity can. The best swordsman in the world doesn't need to fear the second best

swordsman in the world; no, the person for him to be afraid of is some ignorant antagonist who has never had a sword in his hand before; he doesn't do the thing he ought to do, and so the expert isn't prepared for him; he does the thing he ought not to do: and often it catches the expert out and ends him on the spot. Well, how could I, with all my gifts, make any valuable preparation against a nearsighted, cross-eyed, puddingheaded clown who would aim himself at the wrong tree and hit the right one? And that is what he did. He went for the wrong tree, which was of course the right one by mistake, and up he started.

Matters were serious, now. We remained still and awaited developments. The peasant toiled his difficult way up. The king raised himself up and stood; he made a leg ready, and when the comer's head arrived in reach of it there was a dull thud, and down went the man floundering to the ground. There was a wild outbreak of anger, below, and the mob swarmed in from all around, and there we were treed, and prisoners. Another man started up; the bridging bough was detected, and a volunteer started up the tree that furnished the bridge. The king ordered me to play Horatius and keep the bridge. For a while the enemy came thick and fast; but no matter, the head man of each procession always got a buffet that dislodged him as soon as he came in reach. The king's spirits rose, his joy was limitless. He said that if nothing occurred to mar the prospect we should have a beautiful night, for on this line of tactics we could hold the tree against the whole countryside.

However, the mob soon came to that conclusion themselves; wherefore they called off the assault and began to debate other plans. They had no weapons, but there were plenty of stones, and stones might answer. We had no objections. A stone might possibly penetrate to us once in a while, but it wasn't very likely; we were well protected by boughs and foliage, and were not visible from any good aiming point. If they would but waste half an hour in stone throwing, the dark would come to our help. We were feeling very well satisfied. We could smile; almost laugh.

But we didn't; which was just as well, for we should have been interrupted. Before the stones had been raging through the leaves and bouncing from the boughs fifteen minutes, we began to notice a smell. A couple of sniffs of it was enough of an explanation: it was smoke! Our game was up at last. We recognized that. When smoke invites you, you have to come. They raised their pile of dry brush and damp weeds higher and higher, and when they saw the thick cloud begin to roll up and smother the tree, they broke out in a storm of joy-clamors. I got enough breath to say:

"Proceed, my liege; after you is manners."

The king gasped:

"Follow me down, and then back thyself against one side of the trunk, and leave me the other. Then will we fight. Let each pile his dead according to his own fashion and taste."

Then he descended barking and coughing, and I followed. I struck the ground an instant after him; we sprang to our appointed places, and began to give and take with all our might. The powwow and racket were prodigious; it was a tempest of riot and confusion and thick-falling blows. Suddenly some horsemen tore into the midst of the crowd, and a voice shouted:

"Hold—or ye are dead men!"

How good it sounded! The owner of the voice bore all the marks of a gentleman: picturesque and costly raiment, the aspect of command, a hard countenance with complexion and features marred by dis-

sipation. The mob fell humbly back, like so many spaniels. The gentleman inspected us critically, then said sharply to the peasants:

"What are ye doing to these people?"

"They be madmen, worshipful sir, that have come wandering we know not whence, and—"

"Ye know not whence? Do ye pretend ye know them not?"

"Most honored sir, we speak but the truth. They are strangers and unknown to any in this region; and they be the most violent and bloodthirsty madmen that ever—"

"Peace! Ye know not what ye say. They are not mad. Who are ye? And whence are ye? Explain."

"We are but peaceful strangers, sir," I said, "and traveling upon our own concerns. We are from a far country, and unacquainted here. We have purposed no harm; and yet but for your brave interference and protection these people would have killed us. As you have divined, sir, we are not mad; neither are we violent or bloodthirsty."

The gentleman turned to his retinue and said calmly:

"Lash me these animals to their kennels!"

The mob vanished in an instant; and after them plunged the horsemen, laying about them with their whips and pitilessly riding down such as were witless enough to keep the road instead of taking to the bush. The shrieks and supplications presently died away in the distance, and soon the horsemen began to straggle back. Meantime the gentleman had been questioning us more closely, but had dug no particulars out of us. We were lavish of recognition of the service he was doing us, but we revealed nothing more than that we were friendless strangers from a far country. When the escort were all returned, the gentleman said to one of his servants:

"Bring the lead horses and mount these people."

"Yes, my lord."

We were placed toward the rear, among the servants. We traveled pretty fast, and finally drew rein some time after dark at a roadside inn some ten or twelve miles from the scene of our troubles. My lord went immediately to his room, after ordering his supper, and we saw no more of him. At dawn in the morning we breakfasted and made ready to start.

My lord's chief attendant sauntered forward at that moment with indolent grace, and said:

"Ye have said ye should continue upon this road, which is our direction likewise; wherefore my lord, the earl Grip, hath given commandment that ye retain the horses and ride, and that certain of us ride with ye a twenty mile to a fair town that hight Cambenet, whenso ye shall be out of peril."

We could do nothing less than express our thanks and accept the offer. We jogged along, six in the party, at a moderate and comfortable gait, and in conversation learned that my lord Grip was a very great personage in his own region, which lay a day's journey beyond Cambenet. We loitered to such a degree that it was near the middle of the forenoon when we entered the market square of the town. We dismounted, and left our thanks once more for my lord, and then approached a crowd assembled in the center of the square, to see what might be the object of interest. It was the remnant of that old peregrinating band of slaves! So they had been dragging their chains about, all this weary time. That poor husband was gone, and also many others; and some few purchases had been added to the gang. The king was not interested, and wanted to move along,

but I was absorbed, and full of pity. I could not take my eyes away from these worn and wasted wrecks of humanity. There they sat, grouped upon the ground, silent, uncomplaining, with bowed heads, a pathetic sight. And by hideous contrast, a redundant orator was making a speech to another gathering not thirty steps away, in fulsome laudation of "our glorious British liberties!"

I was boiling. I had forgotten I was a plebeian, I was remembering I was a man. Cost what it might, I would mount that rostrum and—

Click! the king and I were handcuffed together! Our companions, those servants, had done it: my lord Grip stood looking on. The king burst out in a fury, and said:

"What meaneth this ill-mannered jest?"

My lord merely said to his head miscreant, coolly:

"Put up the slaves and sell them!"

Slaves! The word had a new sound— and how unspeakably awful! The king lifted his manacles and brought them down with a deadly force; but my lord was out of the way when they arrived. A dozen of the rascal's servants sprang forward, and in a moment we were helpless, with our hands bound behind us. We so loudly and so earnestly proclaimed ourselves freemen, that we got the interested attention of that liberty-mouthing orator and his patriotic crowd, and they gathered about us and assumed a very determined attitude. The orator said:

"If indeed ye are freemen, ye have nought to fear—the God-given liberties of Britain are about ye for your shield and shelter! (Applause.) Ye shall soon see. Bring forth your proofs."

"What proofs?"

"Proof that ye are freemen."

Ah—I remembered! I came to myself; I said nothing. But the king stormed out:

"Thou'rt insane, man. It were better, and more in reason, that this thief and scoundrel here prove that we are *not* freemen."

You see, he knew his own laws just as other people so often know the laws: by words, not by effects. They take a *meaning*, and get to be very vivid, when you come to apply them to yourself.

All hands shook their heads and looked disappointed; some turned away, no longer interested. The orator said—and this time in the tones of business, not of sentiment:

"An ye do not know your country's laws, it were time ye learned them. Ye are strangers to us; ye will not deny that. Ye may be freemen, we do not deny that; but also ye may be slaves. The law is clear: it doth not require the claimant to prove ye are slaves, it requireth you to prove ye are *not*."

I said:

"Dear sir, give us only time to send to Astolat; or give us only time to send to the Valley of Holiness—"

"Peace, good man, these are extraordinary requests, and you may not hope to have them granted. It would cost much time, and would unwarrantably inconvenience your master—"

"*Master*, idiot!" stormed the king. "I have no master, I myself am the m—"

"Silence, for God's sake!"

I got the words out in time to stop the king. We were in trouble enough already; it could not help us any to give these people the notion that we were lunatics.

There is no use in stringing out the details. The earl put us up and sold us at auction. This same infernal law had existed in our own South in my own time, more than thirteen hundred years later, and under it hundreds of freemen who could not prove that they were freemen had been sold into lifelong slavery without the circumstance making any particular impression upon me; but the minute law and the auction block came into my personal experience, a thing which had been merely improper before became suddenly hellish. Well, that's the way we are made.

Yes, we were sold at auction, like swine. In a big town and an active market we should have brought a good price; but this place was utterly stagnant and so we sold at a figure which makes me ashamed, every time I think of it. The King of England brought seven dollars, and his prime minister nine; whereas the king was easily worth twelve dollars and I as easily worth fifteen. But that is the way things always go; if you force a sale on a dull market, I don't care what the property is, you are going to make a poor business of it, and you can make up your mind to it. If the earl had had wit enough to—

However, there is no occasion for my working my sympathies up on his account. Let him go, for the present: I took his number, so to speak.

The slave dealer bought us both, and hitched us onto that long chain of his, and we constituted the rear of his procession. We took up our line of march and passed out of Cambenet at noon; and it seemed to me unaccountably strange and odd that the King of England and his chief minister, marching manacled and fettered and yoked, in a slave convoy, could move by all manner of idle men and women, and under windows where sat the sweet and the lovely, and yet never attract a curious eye, never provoke a single remark. Dear, dear, it only shows that there is nothing diviner about a king than there is about a tramp, after all. He is just a cheap and hollow artificiality when you don't know he is a king. But reveal his quality, and dear me it takes your very breath away to look at him. I reckon we are all fools. Born so, no doubt.

CHAPTER 35

It's a world of surprises. The king brooded; this was natural. What would he brood about, should you say? Why, about the prodigious nature of his fall, of course—from the loftiest place in the world to the lowest; from the most illustrious station in the world to the obscurest; from the grandest vocation among men to the basest. No, I take my oath that the thing that graveled him most, to start with, was not this, but the price he had fetched! He couldn't seem to get over that seven dollars. Well, it stunned me so, when I first found it out, that I couldn't believe it; it didn't seem natural. But as soon as my mental sight cleared and I got a right focus on it, I saw I was mistaken: it *was* natural. For this reason: a king is a mere artificiality, and so a king's feelings, like the impulses of an automatic doll, are mere artificialities; but as a man, he is a reality, and his feelings, as a man, are real, not phantoms. It shames the average man to be valued below his own estimate of his worth; and the king certainly wasn't anything more than an average man, if he was up that high.

Confound him, he wearied me with arguments to show that in anything like a fair market he would have fetched twenty-five dollars, sure—a thing which was plainly nonsense, and full of the baldest conceit; I wasn't worth it myself. But it was tender ground for me to argue on. In fact I had to simply shirk argument and do the diplomatic instead. I had to throw conscience aside, and brazenly concede that he ought to have brought twenty-five dollars; whereas I was quite well aware that in all the ages, the world had never seen a king that was worth half the money, and during the next thirteen centuries wouldn't see one that was worth the fourth of it. Yes, he tired me. If he began to talk about the crops, or about the recent weather, or about the condition of politics, or about dogs, or cats, or morals, or theology—no matter what—I sighed, for I knew what was coming: he was going to get out of it a palliation of that tiresome seven-dollar sale. Wherever we halted, where there was a crowd, he would give me a look which said, plainly: "if that thing could be tried over again, now, with this kind of folk, you would see a different result." Well, when he was first sold, it secretly tickled me to see him go for seven dollars; but before he was done with his sweating and worrying I wished he had fetched a hundred. The thing never got a chance to die, for every day, at one place or another, possible purchasers looked us over, and as often as any other way, their comment on the king was something like this:

"Here's a two-dollar-and-a-half chump with a thirty-dollar style. Pity but style was marketable."

At last this sort of remark produced an evil result. Our owner was a practical person and he perceived that this defect must be mended if he hoped to find a purchaser for the king. So he went to work to take the style out of his sacred majesty. I could have given the man some valuable advice, but I didn't; you mustn't volunteer advice to a slave driver unless you want to damage the cause you are arguing for. I had found it a sufficiently difficult job to reduce the king's style to a peasant's style, even when he was a willing and anxious pupil; now then, to undertake to reduce the king's style to a slave's style—and by force—go to! It was a stately contract. Never mind the details—it will save me trouble to let you imagine them. I will only remark that at the end of a week there was plenty of evidence that lash and club and fist had done their work well; the king's body was a sight to see—and to weep over; but his spirit—why, it wasn't even phased. Even that dull clod of a slave driver was able to see that there can be such a thing as a slave who will remain a man till he dies; whose bones you can break, but whose manhood you can't. This man found that from his first effort down to his latest, he couldn't ever come within reach of the king but the king was ready to plunge for him, and did it. So he gave up, at last, and left the king in possession of his style unimpaired. The fact is, the king was a good deal more than a king, he was a man; and when a man is a man, you can't knock it out of him.

We had a rough time for a month, tramping to and fro in the earth, and suffering. And what Englishman was the most interested in the slavery question by that time? His grace the king! Yes; from being the most indifferent, he was become the most interested. He was become the bitterest hater of the institution I had ever heard talk. And so I ventured to ask once more a question which I had asked years before and had gotten such a sharp answer that I had not thought it prudent to meddle in the matter further. Would he abolish slavery?

His answer was as sharp as before, but it was music this time; I shouldn't ever wish to hear pleasanter, though the profanity was not good, being awkwardly put together, and with the crash word almost in the middle instead of at the end, where of course it ought to have been.

I was ready and willing to get free, now; I hadn't wanted to get free any sooner. No, I cannot quite say that. I had wanted to, but I had not been willing to take desperate chances, and had always dissuaded the king from them. But now—ah, it was a new atmosphere! Liberty would be worth any cost that might be put upon it now. I set about a plan, and was straightway charmed

with it. It would require time, yes, and patience, too, a great deal of both. One could invent quicker ways, and fully as sure ones; but none that would be as picturesque as this; none that could be made so dramatic. And so I was not going to give this one up. It might delay us months, but no matter, I would carry it out or break something.

Now and then we had an adventure. One night we were overtaken by a snowstorm while still a mile from the village we were making for. Almost instantly we were shut up as in a fog, the driving snow was so thick. You couldn't see a thing, and we were soon lost. The slave driver lashed us desperately, for he saw ruin before him, but his lashings only made matters worse, for they drove us further from the road and from likelihood of succor. So we had to stop, at last, and slump down in the snow where we were. The storm continued until toward midnight, then ceased. By this time two of our feebler men and three of our women were dead, and others past moving and threatened with death. Our master was nearly beside himself. He stirred up the living and made us stand, jump, slap ourselves, to restore our circulation, and he helped as well as he could with his whip.

Now came a diversion. We heard shrieks and yells, and soon a woman came running, and crying; and seeing our group, she flung herself into our midst and begged for protection. A mob of people came tearing after her, some with torches, and they said she was a witch who had caused several cows to die by a strange disease, and practiced her arts by help of a devil in the form of a black cat. This poor woman had been stoned until she hardly looked human, she was so battered and bloody. The mob wanted to burn her.

Well, now, what do you suppose our master did? When we closed around this poor creature to shelter her, he saw his chance. He said, burn her here, or they shouldn't have her at all. Imagine that! They were willing. They fastened her to a post; they brought wood and piled it about her; they applied the torch while she shrieked and pleaded and strained her two young daughters to her breast; and our brute, with a heart solely for business, lashed us into position about the stake and warmed us into life and commercial value by the same fire which took away the innocent life of that poor harmless mother. That was the sort of master we had. I took *his* number. That snowstorm cost him nine of his flock; and he was more brutal to us than ever, after that, for many days together, he was so enraged over his loss.

We had adventures, all along. One day we ran into a procession. And such a procession! All the riffraff of the kingdom seemed to be comprehended in it; and all drunk at that. In the van was a cart with a coffin in it, and on the coffin sat a comely young girl of about eighteen suckling a baby, which she squeezed to her breast in a passion of love every little while, and every little while wiped from its face the tears which her eyes rained down upon it; and always the foolish little thing smiled up at her, happy and content, kneading her breast with its dimpled fat hand, which she patted and fondled right over her breaking heart.

Men and women, boys and girls, trotted along beside or after the cart, hooting, shouting profane and ribald remarks, singing snatches of foul song, skipping, dancing—a very holiday of hellions, a sickening sight. We had struck a suburb of London, outside the walls, and this was a sample of one sort of London society. Our master secured a good place for us near the gallows. A priest was in attendance, and he helped the girl climb up, and said comforting words to her, and made the under-

sheriff provide a stool for her. Then he stood there by her on the gallows, and for a moment looked down upon the mass of upturned faces at his feet, then out over the solid pavement of heads that stretched away on every side occupying the vacancies far and near, and then began to tell the story of the case. And there was pity in his voice—how seldom a sound that was in that ignorant and savage land! I remember every detail of what he said, except the words he said it in; and so I change it into my own words:

"Law is intended to mete out justice. Sometimes it fails. This cannot be helped. We can only grieve, and be resigned, and pray for the soul of him who falls unfairly by the arm of the law, and that his fellows may be few. A law sends this poor young thing to death—and it is right. But another law had placed her where she must commit her crime or starve, with her child—and before God that law is responsible for both her crime and her ignominious death!

"A little while ago this young thing, this child of eighteen years, was as happy a wife and mother as any in England; and her lips were blithe with song, which is the native speech of glad and innocent hearts. Her young husband was as happy as she; for he was doing his whole duty, he worked early and late at his handicraft, his bread was honest bread well and fairly earned, he was prospering, he was furnishing shelter and sustenance to his family, he was adding his mite to the wealth of the nation. By consent of a treacherous law, instant destruction fell upon this holy home and swept it away! That young husband was waylaid and impressed, and sent to sea. The wife knew nothing of it. She sought him everywhere, she moved the hardest hearts with the supplication of her tears, the broken eloquence of her despair. Weeks dragged by, she watching, waiting, hoping, her mind going slowly to wreck under the

burden of her misery. Little by little all her small possessions went for food. When she could no longer pay her rent, they turned her out of doors. She begged, while she had strength; when she was starving, at last, and her milk failing, she stole a piece of linen cloth of the value of a fourth part of a cent, thinking to sell it and save her child. But she was seen by the owner of the cloth. She was put in jail and brought to trial. The man testified to the facts. A plea was made for her, and her sorrowful story was told in her behalf. She spoke, too, by permission, and said she did steal the cloth, but that her mind was so disordered of late, by trouble, that when she was overborne with hunger all acts, criminal or other, swam meaningless through her brain and she knew nothing rightly, except that she was *so* hungry! For a moment all were touched, and there was disposition to deal mercifully with her, seeing that she was so young and friendless, and her case so piteous, and the law that robbed her of her support to blame as being the first and only cause of her transgression; but the prosecuting officer replied that whereas these things were all true, and most pitiful as well, still there was much small theft in these days, and mistimed mercy would be a danger to property—oh, my God, is there no property in ruined homes, and orphaned babes, and broken hearts that British law holds precious—and so he must require sentence.

"When the judge put on his black cap, the owner of the stolen linen rose trembling up, his lip quivering, his face as gray as ashes; and when the awful words came, he cried out, 'Oh, poor child, poor child, I did not know it was death!' and fell as a tree falls. When they lifted him up his reason was gone; before the sun was set, he had taken his own life. A kindly man; a man whose heart was right, at bottom; add his murder to this that is to be now done

here; and charge them both where they belong—to the rulers and the bitter laws of Britain. The time is come, my child; let me pray over thee—not *for* thee, dear abused poor heart and innocent, but for them that be guilty of thy ruin and death, who need it more."

After his prayer they put the noose around the young girl's neck, and they had great trouble to adjust the knot under her ear, because she was devouring the baby all the time, wildly kissing it, and snatching it to her face and her breast, and drenching it with tears, and half moaning, half shrieking all the while, and the baby crowing, and laughing, and kicking its feet with delight over what it took for romp and play. Even the hangman couldn't stand it, but turned away. When all was ready the priest gently pulled and tugged and forced the child out of the mother's arms, and stepped quickly out of her reach; but she clasped her hands, and made a wild spring toward him, with a shriek; but the rope—and the undersheriff—held her short. Then she went on her knees and stretched out her hands and cried:

"One more kiss—Oh, my God, one more, one more—it is the dying that begs it!"

She got it; she almost smothered the little thing. And when she got it away again, she cried out:

"Oh, my child, my darling, it will die! It has no home, it has no father, no friend, no mother—"

"It has them all!" said that good priest. "All these will I be to it till I die."

You should have seen her face then! Gratitude? Lord, what do you want with words to express that? Words are only painted fire; a look is the fire itself. She gave that look, and carried it away to the treasury of heaven, where all things that are divine belong.

FOR DISCUSSION

1. What evil is Mark Twain attacking in his account of "a pitiful incident"? What other evils of British law and human nature do the Yankee and the king encounter in these two chapters?

2. How do the king's attitudes change as a result of his enslavement?

3. What are the Yankee's thoughts on the divinity of kings and the dignity of man?

CHAPTER 36

London—to a slave—was a sufficiently interesting place. It was merely a great big village; and mainly mud and thatch. The streets were muddy, crooked, unpaved. The populace was an ever flocking and drifting swarm of rags and splendors, of nodding plumes and shining armor. The king had a palace there; he saw the outside of it. It made him sigh; yes, and swear a little, in a poor juvenile sixth-century way. We saw knights and grandees whom we knew, but they didn't know us in our rags and dirt and raw welts and bruises, and wouldn't have recognized us if we had hailed them, nor stopped to answer, either, it being unlawful to speak with slaves on a chain. Sandy passed within ten yards of me on a mule—hunting for me, I imagined. But the thing which clean broke my heart was something which happened in front of our old barrack in a square, while we were enduring the spectacle of a man being boiled to death in oil for counterfeiting pennies. It was the sight of a newsboy—and I couldn't get at him! Still, I had one comfort; here was proof that Clarence was still alive and banging away. I meant to be with him before long; the thought was full of cheer.

I had one little glimpse of another thing, one day, which gave me a great uplift. It was a wire stretching from housetop to housetop. Telegraph or telephone, sure. I did very much wish I had a little piece of it. It was just what I needed, in order to carry out my project of escape. My idea was, to get loose some night, along with the king, then gag and bind our master, change clothes with him, batter him into the aspect of a stranger, hitch him to the slave chain, assume possession of the property, march to Camelot, and—

But you get my idea; you see what a stunning dramatic surprise I would wind up with at the palace. It was all feasible, if I could only get hold of a slender piece of iron which I could shape into a lockpick. I could then undo the lumbering padlocks with which our chains were fastened, whenever I might choose. But I never had any luck; no such thing ever happened to fall in my way. However, my chance came at last. A gentleman who had come twice before to dicker for me, without result, or indeed any approach to a result, came again. I was far from expecting ever to belong to him, for the price asked for me from the time I was first enslaved was exorbitant, and always provoked either anger or derision, yet my master stuck stubbornly to it—twenty-two dollars. He wouldn't bate a cent. The king was greatly admired, because of his grand physique, but his kingly style was against him, and he wasn't salable; nobody wanted that kind of a slave. I considered myself safe from parting from him because of my extravagant price. No, I was not expecting to ever belong to this gentleman whom I have spoken of, but he had something which I expected would belong to me eventually, if he would but visit us often enough. It was a steel thing with a long pin to it, with which his long cloth outside garment was fastened together in front. There were three of them. He had disappointed me twice, because he did not come quite close enough to me to make my project entirely safe; but this time I succeeded; I captured the lower clasp of the three, and when he missed it he thought he had lost it on the way.

I had a chance to be glad about a minute, then straightway a chance to be sad again. For when the purchase was about to fail, as usual, the master suddenly spoke up and said what would be worded thus—in modern English:

"I'll tell you what I'll do. I'm tired supporting these two for no good. Give me twenty-two dollars for this one, and I'll throw the other one in."

The king couldn't get his breath, he was in such a fury. He began to choke and gag, and meantime the master and the gentleman moved away, discussing.

"An ye will keep the offer open—"

" 'Tis open till the morrow at this hour."

"Then will I answer you at that time," said the gentleman and disappeared, the master following him.

I had a time of it to cool the king down, but I managed it. I whispered in his ear, to this effect:

"Your grace *will* go for nothing, but after another fashion. And so shall I. Tonight we shall both be free."

"Ah! How is that?"

"With this thing which I have stolen, I will unlock these locks and cast off these chains tonight. When he comes about nine-thirty to inspect us for the night, we will seize him, gag him, batter him, and early in the morning we will march out of this town, proprietors of this caravan of slaves."

That was as far as I went, but the king was charmed and satisfied. That evening we waited patiently for our fellow slaves to get to sleep and signify it by the usual sign, for you must not take many chances on those poor fellows if you can avoid it. It is best to keep your own secrets. No doubt they fidgeted only about as usual, but it didn't seem so to me. It seemed to me that they were going to be forever getting down to their regular snoring. As the time dragged on I got nervously afraid we shouldn't have enough of it left for our needs; so I made several premature attempts, and merely delayed things by it; for I couldn't seem to touch a padlock, there in the dark, without starting a rattle out of it which interrupted somebody's sleep and made him turn over and wake some more of the gang.

But finally I did get my last iron off, and was a free man once more. I took a good breath of relief, and reached for the king's irons. Too late! in comes the master, with a light in one hand and his heavy walking staff in the other. I snuggled close among the wallow of snorers, to conceal as nearly as possible that I was naked of irons; and I kept a sharp lookout and prepared to spring for my man the moment he should bend over me.

But he didn't approach. He stopped, gazed absently toward our dusky mass a minute, evidently thinking about something else; then set down his light, moved musingly toward the door, and before a body could imagine what he was going to do, he was out of the door and had closed it behind him.

"Quick!" said the king. "Fetch him back!"

Of course it was the thing to do, and I was up and out in a moment. But dear me, there were no lamps in those days, and it was a dark night. But I glimpsed a dim figure a few steps away. I darted for it, threw myself upon it, and then there was a state of things and lively! We fought and scuffled and struggled, and drew a crowd in no time. They took an immense interest in the fight and encouraged us all they could, and in fact couldn't have been pleasanter or more cordial if it had been their own fight. Then a tremendous row broke out behind us, and as much as half of our audience left us, with a rush, to invest some sympathy in that. Lanterns began to swing in all directions; it was the watch, gathering from far and near. Presently a halberd fell across my back, as a reminder, and I knew what it meant. I was in custody. So was my adversary. We were marched off toward prison, one on each side of the watchman. Here was disaster, here was a fine scheme gone to sudden destruction! I tried to imagine what would happen when the master should discover that it was I who had been fighting him; and what would happen if they jailed us together in the general apartment for brawlers and petty law breakers, as was the custom; and what might—

Just then my antagonist turned his face around in my direction, the freckled light from the watchman's tin lantern fell on it, and by George he was the wrong man!

CHAPTER 37

Sleep? It was impossible. It would naturally have been impossible in that noisome cavern of a jail, with its mangy crowd of drunken, quarrelsome and song-singing rapscallions. But the thing that made sleep all the more a thing not to be dreamed of, was my racking impatience to get out of this place and find out the whole size of what might have happened yonder in the slave quarters in consequence of that intolerable miscarriage of mine.

It was a long night but the morning got around at last. I made a full and frank explanation to the court. I said I was a slave, the property of the great Earl Grip, who had arrived just after dark at the Tabard inn in the village on the other side of the water, and had stopped there overnight, by compulsion, he being taken deadly sick with a strange and sudden disorder. I had been ordered to cross to the city in all haste and bring the best physician; I was doing my best; naturally I was running with all my might; the night was dark, I ran against this common person here, who seized me by the throat and began to pummel me, although I told him my errand, and implored him, for the sake of the great earl my master's mortal peril—

The common person interrupted and said it was a lie; and was going to explain how I rushed upon him and attacked him without a word—

"Silence, sirrah!" from the court. "Take him hence and give him a few stripes whereby to teach him how to treat the servant of a nobleman after a different fashion another time. Go!"

Then the court begged my pardon, and hoped I would not fail to tell his lordship it was in no wise the court's fault that this high-handed thing had happened. I said I would make it all right, and so took my leave. Took it just in time, too; he was starting to ask me why I didn't fetch out these facts the moment I was arrested. I said I would if I had thought of it—which was true—but that I was so battered by that man that all my wit was knocked out of me —and so forth and so on, and got myself away, still mumbling.

I didn't wait for breakfast. No grass

grew under my feet. I was soon at the slave quarters. Empty—everybody gone! That is, everybody except one body—the slave master's. It lay there all battered to pulp; and all about were the evidences of a terrific fight. There was a rude board coffin on a cart at the door, and workmen, assisted by the police, were thinning a road through the gaping crowd in order that they might bring it in.

I picked out a man humble enough in life to condescend to talk with one so shabby as I, and got his account of the matter.

"There were sixteen slaves here. They rose against their master in the night, and thou seest how it ended."

"Yes. How did it begin?"

"There was no witness but the slaves. They said the slave that was most valuable got free of his bonds and escaped in some strange way—by magic arts 'twas thought, by reason that he had no key, and the locks were neither broke nor in any wise injured. When the master discovered his loss, he was mad with despair, and threw himself upon his people with his heavy stick, who resisted and brake his back and in other and divers ways did give him hurts that brought him swiftly to his end."

"This is dreadful. It will go hard with the slaves, no doubt, upon the trial."

"Marry, the trial is over."

"Over!"

"Would they be a week, think you—and the matter so simple? They were not the half of a quarter of an hour at it."

"Why, I don't see how they could determine which were the guilty ones in so short a time."

"*Which* ones? Indeed they considered not particulars like to that. They condemned them in a body. Wit ye not the law—which men say the Romans left behind them here when they went—that if one slave killeth

his master all the slaves of that man must die for it."

"True. I had forgotten. And when will these die?"

"Belike within a four and twenty hours; albeit some say they will wait a pair of days more, if peradventure they may find the missing one meantime."

The missing one! It made me feel uncomfortable.

"Is it likely they will find him?"

"Before the day is spent—yes. They seek him everywhere. They stand at the gates of the town, with certain of the slaves who will discover him to them if he cometh, and none can pass out but he will be first examined."

"Might one see the place where the rest are confined?"

"The outside of it—yes. The inside of it —but ye will not want to see that."

I took the address of that prison, for future reference, and then sauntered off. At the first secondhand clothing shop I came to, up a back street, I got a rough rig suitable for a common seaman who might be going on a cold voyage, and bound up my face with a liberal bandage, saying I had a toothache. This concealed my worst bruises. It was a transformation. I no longer resembled my former self. Then I struck out for that wire, found it and followed it to its den. It was a little room over a butcher's shop—which meant that business wasn't very brisk in the telegraphic line. The young chap in charge was drowsing at his table. I locked the door and put the vast key in my bosom. This alarmed the young fellow, and he was going to make a noise; but I said:

"Save your wind; if you open your mouth you are dead, sure. Tackle your instrument. Lively, now! Call Camelot."

"This doth amaze me! How should such as you know aught of such matters as—"

"Call Camelot! I am a desperate man. Call Camelot, or get away from the instrument and I will do it myself."

"What—you?"

"Yes—certainly. Stop gabbling. Call the palace." He made the call.

"Now then, call Clarence."

"Clarence *who*?"

"Never mind Clarence who. Say you want Clarence; you'll get an answer."

He did so. We waited five nerve-straining minutes—ten minutes—how long it did seem!—and then came a click that was as familiar to me as a human voice; for Clarence had been my own pupil.

"Now, my lad, vacate! They wouldn't have known *my* touch, maybe, and so your call was surest; but I'm all right, now."

He vacated the place and cocked his ear to listen—but it didn't win. I used a cipher. I didn't waste any time in sociabilities with Clarence, but squared away for business, straight off—thus:

"The king is here and in danger. We were captured and brought here as slaves. We should not be able to prove our identity—and the fact is, I am not in a position to try. Send a telegram for the palace here which will carry conviction with it."

His answer came straight back:

"They don't know anything about the telegraph; they haven't had any experience yet, the line to London is so new. Better not venture that. They might hang you. Think up something else."

Might hang us! Little he knew how closely he was crowding the facts. I couldn't think up anything for the moment. Then an idea struck me, and I started it along:

"Send five hundred picked knights with Launcelot in the lead; and send them on the jump. Let them enter by the southwest gate, and look out for the man with a white cloth around his right arm."

The answer was prompt:

"They shall start in half an hour."

"All right, Clarence; now tell this lad here that I'm a friend of yours and a deadhead; and that he must be discreet and say nothing about this visit of mine."

The instrument began to talk to the youth and I hurried away. I fell to ciphering. In half an hour it would be nine o'clock. Knights and horses in heavy armor couldn't travel very fast. These would make the best time they could, and now that the ground was in good condition, and no snow or mud, they would probably make a seven-mile gait; they would have to change horses a couple of times; they would arrive about six, or a little after; it would still be plenty light enough; they would see the white cloth which I should tie around my right arm, and I would take command. We would surround that prison and have the king out in no time. It would be showy and picturesque enough, all things considered, though I would have preferred noonday, on account of the more theatrical aspect the thing would have.

Now then, in order to increase the strings to my bow, I thought I would look up some of those people whom I had formerly recognized, and make myself known. That would help us out of our scrape, without the knights. But I must proceed cautiously, for it was a risky business. I must get into sumptuous raiment, and it wouldn't do to run and jump into it. No, I must work up to it by degrees, buying suit after suit of clothes, in shops wide apart, and getting a little finer article with each change, until I should finally reach silk and velvet, and be ready for my project. So I started.

But the scheme fell through like scat! The first corner I turned, I came plump upon one of our slaves, snooping around with a watchman. I coughed, at the moment, and he gave me a sudden look that bit right into my marrow. I judge he thought he had heard that cough before. I turned immediately into a shop and worked along down the counter, pricing things and watching out of the corner of my eye. Those people had stopped, and were talking together and looking in at the door. I made up my mind to get out the back way, if there was a back way, and I asked the shopwoman if I could step out there and look for the escaped slave, who was believed to be in hiding back there somewhere, and said I was an officer in disguise, and my pard was yonder at the door with one of the murderers in charge, and would she be good enough to step there and tell him he needn't wait, but had better go at once to the further end of the back alley and be ready to head him off when I rousted him out.

She was blazing with eagerness to see one of those already celebrated murderers, and she started on the errand at once. I slipped out the back way, locked the door behind me, put the key in my pocket and started off, chuckling to myself and comfortable.

Well, I had gone and spoiled it again, made another mistake. A double one, in fact. There were plenty of ways to get rid of that officer by some simple and plausible device, but no, I must pick out a picturesque one; it is the crying defect of my character. And then, I had ordered my procedure upon what the officer, being human, would *naturally* do; whereas when you are least expecting it, a man will now and then go and do the very thing which it's *not* natural for him to do. The natural thing for the officer to do, in this case, was to follow straight on my heels; he would find a stout oaken door, securely locked, between him and me; before he could break it down, I should be far away and engaged in slipping into a succession of baffling disguises which would soon get me into a sort of raiment which was a surer protection from meddling law dogs in Britain than any amount of mere innocence and purity of character. But instead of doing the natural thing, the officer took me at my word, and followed my instructions. And so, as I came trotting out of that cul-de-sac, full of satisfaction with my own cleverness, he turned the corner and I walked right into his handcuffs. If I had known it was a cul-de-sac—however, there isn't any excusing a blunder like that, let it go. Charge it up to profit and loss.

Of course I was indignant, and swore I had just come ashore from a long voyage, and all that sort of thing—just to see, you know, if it would deceive that slave. But it didn't. He knew me. Then I reproached him for betraying me. He was more surprised than hurt. He stretched his eyes wide, and said:

"What wouldst have me let thee, of all men, escape and not hang with us, when thou'rt the very *cause* of our hanging? Go to!"

"Go to" was their way of saying "I should smile!" or "I like that!" Queer talkers, those people.

Well, there was a sort of justice in his view of the case, and so I dropped the matter. When you can't cure a disaster by argument, what is the use to argue? It isn't my way. So I only said:

"You're not going to be hanged. None of us are."

Both men laughed, and the slave said:

"Ye have not ranked as a fool—before. You might better keep your reputation, seeing the strain would not be for long."

"It will stand it, I reckon. Before tomorrow we shall be out of prison, and free to go where we will, besides."

The witty officer lifted at his left ear with his thumb, made a rasping noise in his throat, and said:

"Out of prison—yes—ye say true. And free likewise to go where ye will, so ye wander not out of his grace the Devil's sultry realm."

I kept my temper, and said, indifferently:

"Now I suppose you really think we are going to hang within a day or two."

"I thought it not many minutes ago, for so the thing was decided and proclaimed."

"Ah, then you've changed your mind, is that it?"

"Even that. I only *thought,* then; I *know,* now."

I felt sarcastical, so I said:

"Oh, sapient servant of the law, condescend to tell us, then, what you *know.*"

"That ye will all be hanged *today,* at midafternoon! Oho! that shot hit home!

Lean upon me."

The fact is I did need to lean upon somebody. My knights couldn't arrive in time. They would be as much as three hours too late. Nothing in the world could save the King of England; nor me, which was more important. More important, not merely to me, but to the nation—the only nation on earth standing ready to blossom into civilization. I was sick. I said no more, there wasn't anything to say. I knew what the man meant; that if the missing slave was found, the postponement would be revoked, the execution take place today. Well, the missing slave was found.

CHAPTER 38

Nearing four in the afternoon. The scene was just outside the walls of London. A cool, comfortable, superb day, with a brilliant sun; the kind of day to make one want to live, not die. The multitude was prodigious and far-reaching; and yet we fifteen poor devils hadn't a friend in it. There was something painful in that thought, look at it how you might. There we sat, on our tall scaffold, the butt of the hate and mockery of all those enemies. We were being made a holiday spectacle. They had built a sort of grandstand for the nobility and gentry, and these were there in full force, with their ladies. We recognized a good many of them.

The crowd got a brief and unexpected dash of diversion out of the king. The moment we were freed of our bonds he sprang up, in his fantastic rags, with face bruised out of all recognition, and proclaimed himself Arthur King of Britain, and denounced the awful penalties of treason upon every soul there present if hair of his sacred head were touched. It startled and surprised him

to hear them break into a vast roar of laughter. It wounded his dignity, and he locked himself up in silence, then, although the crowd begged him to go on, and tried to provoke him to it by catcalls, jeers, and shouts of:

"Let him speak! The king! The king! his humble subjects hunger and thirst for words of wisdom out of the mouth of their master his Serene and Sacred Raggedness!"

But it went for nothing. He put on all his majesty and sat under this rain of contempt and insult unmoved. He certainly was great in his way. Absently, I had taken off my white bandage and wound it about my right arm. When the crowd noticed this, they began upon me. They said:

"Doubtless this sailorman is his minister —observe his costly badge of office!"

I let them go on until they got tired, and then I said:

"Yes, I am his minister, The Boss; and tomorrow you will hear that from Camelot which—"

I got no further. They drowned me out

with joyous derision. But presently there was silence; for the sheriffs of London, in their official robes, with their subordinates, began to make a stir which indicated that business was about to begin. In the hush which followed, our crime was recited, the death warrant read, then everybody uncovered while a priest uttered a prayer.

Then a slave was blindfolded, the hangman unslung his rope. There lay the smooth road below us, we upon one side of it, the banked multitude walling its other side—a good clear road, and kept free by the police—how good it would be to see my five hundred horsemen come tearing down it! But, no, it was out of the possibilities. I followed its receding thread out into the distance—not a horseman on it, or sign of one.

There was a jerk, and the slave hung dangling; dangling and hideously squirming, for his limbs were not tied.

A second rope was unslung, in a moment another slave was dangling.

In a minute a third slave was struggling in the air. It was dreadful. I turned away my head a moment, and when I turned back I missed the king. They were blindfolding him! I was paralyzed; I couldn't move, I was choking, my tongue was petrified. They finished blindfolding him, they led him under the rope. I couldn't shake off that clinging impotence. But when I saw them put the noose around his neck, then everything let go in me and I made a spring to the rescue—and as I made it I shot one

more glance abroad—by George, here they came, atilting—five hundred mailed and belted knights on bicycles!

The grandest sight that ever was seen. Lord, how the plumes streamed, how the sun flamed and flashed from the endless procession of webby wheels!

I waved my right arm as Launcelot swept in—he recognized my rag—I tore away noose and bandage, and shouted:

"On your knees, every rascal of you, and salute the king! Who fails shall sup in hell tonight!"

I always use that high style when I'm climaxing an effect. Well, it was noble to see Launcelot and the boys swarm up onto that scaffold and heave sheriffs and such overboard. And it was fine to see that astonished multitude go down on their knees and beg their lives of the king they had just been deriding and insulting. And as he stood apart, there, receiving this homage in his rags, I thought to myself, well really there *is* something peculiarly grand about the gait and bearing of a king, after all.

I was immensely satisfied. Take the whole situation all around, it was one of the gaudiest effects I ever instigated.

And presently up comes Clarence, his own self! And winks, and says, very modernly:

"Good deal of a surprise, wasn't it? I knew you'd like it. I've had the boys practicing, this long time, privately; and just hungry for a chance to show off."

FOR DISCUSSION

1. What surprising thing does the Yankee see while watching a man being boiled in oil? This and another thing lift his spirits. What is it?

2. At this time he also thinks of a plan of es-

cape. What is his plan and how does it backfire? What is his second plan? How is it—and its failure—typical of him?

3. What anachronism finally saves the Yankee and the king?

CHAPTER 39

Home again, at Camelot. A morning or two later I found the paper, damp from the press, by my plate at the breakfast table. I turned to the advertising columns, knowing I should find something of personal interest to me there. It was this:

Know that the great lord and illustrious knight SIR SAGRAMOR LE DESIROUS having condescended to meet the King's Minister, Hank Morgan, the which is surnamed The Boss, for satisfaction of offences anciently given, these will engage in the lists by Camelot about the fourth hour of the morning of the sixteenth day of this next succeeding month. The battle will be á l'outrance, since the said offence was of a deadly sort, admitting no composition.

It will be observed, by a glance at our advertising columns that the community is to be favored with a treat of unusual interest in the tournament line. The names of the artists are warrant of good entertainment. The box-office will be open at noon of the 13th; admission 3 cents, reserved seats 5; proceeds to go to the hospital fund. The royal pair and all the Court will be present. With these exceptions, and the press and the clergy, the free list is strictly suspended. Parties are hereby warned against buying tickets of speculators; they will not be good at the door. Everybody knows and likes The Boss, everybody knows and likes Sir Sag.; come, let us give the lads a good sendoff. Remember, the proceeds go to a great and free charity, and one whose broad benevolence stretches out its helping hand, warm with the blood of a loving heart, to all that suffer, regardless of race, creed, condition or color—the only charity yet established in the earth which has no politico-religious topcock on its compassion, but says here flows the stream let all come and drink! Turn out all hands! fetch along your doughnuts and your gum-drops and have a good time. Pie for sale on the grounds, and rocks to crack it with; also circus-lemonade—three drops of lime juice to a barrel of water.

N.B. This is the first tournament under the new law, which allows each combatant to use any weapon he may prefer.

Up to the day set, there was no talk in all Britain of anything but this combat. All other topics sank into insignificance and passed out of men's thoughts and interest. It was not because a tournament was a great matter; it was not because Sir Sagramor had found the Holy Grail, for he had not, but had failed; it was not because the second (official) personage in the kingdom was one of the duelists; no, all these features were commonplace. Yet there was abundant reason for the extraordinary interest which this coming fight was creating. It was born of the fact that all the nation knew that this was not to be a duel between mere men, so to speak, but a duel between two mighty magicians; a duel not of muscle but of mind, not of human skill but of superhuman art and craft; a final struggle for supremacy between the two master enchanters of the age. It was realized that the most prodigious achievements of the most renowned knights could not be worthy of comparison with a spectacle like this; they could be but child's play, contrasted with this mysterious and awful battle of the gods. Yes, all the world knew it was going to be in reality a duel between Merlin and me, a measuring of his magic powers against mine. It was known that Merlin had been busy whole days and nights together, imbuing Sir Sagramor's arms and armor with supernal powers of offense and defense, and that he had procured for him from the spirits of the air a fleecy veil which would render the wearer invisible to his antagonist while still visible to other men. Against Sir Sagramor, so weaponed and protected, a thousand knights could accomplish nothing; against him no known enchantments could prevail. These facts were sure; regarding them there was no doubt, no reason for doubt. There was but one question: might there be still other enchantments, *unknown* to Merlin, which could render Sir Sagramor's veil transparent to me, and make his enchanted mail vulnerable to my weapons? This was the one thing to be decided in the lists. Until then the world must remain in suspense.

So the world thought there was a vast matter at stake here, and the world was right, but it was not the one they had in their minds. No, a far vaster one was upon the cast of this die: *the life of knight-errantry.* I was a champion, it was true, but not the champion of the frivolous black arts, I was the champion of hard unsentimental common sense and reason. I was entering the lists to either destroy knight-errantry or be its victim.

Vast as the showgrounds were, there were no vacant spaces in them outside of the lists, at ten o'clock on the morning of the 16th. The mammoth grandstand was clothed in flags, streamers, and rich tapestries, and packed with several acres of small-fry tributary kings, their suites, and the British aristocracy; with our own royal gang in the chief place, and each and every individual a flashing prism of gaudy silks and velvets—well, I never saw anything to begin with it but a fight between an Upper Mississippi sunset and the aurora borealis. The huge camp of beflagged and gay-colored tents at one end of the lists, with a stiff-standing sentinel at every door and a shining shield hanging by him for challenge, was another fine sight. You see, every knight was there who had any ambition or any caste feeling; for my feeling toward their order was not much of a secret, and so here was their chance. If I won my fight with Sir Sagramor, others would have the right to call me out as long as I might be willing to respond.

Down at our end there were but two tents; one for me, and another for my servants. At the appointed hour the king made a sign, and the heralds, in their tabards, appeared and made proclamation, naming the combatants and stating the cause of quarrel. There was a pause, then a ringing bugle blast, which was the signal for us to come forth. All the multitude caught their breath, and an eager curiosity flashed into every face.

Out from his tent rode great Sir Sagramor, an imposing tower of iron, stately and rigid, his huge spear standing upright in its socket and grasped in his strong hand, his grand horse's face and breast cased in steel, his body clothed in rich trappings that almost dragged the ground—oh, a most noble picture. A great shout went up, of welcome and admiration.

And then out I came. But I didn't get any shout. There was a wondering and eloquent silence, for a moment, then a great wave of laughter began to sweep along that human sea, but a warning bugle blast cut its career short. I was in the simplest and comfortablest of gymnast costumes—flesh-colored tights from neck to heel, with blue silk puffings about my legs, and bareheaded. My horse was not above medium size, but he was alert, slender-limbed, muscled with watch springs, and just a greyhound to go. He was a beauty, glossy as silk, and naked as he was when he was born, except for bridle and ranger saddle.

The iron tower and the gorgeous bed quilt came cumbrously but gracefully pirouetting down the lists, and we tripped lightly up to meet them. We halted; the tower saluted, I responded; then we wheeled and rode side by side to the grandstand and faced our king and queen, to whom we made obeisance. The queen exclaimed:

"Alack, Sir Boss wilt fight naked, and

without lance or sword or—"

But the king checked her and made her understand, with a polite phrase or two, that this was none of her business. The bugles rang again; and we separated and rode to the ends of the lists, and took position. Now old Merlin stepped into view and cast a dainty web of gossamer threads over Sir Sagramor which turned him into Hamlet's ghost; the king made a sign, the bugles blew, Sir Sagramor laid his great lance in rest, and the next moment here he came thundering down the course with his veil flying out behind, and I went whistling through the air like an arrow to meet him—cocking my ear, the while, as if noting the invisible knight's position and progress by hearing, not sight. A chorus of encouraging shouts burst out for him, and one brave voice flung out a heartening word for me—said:

"Go it, slim Jim!"

It was an even bet that Clarence had procured that favor for me—and furnished the language, too. When that formidable lance point was within a yard and a half of my breast I twitched my horse aside without an effort and the big knight swept by, scoring a blank. I got plenty of applause that time. We turned, braced up, and down we came again. Another blank for the knight, a roar of applause for me. This same thing was repeated once more; and it fetched such a whirlwind of applause that Sir Sagramor lost his temper, and at once changed his tactics and set himself the task of chasing me down. Why, he hadn't any show in the world at that; it was a game of tag, with all the advantage on my side; I whirled out of his path with ease whenever I chose, and once I slapped him on the back as I went to the rear. Finally I took the chase into my own hands; and after that, turn, or twist, or do what he would, he was never able to get behind me again; he found himself always

in front, at the end of his maneuver. So he gave up that business and retired to his end of the lists. His temper was clear gone, now, and he forgot himself and flung an insult at me which disposed of mine. I slipped my lasso from the horn of my saddle, and grasped the coil in my right hand. This time you should have seen him come! It was a business trip, sure; by his gait there was blood in his eye. I was sitting my horse at ease, and swinging the great loop of my lasso in wide circles about my head; the moment he was under way, I started for him; when the space between us had narrowed to forty feet, I sent the snaky spirals of the rope a-cleaving through the air, then darted aside and faced about and brought my trained animal to a halt with all his feet braced under him for a surge. The next moment the rope sprang taut and yanked Sir Sagramor out of the saddle! Great Scott, but there was a sensation!

Unquestionably the popular thing in this world is novelty. These people had never seen anything of that cowboy business before, and it carried them clear off their feet with delight. From all around and everywhere, the shout went up—

"Encore! encore!"

I wondered where they got the word, but there was no time to cipher on philological matters, because the whole knight-errantry hive was just humming, now, and my prospect for trade couldn't have been better. The moment my lasso was released and Sir Sagramor had been assisted to his tent, I hauled in the slack, took my station and began to swing my loop around my head again. I was sure to have use for it as soon as they could elect a successor for Sir Sagramor, and that couldn't take long where there were so many hungry candidates. Indeed, they elected one straight off—Sir Hervis de Revel.

Continued on page 658

IDEAS AND THE ARTS

One of the most interesting ideas that has been developed in this century is the idea of culture conflict. To understand it, we must first have some notion of what the term *culture* means. Culture used to refer to the kind of knowledge and activity that requires study, learning, and practice. It referred to things such as philosophy, literature, science, the kind of paintings found in museums, and the kind of music played by symphony orchestras. It still has this meaning, but in the past hundred years it has also been given another meaning. *Culture* now refers also to whatever human beings do that is learned from other human beings, as opposed to what human beings do that is done "naturally." By *naturally* we refer to behavior that people supposedly do not have to learn.

Thousands of people have been busy studying human behavior all over the world. They have studied the most primitive of human beings now living, and they have studied the most civilized human beings. And they have come to a definite conclusion: man has learned to do almost everything he does. Almost nothing he does is natural. Almost everything is a matter of culture.

You might say that it is natural to eat, and that is undoubtedly true. But the ways different people eat are so various that about all they have in common is putting into the mouth something the culture thinks is edible and swallowing it. *Edible* refers to what a culture thinks ought to be eaten, and here there is great disagreement. What one culture thinks is delicious, another culture regards as inedible, or even horrible and repulsive. We eat what we have been taught to eat.

Culture, then, is what you are taught to expect and what you are taught to do in any situation. You learn these things from your parents, your friends, your teachers, your minister or priest or rabbi, and from everyone else you meet, as well as from mass media.

But even with all these instructions there will be situations in which you will not know how to act. Suppose you have always gone to school in classrooms where the desks and chairs are arranged in neat rows facing the teacher's desk. Now suppose you move to a new school where the desks and chairs are arranged in small separate groups with desks facing each other. There is no teacher's desk, and there is no regular teacher. Teachers come and go. Instead of all students doing the same thing, each group of students is doing something different. And some students are doing things no other student is doing. When you enter this classroom, after having been used to a different kind, you will not know what to do or what to expect. You will experience "culture shock." Now suppose you find that you do not like the new classroom. You prefer the old one. You will experience "culture conflict," which arises when there are two sets of instructions and expectations for the same situation.

Mark Twain's *A Connecticut Yankee at King Arthur's Court* is a serious, though funny, novel about culture shock and culture conflict. It seems to be about the shock of encountering a different culture and the conflict between two cultures. Actually it is about Mark Twain's own culture shock and about the conflict within his own culture. Mark Twain sees the old values still in his own society, but he sees them disappearing. And he feels that something important and valuable might be lost.

Morse Peckham

ART

It is hard to believe how popular stories of King Arthur and his knights were during the Middle Ages. In the libraries of Europe and America there are so many manuscripts containing these stories that it would take at least three hundred and fifty ordinary modern books to print them all. It is impossible to guess how many manuscripts have been destroyed, but it is probable that at least as many have been destroyed as have been preserved. Of course we must remember that it took at least four hundred years to produce all these manuscripts. Still, the population of Europe was very small compared to what it is now, and only a tiny number of people could read. The number of people who heard the stories, however, was quite large. The manuscripts were read aloud, over and over again, and there were wandering story tellers who told stories from memory.

Hundreds of these manuscripts are illustrated. The proper word for manuscript illustration is *illumination.* A few pictures from these illuminated manuscripts will show how people have thought about the Arthurian stories.

The first example, *Perceval Meets Arthur's Knights,* shows the beginning of the career of one of Arthur's greatest knights, Perceval. According to some versions of his story, he at last found the Holy Grail, the object of many of Arthur's knights. Perceval's mother brought him up carefully so that he would not know about knights and battles. One day, however, he saw a couple of Arthur's knights, and he knew at once that he too must become a knight. At the top of the manuscript, which was done about 1330, we see him meeting the knights, and at the left he says good-bye to his mother. At the bottom his mother dies of a broken heart. But Perceval sets out, and in his first fight he kills the Red Knight.

The manuscript picturing the story of Perceval was painted in France. The next one, *Arthur in Camelot,* was done in Italy about twenty or thirty years later. This one shows Arthur himself in a procession in his city of Camelot. This example shows how the illuminations were not often set apart from the text on a separate page or framed in any way on the same page. Here the illumination is combined with the text of the story. Since the painter was Italian, the buildings are in Italian style.

The third illumination, *Sports at Caerleon,* was done in Flanders a little more than a hundred years later. By this time printing had been invented, but many people still preferred hand-done manuscripts, just as today many people prefer hardbound books to paperbacks. A manuscript was felt somehow or other to be the real thing. This illumination shows no particular scene from the Arthurian stories. It shows instead a typical day at Caerleon, another name for Arthur's city. The architecture and the costumes are typical of the time the manuscript was painted, about 1468. The knights are exercising and practicing fighting. Some are jousting on horseback. Others are fighting on foot. One is lifting a heavy weight, and another is throwing a spear.

One reason people in the Middle Ages loved the Arthurian stories was that they were stories about people like themselves and the world they knew. To the people of the time the pictures accompanying the stories were familiar and realistic, as familiar and realistic as newspaper comic strips of today. But by the nineteenth century, the legend of Arthur had become a legend of a remote, mysterious, magical, and idealized world. Many nineteenth-century artists painted subjects from the Arthurian legends, but they did not see the world of Arthur as people of the Middle Ages did. These later artists saw a world that was more beautiful, more moral, more religious, and in every way more desirable than the industrialized world of the nineteenth century. And they portrayed that world as they saw it. Mark Twain attacked this attitude toward the world of Arthur and the Middle Ages in *A Connecticut Yankee at King Arthur's Court*. He, too, felt the attractiveness of Arthur's world, but he thought that idealizing the Middle Ages was a way of avoiding the real problems of modern life.

G. F. Watts painted *Sir Galahad* in 1862. It represents exactly the kind of impossible idealism that Mark Twain disliked. Dante Gabriel Rossetti's *Sir Galahad at the Ruined Castle* is another example of the longing for the medieval, the remote, and the impossible. It represents a world too beautiful ever to have existed. *The Beguiling of Merlin* by Sir Edward Burne-Jones was strongly influenced by Rossetti's work. It illustrates the story of the beautiful but evil Vivien who lured Arthur's magician and adviser, Merlin, away from Camelot. She persuaded him to tell her his secrets of enchantment. Her success is shown by the book she holds, which seems to half float in air. She used Merlin's secrets to enchant him into sleep, and she locked him up forever in a hollow tree. Here again the world is too beautiful to be real.

Morse Peckham

FRENCH SCHOOL (c.1330) *PERCEVAL MEETS ARTHUR'S KNIGHTS,* from the *CONTE DEL GRAAL,* Ms.Fr.12577. Bibliotheque
Nationale, Paris.

ITALIAN SCHOOL (1352-1362) *ARTHUR IN CAMELOT,* from *MELIADUS,* Ms.Add.12228, 305. f.221^V. British Museum, London.

FLEMISH SCHOOL (1468) *SPORTS AT CAERLEON,* from *CHRONIQUES DE HAINAUT,* Ms.9243, f.45ʳ. Bibliothèque Royale de Belgique, Brussels.

SIR GEORGE FREDERICK WATTS (1817-1904) *SIR GALAHAD.* Fogg Art Museum, Harvard
University, Cambridge, Massachusetts.

DANTE GABRIEL ROSSETTI (1828-1882) *SIR GALAHAD AT THE RUINED CASTLE.* Birmingham Museum and Art Gallery, Birmingham, England.

SIR EDWARD BURNE-JONES (1833-1898) *THE BEGUILING OF MERLIN.* Lady Lever Art Gallery,
Port Sunlight, Cheshire, England.

656

MUSIC

ARNOLD SCHOENBERG:
THREE PIANO PIECES, *OPUS 11*
[A number of recordings available]

Culture can be defined as "directions for our behavior." When we receive two different sets of directions for our behavior in the same situation, we feel culture conflict.

At the present time many boys and young men like to wear their hair long, but many people object strongly to this. These objections have forced some young people away from school or jobs until they cut their hair. Often the question has been taken to court, and judges have sometimes supported one side and sometimes the other. What is happening there is a culture conflict created by differing sets of directions.

A few years ago there was no problem. The culture said that men's hair should be short, and no one questioned it. Short hair was considered "right" and long hair was considered "wrong." But then the culture began to change, and some people, especially the young, decided that long hair was "right." At this point young people were faced with two different sets of directions about how to wear their hair. One said that short hair was "right," and the other said that long hair was "right." No matter what one did, he got into trouble with somebody. A culture conflict had come into existence, and culture conflict always creates strong feelings.

The music of Arnold Schoenberg points to another example of culture conflict. It has made many people very angry, although others regard it as great music. About sixty years ago Schoenberg became very dissatisfied with the way composers had been composing music for more than three hundred years. He felt it was too limited. He was sure that there were things music could say that could not be said in the traditional way of composing music. He felt that the traditional way did not allow him to express his unique way of feeling. He was caught in a culture conflict.

The traditional way was to write music that people were used to and could find beautiful. This meant that beautiful music could be written only in certain and definite ways. Long before Schoenberg, however, a new attitude toward music had come into being. This was the belief that the composer should express his own individuality in his music. On the one hand, then, was the cultural direction that music should be written according to a great tradition, and, on the other, that the composer's individuality was more important than the tradition. By sacrificing tradition to his individuality, Schoenberg brought this culture conflict out into the open.

When you first hear Schoenberg's *Three Piano Pieces, Opus 11,* you might think that he wrote them because he could not write traditional music. Actually he had already written a great deal of very fine traditional music. His new music made people furious. When it was performed in public it actually caused riots. This new music at first sounds as if it had no melody. On first hearing, it is very difficult to know when one piece ends and the next begins. The second piece begins with a rocking motion in the bass. The third begins with loud and fast discords. After a few hearings you will be able to hear the melodies. Then it will become clear that extraordinary and valuable new things can result from culture conflict.

Morse Peckham

Bzz! Here he came, like a house afire; I dodged; he passed like a flash, with my horsehair coils settling around his neck; a second or so later, *fst!* his saddle was empty.

I got another encore; and another, and another, and still another. When I had snaked five men out, things began to look serious to the ironclads, and they stopped and consulted together. As a result, they decided that it was time to waive etiquette and send their greatest and best against me. To the astonishment of that little world, I lassoed Sir Lamorak de Galis, and after him Sir Galahad. So you see there was simply nothing to be done, now, but play their right bower—bring out the superbest of the superb, the mightiest of the mighty, the great Sir Launcelot himself!

A proud moment for me? I should think so. Yonder was Arthur, King of Britain; yonder was Guenever; yes, and whole tribes of little provincial kings and kinglets; and in the tented camp yonder, renowned knights from many lands; and likewise the selectest body known to chivalry, the Knights of the Table Round, the most illustrious in Christendom; and biggest fact of all, the very sun of their shining system was yonder couching his lance, the focal point of forty thousand adoring eyes; and all by myself, here was I laying for him. Across my mind flitted the dear image of a certain hello-girl of West Hartford, and I wished she could see me now. In that moment, down came the Invincible, with the rush of a whirlwind—the courtly world rose to its feet and bent forward— the fateful coils went circling through the air, and before you could wink I was towing Sir Launcelot across the field on his back, and kissing my hand to the storm of waving kerchiefs and the thundercrash of applause that greeted me!

Said I to myself, as I coiled my lariat and hung it on my saddle horn, and sat there drunk with glory, "The victory is perfect— no other will venture against me—knight-errantry is dead." Now imagine my astonishment—and everybody else's too—to hear the peculiar bugle call which announces that another competitor is about to enter the lists! There was a mystery here; I couldn't account for this thing. Next, I noticed Merlin gliding away from me; and then I noticed that my lasso was gone! The old sleight-of-hand expert had stolen it, sure, and slipped it under his robe.

The bugle blew again. I looked, and down came Sagramor riding again, with his dust brushed off and his veil nicely rearranged. I trotted up to meet him, and pretended to find him by the sound of his horse's hoofs. He said:

"Thou'rt quick of ear, but it will not save thee from this!" and he touched the hilt of his great sword. "An ye are not able to see it, because of the influence of the veil, know that it is no cumbrous lance, but a sword—and I ween ye will not be able to avoid it."

His visor was up; there was death in his smile. I should never be able to dodge his sword, that was plain. Somebody was going to die, this time. If he got the drop on me, I could name the corpse. We rode forward together, and saluted the royalties. This time the king was disturbed. He said:

"Where is thy strange weapon?"

"It is stolen, sire."

"Hast another at hand?"

"No, sire, I brought only the one."

Then Merlin mixed in:

"He brought but the one because there was but the one to bring. There exists none other but that one. It belongeth to the king of the Demons of the Sea. This man is a pretender, and ignorant; else he had known that that weapon can be used in but eight bouts only, and then it vanisheth away to its home under the sea."

"Then is he weaponless," said the king. "Sir Sagramor, ye will grant him leave to borrow."

"And I will lend!" said Sir Launcelot, limping up. "He is as brave a knight of his hands as any that be on live, and he shall have mine."

He put his hand on his sword to draw it, but Sir Sagramor said:

"Stay, it may not be. He shall fight with his own weapons; it was his privilege to choose them and bring them. If he has erred, on his head be it."

"Knight!" said the king. "Thou'rt overwrought with passion; it disorders thy mind. Wouldst kill a naked man?"

"An he do it, he shall answer it to me," said Sir Launcelot.

"I will answer it to any he that desireth!" retorted Sir Sagramor hotly.

Merlin broke in, rubbing his hands and smiling his lowdownest smile of malicious gratification:

" 'Tis well said, right well said! And 'tis enough of parleying, let my lord the king deliver the battle signal."

The king had to yield. The bugle made proclamation, and we turned apart and rode to our stations. There we stood, a hundred yards apart, facing each other, rigid and motionless, like horsed statues. And so we remained, in a soundless hush, as much as a full minute, everybody gazing, nobody stirring. It seemed as if the king could not take heart to give the signal. But at last he lifted his hand, the clear note of the bugle followed, Sir Sagramor's long blade described a flashing curve in the air, and it was superb to see him come. I sat still. On he came. I did not move. People got so excited that they shouted to me:

"Fly, fly! Save thyself! This is murther!"

I never budged so much as an inch, till that thundering apparition had got within fifteen paces of me; then I snatched a dragoon revolver out of my holster, there was a flash and a roar, and the revolver was back in the holster before anybody could tell what had happened.

Here was a riderless horse plunging by, and yonder lay Sir Sagramor, stone dead.

The people that ran to him were stricken dumb to find that the life was actually gone out of the man and no reason for it visible, no hurt upon his body, nothing like a wound. There was a hole through the breast of his chain mail, but they attached no importance to a little thing like that; and as a bullet wound there produces but little blood, none came in sight because of the clothing and swaddlings under the armor. The body was dragged over to let the king and the swells look down upon it. They were stupefied with astonishment, naturally. I was requested to come and explain the miracle. But I remained in my tracks, like a statue, and said:

"If it is a command, I will come, but my lord the king knows that I am where the laws of combat require me to remain while any desire to come against me."

I waited. Nobody challenged. Then I said:

"If there are any who doubt that this field is well and fairly won, I do not wait for them to challenge me, I challenge them."

"It is a gallant offer," said the king, "and well beseems you. Whom will you name, first?"

"I name none, I challenge all! Here I stand, and dare the chivalry of England to come against me—not by individuals, but in mass!"

"What!" shouted a score of knights.

"You have heard the challenge. Take it, or I proclaim you recreant knights and vanquished, every one!"

It was a "bluff" you know. At such a

time it is sound judgment to put on a bold face and play your hand for a hundred times what it is worth; forty-nine times out of fifty nobody dares to "call," and you rake in the chips. But just this once—well, things looked squally! In just no time, five hundred knights were scrambling into their saddles, and before you could wink, a widely scattering drove were under way and clattering down upon me. I snatched both revolvers from the holsters and began to measure distances and calculate chances.

Bang! One saddle empty. Bang! another one. Bang—bang! and I bagged two. Well it was nip and tuck with us, and I knew it. If I spent the eleventh shot without convincing these people, the twelfth man would kill me, sure.

And so I never did feel so happy as I did when my ninth downed its man and I detected the wavering in the crowd which is premonitory of panic. An instant lost now, could knock out my last chance. But I didn't lose it. I raised both revolvers and pointed them—the halted host stood their ground just about one good square moment, then broke and fled.

The day was mine. Knight-errantry was a doomed institution. The march of civilization was begun. How did I feel? Ah, you never could imagine it.

And Brer Merlin? His stock was flat again. Somehow, every time the magic of folderol tried conclusions with the magic of science, the magic of folderol got left.

CHAPTER 40

When I broke the back of knight-errantry that time, I no longer felt obliged to work in secret. So, the very next day I exposed my hidden schools, my mines, and my vast system of clandestine factories and workshops to an astonished world. That is to say, I exposed the nineteenth century to the inspection of the sixth.

Well, it is always a good plan to follow up an advantage promptly. The knights were temporarily down, but if I would keep them so I must just simply paralyze them—nothing short of that would answer. You see, I was "bluffing" that last time, in the field; it would be natural for them to work around to that conclusion, if I gave them a chance. So I must not give them time: and I didn't.

I renewed my challenge, engraved it on brass, posted it up where any priest could read it to them, and also kept it standing, in the advertising columns of the paper.

I not only renewed it, but added to its proportions. I said, name the day, and I would take fifty assistants and stand up *against the massed chivalry of the whole earth and destroy it.*

I was not bluffing this time. I meant what I said; I could do what I promised. There wasn't any way to misunderstand the language of that challenge. Even the dullest of the chivalry perceived that this was a plain case of "put up, or shut up." They were wise and did the latter. In all the next three years they gave me no trouble worth mentioning.

Consider the three years sped. Now look around on England. A happy and prosperous country, and strangely altered. Schools everywhere, and several colleges; a number of pretty good newspapers. Even authorship was taking a start; Sir Dinadan the Humorist was first in the field, with a volume of gray-headed jokes which I had been familiar with during thirteen centuries. If he had left out that old rancid one about the lecturer I wouldn't have said anything; but I couldn't stand that one. I suppressed the book and hanged the author.

Slavery was dead and gone; all men were equal before the law; taxation had been equalized. The telegraph, the telephone, the phonograph, the typewriter, the sewing machine, and all the thousand willing and handy servants of steam and electricity were working their way into favor. We had a steamboat or two on the Thames, we had steam warships, and the beginnings of a steam commercial marine; I was getting ready to send out an expedition to discover America.

We were building several lines of railway, and our line from Camelot to London was already finished and in operation. I was shrewd enough to make all offices connected with the passenger service places of high and distinguished honor. My idea was to attract the chivalry and nobility, and make them useful and keep them out of mischief. The plan worked very well, the competition for the places was hot. The conductor of the 4:33 express was a duke, there wasn't a passenger conductor on the line below the degree of earl. They were good men, every one, but they had two defects which I couldn't cure, and so had to wink at: they wouldn't lay aside their armor, and they would "knock down" fares—I mean rob the company.

There was hardly a knight in all the land who wasn't in some useful employment. They were going from end to end of the country in all manner of useful missionary capacities; their penchant for wandering, and their experience in it, made them altogether the most effective spreaders of civilization we had. They went clothed in steel and equipped with sword and lance and battle-ax, and if they couldn't persuade a

person to try a sewing machine on the installment plan, or a melodeon, or a barbed wire fence, or a prohibition journal, or any of the other thousand and one things they canvassed for, they removed him and passed on.

I was very happy. Things were working steadily toward a secretly longed-for point. You see, I had two schemes in my head which were the vastest of all my projects. The one was, to overthrow the Catholic Church and set up the Protestant faith on its ruins—not as an Established Church, but a go-as-you-please one; and the other project was, to get a decree issued by and by, commanding that upon Arthur's death unlimited suffrage should be introduced, and given to men and women alike—at any rate to all men, wise or unwise, and to all mothers who at middle age should be found to know nearly as much as their sons at twenty-one. Arthur was good for thirty years yet, he being about my own age—that is to say, forty—and I believed that in that time I could easily have the active part of the population of that day ready and eager for an event which should be the first of its kind in the history of the world—a rounded and complete governmental revolution without bloodshed. The result to be a republic. Well, I may as well confess, though I do feel ashamed when I think of it: I was beginning to have a base hankering to be its first president myself. Yes, there was more or less human nature in me; I found that out.

Clarence was with me as concerned the revolution, but in a modified way. His idea was a republic, without privileged orders but with a hereditary royal family at the head of it instead of an elective chief magistrate. He believed that no nation that had ever known the joy of worshiping a royal family could ever be robbed of it and not fade away and die of melancholy. I urged that kings were dangerous. He said, then have cats. He was sure that a royal family of cats would answer every purpose. They would be as useful as any other royal family, they would know as much, they would have the same virtues and the same treacheries, the same disposition to get up shindies with other royal cats, they would be laughably vain and absurd and never know it, they would be wholly inexpensive; finally, they would have as sound a divine right as any other royal house, and "Tom VII, or Tom XI, or Tom XIV by the grace of God King," would sound as well as it would when applied to the ordinary royal tomcat with tights on. "And as a rule," said he, in his neat modern English, "the character of these cats would be considerably above the character of the average king, and this would be an immense moral advantage to the nation, for the reason that a nation always models its morals after its monarch's. The worship of royalty being founded in unreason, these graceful and harmless cats would easily become as sacred as any other royalties, and indeed more so, because it would presently be noticed that they hanged nobody, beheaded nobody, imprisoned nobody, inflicted no cruelties or injustices of any sort, and so must be worthy of a deeper love and reverence than the customary human king, and would certainly get it. The eyes of the whole harried world would soon be fixed upon this humane and gentle system, and royal butchers would presently begin to disappear; their subjects would fill the vacancies with catlings from our own royal house; we should become a factory; we should supply the thrones of the world; within forty years all Europe would be governed by cats, and we should furnish the cats. The reign of universal peace would begin then, to end no more forever. . . . *Me-e-e-yow-ow-ow-ow—fzt—wow!*"

Hang him, I supposed he was in earnest, and was beginning to be persuaded by him,

until he exploded that cathowl and startled me almost out of my clothes. But he never could be in earnest. He didn't know what it was. He had pictured a distinct and perfectly rational and feasible improvement upon constitutional monarchy, but he was too featherheaded to know it, or care anything about it, either. I was going to give him a scolding, but Sandy came flying in at that moment, wild with terror, and so choked with sobs that for a minute she could not get her voice. I ran and took her in my arms, and lavished caresses upon her and said, beseechingly:

"Speak, darling, speak! What is it?"

Her head fell limp upon my bosom, and she gasped, almost inaudibly:

"Hello-Central!"

"Quick!" I shouted to Clarence; "telephone the king's homeopath to come!"

In two minutes I was kneeling by the child's crib, and Sandy was dispatching servants here, there, and everywhere, all over the palace. I took in the situation almost at a glance—membranous croup! I bent down and whispered:

"Wake up, sweetheart! Hello-Central!"

She opened her soft eyes languidly, and made out to say—

"Papa."

That was a comfort. She was far from dead, yet. I sent for preparations of sulphur, I rousted out the croup kettle myself; for I don't sit down and wait for doctors when Sandy or the child is sick. I knew how to nurse both of them, and had had experience. This little chap had lived in my arms a good part of its small life, and often I could soothe away its troubles and get it to laugh through the tear-dews on its eyelashes when even its mother couldn't.

Sir Launcelot, in his richest armor, came striding along the great hall, now, on his way to the stock board; he was president of the stock board, and occupied the Siege Perilous, which he had bought of Sir Galahad; for the stock board consisted of the Knights of the Round Table, and they used the Round Table for business purposes, now. Seats at it were worth—well, you would never believe the figure, so it is no use to state it. Sir Launcelot was a bear, and he had put up a corner in one of the new lines, and was just getting ready to squeeze the shorts today; but what of that? He was the same old Launcelot, and when he glanced in as he was passing the door and found out that his pet was sick, that was enough for him; bulls and bears might fight it out their own way for all him, he would come right in here and stand by little Hello-Central for all he was worth. And that was what he did. He shied his helmet into the corner, and in half a minute he had a new wick in the alcohol lamp and was firing up on the croup kettle. By this time Sandy had built a blanket canopy over the crib, and everything was ready.

Sir Launcelot got up steam, he and I loaded up the kettle with unslaked lime and carbolic acid, with a touch of lactic acid added thereto, then filled the thing up with water and inserted the steam spout under the canopy. Everything was shipshape, now, and we sat down on either side of the crib to stand our watch. Sandy was so grateful and so comforted that she charged a couple of churchwardens with willow-bark and sumac tobacco for us, and told us to smoke as much as we pleased, it couldn't get under the canopy, and she was used to smoke, being the first lady in the land who had ever seen a cloud blown. Well, there couldn't be a more contented or comfortable sight than Sir Launcelot in his noble armor sitting in gracious serenity at the end of a yard of snowy churchwarden. He was a beautiful man, a lovely man, and was just intended to make a wife and children happy. But of course, Guenever— however, it's no use to cry over what's done and can't be helped.

Well, he stood watch and watch with me, right straight through, for three days and nights, till the child was out of danger; then he took her up in his great arms and kissed her, with his plumes falling about her golden head, then laid her softly in Sandy's lap again and took his stately way down the vast hall, between the ranks of admiring men-at-arms and menials, and so disappeared. And no instinct warned me that I should never look upon him again in this world! Lord, what a world of heart-break it is.

The doctors said we must take the child away, if we would coax her back to health and strength again. And she must have sea air. So we took a man-of-war, and a suite of two hundred and sixty persons, and went cruising about, and after a fortnight of this we stepped ashore on the French coast, and the doctors thought it would be a good idea to make something of a stay there. The little king of that region offered us his hospitalities, and we were glad to accept. If he had had as many conveniences as he lacked, we should have been plenty comfortable enough; even as it was, we made out very well, in his queer old castle, by the help of comforts and luxuries from the ship.

At the end of a month I sent the vessel home for fresh supplies, and for news. We expected her back in three or four days. She would bring me, along with other news, the result of a certain experiment which I had been starting. It was a project of mine to replace the tournament with something which might furnish an escape for the extra steam of the chivalry, keep those bucks entertained and out of mischief, and at the same time preserve the best thing in them, which was their hardy spirit of emulation. I had had a choice band of them in private training for some time, and the date was now arriving for their first public effort.

This experiment was baseball. In order to give the thing vogue from the start, and place it out of the reach of criticism, I chose my nines by rank, not capacity. There wasn't a knight in either team who wasn't a sceptered sovereign. As for material of this sort, there was a glut of it, always, around Arthur. You couldn't throw a brick in any direction and not cripple a king. Of course I couldn't get these people to leave off their armor; they wouldn't do that when they bathed. They consented to differentiate the armor so that a body could tell one team from the other, but that was the most they would do. So, one of the teams wore chain-mail ulsters, and the other wore plate armor made of my new Bessemer steel. Their practice in the field was the most fantastic thing I ever saw. Being ballproof, they never skipped out of the way, but stood still and took the result; when a Bessemer was at the bat and a ball hit him, it would bound a hundred and fifty yards, sometimes. And when a man was running, and threw himself on his stomach to slide to his base, it was like an ironclad coming into port. At first I appointed men of no rank to act as umpires, but I had to discontinue that. These people were no easier to please than other nines. The umpire's first decision was usually his last; they broke him in two with a bat, and his friends toted him home on a shutter. When it was noticed that no umpire ever survived a game, umpiring got to be un-popular. So I was obliged to appoint somebody whose rank and lofty position under the government would protect him.

Here are the names of the nines:

BESSEMERS.

KING ARTHUR.
KING LOT OF LOTHIAN.
KING OF NORTHGALIS.
KING MARSIL.
KING OF LITTLE BRITAIN.
KING LABOR.
KING PELLAM OF LISTENGESE.
KING BADGEMAGUS.
KING TOLLEME LA FEINTES.

ULSTERS

EMPEROR LUCIUS.
KING LOGRIS.
KING MARHALT OF IRELAND.
KING MORGANORE.
KING MARK OF CORNWALL.
KING NENTRES OF GARLOT.
KING MELIODAS OF LIONES.
KING OF THE LAKE.
THE SOWDAN OF SYRIA.

Umpire—CLARENCE

The first public game would certainly draw fifty thousand people; and for solid fun would be worth going around the world to see. Everything would be favorable; it was balmy and beautiful spring weather, now, and Nature was all tailored out in her new clothes.

FOR DISCUSSION

1. Show how Mark Twain uses incongruity, exaggeration, and understatement to make the description of his "baseball experiment" humorous.

2. In the fight with Sir Sagramor, what larger goal does the Yankee seek beyond defeating his opponent? What techniques enable him to overcome the knights' strength and Merlin's trickery?

3. On what basis can the Yankee boast that "The march of civilization was begun"? How does he persuade the knights to leave him in peace, the nobility to become passenger conductors, and the country people to try his new inventions?

4. "I had two schemes in my head which were the vastest of all my projects." Explain what the Yankee's schemes are, and why he thinks them most important.

5. Clarence presents an ironic scheme for a royal family of cats. What "advantages" would they offer over human rulers? What is Mark Twain satirizing through this proposal?

CHAPTER 41

However, my attention was suddenly snatched from such matters; our child began to lose ground again, and we had to go to sitting up with her, her case became so serious. We couldn't bear to allow anybody to help, in this service, so we two stood watch and watch, day in and day out. Ah, Sandy, what a right heart she had, how simple, and genuine, and good she was! She was a flawless wife and mother; and yet I had married her for no particular reason, except that by the customs of chivalry she was my property until some knight should win her from me in the field. She had hunted Britain over for me; had found me at the hanging-bout outside of London, and had straightway resumed her old place at my side in the placidest way and as of right. I was a New Englander, and in my opinion this sort of partnership would compromise her, sooner or later. She couldn't see how, but I cut argument short and we had a wedding.

Now I didn't know I was drawing a prize, yet that was what I did draw. Within the twelvemonth I became her worshiper; and ours was the dearest and perfectest comradeship that ever was. People talk about beautiful friendships between two persons of the same sex. What is the best of that sort, as compared with the friendship of man and wife, where the best impulses and highest ideals of both are the same? There is no place for comparison between the two friendships; the one is earthly, the other divine.

In my dreams, along at first, I still wandered thirteen centuries away, and my unsatisfied spirit went calling and harking all up and down the unreplying vacancies of a vanished world. Many a time Sandy heard that imploring cry come from my lips in my sleep. With a grand magnanimity she saddled that cry of mine upon our child, conceiving it to be the name of some lost darling of mine. It touched me to tears, and it also nearly knocked me off my feet, too, when she smiled up in my face for an earned reward, and played her quaint and pretty surprise upon me:

"The name of one who was dear to thee is here preserved, here made holy, and the music of it will abide always in our ears. Now thou'll kiss me, as knowing the name I have given the child."

But I didn't know it, all the same. I hadn't an idea in the world; but it would have been cruel to confess it and spoil her pretty game; so I never let on, but said:

"Yes, I know, sweetheart—how dear and good it is of you, too! But I want to hear these lips of yours, which are also mine, utter it first—then its music will be perfect."

Pleased to the marrow, she murmured—

"Hello-Central!"

I didn't laugh—I am always thankful for that—but the strain ruptured every cartilage in me, and for weeks afterward I could hear my bones clack when I walked. She never found out her mistake. The first time she heard that form of salute used at the telephone she was surprised; and not pleased; but I told her I had given order for it: that henceforth and forever the telephone must always be invoked with that reverent formality, in perpetual honor and remembrance of my lost friend and her small namesake. This was not true. But it answered.

Well, during two weeks and a half we watched by the crib, and in our deep solicitude we were unconscious of any world outside of that sickroom. Then our reward came: the center of the universe turned the corner and began to mend. Grateful? It isn't the term. There *isn't* any term for it. You know that, yourself, if you've watched your child through the Valley of the Shadow and seen it come back to life and sweep night out of the earth with one all-illuminating smile that you could cover with your hand.

Why, we were back in this world in one instant! Then we looked the same startled thought into each other's eyes at the same moment: more than two weeks gone, and that ship not back yet!

In another minute I appeared in the presence of my train. They had been steeped in troubled bodings all this time—their faces showed it. I called an escort and we galloped five miles to a hilltop overlooking the sea. Where was my great commerce that so lately had made these glistering expanses populous and beautiful with its white-winged flocks? Vanished, every one! Not a sail, from verge to verge, not a smoke bank—just a dead and empty solitude, in place of all that brisk and breezy life.

I went swiftly back, saying not a word to anybody. I told Sandy this ghastly news. We could imagine no explanation that would begin to explain. Had there been an invasion? An earthquake? A pestilence? Had the nation been swept out of existence? But guessing was profitless. I must go—at once. I borrowed the king's navy—a "ship" no bigger than a steam launch—and was soon ready.

The parting—ah, yes, that was hard. As I was devouring the child with last kisses, it brisked up and jabbered out its vocabulary—the first time in more than two weeks, and it made fools of us for joy. The darling mispronunciations of childhood! Dear me, there's no music that can touch it; and how one grieves when it wastes away and dissolves into correctness, knowing it will never visit his bereaved ear again. Well, how good it was to be able to carry that gracious memory away with me!

I approached England the next morning, with the wide highway of salt water all to myself. There were ships in the harbor, at Dover, but they were naked as to sails, and there was no sign of life about them. It was Sunday; yet at Canterbury the streets were empty; strangest of all, there was not even a priest in sight, and no stroke of a bell fell upon my ear. The mournfulness of death was everywhere. I couldn't understand it. At last, in the further edge of that town I saw a small funeral procession—just a family and a few friends following a coffin—no priest; a funeral without bell, book, or candle; there was a church there, close at hand, but they passed by it, weeping, and did not enter it; I glanced up at the belfry, and there hung the bell, shrouded in black, and its tongue tied back. Now I knew! Now I understood the stupendous calamity that had overtaken England. Invasion? Invasion is a triviality to it. It was the INTERDICT!

I asked no questions; I didn't need to ask

any. The Church had struck; the thing for me to do was to get into a disguise, and go warily. One of my servants gave me a suit of his clothes, and when we were safe beyond the town I put them on, and from that time I traveled alone; I could not risk the embarrassment of company.

A miserable journey. A desolate silence everywhere. Even in London itself. Traffic had ceased; men did not talk or laugh, or go in groups, or even in couples; they moved aimlessly about, each man by himself, with his head down, and woe and terror at his heart. The Tower showed recent war scars. Verily, much had been happening.

Of course I meant to take the train for Camelot. Train! Why, the station was as vacant as a cavern. I moved on. The journey to Camelot was a repetition of what I had already seen. The Monday and the Tuesday differed in no way from the Sunday. I arrived, far in the night. From being the best electric-lighted town in the kingdom and the most like a recumbent sun of anything you ever saw, it was become simply a blot—a blot upon darkness—that is to say, it was darker and solider than the rest of the darkness, and so you could see it a little better; it made me feel as if maybe it was symbolical—a sort of sign that the Church was going to *keep* the upper hand, now, and snuff out all my beautiful civilization just like that. I found no life stirring in the somber streets. I groped my way with a heavy heart. The vast castle loomed black upon the hilltop, not a spark visible about it. The drawbridge was down, the great gate stood wide, I entered without challenge, my own heels making the only sound I heard—and it was sepulchral enough, in those huge vacant courts.

CHAPTER 42

I found Clarence, alone in his quarters, drowned in melancholy; and in place of the electric light, he had reinstituted the ancient rag-lamp, and sat there in a grisly twilight with all curtains drawn tight. He sprang up and rushed for me eagerly, saying:

"Oh, it's worth a billion milrays to look upon a live person again!"

He knew me as easily as if I hadn't been disguised at all. Which frightened me; one may easily believe that.

"Quick, now, tell me the meaning of this fearful disaster," I said. "How did it come about?"

"Well, if there hadn't been any Queen Guenever, it wouldn't have come so early; but it would have come, anyway. It would have come on your own account, by and by; by luck, it happened to come on the queen's."

"*And* Sir Launcelot's?"

"Just so."

"Give me the details."

"I reckon you will grant that during some years there has been only one pair of eyes in these kingdoms that has not been looking steadily askance at the queen and Sir Launcelot—"

"Yes, King Arthur's."

"—and only one heart that was without suspicion—"

"Yes—the king's; a heart that isn't capable of thinking evil of a friend."

"Well, the king might have gone on, still happy and unsuspecting, to the end of his days, but for one of your modern improvements—the stock board. When you left, three miles of the London, Canterbury and Dover were ready for the rails, and also ready and ripe for manipulation in the stock market. It was wildcat, and everybody knew it. The stock was for sale at a giveaway. What does Sir Launcelot do, but—"

"Yes, I know; he quietly picked up nearly all of it, for a song; then he bought about twice as much more, deliverable upon call; and he was about to call when I left."

"Very well, he did call. The boys couldn't deliver. Oh, he had them—and he just settled his grip and squeezed them. They were laughing in their sleeves over their smartness in selling stock to him at fifteen and sixteen and along there, that wasn't worth ten. Well, when they had laughed long enough on that side of their mouths, they rested up that side by shifting the laugh to the other side. That was when they compromised with the Invincible at two hundred eighty-three!"

"Good land!"

"He skinned them alive, and they deserved it—anyway, the whole kingdom rejoiced. Well, among the flayed were Sir Agravaine and Sir Mordred, nephews to the king. End of the first act. Act second, scene first, an apartment in Carlisle castle, where the court had gone for a few days' hunting. Persons present, the whole tribe of the king's nephews. Mordred and Agravaine propose to call the guileless Arthur's attention to Guenever and Sir Launcelot. Sir Gawaine, Sir Gareth, and Sir Gaheris will have nothing to do with it. A dispute ensues, with loud talk; in the midst of it, enter the king. Mordred and Agravaine spring their devastating tale upon him. *Tableau.* A trap is laid for Launcelot, by the king's command, and Sir Launcelot walks into it. He made it sufficiently uncomfortable for the ambushed witnesses—

to wit, Mordred, Agravaine, and twelve knights of lesser rank, for he killed every one of them but Mordred; but of course that couldn't straighten matters between Launcelot and the king, and didn't."

"Oh, dear, only one thing could result— I see that. War, and the knights of the realm divided into a king's party and a Sir Launcelot's party."

"Yes—that was the way of it. The king sent the queen to the stake, proposing to purify her with fire. Launcelot and his knights rescued her, and in doing it slew certain good old friends of yours and mine —in fact, some of the best we ever had, to wit: Sir Belias le Orgulous, Sir Segwarides, Sir Griflet le Fils de Dieu, Sir Brandiles, Sir Aglovale—"

"Oh, you tear out my heartstrings."

"—wait, I'm not done yet—Sir Tor, Sir Gauter, Sir Gillimer—"

"The very best man in my subordinate nine. What a handy right fielder he was!"

"—Sir Reynolds three brothers, Sir Damus, Sir Priamus, Sir Kay the Stranger—"

"My peerless shortstop! I've seen him catch a daisy cutter in his teeth. Come, I can't stand this!"

"—Sir Driant, Sir Lambegus, Sir Herminde, Sir Pertilope, Sir Perimones, and —whom do you think?"

"Rush! Go on."

"Sir Gaheris, and Sir Gareth—both!"

"Oh, incredible! Their love for Launcelot was indestructible."

"Well, it was an accident. They were simply onlookers; they were unarmed, and were merely there to witness the queen's punishment. Sir Launcelot smote down whoever came in the way of his blind fury, and he killed these without noticing who they were. Here is an instantaneous photograph one of our boys got of the battle; it's for sale on every newsstand. There—the figures nearest the queen are Sir Launcelot with his sword up, and Sir Gareth gasping his last breath. You can catch the agony in the queen's face through the curling smoke. It's a rattling battle picture."

"Indeed it is. We must take good care of it; its historical value is incalculable. Go on."

"Well, the rest of the tale is just war, pure and simple. Launcelot retreated to his town and castle of Joyous Gard, and gathered there a great following of knights. The king, with a great host, went there, and there was desperate fighting during several days, and as a result, all the plain around was paved with corpses and cast iron. Then the Church patched up a peace between Arthur and Launcelot and the queen and everybody—everybody but Sir Gawaine. He was bitter about the slaying of his brothers, Gareth and Gaheris, and would not be appeased. He notified Launcelot to get him thence, and make swift preparation, and look to be soon attacked. So Launcelot sailed to his Duchy of Guienne, with his following, and Gawaine soon followed, with an army, and he beguiled Arthur to go with him. Arthur left the kingdom in Sir Mordred's hands until you should return—"

"Ah—a king's customary wisdom!"

"Yes. Sir Mordred set himself at once to work to make his kingship permanent. He was going to marry Guenever, as a first move; but she fled and shut herself up in the Tower of London. Mordred attacked; the Bishop of Canterbury dropped down on him with the Interdict. The king returned; Mordred fought him at Dover, at Canterbury, and again at Barnham Down. Then there was talk of peace and a composition. Terms, Mordred to have Cornwall and Kent during Arthur's life, and the whole kingdom afterward."

"Well, upon my word! My dream of a republic to *be* a dream, and so remain."

"Yes. The two armies lay near Salisbury. Gawaine—Gawaine's head is at Dover Castle, he fell in the fight there—Gawaine appeared to Arthur in a dream, at least his ghost did, and warned him to refrain from conflict for a month, let the delay cost what it might. But battle was precipitated by an accident. Arthur had given order that if a sword was raised during the consultation over the proposed treaty with Mordred, sound the trumpet and fall on! for he had no confidence in Mordred. Mordred had given a similar order to *his* people. Well, by and by an adder bit a knight's heel; the knight forgot all about the order, and made a slash at the adder with his sword. Inside of half a minute those two prodigious hosts came together with a crash! They butchered away all day. Then the king—however, we have started something fresh since you left —our paper has."

"Yes, the paper was booming right along, for the Interdict made no impression, got no grip, while the war lasted. I had war correspondents with both armies. I will finish that battle by reading you what one of the boys says:

Then the king looked about him, and then was he ware of all his host and of all his good knights were left no more on live but two knights, that was Sir Lucan de Butlere, and his brother Sir Bedivere: and they were full sore wounded. Jesu mercy, said the king, where are all my noble knights becomen? Alas that ever I should see this doleful day. For now, said Arthur, I am come to mine end. But would to God that I wist where were that traitor Sir Mordred, that hath caused all this mischief. Then was King Arthur ware where Sir Mordred leaned upon his sword among a great heap of dead men. Now give me my spear, said Arthur unto Sir Lucan, for yonder I have espied the traitor that all this woe hath wrought. Sir, let him be, said Sir Lucan, for he is unhappy; and if ye pass this unhappy

day, ye shall be right well revenged upon him.
Good lord, remember ye of your night's dream,
and what the spirit of Sir Gawaine told you
this night, yet God of his great goodness hath
preserved you hitherto. Therefore, for God's
sake, my lord, leave off by this. For blessed be
God ye have won the field: for here we be
three on live, and with Sir Mordred is none
on live. And if ye leave off now, this wicked
day of destiny is past. Tide me death, betide
me life, saith the king, now I see him yonder
alone, he shall never escape mine hands, for
at a better avail shall I never have him. God
speed you well, said Sir Bedivere. Then the
king gat his spear in both his hands, and ran
toward Sir Mordred, crying, Traitor, now is
thy death day come. And when Sir Mordred
heard Sir Arthur, he ran until him with his
sword drawn in his hand. And then King
Arthur smote Sir Mordred under the shield,
with a foin of his spear throughout the body
more than a fathom. And when Sir Mordred
felt that he had his death's wound, he thrust
himself, with the might that he had, up to the
butt of King Arthur's spear. And right so he
smote his father Arthur with his sword holden
in both his hands, on the side of the head,
that the sword pierced the helmet and the
brain-pan, and therewithal Sir Mordred fell
stark dead to the earth. And the noble Arthur
fell in a swoon to the earth, and there he
swooned ofttimes."

"That is a good piece of war correspon-
dence, Clarence; you are a first-rate newspaper man. Well—is the king all right?
Did he get well?"

"Poor soul, no. He is dead."

I was utterly stunned; it had not seemed
to me that any wound could be mortal to
him.

"And the queen, Clarence?"

"She is a nun, in Almesbury."

"What changes! and in such a short
while. It is inconceivable. What next, I
wonder?"

"I can tell you what next."

"Well?"

"Stake our lives and stand by them!"

"What do you mean by that?"

"The Church is master, now. The Interdict included you with Mordred; it is not
to be removed while you remain alive. The
clans are gathering. The Church has gathered all the knights that are left alive, and
as soon as you are discovered we shall have
business on our hands."

"Stuff! With our deadly scientific war
material; with our hosts of trained—"

"Save your breath—we haven't sixty
faithful left!"

"What are you saying? Our schools, our
colleges, our vast workshops, our—"

"When those knights come, those estab-
lishments will empty themselves and go
over to the enemy. Did you think you had
educated the superstition out of those
people?"

"I certainly did think it."

"Well, then you may unthink it. They
stood every strain easily—until the Interdict. Since then, they merely put on a bold
outside—at heart they are quaking. Make
up your mind to it—when the armies come,
the mask will fall."

"It's hard news. We are lost. They will
turn our own science against us."

"No they won't."

"Why?"

"Because I and a handful of the faithful
have blocked that game. I'll tell you what
I've done, and what moved me to it. Smart
as you are, the Church was smarter. It was
the Church that sent you cruising—through
her servants the doctors."

"Clarence!"

"It is the truth. I know it. Every officer
of your ship was the Church's picked servant, and so was every man of the crew."

"Oh, come!"

"It is just as I tell you. I did not find out
these things at once, but I found them out
finally. Did you send me verbal information, by the commander of the ship, to the
effect that upon his return to you, with

supplies, you were going to leave Cadiz—"

"Cadiz! I haven't been at Cadiz at all!"

"—going to leave Cadiz and cruise in distant seas indefinitely, for the health of your family? Did you send me that word?"

"Of course not. I would have written, wouldn't I?"

"Naturally. I was troubled and suspicious. When the commander sailed again I managed to ship a spy with him. I have never heard of vessel or spy since. I gave myself two weeks to hear from you in. Then I resolved to send a ship to Cadiz. There was a reason why I didn't."

"What was that?"

"Our navy had suddenly and mysteriously disappeared! Also as suddenly and as mysteriously, the railway and telegraph and telephone service ceased, the men all deserted, poles were cut down, the Church laid a ban upon the electric light! I had to be up and doing—and straight off. Your life was safe—nobody in these kingdoms but Merlin would venture to touch such a magician as you without ten thousand men at his back—I had nothing to think of but how to put preparations in the best trim against your coming. I felt safe myself—nobody would be anxious to touch a pet of yours. So this is what I did. From our various works I selected all the men—boys I mean—whose faithfulness under whatsoever pressure I could swear to, and I called them together secretly and gave them their instructions. There are fifty-two of them; none younger than fourteen, and none above seventeen years old."

"Why did you select boys?"

"Because all the others were born in an atmosphere of superstition and reared in it. It is in their blood and bones. We imagined we had educated it out of them; they thought so, too; the Interdict woke them up like a thunderclap! It revealed them to themselves, and it revealed them to me, too. With boys it was different. Such as have

been under our training from seven to ten years and have had no acquaintance with the Church's terrors, and it was among these that I found my fifty-two. As a next move, I paid a private visit to that old cave of Merlin's—not the small one—the big one—"

"Yes, the one where we secretly established our first great electric plant when I was projecting a miracle."

"Just so. And as that miracle hadn't become necessary then, I thought it might be a good idea to utilize the plant now. I've provisioned the cave for a siege—"

"A good idea, a first rate idea."

"I think so. I placed four of my boys there, as a guard—inside, and out of sight. Nobody was to be hurt—while outside; but any attempt to enter—well, we said just let anybody try it! Then I went out into the hills and uncovered and cut the secret wires which connected your bedroom with the wires that go to the dynamite deposits under all our vast factories, mills, workshops, magazines, etc., and about midnight I and my boys turned out and connected that wire with the cave, and nobody but you and I suspects where the other end of it goes to. We laid it under ground, of course, and it was all finished in a couple of hours or so. We shan't have to leave our fortress, now, when we want to blow up our civilization."

"It was the right move—and the natural one; a military necessity, in the changed condition of things. Well, what changes *have* come! We expected to be besieged in the palace some time or other, but—however, go on."

"Next, we built a wire fence."

"Wire fence?"

"Yes. You dropped the hint of it yourself, two or three years ago."

"Oh, I remember—the time the Church tried her strength against us for the first time, and presently thought it wise to wait for a hopefuler season. Well, how have you arranged the fence?"

"I start twelve immensely strong wires —naked, not insulated—from a big dynamo in the cave—dynamo with no brushes except a positive and a negative one—"

"Yes, that's right."

"The wires go out from the cave and fence-in a circle of level ground a hundred yards in diameter; they make twelve independent fences, ten feet apart—that is to say, twelve circles within circles—and their ends come into the cave again."

"Right; go on."

"The fences are fastened to heavy oaken posts only three feet apart, and these posts are sunk five feet in the ground."

"That is good and strong."

"Yes. The wires have no ground connection outside of the cave. They go out from the positive brush of the dynamo; there is a ground connection through the negative brush; the other ends of the wire return to the cave, and each is grounded independently."

"No-no, that won't do!"

"Why?"

"It's too expensive—uses up force for nothing. You don't want any ground connection except the one through the negative brush. The other end of every wire must be brought back into the cave and fastened independently, and *without* any ground connection. Now, then, observe the economy of it. A cavalry charge hurls itself against the fence; you are using no power, you are spending no money, for there is only one ground connection till those horses come against the wire; the moment they touch it they form a connection with the negative brush *through the ground*, and drop dead. Don't you see— you are using no energy until it is needed; your lightning is there, and ready, like the load in a gun; but it isn't costing you a cent till you touch it off. Oh, yes, the single ground connection—"

"Of course! I don't know how I overlooked that. It's not only cheaper, but it's more effectual than the other way, for if wires break or get tangled, no harm is done."

"No, especially if we have a telltale in the cave and disconnect the broken wire. Well, go on. The gatlings?"

"Yes—that's arranged. In the center of the inner circle, on a spacious platform six feet high, I've grouped a battery of thirteen gatling guns, and provided plenty of ammunition."

"That's it. They command every approach, and when the Church's knights arrive, there's going to be music. The brow of the precipice over the cave—"

"I've got a wire fence there, and a gatling. They won't drop any rocks down on us."

"Well, and the glass-cylinder dynamite torpedoes?"

"That's attended to. It's the prettiest garden that was ever planted. It's a belt forty feet wide, and goes around the outer fence—distance between it and the fence one hundred yards—kind of neutral ground, that space is. There isn't a single square yard of that whole belt but is equipped with a torpedo. We laid them on the surface of the ground, and sprinkled a layer of sand over them. It's an innocent looking garden, but you let a man start in to hoe it once, and you'll see."

"You tested the torpedoes?"

"Well, I was going to, but—"

"But what? Why, it's an immense oversight not to apply a—"

"Test? Yes, I know; but they're all right; I laid a few in the public road beyond our lines and they've been tested."

"Oh, that alters the case. Who did it?"

"A Church committee."

"How kind!"

"Yes. They came to command us to make submission. You see they didn't really come to test the torpedoes; that was merely an incident."

"Did the committee make a report?"

"Yes, they made one. You could have heard it a mile."

"Unanimous?"

"That was the nature of it. After that I put up some signs, for the protection of future committees, and we have had no intruders since."

"Clarence, you've done a world of work, and done it perfectly."

"We had plenty of time for it; there wasn't any occasion for hurry."

We sat silent awhile, thinking. Then my mind was made up, and I said:

"Yes, everything is ready; everything is shipshape, no detail is wanting. I know what to do, now."

"So do I: sit down and wait."

"No, *sir!* rise up and *strike!*"

"Do you mean it?"

"Yes, indeed! The *defensive* isn't in my line, and the *offensive* is. That is, when I hold a fair hand—two-thirds as good a hand as the enemy. Oh, yes, we'll rise up and strike; that's our game."

"A hundred to one, you are right. When does the performance begin?"

"*Now!* We'll proclaim the Republic."

"Well, that *will* precipitate things, sure enough!"

"It will make them buzz, *I* tell you! England will be a hornet's nest before noon tomorrow, if the Church's hand hasn't lost

its cunning—and we know it hasn't. Now you write and I'll dictate—thus:

PROCLAMATION.

BE IT KNOWN UNTO ALL. Whereas the king having died and left no heir, it becomes my duty to continue the executive authority vested in me, until a government shall have been created and set in motion. The monarchy has lapsed, it no longer exists. By consequence, all political power has reverted to its original source, the people of the nation. With the monarchy, its several adjuncts died also; wherefore there is no longer a nobility, no longer a privileged class, no longer an Established Church: all men are become exactly equal, they are upon one common level, and religion is free. *A Republic is hereby proclaimed*, as being the natural estate of a nation when other authority has ceased. It is the duty of the British people to meet together immediately, and by their votes elect representatives and deliver into their hands the government.

I signed it "The Boss," and dated it from Merlin's Cave. Clarence said:

"Why, that tells where we are, and invites them to call right away."

"That is the idea. We *strike*—by the Proclamation—then it's their innings. Now have the thing set up and printed and posted, right off; that is, give the order; then, if you've got a couple of bicycles handy at the foot of the hill, ho for Merlin's Cave!"

"I shall be ready in ten minutes. What a cyclone there is going to be tomorrow when this piece of paper gets to work! . . . It's a pleasant old palace, this is; I wonder if we shall ever again—but never mind about that."

FOR DISCUSSION

1. Review the series of events beginning with Sir Launcelot's killing on the stock market and ending with the Yankee's proclamation of a Republic. How was the Church able to destroy the Yankee's civilization so easily? Why didn't the people resist?

2. What is Clarence's plan of defense? How had the Church Committee helped him with his preparations?

3. How has the Yankee's attitude toward Sandy changed since their first meeting? What is responsible for the change? Explain how their child came to have the incongruous name "Hello-Central."

CHAPTER 43

In Merlin's Cave—Clarence and I and fifty-two fresh, bright, well-educated, clean-minded young British boys. At dawn I sent an order to the factories and to all our great works to stop operations and remove all life to a safe distance, as everything was going to be blown up by secret mines, *"and no telling at what moment—therefore, vacate at once."* These people knew me, and had confidence in my word. They would clear out without waiting to part their hair, and I could take my own time about dating the explosion. You couldn't hire one of them to go back during the century, if the explosion was still impending.

We had a week of waiting. It was not dull for me, because I was writing all the time. During the first three days, I finished turning my old diary into this narrative form; it only required a chapter or so to bring it down to date. The rest of the week I took up in writing letters to my wife. It was always my habit to write to Sandy every day, whenever we were separate, and now I kept up the habit for love of it, and of her, though I couldn't do anything with the letters, of course, after I had written them. But it put in the time, you see, and was almost like talking; it was almost as if I was saying, "Sandy, if you and Hello-Central were here in the cave, instead of only your photographs, what good times we could have!" And then, you know, I could imagine the baby goo-gooing something out in reply, with its fists in its mouth and itself stretched across its mother's lap on its back, and she a-laughing and admiring and worshiping, and now and then tickling under the baby's chin to set it cackling, and then maybe throwing in a word of answer to me herself—and so on and so on—well, don't you know, I could sit there in the cave with my pen, and keep it up, that way, by the hour with them. Why, it was almost like having us all together again.

I had spies out, every night, of course, to get news. Every report made things look more and more impressive. The hosts were gathering, gathering; down all the roads and paths of England the knights were riding, and priests rode with them, to hearten these original Crusaders, this being the Church's war. All the nobilities, big and little, were on their way, and all the gentry. This was all as was expected. We should thin out this sort of folk to such a degree that the people would have nothing to do but just step to the front with their republic and—

Ah, what a donkey I was! Toward the end of the week I began to get this large and disenchanting fact through my head: that the mass of the nation had swung their caps and shouted for the republic for about one day, and there an end! The Church, the nobles, and the gentry then turned one grand, all-disapproving frown upon them and shriveled them into sheep! From that moment the sheep had begun to gather to the fold—that is to say, the camps—and offer their valueless lives and their valuable wool to the "righteous cause." Why, even the very men who had lately been slaves were in the "righteous cause," and glorifying it, praying for it, sentimentally slabbering over it, just like all the other commoners. Imagine such human muck as this; conceive of this folly!

Yes, it was now "Death to the Republic!" everywhere—not a dissenting voice. All England was marching against us! Truly this was more than I had bargained for.

I watched my fifty-two boys narrowly; watched their faces, their walk, their unconscious attitudes: for all these are a language—a language given us purposely that it may betray us in times of emergency, when we have secrets which we want to keep. I knew that that thought would keep saying itself over and over again in their minds and hearts, *All England is marching against us!* and evermore strenuously imploring attention with each repetition, ever more sharply realizing itself to their imaginations, until even in their sleep they would find no rest from it, but hear the vague and flitting creatures of their dreams say, *All England*—ALL ENGLAND—*is marching against you!* I knew all this would happen; I knew that ultimately the pressure would become so great that it would compel utterance; therefore, I must be ready with an answer at that time—an answer well chosen and tranquilizing.

I was right. The time came. They *had* to speak. Poor lads, it was pitiful to see, they were so pale, so worn, so troubled. At first their spokesman could hardly find voice or words; but he presently got both. This is what he said—and he put it in the neat modern English taught him in my schools:

"We have tried to forget what we are—English boys! We have tried to put reason before sentiment, duty before love; our minds approve, but our hearts reproach us.

While apparently it was only the nobility, only the gentry, only the twenty-five or thirty thousand knights left alive out of the late wars, we were of one mind, and undisturbed by any troubling doubt; each and every one of these fifty-two lads who stand here before you, said, 'They have chosen—it is their affair.' But think—the matter is altered—*all England is marching against us!* Oh, sir, consider! Reflect! These people are our people, they are bone of our bone, flesh of our flesh, we love them—do not ask us to destroy our nation!"

Well, it shows the value of looking ahead, and being ready for a thing when it happens. If I hadn't foreseen this thing and been fixed, that boy would have had me—I couldn't have said a word. But I *was* fixed. I said:

"My boys, your hearts are in the right place, you have thought the worthy thought, you have done the worthy thing. You are English boys, you will remain English boys, and you will keep that name unsmirched. Give yourselves no further concern, let your minds be at peace. Consider this: while all England *is* marching against us, who is in the van? Who, by the commonest rules of war, will march in the front? Answer me."

"The mounted host of mailed knights."

"True. They are 30,000 strong. Acres deep, they will march. Now, observe: none but *they* will ever strike the sand belt! Then there will be an episode! Immediately after, the civilian multitude in the rear will retire, to meet business engagements elsewhere. None but nobles and gentry are knights, and *none but these* will remain to dance to our music after that episode. It is absolutely true that we shall have to fight nobody but these thirty thousand knights. Now speak, and it shall be as you decide. Shall we avoid the battle, retire from the field?"

"NO!!!"

The shout was unanimous and hearty.

"Are you—are you—well, afraid of these thirty thousand knights?"

That joke brought out a good laugh, the boys' troubles vanished away, and they went gaily to their posts. Ah, they were a darling fifty-two! As pretty as girls, too.

I was ready for the enemy, now. Let the approaching big day come along— it would find us on deck.

The big day arrived on time. At dawn the sentry on watch in the corral came into the cave and reported a moving black mass under the horizon, and a faint sound which he thought to be military music. Breakfast was just ready; we sat down and ate it.

This over, I made the boys a little speech, and then sent out a detail to man the battery, with Clarence in command of it.

The sun rose presently and sent its unobstructed splendors over the land, and we saw a prodigious host moving slowly toward us, with the steady drift and aligned front of a wave of the sea. Nearer and nearer it came, and more and more sublimely imposing became its aspect; yes, all England were there, apparently. Soon we could see the innumerable banners fluttering, and then the sun struck the sea of armor and set it all a-flash. Yes, it was a fine sight; I hadn't ever seen anything to beat it.

At last we could make out details. All the front ranks, no telling how many acres deep, were horsemen—plumed knights in armor. Suddenly we heard the blare of trumpets; the slow walk burst into a gallop, and then—well, it was wonderful to see! Down swept that vast horseshoe wave— it approached the sand belt—my breath stood still; nearer, nearer—the strip of green turf beyond the yellow belt grew narrow—narrower still—became a mere ribbon in front of the horses—then disap-

peared under their hoofs. Great Scott! Why, the whole front of that host shot into the sky with a thundercrash, and became a whirling tempest of rags and fragments; and along the ground lay a thick wall of smoke that hid what was left of the multitude from our sight.

Time for the second step in the plan of campaign! I touched a button, and shook the bones of England loose from her spine!

In that explosion all our noble civilization-factories went up in the air and disappeared from the earth. It was a pity, but it was necessary. We could not afford to let the enemy turn our own weapons against us.

Now ensued one of the dullest quarter hours I had ever endured. We waited in a silent solitude enclosed by our circles of wire, and by a circle of heavy smoke outside of these. We couldn't see over the wall of smoke, and we couldn't see through it. But at last it began to shred away lazily, and by the end of another quarter hour the land was clear and our curiosity was enabled to satisfy itself. No living creature was in sight! We now perceived that additions had been made to our defenses. The dynamite had dug a ditch more than a hundred feet wide, all around us, and cast up an embankment some twenty-five feet high on both borders of it. As to destruction of life, it was amazing. Moreover, it was beyond estimate. Of course we could not *count* the dead, because they did not exist as individuals, but merely as homogeneous protoplasm, with alloys of iron and buttons.

No life was in sight, but necessarily there must have been some wounded in the rear ranks, who were carried off the field under cover of the wall of smoke; there would be sickness among the others—there always is, after an episode like that. But there would be no reinforcements; this was the last stand of the chivalry of England; it was all that was left of the order, after the recent annihilating wars. So I felt quite safe in believing that the utmost force that could for the future be brought against us would be but small; that is, of knights. I therefore issued a congratulatory proclamation to my army in these words:

SOLDIERS, CHAMPIONS OF HUMAN LIBERTY AND EQUALITY: Your General congratulates you! In the pride of his strength and the vanity of his renown, an arrogant enemy came against you. You were ready. The conflict was brief; on your side, glorious. This mighty victory having been achieved utterly without loss, stands without example in history. So long as the planets shall continue to move in their orbits, the BATTLE OF THE SAND BELT will not perish out of the memories of men.

THE BOSS.

I read it well, and the applause I got was very gratifying to me. I then wound up with these remarks:

"The war with the English nation, as a nation, is at an end. The nation has retired from the field and the war. Before it can be persuaded to return, war will have ceased. This campaign is the only one that is going to be fought. It will be brief—the briefest in history. Also the most destructive to life, considered from the standpoint of proportion of casualties to numbers engaged. We are done with the nation; henceforth we deal only with the knights. English knights can be killed, but they cannot be conquered. We know what is before us. While one of these men remains alive, our task is not finished, the war is not ended. We will kill them all." [Loud and long continued applause.]

I picketed the great embankments thrown up around our lines by the dynamite explosion—merely a lookout of a couple of boys to announce the enemy when he should appear again.

Next, I sent an engineer and forty men to a point just beyond our lines on the south, to turn a mountain brook that was there, and bring it within our lines and under our command, arranging it in such a way that I could make instant use of it in an emergency. The forty men were divided into two shifts of twenty each, and were to relieve each other every two hours. In ten hours the work was accomplished.

It was nightfall, now, and I withdrew my pickets. The one who had had the northern outlook reported a camp in sight, but visible with the glass only. He also reported that a few knights had been feeling their way toward us, and had driven some cattle across our lines, but that the knights themselves had not come very near. That was what I had been expecting. They were feeling us, you see; they wanted to know if we were going to play that red terror on them again. They would grow bolder in the night, perhaps. I believed I knew what project they would attempt, because it was plainly the thing I would attempt myself if I were in their places and as ignorant as they were. I mentioned it to Clarence.

"I think you are right," said he; "it is the obvious thing for them to try."

"Well, then," I said, "if they do it they are doomed."

"Certainly."

"They won't have the slightest show in the world."

"Of course they won't."

"It's dreadful, Clarence. It seems an awful pity."

The thing disturbed me so, that I couldn't get any peace of mind for thinking of it and worrying over it. So, at last, to quiet my conscience, I framed this message to the knights:

TO THE HONORABLE THE COMMANDER OF THE INSURGENT CHIVALRY OF ENGLAND: You fight in vain. We know your strength—if one may call it by that name. We know that at the utmost you cannot bring against us above five and twenty thousand knights. Therefore, you have no chance—none whatever. Reflect: we are well equipped, well fortified, we number fifty-four. Fifty-four what? Men? No, *minds*—the capablest in the world; a force against which mere animal might may no more hope to prevail than may the idle waves of the sea hope to prevail against the granite barriers of England. Be advised. We offer you your lives; for the sake of your families, do not reject the gift. We offer you this chance, and it is the last: throw down your arms; surrender unconditionally to the Republic, and all will be forgiven.

(Signed)   THE BOSS.

I read it to Clarence, and said I proposed to send it by a flag of truce. He laughed the sarcastic laugh he was born with, and said:

"Somehow it seems impossible for you to ever fully realize what these nobilities are. Now let us save a little time and trouble. Consider me the commander of the knights yonder. Now then, you are the flag of truce; approach and deliver me your message, and I will give you your answer."

I humored the idea. I came forward under an imaginary guard of the enemy's soldiers, produced my paper, and read it through. For answer, Clarence struck the paper out of my hand, pursed up a scornful lip and said with lofty disdain—

"Dismember me this animal, and return him in a basket to the baseborn knave who sent him; other answer have I none!"

How empty is theory in presence of fact! And this was just fact, and nothing else. It was the thing that would have happened, there was no getting around that. I tore up the paper and granted my mistimed sentimentalities a permanent rest.

Then, to business. I tested the electric signals from the gatling platform to the cave, and made sure that they were all right; I tested and retested those which commanded the fences—these were signals whereby I could break and renew the electric current in each fence independently of the others, at will. I placed the brook connection under the guard and authority of three of my best boys, who would alternate in two-hour watches all night and promptly obey my signal, if I should have occasion to give it—three revolver-shots in quick succession. Sentry duty was discarded for the night, and the corral left empty of life; I ordered that quiet be maintained in the cave, and the electric lights turned down to a glimmer.

As soon as it was good and dark, I shut off the current from all of the fences, and then groped my way out to the embankment bordering our side of the great dynamite ditch. I crept to the top of it and lay there on the slant of the muck to watch. But it was too dark to see anything. As for sounds, there were none. The stillness was deathlike. True, there were the usual night-sounds of the country—the whir of night birds, the buzzing of insects, the barking of distant dogs, the mellow lowing of far-off kine—but these didn't seem to break the stillness, they only intensified it, and added a gruesome melancholy to it into the bargain.

I presently gave up looking, the night shut down so black, but I kept my ears strained to catch the least suspicious sound, for I judged I had only to wait and I shouldn't be disappointed. However, I had to wait a long time. At last I caught what you may call indistinct glimpses of sound—dulled metallic sound. I pricked up my ears, then, and held my breath, for this was the sort of thing I had been waiting for. This sound thickened, and approached—from toward the north. Presently I heard it at my own level—the ridgetop of the opposite embankment, a hundred feet or more away. Then I seemed to see a row of black dots appear along that ridge—human heads? I couldn't tell; it mightn't be anything at all; you can't depend on your eyes when your imagination is out of focus. However, the question was soon settled. I heard that metallic noise descending into the great ditch. It augmented fast, it spread all along, and it unmistakably furnished me this fact: an armed host was taking up its quarters in the ditch. Yes, these people were arranging a little surprise party for us. We could expect entertainment about dawn, possibly earlier.

I groped my way back to the corral, now; I had seen enough. I went to the platform and signaled to turn the current onto the two inner fences. Then I went into the cave, and found everything satisfactory there—nobody awake but the working watch. I woke Clarence and told him the great ditch was filling up with men, and that I believed all the knights were coming for us in a body. It was my notion that as soon as dawn approached we could expect the ditch's ambuscaded thousands to swarm up over the embankment and make an assault, and be followed immediately by the rest of their army.

Clarence said:

"They will be wanting to send a scout or two in the dark to make preliminary observations. Why not take the lightning off the outer fences, and give them a chance?"

"I've already done it, Clarence. Did you ever know me to be inhospitable?"

"No, you are a good heart. I want to go and—"

"Be a reception committee? I will go, too."

We crossed the corral and lay down together between the two inside fences. Even the dim light of the cave had disordered our eyesight somewhat, but the focus straightway began to regulate itself and soon it was adjusted for present circumstances. We had had to feel our way before, but we could make out to see the fence posts now. We started a whispered conversation, but suddenly Clarence broke off and said:

"What is that?"

"What is what?"

"That thing yonder?"

"What thing—where?"

"There beyond you a little piece—a dark something—a dull shape of some kind—against the second fence."

I gazed and he gazed. I said:

"Could it be a man, Clarence?"

"No, I think not. If you notice, it looks a lit—why, it *is* a man—leaning on the fence!"

"I certainly believe it is; let's us go and see."

We crept along on our hands and knees until we were pretty close, and then looked up. Yes, it was a man—a dim great figure in armor, standing erect, with both hands on the upper wire—and of course there was a smell of burning flesh. Poor fellow, dead as a doornail, and never knew what hurt him. He stood there like a statue—no motion about him, except that his plumes swished about a little in the night wind. We rose up and looked in through the bars of his visor, but couldn't make out whether we knew him or not—features too dim and shadowed.

We heard muffled sounds approaching, and we sank down to the ground where we were. We made out another knight vaguely; he was coming very stealthily, and feeling his way. He was near enough, now, for us to see him put out a hand, find an upper wire, then bend and step under it and over the lower one. Now he arrived at the first knight—and started slightly

when he discovered him. He stood a moment—no doubt wondering why the other
one didn't move on; then he said, in a low
voice, "Why dreamest thou here, good Sir
Mar—" then he laid his hand on the
corpse's shoulder—and just uttered a little
soft moan and sunk down dead. Killed by
a dead man, you see—killed by a dead
friend, in fact. There was something awful
about it.

These early birds came scattering along
after each other, about one every five
minutes in our vicinity, during half an
hour. They brought no armor of offense
but their swords; as a rule they carried
the sword ready in the hand, and put it
forward and found the wires with it. We
would now and then see a blue spark when
the knight that caused it was so far away
as to be invisible to us; but we knew what
had happened, all the same, poor fellow;
he had touched a charged wire with his
sword and been elected. We had brief intervals of grim stillness, interrupted with
piteous regularity by the clash made by the
falling of an ironclad; and this sort of thing
was going on, right along, and was very
creepy, there in the dark and lonesomeness.

We concluded to make a tour between
the inner fences. We elected to walk upright, for convenience sake; we argued that
if discerned, we should be taken for friends
rather than enemies, and in any case we
should be out of reach of swords, and
these gentry did not seem to have any
spears along. Well, it was a curious trip.
Everywhere dead men were lying outside
the second fence—not plainly visible, but
still visible; and we counted fifteen of those
pathetic statues—dead knights standing
with their hands on the upper wire.

One thing seemed to be sufficiently
demonstrated: our current was so tremendous that it killed before the victim could
cry out. Pretty soon we detected a muffled

and heavy sound, and next moment we
guessed what it was. It was a surprise in
force coming! I whispered Clarence to go
and wake the army, and notify it to wait
in silence in the cave for further orders.
He was soon back, and we stood by the
inner fence and watched the silent lightning do its awful work upon that swarming host. One could make out but little of
detail; but he could note that a black mass
was piling itself up beyond the second
fence. That swelling bulk was dead men!
Our camp was enclosed with a solid wall
of the dead—a bulwark, a breastwork, of
corpses, you may say. One terrible thing
about this thing was the absence of human voices; there were no cheers, no war
cries: being intent upon a surprise, these
men moved as noiselessly as they could;
and always when the front rank was near
enough to their goal to make it proper for
them to begin to get a shout ready, of
course they struck the fatal line and went
down without testifying.

I sent a current through the third fence,
now; and almost immediately through the
fourth and fifth, so quickly were the gaps
filled up. I believed the time was come,
now, for my climax; I believed that that
whole army was in our trap. Anyway, it
was high time to find out. So I touched a
button and set fifty electric suns aflame on
the top of our precipice.

Land, what a sight! We were enclosed in
three walls of dead men! All the other
fences were pretty nearly filled with the
living, who were stealthily working their
way forward through the wires. The sudden glare paralyzed this host, petrified
them, you may say, with astonishment;
there was just one instant for me to utilize
their immobility in, and I didn't lose the
chance. You see, in another instant they
would have recovered their faculties, then
they'd have burst into a cheer and made

a rush, and my wires would have gone down before it; but that lost instant lost them their opportunity forever; while even that slight fragment of time was still unspent, I shot the current through all the fences and struck the whole host dead in their tracks! *There* was a groan you could *hear!* It voiced the death pang of eleven thousand men. It swelled out on the night with awful pathos.

A glance showed that the rest of the enemy—perhaps ten thousand strong— were between us and the encircling ditch, and pressing forward to the assault. Consequently we had them *all!* and had them past help. Time for the last act of the tragedy. I fired the three appointed revolver shots—which meant:

"Turn on the water!"

There was a sudden rush and roar, and in a minute the mountain brook was raging through the big ditch and creating a river a hundred feet wide and twenty-five deep.

"Stand to your guns, men! Open fire!"

The thirteen gatlings began to vomit death into the fated ten thousand. They halted, they stood their ground a moment against that withering deluge of fire, then they broke, faced about and swept toward the ditch like chaff before a gale. A full fourth part of their force never reached the top of the lofty embankment; the three-fourths reached it and plunged over—to death by drowning.

Within ten short minutes after we had opened fire, armed resistance was totally annihilated, the campaign was ended, we fifty-four were masters of England! Twenty-five thousand men lay dead around us.

But how treacherous is fortune! In a little while—say an hour—happened a thing, by my own fault, which—but I have no heart to write that. Let the record end here.

CHAPTER 44

I, Clarence, must write it for him. He proposed that we two go out and see if any help could be afforded the wounded. I was strenuous against the project. I said that if there were many, we could do but little for them; and it would not be wise for us to trust ourselves among them, anyway. But he could seldom be turned from a purpose once formed; so we shut off the electric current from the fences, took an escort along, climbed over the enclosing ramparts of dead knights, and moved out upon the field. The first wounded man who appealed for help was sitting with his back against a dead comrade. When the Boss bent over him and spoke to him, the man recognized him and stabbed him. That knight was Sir Meliagraunce, as I found

out by tearing off his helmet. He will not ask for help any more.

We carried the Boss to the cave and gave his wound, which was not very serious, the best care we could. In this service we had the help of Merlin, though we did not know it. He was disguised as a woman, and appeared to be a simple old peasant goodwife. In this disguise, with brown-stained face and smooth-shaven, he had appeared a few days after the Boss was hurt, and offered to cook for us, saying her people had gone off to join certain new camps which the enemy were forming, and that she was starving. The Boss had been getting along very well, and had amused himself with finishing up his record.

We were glad to have this woman, for

we were shorthanded. We were in a trap, you see—a trap of our own making. If we stayed where we were, our dead would kill us; if we moved out of our defenses, we should no longer be invincible. We had conquered; in turn we were conquered. The Boss recognized this; we all recognized it. If we could go to one of those new camps and patch up some kind of terms with the enemy—yes, but the Boss could not go, and neither could I, for I was among the first that were made sick by the poisonous air bred by those dead thousands. Others were taken down, and still others. Tomorrow—

Tomorrow. It is here. And with it the end. About midnight I awoke, and saw that hag making curious passes in the air about the Boss's head and face, and wondered what it meant. Everybody but the dynamo-watch lay steeped in sleep; there was no sound. The woman ceased from her mysterious foolery, and started tiptoeing toward the door. I called out—

"Stop! What have you been doing?"

She halted, and said with an accent of malicious satisfaction:

"Ye were conquerors; ye are conquered! These others are perishing—you also. Ye shall all die in this place—every one—except *him.* He sleepeth, now—and shall sleep thirteen centuries. I am Merlin!"

Then such a delirium of silly laughter overtook him that he reeled about like a drunken man, and presently fetched up against one of our wires. His mouth is spread open yet; apparently he is still laughing. I suppose the face will retain that petrified laugh until the corpse turns to dust.

The Boss has never stirred—sleeps like a stone. If he does not wake today we shall understand what kind of a sleep it is, and his body will then be borne to a place in one of the remote recesses of the cave where none will ever find it to desecrate it. As for the rest of us—well, it is agreed that if any one of us ever escapes alive from this place, he will write the fact here, and loyally hide this Manuscript with the Boss, our dear good chief, whose property it is, be he alive or dead.

END OF THE MANUSCRIPT

FINAL P.S. BY M.T.

The dawn was come when I laid the manuscript aside. The rain had almost ceased, the world was gray and sad, the exhausted storm was sighing and sobbing itself to rest. I went to the stranger's room, and listened at his door, which was slightly ajar. I could hear his voice, and so I knocked. There was no answer, but I still heard the voice. I peeped in. The man lay on his back, in bed, talking brokenly but with spirit, and punctuating with his arms, which he thrashed about, restlessly, as sick people do in delirium. I slipped in softly and bent over him. His mutterings and ejaculations went on. I spoke—merely a word, to call his attention. His glassy eyes and his ashy face were alight in an instant with pleasure, gratitude, gladness, welcome:

"O, Sandy, you are come at last—how I have longed for you! Sit by me—do not leave me—never leave me again, Sandy, never again. Where is your hand—give it me, dear, let me hold it—there—now all is well, all is peace, and I am happy again— *we* are happy again, isn't it so, Sandy? You

are so dim, so vague, you are but a mist, a cloud, but you are *here,* and that is blessedness sufficient; and I have your hand; don't take it away—it is for only a little while, I shall not require it long. . . . Was that the child? . . . Hello-Central! . . . She doesn't answer. Asleep, perhaps? Bring her when she wakes, and let me touch her hands, her face, her hair, and tell her good-bye. . . . Sandy! . . . Yes, you are there. I lost myself a moment, and I thought you were gone. . . . Have I been sick long? It must be so; it seems months to me. And such dreams! Such strange and awful dreams, Sandy! Dreams that were as real as reality— delirium, of course, but *so* real! Why, I thought the king was dead, I thought you were in Gaul and couldn't get home, I thought there was a revolution; in the fantastic frenzy of these dreams, I thought that Clarence and I and a handful of my cadets fought and exterminated the whole chivalry of England! But even that was not the strangest. I seemed to be a creature out of a remote unborn age, centuries hence, and even *that* was as real as the rest! Yes, I seemed to have flown back out of that age into this of ours, and then forward

to it again, and was set down, a stranger and forlorn in that strange England, with an abyss of thirteen centuries yawning between me and you! between me and my home and my friends! between me and all that is dear to me, all that could make life worth the living! It was awful—awfuler than you can ever imagine, Sandy. Ah, watch by me, Sandy—stay by me every moment—*don't* let me go out of my mind again; death is nothing, let it come, but not with those dreams, not with the torture of those hideous dreams—I cannot endure *that* again. . . . Sandy? . . ."

He lay muttering incoherently some little time; then for a time he lay silent, and apparently sinking away toward death. Presently his fingers began to pick busily at the coverlet, and by that sign I knew that his end was at hand. With the first suggestion of the death rattle in his throat he started up slightly, and seemed to listen; then he said:

"A bugle? . . . It is the king! The drawbridge, there! Man the battlements—turn out the—"

He was getting up his last "effect"; but he never finished it.

FOR DISCUSSION

1. How is the Yankee returned to his own time? What is the irony of his last speech?

2. What happens to the Yankee's dream of a people's uprising? How is he able to persuade

his boys to fight when "all England is marching" against them?

3. Diagram the plan by which the cave is defended. How are the conquerors defeated by their own success?

In Summary

FOR DISCUSSION

1. Mark Twain does not paint a very rosy picture of life in sixth-century England. Do you think his purpose in writing *A Connecticut Yankee at King Arthur's Court* was only to attack medieval customs, or was he satirizing modern man as well? How much of the evil and foolish behavior that he satirized is still common? Has human behavior changed much since the "savages" of King Arthur's time?

2. One of the institutions which the Yankee criticizes most often is the Church. Is he against all religion, or only certain aspects of it? What in particular does he object to? Find specific passages that demonstrate his religious attitudes.

3. The Connecticut Yankee sees himself as a missionary bringing the light of civilization to a savage land. From another point of view he might seem to be an "ugly American," selfishly imposing his values on a foreign culture. Which point of view seems more accurate to you? Reading *The Ugly American* by Eugene Burdick and W. H. Lederer might help you to decide.

4. The Yankee seems to have unlimited faith in democracy, reason, and technology. Is there anything in the novel to suggest that Mark Twain didn't share this faith completely? According to Mark Twain's view, what dangers must a democratic, technological society guard against?

5. Mark Twain uses many satirical methods in this novel. Sometimes he gives the Yankee long, angry speeches directly attacking some evil; other times he paints pathetic pictures of human suffering; other times he uses more subtle techniques of humor and irony. Which methods do you find most effective and least effective? If you were hiring him as a writer to help you protest some injustice, which methods would you ask him to use? Find example passages that you think accomplish his satirical purpose especially well.

OTHER THINGS TO DO

1. How accurate is Mark Twain's picture of medieval England? Contrast it with a more romantic version of King Arthur's Court (such as *Camelot and Idylls of the King),* then consult a more objective source, such as an encyclopedia or history book, to learn more about the Arthurian legend and daily life in the Middle Ages.

2. Find out all you can about costumes in sixth-century England, then make sketches of clothes that the Yankee, Sandy, King Arthur, the Knights and their ladies, freemen, and slaves might have worn.

3. Illustrate some scenes from the book. You will have to do research on medieval architecture, furnishings, and weapons. Or prepare a report on armor and weapons, making models of some of those mentioned in the book.

4. Make a newspaper such as might have been printed during the Boss's reign. A group could make one several pages long, including news, editorials, sports, features, and advertisements.

5. Make a crossword puzzle using vocabulary words, characters, and events from the book.

6. Rewrite one scene from the book as a film script. Since everything on film has to be *shown,* choose a scene that emphasizes action and vivid description. Shorten long speeches or tie them to images in some way.

7. Write a short story about a modern American who, like the Connecticut Yankee, is transported to another place and time—past or future. (H. G. Wells's *The Time Machine* might be helpful if you choose the future.) Decide whether it will be humorous, satirical, historical, or just fantastic.

The World of Words

A CONNECTICUT YANKEE AT KING ARTHUR'S COURT

1. The word *Yankee* has at least three different meanings, depending on the context in which the word is used. What does the word mean in each of the following sentences? (1) He was a Yankee from Vermont. (2) The Yankee forces won the battle of Gettysburg. (3) The Yankees fought in France during World War I.

2. The Yankee in Mark Twain's story is referred to as "The Boss." The meaning of the word *boss* in the sense of "someone in authority who makes decisions" is clear enough here. But the word has another meaning. This second meaning is part of the verb *emboss*. What is the second meaning of *boss*? What does *emboss* mean?

3. The narrator of the story speaks of "knight errantry." In this context the word *errant* means "roving or wandering in search of adventure." This is what Arthur's knights did, and the practice was called "knight errantry." The whole matter of knighthood, what knights were like and what they did, is known as "*chivalry*." But the word *chivalry* also refers to the ways in which knights were expected to behave. What kind of behavior does the word *chivalry* refer to? Is the word ever used today? The words *chivalry, cavalcade,* and *cavalry* all go back to the same source in Latin. Look up the source of these words, and explain how they are related.

4. The newspaper, telephone, telegraph, and other devices that "The Boss" introduces into Arthur's kingdom are called "anachronisms." The word *anachronism* is made up of *ana-,* meaning "backward or reversed," and *khroni-zein* which comes from the Greek word *khronos,* meaning "time." What, then, is the meaning of *anachronism*? Other words that come from *khronos* are *chronic, chronicle, chronological,* and *chronometer.* What are the meanings of these words?

Reader's Choice

Animal Farm, *by George Orwell.*

"Four legs good, two legs bad." Weary of their life under Farmer Jones, the animals of Manor Farm overthrow his rule—only to find animal dictators rising to take his place. Orwell's satirical story is a long fable in which each character symbolizes a political type. It contains important lessons about political power, revolution, and dictatorship.

Brave New World, *by Aldous Huxley.*

Huxley imagines a future in which babies are manufactured in test tubes and unhappiness is eliminated through drugs. His hero is a "savage" who opposes technology's completely controlled, inhuman system.

Camelot and Idylls of the King, *by Alan Jay Lerner and Alfred, Lord Tennyson.*

The legends of King Arthur have fascinated many authors—including a nineteenth-century poet and the writer of a modern Broadway musical. This book brings together these two very different versions of the old story.

Candide, *by Voltaire.*

"Everything is for the best in this best of all possible worlds." Armed with this optimistic philosophy, young Candide sets out into a world full of horrors, determined to see the bright side of everything. Voltaire's classic is one of the most bitterly ironic satires ever written.

Gulliver's Travels, *by Jonathan Swift.*

On his strange travels Gulliver encounters pygmies, giants, and a nation of horses—all bearing uncanny resemblances to "normal" men. This novel, sometimes read as a children's story, has deeper satirical meanings for adults.

The Mouse on the Moon, *by Leonard Wibberley.*

The world's smallest nation, the Duchy of Grand Fenwick, beats all the world powers in getting the first man on the moon. Using a secret fuel based on a special vintage of wine, they throw the great nations into a panic. This is a lighthearted satire on science, politics, and diplomacy.

Nineteen Eighty-four, *by George Orwell.*

In the totalitarian state of 1984, every citizen's every move is watched by "Big Brother," and the Ministry of Truth publishes slogans like "War is peace," and "Freedom is slavery." When Winston Smith decides to think for himself he learns how terrible the control of an absolute government can be.

The Sword in the Stone, *by T. H. White.*

T. H. White's version of young King Arthur's growing up is humorous and fantastic. Unaware of his destiny, Arthur "the Wart" thinks he is preparing to be a page—but Merlin prepares him for kingship by turning him into various kinds of animals. Students who enjoy White's style can read more of his Round Table stories in *The Once and Future King*.

The Time Machine, *by H. G. Wells.*

The Time Traveler, arriving in the year 802,000, finds men divided into two species: the workers and the leisure class. In a world where the environment has become entirely controlled, man has lost all of his creativity; nothing ever changes. Wells's grim vision of the future provides comparisons with Mark Twain's grim vision of the past.

ABOUT THE AUTHORS

Franklin P. Adams (1881–1960) A Midwesterner, Adams, or F. P. A., became known to the entire country in the 1930s, not only through his famous newspaper column, *The Conning Tower,* but also through his participation as a regular panelist on one of the first of the national quiz shows. *Information Please* was broadcast on radio for many years, and during that time Adams' sharp wit and Chicago accent became familiar to millions.

W. H. Auden (1907–1973) In 1939, the already distinguished English poet Wystan Hugh Auden came to the United States, where within a few years he became an American citizen. He had been born in the English city of York, and while still a very young writer had made a name for himself in a variety of forms; he had written stories, plays, travel books, and an impressive amount of poetry. That youthful poetry was filled with what one critic has called a "crazy wit" and a "delight in playing with words." But as he grew older, Auden became more serious (though hardly less witty). *The Age of Anxiety* appeared in 1947—and gave a name to a whole generation. By the time of his death, this Anglo-American was generally regarded as unsurpassed by any other poet then writing in English.

Isaac Babel (1894–) Russian-born Isaac Babel graduated from the University of Saratov in Kiev and moved to St. Petersburg (now Leningrad) in Russia. There he had a difficult time, for the city was officially banned to Jews.

Babel met Maxim Gorky, Russian author, who helped start his career by publishing some of his stories. But Babel was then arrested. Later he became a soldier and traveled extensively. His travels and experiences were later to add greatly to the quality of his works.

Ambrose Bierce (1842–1914?) A Union soldier during the Civil War, Ambrose Bierce was the kind of man who could stake his future on the flip of a coin. When the war ended, he did just that to decide whether to accept a commission in the regular army or to write. The coin was responsible for his becoming a journalist. At first the stories and sketches he produced as a civilian were not well received. In fact, his outspoken satire earned the author the name of Bitter Bierce. Yet, even in his lifetime, a few discriminating people did respond warmly to what he was writing. About "An Occurrence at Owl Creek Bridge," Stephen Crane commented that "nothing better exists. That story contains everything." Before Bierce disappeared on an expedition into Mexico, where he was presumably shot by bandits, he had produced a large body of work.

Hal Borland (1900–) "I grew up on the American frontier," writes Hal Borland. "I was born . . . ninety-six years to the day after Lewis and Clark left St. Louis on their expedition." In terms of historical progress, he continues, "I have lived close to 150 years, simply because I grew up . . . during the tag end of the big cattle-ranch and sod-house days." Completing high school in three years, he earned his way through the University of Colorado by working as a newspaper correspondent and ever since graduation has combined newspaper work with the writing of books. Mr. Borland is known for his nature writing in particular. On his hundred-acre farm he has written the "outdoor" editorials that have been appearing in Sunday editions of *The New York Times* for more than twenty years. *High, Wide and Lonesome* derives its name from the author's description of the country he knew as a boy.

Ray Bradbury (1920–   )   Comic-strip adventures gave Ray Bradbury his first taste of what he calls "the fabulous world of the future, and the world of fantasy." As a boy in Illinois he soon became absorbed in learning magic tricks and writing space stories of his own. After graduation from high school he sold newspapers on a street corner for three years, all the while writing at the rate of 2000 words a day—most of which he later burned. Since then he has published a great many stories and a few novels as well, including the eerie *Something Wicked This Way Comes.* Now one of the foremost science-fiction writers, Bradbury confessed that although his characters fly from planet to planet without turning a hair, he himself has never been in an airplane.

Gwendolyn Brooks (1917–   )   Awarded the Pulitzer Prize in 1950 for *Annie Allen,* her second book of poetry, Gwendolyn Brooks is also a fine novelist. Both her fiction and her poetry are characterized by a directness and restraint that make all the more moving the seemingly uneventful lives she explores. Although her own life has been comfortable, she writes frequently and sympathetically of the poor, doomed to squalor while dreaming of something better. Her verse, as one critic has noted, draws on the world she understands but records insights about that world in such a way that they become "not merely personal or racial but universal in their implications."

Heywood Broun (1888–1939)   Heywood Broun lived an active life. Primarily he was a journalist—and a courageous and controversial one. After college at Harvard, he became a sports writer for a New York newspaper. Later he earned a reputation as a drama critic. In the 1930s Broun crowned a long interest in politics by running for Congress—and being defeated. Then he became a good painter; on several occasions his paintings were exhibited in museums. In his spare time he wrote novels, biographies, and short stories.

Whit Burnett (1899–1973)   From Salt Lake City, Utah, Burnett began his career as a newspaperman. He became a foreign correspondent and his work took him to places such as Paris, Vienna, and Geneva. Later Burnett and his wife, Martha Foley, founded *Story* magazine, which is devoted to publishing stories of excellence. Many young authors receive their first recognition through this magazine. In addition to his interest in writing, Burnett was an avid trout fisherman and viola player.

Witter Bynner (1881–1968)   Witter Bynner traveled far from his Brooklyn, New York, birthplace. In China he became the first American to translate a volume of Chinese poetry into English. Later he lived in Santa Fe, New Mexico, where he studied American Indian poetry. Some of his own poems describe the Pueblo ritual dances.

Morley Callaghan (1903–   )   After graduating from college and before attending law school, Morley Callaghan worked as a reporter for his hometown newspaper, the Toronto *Daily Star.* While working there he met Ernest Hemingway, who encouraged Callaghan in his efforts to become a writer. Later when Callaghan went to Paris he met, through Hemingway, people who published his first stories. Callaghan later did become a lawyer but still devoted time to writing.

William Childress A resident of California, Mr. Childress is both a teacher and a poet. He is a recent Stephen Vincent Benét Award winner for his poetry. His first published collection of poems is called *The Weighing-Tree.*

W. H. Auden

John Ciardi (1916–   ) As poet, critic, lecturer, and translator, Ciardi (pronounced *Char*-dee) has made a distinguished name for himself in recent years. For many years he spoke to a wide audience in the pages of *The Saturday Review,* where his reactions to new books often stirred controversy. He never wrote as one "meek by trade" (see his poem in this volume, page 273). But while insisting bluntly that a poem must be "understandable," he also reminded us as readers that when a poet fails to communicate, the fault may be ours for not reading carefully.

Ray Bradbury

John Bell Clayton Mr. Clayton grew up on a Virginia farm, west of the Blue Ridge Mountains. He studied for a time at the University of Virginia and eventually became a newspaper man. About his work, Mr. Clayton says, "A man trying to tell stories can only say about himself that he has some stories he wants to tell, some short ones and some long ones, and then sit down and—try his level best to tell them honestly and well." Among Clayton's best-known works are *Six Angels at My Back* and *Wait Son, October Is Near.*

John Ciardi

John Collier (1901–   ) English author John Collier began his literary career by writing poetry. But he later switched to novels. His first, the satirical *His Monkey Wife,* won high praise. Perhaps his most interesting novel is *Full Circle,* a story about England in 1995 after it has been destroyed by war. John Collier has served as poetry editor for a leading British magazine.

Stephen Crane (1871–1900)   Crane was only twenty-four when he published his master-piece, *The Red Badge of Courage*. Although he had never witnessed a battle himself, he recreated in his imagination the physical and psychological experiences of a common soldier during the Civil War. The novel, the literary success of 1895, has influenced many later writers. Still only in his mid-twenties, Crane then served as a war correspondent in Turkey and in Cuba. But his roving adventures ruined his health; after two years in England he died of tuberculosis before his thirtieth birthday.

E. E. Cummings (1894–1962)   One of the most discussed of modern poets, E. E. Cummings was born in Cambridge, Massachusetts, the son of a Harvard professor. During World War I, Cummings was confined briefly to a concentration camp. Later he went to Paris and became a painter, a draftsman, and a writer. His first volume of poems, *Tulips and Chimneys*, appeared in 1923. However strange his poems may appear at first reading, what they actually say is usually simple and familiar —celebrations of the wonder of love, the beauty of spring, the triumph of the individual over man in the mass. But with Cummings, the way a thing is said made all the difference and at its best his way is fresh, astonishingly vigorous, and unforgettable.

Roald Dahl (1916–   )   Born of Norwegian parents in Wales, Dahl is one of the contemporary short story masters of the English language. His wildly improbable plots, unique characters, and acid humor have gained him international acclaim. His collections, *Kiss Kiss*, and *Someone Like You*, consist of bizarre stories a reader is not likely ever to forget.

Borden Deal (1922–   )   A writer of novels as well as short stories, Borden Deal has also fought forest fires, worked for a circus, and been a government skip tracer (tracer of peo-ple who fail to pay bills). Born and raised in Mississippi, he served in the navy during World War II and now lives in Florida. Mr. Deal began his writing career when he won first prize in a short-story contest while a student at the University of Alabama.

Sir Arthur Conan Doyle (1859–1930)   Sherlock Holmes came into being while a struggling young doctor waited vainly for patients. Scottish-born Sir Arthur Conan Doyle amused himself during those long hours by writing stories about a "scientific" detective who solved cases by his amazing powers of deduction. The physician modeled Holmes on a real person, a tall, wiry surgeon who had the reputation of being able to tell a person's occupation just by looking at him. Later, growing tired of writing Holmes stories, Sir Arthur Conan Doyle wrote a story in which the detective was killed by a Professor Moriarty. But Holmes was so popular that public demand forced the author to bring him back to life.

Robert Frost (1874–1963)   The only American poet to be awarded the Pulitzer Prize four times was Robert Frost. For half a century, he has charmed and challenged the readers of poetry. His poems, often set against a rural New England landscape, are notable for their conversational style and realistic portraits. Beneath their seeming simplicity, however, lies an irony and subtlety which exemplify Frost's belief that poetry is a question of "saying one thing and meaning another."

Thom Gunn (1929–   )   Thom Gunn was still a university student in his native England when he began writing poetry. He soon won quite a reputation for himself among his fellow countrymen and later in the United States. He has been an instructor at several American colleges and universities, most recently, the University of California.

Thomas Hardy (1840–1928) Thomas Hardy was an architect before he wrote *The Return of the Native* and the other novels that made him a widely talked about figure in the England of Queen Victoria. Then, not long before the beginning of a new century, Hardy abandoned novel-writing. He turned to a more compelling interest, poetry. In his poems, as in his novels, he wrote of the farm people and villagers in Wessex—the historic name he used in his books for the southwestern part of England where he had grown up.

Robert Hayden (1913–   ) Both a student and teacher in Michigan where he was born Robert Hayden taught at the University of Michigan. He later joined the faculty of Fisk University in Nashville, Tennessee, where he is currently a professor. He has had several volumes of poetry published and has won many honors. In 1966 he earned first prize at the First World Festival of Negro Arts at Dakar, Senegal, for a book entitled *A Ballad of Remembrance.* He has also been the recipient of a Ford Foundation Fellowship for travel and writing in Mexico.

Homer. Probably it will never be known whether a single poet named Homer really wrote the greatest of all epics in Western culture. Traditionally, the authorship of the *Iliad* and the *Odyssey,* poems that tell of the ten years' seige of Troy and of Odysseus's wanderings for ten years after Troy fell, has been assigned to a poet whom legend says was blind—but about whom nothing in fact is known. The poems may have been written anytime between the twelfth and the ninth century B. C., and they may have been composed by more than one poet. Whoever wrote them though, their imaginative appeal continues to this day.

A. E. Housman (1859–1936) Alfred Edward Housman worked for a while in a London patent office until he became a professor of classics at University College, London. In 1896

E. E. Cummings

Roald Dahl

Robert Frost

Housman published his first book of poems, *A Shropshire Lad*, written in a period of "continuous excitement." *Last Poems* was not published until twenty-six years later, while Housman was teaching at Trinity College, Cambridge. Lonely and reserved, this distinguished scholar and poet refused several honorary degrees as well as the Order of Merit.

Langston Hughes (1902–1967)   From Joplin, Missouri, Langston Hughes was a young sailor returning from Europe when he determined to break free from his past; one night he stood on the deck of the ship and, one by one, threw his books into the ocean. Back in America in 1926 Hughes published his first book of poems. That work won both wide acclaim and a college scholarship for him. Once he finished college he began writing seriously for a living. A versatile as well as a talented writer, he published poems, short stories, novels, plays, movie scripts, songs, and several nonfiction studies of the American Negro.

Margaret Jackson (1895–1974)   Margaret Weymouth Jackson spent most of her adult years in Indiana. Her writing career began when at the age of 17 she sold a story to *The Chicago Tribune*. During the rest of her long life she published more than 200 stories and articles, as well as several books.

Doris Lessing (1919–   )   Born of British parents in Iran, Doris Lessing grew up in Southern Rhodesia and never even visited England until 1949. Her writings express her concern with two major issues: the conflict between the races in Africa and the problems of an intelligent woman seeking to maintain her identity in a man's world. Her *African Stories*, according to one reviewer, are beautifully wrought "by a sensitive and thoughtful but fiercely honest writer. . . ." Playwright,

poet, journalist, writer of fiction, Doris Lessing has been called by the *London Times* "not only the best woman novelist we have, but one of the most serious, intelligent, and honest writers of the whole post-war generation."

Luis Llórens Torres   Llórens Torres, the well-known Puerto Rican poet, was for many years a very successful lawyer. But he suddenly decided he wanted to become a poet, even if it also meant becoming quite poor. Llórens Torres was especially interested in the plight of the *jibaro,* or peasant, whose problems seemed to be at their height during the 1930s when many Puerto Ricans were advocating statehood.

Jack London (1876–1916)   Before he was nineteen years old, Jack London had worked in a cannery, in a jute mill, and on an ice wagon. He had shipped on a sealing vessel to Siberia and—by robbing the nets of other fishermen—earned the title Prince of the Oyster Pirates. He had bummed his way across America and back, spending a month in jail as a vagrant in Niagara Falls. Then he decided to go to high school. Shortly after London began his college career, gold was discovered in California. London followed the prospectors, but found no gold. He did find a wealth of experiences which formed the basis for many of his short stories. Until he died at age forty, Jack London traveled and wrote continuously. He exemplified for many Americans what he considered "the proper function of man . . . to live, not to exist."

Don Marquis (1878–1937)   "It would be one on me," Marquis wrote, "if I should be remembered for creating a cockroach character." He had worked ten years on a drama of the Crucifixion, and wrote many other volumes of serious poetry and prose. But now those are forgotten, while his cockroach "archy" lives on.

John Masefield (1878–1967)   While still in his teens John Masefield sailed to Chile as an apprentice in the merchant marine. Besides being a seaman and later an officer, he worked in a livery stable and a factory before making a career of writing. His reputation as a poet grew until he was appointed Poet Laureate, or national poet, of Great Britain.

Somerset Maugham (1874–1965)   "In one way and another," said Somerset Maugham, "I have used in my writings whatever has happened to me in the course of my life. . . . Fact and fiction are so intermingled that now, looking back on it, I can hardly distinguish one

Jack London

A.E. Housman

John Masefield

Langston Hughes

Somerset Maugham

from the other." He wrote of the early years in *Of Human Bondage,* which he once described as an autobiographical novel. Orphaned at ten, he had been sent to live with a stern, unsympathetic uncle. At eighteen he refused to attend college and instead began the study of medicine at a London hospital. He read and wrote whenever he could. By the time he was twenty-three, Maugham was both a qualified doctor and the author of a successful novel. He then abandoned medicine, leaving England to live on the European continent as a struggling young writer. For the rest of his life he continued to write, pausing only for British Intelligence work during World War I and for the travels which took him all over the world.

Guy de Maupassant (1850–1893) Guy de Maupassant was born in France, the son of a Paris stockbroker. His parents' separation when he was eleven left the young boy to grow up in the care of his mother, through whom he met the literary circle that was later to have a great influence on his writing career. Maupassant's education was interrupted by army service during the Franco-Prussian War. After the war he began to take an interest in writing, soon finding that his talent lay in the short story. Before illness cut short his career, Maupassant's many books had earned him a place among the world's best short-story writers.

Agnes Maxwell-Hall (1894–   ) Born in Jamaica in the British West Indies, Miss Maxwell-Hall was educated on both sides of the Atlantic—in London, Boston, and New York. At Columbia University she studied short-story writing. For more than two decades her stories and poems have been appearing in both English and American magazines. Her best poetry has been anthologized in such books as *The Poetry of the Negro.*

Carson McCullers (1917–1967) Mrs. McCullers began writing when she was sixteen. She

had wanted to be a concert pianist, but then, greatly admiring the playwright Eugene O'Neill, she tried to write a play. It was later performed by and for her family. Carson then went to New York to attend school but on the subway one day she lost her tuition money. Working during the day, she went to school at night. She was not able to concentrate on her studies however, for she found New York a fascinating place, very different from her native Georgia. Soon one of her short stories was published in *Story* magazine. It was the beginning of her long career as an author. Her best-known works include *Member of the Wedding* and *The Heart Is a Lonely Hunter.*

Phyllis McGinley (1905–   ) "The vanishing West had not quite vanished," recalls Phyllis McGinley about her childhood on a Colorado ranch. She and her brother rode ponies three miles to a school at which they were sometimes the only students. Later Miss McGinley spent a year in Utah as a teacher. Today, however, she and her husband live in the suburbs of New York City. Much of her poetry, which has been collected in *Times Three,* she describes as "outwardly amusing, but inwardly serious."

Edna St. Vincent Millay (1892–1950) By the time she was twenty, Edna St. Vincent Millay had achieved fame with "Renascence." The poem marked the beginning of a career that was to see her become probably the most popular poet in America between the two World Wars. Her poems expressed the disillusionment of the postwar generation and struck a tone that appealed to public tastes. Although usually working within traditional stanza forms, she often expressed a romantic protest against traditions and conventions. Her early concern with her own identity—her relationship to others and to the universe—gradually shifted to a concern with broader social issues.

N. Scott Momaday (1935–   )   A Kiowa Indian, N. Scott Momaday spent his childhood on reservations in the Southwest. Having earned his Ph.D. from Stanford University, Momaday is now Associate Professor of English and Comparative Literature at the University of California at Berkeley. Much of his writing is concerned with the problem of the dual culture faced by the American Indian. Momaday's novel *House Made of Dawn* received the 1969 Pulitzer Prize.

Liam O'Flaherty (1896–   )   The Irish author Liam O'Flaherty was born in the Aran Islands, tiny windswept points of land off the west coast, where fishermen and farmers struggle against the violence of nature and still speak the ancient language of their ancestors. His first language was Gaelic (Irish), not English. Leaving college to enlist in the British army during World War I, O'Flaherty was seriously injured in action. After his discharge he knocked about the world, working for a while in the United States as a Western Union messenger, factory hand, and fisherman. O'Flaherty was in Ireland during part of the political upheaval of the early 1920s. *The Informer*, his best-known novel, is set in Dublin during the same period as "The Sniper."

Carson McCullers

Edna St. Vincent Millay

Guy de Maupassant

N. Scott Momaday

Edgar Allan Poe (1809–1849)   Poe was one of the first American writers to gain international fame. He is the originator of the modern detective story. In his short stories and poetry, he sought to establish a mood and single overall effect. Beauty—not moral wisdom—he felt should be the concern of poetry. The music of his poetry, with its unique use of meter, rhythm, and rhyme, has retained its freshness and popularity through the years.

Ralph Pomeroy   No biographical information available.

Theodore Roethke (1908–1963)   A teacher throughout much of his adult life, Theodore Roethke was also a fine athlete and excellent coach. "It took me ten years to complete one little book," he confessed about his first volume of verse. That book and the six that followed earned him many literary honors, including the 1954 Pulitzer Prize. Many of his poems reflect his professional knowledge of flowers, gained from a childhood spent in and around a greenhouse owned by his father and uncle. "Who else," a reviewer commented in amazement, "would know that tulips 'creak'?" Roethke's style is original and powerful, striving—as he once explained—to "permit many ranges of feeling, including humor."

Larry Rubin (1930–   )   From Bayonne, New Jersey, Rubin is a graduate of Columbia and Emory Universities. He is with the English Department at the Georgia Institute of Technology. Winner of numerous awards for his poetry, Rubin has published two collections: *The World's Old Way* and *Lanced in Light*. He has also written several short stories and is at work on a novel.

Buffy Sainte-Marie (1942?–   )   Of Cree Indian descent, Buffy Sainte-Marie was born in Canada but moved to the United States when, after her parents' death, she was adopted by an American couple. Buffy grew up in Wakefield, Massachusetts, where she wrote poetry that later became the lyrics for many of her songs. She taught herself to play the guitar and began her singing career while still in college. She graduated from the university with honors and went to New York to pursue her career as a folk singer. Her best-known songs include "The Universal Soldier" and "Cripple Creek."

Saki (1870–1916)   Saki was the pen name of an Englishman named H. H. Munro. Born in Burma, Munro was sent to England as a child and grew up there. He traveled widely during his youth before starting a career as news writer and foreign correspondent. In time he began writing novels and the famous Saki short stories which contain a unique blend of horror and humor and that has made them favorites with readers ever since they first appeared in print. When World War I began, Munro—at forty-four—enlisted as a private. Refusing the chance to be an officer, he went to France as a corporal, and met his death in action.

Carl Sandburg (1878–1967)   Milkman, dishwasher, harvest hand, sign painter, brickmaker, and barbershop porter—all these jobs Carl Sandburg had tried before enrolling in Lombard College not far from his Illinois home. With the publication of "Chicago" in 1914, Sandburg at last found the role for which he had unconsciously been preparing all his life. In many books which followed, Sandburg demonstrated his remarkable command of American speech, rhythms, and colloquial idiom, as well as an uncanny ability to convey what it feels like to live in a modern industrial civilization.

William Saroyan (1908–   )   Born in California of Armenian parents, William Saroyan

Edgar Allan Poe

Saki

Theodore Roethke

Carl Sandburg

Buffy Saint-Marie

William Saroyan

early displayed a spirit of independence. Before he went to work to help his mother support the family, he earned himself a reputation for playing hookey from school. But books appealed to him, even if school did not, and his wide reading encouraged him to write his own stories. Saroyan has tried almost every kind of writing: stories, plays, novels. It is the writing itself, not the various forms, that interests him: "What difference does it make what you call it, just so it breathes?" he once asked.

Jack Schaefer (1907–   ) Born in Cleveland, Ohio, Jack Schaefer graduated from Oberlin College, then traveled East, where he studied at Columbia University and went into newspaper work. For a time he served as education director at a state reformatory. Today, however, Mr. Schaefer is known as the author of unusually fine stories of the West, based on his study of Western history. His novel *Shane* was made into a highly successful movie. As a setting for *Old Ramon*, a more recent short novel, he chose the New Mexico range country where he himself lives on a ranch.

William Shakespeare (1564–1616) Shakespeare is the best-known author in any language. Born in the provincial town of Stratford-on-Avon, he went to London as a young man, apparently to seek his fortune. During two decades there he wrote thirty-seven plays. They include histories and comedies as well as such unsurpassable tragedies as *Hamlet, King Lear, Othello, Antony and Cleopatra,* and *Macbeth*. In addition to his plays, Shakespeare wrote two narrative poems and a collection of sonnets. And he was a successful actor and businessman as well. For the last few years of his life he retired to Stratford with his family and lived the life of a gentleman. Shakespeare died at the age of fifty-two and was buried in the church of the village in which he was born.

Irwin Shaw (1913–   ) Irwin Shaw was born and educated in Brooklyn, New York. During his three years in the Army in World War II, he wrote for *Stars and Stripes* and traveled over North Africa and the Middle East as well as Europe. Of his several novels, the most celebrated is *The Young Lions,* a long and interesting story set during World War II. The author now lives in Switzerland with his family.

Paul Simon (1942–   ) One half of the popular recording team of Simon and Garfunkel, Paul Simon is responsible for the words of such songs as "Homeward Bound," "The Dangling Conversation," "Sound of Silence," and "Bridge over Troubled Water." In songs that often deal with loneliness, alienation, and man's inability to communicate, Simon has clearly communicated with a younger generation committed to humanity, not technology.

Sophocles (496?–406? B.C.) Sophocles was born near Athens, Greece, and lived there all his life. He lived during one of Athens' greatest cultural periods. His drama won great acclaim and received numerous awards. Sophocles himself was held in extremely high regard by the Greeks. He wrote over a hundred plays, three of which are referred to as the Theban plays. They are "King Oedipus," "Oedipus at Colonus," and "Antigone." All three were written about the legend of the royal house of Thebes, but they were written at different times. One of them was written when Sophocles was nearly ninety.

William Stafford (1914–   ) William Stafford is both an author and an educator. He was born in Kansas, holds his doctorate of philosophy from the State University of Iowa, and has taught both in the Midwest and on the West Coast. In 1963, he was given the National Book Award for *Traveling Through* *the Dark.* His books of poetry include *West of Your City* and *The Rescued Year.* At present he teaches at Lewis and Clark College in Portland, Oregon.

John Steinbeck (1902–1968) Much of Steinbeck's writing is concerned with social injustices that blight the lives of the poor and the ignorant. Born in Salinas, California, he first worked as a hod carrier, painter, chemist, surveyor, and fruit picker before finally achieving success as a novelist. His rich background of experience on different social levels gave him compassionate insight into the lives of all kinds of people, a compassion that is especially evident in such books as *Of Mice and Men* and *The Grapes of Wrath.* When he was awarded the Nobel Prize for literature in 1962, the citation noted that "his sympathies always go out to the oppressed, the misfits, and the distressed."

May Swenson (1919–   ) May Swenson was born in Logan, Utah, the child of Swedish immigrants. She graduated from Utah State University and later moved to New York City where she lives and works. Her work has not been limited to writing poetry as she has also served as an editor in a publishing firm. Miss Swenson says that she has written many of her poems "directly on the scene . . . in much the same way a painter sketches from life."

Hernando Tellez No biographical information available.

Mark Twain (1835–1910) Born in Missouri, Samuel Clemens made his famous trip West after the Civil War cut short his career as a steamboat pilot on the Mississippi River. Taking the pen name Mark Twain from a river expression meaning "safe water," he wrote newspaper sketches in Nevada and California. In 1870, already a successful author, he mar-

William Shakespeare

Paul Simon

Sophocles

ried and moved to Hartford, Connecticut. Books such as *Tom Sawyer* soon made him a national celebrity, and huge crowds came to hear him speak on his lecture tours around the country. Although illness and death in his family embittered the last years of his life, his stature as a writer continued to grow, placing Mark Twain finally among the best in American literature.

Kurt Vonnegut, Jr. (1922–   ) Most of Vonnegut's writing attacks man's dependence on the products of modern technology, a dependence which he feels is destroying our creativity, sensitivity, and compassion—traits that make us human. Our increasing numbness serves to feed greater wars and greater cruelties. "All writers are going to have to learn more about science," claims Vonnegut, "simply because the scientific method is such an important part of our environment." Often mislabeled as a science-fiction writer, Vonnegut seeks deeper levels in his stories and novels. Among his published works are *Cat's Cradle, Welcome to the Monkey House,* and *Slaughterhouse-Five.*

Walt Whitman (1819–1892) In 1855 Walt Whitman published a slender volume of poetry entitled *Leaves of Grass.* The poet may well have expected his book to cause wide critical comment, for he had abandoned regular rhymes, meters, and stanza patterns, aiming instead for a free verse form that grew out of content, "as loosely as lilacs or roses on a bush." For a long time the book was scarcely noticed, but Whitman—a former office-boy, printer, teacher, builder, and newspaper editor—determined to make his book his life's work. From then until his death he continued to revise and add to it. Today, Whitman's poems are considered a major achievement in American poetry.

Keith Wilson (1927–   ) Keith Wilson is a widely published modern poet who is best known for his powerful war poetry and poems of his native Southwest. A graduate of the U.S. Naval Academy, Wilson turned to poetry after the Korean War. He received a Master's degree in English from the University of New Mexico, and is now a resident poet and associate professor of English at New Mexico State University. He has published many volumes of poetry and has given readings of his work throughout the West.

Chiang Yee (1903–   ) Son of the painter Chiang Ho-an, Chiang Yee was born in Kiukiang, China. In 1935 he became a lecturer in Chinese at London University. It was at that time that he also gained recognition as an artist of some renown. Some years later Chiang Yee came to the United States. He is the author of many novels, children's books, and poems. Perhaps his most well-known book is *The Silent Traveller,* which contains poems, paintings, and comments on the author's travels.

Yevgeny Yevtushenko (1933–   ) After the death of Stalin in 1953, the Soviet Union for a time underwent a period of liberalization in the arts known as "the Thaw." One of the youngest and most vigorous of the new Soviet poets was Yevtushenko, who, before he was thirty, was internationally known as the voice of the post-Stalin generation in Russia. "Let us be extremely outspoken," he proclaimed. In a famous poem, "Babi Yar," named after a place where the Nazis killed thousands of Jews during World War II, he condemns by implication anti-Semitism in Soviet Russia. In recent years Yevtushenko's voice has been heard less often, but his vigorous and lyrical poetry and his *Precocious Autobiography* continue to circulate widely in his own country and in the West.

Mark Twain

Chiang Yee

Kurt Vonnegut, Jr.

Walt Whitman

ABOUT THE MAJOR ARTISTS

John Constable (1776–1837) The peaceful, pastoral countryside where Constable grew up became the major subject of the paintings of this innovative landscape artist. His artistic growth was painfully slow, and for many years he attempted unsuccessfully to imitate the important artists of his day. It wasn't until he found his own fresh, original style that his talent was recognized. He was elected to the Royal Academy of Arts in 1829, but his fame reached its height only after his death.

Hilaire Germain Edgar Degas (1834–1917) His French *bourgeois* parents hoped he would study law, but Edgar Degas enrolled in the École des Beaux Arts in Paris at the age of 19. As a student of Ingres, it seems likely that the young Degas hoped to succeed as a classical painter in the true French tradition. But after painting historical subjects for a while, he became fascinated by the human figure in movement. He experimented with groupings of figures and unusual angles, and in the 1870s was influenced by Impressionism. In later life, his eyesight failed, and he was nearly blind at the time of his death in 1917.

Piero della Francesca (c. 1420–1492) Known today as one of the great masters of fifteenth-century Italian painting, Piero della Francesca was also a capable mathematician. His mathematical interests led him to expand Italian knowledge of perspective. Born in Borgo, Francesca worked in Florence, Rome, and Urbino. His most famous frescoes, noted for their calmness and severe geometry, were painted during his height between 1450 and 1460. After 1460, few paintings are ascribed to him, and it has been suggested that he devoted his time increasingly to architecture and mathematics.

Giorgione (1477 or 1478–1510) There are very few actual documents available about this Italian Renaissance painter, but there are so many legends that it is difficult to sift out the truth. He apparently was of humble origin and received acclaim at an early age for his innovative use of color and light. His small number of documented works now stand as a turning point between fifteenth- and sixteenth-century art.

Jean Auguste Dominique Ingres (1780–1867) Son of a sculptor, Ingres was encouraged to become an artist and went to Paris to study at the age of eleven. By the age of seventeen, as a student of David, Ingres was beginning to win prizes. He spent the rest of his life in Italy and France, painting primarily classical and historical subjects. He became the leader of the French classical tradition, and all his works show an interest in line and form rather than color.

Rembrandt van Rijn (1609–1669) Landscapes, religious subjects, scenes from everyday life, portraits, historical and mythological subjects

—all of these were captured by the Netherlands' greatest artist. This seventeenth-century artist had a tremendous output (he made about 100 self-portraits) but his reputation rests on his power as a story teller, his warm sympathy, and his ability to reveal the innermost feelings of his subjects. He is known for his palette of warm golds and browns and most of his paintings seem to glow with a yellowy warmth or to advance from a shadowy background. During his lifetime Rembrandt received wide acclaim, but later in life, his popularity and fortunes waned, and he was beset by personal misfortune. However, it was in the last years of his life that he reached final maturity and depth of feeling.

Joseph M. W. Turner (1775–1851) Turner as a boy is said to have displayed his drawings in his father's store next to the wigs as marketable merchandise. He was a prolific artist, the creator of 282 paintings and over 19,000 drawings. Most famous are his landscapes (see page 448), which he often rearranged from nature to suit himself—moving mountains and adding waterfalls—and his sea pieces, which include the familiar *The Slave Ship* and *The Fighting Temeraire*, the latter commemorating a famous battleship. Turner left a huge fortune for, as he said, "the maintenance and support of male decayed artists, being born in England . . . and of lawful issue."

Vincent Van Gogh (1853–1890) He sold only one painting during his entire lifetime, but today Van Gogh's works are among the most popular paintings in the world. This Dutch artist had an extremely short artistic career; his most productive period being the six years before his suicide. Although his earlier paintings use shades of brown, Van Gogh's later works are alive with color, which seems to vibrate from his swirling trees, skies and flowers. His approach to painting was revolutionary. The thickness, shape, and direction of his brush strokes create a three dimensional counterpart to his glowing colors.

Jan Vermeer (1632–1675) Little is known about the Dutch painter Jan Vermeer, so we must look to the few records and his paintings in order to find out what sort of man he was. Sparse records in the city archives in Delft, where he lived all his life, indicate the dates of his marriage and death, and that he had died penniless. In fact, his widow was forced to sell two of his paintings to settle a baker's debt. He seems to have been principally an art dealer, which may account for the fact that he painted very few pictures (only thirty-five survive). His paintings are usually of common people and he had a sharp eye for the effects of daylight and color. The paintings show great objectivity and moving accounts of simple life.

James Abbott McNeill Whistler (1834–1903) Although he was born in Lowell, Massachusetts, Whistler spent little of his life in the United States. As a boy, he lived in St. Petersburg, Russia (now Leningrad) where his father was supervising railway building for the czar. After a short time at West Point, Whistler went to Paris to study art. In 1859, he settled in London. Although he was in conflict most of his life with the ideas of Impressionism popular at the period, his work still received acceptance. Late in life he became quite popular in both France and England, and as President of the Royal Society of Artists, was able to bridge the gap between British and French artists.

John Constable

Edgar Degas

Joseph M. W. Turner

Jean Ingres

Vincent Van Gogh

Rembrandt

James McNeill Whistler

GLOSSARY OF LITERARY TERMS

Alliteration. Repetition of consonants (generally initial consonants) in words close together. The letter *d* is alliterated in the following line:

> I am in *d*anger of *d*isappearing into the sunny *d*ust.
> (Pomeroy, "Corner")

The following lines alliterate *p*:
> ... the *p*ommel and yet the *p*oll
> of my nickering *p*ony's head ...
> (Swenson, "The Centaur")

Autobiography. Nonfiction that records the life of an individual written by the individual himself. *Life on the Mississippi* (page 29), recounting in his own words the childhood experiences of Mark Twain, is autobiographical.

Characterization. The means by which an author creates lifelike people in his writing. An accurate and believable characterization is developed through the manner in which a character speaks and acts, and through the way in which others act toward him and speak about him. We come to understand Jody in "The Gift" (page 52) partly by how he acts toward his pony, partly by what he says, partly by how others speak and act toward him. For instance, we are convinced of the depth of feeling the boy has for his pony in part by his irrational attack on the buzzard at the end of the story, though his actions throughout—caring for the pony in health and sickness—have already indicated his deep love.

In addition, the writer of a short story or novel may make direct comments about his characters. In Somerset Maugham's story on page 132, the author tells us directly that the verger "was tolerant," and that "his deportment was irreproachable." Moreover, "He had tact, firmness and self-assurance. His character was unimpeachable." A playwright, by contrast, would have to express those qualities indirectly, through actions that Mr. Foreman does or words he says on stage; for a playwright has no way of commenting on his characters or revealing their feelings directly to an audience in a theater. As a consequence, his characterization must be limited to recording how a person talks and moves about the stage, and how others speak about him and behave toward him.

Climax. The high point in the action of a play, narrative poem, or story, marking the decisive moment of the plot. Before the climax, the action may develop in many ways; at the climax, alternatives are removed, and the narrative proceeds toward the single logical ending. The climax of "Lather and Nothing Else" (page 26) occurs when the barber decides not to slit the throat of his customer; before then the action might have developed in a number of ways, whereas afterward the ending is all but inevitable. The climax of "The Necklace" (page 92) occurs when the Loisels, having replaced the lost necklace with a new one, return it to Mme. Forestier. Before then, they might have told her the truth about the loss, or replaced the jewels with fake ones, or fled Paris, or done any one of a number of other things. But after having returned the necklace, given their characters, what follows is virtually inevitable.

Notice that a climax is by no means always at or even near the end of a story. The climax of a race occurs not when one person actually wins, but at that instant—perhaps quite early in the race—when it becomes apparent who will win.

Dialogue. In literature, conversation directly quoted as taking place among characters. Except for *stage directions,* the body of a play is made up entirely of dialogue. It is the playwright's chief means of characterization, and it is also the principal way in which he unfolds the plot. Short stories and novels use dialogue, too; the way in which a particular character speaks helps reveal the kind of person he is. The personality and mood of Romeo in Shakespeare's play is revealed to some extent before he ever appears on stage, by the words of Benvolio and Montague (page 290), discussing his behavior: "My heavy son," "private in his chamber," his window shut up, his room in darkness, his humor "Black and portentous" (I, i, 125–129). The commonsensical Boss in *A Connecticut Yankee at King Arthur's Court* (page 538) reveals his character to some extent by how he speaks, as well as by what he does.

Dramatic poetry. see LYRIC.

Epic. A long poem on a noble subject, narrated in an elevated style, and generally celebrating the feats of a hero representative of a race or nation. The *Odyssey* (page 490) is an example of an epic from ancient Greece.

Figurative language. The opposite of literal language. Frequent in literature, figurative language takes many forms, but it always calls on the reader to use his imagination to complete the author's meaning. For example, the reader does not concentrate exclusively on the literal meaning of "den" and "braille" in order to understand the figures that William Childress develops in "The Dreamer" (page 242):

He spent his childhood hours in a den of rushes, watching the gray rain braille the surface of the river . . .

Instead, the reader thinks of figurative meanings—a den as a cozy haunt rather than literally a place where foxes live, and braille as a surface made rough, rather than literally as a page with bumps on it for a blind man to read with his fingers. Notice, however, that the literal meanings do add to the effect of the images, making the boy like some wild creature at home in nature, and the river like a surface expressing something to be comprehended, if one only knows how to read it. Metaphors, similes, and personifications are all examples of figurative language.

Flashback. A narrative device in which the orderly sequence of chronological events is interrupted by an event that has occurred earlier in time. Such an event is often a reminiscence, as is the case in "Sucker," where all the opening action is remembered two or three months after it occurred: "All of that was two or three months ago. Since then . . ." (page 14).

Foot. See METER.

Free verse. Verse with an irregular rhythm. The meaning and emotion of the poem create a rise and fall of sound not fixed by any metrical pattern. Like meter, rhyme appears seldom in free verse, but other poetic devices such as alliteration are often used. Examples include "Beach along L Street" (page 246), "Traveling Through the Dark" (page 255), and "When I Heard the Learn'd Astronomer" (page 263).

Imagery. Word pictures. The term is often used to signify nothing more than literal descriptive passages in poetry. The following creates images in the mind's eye:

There are birds of many colors—red, blue, green, yellow . . .
(Sandburg, from "The People, Yes")

The appeal of the image need not be limited

to the sense of sight. The following, from "High, Wide and Lonesome" (page 16), appeals to the sense of hearing as well as that of sight:

Two little owls were bobbing and screaming at each other . . . Similarly, images may appeal to the senses of taste, smell, and touch. The term is used, in addition, to refer to figurative language, especially to metaphors and similes. The following image is figuratively expressed:

Life is hard; be steel; be a rock.
(Sandburg, "A Father Sees
a Son Nearing Manhood")

The father is advising his son to have the strong qualities of steel and stone—something different from advising someone to become steel or rock literally.

Irony. The effect of implying a meaning quite different from the apparent or surface meaning. Since we usually think of words like "horrible," "bloody," and "cruel" to describe war, there is irony in calling war "Quaint and curious." Yet the context of "The Man He Killed" (page 28) justifies those unexpected, ironical adjectives. Montresor's several expressions of concern for Furtunato's well-being in "The Cask of Amontillado" (page 171) are ironical—"We will go back; you will be ill, and I cannot be responsible"—since he intends to kill the man at the earliest opportunity. Situations can be ironical. For example, it is ironical that Mme. Loisel in "The Necklace" (page 92) slaves ten years to repay the cost of borrowed jewels that she has lost and that in fact (though she does not know it) are worth very little, being false. It is ironical that at the very time Peter Two (page 152) feels most confident about his fearlessness, he is presented with an extraordinary situation that fills him with terror.

Lyric. One of the three general types of poetry. DRAMATIC POETRY appears in verse plays, such as *Romeo and Juliet* (page 286) and *Antigone* (page 387). NARRATIVE POETRY, such as The *Odyssey* (page 490),

tells a story. Lyric poetry—the most common type—includes all other verse forms. Lyrics were originally sung to the accompaniment of a musical instrument called a lyre, from which the word *lyric* is derived. Often lyrics are intensely personal; often they are brief and charged with emotion; often they are unified in the effect they achieve. All of the poems in Unit Three are lyrics.

Metaphor. An implied comparison between two dissimilar objects. Metaphors abound in everyday speech: "She has a sunny disposition"; "He's a lot of hot air." In each case, the meaning intended is not the literal one: the person referred to in the second example is not literally made up of hot air, but instead is full of empty talk (which is itself a metaphor: talk as empty rather than full). Metaphors appear in the following lines:

Bridges of iron lace . . .
And gullies washed with light
(Roethke, "Night Journey")

The bridges look as delicate as lace; the gullies look as though dawn is making them clean. In the following, a cold room being warmed by a fire in the fireplace is being imagined as though the cold air were literally ice:

I'd wake and hear the cold splintering, breaking.
(Hayden, "Those Winter Sundays")

A figure of speech that uses "like" or "as" to state a comparison directly is called a SIMILE. The following simile describes shoppers at a department-store sale:

Clustered like flies in honeyed snare,
Shrill, cross, and well entangled.
(McGinley, "Sale Today")

The following describes planes in the sky:

Like skaters on a lake
combined into a perfect arrowhead up there
(Swenson, "Three Jet Planes")

The figure of skaters is a simile; that of an arrowhead is a metaphor. Both metaphor (an implied comparison) and simile (a stated comparison) help picture scenes vividly and express feeling accurately.

Meter. The measurement of verse according to its pattern of stressed and unstressed syllables. A certain number of metrical FEET make up a line of verse; each foot is composed of one accented syllable and one or more unaccented syllables. For example, the most frequently encountered foot in English verse is the *iamb,* one unstressed syllable followed by a stressed syllable, as in a*live,* con*fer,* pre*dict.* In the following lines the basic meter is iambic, and there are four feet in each line:

A *mo-* / ther's *hard-* / est to / for-*give.*
Life is / the *fruit* / she *longs* / to *hand* you,
Ripe on / a *plate.* / And *while* / you *live,*
Re-*lent* / less-*ly* / she un- / der-*stands* you.
   (McGinley, "The Adversary")

Narrative poetry. See LYRIC.

Narrator. One who tells a story. The narrator in the excerpt from *Life on the Mississippi* (page 29) is the author himself, Mark Twain. In Poe's "The Cask of Amontillado" (page 171) the narrator is the principal character, the fiendish Montresor. In "The Adventure of the Speckled Band" (page 72), the narrator is not the major character, Sherlock Holmes, but a minor one, Dr. Watson.

Onomatopoeia. The making of words out of sounds that suggest their meaning. *Zoom, knock, clank,* and *roar* are examples. Other examples occur in the following:

The way he *creaks* in his saddle
   (Pomeroy, "Corner")

We rush into a rain
That *rattles* double glass.
   (Roethke, "Night Journey")

As of someone gently *rapping* . . .
   (Poe, "The Raven")

A phrase or whole sentence may be ono-matopoetic, when the sounds of the line taken together echo the sense:

Sling your knuckles on the bottoms of
   the happy tin pans, let your trombones
   ooze, and go husha-husha-hush with
   slippery sandpaper.
      (Sandburg, "Jazz Fantasia")

Paradox. See IRONY.

Personification. A special kind of metaphor in which human characteristics are given to abstract ideas or non-human objects. In the following example, trees are seen as human beings standing by the roadside and dressed in white for Easter:

Loveliest of trees, the cherry now
Is hung with bloom along the bough.
And stands about the woodland ride
Wearing white for Eastertide.
   (Housman, "Loveliest of Trees")

In the following, night and morning are personified as two people:

The gray-eyed morn smiles on the
   frowning night.
      (Shakespeare, *Romeo and Juliet)*

Plot. Arrangement of the action in fiction or drama. Plot refers to what takes place in bare outline from the beginning to the end of the story. The plot of "Thank You, M'am" (page 149) begins when a boy attempts unsuccessfully to snatch the purse of a woman one evening around eleven o'clock. The woman grabs the boy and takes him back to her furnished room, where she feeds him and talks to him and finally gives him money to buy the pair of shoes for which he had tried to steal the purse in the first place. The boy leaves, unable to thank the woman adequately for her kindness and understanding. Notice that such a summary does not develop the setting in any detail or attempt to explain why the characters do what they do. At its simplest, the plot is merely what the story is about.

Point of view. The position from which a story is told. To tell a story, whether in verse or prose, an author may put himself figuratively into the body and mind of some character taking part in the story's action. For example, Sherrel's brother, a participant in the events, tells what happened in the story "Sherrel" (page 2). Alternatively, an author may stand outside his story, knowing what each of his characters is doing and thinking at any moment. Saki uses that method in "The Interlopers" (page 88), which is told from the author's point of view.

Rhyme. Repetition of the same stressed sound or sounds at the end of words. "Strange" rhymes with "change"; "token" rhymes with "broken." Usually when rhyme is used in a poem, the end of one line will rhyme with the end of another line nearby:

> As I listened from a beach-chair in the *shade*
> To all the noises that my garden *made,*
> It seemed to me only proper that *words*
> Should be withheld from vegetables and *birds.*
> (Auden: "Their Lonely Betters")

Lines 1 and 2 rhyme, and lines 3 and 4 rhyme.

Rhythm. Melody of language—the flowing sound of words together, as distinguished from their meaning. Rhythm in this sense includes not only meter, but alliteration, onomatopoeia, and the harshness or softness of sounds within words and phrases. Rhythms may be subdued and gentle:

> Till rising and gliding out I wandered off by myself,
> In the mystical moist night-air, and from time to time
> Looked up in perfect silence at the stars.
> (Whitman, "When I Heard the Learn'd Astronomer")

or abrupt:

> A man said to the universe:
> "Sir, I exist!"

(Crane, "A Man Said to the Universe")

or hurried and intense:

> What, drawn, and talk of peace! I hate the word
> As I hate hell, all Montagues, and thee.
> Have at thee, coward!
> (Shakespeare, *Romeo and Juliet*)

or light and lilting:

> And since to look at things in bloom
> Fifty springs are little room,
> About the woodlands I will go
> To see the cherry hung with snow.
> (Housman, "Loveliest of Trees")

Rhythmic variations, in fact, are virtually endless. *Meter* is a fixed measure or beat; *rhythm* includes meter plus all variations of sound that keep meter from becoming monotonous.

Satire. Verse or prose that makes fun of popular institutions, customs, or beliefs. Generally satire is humorous; its tone may be scornful or wryly amused. Like a cartoon, it depends for its effect more on exaggeration than photographic accuracy or truth. "The Fifty-First Dragon" (page 193) contains some gentle satire at the expense of higher education, specifically the customs and practices of universities that profess to teach their students to "slay the dragons" threatening contemporary society.

Setting. The time and place of a story, play, or narrative poem. "The Sniper" (page 176) is set in Dublin, Ireland, early in the twentieth century. "Jacob" (page 138) is set in Montana in the 1870s. *Antigone* (page 387) is set in ancient Thebes, in what is now Greece.

Simile. See METAPHOR.

Soliloquy. In a play, a speech delivered by an actor alone on the stage. A soliloquy resembles a character's thoughts spoken aloud. An example is Juliet's speech in Act IV, scene iii, of *Romeo and Juliet,* beginning

"Farewell! God knows when we shall meet again," and ending "This do I drink to thee" (pages 366–367).

Sonnet. A lyric of fourteen lines, usually written in iambic meter, with five feet to each line. Auden's "Sonnet XV: *Sonnets from China*" (page 267) is an example. See METER.

Stanza. Verses grouped systematically together. In conventional poetry, stanzas are usually parallel. For example, "Stopping by Woods on a Snowy Evening" (page 256) is composed of four stanzas of four lines each. Each line has eight syllables with alternating stress. The first three stanzas make use of one rhyme, with the third line in each stanza unrhymed, but carried over to form the sound for the rhyme of the following stanza. The final stanza concludes the pattern by having the third line identical with the final line of the poem.

Style. An author's characteristic arrangement of words. A style may be colloquial, formal, terse, wordy, subdued, colorful, poetic, or highly individual in any number of ways. Cummings' style, as seen in a poem like "old age sticks" (page 470), is made up of unconventional punctuation, breaking of words in unusual places, and printing syllables or even two consonants ("gr") as words. Poe's style, as exemplified by "The Raven" (page 215), is characterized by a fondness for italics, for exclamation points, for melodic effects with rhyme and alliteration, and for somber choices of words: *loneliness, desolate, dreary, grim, ghastly,* and so on. The style of "To Build a Fire" (page 40) is clear and sharp and exceptionally vivid, in part because of London's gift for choosing effective, concrete nouns and active verbs.

Theme. The generalized meaning of a literary work. One theme of "Peter Two" (page 152) has to do with a boy's maturing understanding of life and himself—life as complex and mysterious, himself as often helpless to cope with its complexities. That theme arises out of a specific experience of a boy left by himself one evening in a New York apartment building. *Antigone* (page 387) develops a thematic consideration of loyalty as a concept. Where should one's first loyalty lie? In the end, Creon's loyalties to the state above all are seen to support hate and vindication, whereas Antigone's—to her family at the expense of the state—are seen to support forgiveness and love. Themes are general; subjects are specific. Often, of course, themes are difficult to state briefly and precisely.

Tone. In a literary work, the attitude the speaker takes toward his subject. That attitude is revealed through choice of details, through diction and style, and through the emphasis and comments that are made. The tone of Millay's "Apostrophe to Man" (page 268) is filled with contempt and loathing. The tone of "The Fifty-First Dragon" (page 193) is humorous. The tone of "Now that the Buffalo's Gone" (page 21) is nostalgic and bitter. Often tone varies within a single literary work. In *Romeo and Juliet,* the tone changes from speech to speech, depending on the different attitudes each character takes toward what he is saying.

Tragedy. A dramatic form in which a person or persons struggle against forces that in the end prove overpowering. Sometimes the adverse forces are exterior ones, such as war. Sometimes the forces struggled against are flaws of character. Often a combination of fate and character brings about the defeat of the protagonist, or hero of the drama. Though a tragedy ends in defeat, the reader or spectator is nevertheless made aware of the nobility with which defeat may be met. Thus the effect on the reader is finally more ennobling than saddening. Both *Antigone* and *Romeo and Juliet* are tragedies.

Verse. The proper term for a line of poetry. Two or more verses grouped together in a pattern make up a STANZA.

INDEX OF AUTHORS, ARTISTS, AND TITLES

ACKNOWLEDGMENTS

Illustrations for this book were obtained from the following sources: p. ii: Jim Hodgson; p. xvi: Frank James; p. 5: "Sleepers II" by George Tooker, collection, the Museum of Modern Art, Larry Aldrich Foundation Fund; p. 12: Frank James; p. 19: Michael Mathers; p. 21: Derrick Te Paske; p. 25: Richard Rogers; pp. 34–35: photo by George Barker, courtesy of the Library of Congress; p. 38: The Granger Collection; p. 41: Derrick Te Paske; p. 59: Michael Mathers; p. 70: Pamela R. Schuyler; p. 106: "The Laundress" by Henri de la Toulouse-Lautrec, Cleveland Museum of Art, Gift of Hanna Fund; p. 111: Barbara Marshall; p. 120: Frank James; p. 127: Mark Silber; p. 130: Philip Jon Bailey; p. 136: Mark Silber; p. 142: The Granger Collection; p. 150: Frank James; p. 156: Philip Jon Bailey; p. 165: Empire of Light by René Magritte, collection, the Museum of Modern Art; p. 180: "Albert's Son" by Andrew Wyeth, Nasjonalgalleriet, Oslo; p. 188: Monkmeyer Press Photo Service; p. 190: United Press International; p. 197: Detail from the Nine Dragon Scroll, Ch'en Jung, the Boston Museum of Fine Arts; Frances Gardner Curtis Fund; p. 206: "Silence" by Odilon Redon, The Museum of Modern Art, Lillie P. Bliss Collection; p. 209: Charles Gatewood; p. 213: Michael Mathers; p. 217: lithograph by Edouard Manet, the New York Public Library, Astor, Lennox and Tilden Foundations; p. 221: Jon Diele; p. 225: Michael Mathers; p. 227: Candy Cochrane; p. 228: Donald Dietz; p. 243: Jon Diele; p. 247: John Urban; p. 248: Candy Cochrane; p. 251: Jon Diele; p. 255: Seraphim Karalexis; p. 257: Jon Diele; p. 259: Margot Niederland; p. 264: Candy Cochrane; p. 269: Michael Mathers; p. 271: Albert Gregory; p. 275: Donald Dietz; p. 277: Candy Cochrane; p. 279: Mark Silber; p. 281: Mark Silber; p. 284: Karin Rosenthal; pp. 306, 325, 329, 348, 381: Paramount Pictures; p. 389: Inge Morath, Magnum Photos, Inc.; p. 395: David Seymour, Magnum Photos, Inc.; p. 413: Erich Lessing, Magnum Photos, Inc.; p. 426: George Gardner; p. 431: Philip Jon Bailey; p. 451: Derrick Te Paske; p. 459: "Woman I" by Willem de Kooning, collection, the Museum of Modern Art, Purchase; p. 474: Eric Simmons; p. 480: Candy Cochrane; p. 483: Donald Dietz; p. 488: Boston Museum of Fine Arts; p. 501: Nationalbibliothek, Bildarchiv d. ost., photo Art Reference Bureau; p. 506: Museo Archaeologico, Florence, photo Hirmer, Art Reference Bureau; p. 526: Museum Antiker Kleinkunst, Munchen, photo Hirmer, Art Reference Bureau; p. 529: Museum Antiker Kleinkunst, Munchen, photo Hirmer, Art Reference Bureau; pp. 536, 541, 563, 581, 599, 613, 635, 683: Tobi Zausner; p. 691: top, Jerry Bauer, center, Brown Brothers; bottom, Houghton Mifflin Company; p. 693: top, Marion Morehouse; center, Leonard McCombe, LIFE Magazine © Time Inc.; bottom, NET; p. 695: left top, National Portrait Gallery, London; left bottom, Culver Pictures; right top, Appleton-Century-Crofts; right center, Macmillan; right bottom, The Bettmann Archive; p. 697: left, Brown Brothers; right top, Louise Dahl Wolfe; right center, Mishkin; right bottom, Bob Dauner, University of New Mexico Press; p. 699: left top, F. T. Stuart; left center, Mary Randlett; left bottom, Vanguard; right top, H. W. Wilson Company; right center, William A. Smith; right bottom, Harcourt, Brace & World; p. 701: top, Shakespeare Memorial Picture Gallery; center, Columbia Records; bottom, Houghton Mifflin Company; p. 703: left top, Milton Meltzer; left center, Henry Grossman, LIFE Magazine © Time Inc.; left bottom, Culver Pictures; right top, Budd, W. W. Norton & Co.; p. 706: Culver Pictures; p. 707: left top, center bottom, Culver Pictures; right top and bottom, Culver Pictures; right center, The Bettmann Archive.

Cover photo: David Cavagnaro

FGHIJ–RM–8210/7987